UNITED STATES ARMY IN WORLD WAR II

The European Theater of Operations

THE LAST OFFENSIVE

By
Charles B. MacDonald

MILITARY INSTRVCTION

OFFICE OF THE CHIEF OF MILITARY HISTORY
UNITED STATES ARMY
WASHINGTON, D.C., 1973

This volume, one of the series UNITED STATES ARMY IN WORLD WAR II, is the ninth to be published in the subseries THE EUROPEAN THEATER OF OPERATIONS. The volumes in the over-all series are closely related and present a comprehensive account of the activities of the Military Establishment during World War II. A list of subseries is appended at the end of this volume.

Library of Congress Catalog Card Number: 71–183070

First Printing

For sale by the Superintendent of Documents, U.S. Government Printing Office
Washington, D.C. 20402 – Price $15.20   Stock Sumber 0829–0087

UNITED STATES ARMY IN WORLD WAR II

Maurice Matloff, General Editor

Advisory Committee
(As of 1 February 1972)

Office of the Chief of Military History
Brig. Gen. James L. Collins, Jr., Chief of Military History

The History of

THE EUROPEAN THEATER OF OPERATIONS

prepared under the direction of

Hugh M. Cole and Charles B. MacDonald

Cross-Channel Attack
Breakout and Pursuit
The Lorraine Campaign
The Siegfried Line Campaign
The Riviera to the Rhine
The Ardennes: Battle of the Bulge
The Last Offensive
The Supreme Command
Logistical Support of the Armies (2 volumes)

. . . to Those Who Served

Foreword

Recovering rapidly from the shock of German counteroffensives in the Ardennes and Alsace, Allied armies early in January 1945 began an offensive that gradually spread all along the line from the North Sea to Switzerland and continued until the German armies and the German nation were prostrate in defeat. This volume tells the story of that offensive, one which eventually involved more than four and a half million troops, including ninety-one divisions, sixty-one of which were American.

The focus of the volume is on the role of the American armies—First, Third, Seventh, Ninth, and, to a lesser extent, Fifteenth—which comprised the largest and most powerful military force the United States has ever put in the field. The role of Allied armies—First Canadian, First French, and Second British—is recounted in sufficient detail to put the role of American armies in perspective, as is the story of tactical air forces in support of the ground troops.

This is the ninth volume in a subseries of ten designed to record the history of the United States Army in the European Theater of Operations. One volume, The Riviera to the Rhine, remains to be published.

Washington, D.C.   JAMES L. COLLINS, JR.
5 June 1972   Brigadier General, USA
                                                     Chief of Military History

The Author

Charles B. MacDonald is the author of *The Siegfried Line Campaign* and co-author of *Three Battles: Arnaville, Altuzzo, and Schmidt,* both in the official series UNITED STATES ARMY IN WORLD WAR II. He has supervised the preparation of other volumes in the European and Mediterranean theater subseries and is a contributor to *Command Decisions* and *American Military History.* He is also the author of *Company Commander* (Washington: 1947), *The Battle of the Huertgen Forest* (Philadelphia: 1963), *The Mighty Endeavor* (New York: 1969), and *Airborne* (New York: 1970). A graduate of Presbyterian College, he also holds the Litt.D. degree from that institution. In 1957 he received a Secretary of the Army Research and Study Fellowship and spent a year studying the interrelationship of terrain, weapons, and tactics on European battlefields. A colonel in the Army Reserve, he holds the Purple Heart and Silver Star. As Deputy Chief Historian for Southeast Asia, he is currently engaged in preparing the official history of the United States Army in Vietnam.

Preface

The American armies that absorbed the shock of the German counter-offensives in the Ardennes and Alsace in the winter of 1944–45 were the most powerful and professional that the United States had yet put in the field. That this was the case was abundantly demonstrated as the final campaign to reduce Nazi Germany to total defeat unfolded.

The campaign was remarkably varied. As it gathered momentum in the snows of the Ardennes and the mud and pillboxes of the West Wall, the fighting was often as bitter as any that had gone before among the hedgerows of Normandy and the hills and forests of the German frontier. Yet the defense which the Germans were still able to muster following the futile expenditure of lives and means in the counteroffensives was brittle. The campaign soon evolved into massive sweeps by powerful Allied columns across the width and breadth of Germany. That the Germans could continue to resist for more than two months in the face of such overwhelming power was a testament to their pertinacity but it was a grim tragedy as well. To such an extent had they subjugated themselves to their Nazi leaders that they were incapable of surrender at a time when defeat was inevitable and surrender would have spared countless lives on both sides.

It was a dramatic campaign: the sweep of four powerful U.S. armies to the Rhine; the exhilarating capture of a bridge at Remagen; assault crossings of the storied Rhine River, including a spectacular airborne assault; an ill-fated armored raid beyond Allied lines; the trapping of masses of Germans in a giant pocket in the Ruhr industrial region; the uncovering of incredible horror in German concentration camps; a dashing thrust to the Elbe River; juncture with the Russians; and a Wagnerian climax played to the accompaniment of Russian artillery fire in the *Fuehrerbunker* in Berlin.

This volume is chronologically the final work in the European theater subseries of the UNITED STATES ARMY IN WORLD WAR II. In point of time, it follows *The Ardennes: Battle of the Bulge,* previously published, and The Riviera to the Rhine, still in preparation.

Even more than most of the volumes in the official history, this one is the work of many people. The author is particularly indebted to two historians who earlier worked on the project: Gordon A. Harrison, author of *Cross-Channel Attack,* whose felicity of phrase may still be apparent in some of the early chapters, and Fred J. Meyer, who prepared a preliminary draft of the entire work. The volume as it stands owes much to their contributions. Mrs. Magna E. Bauer prepared a number of detailed and valuable studies on the German side. As always, Mrs. Lois Aldridge of the World War II Records Division, National Archives and Records Service, displayed remarkable patience in assisting the author's exploration of mountains of records. More than forty senior American officers, including Generals of the Army Dwight D. Eisenhower and Omar N. Bradley, Generals Jacob L. Devers and William H. Simpson, and four senior German officers, including General Hasso von Manteuffel, gave generously of their time in reading and commenting on all or parts of the manuscript. Assistance was also received from the Cabinet Office Historical Section, London; the Directorate of History, Canadian Forces Headquarters, Ottawa; and the *Militaergeschichtliches Forschungsamt,* Freiburg.

Within the editorial staff, I am particularly grateful for the assistance of Mrs. Loretto C. Stevens; the copy editors were Mrs. Stephanie B. Demma, Mr. Alfred M. Beck, and Mrs. Joyce W. Hardyman. Mr. Elliot Dunay and his staff, Mr. Howell C. Brewer and Mr. Roger D. Clinton, prepared the maps. The cartographic staff was supplemented by men of the United States Army to whom I am especially grateful: Specialist 5 Arthur S. Hardyman, Specialist 5 Edward S. Custer, Specialist 4 Daryl L. DeFrance, and Specialist 5 Mark C. Finnemann. Miss Margaret L. Emerson made the index.

The author alone is responsible for interpretations and conclusions, as well as for any errors that may appear.

Washington, D.C.   CHARLES B. MacDONALD
5 June 1972

Contents

Maps

Illustrations

Illustrations are from Department of Defense files.

470-926 O - 73 - 2

THE LAST OFFENSIVE

CHAPTER I

Prelude to Victory

By the third day of January 1945, the Germans in the snow-covered Ardennes region of Belgium and Luxembourg had shot their bolt. The winter counteroffensive, one of the more dramatic events of World War II in Europe, was not over in the sense that the original front lines had been restored, but the outcome could no longer be questioned. A week earlier the Third U.S. Army had established contact with an embattled American force at the road center of Bastogne, well within the southern shoulder of the German penetration. At this point it could be only a matter of time before the Third Army linked with the First U.S. Army driving down from the northern shoulder. Adolf Hitler, the German Fuehrer, himself admitted on 3 January that the Ardennes operation, under its original concept, was "no longer promising of success." [1]

On this third day of January the First Army began its attack to link with the Third Army, to push in what had become known as the "bulge," and to reach the Rhine River. It was an attack destined to secure the tactical initiative that the Allied armies had lost temporarily in the December fighting but which, once regained, they would hold until after Hitler was dead and the German armed forces and nation were prostrate. One day later on the fourth, the Third Army, which had been attacking in the Ardennes since 22 December, was to start a new phase in its campaign to push in the southern portion of the bulge.

On these two days in early January, deep in the Ardennes, the Allies began, in effect, their last great offensive of the war in Europe. (*Map I*) *

Not that the entire front—stretching some 450 airline miles from the North Sea to the Swiss border—burst immediately into flame. (*Map II*) Indeed, the Germans no longer ago than New Year's Eve had launched a second counteroffensive—Operation *NORDWIND*—near the southern end of the Allied line in Alsace. This would take more than a fortnight to subdue.[2] Yet the fighting in Alsace, no matter how real and trying to the men and units involved, was a secondary effort. The true turn the war was taking was more apparent in the north, where the last offensive materialized slowly, even gropingly, as the First and Third Armies sought to eradicate the last vestiges of the enemy's thrust in the Ardennes. One by one the other Allied armies would join the fight.

---

* Maps numbered in Roman are placed in inverse order inside the back cover.

[2] Robert Ross Smith, The Riviera to the Rhine, a volume in preparation for the series UNITED STATES ARMY IN WORLD WAR II.

---

[1] Magna E. Bauer, MS # R-15, Key Dates During the Ardennes Offensive 1944, Part 1, annotated copy in OCMH.

Allied Strategy

As soon as the Western Allies could repair their ruptured line, they could get back to what they had been about that cold, mist-clad morning of 16 December when the Germans had appeared without warning in the forests of the Ardennes.[3] Not only could the attacks and preparations that had been in progress be resumed in somewhat altered form but also a lively debate could be renewed among Allied commanders as to the proper course for Allied strategy. The debate had begun in August after the extent of the enemy's defeat in Normandy had become apparent.

In planning which preceded the invasion of Europe, General Dwight D. Eisenhower, Supreme Commander, Allied Expeditionary Force, and his advisers had agreed to build up strength in a lodgment area in France, then to launch two major thrusts into Germany. One was to pass north of the Ardennes to seize the Ruhr industrial region, Germany's primary arsenal, the other south of the Ardennes to assist the main drive and at the same time eliminate the lesser Saar industrial area.[4]

---

[3] Hugh M. Cole, *The Ardennes: Battle of the Bulge,* UNITED STATES ARMY IN WORLD WAR II (Washington, 1965).

[4] SHAEF Planning Staff draft, Post-NEPTUNE Courses of Action After Capture of the Lodgment Area, Main Objectives and Axis of Advance, I, 3 May 1944, SHAEF SGS 381, Post-OVERLORD Planning, I. The preinvasion plan and the debate are discussed in some detail in four volumes of the European theater subseries of the UNITED STATES ARMY IN WORLD WAR II: Hugh M. Cole, *The Lorraine Campaign* (Washington, 1950); Forrest C. Pogue, *The Supreme Command* (Washington, 1954); Martin Blumenson, *Breakout and Pursuit* (Washington, 1961); and Charles B. MacDonald, *The Siegfried Line Campaign* (Washington, 1963).

In the event, the extent of German defeat in Normandy had exceeded anything the preinvasion planners had foreseen; the Allies had gained the proposed limits of the lodgment area and had kept going in an uninterrupted drive against a fleeing enemy. When it appeared likely that failing to pause to allow the armies' logistical tails to catch up soon would limit operations, the senior British field commander in the theater, Field Marshal Sir Bernard L. Montgomery, had asked Eisenhower to abandon the secondary thrust. Concentrate everything, Montgomery urged, on one bold, end-the-war offensive north of the Ardennes, to be conducted primarily by Montgomery's command, the 21 Army Group. The commander of the 12th U.S. Army Group, Lt. Gen. Omar N. Bradley, favored instead a thrust by his First and Third U.S. Armies generally south of the Ardennes along the shortest route into Germany. One of Bradley's subordinates, Lt. Gen. George S. Patton, Jr., had insisted that his command alone, the Third Army, could do the job.

Unmoved by the arguments, General Eisenhower had continued to favor the preinvasion plan. While granting concessions to the main thrust in the north, including support from the First U.S. Army and the First Allied Airborne Army and a temporary halt in offensive operations by the Third Army, he had held to the design of advancing on a broad front.

As operations developed, the 21 Army Group with the First Canadian and Second British Armies had advanced generally north of the Ardennes through the Belgian plain into the Netherlands, while the First U.S. Army had provided

GENERALS EISENHOWER (*center*), BRADLEY (*left*), AND PATTON CONFER IN THE
ARDENNES

support with a drive across eastern Belgium into what became known as the Aachen Gap. The Third Army, meanwhile, had moved across northern France into Lorraine. In the south a new Allied force, the 6th Army Group, commanded by Lt. Gen. Jacob L. Devers and composed of the Seventh U.S. and First French Armies, had come ashore in southern France and extended the Allied front into Alsace.

At that point the Germans, strengthened along their frontier by inhospitable terrain and concrete fortifications (the West Wall, or, as Allied troops called it, the Siegfried Line), and by proximity to their sources of supply as opposed to ever-lengthening Allied supply lines, had turned to fight back with surprising effect. Through the fall of 1944 they had limited Allied gains in the south to the German frontier along the Saar River and the upper Rhine. In the north, despite a spectacular airborne assault in the Netherlands by the First Allied Airborne Army, they had held the 21 Army Group generally south and west of the Maas River and the First Army west of the Roer River, less than 23 miles inside Germany.

Through the fall campaign, debate over a concentrated thrust in the north as opposed to Eisenhower's broad-front strategy had continued to arise from time to time in one form or another. Tied in with it was a long-standing tenet of Field Marshal Montgomery's that Eisenhower should designate a single, over-all ground commander, presumably Montgomery himself. To both arguments, Eisenhower had continued to say no. The front was too long, he said, for one man to control it all; that was the

reason for having army groups and armies. As to advance on a broad front, he believed it would be "very important to us later on to have two strings to our bow." [5]

Yet what persuasion could not effect, the enemy counteroffensive in part had wrought. With the German drive threatening to split the 12th Army Group, Eisenhower had given Montgomery temporary command of all forces north of the penetration. Not only was the First Army included but also the Ninth U.S. Army, which had entered the line in October north of Aachen between the First Army and the British.

The debate had arisen again as the year 1944 came to a close. As soon as the Ardennes breach could be repaired, General Eisenhower revealed, he intended to return the First Army to General Bradley's command and to resume operations within the framework of the broad-front strategy. The First and Third Armies were to drive from the Ardennes through the Eifel to reach the Rhine south of the Ruhr, while the 21 Army Group was to retain the Ninth Army and make a major drive to the Rhine north of the Ruhr. [6]

Even as the fighting to eliminate the enemy in the Ardennes developed momentum, the British Chiefs of Staff emerged in clear disagreement with Eisenhower's views. On 10 January they asked formally for a strategy review by the Combined Chiefs of Staff (U.S. and British), under whose direction General Eisenhower served. In reply to inquiry

---

[5] Ltrs, Eisenhower to Montgomery, 10 and 13 Oct 44 and 1 Dec 44, as cited in Pogue, *The Supreme Command*, pp. 297, 314.

[6] Ltr, Eisenhower to Montgomery, 31 Dec 44, as cited in Pogue, *The Supreme Command*, p. 409.

from General George C. Marshall, Chief of Staff of the U.S. Army and a member of the Combined Chiefs, Eisenhower insisted that in order to concentrate a powerful force north of the Ruhr for the invasion of Germany, he had to have a firm defensive line (the Rhine) that could be held with minimum forces. Once he had concentrated along the Rhine, the main thrust would be made in the north on the north German plain over terrain conducive to the mobile warfare in which the Allies excelled. A secondary thrust was to be made south of the Ruhr, not in the vicinity of Bonn and Cologne, as the British wanted, because the country east of the Rhine there is tactically unfavorable, but farther south near Frankfurt, where a terrain corridor that runs south of the Ardennes extends across the Rhine through Frankfurt to Kassel.

Stopping off at Malta en route to top-level discussions with the eastern ally, the Soviet Union, the Chiefs of Staff of the British and American services—sitting as the Combined Chiefs of Staff—would on 2 February accept the Supreme Commander's plan. They would do so with the assurance that the main effort would be made north of the Ruhr and that this main thrust would not necessarily await clearing the entire west bank of the Rhine.[7]

For all its aspects of finality, this decision was not to end the matter. As plans for broadening the last offensive progressed, various ramifications of the controversy would continue to arise. Yet for the moment, at least, the air was clear.

Allied Versus German Strength

In returning to the offensive, General Eisenhower and his Allied command were dealing from overwhelming strength. By 3 January 3,724,927 Allied soldiers had come ashore in western Europe.[8] They were disposed tactically in 3 army groups, 9 armies (including one not yet assigned divisions), 20 corps, and 73 divisions. Of the divisions, 49 were infantry, 20 armored, and 4 airborne.[9] Six tactical air commands and thousands of medium and heavy bombers backed up the armies. A highly complex, technical, and skilled logistical apparatus, recovered at last from the strain imposed by the pursuit to the German frontier, rendered support; behind the U.S. armies, this went by the name of the Communications Zone. The Allies would be striking with one of the strongest, unquestionably the best-balanced, military forces of all time.

At first glance German ground strength available to the Commander in Chief West (_Oberbefehlshaber West_),[10] Generalfeldmarschall Gerd von Rundstedt, appeared equal, even superior, to that of the Allies, for Rundstedt controlled, nominally, eighty divisions. In reality, many of these had been drastically reduced in the fighting. The _26th_

---

[7] For a full discussion of this subject, see Pogue, _The Supreme Command_, pp. 409–16.

[8] SHAEF G–3 War Room Daily Summaries, 214–18. Casualties through 3 January totaled 516,244, though many of these men had returned to duty. U.S. forces had incurred 335,090 casualties, including 55,184 killed.

[9] Twelve divisions were British, 3 Canadian, 1 Polish, 8 French, and 49 American. There were, in addition, a Polish brigade and contingents of Dutch, Belgian, and Czechoslovakian troops.

[10] _Oberbefehlshaber West_ means either the Commander in Chief West or his headquarters. In this volume, the abbreviated form, _OB WEST_, will be used to refer to the headquarters.

FIELD MARSHAL VON RUNDSTEDT

Volks Grenadier Division, for example, which had fought in the Ardennes, had a "present for duty" (*Tagesstaerke*) strength of 5,202 but a "combat effective" (*Kampfstaerke*) strength of only 1,782; this against a table of organization calling for approximately 10,000 men. Nor did the Germans have the trained replacements to bring units back to full strength.[11]

By contrast, Allied units, despite losses in the Ardennes and despite a pinch in American infantry replacements, would

quickly be reconstituted. The 28th Infantry Division, for example, literally shattered by the opening blows of the enemy thrust in December, would be virtually at full strength again by the end of January, even though Allied tables of organization called for from two to four thousand more men per division than did German tables. Only the 106th Infantry Division, which had had two regiments captured early in the fighting, would not be returned to full strength.

The German forces opposing the Western Allies were organized into four army groups. In the north, *Army Group H* (Generaloberst Kurt Student) held the line from the Dutch coast to Roermond with the *Twenty-fifth* and *First Parachute Armies,* its boundaries roughly coterminous with those of the 21 Army Group's First Canadian and Second British Armies. From Roermond south to the Moselle River near Trier, including the Ardennes bulge, stood *Army Group B* (Generalfeldmarschall Walter Model), the strongest—by virture of having been beefed up for the Ardennes operation—of the German army groups. *Army Group B* controlled the *Fifth* and *Sixth Panzer Armies* and the *Seventh* and *Fifteenth Armies,* generally opposing the First, Third, and Ninth U.S. Armies. Extending the front to the northeast corner of France was *Army Group G* (Generaloberst Johannes Blaskowitz) with only one army, the *First,* opposite portions of the Third and Seventh U.S. Armies. Also controlling only one army, the *Nineteenth, Army Group Oberrhein* (Reichsfuehrer SS Heinrich Himmler) was responsible for holding the sector extending south to the Swiss border and for conducting the other winter counterblow, Operation

---

[11] *OB WEST Wochenmeldungen,* 1944–45, # H 22/287. *Volks Grenadier* was an honorific, selected to appeal to the pride of the German people, *das Volk,* which Hitler accorded to certain infantry divisions.

NORDWIND. For various reasons, among them the fact that an exalted personage of the Nazi party such as Himmler hardly could submit to the command of an army leader, *Army Group Oberrhein* was tactically independent, in effect, a separate theater command.[12]

Unusual command arrangements, which in this particular case would not last beyond mid-January, were nothing new on the German side. The Commander in Chief West himself, for example, never had been a supreme commander in the sense that General Eisenhower was. The real supreme commander was back in Berlin, Adolf Hitler. To reach Hitler, Rundstedt's headquarters, *OB WEST,* had to go through a central headquarters in Berlin, the *Oberkommando der Wehrmacht* (OKW), which was charged with operations in all theaters except the east. (*Oberkommando des Heeres*—OKH— watched over the Eastern Front.) Jealousies playing among the Army, Navy, Luftwaffe (air force), *Waffen-SS* (military arm of the Nazi party), and Nazi party political appointees further circumscribed *OB WEST's* authority.[13]

There could be no question as to the overwhelming nature of Allied strength as compared with what the Germans, fighting a three-front war, could muster in the west. Allied superiority in the west was at least 2½ to 1 in artillery,

roughly 10 to 1 in tanks, more than 3 to 1 in aircraft, and 2½ to 1 in troops. Nor could there be any question that long-range Allied capabilities also were immensely superior, since much of the great natural and industrial potential of the United States was untapped. German resources in January 1945 still were considerable nevertheless. If adroitly handled, some believed, these resources might enable the Germans to prolong the war and—should Hitler's secret weapons materialize—might even reverse the course of the war.

Despite the demands of five years of war and saturation attacks by Allied bombers, German production had reached a peak only in the fall of 1944. During September 1944, for example, Germany had produced 4,103 aircraft of all types. As late as November 1944, the Luftwaffe had more planes than ever before—8,103 (not counting transports), of which 5,317 were operational. On New Year's Day 1,035 planes had taken to the air over the Netherlands, Belgium, and northern France in support of the Ardennes fighting. Some 25 new submarines—most equipped with a snorkel underwater breathing device—had been completed each month through the fall. Tank and assault gun output would stay at a steady monthly level of about 1,600 from November 1944 to February 1945.[14] A few newly developed jet-propelled aircraft already had appeared over the Western Front. In light of V–1 flying bombs and V–2 supersonic missiles that had for months been bombarding British and Continental cities, a report that soon

[12] *Oberkommando der Wehrmacht* (OKW) *Wehrmachtfuehrungsstab* (*WFSt*) situation maps for the period; Magna E. Bauer, MS # R–64, The Western Front in Mid-January 1945, prepared in OCMH to complement this volume, copy in OCMH.

[13] MSS # T–121, T–122, and T–123, *OB WEST,* A Study in Command (Generalleutnant Bodo Zimmerman, G–3, *OB WEST,* and other officers).

[14] Magna E. Bauer, MS # R–61, Effects of the Ardennes Offensive: Germany's Remaining War Potential, prepared to complement this volume, annotated copy in OCMH.

the Germans would possess an intercontinental missile was not lightly dismissed.[15]

In manpower the Germans still had reserves on which to draw. Of a population within prewar boundaries of some 80 million, close to 13 million had been inducted into the armed forces, of whom 4 million had been killed, wounded, or captured in five years of war. Yet not until January 1945 would Hitler decree that older men up to forty-five years of age be shifted from industry to the armed forces. As late as February, eight new divisions would be created, primarily from youths just turned seventeen. As the roles of the Navy and Luftwaffe declined, substantial numbers of their men could be transferred to the Army.[16]

To these points on the credit side of the German ledger would have to be added the pertinacity of the German leader, Adolf Hitler. Although shaken by an attempt on his life in the summer of 1944 and sick from overuse of sedatives, Hitler in January 1945 still was a man of dominant personality and undiluted devotion to the belief that even though a German military victory might be impossible, the war somehow could be brought to a favorable end. His distrust of nearly everybody around him had served to feed his conviction that he alone was capable of correctly estimating the future course of the war. He would tolerate no dissenting voices.

To a varying degree, depending on individual insight, the German soldiers and their leaders accepted the promises and assurances of their Fuehrer that, given time, political *démarches,* dissent among the Allies, even continued conventional military efforts, Germany could anticipate some kind of salvation. Given time alone, the Third Reich could develop new miracle weapons and improve existing weapons so that the enemy, if he could not be beaten, still could be forced to compromise, or else the "Anglo-Saxons," as Hitler called the Western Allies, might be persuaded to join with Germany in the war against bolshevism. The time to achieve all this could be gained only by stubborn combat. If some preferred to give up the fight and surrender, the great majority would continue the battle with determination.[17]

It is difficult, in retrospect, to comprehend how any thinking German could have believed genuinely in anything other than defeat as 1945 opened, despite the credits on the ledger, for entries on the debit side were almost overwhelming. North Africa, France, Belgium, Luxembourg, Crete, Russia, much of the Balkans, much of Italy and Poland, parts of the Netherlands, Czechoslovakia, Yugoslavia, and even East Prussia—all had been lost, together with the Finnish and Italian allies. The nation's three major industrial regions—the Ruhr, Saar, and Silesia—lay almost in the shadow of the guns of either the Western Allies or the Russians. The failure in the Ardennes was all the more disheartening because so much had been expected of the campaign. The impressive numbers of aircraft were almost meaningless when

[15] Wesley Frank Craven and James Lea Cate, eds., "The Army Air Forces in World War II," III, *Europe: Argument to V-E Day* (Chicago: The University of Chicago Press, 1951) (Hereafter cited as *AAF III*), 84, 545, and 659.

[16] MS # R–61 (Bauer).

[17] *Ibid.*

measured against shortages in trained pilots and aviation fuel, the latter so lacking that few new pilots could be trained. Although Hitler time after time promised to introduce a fleet of jet-propelled fighters to set matters right in the skies, his insistence back in 1943 that the jet be developed not as a fighter but as a bomber in order to wreak revenge on the British had assured such a delay in jet fighter production that jets would play only a peripheral role in the war.

Tank and assault gun production figures also had to be considered against the background of fuel shortages and a crippled transportation system that made it increasingly difficult to get the weapons from assembly line to front line. An Allied air offensive against oil and transportation, for example, begun during the summer of 1944, had had severe repercussions in more than one segment of the war economy. Shipment of coal by water and by rail (normally 40 percent of traffic) had fallen from 7.4 million tons in August to 2.7 million tons in December. Production in synthetic fuel plants, responsible for 90 percent of Germany's aviation gasoline and 30 percent of the nation's motor gasoline, had dropped from an average of 359,000 tons in the four months preceding the attacks to 24,000 tons in September.[18] The atmosphere of impending doom was further heightened by knowledge that even if the Ardennes fighting did delay another major Allied offensive for a month or so, the Russians were readying an all-out strike that was sure to come, if not in days then in weeks.

[18] The United States Strategic Bombing Survey, Report 3, European War, The Effects of Strategic Bombing on the German War Economy, 31 October 1945, pp. 12–13.

Nor was the German Army that stood in the east, in Italy, and in the west in any way comparable to the conquering legions of the early months of the war. The long, brutal campaign against the Russians had crippled the Army even before Allied troops had forced their way ashore in Normandy. Units that at one time had boasted of their all-German "racial purity" were now laced with *Volksdeutsche* ("racial Germans" from border areas of adjacent countries), and *Hilfswillige* (auxiliaries recruited from among Russian prisoners of war), and physical standards for front-line service had been sharply relaxed. Many of the German divisions had only two infantry regiments of two battalions each, and some had only two light artillery battalions of two batteries each and one medium battalion.

The Army faced a further handicap in the stultifying effect of a long-standing order from Hitler forbidding any voluntary withdrawal. Having apparently forestalled a disastrous retreat before the Russian counteroffensive in front of Moscow in the winter of 1941–42 by ordering that positions be held even when bypassed or surrounded, Hitler saw a policy of "hold at all costs" as a panacea for every tactical situation. Not a single concrete pillbox or bunker of the western border fortifications, the West Wall, was to be relinquished voluntarily. Hitler also constantly delayed granting authority for preparing rear defensive positions lest these serve as a magnet pulling the troops back.

For all these negative factors, many Germans continued to believe if not in victory, then in a kind of nihilistic syllogism which said: Quit now, and all is lost; hold on, and maybe something will happen to help—a process of inductive reasoning that Allied insistence on unconditional surrender may not have promoted but did nothing to dissuade. Already the Germans had demonstrated amply an ability to absorb punishment, to improvise, block, mend, feint, delay.

Weapons and Equipment

Making up approximately three-fourths of the total Allied force engaged in the last offensive, the American soldier was perhaps the best-paid and best-fed soldier of any army up to that time. Except for a few items of winter clothing, he was also as well or better clothed than any of his allies or his enemy. In the matter of armament and combat equipment, American research and production had served him well. On the other hand, his adversary possessed, qualitatively at least, battle-worthy equipment and an impressive arsenal.[19]

The basic shoulder weapon of the U.S. soldier was the .30-caliber M1 (Garand) rifle, a semiautomatic piece, while the German soldier employed a 7.92-mm. (Mauser) bolt-action rifle. Two favorite weapons of the American were outgrowths of World War I, the .30-caliber Browning automatic rifle (BAR) and the .30-caliber Browning machine gun in both light (air-cooled) and heavy (water-cooled) models. The German soldier had no widely used equivalent of the BAR, depending instead on a machine pistol that the Ameri-

cans called, from an emetic sound attributable to a high cyclic rate of fire, a "burp gun." The burp gun was similar, in some respects, to the U.S. Thompson submachine gun. The standard German machine gun was the M1942, which had a similarly high cyclic rate of fire.

In the two arsenals of antitank weapons, the most effective close-range weapons were the German one-shot, shaped-charge piece called a *Panzerfaust,* and the American 2.36-inch rocket launcher, the bazooka. Late in the campaign the Americans would introduce a new antitank weapon, the recoilless rifle in 57- and 75-mm. models, but the war would end before more than a hundred reached the European theater. The conventional towed 57-mm. antitank gun most American units at this stage of the war had come to view as excess baggage; but in the defensive role in which the Germans would find themselves, towed pieces still would be used. In general, the basic antitank weapon was the tank itself or a self-propelled gun, called by the Americans a tank destroyer, by the Germans an assault gun. German assault guns usually were either 76- or 88-mm. Most American tank destroyers were M10's with 3-inch guns, though by November substantial numbers of M36's mounting a high-velocity 90-mm. piece had begun to arrive. Because the tank destroyer looked much like a tank, many commanders tried to employ it as a tank, but since it lacked heavy armor plate, the practice often was fatal.

The standard American tank, the M4 Sherman, a 33-ton medium, was relatively obsolescent. Most of the Shermans still mounted a short-barreled 75-mm. gun, which repeatedly had proved inca-

---

[19] A comprehensive study and comparison of American and German weapons and equipment will be found in Lida Mayo, *The Ordnance Department: On Beachhead and Battlefront,* UNITED STATES ARMY IN WORLD WAR II (Washington, 1968).

M4 Sherman Tank in the Ardennes

pable of fighting German armor on equal terms. They plainly were outgunned, not necessarily by the enemy's medium (Mark IV) tank but unquestionably by the 50-ton Mark V (Panther) and the 54-ton Mark VI (Tiger), the latter mounting a high-velocity 88-mm. gun.[20] The Panther and Tiger also surpassed the Sherman in thickness of armor and width of tracks.

Although modifications of the M4 had begun to reach the theater in some quantity in late fall and early winter, most equipped with a 76-mm. gun, some with

increased armor plate, the old Sherman remained the basic tank. As late as the last week of February 1945, for example, less than one-third of the mediums in the Ninth Army were equipped with a 76-mm. piece. The best of the modifications of the M4 to reach the theater in any quantity was the M4A3, 76-mm. gun, Wet Series, familiarly known as the "Jumbo." Its high-velocity gun had a muzzle brake, and the tank had a new suspension system and 23-inch steel tracks in place of the old 16 9/16-inch rubber block tracks. Neither a radically designed medium tank (the M26, mounting a 90-mm. gun) nor a heavy tank would reach the theater before the

---

[20] A souped-up version of the Tiger, called the King Tiger or Tiger Royal, appeared in small numbers.

end of hostilities in other than experimental numbers.[21]

The basic German mortars were of 50- and 81-mm. caliber, comparable to the American 60- and 81-mm., but the little 50 had fallen into disfavor as too small to be effective. Unlike the Americans, the Germans also employed heavier mortars, some up to 380-mm. The *Nebelwerfer,* or "Screaming Meemie," as the U.S. soldier called it, was a multiple-barrel 150-mm. mortar or rocket launcher mounted on wheels and fired electrically. The Americans had a similar weapon in the 4.5-inch rocket launcher.

The most widely used artillery pieces of both combatants were light and medium howitzers, German and American models of which were roughly comparable in caliber and performance. The German pieces were gun-howitzers (105-mm. light and 150-mm. medium); the American pieces, howitzers (105- and 155-mm.). The German infantry division, like the American, was supposed to have four artillery battalions, three light and one medium. As was standard practice in the U.S. Army, additional artillery, some of it of larger caliber, operated under corps and army control.

German artillery doctrine and organization for the control and delivery of fire differed materially from the American only in that the German organic divisional artillery was less well equipped for communication. Excellent American communications facilities down to bat-

M4A3 Sherman Tank With 76–mm. Gun

tery level and effective operation of fire direction centers permitted more accurate fire and greater concentration in a shorter time. Yet the shortcomings of the enemy in the matter of effective concentrations were attributable less to deficiencies of doctrine and organization than to shortages of ammunition and other ravages of war. Except that of the panzer and panzer grenadier divisions, almost all German artillery, for example, was at this stage horse-drawn.[22]

Controlling the air, the Americans could employ with tremendous effect artillery spotter planes which greatly extended the effective visual distance of artillery observers. A simple little monoplane (L–4 or L–5), known variously as

---

[21] Cole, in *The Lorraine Campaign,* pages 603–04, and *The Ardennes,* pages 651–52, compares characteristics of German and U.S. tanks. See also Constance McLaughlin Green, Harry C. Thomson, and Peter C. Roots, *The Ordnance Department: Planning Munitions for War,* UNITED STATES ARMY IN WORLD WAR II (Washington, 1955), ch. X.

[22] Charles V. P. von Luttichau, Notes on German and U.S. Artillery, MS in OCMH; Gen. Hasso von Manteuffel, comments on draft MS for this volume.

a Piper Cub, cub, liaison plane, grass-hopper, or observation plane, it had more than proved its worth—particularly in counterbattery fires—long before the last offensive began. Although the Germans had a similar plane—the *Storck*—overwhelming Allied air superiority had practically driven it from the skies.

American artillery also gained a slight advantage from a supersecret fuze, called variously the VT (variable time), POZIT, or proximity fuze, by means of which artillery shells exploded from external influences in the air close to the target, an improvement on time fire. Long employed in antiaircraft fire but first used by ground artillery during the defensive phase of the Ardennes fighting, the fuze was undoubtedly effective, though the limited extent of its use could hardly justify extravagant claims made for it by enthusiastic scientists.[23]

Other than tanks, the German weapon which most impressed the American soldier was the "88," an 88-mm. high-velocity, dual-purpose antiaircraft and antitank piece. So imbued with respect for the 88 had the American become from the fighting in North Africa onward that a shell from almost any high-velocity German weapon he attributed to the 88.

In the vital field of signal communications, the Americans held an advantage at tactical levels because of the inroads battle losses and substitute materials had made in the German system and because of widespread American use of frequency modulation (FM) in radio communications. Both armies operated on the same theory of two networks of radio and two of telephone communications within the

division, one for infantry or armor, one for artillery; but at this stage of the war the German system often failed to reach as low as company level. By use of sound-powered telephone, the Americans gained telephonic communication down to platoons and even squads. They also had a good intracompany radio system with the use of an amplitude modulated (AM) set, the SCR–536, or handie-talkie.

In the offensive, radio usually served as the communications workhorse in forward areas. Here the Americans held advantages with the handie-talkie and with FM. One of the communications standbys of the war was the SCR–300, the walkie-talkie, an FM set of commendable performance, used primarily at company and battalion levels. German sets, all of which were AM, were subject to interference by the sheer volume of their own and Allied traffic. Perhaps because of the lack of intracompany wire or radio, the Germans used visual signals such as colored lights and pyrotechnics more often than did the Americans.[24]

The air support which stood behind the Allied armies was tremendously powerful. In close support of the ground troops were six tactical air commands, but also available for tactical support were eleven groups of medium and light bombers (B–26 Marauders, A–20 Havocs, and A–26 Invaders) of the IX U.S. Bomber Command and other mediums under British

[23] Cole, *The Ardennes,* pp. 655–56.

[24] For detailed discussion of American and German communications, see two volumes in the series, UNITED STATES ARMY IN WORLD WAR II: George R. Thompson, Dixie R. Harris, Pauline M. Oakes, and Dulany Terrett, *The Signal Corps: The Test* (Washington, 1957), and George R. Thompson and Dixie R. Harris, *The Signal Corps: The Outcome* (Washington, 1966).

control. On occasion, the devastating heavy bombers of the U.S. Eighth Air Force and the Royal Air Force Bomber Command were called in. Not counting Allied aircraft based in Italy, the Allies could muster more than 17,500 first-line combat aircraft, including approximately 5,000 British aircraft of all types, 6,881 U.S. bombers, and 5,002 U.S. fighters, plus hundreds of miscellaneous types for reconnaissance, liaison, and transport.[25]

The tactical air commands were the British Second Tactical Air Force, in support of the Second British and First Canadian Armies; the First French Air Corps, in support of the First French Army; and four American forces, the IX, XI, XIX, and XXIX Tactical Air Commands, in support, respectively, of the First, Seventh, Third, and Ninth Armies. All American tactical support aircraft—mediums and fighter-bombers—were a part of the Ninth Air Force (Maj. Gen. Hoyt Vandenberg).

Like divisions attached to ground corps and armies, the number of fighter-bomber groups assigned to tactical air commands often varied, though the usual number was six. A group normally had three squadrons of twenty-five planes each: P–38's (Lightnings), P–47's (Thunderbolts), P–51's (Mustangs), or, in the case of night fighter groups, P–61's (Black Widows). The French used American planes, while the basic British tactical fighters were rocket-firing Hurricanes and Typhoons.

Requests for air support passed from the air support officer at division head-

quarters to the G–3 Air Section at army headquarters for transmission to the tactical air command, with an air support officer at corps merely monitoring the request. Usually set up close to the army headquarters, the air headquarters ruled on the feasibility of a mission and assigned the proper number of aircraft to it. Since air targets could not always be anticipated, most divisions had come to prefer a system of "armed reconnaissance flights" in which a group assigned to the division or corps for the day checked in by radio directly with the appropriate air support officer. Thus the planes could be called in as soon as a target appeared without the delay involved in forwarding a request through channels. Requests for support from mediums had to be approved by the G–3 Air Section at army group headquarters and took appreciably longer.[26]

In the matter of logistics, the pendulum had swung heavily to the Allied side. Although logistical difficulties had contributed in large measure to the Allied bog-down along the German border in the fall of 1944, opening of the great port of Antwerp in late November, plus the use of major ports in southern France, had speeded recovery of the logistical apparatus. Supply losses in the early Ardennes fighting, while locally painful, were no problem in the long run. The Germans, for their part, had expended carefully hoarded reserves in the Ardennes. Although they still derived some benefit from proximity to their sources of supply, they would find that the traditional advan-

---

[25] Army Air Forces Statistical Digest, World War II, with supplement, p. 156.

[26] Craven and Cate, *AAF III*, pp. 107–37; The Ninth Air Force and Its Principal Commands in the ETO, vol. I, ch. VII, and vol. II, part 1.

tage of inner lines had lost some of its effect in the air age.[27]

Organization and Command

With the exception of a few new divisions, the American force participating in the last offensive was experienced in the ways of battle, a thoroughly professional force scarcely comparable to the unseasoned soldiery that had taken the field even such a short time before as D-day in Normandy. That the Americans had come fully of age had been amply demonstrated in the stalwart defense of the American soldier against the surprise onslaught in the Ardennes and in the swift reaction of the American command.

Having moved three months before from England, General Eisenhower's Supreme Headquarters, Allied Expeditionary Force (SHAEF Main) was established in Versailles with adequate radio and telephone communications to all major commands. A small tent and trailer camp at Gueux, near Reims, served the Supreme Commander as a forward headquarters. In addition to the three Allied army groups—6th, 12th, and 21—General Eisenhower exercised direct command over the First Allied Airborne Army (Lt. Gen. Lewis H. Brereton), U.S. and British tactical air forces, and the Communications Zone (Lt. Gen. John C. H. Lee). Although the Allied strategic air forces operated directly under the Combined Chiefs of Staff rather than under Eisenhower, the Supreme Commander had first call upon them when he required their direct support for ground operations.

The two American army groups represented, in effect, a new departure in American military experience in that the only previous U.S. army group had existed only briefly near the end of World War I when General John J. Pershing had grouped two American armies under his own command. With little precedent as a guide, the way the two army group commanders, Generals Bradley and Devers, organized their headquarters and exercised command reflected much of their own individual concepts. Although both retained the usual "G" and Special Staff organization, Devers ran his army group with a staff of only about 600 officers and men, while Bradley employed double that number. The numbers told much about the way each interpreted the role of the army group commander: Devers played it loosely, leaving planning mainly to his army commanders and authorizing his staff to seek information at lower levels and make changes on the spot. Much as when he had commanded the First Army, Bradley exercised much closer control over his army commanders and employed his staff in intricate, detailed planning. General Bradley after the war liked to point out that he had intimate foreknowledge of every move of his armies except in one case when General Patton set out on an operation that he came to rue.[28]

Under the American system, both army group and army exercised command and logistical functions, while at

---

[27] A detailed account of logistics in the European theater may be found in Roland G. Ruppenthal, *Logistical Support of the Armies I*, UNITED STATES ARMY IN WORLD WAR II (Washington, 1955), and *II* (Washington, 1959).

[28] Interviews, author with Bradley, 30 Jun 67, and Devers, 7 Dec 67.

the level of corps the commander was free of the latter. This system afforded the corps commander time to concentrate on tactical matters and established the corps as a strong component in the command structure. Equipped with modern means of communication and transportation, the corps commander had regained a measure of the control and influence over the actions of his divisions that the advent of mass armies and rapid-fire weapons had originally taken away.

The American division in World War II reflected an early decision to keep the army in the field lean, to avoid duplicating the powerful but ponderous 28,000-man division that had fought in the trenches with Pershing. The theory was that if all the engineer, medical, transport, quartermaster, and other support troops that were needed to meet any contingency were an integral part of the division, not only would the division be difficult to control and maneuver but many of the troops would often be idle while awaiting a call on the specialties for which they were trained. Better to let infantrymen themselves double as drivers, radio operators, mechanics, and the like, while specialized units of heavy artillery, transport, construction engineers, signalmen, tank destroyers, tanks, and other support could be attached as required. The method had the added virtue of eliminating the need for a variety of specialized divisions since infantry divisions could be tailored by attachments to fit various requirements.

Because the fighting in Europe posed an almost constant demand for close-support firepower and antitank defense, attachment of a tank and a tank de-

stroyer battalion to the infantry division became customary, bringing the size of the division to about 16,000 men. Similarly, a separate tank destroyer battalion was nearly always attached to the armored division.

After a first rush to create a "heavy" armored division comparable to the early German panzer division, the U.S. Army had scaled down the medium tank strength of the armored division from 250 to 154 and added more infantry to provide staying power. The new organization had dispensed with armored and armored infantry regiments, providing instead battalions that could be grouped in various "mixes" under combat commands. While lacking some of the shock power of the old heavy division, the new formation had proven flexible, maneuverable, and fully capable of meeting the German panzer division of 1944-45 on at least equal terms. Three of the heavy armored divisions remained—the 1st in Italy and the 2d and 3d in Eisenhower's command.

The armored division usually operated in three combat commands, A, B, and R (Reserve), each built around a battalion of medium tanks and a battalion of armored infantry, with added increments of engineers, tank destroyers, medics, and other services plus artillery support commensurate with the combat command's assignment. Thus each combat command was approximately equal in power and interchangeable in terms of combat mission, while in the old heavy division Combat Commands A and B almost always bore the major assignments since the reserve consisted usually of some contingent pulled from either or both of the larger commands to afford the commander a maneuver or reinforcing element. In both type divisions combat commands usually operated under an arrangement of two or more "task forces."

Much like armor with its combat commands, infantry divisions almost always employed regimental combat teams. Each of the division's three infantry regiments was supported by a 105-mm. howitzer battalion and increments of divisional support troops while the division's 155-mm. howitzer battalion was available for reinforcing fires as needed.

The corps usually consisted of a minimum of three divisions—two infantry, one armored. Never did the U.S. Army employ an armored corps of the type the Germans used in early breakthroughs in Poland and on the Western Front, partly because of the antipathy toward specialization and partly because the American infantry division with a high mobility and with attached tanks and tank destroyers was essentially the equivalent of the German panzer grenadier division. Thus a regular corps was considerably heavier in armor than the presence of one armored and two infantry divisions might otherwise indicate. The only specialized U.S. corps was the XVIII Airborne Corps, which like U.S. airborne divisions was destined to spend more time in straight ground combat than in its specialized role.

Heading this American force in Europe was a group of senior commanders who had come to know each other intimately during the lean years of the small peacetime Army and who all had absorbed the same doctrinal concepts from the service schools and the Command and General Staff College. General Eisenhower and two of his top American subordinates, Bradley and Patton, had been closely associated in battle since the campaign in North Africa, and Lt. Gen. Courtney H. Hodges of the First Army, who had come to France as Bradley's deputy in the First Army, and Lt. Gen. William H. Simpson of the Ninth Army had developed a close command association with the others through the fighting of the fall and early winter. General Devers and his one American army commander, Lt. Gen. Alexander M. Patch of the Seventh Army, were less fully integrated in the command team, partly because they had entered the fight separately by way of southern France rather than Normandy, partly because they functioned in a supporting role on a flank and thus commanded less direct attention from the Supreme Commander, and partly because General Devers had not been Eisenhower's selection but that of the Chief of Staff, General Marshall, and Patch had been Dever's choice. Yet the military schooling and experience of these two was much the same as that of the others, and the fall and early winter campaigns had already produced a strong measure of understanding.

A potentially divisive element was present in the American command in the person of the Third Army commander, General Patton. A charismatic leader, Patton was also impetuous and had come close on several occasions to summary relief. While General Eisenhower had in each case decided finally against that discipline, Patton had sorely tried his patience, and as a result of slapping incidents involving two hospitalized soldiers in Sicily, he had vowed never to elevate Patton above army command. Respecting Bradley, Patton had agreed without rancor to serve under Bradley, one who in North Africa and Sicily had been his subordinate. Aware that Patton was impetuous and that grim, slugging warfare tried his thin patience, Eisenhower and Bradley kept a close rein on the Third Army commander but so unobtrusively that Patton himself often thought he was putting things over on his superiors when actually they were fully informed. Aware also of Patton's superior abilities in more fluid warfare, Eisenhower and Bradley consciously loosened their hold on the rein when breakthrough and pursuit were the order of the day.[29]

In the over-all command structure, two other potentially abrasive elements were present in the persons of the 21 Army Group commander, Field Marshal Montgomery, and the First French Army commander, General Jean de Lattre de Tassigny. Although Montgomery and de Lattre commanded forces considerably smaller than those fielded by the Americans, each was a dominant personality and as the senior field representative of one of the major allies sought a strong voice in command deliberations. Nor was either reluctant in the face of controversy to call in the persuasive force of his head of state.

Terrain and the Front Line

At the closest point, the Allied front line in early January was some twenty-five miles from the Ruhr industrial area. Although Berlin, the political heart of Germany, might constitute the

final objective of the Allied armies, the Ruhr with its coal mines, blast furnaces, and factories, the muscle with which Germany waged war, was the more vital objective. Without the Ruhr, Germany's case would fast become hopeless; taking Berlin and all other objectives then would be but a matter of time.[30]

No political or geographical entity, the Ruhr can be fairly accurately described as a triangle with its base along the east bank of the Rhine River from Cologne northward to Duisburg, a distance of some thirty-five miles. One side of the triangle extends eastward from Duisburg along the Lippe River to Dortmund, for thirty-five to forty miles; the other side about the same distance southwestward from Dortmund to the vicinity of Cologne along the Ruhr River. The region embraces major cities such as Essen, Duesseldorf, and Wuppertal.

The trace of the front line in early January clearly reflected Allied preoccupation with the Ruhr as an objective and General Eisenhower's broad-front strategy, plus the accident of the Ardennes counteroffensive. Starting at the Dutch islands of Noord Beveland and Tholen, the line followed the Maas and Waal Rivers eastward to Nijmegen, where the Allies maintained a small bridgehead north of the Waal, thence southward along the west bank of the Maas to Maeseyck. There the line turned southeastward across the Maas to reach the Roer River near Heinsberg, thence south and southwestward to the headwaters of the Roer at Monschau. The sector along the Roer—some forty

---

[29] Interviews, author with Eisenhower, 23 Jun 67; Bradley, 30 Jun 67; and Devers, 7 Dec 67.

[30] SHAEF Planning Staff, Post-NEPTUNE Courses of Action After Capture of Lodgment Area, SHAEF SGS file, 381, I.

miles long—represented the only major breach of the West Wall fortifications.

At Monschau began what was left of the Ardennes bulge. The line ran sharply southwest as far as Marche, some forty miles west of the German frontier, thence southeast to rejoin the frontier a few miles northwest of Trier. It then followed the Moselle River to the southern border of Luxembourg, there to swing east and parallel the Franco-German border to the vicinity of Sarreguemines. From there to Gambsheim on the west bank of the Rhine a few miles north of Strasbourg the front was in a state of flux as a result of the *NORDWIND* counteroffensive. A few miles south of Strasbourg, it again veered west to encompass a portion of Alsace still held by the Germans, called by Allied soldiers the Colmar pocket. The front line reached the Rhine again east of Mulhouse and followed the river to the Swiss border.

The terrain immediately in front of the Allied positions could be divided into four general classifications: the flatlands of the Netherlands and the Cologne plain, crisscrossed by waterways and studded with towns and villages; the Ardennes-Eifel, a high plateau so deeply cut by erosion that it appears mountainous; the Saar-Palatinate, another plateau, sprinkled with coal mines and steel processing plants, separated from the Ardennes-Eifel by the trench of the Moselle; and the Vosges Mountains-Black Forest massif, two sharply defined mountain regions belonging to the same geological age but separated by the trench of the Rhine.

The flatlands in the north were the responsibility of the First Canadian Army (Lt. Gen. Henry D. G. Crerar),

the Second British Army (Lt. Gen. Sir Miles C. Dempsey), and the Ninth U.S. Army (General Simpson). Soon after the Germans had struck in the Ardennes, the Ninth Army had extended its boundary southward to encompass much of the area originally held by the First U.S. Army, so that the boundary ran in the vicinity of Monschau. With the exception of the western portion of the Netherlands, where canals, rivers, dikes, and deep drainage ditches sharply compartment the land, this region offered the best route to the primary Allied objective, the Ruhr. The Ninth Army might strike directly toward the western base of the Ruhr, while the British and Canadians crossed the Rhine and gained access to the north German plain, thereby outflanking the Ruhr and at the same time opening a way toward Berlin.

The Ardennes-Eifel, with its high ridges, deep-cut, serpentine streams, and dense forests, had never been tested by an army moving against opposition from west to east except during September 1944, when an American corps had pushed as far as the German frontier. Even should the Allies elect to avoid the Eifel as a route of major advance, that portion of the high plateau known as the Ardennes still would have to be cleared of the enemy. The responsibility belonged to General Hodges' First Army, operating temporarily under the 21 Army Group, and the Third Army (General Patton).

The Third Army's sector, some of which upon the start of the Ardennes counteroffensive had been relinquished to the adjacent Seventh U.S. Army (General Patch), included, in addition to the Ardennes, a small portion of the line facing the Saar-Palatinate. This included the trough of the Moselle, a poor route of advance because it is narrow and meandering. That part of the Saar-Palatinate most open to attack lay opposite the Seventh Army from Saarlautern southeastward to the Rhine and encompassed two corridors leading northeast that have seen frequent use in wartime. Separated by a minor mountain chain called the Haardt, these are known usually as the Kaiserslautern and Wissembourg Gaps. Both lead to the Rhine near Mainz, where, after converging, they continue as one past Frankfurt to Kassel.

That part of the Allied line touching the Rhine—from Gambsheim to a point above Strasbourg—was the responsibility of the First French Army (General de Lattre). From the vicinity of Strasbourg the French line swung southwest into the most rugged terrain on the Western Front, the high Vosges Mountains. Rising almost like a wall from the Alsatian Plain, the Vosges reach a height of almost 5,000 feet and in winter are covered with deep snows. In the Vosges and on the plain, the German-held Colmar pocket measured on its periphery about 130 miles. Even after clearing this pocket, the French would face terrain hardly less formidable; just across the Rhine stands the Schwarzwald, or Black Forest, which guards Germany much as the Vosges protect France.

All along the front, with the exception of the Maas-Waal line in the Netherlands and the 40-mile gap along the Roer, the Germans drew strength from their concrete border fortifications, the West Wall. Construction of this fortified line had begun in 1936, first to counter France's Maginot Line opposite the Saar, subsequently to protect almost the full length of Germany's western frontier. No thin line of elaborate, self-contained forts like the Maginot Line, the West Wall was a series of more than 3,000 relatively small, mutually supporting pillboxes or blockhouses arranged in one or two bands, depending on the critical nature of the terrain. Either natural antitank obstacles such as rivers or monolithic concrete projections called dragon's teeth ran in front of the pillboxes. The strongest sectors of the line were around Aachen—already breached—and in front of the Saar. Based on the principle of delaying an attacker, then ejecting him with mobile reserves, the West Wall by 1945 had lost much of its effectiveness, both from a lack of reserves and from the fact that many of the emplacements could not accommodate contemporary weapons. Yet as many an Allied soldier already had learned, concrete in almost any form can lend real substance to a defense.[31]

Before the entire Allied front would rest on reasonably economical natural obstacles, and thus before the last offensive could develop in full force, four matters of unfinished business in addition to reconquest of the Ardennes remained to be dealt with. First, the enemy's second winter counteroffensive, which had started on New Year's Eve in Alsace, would have to be contained and any gains wiped out. Second, the enemy's hold-out position around Colmar would have to be erased. Third, the Germans would have to be driven from an angle formed by confluence of the Saar and Moselle Rivers, known as the Saar-Moselle triangle. And fourth, an-

---

[31] For a detailed description of the West Wall, see MacDonald, *The Siegfried Line Campaign.*

other hold-out position in the north in an angle formed by juncture of the Roer and Maas Rivers, a so-called Heinsberg pocket, would have to be eliminated.

Execution of the first two tasks, both in Alsace, would so occupy the Seventh U.S. and First French Armies, operating under General Devers's 6th Army Group, all through January and February that only in March would these two armies be able to join the final drive.[32] Elimination of the Saar-Moselle triangle, on the other hand, the Third Army would accomplish as a logical ex-

pansion of its developing role in the last offensive. Meanwhile, the British would eliminate the Heinsberg pocket before their assignment in the last offensive came due.

Thus the birth of the last offensive occurred in January in the Ardennes. There the First Army at last could strike back at the forces that had hit without warning in December, and there the Third Army might reorient its operations away from the local objective of succoring Bastogne to the broader assignment of pushing in the bulge and driving to the Rhine.

---

[32] Smith, The Riviera to the Rhine.

CHAPTER II

Victory in the Ardennes

"If you go into that death-trap of the Ardennes," General Charles Louis Marie Lanzerac reputedly told a fellow French officer in 1914, "you will never come out." [1] This remark for a long time typified the attitude of the French and their allies toward the Ardennes. It was a region to be avoided.

For centuries before 1914, warfare, like commerce, had skirted the Ardennes to north or south; yet at the start of the Great War, Helmuth von Moltke, under influence of the Schlieffen Plan, had sent three armies totaling almost a million men directly through the Ardennes. Although not constituting the German main effort, these armies contributed to it by outflanking hasty Allied attempts to form a line against the main blow on the Belgian plain. In 1940, expecting a repetition of the 1914 maneuver, the French had entrusted defense of the Ardennes to reserve divisions while concentrating their battle-worthy forces across the gateway to the plain. That had led to breakthrough by panzer columns at Sedan and Dinant.

Although made against scattered opposition consisting sometimes of nothing more imposing than horse cavalry, these speedy German conquests tended to obscure the fact that the Ardennes is a major barrier presenting the most rugged face of any terrain from the Vosges Mountains to the North Sea. While the highest elevations are less than 2,500 feet above sea level, deep and meandering defiles cut by myriad creeks and small rivers sharply restrict and canalize movement either along or across the grain of the land. (*Map III*)

Properly a part of a vast, high plateau lying mostly inside Germany, the Ardennes and its contiguous region, the Eifel, are separated from the rest of the plateau by the accidents of the Moselle and Rhine Rivers. The Ardennes and Eifel are divided only by the artificial barrier of an international frontier. It was back across this frontier into the casemates of the West Wall and the forests cloaking them that the Allies had to drive the Germans before victory in the Ardennes might be consummated and the final offensive in Europe begun in earnest.

The Ardennes encompasses all the grand duchy of Luxembourg, that part of southern and eastern Belgium bounded on the west and north by the gorge of the Meuse River, and a small portion of northern France. It can be divided into two unequal parts, the smaller Low Ardennes in the northwest, into which the winter counteroffensive had achieved only minor penetration, and the High

---

[1] For details on the military history and terrain of the Ardennes, see Charles B. MacDonald, "The Neglected Ardennes," *Military Review*, Vol. 43, No. 4 (April 1963), pp. 74–89.

or True Ardennes in the northeast, center, and south, covering some three-fourths of the entire region.

Stretching westward from the German frontier in something of the shape of an isosceles triangle, the High Ardennes encompasses in its northern angle a marshy ridgeline near Spa and Malmédy called the Hohe Venn or Hautes Fanges, meaning high marshland. The highest point in the Ardennes is here (2,276 feet). Southwest of the Hohe Venn along the northwestern edge of the triangle is another stretch of high, marshy ground containing the headwaters of three picturesque rivers, the Plateau des Tailles. The central portion of the triangle, around Bastogne and Neufchâteau, is high but less sharply incised than other portions. In the southwestern corner stands the Forêt des Ardennes, or Ardennes Forest, a name which Americans with a penchant for generalized inaccuracy gave to the entire region of the Ardennes. Across the border in Luxembourg lies sharply convoluted terrain that the natives with an eye toward tourism call la Petite Suisse or Little Switzerland.

A picture-postcard pastoral region marked by few towns with populations of more than a few thousand, the Ardennes nevertheless has an extensive network of improved roads knotted together at critical points such as Bastogne and St. Vith, the latter in the northeast close to the German border. Like the general lay of the land, the major roads favor military movement from northeast to southwest, or the reverse. By holding fast in front of the Hohe Venn, American troops in December 1944 had denied the Germans roads in the north with more favorable

orientation toward the German goal of Antwerp, forcing them into an all-out fight for Bastogne and roads emanating from that town to the northwest. As the Americans headed back toward the German frontier, the orientation of the roadnet would afford some advantage.

In plunging out of the Eifel, the Germans had attained their deepest penetration on Christmas Eve when armored spearheads got within four miles of the Meuse River. The bulge in American lines reached a maximum depth of not quite sixty miles. At the base, the bulge extended from near Monschau in the north to the vicinity of Echternach in the south, just under fifty miles. It encompassed much of Little Switzerland, the Plateau des Tailles, and some of the more open highland around Bastogne; but it fell short of the two vital objectives, the Meuse and the Hohe Venn.

American offensive reaction to the German blow had begun even before the penetration reached its high-water mark. As early as dawn of 22 December one division of the Third Army had opened limited objective attacks to stabilize the southern shoulder of the bulge near its base while an entire corps began a drive toward Bastogne. On Christmas Day an armored division of the First Army had wiped out the spearhead near the Meuse.

As General Eisenhower on 19 December had met with his top subordinates to plan opening countermoves, the obvious method was to attack simultaneously from north and south to saw off the penetration at its base close along the German border; but several considerations denied this approach. Still heavily involved trying to prevent expansion of the bulge to north and northwest, the First Army was in no position yet to hit the northern flank. Nor could the Third Army, which had to provide the troops for striking the southern flank, make available immediately enough divisions to do more than stabilize the southern flank and possibly relieve Bastogne. Because Bastogne was the key to the roadnet not only to the northwest but to southwest and south as well, and since nobody knew for sure at the time which way the Germans wanted to go, the need to hold Bastogne never came into question.[2]

This early commitment to relieving and reinforcing Bastogne in large measure dictated the way the Allied command would go about eliminating the penetration, a drive to squeeze the bulge at its waist rather than its base, then a turn to push in what was left. It was a conservative approach but one necessitated, at least in the opening moves, by the surprise, early success, and persisting strength of the German assault.

Yet once Bastogne was relieved on the 26th, the way was open for another solution, the classic though venturesome maneuver for eliminating a deep penetration, cutting it off at its base. This the Third Army commander, General Patton, proposed, a drive by his army north and northeast from Luxembourg City into a westward-protruding portion of the Eifel to link with a complementary thrust by the First Army in the vicinity of Pruem, a road center a little over ten miles inside Germany, southeast of St. Vith.[3]

Although Patton's opposite on the

north flank, General Hodges of the First Army, agreed with this approach in principle, he advised against it because he deemed the roadnet close to the border in the north inadequate to sustain the large force, heavy in armor, that would be necessary for the cleaving blow essential to a successful amputation. Nor did the 12th Army Group commander, General Bradley, endorse it. Bradley was concerned about the effect of winter weather, both on the counterattack itself and on air support, and of the inhospitable terrain. He was worried too about a lack of reserves. Already the 6th Army Group had extended its lines dangerously to release the bulk of the Third Army for the fight in the Ardennes. Although the matter of reserves might have been remedied by greater commitment of British troops, the British commander who also controlled the First U.S. Army, Field Marshal Montgomery, wanted to avoid major realignment of British forces lest it unduly delay return to the scheduled main effort in the north against the Ruhr.

On 28 December General Eisenhower met with Montgomery to plot the role of the First Army in the offensive. Already in hand was General Bradley's view that the Third Army should strike not at the base of the bulge but from Bastogne generally northeast toward St. Vith. As formulated after earlier conversations with General Hodges and corps commanders of the First Army, Montgomery's decision was for the First Army to link with the Third Army at Houffalize, nine miles northeast of Bastogne, then broaden the attack to drive generally east on St. Vith. Noting that he was moving British units against the tip of the bulge to assist the First Army to con-

---

[2] For an account of early decisions, see Cole, *The Ardennes*, pp. 487–88, 509–10.

[3] Cole, *The Ardennes*, pp. 610–13, provides a detailed discussion of the deliberations. See also Pogue, *The Supreme Command*, pp. 383, 393.

centrate, Montgomery indicated that the attack was to begin within a day or two of the New Year.

As the old year neared an end and the two American armies prepared their offensives, this was the picture around the periphery of the German penetration:

From a point north of Monschau marking the boundary between the First and Ninth Armies, the sector of the V Corps (Maj. Gen. Leonard T. Gerow) extended southward as far as Elsenborn, thereby encompassing high ground serving as an outpost for the Hohe Venn, then swung west along a deep-cut creek to Waimes, where V Corps responsibility yielded to the XVIII Airborne Corps (Maj. Gen. Matthew B. Ridgway). The line continued to follow the creek through Malmédy to Stavelot, thence along the Ambleve River for a mile or two to Trois Ponts. At that point, the forward trace extended cross-country to the southwest along no clearly defined feature. Where it cut across the Lienne River near Bra, the sector of the VII Corps (Maj. Gen. J. Lawton Collins) began. The VII Corps line extended southwest across the Bastogne-Liège highway to the Ourthe River near Hotton.

The Ourthe was, temporarily, the First Army's right boundary. On the other side Field Marshal Montgomery had inserted under his direct command contingents of the 30 British Corps. Running from the Meuse south of Dinant generally eastward to Houffalize, the boundary between the 21 and 12th Army Groups split the bulge roughly in half.

From the army group boundary southeast to St. Hubert, fifteen miles west of Bastogne, no formal line existed. Patrols of an American regiment hard hit early

in the fighting, a reconnaissance squadron, and a French parachute battalion covered the sector, while a fresh American airborne division backed it up from positions along the Meuse. The sector was part of the responsibility of the VIII Corps (Maj. Gen. Troy H. Middleton), the corps that had been hardest hit by the opening blows of the counteroffensive. Serving at this point under the Third Army, the main body of the VIII Corps was located between St. Hubert and Bastogne.

In the sector of the VIII Corps, at Bastogne itself, and southeast of the town, the front was in a state of flux because here General Patton had begun opening moves in his part of the offensive two days before the New Year. Charged with reaching the First Army at Houffalize, the VIII Corps was to pass to the west of Bastogne, then swing northeast on Houffalize. East and southeast of Bastogne, the III Corps (Maj. Gen. John Millikin) was to broaden to the east the corridor its armor had forged into the town, then continue northeast toward St. Vith. Holding the south flank of the bulge generally along the Sûre River east to the German border, the XII Corps (Maj. Gen. Manton S. Eddy) was to join the offensive later.[4]

That these opening blows by the Third Army collided head on with a major German effort to sever the corridor into Bastogne, again encircle the town, and take it, contributed to the fluid situation prevailing there. Night was falling on the second day of the new year before the Americans around Bastogne could claim that they had parried

---

[4] A detailed account of the first four days of the Third Army's offensive is provided in Cole, *The Ardennes*, ch. XXIV.

what would turn out to be the stronger of two final German blows aimed at seizing the town.

German dispositions within the bulge reflected the broad pattern shaped by early stages of the counteroffensive, plus the recent emphasis on taking Bastogne. Three infantry divisions on the south wing of the *Fifteenth Army* (General der Infanterie Gustav von Zangen) opposed the V Corps in the angle at the northern base of the bulge. The *Sixth Panzer Army* (Generaloberst der Waffen-SS Josef "Sepp" Dietrich), comprising six divisions, opposed the XVIII Airborne Corps and the VII Corps. Opposite the British in the tip of the bulge and part of the VIII Corps were contingents of three divisions of the *Fifth Panzer Army* (General der Panzertruppen Hasso von Manteuffel), while as a result of the efforts to capture Bastogne the bulk of that army—nine other divisions and a special armored brigade—was concentrated around Bastogne and to the southeast of the town. The remainder of the southern flank was the responsibility of the *Seventh Army* (General der Panzertruppen Erich Brandenberger), whose five divisions and several separate units of battalion or *Kampfgruppe* (task force) size extended the line to the border near Echternach and southward along the frontier as far as the Moselle.[5]

The First Army's Attack

As finally determined by Field Marshal Montgomery, the First Army's attack was to begin on 3 January. Since the troops around Bastogne had stopped a major German effort to take that town

---

[5] Situation Map, *OKW/WFSt Op (H) West (3)*, 4 Jan 45.

late on 2 January, the Third Army might be able to renew its offensive in earnest on the same day.

A veteran force that had come ashore on the beaches of Normandy, liberated Paris, and penetrated the West Wall around Aachen, the First Army on the eve of resuming the offensive contained thirteen divisions. Included were three armored divisions, one of which had been badly mauled in a heroic defense of St. Vith and two of which had given as good as they took in later stages of the Ardennes fight. These two were old-style heavy divisions, the 2d and 3d. A loan of 200 British Shermans had helped replace tank losses incurred in the December fighting, and all except a few files had been filled in infantry ranks.

A calm—almost taciturn—infantryman, General Hodges had assumed command of the First Army in Normandy when General Bradley had moved up to army group. Shaken in the early days of the counteroffensive by what had happened to his troops, Hodges had come back strong in a manner that drew praise from his British superior, Montgomery. Reflecting both Bradley's interest and his own, Hodges' staff was heavy on infantrymen, including the chief of staff, Maj. Gen. William G. Kean. Two of the three corps commanders then under the army, Generals Gerow and Collins, had long been members of the First Army's team, and both enjoyed a close rapport with Hodges.

The burden of the First Army's attack was to fall on General Collins's VII Corps, which Montgomery had been carefully hoarding since early in the counteroffensive for just such a role. General Hodges directed this corps to advance generally southeast between the

Ourthe and Lienne Rivers to seize forward slopes of the high marshland of the Plateau des Tailles, which command the town of Houffalize. General Ridgway's XVIII Airborne Corps meanwhile was to advance its right flank to conform with progress of the VII Corps while Gerow's V Corps held in place. Parts of two British divisions were to push in the bulge from the west, eventually to be pinched out short of Houffalize by the converging First and Third Armies.[6]

Heavily reinforced, the VII Corps contained almost a hundred thousand men, including the two armored divisions, three infantry divisions, and twelve field artillery battalions in addition to divisional artillery. Each infantry division had the normal attachments of a medium tank battalion and a tank destroyer battalion.

Two of the infantry divisions, the 75th and 84th, held a 14-mile corps front extending from the vicinity of Bra southwestward to the Ourthe near Hotton. In an attempt to trap those German troops still in the tip of the bulge, General Collins planned to open the attack with his two powerful armored divisions in hope of a swift penetration across the high marshland to his objective twelve miles to the southeast. As the armor passed through the infantry line, the 84th Division was to follow the 2d Armored Division to mop up while the 83d Infantry Division did the same for the 3d Armored. The 75th Division was to pass into corps reserve.[7]

The estimate of the enemy situation

GENERAL HODGES

by the VII Corps G–2, Col. Leslie D. Carter, was basically correct. First concern of the Germans, Colonel Carter believed, was Bastogne. Until the south flank could be stabilized there, the Germans to the west were liable to entrapment. A number of divisions that earlier had fought the VII Corps had moved south to help at Bastogne, their departure leaving *Sixth Panzer Army* a blunted residue of what had once been the steel skewer of the counteroffensive. Of the panzer army's six remaining divisions, three under the *II SS Panzer Corps* (General der Waffen-SS Willi Bittrich) confronted the VII Corps: the *12th Volks Grenadier Division* opposite the left wing of the corps, the *560th Volks Grenadier Division* in the center, and the *2d SS Panzer Division* opposite the right wing. First-line German units,

---

[6] FUSA Ltr of Instrs, 1 Jan 45, FUSA Ltrs of Instrs file, Jan 45; First Army Rpt of Opns, 1 Aug 44–22 Feb 45, pp. 126–27.

[7] VII Corps FO 14, 2 Jan 45, VII Corps FO file, Jan 45.

these divisions had taken sizable losses
during the counteroffensive; strengths
varied from 2,500 men in the *560th* to
6,000 in the panzer division. Preoccupation with the Bastogne sector and with
the new counteroffensive (*NORD-
WIND*) in Alsace would restrict severely, Colonel Carter noted, the reserves
that might oppose the American attack.[8]

What Colonel Carter could not know
was that on the very eve of the First
Army's attacks, German field commanders were conceding defeat, not only in
terms of the broad objectives of the
counteroffensive, which as early as
Christmas Eve they had come to accept,
but also of the limited objective of taking
Bastogne. The failure to sever the
American corridor to Bastogne had convinced the commander of the *Fifth Panzer Army,* General von Manteuffel, that
the time had come to abandon all
thought of continuing the offensive in
the Ardennes. Lest the troops farthest
west be trapped, Manteuffel appealed
late on 2 January to Field Marshal
Model, commander of *Army Group B,*
for permission to pull back to a line anchored on Houffalize.

Although Model apparently agreed
professionally with Manteuffel, he was
powerless to act because of Hitler's long-
professed decree that no commander give
up ground voluntarily unless Hitler himself endorsed the move in advance, something that seldom happened. Since the
unsuccessful attempt on his life the preceding July, the Fuehrer had come to
accept any indication of withdrawal as

evidence of defeatism, even treason.
Model and even the Commander in
Chief West, Field Marshal von Rundstedt, had to live with the fiction that
nobody ever withdrew.

Even though Hitler himself the next
day, 3 January, would issue his qualified
admission of failure under the original
concept in the Ardennes, he had arrived
by this time at definite ideas of how the
salient still might be turned to German
advantage, and withdrawal had no part
in the plan. Taking Bastogne did. Despite the failure of the latest attempt,
Model and his staff at *Army Group B*
were compelled to continue planning for
yet another attack on Bastogne, this to
begin on 4 January.[9]

As the hour for American attack
neared, the weather augury was anything
but encouraging. It was bitterly cold.
The ground was frozen and covered with
snow. Roads were icy. A low, foglike
overcast so restricted visibility that
planned support from fighter-bombers of
the IX Tactical Air Command (Maj.
Gen. Elwood R. Quesada) was hardly to
be assured. Yet since hope of improvement in the weather was dim, the attack
was to proceed. Top commanders in the
First Army had for some time been
chafing to shift to the offensive lest the
Third Army be called upon to do it all,
and delay would give the Germans in the
tip of the bulge that much more time
to escape.[10]

---

[8] VII Corps Annex 2 to FO 14 and Incl 1, VII
Corps FO file, Jan 45; MS # A-924, Operation of
Sixth Panzer Army, 1944-45 (Generalmajor der
Waffen-SS Fritz Kraemer, CofS, *Sixth Panzer
Army*).

[9] German material is from Cole, *The Ardennes,*
pp. 647-48. See also MS # A-858, The Course of
Events of the German Offensive in the Ardennes,
16 Dec 1944-14 Jan 1945 (Maj. Percy E. Schramm,
keeper of the *OKW/WFSt* War Diary).

[10] VII Corps AAR, Jan 45; Ltr, Bradley to
Hodges, 26 Dec 44, 12th AGp 371.3, Military Objectives, vol. IV; Diary of Maj. William C. Sylvan,
aide-de-camp to Gen Hodges (hereafter cited as
Sylvan Diary), entry of 2 Jan 45, copy in OCMH.

Stretching all the way across the zone of attack of the VII Corps, the high marshes of the Plateau des Tailles added a third dimension to the obstacles of woods and deep-cut streambeds that are common in the Ardennes, thus making the roadnet the number one tactical objective. Only one major road, the Liège-Houffalize-Bastogne highway, led directly to any part of the objective. A web of secondary roads connecting the villages in the region would have to serve as main avenues of advance despite numerous bridges, defiles, and hairpin turns.

Preoccupation with roads was apparent from the first objectives assigned the armored divisions. Both were to aim at high ground commanding roads leading approximately four miles to the southeast to the La Roche–Salmchâteau highway, a lateral route from which a number of local roads in addition to the Liège-Bastogne highway provide access to the forward slopes of the Plateau des Tailles. On the left the 3d Armored Division (Maj. Gen. Maurice Rose) would have only one road at the start, while on the right the 2d Armored Division (Maj. Gen. Ernest N. Harmon) could employ both the main highway leading to Houffalize and a secondary route to the southwest. Cutting the lateral La Roche–Salmchâteau highway would eliminate one of only two escape routes left in this sector to the Germans still standing to the west. Seizing the high ground overlooking Houffalize would eliminate the other.[11]

Hardly had the van of the armor passed through the infantry line early on

GENERAL COLLINS

3 January when the hostile weather and terrain began to have effect. So foggy was the atmosphere that not a single tactical plane could support the attack at any time during the day. Observation by artillery planes was possible for no more than an hour. It was a pattern that would undergo little change for the next fortnight. On only one day in two weeks would visibility allow tactical aircraft to operate all day; on only two other days would fighter-bombers be able to take to the air at all.

Much of the time infantry and armor advanced through snow flurries interspersed with light rain on a few occasions when temperatures rose above freezing. During late afternoon and evening of 7 January, a heavy snowfall added several inches to the cover already on the ground. Drifts piled in some places to a depth of three to four feet.

On the first day, the enemy from his

---

[11] Unless otherwise noted, the tactical story is based on the field orders, after action reports, and journals of the VII Corps and subordinate units.

GENERAL VON MANTEUFFEL

on the ice. Two antitank guns of the 84th Division and their prime movers skidded, jackknifed, collided, and effectively blocked a road for several hours. Two trucks towing 105-mm. howitzers skidded and plunged off a cliff.

FIELD MARSHAL MODEL

outposts offered relatively light resistance, though antitank minefields hidden by the snow caused several delays and in late afternoon a force of infantry supported by from six to ten tanks of the *2d SS Panzer Division* counterattacked forward units on the right wing. On the next and succeeding days, resistance stiffened. Artillery, antitank, mortar, and *Nebelwerfer* fire increased. Battalion-size counterattacks supported by a few tanks or self-propelled guns increased too, though seldom did they accomplish more than to delay local advances for a few hours.

The terrain and the weather were the big obstacles. Whenever the tanks found fairly level terrain, they could move cross-country over the frozen ground with some facility, but more often than not the ground was hilly, wooded, or marshy, confining the tanks to the icy roads. In advancing up a steep hill on 5 January, eight tanks of a task force of the 2d Armored Division stalled in a row

Deliberate roadblocks consisting of felled trees with antitank mines embedded on the approaches usually could be eliminated only by dismounted infantry making slow, sometimes costly flanking moves through adjacent woods. In other cases, blown bridges blocked the routes. Sometimes fords or bypasses to other roads were available, but usually infantrymen had to wade an icy stream and create a small bridgehead while tanks awaited construction of a new bridge. Because bridge sites seldom could be cleared immediately of enemy fire, engineers did most of their work after darkness blinded German gunners.

Advances on the first day against the enemy's outposts averaged about two miles, but progress slowed on succeeding days. Facing the bulk of the German armor in this sector, the 2d Armored Division on the right encountered particularly stubborn German stands on both its routes of advance. When the neighboring 3d Armored on the third day, 6 January, cut the lateral La Roche–Salmchâteau highway, General Collins sent part of the division westward to seize the intersection with the main highway to Houffalize in an effort to loosen the opposition in front of the other division. It was late the next day before the Americans gained the intersection, which they knew as Parker's Crossroads after the commander of a task force that had made an epic stand there during the winter counteroffensive. This did the job expected; late on the same day, the 7th, a task force of the 2d Armored Division also cut the La Roche–Salmchâteau road.

Artillery was hamstrung throughout by poor observation resulting from the weather, the woods, and the broken ground. Since weather denied air support on the opening day, General Collins canceled a preliminary artillery bombardment as well in hope of gaining some advantage from surprise. Artillery subsequently averaged about 19,000 rounds a day. Each armored division expended about 7,000 rounds daily, corps guns fired another 3,500 rounds, and infantry divisional artillery and British pieces west of the Ourthe provided additional support.

While the role of the infantry divisions was nominally supporting, it turned out to be more than that. In the main the 83d and 84th Divisions were to mop up bypassed resistance, but when the first shock of the armor failed to produce a penetration, the role of the infantry increased. Both divisions from the first contributed a regiment each for attachment to the armor, and before the fighting was over both would incur appreciably greater casualties than either of the armored divisions.

For all the grudging nature of the defense, the enemy produced few surprises. Through the first week, full responsibility for defense lay with the three units of the *Sixth Panzer Army* previously identified, the *2d SS Panzer* and *12th* and *560th Volks Grenadier Divisions*. At times, the panzer division loaned some of its tanks to neighboring infantry units, as on 5 January when four tanks reinforced a battalion of the *12th Volks Grenadier Division* in an effort to retake a hill from the 3d Armored Division. The only outside help came from assorted engineer and low-grade replacement battalions. By the end of the week all three German divisions were reduced on occasion to using artillerymen and other supporting troops as infantry.

Near the end of the first week, on 8 January, Hitler at last authorized a withdrawal, not all the way back to a line anchored on Houffalize as General von Manteuffel had urged but only out of the extreme tip of the bulge to a line anchored on a great eastward loop of the Ourthe River some five miles west of Houffalize. Because of the point at which Hitler drew the withdrawal line, only a few troops of the *Sixth Panzer Army,* those on the extreme west wing near La Roche, were involved. Those authorized to withdraw were mainly contingents of the *Fifth Panzer Army* facing the British and the U.S. VIII Corps west of Bastogne.

While the units of the *Sixth Panzer Army* were to continue to hold, Dietrich's headquarters was to pull out, gradually relinquishing control to the *Fifth Panzer Army.* Thereupon, the two SS panzer corps headquarters and four SS panzer divisions that originally had belonged to the *Sixth Panzer Army* were to join Dietrich's headquarters in the rear near St. Vith, there to form a reserve to guard against attacks near the base of the bulge. This was, in effect, tacit admission—Hitler's first—that the Ardennes counteroffensive had failed utterly.[12]

Reflecting the withdrawal, resistance on the right wing of the VII Corps gradually slackened. Patrols on the 10th entered La Roche, while British troops on the opposite bank of the Ourthe reported no contact with the enemy. Although the British re-established contact on subsequent days, they met only light covering detachments and, in keeping with Montgomery's desire to avoid major British commitment, pressed their advance only enough to spare the Americans flanking fire from Germans west of the Ourthe.

The fight was as dogged as ever on the other wing, where in deference to marshy ground and an impoverished roadnet leading to the final objectives on the southeastern slopes of the Plateau des

Tailles, the 83d Division (Maj. Gen. Robert C. Macon) on 9 January assumed the assault role on the left wing of the VII Corps. It took the infantry two days to break into and clear a village south of the La Roche–Salmchâteau highway and another day to beat off counterattacks. Not until forcibly rooted out would the Germans budge from any position.

At the same time, the 82d Airborne Division (Maj. Gen. James M. Gavin) of General Ridgway's XVIII Airborne Corps had the job of protecting the left flank of the VII Corps. To do this, the airborne division was to press forward to the line of the Salm River, which like the Lienne and the Ourthe has its source in the Plateau des Tailles.[13]

Assisted by an attached separate regiment, the 517th Parachute Infantry, the airborne division jumped off along with the VII Corps on 3 January. Like the armored divisions, the paratroopers and glidermen met resistance immediately from the weather, the terrain, and, to a lesser extent, the enemy. The roadnet was even more restricted than in front of the VII Corps, and a thick forest stretched across the center of the division's zone.

Possibly because the enemy relied too heavily on the forest as an obstacle, the 82d's 505th Parachute Infantry found relatively few defenders. In three days the paratroopers advanced four miles to reach the far edge of the forest overlooking the valley of the Salm.

Close alongside the boundary with the VII Corps, the 517th Parachute Infantry made only limited progress until it turned abruptly on 7 January to take the enemy in flank. The next day the para-

---

[12] Magna E. Bauer, The German Withdrawal From the Ardennes, prepared to complement this volume, annotated copy in OCMH.

[13] The tactical story is from official records of the XVIII Airborne Corps and subordinate units.

troopers drove all Germans before them east of the Salm and sent patrols to range as far as two miles beyond the river. On the 9th they established a small bridgehead across the Salm to be used as a stepping stone when the offensive turned in the direction of St. Vith.

Another division of the XVIII Airborne Corps, the 30th (Maj. Gen. Leland S. Hobbs) did much the same thing. On 6 January the division began limited objective attacks with an attached regiment, the 28th Division's 112th Infantry, to forge a bridgehead two miles deep in an angle formed by the joining of the Salm and Ambleve Rivers.

Resistance in the zone of the VII Corps continued stiffest opposite the left wing along a land bridge between headwaters of the Salm and the Ourthe. There the Germans occupied a forest mass in strength with contingents of the *9th SS Panzer Division* moving in to support a faltering *12th Volks Grenadier Division.* The infantry of the 83d Division still was finding the going slow when the 3d Armored Division's Reconnaissance Battalion discovered a network of back roads and trails less staunchly defended.

The reconnaissance troops having shown the way, the division commander, General Rose, early on 13 January sent a combat command to trace the route, break out of the woods, and cut the lateral highway that follows the forward slopes of the Plateau des Tailles en route from Houffalize toward St. Vith. Although the Germans still made a fight of it for towns along the highway, the cut by the armor effectively blocked this last major route of escape for German troops in the vicinity of Houffalize.

As night fell on the 13th, men of the VII Corps could see to the south light-ninglike flashes of artillery pieces supporting the Third Army. Patrols prepared to probe in that direction the next day, eager to end the separation the counteroffensive had imposed between the First and Third Armies.

Getting this far had cost the VII Corps almost 5,000 casualties, a high but hardly alarming figure in view of the harsh weather and terrain. Although fighting a deliberate withdrawal action with determination and skill, the Germans had lost several hundred more than that in prisoners alone.

A Grim Struggle Around Bastogne

Having collided head on with another German effort to capture Bastogne, the Third Army's four-day-old offensive had reached, on the eve of the First Army's attack, positions that mirrored a combination of American and German intentions. Making a main effort against the corridor southeast of Bastogne, Manteuffel's *Fifth Panzer Army* with some help from the right wing of Brandenberger's *Seventh Army* had managed to retain or establish positions that formed a salient four miles wide and four miles deep into lines of the Third Army's III Corps. That the salient was no deeper represented a defensive triumph for the III Corps but at the same time marked a failure thus far of this phase of General Patton's offensive. East and north of Bastogne, a line roughly three miles from the town that stalwart soldiers of the 101st Airborne Division and assorted lesser units had established and held through the days of encirclement remained intact. Against a German attack west and southwest of Bastogne, troops of the VIII Corps had managed not only to contain the thrust but also to make gains of their own, so that by nightfall of 2 January the front line ran generally west from Bastogne toward St. Hubert.[14]

As the Third Army prepared to continue its offensive, the original plan remained unchanged. While the III Corps advanced generally northeast, in the process eliminating the salient southeast of Bastogne, the VIII Corps was to pivot on the town and swing northeast to establish contact with the First Army's VII Corps at Houffalize.

Intending to return to the offensive on 4 January, the Germans proposed a change in their approach. Although Rundstedt at *OB WEST* ordered another attempt to sever the corridor into Bastogne, Field Marshal Model at *Army Group B* pleaded that the Americans had become so strong around the salient southeast of the town and had confined it so tightly that no additional German units could be inserted. Model suggested instead an attack to push in the northern and northeastern periphery of the Bastogne defense. There the ground was more suited to tank warfare and General von Manteuffel might employ the *I SS Panzer Corps* (Generalleutnant der Waffen-SS Hermann Priess) with the *9th* and *12th SS Panzer Divisions* and the *Fuehrer Grenadier Brigade,* the last an elite unit originally drawn from Hitler's household guard, consisting of a battalion each of tanks, panzer grenadiers, and foot soldiers.[15]

Possibly because Model was one of the Fuehrer's more faithful disciples among top commanders, Hitler listened to this change. What mattered to the Fuehrer was not how Bastogne was taken but that

it be taken. As revealed on 3 January when he acknowledged that the counteroffensive would not gain Antwerp or even the Meuse, Hitler required Bastogne as a vital anchor for holding the bulge. Bastogne's nexus of roads was essential for securing the southern flank and thus for helping the *Sixth Panzer Army* to resist the American offensive from the north that had begun that day.

In creating the bulge in the Ardennes, Hitler reasoned, he had forced General Eisenhower to employ almost all his resources. The desperate commitment of elite airborne divisions to brutal defensive battles was in Hitler's mind proof enough of that. By holding the bulge, the Germans might keep the Allies widely stretched while pulling out some of their own units to attack at weak points along the extended Western Front and thereby prevent the Allies from concentrating for a major drive. Operation *NORDWIND* in Alsace, Hitler rationalized, was the first of these intended strikes; yet only with Bastogne in hand was the new stratagem practical in the long run.[16]

As finally determined, the main effort of the new attack on Bastogne by the *I SS Panzer Corps* was to be made astride the Houffalize highway. Since some units would arrive too late to attack early on the 4th, only the *9th Panzer* and *26th Volks Grenadier Divisions* west of the highway were to attack at first, this in midmorning, while the *12th SS Panzer Division* and a unit that only recently had been brought into the Ardennes from the Aachen sector, the *340th Volks Grenadier Division,* attacked at noon along the east side of the highway. The

---

[14] See Cole, *The Ardennes,* ch. XXIV and Map X.
[15] MS # A-858 (Schramm).

---

[16] *Ibid.*

Fuehrer Grenadier Brigade was to serve as a reserve. The *XLVII Panzer Corps* (General der Panzertruppen Heinrich Freiherr von Luettwitz) west of Bastogne and the divisions in the salient southeast of the town were to hold in place, counterattacking in strength where necessary to maintain their positions or assist the main attack.[17]

Having fought through early stages of the counteroffensive as part of the *Sixth Panzer Army,* all divisions of General Priess's *I SS Panzer Corps* except the *340th* had taken heavy losses. Between them the two SS panzer divisions had 55 tanks, only one more than normally supported every U.S. infantry division. Although one of the so-called *Volks Artillery Corps* that Hitler had created especially for the counteroffensive was to be moved in to strengthen existing artillery, a shortage of gasoline made it problematical when this force and even some of the subordinate units of the panzer and volks grenadier divisions would arrive.

Top commanders hid their concern, but neither Manteuffel, who already had recommended stopping all attacks in the Ardennes, nor his superior, Model, held out much hope for the new attack. This state of mind was clearly indicated when they released without protest to *OB WEST* for transfer to Alsace the corps headquarters that had been controlling the divisions in the salient southeast of Bastogne. If the superior forces the Germans previously had employed at Bastogne against limited American strength

had failed, what hope with makeshift forces now that the Americans had sharply increased their commitment? [18]

For renewing the Third Army's offensive around Bastogne, General Patton had eight divisions. East and southeast of the town, Millikin's III Corps had three veteran units, the 6th Armored and 26th and 35th Infantry Divisions. Holding part of Bastogne's old perimeter defense to north and northwest, the 101st Airborne Division with an attached combat command of the 10th Armored Division was the only readily available experienced force in Middleton's VIII Corps. Middleton had in addition the 17th Airborne Division and two newcomers to the front, the 11th Armored and 87th Divisions, which General Bradley had specifically directed to be employed at Bastogne lest Patton stint the offensive there in favor of his cherished drive near the base of the bulge.[19] In the four days of fighting preceding renewal of the offensive on 3 January, the 87th and the armor had taken substantial losses, leaving the armored division "badly disorganized" after loss of a third of its tanks.[20] To enable the armor to catch its breath, the new airborne division was to enter the line on 3 January. Meanwhile, an eighth division, the veteran 4th Armored, had been pulled into

---

[17] MS # B-779, The *I SS Panzer Corps* During the Ardennes Offensive, 15 December 1944–25 January 1945 (Col Rudolf Lehmann, CofS); MS # A-939, The Assignment of the *XLVII Panzer Corps* in the Ardennes, 1944–45 (General der Panzertruppen Heinrich von Luettwitz).

[18] MSS # B-779 (Lehmann); # B-151a, *Fifth Panzer Army,* Ardennes Offensive (General der Panzertruppen Hasso von Manteuffel); # A-940, *XLVII Panzer Corps* in the Ardennes Offensive (General der Panzertruppen Heinrich von Luettwitz). See also Charles von Luttichau, Key Dates During the Ardennes Offensive 1944, Part II, MS prepared to complement this volume, copy in OCMH.

[19] On this point, see Cole, *The Ardennes,* pp. 612–13.

[20] Army Commander's Notes on the Bastogne Operation, TUSA AAR, 1 Aug 44–8 May 45.

reserve after its tank strength had fallen dangerously low as a result of heavy fighting through much of December.

The remaining six of a total of fourteen divisions in the Third Army were split equally between Eddy's XII Corps along the generally quiescent line of the Sûre River running eastward to the German frontier and Maj. Gen. Walton H. Walker's XX Corps. The latter had not been drawn into the Ardennes fight and continued to hold positions in Lorraine.[21]

The Third Army and its veteran commander, George Patton, had entered the campaign in France in early August to exploit the breakout from Normandy engineered by Hodges' First Army. While one corps turned westward against the ports of Brittany, the bulk of the army had driven swiftly eastward across northern France until a gasoline drought forced a halt at the border of Lorraine. Through the fall Patton's troops had fought doggedly across water-logged terrain to gain a small foothold within the West Wall at Saarlautern just as the Ardennes counteroffensive began. While the XX Corps continued to hold that position, Patton had turned the rest of his army toward Bastogne.

Despite General Patton's affinity for armor, most of his staff and his corps commanders were infantrymen, including Eddy of the XII Corps, an old-timer with the Third Army; Walker of the XX Corps, another old-timer; and Middleton of the VIII Corps, whose command had made the sweep into Brittany before joining the First Army for a rendezvous with fate in the Ardennes and then a

return to the Third Army. Only Patton's chief of staff, Maj. Gen. Hobart R. Gay, and General Millikin of the III Corps, a relative newcomer to the Third Army, had been commissioned as cavalrymen.

Bitterly cold, stung by biting winds and driving snow, American troops on the frozen ground around Bastogne saw little change on 3 January in a pattern too long familiar. Many of the German units had fought here since before Christmas, such respected names as the *3d* and *15th Panzer Grenadier Divisions,* the *5th Parachute Division,* the *1st SS Panzer Division,* and the *Panzer Lehr Division,* the last so called because it originally had been a training unit. The place names too, after more than a fortnight of grim combat, were accustomed: Marvie, Wardin, Mageret, Longvilly, Oubourcy, Noville, Longchamps. So was the tactic of almost every attack followed by an immediate German riposte, intense shelling preceding a seemingly inevitable tank-supported counterattack.[22]

Early on the 3d the Germans surrounded a company of the 87th Division (Brig. Gen. John M. Lentz) on the west flank of the VIII Corps, though a relief column broke through before the day was out. In the afternoon tanks and infantry hit the 101st Airborne Division (Maj. Gen. Maxwell D. Taylor) at Longchamps and south of Noville, achieving some penetration at both places before the paratroopers rallied to re-establish their lines. Only the 6th Armored Division (Maj. Gen. Robert W. Grow) on the left wing of the III Corps generally east of Bastogne made any appreciable gain, an advance of from one to two

---

[21] The depleted 28th Division and a combat command of the 9th Armored Division were awaiting transfer from the Third Army.

[22] This account is from official unit records. German material is from manuscripts previously cited.

WIND-SWEPT SNOW IN THE ARDENNES

miles that took the battered villages of Oubourcy, Mageret, and Wardin.

The renewed German attempt to seize Bastogne began before dawn on the 4th when a regiment of the *15th Panzer Grenadier Division* attacked Longchamps in a token assist by Leuttwitz's *XLVII Panzer Corps* to a main assault that began a few hours later close by the road from Houffalize. Combat raged in this sector all morning, but at noon counterattacking paratroopers still maintained their hold on Longchamps, and intense artillery fire delivered in open, snow-covered fields had driven back

tanks and assault guns of the *9th SS Panzer Division*. The airborne troops and their armored support claimed to have destroyed during the day thirty-four German tanks.

East of the Houffalize highway and east of Bastogne, the *12th SS Panzer* and *340th Volks Grenadier Divisions* achieved greater success in the main German assault. Tank against tank, the German armor forced the 6th Armored Division to relinquish all three villages taken the day before, but once the American tanks had pulled back to high ground west of the villages the Germans could make no more headway. Here and elsewhere artillery pieces of the III and VIII Corps shared their power in moments of crisis to deal telling blows whenever the Germans massed and moved into the open.

From the moment the 6th Armored Division halted the panzers, the fighting around Bastogne again reverted to pattern. In combat as bitter as any during the counteroffensive, attack followed counterattack on both sides until it was scarcely possible to distinguish which was which.

Handicapped by piecemeal commitment of tardily arriving subordinate units, the I SS Panzer Corps could do little more than maintain the minor gains achieved against American armor on the 4th. West of Bastogne the XLVII Panzer Corps reacted so strongly to American efforts to renew the attack on the 4th with the inexperienced 17th Airborne Division (Maj. Gen. William M. Miley) that the division had to spend the next two days reorganizing and adjusting its positions. ("God, how green we are," said one regimental commander, "but we are learning fast and the next time we will beat them.") [23]

Nor could the infantry divisions of General Millikin's III Corps make any headway against the salient southeast of Bastogne. Late on the 5th Maj. Gen.

Paul W. Baade reluctantly asked and received permission to call off the attack in the southern part of his 35th Division's front; such a battle of attrition had it become that his men could hope to do no more for the moment than hold their own.

As was the case with the First Army, the Third Army could count on little help from its supporting aircraft of the XIX Tactical Air Command (Brig. Gen. Otto P. Weyland). So dismal was the weather that only briefly on one day, 5 January, were planes able to operate. In one way this was a blessing, since the weather also cut short a resurgence that had begun around Bastogne a few days earlier by a long-dormant Luftwaffe.

For all the success in blunting the German thrust on the 4th, few Americans viewed the situation with any complacency. Visiting the front late on the 4th during a German artillery bombardment, the army commander, General Patton, noted to himself glumly, "We can still lose this war." [24] The commander of the VIII Corps, General Middleton, kept close personal rein on his division commanders and alerted the depleted 4th Armored and the 11th Armored Divisions to be prepared to move swiftly to the aid of either or both of the airborne divisions.

Unknown to the American command, any crisis engendered by the German attack had passed by nightfall of 5 January. Late on that day Field Marshal Model tacitly admitted failure at Bastogne by ordering General von Manteuffel to release the 9th SS Panzer Division to go to the aid of the Sixth Panzer Army

---

[23] Third Army Diary kept by Gen Gay, entry of 5 Jan 45, quoting Col James R. Pierce, 194th Glider Infantry. As two German tanks counterattacked a company of the 513th Parachute Infantry on 4 January, Staff Sgt. Isadore S. Jachman seized a bazooka from a fallen comrade, ran to a position close to the tanks, and opened fire. He damaged one and prompted both to retire but himself died of wounds incurred in the fight. A German-born U.S. citizen, Sergeant Jachman was awarded the Medal of Honor posthumously.

[24] George S. Patton, Jr., War As I Knew It (Boston: Houghton Mifflin Co., 1947), p. 213.

in its hour of trial against the American offensive from the north. The next day Manteuffel took it upon himself to order the *12th Panzer Division* to pull out of the line the night of the 7th to constitute a reserve.

Sensing as early as the 6th that the Germans soon might begin to withdraw, General Patton for all his concern about the bitterness of the fight deplored the possibility. Only the day before he had acquiesced in the artful persuasion of General Bradley to move a newly available division from the XX Corps to the salient southeast of Bastogne rather than to use it in a strike against the base of the bulge. Still hoping to mount an attack against the base, Patton worried now lest the Germans make good their escape before he could act.[25]

Despite the exodus of German armor, American troops found no evidence on 7 and 8 January of German intent to withdraw. Although the U.S. divisions around the salient postponed further attacks to await arrival of the new division, patrols found the enemy as full of fight as ever. The 17th Airborne and 87th Divisions meanwhile renewed their attacks on both days with the usual violent German reaction.

For the 87th, trying to break into the crossroads settlement of Tillet, midway between Bastogne and St. Hubert, the fighting proved bitterly frustrating as every attempt met sharp riposte from the *Fuehrer Begleit Brigade*, another elite unit heavy in armor that also had been

created from Hitler's household guard.[26] Although a regiment of the 17th Airborne Division entered Flamierge along a major highway leading northwest from Bastogne, the *3d Panzer Grenadier Division* counterattacked late on the 7th and again early on the 8th, trapping the bulk of a battalion in the town. Most of the able-bodied paratroopers eventually escaped by infiltrating to the rear, but they had to leave their wounded behind.

As divisions of the III Corps rejoined the offensive on the 9th, any evidence of German withdrawal still was hard to come by, despite Hitler's approval on the 8th for troops in the tip of the bulge to pull back. Hitler's authorization affected only units west of Bastogne in any case, since the new line he ordered to be held ran generally northwest from Longchamps toward the eastward bend of the Ourthe. Even the affected units made no precipitate exodus but instead executed the kind of gradual, grudging withdrawal that nobody did better than the Germans with their penchant for counterattack whenever and wherever a position approached the untenable.

Not until the third day of the renewed offensive, 11 January, did any firm indications of withdrawal develop. On the west wing of the VIII Corps, the 87th Division after finally having entered Tillet the night before found the Germans pulling back, abandoning St. Hubert and several smaller towns but leaving behind rear guards, roadblocks,

---

[25] *Ibid.;* Army Commander's Notes on the Bastogne Operation.

[26] Near Tillet, Staff Sgt. Curtis F. Shoup of the 87th Division's 346th Infantry charged head on against a German machine gun, firing his automatic rifle as he went. Although German fire cut him down, he mustered strength as he died to hurl a hand grenade that knocked out the enemy gun. He was awarded the Medal of Honor posthumously.

and deadly quilts of mines. At the same time, southeast of Bastogne, men of the III Corps saw their enemy also beginning to give ground in the face of an enveloping movement against his salient that imposed a forced rather than intentional retreat.

On 9 January a newly arrived but veteran 90th Infantry Division (Maj. Gen. James A. Van Fleet) attacked to the northeast through positions of the 26th Division (Maj. Gen. Willard S. Paul) along the southeastern fringe of the German salient, while the 6th Armored Division, later reinforced by a regiment of the 35th Division, tried a converging attack from the northwest. The axis of advance for both drives was a ridge road running southeast from Bastogne that served as a watershed for the little Wiltz River along the base of the salient.

Having arrived under a heavy cloak of secrecy, the 90th Division on the first day took the enemy's *5th Parachute Division* by surprise. Even though a snowstorm denied air support and turned roads into slick chutes, the attack on the 9th carried just over a mile and the next day reached high ground commanding the only road leading out of the salient. The Germans, despite a stalwart stand denying progress in the converging attack from the northwest, had no choice but to abandon the salient.

They began to retire the night of the 10th. On the 11th and again on the 12th, as infantrymen of the 90th Division shook hands with colleagues of the 35th Division on the other side of the salient, the Americans took over a thousand prisoners. Pulling back to the Wiltz River where the cuts, fills, and tunnels of a railroad aided the defense along a natural extension of the line of the Sûre

River, the survivors of the salient joined a hastily committed reserve, the *Fuehrer Grenadier Brigade,* to hold fast.[27] From the American viewpoint, this mattered little, since emphasis shifted at this point to the left wing of the III Corps where Millikin's troops were to aid the drive of the VIII Corps toward a linkup with the First Army at Houffalize.[28]

Despite German withdrawal on the extreme west wing of the VIII Corps, the going was slow. Disorganized in the bitter give-and-take west of Bastogne to the extent that the corps commander had asked Patton to delay renewed attack, the 17th Airborne and 87th Divisions pushed forward with little verve. Yet their snail-like pace made small difference in the end, because the veteran 101st Airborne Division could make only measured progress astride the road to Houffalize, where advance had to be swift if any Germans were to be trapped farther west. A relatively fresh *340th Volks Grenadier Division,* plus counterattacking contingents of the *3d Panzer Grenadier* and *12th SS Panzer Divisions,* insured not only firm but often dogged resistance.

The most encouraging progress on the direct route toward Houffalize appeared about to develop on 10 January east of the main highway as General Middleton inserted a combat command of the 4th

---

[27] MS # A-876, Ardennes Offensive of *Seventh Army,* 16 December 1944–25 January 1945 (General der Panzertruppen Erich Brandenberger).

[28] In an attack in this sector on 11 January, a squad leader in the 6th Armored Division's 9th Armored Infantry Battalion, Staff Sgt. Archer T. Gammon, charged ahead of his platoon to knock out two German machine guns and to close in with such daring on a German tank that the tank began to withdraw. Firing its 88-mm. gun as it retired, the tank killed the intrepid soldier with a direct hit. Sergeant Gammon was awarded the Medal of Honor posthumously.

Armored Division (Maj. Gen. Hugh J. Gaffey) along the corps boundary to seize Bourcy. Located on high ground commanding the highway to Houffalize where it passed through Noville, an enemy strongpoint, Bourcy in American hands might unhinge the defenses along the highway. Yet hardly had the armor begun to advance early on the 10th when General Patton called a halt.

Having shared in the failure to guess the enemy's intent to launch a counter-offensive in the Ardennes, intelligence staffs at SHAEF and the 12th Army Group these days were seeing burglars under every bed. They were concerned lest the Germans spoil the American offensive by counterattacking from positions near the base of the bulge south-ward toward Luxembourg City or at some point to the southeast where American lines had been thinned to provide forces for the Ardennes. General Bradley ordered Patton to pull out an armored division to guard against this threat. Seeing no burglars himself, General Patton filled the requirement by selecting the 4th Armored Division, which needed a rest for refitting anyway.[29]

General Bradley directed further that Patton halt the attack of the VIII Corps immediately and that of the III Corps when it reached a logical stopping point. Only after the German threat (based, Patton believed, more on rumor than solid intelligence) failed to materialize did Bradley on the 12th give approval for the Third Army to resume the of-

fensive, this time with the 11th Armored Division (Brig. Gen. Charles S. Kilburn) inserted between the two airborne divisions of the VIII Corps.[30]

Progress of the renewed drive reflected less of American intent than of German. On the west, in the sector included in Hitler's authorization to German units to withdraw, patrols of the 87th Division reached the Ourthe River the first day, the 13th, those of the 17th Airborne Division the next. The armor, meanwhile, attacking generally astride the line Hitler had designated as stopping point for the withdrawal, had to fight hard for every objective and as late as the 15th beat off a counterattack by some twenty tanks supported by a covey of fighter aircraft. Concurrently, the 101st Airborne Division astride the road to Houf-falize encountered the same determined stand as before. At Foy, south of Noville, for example, the Germans counter-attacked three times, retaking the town at dawn on the 14th with a battalion of infantry supported by a company of tanks.

Yet the airborne troops, too, were destined soon to experience softening resistance. On the 14th, the Commander in Chief West, Field Marshal von Rund-stedt, appealed to Hitler to authorize a further withdrawal: the line Hitler earlier had specified west of Houffalize already had been compromised in the north and was being rolled up in the south. He asked approval to pull back farther to anchor a new line on high ground just east of Houffalize, extending it northward behind the Salm River and southward through existing positions east of Bastogne.

[29] Patton, *War As I Knew It*, p. 217; Gay Diary, entry of 10 Jan 45; Leonard Rapport and Arthur Northwood, Jr., *Rendezvous With Destiny—A History of the 101st Airborne Division* (Washington: Infantry Journal Press, 1948), p. 643. The last is one of the better unofficial unit histories.

[30] Gay Diary, entries of 10, 11, 12 Jan 45.

PATROLS OF THE FIRST AND THIRD ARMIES MEET AT HOUFFALIZE

Having accepted by this time the inevitability of losing the bulge, Hitler agreed, but he refused to listen to ardent pleas by both Rundstedt and the *Army Group B* commander, Field Marshal Model, that they be allowed to withdraw by stages all the way to the Rhine, the only line, they believed, that the Germans in the west still might hope with any assurance to hold. They could withdraw, Hitler said, but only under pressure and only as far as the West Wall. There they were to make their stand.[31]

On the 15th, men of the 101st Airborne Division entered Noville, five miles south of Houffalize.[32] Early the next morning, the 11th Armored Division seized high ground along the high-

---

[31] Bauer, The German Withdrawal From the Ardennes; MS # A–858 (Schramm).

[32] In a complementary attack by the 6th Armored Division on this same day, a gunner in the attached 603d Tank Destroyer Battalion, Cpl. Arthur O. Beyer, dismounted from his vehicle to capture two Germans. When a German machine gun opened fire on him, he rushed forward to knock it out with a grenade, then worked his way along a German defense line, wiping out the occupants of one foxhole after another. In his one-man assault, he destroyed 2 machine guns, killed 8 Germans, and captured 18. For this feat, Corporal Beyer received the Medal of Honor.

way immediately south of Houffalize. Southwest of the town, a patrol commanded by Maj. Joseph M. L. Greene met a patrol from the 2d Armored Division of the First Army's VII Corps.

Rent by the counteroffensive, the First and Third Armies at last had linked at the waist of the bulge. In one way, it was an empty accomplishment; so measured had been the advance, such delays had the Germans imposed, that most of the troops in what might have been a sizable pocket had escaped.

Juncture at Houffalize nevertheless marked completion of the first phase of the campaign to push in the bulge. It also meant that the break in communications between American armies, which had caused General Eisenhower to put the First Army under Montgomery's command, no longer existed. At midnight the next day, 17 January, the First Army returned to Bradley's 12th Army Group.

The Drive on St. Vith

From the viewpoint of the First Army, the juncture at Houffalize marked no interval in the offensive to erase the bulge, but it pointed up a shift in emphasis that had gradually been evolving as linkup neared. Having begun to attack early in January in support of the VII Corps, General Ridgway's XVIII Airborne Corps took over the main assignment, a drive eastward on the road center of St. Vith. Collins's VII Corps was to support this drive briefly by also turning east; but because of the northeastward orientation of Patton's Third Army, the VII Corps soon would be pinched out of the line.

A more important supporting role was to be performed by the V Corps. From the northern shoulder of the bulge close by its base, the V Corps was to seize a defile along upper reaches of the little Ambleve River, thereby springing loose an armored division for a direct thrust southward on St. Vith. The armor, once free, was to come under command of the airborne corps to constitute the northern arm of a two-pronged thrust on St. Vith.[33]

For the Third Army, the juncture at Houffalize did represent a distinct break in the offensive, since it gave Patton an opportunity he would embrace with relish—to return to his original concept of an attack close to the southern base of the bulge. Patton intended to launch this thrust across the Sûre River with General Eddy's XII Corps.

It was too late at this point (if it had ever been feasible) to try seriously the maneuver Patton had talked about in December, a full-blooded attack northeastward across the German frontier to Pruem to cut off and destroy the Germans in the bulge. The rationale now for an attack from the south, directed almost due northward in the direction of St. Vith, was precisely the opposite of envelopment, a hope that threat from the south would prompt the Germans to shift enough strength from the vicinity of Houffalize and Bastogne to enable Millikin's III Corps and Middleton's VIII Corps to advance with relative ease toward the northeast. Yet against the slim possibility that the XII Corps might achieve a breakthrough, despite sharply compartmented terrain and heavy snow, General Eddy held an armored division in reserve. The 12th Army Group commander, General Bradley, also proposed

[33] FUSA Report of Operations, 1 Aug 44–22 Feb 45.

that once the First Army took St. Vith, General Hodges should send a corps south to link with the Third Army's XII Corps, a shallow envelopment that might trap any German forces still remaining farther west.[34]

Having at last gained Hitler's permission to withdraw from the bulge, German commanders faced the problem of how to get out before converging American attacks at the base cut them off. They had to make their withdrawal either on those days when weather cloaked them from the *Jabo,* as German troops called Allied fighter-bombers, or by night. A shortage of gasoline, that had developed early in the counteroffensive as the logistical pipeline over snow-drenched Eifel roads broke down, was at this point acute; and the prospects of bottlenecks at the few tactical bridges in the snow-slick gorge of the Our River along the frontier filled many a commander with dread.[35]

German commanders now faced their number one task of holding the shoulders of their salient without the services of the two SS panzer corps headquarters and four SS panzer divisions that Hitler had directed to assemble near St. Vith under the *Sixth Panzer Army.* The Fuehrer was becoming increasingly piqued that field commanders had not taken these divisions immediately out of the line and were still using portions of them as fire brigades in threatened sectors. That the SS divisions soon would be totally out of reach of the western commanders became apparent on the

14th when Hitler ordered two volks artillery corps shifted hurriedly from the Ardennes to the east in response to the new Russian offensive and alerted the SS divisions for a similar move. All that would be left to hold in the Ardennes would be men who not only had seen the grandiose prospects of the counteroffensive dashed to bits but who also were embittered by Hitler's pulling out the SS divisions for what looked to the men in the foxhole like a rest.[36]

The new main effort by General Hodges' First Army had begun even before the linkup at Houffalize and a day before Hitler authorized withdrawal to a new line east of Houffalize. This line was already breached along its northward extension, for even while acting in a supporting role to the VII Corps General Ridgway's XVIII Airborne Corps had established a bridgehead across the Salm River and another over the Ambleve near where the two rivers come together.

Beginning on 13 January, as a first step in the drive on St. Vith, the XVIII Airborne Corps attacked to flatten the corner formed by the meeting of the Ambleve and the Salm. At General Ridgway's insistence, this drive was to be no measured blunting of the angle all along the line; emphasis instead fell to the 30th Division from positions on the northern shoulder some three miles north of the meandering Ambleve River at Malmédy to drive southward, thereby posing threat of envelopment to Germans in the Salm-Ambleve angle to the west.[37] Having replaced the 82d Airborne Division along the Salm on the right flank of the corps,

---

[34] Gay Diary, entry of 15 Jan 45; TUSA AAR, Jan 45.

[35] MS # B–151a (Manteuffel); MS # A–876 (Brandenberger); Bauer, The German Withdrawal From the Ardennes.

[36] MS # A–858 (Schramm); Bauer, The German Withdrawal From the Ardennes.

[37] Sylvan Diary, entries of 4, 9 Jan 45.

General S. L. A. Marshall
Military Editor
The Washington Post
1515 L, N. W.
Washington, D.C. 20005
card sent 5-6-74.

4-74 MA

MacDONALD, Charles B.

THE Last Offensive. Washington, D.C. :
U.S. Government Printing Office, 1973. $15.20.

the 75th Division (Maj. Gen. Fay B. Prickett) attacked in an easterly direction toward St. Vith to form the second arm of a pincers threatening the Germans in the corner. The 106th Division (Brig. Gen. Herbert T. Perrin) pressed forward in the angle itself with the separate 517th Parachute Infantry and the division's sole surviving regiment (the others had been destroyed early in the counteroffensive).

Nowhere was there a solid German line. Although defense was stubborn and included small counterattacks, it centered primarily in villages and on occasional key high ground. On the first day and again on the second, the 30th Infantry Division south of Malmédy made the most gains, advancing up to four miles to take high ground that guarded approach to the west shoulder of the defile through which armor of the V Corps later was to debouch.

Part of the 30th Infantry Division's success was attributable to hitting near a boundary between major German units —to the east the *LXVII Corps* (General der Infanterie Otto Hitzfeld) of Zangen's *Fifteenth Army* and to the west the *XIII Corps* (General der Infanterie Hans Felber), which was still under control of Dietrich's *Sixth Panzer Army.* Pushing back and occasionally overrunning portions of a depleted volks grenadier division of Felber's *XIII Corps,* the infantrymen cut into the flank and rear of the *3d Parachute Division* of Hitzfeld's *LXVII Corps,* prompting Hitzfeld to bring up another understrength volks grenadier division in hope of filling the breach.[38]

GENERAL RIDGWAY

The big disappointment to the Americans was slow progress by the 75th Division, whose advance across the Salm toward St. Vith was so limited that it took much of the threat out of General Ridgway's intended envelopment of the Germans in the Ambleve-Salm angle. While trying to make allowance for the fact that the division had seen its first combat only a day before Christmas, both Ridgway and the First Army commander, General Hodges, feared all offensive punch temporarily gone. On the 19th, patrols of the 75th and 30th Divisions at last met to pinch out the 106th Division and seal off the corner, but so slow had been the 75th's advance that two divisions of Felber's *XIII Corps* had escaped with little difficulty. Seeing the problem as one of command, General

---

[38] German material is from Bauer, The German Withdrawal From the Ardennes.

Hodges recommended the division commander's relief.[39]

The main fight centered in the meantime on the defile through which armor under the V Corps was to drive in order to come upon St. Vith from the north. Named for a town on the northern approach, this was known as the Ondenval defile.

As the V Corps began its drive early on 15 January, a new commander took over while General Gerow left to head an army headquarters newly arrived from the United States, the Fifteenth, destined to serve primarily as an occupation force as the Allies swept across Germany.[40] The new corps commander was Maj. Gen. C. Ralph Huebner, who had guided the veteran 1st Infantry Division since the end of the campaign in Sicily.

General Huebner's former command, headed now by the former division artillery commander, Brig. Gen. Clift Andrus, drew the assignment of opening the Ondenval defile for the armor. While the regiments of the 1st Division took high ground east of the defile and contingents of the 30th Division wooded high ground to the west, the 2d Division's 23d Infantry, attached to the 1st Division, moved south through Ondenval directly against the defile.

A five-day fight developed, primarily against the *3d Parachute Division*. Sensing the full import of the attack as a threat to St. Vith and those German units still west of the town, Field Marshal Model at *Army Group B* on the 17th unified command in the sector by transferring Hitzfeld's *LXVII Corps* to Die-

trich's *Sixth Panzer Army*. Two days later, in an effort to shore up a faltering defense all along the line, General Dietrich risked Hitler's wrath by recommitting artillery of the *I SS Panzer Corps* to reinforce fires at the Ondenval defile and small contingents of tanks from three of his four SS panzer divisions to reinforce local counterattacks.

Dietrich might slow the advance but neither he nor cruel winter weather with waist-high drifts of snow could stop it. Sometimes the weather was more of a problem than the enemy. On one occasion two men stopping to rest dropped unconscious from exhaustion. "We are fighting the weather," said General Hobbs, commanding the 30th Division, "and losing about one hundred a day. . . . It is a hell of a country."[41]

The state of the weather gave the little Ardennes towns an added dimension as prizes of war. Not only did the towns control the roads needed for tanks and trucks but they also afforded shelter, a chance for the men to thaw out and dry out, to get a night's sleep under cover. The towns, unfortunately, were almost always in a draw or on a reverse slope, making it necessary to seize the high ground beyond and hold it from foxholes blasted out of frozen earth with small explosive charges. It became a matter of constant nagging concern to forward commanders to rotate their men and allow all at least brief respite from the cold.

Partly because the German soldiers,

[39] Sylvan Diary, entries of 16, 17, 20 Jan 45.

[40] *History of the Fifteenth United States Army* (no publisher, no date), an unofficial unit history. See also below, ch. XV.

[41] 30th Div G-3 Jnl, 22 Jan 45. This division's journal contains valuable verbatim records of telephone conversations. See also Robert P. Hewitt, *Workhorse of the Western Front* (Washington: Infantry Journal Press, 1946), an excellent unit history.

MEDICS USE A "LITTER JEEP" TO EVACUATE PATIENTS

too, wanted shelter, and partly because buildings made good strongpoints, the villages and small settlements at critical road junctions were hardest to get at. Although sometimes delayed by mines hidden by the deep snow, tanks and tank destroyers proved almost essential for blasting the Germans from the houses. Artillery could chase the defenders into the cellars, but it could not keep them there. As men of one battalion of the 23d Infantry entered a village close behind an artillery preparation, Germans emerged in their midst to promote a fight so intimate that at one point an American soldier reputedly engaged a German with his fists.[42]

The enemy, fortunately, was not so consistently persistent as was the weather. Nearly all units had the experience of advancing for an hour or sometimes even half a day without a round fired at them; then, suddenly, at a stream bank, a farmhouse, the edge of a wood or a village, a flurry of fire from automatic weapons or shelling from artillery and mortars, or both, might erupt. Sometimes this signaled start of a counterattack, usually in

---

[42] 1st Div G–3 Jnl, 19 Jan 45.

no more than company strength, precipitating a sharp but usually short engagement.

The 23d Infantry finally cleared the Ondenval defile on the 17th, held it with the help of massed artillery fires against a battalion-size counterattack supported by three tanks on the 18th, then passed on in a blinding snowstorm on the 19th to seize the first tier of towns beyond. Through the defile and along another road to the west in the 30th Division's zone, tanks, tank destroyers, and half-tracks of the 7th Armored Division (Maj. Gen. Robert W. Hasbrouck) began to pass early on the 20th, headed for the rubble that St. Vith had become after this same division had fought gallantly for the town in December.

Northward Across the Sûre

Patton's Third Army resumed its role in pushing the Germans back with surprise crossings of the Sûre River before daylight on 18 January. Close by the German frontier, a regiment of the 4th Infantry Division (Brig. Gen. Harold W. Blakeley) began to cross into an angle formed by confluence of the Sûre and the Our, while two regiments of the 5th Infantry Division (Maj. Gen. S. LeRoy Irwin) crossed on either side of Diekirch, less than five miles west of the frontier. While the men of the 4th Division protected the 5th Division's right flank and took out the enemy's bridges across the Our below the Luxembourg frontier town of Vianden, four miles north of the Sûre, the men of the 5th were to drive north along a highway that runs within several miles of the frontier. Because the highway follows the crest of a ridgeline through semimountainous

countryside (la Petite Suisse), American soldiers long ago had christened it the "Skyline Drive."

Even more than in the vicinity of St. Vith, it was imperative for the Germans to hold firm along the Sûre River, because the heaviest concentration of German force remaining in the bulge, that which had fought around Bastogne, was peculiarly susceptible to a thrust from the south. Four divisions of General Brandenberger's *Seventh Army,* charged with defending the southern flank, and at least nine of General von Manteuffel's *Fifth Panzer Army* in the vicinity of Bastogne had to withdraw through this southern portion of the bulge. The east-west roads they had to use were markedly inferior to the north-south routes that beckoned an attacker from the south; and the Germans had only five tactical bridges over the Our River, three of which, at and south of Vianden, were dangerously close to the existing American line along the Sûre. The bridges in any case inevitably meant congestion, slowing the withdrawal and inviting attack from the air.[43]

Toward the end of December, the presence in reserve south of the Sûre of the 6th U.S. Armored Division had alarmed General Brandenberger lest the Americans strike while the bulk of his strength was trying to help the *Fifth Panzer Army* break Bastogne; but with the shift of the armor to Bastogne and the beginning of American attacks there, Brandenberger had begun to view his vulnerable positions along the Sûre with greater equanimity. If his *Seventh Army* was to be hit any time soon, Brandenberger deduced, the strike would come

---

[43] German material is from Bauer, The German Withdrawal From the Ardennes.

not along the Sûre close to the base of the bulge but farther west where his troops still held positions between Ettelbruck at the southern terminus of the Skyline Drive, and Wiltz, positions that were south and west of the Sûre in one place and between the Sûre and Wiltz Rivers in another.

Brandenberger was seeing American intentions in terms of his own dispositions. He was stronger west and northwest of Ettelbruck, where three volks grenadier divisions under the *LIII Corps* (General der Kavallerie Edwin Graf Rothkirch und Trach) held the line. Along the Sûre between Ettelbruck and the frontier, he had only one volks grenadier division, which with another that was holding a 30-mile stretch of the West Wall along the frontier to the southeast, made up the *LXXX Corps* (General der Infanterie Franz Beyer).

Although the little Sûre River is fordable at many points, the weather was too cold for wading. Nor was American artillery to forewarn the enemy with a preparatory barrage. The night was black, cold, and silent as men of the 4th and 5th Divisions moved assault boats and three-man canvas rafts to the ice-crusted edge of the stream.[44]

The troops gained the surprise they sought. Hardly a shot sounded along the Sûre that night before the first waves of infantrymen touched down on the north bank. Only at a place just west of Diekirch, where a machine gun opened up on an assault company of the 5th Di-

vision's 2d Infantry, was there troublesome German fire; and there the infantrymen were able to pull back and cross in an adjacent sector.

Just east of Diekirch, a battalion of the same division's 10th Infantry turned the icy, snow-covered river bank to advantage by loading men into the assault boats at the top of the slope and shoving the boats downhill like toboggans. At another point engineers tied 150-foot ropes to either end of the boats so that, once the first wave had passed, they could pull the boats back and forth across the little river. In two places infantrymen crossed on footbridges that engineers had quietly shoved into place just before H-hour.

The night was so dark and the early morning made so obscure by a combination of mist in the river bottom and American smoke pots that the Germans were hard put at first to determine the extent of the threat posed against them. In many cases U.S. troops passed unseen by German machine gun and mortar crews. Already seriously weakened by loss of field pieces earlier in the Ardennes fighting and by ammunition shortages, German artillery was "as good as blinded." [45] Some three hours passed before the first artillery shells struck along the river.

By the end of the first day a vehicular ford and several treadway bridges were operating to enable supporting tanks and tank destroyers to cross the Sûre. A bridgehead up to two miles deep was solidly established, in enough depth to bring the two German bridges over the Our downstream from Vianden under punishing artillery fire. German troubles

---

[44] For an annotated account of this attack at a small-unit level, see Maj. Dello G. Dayton, The Attack by XII Corps 18–29 January 1945, unpublished MS in OCMH, prepared in the European Theater of Operations Historical Section soon after the war. See also combat interviews with men of the 5th Division.

[45] MS # A–876 (Brandenberger).

had been further compounded when in midmorning the 80th Infantry Division (Maj. Gen. Horace L. McBride) had begun to attack to the northeast to drive General Rothkirch's *LIII Corps* behind the Wiltz and another stretch of the Sûre between Ettelbruck and the Wiltz River and to facilitate the 5th Division's advance up the Skyline Drive.[46]

As surprised by the American thrust as were the volks grenadiers on the ground, the *Seventh Army* commander, General Brandenberger, ordered most of the supporting army artillery and engineer units that had been grouped behind the *LIII Corps* to shift to the more seriously menaced *LXXX Corps*. He also directed a volks grenadier division to fall back from the western tip of the *LIII Corps* to establish a blocking position astride the Skyline Drive along a cross-ridge northwest of Vianden, there to form a mask for the two tactical bridges upstream from Vianden.

Field Marshal Model at *Army Group B* provided help by ordering first a *Kampfgruppe,* then all that was left of the *Panzer Lehr Division,* transferred from the *Fifth Panzer Army*. He followed this with an order for a severely depleted *2d Panzer Division* also to turn south, then headquarters of the *XLVII*

Panzer Corps to command the two panzer divisions. Behind the *Fifth Panzer Army,* engineers began building another bridge over the Our.

It would have required long hours under ideal conditions for any of these expedients to have effect. In view of crippling gasoline shortages and the heavy snowstorm of 19 January, it would take not hours but days.

The 5th Division in the meantime fought steadily up the Skyline Drive to reach a point almost due west of Vianden on the 21st; there the division paused amid rumors of impending armored counterattack. Several observers having reported heavy German troop movements around Vianden, the division commander, General Irwin, was disturbed that the 4th Division had been unable to keep pace on his division's right. There the original defenders, their positions compressed and their backs to the Our, kept the 4th Division's 12th Infantry at a respectable distance from Vianden and its vital bridge.

The situation was less disturbing on the 5th Division's other flank. There the advance up the Skyline Drive had posed such a threat of entrapment to the Germans of Rothkirch's *LIII Corps* that on 21 January they began to pull out, leaving only strong rear guards to oppose the 80th Division's attack to the northeast. So precipitate was the exodus that much of it took place in full view of men of the 5th Division on the high ground. The infantrymen cheered to see the Germans run. They cheered, too, at the rich gunnery targets presented by long columns of trucks, tanks, and horse-drawn artillery. "Let her go, boys" one artillery observer radioed to his gunners; "you

---

[46] Ten days before, on 8 January, in the village of Dahl, near Wiltz, a 9-man squad of the 80th Division's 319th Infantry commanded by Sgt. Day G. Turner fought savagely for four hours to hold a house on the fringe of the village against a local German attack. Turner himself bayoneted two Germans, threw a can of flaming oil at others, and, when his ammunition was exhausted, used enemy weapons to continue the fight. Only three of his men still were alive and unhurt when the Germans broke, leaving behind 11 dead and 25 captured. Sergeant Turner received the Medal of Honor.

can't miss a Jerry wherever you land them." [47]

Other observers demanded to know, "Where is the air?" [48] Yet as on so many days of the foggy, snowbound January, there was no air. During the morning, ice and snow on runways prevented most squadrons of the XIX Tactical Air Command from taking off, and during the afternoon pilots of the few planes that got up found ground haze too thick for them to spot the targets.

That changed dramatically the next day, the 22d. A brilliant sun came up, its rays glistening on the new snow cover.

Four groups of fighter-bombers assigned to support the XII Corps began early to attack, then quickly called for help until eventually the entire XIX Tactical Air Command joined the hunt. The snow-drenched roads were thick with German traffic—much of Rothkirch's LIII Corps pulling back to the northeast, rear elements of the Fifth Panzer Army seeking the east bank of the Our, and the XLVII Panzer Corps with the 2d Panzer and Panzer Lehr Divisions cutting across the grain of the withdrawal to go to the Seventh Army's aid. Snarled by the snow and the deep canyon of the Our, vehicles at the Our bridges were stalled bumper-to-bumper.

American pilots were jubilant, reminded of the days in August when so many of the Germans fleeing France had been squashed along the roads like insects. "For the first time [in the Ardennes]," noted General Brandenberger, "the situation in the air was similar to that which had prevailed in Normandy." [49] When the day came to an end, 25 squadrons had flown 627 sorties. Although the pilots as usual made unrealistically high estimates of their accomplishments, the day's strikes caused considerable damage and compounded the delays that terrain, weather, and gasoline shortages already had imposed on the German withdrawal. [50]

The day of 22 January was notable for another development as well. On that day Hitler ordered the Sixth Panzer Army to quit the Ardennes entirely and to transfer with all speed to the east to oppose a broadening Russian offensive, an unqualified admission not only that the counteroffensive had failed but also that the Eastern Front again had priority on resources. In addition to headquarters of the two SS panzer corps and the four SS panzer divisions, the shift included the Fuehrer Begleit and Fuehrer Grenadier Brigades and assorted supporting units. General von Manteuffel's Fifth Panzer Army assumed control of the two corps in the north that General Dietrich had been directing in opposing the American drive on St. Vith.

The next day, 23 January, was notable, too, not in the air, since the weather closed in again, but in three places on the ground. In the north, General Hasbrouck's 7th Armored Division came back to St. Vith, signaling the approximate end of the First Army's role in flattening the bulge. Along the Skyline Drive, General Brandenberger on the same day turned over defense of the

---

[47] 5th Div G–3 Jnl, 21 Jan 45.

[48] Ibid.

[49] MS # A–876 (Brandenberger).

[50] For various reasons, claims of enemy losses from air action almost always were high. One study conducted by the British proved by ground check that air force claims of German tanks destroyed in the Ardennes were at least ten times too high. See Directorate of Tactical Investigation, War Office, The German Counter-Offensive in the Ardennes, MS in OCMH.

blocking position northwest of Vianden to the *XLVII Panzer Corps* with assistance on the west from Rothkirch's *LIII Corps.* There would be no armored counterattack, if indeed the depleted, gasoline-short panzer corps had ever seriously considered one, only a continuing passive defense to keep the Americans away from the Our bridges until the last of the *Fifth Panzer Army* could pull out. Also on the 23d, General Middleton's VIII Corps and General Millikin's III Corps got back into the fight even as the 12th Army Group commander, General Bradley, came up with the genesis of a new plan destined to affect employment of these corps.

As early as 19 January, General Patton had detected enough indications that the northward drive by Eddy's XII Corps would prompt German withdrawal from the eastward-facing line of the bulge to justify ordering Middleton and Millikin to resume their advance. Although Patton specified 21 January for the push to begin, patrols all along the front made so little enemy contact during the afternoon of the 19th that both corps commanders feared delaying another day lest they collapse a bag filled only with air. They ordered their divisions to put out strong patrols and follow them up in strength if resistance failed to develop.

It failed to develop for three days. A tank-supported ambush in a village mangled a company of the 90th Division in the center of the III Corps, but other than that, few units encountered any of the enemy except stragglers. Although some of these fired before surrendering, none represented a true rear guard. So heterogeneous was the mixture that the 6th Armored Division alone took prisoners from ten different divisions. The 11th

Armored Division on the north wing of the VIII Corps was pinched out of the line before ever catching up with the enemy.

Yet for all the lack of resistance, the pursuit was slow. The deep snow and slick roads saw to that. Protecting the right flank of the III Corps, the 6th Cavalry Group most of the time had to advance dismounted. To find suitable roads, the 6th Armored Division often had to impinge on the zone of the neighboring 90th Division.

When coupled with staunch defense against the attack of Eddy's XII Corps from the south, the German withdrawal meant an end to any hopes General Patton still might have entertained for trapping his enemy with a drive close along the base of the bulge. Nor was there any point in implementing General Bradley's earlier suggestion that the First Army send a corps southward from St. Vith.

On the 23d Bradley called Patton to his headquarters, there to propose a plan that he had been contemplating for more than a fortnight, a plan designed to parlay the attack to flatten the bulge into a major drive through the Eifel to gain the Rhine.[51] Since Bradley's plan involved use of a strong corps of the Third Army close along the flank of the First Army around St. Vith, Patton decided to employ Middleton's VIII Corps. Like the First Army's VII Corps, which was pinched out of the fight after only one day of the renewed attack (22 January), the VIII Corps had been scheduled to be pinched out by the northeastward orientation of the III Corps; but because Middleton and his staff knew the terrain

---

[51] Gay Diary, entry of 23 Jan 45; ch. III, below.

around St. Vith from earlier fighting, Patton altered boundaries to change this.[52] Turning the III Corps eastward to pass directly across the front of Eddy's XII Corps, he made room for Middleton's command.

While the VIII Corps with only one division still forward adjusted to the boundary change, the divisions of the III Corps ran into a shooting war again. After having fallen back approximately nine miles, the Germans paused to attempt a new stand behind the little Clerf River, just over two miles west of the Skyline Drive. Yet the resistance, though strong in places, was spotty and depended largely on infantry weapons. Both the 6th Armored and 90th Divisions crossed the Clerf on the 23d, while the 26th Division jumped the stream the next day. By the 25th the hasty German line had ceased to exist, and the defense reverted to delaying action by isolated groups chiefly in a row of villages along the Skyline Drive.

Although some fighting to clear the west bank of the Our continued through 28 January, it was a mop-up operation occupying only a fraction of the Third Army's troops. The focus shifted to shuffling units and boundaries in preparation for the new offensive General Bradley had outlined on the 23d. With the Germans at last driven back into the West Wall, the bulge created by the futile counteroffensive that had cost Germans and Americans alike so heavily was erased.

The drive from 3 through 28 January to flatten the bulge in the Ardennes added 39,672 battle casualties to an American total of 41,315 incurred during

that phase of the fighting when the Germans were on the offensive. Of the additional losses, 6,138 were killed or died of wounds and 6,272 were missing or known captured.[53] Just how many more losses the combat in January produced on the German side is difficult to say. Estimates of enemy losses for all the fighting in the Ardennes have ranged from 81,834 (lowest German estimate) to 103,900 (highest Allied estimate).[54] Possibly as many as 30 to 40 percent of these occurred during the January campaign.

That the Germans were forced to retire to the positions whence they had emerged from the mists of the Eifel on 16 December was testament enough to a victory for American arms. Yet a combination of an American drive to push in rather than cut off the bulge and an adroit German withdrawal had enabled the Germans to escape with losses no greater than might be considered normal in any deliberate delaying action under harsh conditions of weather and terrain. The Germans did it under the handicaps of an acute shortage of gasoline and a vastly superior, almost predominant, Allied air force. In the process, they saved most of their arms and equipment too, although large numbers of tanks and artillery pieces had to be destroyed near the end for lack of spare parts and gasoline.

To the Germans, American tactics appeared to consist of a series of quickly shifting attacks that probed for weak spots to take individual divisions in flanks or rear. Noting that their adversary eschewed night attacks, stopping

---

[52] Patton, *War As I Knew It*, pp. 224–25.

[53] 12th AGp, G–1 Daily Summary, master file, 1 Jan–28 Feb 45. Figures for the earlier period are from Cole, *The Ardennes*, p. 674.
[54] Pogue, *The Supreme Command*, p. 396.

with almost clocklike regularity as darkness fell, the Germans deemed him slow
in following up retrograde movements
but doggedly determined. A constant
nibbling away at German positions
forced German commanders to weaken
one spot to shore up another, only to see
a new penetration develop elsewhere.
What saved them in numbers of instances, the Germans believed, was an
American tendency to stop at a given
objective rather than to exploit an advantage fully and quickly. American
fighter-bombers, the Germans also noted,
failed to hit traffic bottlenecks such as
road intersections and bridges as hard as
the Germans thought they might.[55]

Against these observations would have
to be weighed American difficulties. The
same cruel weather, the same slick roads
affected American operations, probably
more than the Germans', since the offensive force is normally the more exposed.
Like the Germans, too, American units
had problems with replacements. Even
the manpower well in the United States
was showing signs of going dry, and at

the height of the Ardennes fighting General Eisenhower directed both a comb-
out of rear echelon units and a program
whereby Negro service troops might volunteer for the infantry. The Third Army
was particularly short of infantry replacements until well along in the January
campaign, and in all cases replacements
in terms of experience hardly could
equal the fallen.

The question of whether the counteroffensive in the Ardennes had any
chance, however slim, of succeeding and
thus of whether Hitler was justified in
gambling major resources on the Western Front would forever remain unan-
swered, one of those imponderables that
each student of warfare is apt to decide
only for himself.[56] As for the effect of
the counteroffensive and the heavy losses
it entailed on subsequent operations and
the final quest for victory in Europe, that
remained to be demonstrated as a last
offensive born in the cold and snow of
the Ardennes gradually expanded, eventually to encompass Allied armies all
along the line.

---

[55] See Bauer, The German Withdrawal From the
Ardennes.

[56] For a discussion of this point, see Cole, *The
Ardennes*, pp. 673–76.

CHAPTER III

Main Effort in the Eifel

In early December, before the Germans struck in the Ardennes, the Supreme Commander had intended to maintain unremitting pressure on the enemy through the winter in hope of forcing him back to the Rhine. Converging attacks by the 21 and 12th Army Groups across the Rhine were to be launched in early summer, 1945. To criticism that pressure all along the line, the broad-front strategy, was indecisive, General Eisenhower had replied: "It appears to me that wars are won in successive stages and until we get firmly established on the Rhine we are not in position to make the attack which we hope will be fatal to the other fellow." [1]

That the Allies were not indeed in such a position seemed fully attested by the German counteroffensive. Studying possible courses of action to follow after eliminating the German gains, the planning staff at SHAEF drew a plan that one critic called "almost a painstaking, uninspired, plodding way through to Berlin." [2] The plan actually did call for more methodical moves than before, but the timetable, as events were to prove, embodied considerable optimism.

Pointing out that even before the counteroffensive, Allied forces north and south of the Ardennes had been insufficient to insure reaching the Rhine, the planners advocated concentrating on one section of the front at a time, starting with elimination of the Colmar pocket in the French sector, and forming a SHAEF reserve of six divisions. The planners proposed then to turn to an offensive north of the Ardennes while assuming the defensive elsewhere. Not until the 21 and 12th Army Groups had reached the Rhine from Wesel south to Bonn were attacks to be resumed in the south. Not until March, after Allied forces had reached the Rhine all along the front, was anybody to cross the Rhine. [3]

Although never formally approved, this plan fairly represented the new emphasis on defeating the Germans west of the Rhine by stages. As General Eisenhower wrote to Field Marshal Montgomery:

We must substantially defeat the German forces west of the Rhine if we are to make a truly successful invasion [of the interior of Germany] with all forces available. . . . As I see it, we simply cannot afford the large defensive forces that would be necessary if we allow the German to hold great

---

[1] Msg, Eisenhower to the Prime Minister, CPA–90357, 26 Nov 44, SHAEF Msg File, Plans and Opns, A49–70, Folder 27.

[2] Memo, G. H. Phillimore for Chief Plans Sec, GCT/370–47/, sub: Plans, Future Opns—1945, 2 Jan 45, SHAEF G–3 file (Future Operations—1945).

[3] Memo by Planning Staffs, sub: Future Opns—1945, 23 Dec 44, SHAEF G–3 file (Future Opns—1945).

bastions sticking into our lines at the same time that we try to invade his country.[4]

Of eighty-five Allied divisions expected to be available in early summer, Eisenhower estimated that forty-five would be needed in defense and reserve if the Allies were at that time holding a line similar to the one actually held on 15 January, but only twenty-five if the line followed the Rhine.[5]

It was the SHAEF plan for cleaning up the area west of the Rhine before beginning a decisive thrust deep into Germany that incited objections from the British Chiefs of Staff. The British Chiefs feared that the plan meant a dispersion of strength and considered that Eisenhower had only enough superiority on the ground to make a single powerful thrust, backed by enough fresh divisions to maintain momentum. This was the basic point at issue when the British Chiefs on 10 January asked formally for a review of strategy by the Combined Chiefs which led to the Supreme Commander's plan being discussed at the end of January at Malta.[6]

Convinced of the soundness of the plan and assured of backing by the U.S. Chiefs of Staff, General Eisenhower continued to lay the groundwork for a renewed offensive even while waiting for the Combined Chiefs to rule, though an element of the provisional hung over all plans made during the period. The Supreme Commander directed specific at-

tention to what he considered the main effort, a drive to reach the Rhine north of the Ardennes in preparation for an eventual attack north of the Ruhr industrial area. On 18 January he ordered the 21 Army Group commander, Montgomery, to prepare plans for such an offensive.[7]

General Bradley's Proposal

Through the course of the Ardennes fighting, the 12th Army Group commander, General Bradley, had been aware that General Eisenhower intended a return to a main effort in the north. Since the Ninth Army was to remain under Montgomery's command and participate in that drive, Bradley eventually would have to relinquish divisions to bring the Ninth Army to a strength at least equal to that which had existed before General Simpson had released divisions to fight in the Ardennes. General Bradley nevertheless hoped to be able to continue to attack with his army group beyond the Ardennes to cut through northern reaches of the Eifel to the Rhine.[8]

Against the obvious difficulties of attacking in winter over countryside equally as inhospitable as that of the Ardennes and through the West Wall, Bradley could argue that an offensive in the Eifel fitted best as a continuation of the attack to reduce the bulge. It would avoid a pause to regroup; it would insure a constant and mounting pressure against the Germans; it would capitalize on probable German expectation of an Al-

---

[4] Ltr, Eisenhower to Montgomery, 17 Jan 45, in Pogue files. (These files consist of notes and extracts from documents in General Eisenhower's personal files, assembled by Dr. Pogue when he was preparing his volume, *The Supreme Command*.)

[5] Msg, Eisenhower to Marshall, S–75090, 15 Jan 45, War Dept Cable Log.

[6] See above, ch. I.

[7] Msg, SHAEF to CG's AGp's, 18 Jan 45, SHAEF SGS 381, Post-Overlord Planning file, vol. III.

[8] 12th AGp Ltr of Instrs 12, 4 Jan 45, 12th AGp Rpt of Opns, vol. V.

lied return to the offensive in the north; and it would put the 12th Army Group in a position to unhinge the Germans in front of the 21 Army Group. To at least some among the American command, rather delicate considerations of national prestige also were involved, making it advisable to give to American armies and an American command that had incurred a reverse in the Ardennes a leading part in the new offensive.[9]

Attacking through the Eifel also would avoid directly confronting an obstacle that had plagued Bradley and the First Army's General Hodges all through the preceding autumn, a series of dams known collectively as the Roer River dams in rugged country along headwaters of the river near Monschau. So long as the Germans retained control of these dams, they might manipulate the waters impounded by the dams to jeopardize and even deny any Allied crossing of the normally placid Roer downstream to the north.

By pursuing an offensive that the 12th Army Group's planning staff had first suggested in November, General Bradley saw a way to bypass and outflank the dams and still retain his ability to support a main effort farther north.[10] Bradley intended to attack northeastward from a start line generally along the German frontier between Monschau and St. Vith and seize the road center of Euskirchen, not quite thirty miles away, where the Eifel highlands merge with the flatlands of the Cologne plain. This would put American forces behind the

enemy's Roer River defenses in a position to unhinge them.

To the Supreme Commander, General Eisenhower, Bradley's proposal had the double virtue of being a logical follow-up to the job of reducing the bulge and of accomplishing part of the general buildup along the Rhine that he intended before launching a major offensive deep into Germany. Yet Eisenhower saw a 12th Army Group offensive as no substitute for a main effort later by the 21 Army Group. Since Montgomery had considerable regrouping to do before his offensive would be ready, Eisenhower agreed to let Bradley hold on temporarily to the divisions earmarked for the Ninth Army and take a stab at the Eifel.

General Eisenhower nevertheless sharply qualified his approval. If the attack failed to show early promise of a "decisive success," he intended halting it and shifting strength to the Ninth Army.[11] The definition of decisive success was apparently a quick, broad penetration of the West Wall.[12] Even beyond that the operation was to be subject to review at any time, and General Bradley was to be prepared to pass quickly to the defensive, relinquishing divisions to the Ninth Army.[13]

The Eifel Highlands

Terrain would set even narrower limits on tactics in the Eifel than in the Ardennes. Streams in the Eifel have cut even deeper into the surface of the old plateau, and unlike the patchwork pat-

[9] On the last point, see Gay Diary, entry of 24 Jan 45.

[10] For the early planning, see 12th AGp, Estimate of the Situation, 29 Nov 44, 12th AGp G–3 file. Memo by Planning Staffs, sub: Future Opns—1945, 23 Dec 44.

[11] SHAEF to CG's AGp's, 18 Jan 45.

[12] Lt Col T. F. Foote, Staff Rpt. Visit to EAGLE (12th AGp) TAC, 18 Jan 45, in 12th AGp 371.3, Military Objectives, V.

[13] SHAEF to CG's AGp's, 18 Jan 45.

terns in the Ardennes, the forests are vast. Although roads are fairly extensive, they twist and climb in and out of the stream valleys and through the narrow confines of farm villages.

Well defined on the southeast by the convolutions of the Moselle River, the Eifel in the north and northeast merges irregularly into the Cologne plain, roughly on a line from Aachen through Euskirchen to the Rhine some fifteen miles south of Bonn. From the Belgian border to the Rhine the greatest depth of the Eifel is about forty-five miles. In width, the region extends along the frontiers of Belgium and Luxembourg from Aachen to Trier, a distance of some seventy-five miles.

Close to the frontier, two hill masses or ridges stand out. Most prominent is the Schnee Eifel, a forested ridge some ten miles long, roughly parallel to the Belgian border east of St. Vith, rising abruptly from the surrounding countryside to a height of just over 2,000 feet. The other is an L-shaped ridgeline or hill mass forming a bridge between the Hohe Venn and the Schnee Eifel, which may be called from its highest point at the angle of the L, the Weisserstein. This ridgeline generally defines the Belgian-German border southeast of Monschau, then swings to the northeast. Part of the north-south watershed for the region, the Weisserstein in conjunction with the Hohe Venn and the Schnee Eifel also serves as the watershed between Eifel and Ardennes.

Except for the Moselle the rivers of the Eifel are relatively minor streams, but they are important militarily because of their deep, twisting cuts. The main ones are the Our, running along the frontier and joining the Sauer before entering the Moselle; the Pruem, forming another north-south barrier a few miles beyond the Schnee Eifel; the Ahr, draining from the Hohe Eifel northeastward to the Rhine; and the Roer. Two of the more important towns within the generally pastoral region are Pruem and Bitburg, the latter in a relatively open stretch of countryside southeast of Pruem.

The northernmost reaches of the Eifel, the region that General Bradley hoped to avoid by making his attack south of the Roer dams, has no general geographical name, but American soldiers who had fought there had come to know it as the Huertgen Forest. Although not so high as other parts of the Eifel, this is one of the more sharply compartmented sectors and at the time was almost completely covered with forest and the debris of the September to December battles.

The route that General Bradley chose for his main attack cut across the narrow northwestern corner of the Eifel, avoiding the rugged Huertgen Forest. From the Weisserstein several radial ridges stretch northeastward toward Euskirchen and Bonn, and along two of these run good roads that converge at Euskirchen. Although the Roer reservoirs and the Schnee Eifel would confine the frontage of the main effort to a narrow ten to twelve miles, the advantages outweighed this factor.

Athwart the selected route ran the belt of concrete pillboxes, minefields, concrete antitank obstacles (dragon's teeth), and entrenchments of the West Wall. From the Moselle to the northern tip of the Schnee Eifel, the fortified zone was relatively shallow, usually not as much as a mile, but it drew strength from the difficult terrain, including the gorges of the Our and the Sauer and the heights of the Schnee Eifel. Farther north the line split into two bands that diverged as much as eleven miles. Pillboxes in the second band were considerably fewer than in the first.

The Enemy in the Eifel

It was peculiarly difficult to guess in January how strongly the Germans might defend the West Wall, though the 12th Army Group's intelligence staff assumed that the enemy would make as stalwart a stand as possible, both because of a need to hold the Allies at arm's length from the Ruhr and because of Hitler's seemingly fanatic refusal to yield ground voluntarily. The large-scale Russian offensive that had begun on 12 January increased the likelihood of a determined defense of the West Wall even though the means were slipping away into the eastern void.[14]

Still operating under the Fuehrer's directive of 22 January to complete an orderly withdrawal from the Ardennes into the West Wall, German commanders were, as expected, pledged to defend the fortifications, but they were looking forward to at least temporary respite once they gained the fortified line. Detected shifts of some Allied units already had reinforced the generally accepted view that the Allies would return to a major thrust in the north in the direction of Cologne, so that the Germans naturally expected pressure to ease in the center. Because the V U.S. Corps appeared to be readying an attack from positions southeast of Monschau, the *Fifth Panzer Army* assumed that the

Americans intended a limited attack to gain the Roer dams. Remarking relatively favorable terrain for armor around Bitburg, the *Seventh Army* believed that the Third U.S. Army might try to establish a bridgehead over the Our River pointing toward Bitburg but anticipated some delay before any attempt to exploit. No one at the time expected a major thrust through the Eifel.[15]

As January neared an end, the Germans would require another week to get the bulk of the *Sixth Panzer Army* loaded on trains and moving toward the east, but so occupied were the designated divisions with the move that no longer could they provide assistance in the line. Full responsibility for the defense lay with Manteuffel's *Fifth Panzer Army* on the north and Brandenberger's *Seventh Army* on the south.

Even as the Americans argued the merits of a thrust through the Eifel, the German command was making the first of three adjustments designed to counter the expected Allied return to a main effort in the north. The commander of *Army Group B*, Field Marshal Model, transferred the *XIII Corps* to the *Seventh Army*, in the process drawing a new interarmy boundary running eastward from a point south of St. Vith through Pruem, a northward extension of responsibility for the *Seventh Army*. Although the boundary with the *Fifteenth Army* remained for the moment about three miles south of Monschau, this boundary too was to be adjusted northward on 5 February to give the southernmost corps of the *Fifteenth Army* to Manteuffel's command, again a side-

---

[14] FUSA G–2 Estimate No. 64, 21 Jan 45.

[15] Material on the German side is from Bauer, The German Withdrawal From the Ardennes and the Western Front in Mid-January.

slipping to the north. The third step, an exchange of sectors between headquarters of the *Fifth Panzer* and *Fifteenth Armies* in order to put a panzer command in the path of the expected Allied main effort, was destined to be delayed by the attack in the Eifel.

As events developed, early stages of the American drive into the Eifel would pass north of the *Seventh Army,* striking primarily at the front of the *Fifth Panzer Army,* manned by the *LXVI Corps* (General der Artillerie Walter Lucht) and the *LXVII Corps.* It would later involve also the extreme south wing of the *Fifteenth Army,* a responsibility of the *LXXIV Corps* (General der Infanterie Karl Puechler).

Although the divisions committed in this sector still included such illustrious names as the *3d Parachute* and *9th Panzer,* these were in reality little more than remnants of true divisions; and while they still fought, the German command would make little effort to rebuild them. The Germans planned instead to pull these once-elite formations from the line for rehabilitation in keeping with the theory that some respite would follow withdrawal into the West Wall. The Eastern Front had priority on replacements at this point in any case, and such replacements as did reach the west went to the infantry and volks grenadier divisions that were to stay behind to hold the fortifications.

In a general way, Allied intelligence anticipated this policy. It meant, in sum, that in an effort to create a reserve, the Germans would have to thin their ranks in the Eifel to a point where no coherent line would exist. Defense would have to be by strongpoints, relying of necessity on scraps and scratch outfits. The ragged

ranks might be stiffened a little with concrete and barbed wire, their task eased by bad weather and rugged terrain, but the balance of forces remained hopelessly against them. Recognizing this situation, the First U.S. Army's G–2, Col. Benjamin A. Dickson, expressed some optimism about the chances of swiftly cracking the West Wall and piercing the Eifel.[16]

In the last analysis, as the Third Army staff pointed out, quick success depended primarily on the enemy's will to fight. Poorly trained and ill-equipped troops could give good accounts of themselves even in the fortifications of the West Wall and the snowbound compartments of the Eifel only if they wanted to.[17] As the drive toward Euskirchen got under way, just how much the individual German soldier still wanted to fight was the question.

A Try for Quick Success

The first phase of the offensive was to be a frontal attack aimed at penetrating the West Wall on a 25-mile front from Monschau to Luetzkampen, near the northern tip of Luxembourg. (*Map 1*) General Ridgway's XVIII Airborne Corps on the right wing of the First Army was to make the main effort. Holding two infantry divisions in reserve for exploitation, Ridgway was to strike with two others to pierce the fortified line between the Schnee Eifel and the Weisserstein astride the Losheim Gap. Named after a town along the border, the gap is a narrow corridor that in 1914, 1940, and 1944 had served German armies well as

---

[16] See, for example, FUSA G–3 Estimate No. 63, 16 Jan 45.

[17] TUSA G–3 Periodic Rpt, 27 Jan 45.

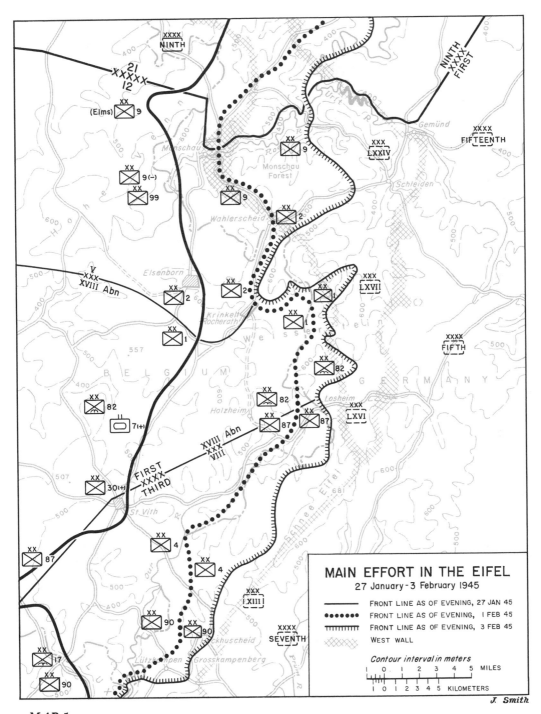

MAIN EFFORT IN THE EIFEL
27 January - 3 February 1945

| | FRONT LINE AS OF EVENING, 27 JAN 45 |
| FRONT LINE AS OF EVENING, 1 FEB 45 |
| FRONT LINE AS OF EVENING, 3 FEB 45 |
| WEST WALL |

Contour interval in meters

MILES

KILOMETERS

J. Smith

MAP 1

MEN OF THE 82D AIRBORNE DIVISION *pull sleds in advancing through the Ardennes snow.*

a débouché. Once through the gap, the airborne corps would have access to one of the main routes leading to Euskirchen.

At the same time, General Huebner's V Corps on the north was to penetrate the western spur of the West Wall in the Monschau Forest and protect the army's left flank by crossing northern reaches of the Weisserstein and seizing Schleiden and Gemuend, both important road centers astride a more circuitous but usable route to Euskirchen. To exploit success by either Huebner or Ridgway, the First Army's General Hodges held in reserve

Collins's VII Corps with two infantry and two armored divisions.[18]

The Third Army's role in this first phase of the operation was to protect the First Army's right flank. General Patton planned to attack at first only with Middleton's VIII Corps, whose northernmost division, the 87th, was to advance abreast of the XVIII Airborne Corps to the vicinity of Losheim while the 4th and 90th Divisions to the south broke

---

[18] 12th AGp Ltr of Instrs 12, 4 Jan 45; SHAEF Liaison Rpt 432, Intentions, 28 Jan 45, in 12th AGp 371.3, Military Objectives, V.

through the West Wall along and just south of the Schnee Eifel. These two divisions then were to block to the southeast, whereupon Patton intended to insert a fourth division on the right of the 87th to advance northeast with the 87th. With protection of the First Army assured, Patton then might advance with three corps abreast northeast to the Rhine or turn southeast to take the West Wall in flank and roll it up southward to Trier.[19]

The line of departure for the attack was irregular. In the north, where units of the V Corps still held the positions on which they had stabilized the northern shoulder of the counteroffensive some weeks earlier, it ran from Monschau south to the ridgeline that served as an outpost of the Hohe Venn near Elsenborn. Below that point, the attack would begin from positions gained during the last few days of fighting. Those generally followed the highway leading into St. Vith from the north. Beyond St. Vith the line retracted to the southeast generally along the trace of the Our River and the German frontier.

Thus the XVIII Airborne Corps still was from eight to twelve miles away from the forward pillboxes of the West Wall, which followed the eastward-bulging contour of the Belgian-German border. Since the countryside in this bulge is either heavily wooded or studded with villages, the troops making the main effort faced a difficult task even to reach the fortified line.

The 1st Infantry and 82d Airborne Divisions of the XVIII Airborne Corps opened the attack on 28 January. The next day the VIII Corps attacked with

the 87th, 4th, and 90th Divisions. On the 30th, the V Corps jumped off in the north.

The story of all these first attacks could be told almost in a word: weather. By the end of January the month's unusually heavy snowfall and low temperatures had left a snow cover one to two feet deep everywhere and in some places drifts up to a man's waist. Snow glazed the hills, choked the valleys and the roads, and hid the enemy's mines. On the first day, it snowed again all day and into the night.[20]

Plowing through the deep snow, the two divisions of the XVIII Airborne Corps encountered only sporadic opposition, often taking the form of occasional patrols or scattered rifle fire. Yet men marching all day through the snow even without sight or sound of the enemy were exhausted when night came from sheer physical exertion. It would take the two divisions four full days to traverse the eight to twelve miles from their jump-off positions to the high ground confronting the West Wall in the Losheim Gap.

It was in some ways a curious twilight war. One night, for example, a patrol from the 82d Airborne Division, sent to investigate a report that the adjacent 87th Division had occupied a village near Losheim, found no soldiers, American or German. Behind blackout curtains the villagers had their lights on. Now and then a shell crashed nearby, and between times the paratroopers could hear babies crying.

On the other hand, an enemy who was nowhere in particular might be any-

---

[19] TUSA Opnl Dir, 26 Jan 45.

[20] Unless otherwise noted, the tactical story is based on official unit records and combat interviews conducted soon after the action by historians of the European Theater Historical Section.

TRAFFIC JAM ON A SLICK ARDENNES ROAD

where. As happened at the village of Holzheim, where on 29 January a company of the 82d Airborne's 508th Parachute Infantry seized 80 prisoners while overrunning the village. Leaving the prisoners under a 4-man guard, the bulk of the company had moved on when a German patrol sneaked back into the village, overpowered the guards, and freed the prisoners. Onto this scene stumbled the company's first sergeant, Leonard A. Funk, Jr. Surprised, he pretended to surrender, but as the Germans moved to disarm him, he swung his submachine gun from his shoulder and opened fire. Seizing German weapons, the 4-man guard joined the fight. In the melee that ensued, 21 Germans were killed and the rest again surrendered.[21]

Or as happened one night early in the attack when a platoon of paratroopers advanced down a narrow road between three-foot banks of snow thrown up by German plows. Three tanks rumbled between the files of riflemen. Out of the darkness, dead ahead, suddenly appeared a German company, marching forward in close formation. The banks of hard snow

[21] Sergeant Funk was awarded the Medal of Honor.

on either side of the road meant no escape for either force. The paratroopers opened fire first, their accompanying tanks pouring withering machine gun fire into the massed enemy. Surprised and without comparable fire support, unable to scatter or retreat, the Germans had no chance. Almost 200 were killed; a handful surrendered. Not an American was hurt.

Foot troops moved slowly, but they could always move. Behind them artillery, supply, service, and armored vehicles jammed the few cleared roads. Especially congested was the zone of the 1st Division where every few hundred yards a partially destroyed village knotted the roadnet. When leading riflemen of the 1st Division reached the West Wall, only one artillery battalion had managed to displace far enough forward to provide support. Trucks bringing food and ammunition often failed to get through. Had the opposition been determined, the traffic snarls could have proved serious; as it was, the only tactical result was to slow the advance.

It was 1 February—the fifth day of the attack—before the two divisions of the XVIII Airborne Corps could begin to move against the West Wall itself. Close by on the right, reflecting the day's delay in starting to attack, the Third Army's 87th Division needed yet another day to reach the pillboxes.

North and south of the main effort, the V Corps and the bulk of the VIII Corps hit the West Wall earlier. One division near Monschau, the 9th, northernmost unit of the V Corps, was already inside the fortified zone at the time of the jump-off on 30 January.

The 9th Division (Maj. Gen. Louis A. Craig), moving southeast from Mon-

schau, and the 2d Division (Maj. Gen. Walter M. Robertson), striking north through the twin border villages of Krinkelt-Rocherath, near Elsenborn, were to converge at a road junction within the Monschau Forest astride the northern end of the Weisserstein at a customs house called Wahlerscheid. Both divisions would have to pass through Wahlerscheid, a pillbox-studded strongpoint, before parting ways again to continue toward Schleiden and Gemuend. Contingents of the 99th Division meanwhile were to clear the Monschau Forest west of the converging thrusts, and the Ninth Army's southernmost division was to make a limited objective attack to protect the left flank of the attacking corps.

In the long run, the V Corps would benefit from the fact that its attack struck along the boundary between the *Fifth Panzer* and *Fifteenth Armies,* but in the early stages the presence of West Wall pillboxes would mean stiffer resistance than that against the main effort. Yet nowhere was the resistance genuinely determined. The Germans of General Puechler's *LXXIV Corps* and General Hitzfeld's *LXVII Corps* simply had not the means for that kind of defense. As elsewhere, deep snow was the bigger problem, while ground fog and low overcast restricted observation for artillery and denied participation by tactical aircraft altogether.

Approaching within a few hundred yards of the Wahlerscheid road junction late on 31 January, the 9th Division repulsed a counterattack by an understrength German battalion. Soon thereafter patrols discovered that the pillboxes at Wahlerscheid were organized for defense only to the south, a response to the fact that the 2d Division in December had hit these same pillboxes from the south in the abortive attack toward the Roer dams. The 9th Division's 39th Infantry moved in on the rear of the fortifications early on 1 February. The 2d Division in the meantime was fighting its way through Krinkelt-Rocherath, scene of an epic stand by the same division during the counteroffensive, and then moving into the Monschau Forest to come upon Wahlerscheid from the south.

As night came on 1 February, both the 2d and 9th Divisions were ready to file past Wahlerscheid. In three days the attack of the V Corps had begun to show genuine promise.

On the south wing of the offensive, the 4th (General Blakeley) and 90th Divisions (Maj. Gen. Lowell W. Rooks) of the VIII Corps at the same time had run into the stiffest fighting of all, partly because of the obstacle of the Our River. The lines of departure of the two divisions lay close to the Our, and for the 90th and the right regiment of the 4th, crossing the river was the first order of business. Narrow and shallow, the Our was frozen solid at some points and easily fordable at others, but steep, slippery banks were a barrier to wheeled traffic and, as it turned out, to tracked vehicles as well. Yet what made the river most difficult was that it was tied into the West Wall defenses. Although the main line lay two to three miles behind the river, the Germans had erected at every likely crossing point fortified outpost positions.

Aiming at the southern end of the Schnee Eifel, one regiment of the 4th Division on the first day, 29 January, tried to cross the Our four miles southeast of St. Vith. As the leading battalion approached the crossing site, a fury of small arms fire erupted from the east bank. Although one rifle platoon got across before the worst of the firing began, the rest of the battalion backed off to look for another site. Casualties were relatively light—for the entire regiment for two days, 9 killed, 29 wounded—but it was noon the next day before all men of the leading battalion were across the Our.

A few miles to the south two regiments of the 90th Division had much the same experience. The leading battalions of each regiment came under intense fire at the selected crossing sites opposite the German outposts, but individual companies managed to maneuver to the south to cross the river and come upon the opposition from the rear.

Despite these successes, the 4th and 90th Divisions advanced only slowly through deep snow against scattered but determined nests of resistance for the next three days. Partial explanation lay in that both divisions were facing the *9th Panzer Division,* a shell of a unit but one still capable of steadfast defense at selected points. By 1 February the 90th Division was in sight of the West Wall around the villages of Heckhuscheid and Grosskampenberg, while the 4th Division still had several villages to clear before climbing the slopes of the Schnee Eifel.[22]

---

[22] In advancing on Heckhuscheid just after nightfall on 1 February, Cpl. Edward A. Bennett's company of the 90th Division's 358th Infantry came under heavy machine gun fire from a house on the edge of the village. Bennett crawled forward alone, dispatched a guard outside the house with a trench knife, then charged into the house and killed three Germans with his rifle, eliminated three more with a .45-caliber pistol, and clubbed a seventh to death. He was awarded the Medal of Honor.

These two divisions were destined to continue their attacks into the West Wall but as part of another operation. On 1 February, the Damocles sword that had hung over the 12th Army Group's offensive from its inception suddenly fell.

A Shift to the North

On 1 February General Eisenhower ordered General Bradley to cancel the 12th Army Group's drive on Euskirchen and shift troops north to the Ninth Army.[23] He made the decision even though Bradley's thrust, while slowed by weather and terrain, was encountering no major opposition from the Germans. Only a complete breakthrough could have saved Bradley's offensive, and that was yet to come.

Several considerations prompted the Supreme Commander's decision. Continuing pressure from Field Marshal Montgomery, some feeling of pressure emanating from the meeting of the Combined Chiefs at Malta, Eisenhower's own unswerving conviction that the best way to victory was in the north against the Ruhr—all played a part. Also, Eisenhower in mid-January apparently had given Montgomery at least an implicit promise that he would make a decision on Bradley's offensive by the first day of February.[24]

Eisenhower's order halting the Eifel offensive was in its formal, written form clear-cut. "It is of paramount importance," the directive said, " . . . to close

the Rhine north of Duesseldorf with all possible speed." [25] To achieve this, the First Canadian Army was to attack not later than 8 February and the Ninth Army not later than 10 February. The Ninth Army was to receive the equivalent of the resources loaned the 12th Army Group at the start of the Ardennes counteroffensive, or at least five divisions. With thinned ranks, Bradley's armies were to go on the defensive except in the north where the First Army was to seize the Roer River dams and, subsequently, to jump the Roer to protect the Ninth Army's right flank.

Informally, General Eisenhower modified these terms considerably. Even though Bradley was to relinquish troops immediately to the Ninth Army, the Supreme Commander would allow his offensive in the Eifel to continue until 10 February with the declared objective of gaining a line from Gemuend to Pruem that would include the Weisserstein and the Schnee Eifel and thus afford control of the Losheim Gap for possible future operations. Yet no matter how far this attack had progressed by 10 February, the First Army from that time was to concentrate on a primary mission of attacking across the Roer to protect the Ninth Army's flank.[26]

Disappointed with the Supreme Commander's decision, General Bradley nevertheless took hope in the possibility that he later might turn the First Army's attack across the Roer to the south, perhaps to join in a thrust by the Third Army to clear the entire Eifel region. In that General Eisenhower granted the Third Army permission to "continue the

---

[23] Msg, SHAEF to CG's 12th and 21 AGp's, S–77434, 1 Feb 45, 12th AGp 371.3, Military Objectives, V.

[24] Ltr, Montgomery to Eisenhower, 12 Jan 45, Pogue files; Memo for Record, Bradley for G–3, 17 Jan 45; 21 AGp Dir, M–548, 21 Jan 45. The last two in 12th AGp 371.3, Military Objectives, V.

[25] S–77434, 1 Feb 45.

[26] Notes on Conference with Army Comdrs, 2 Feb 45, in 12th AGp, 371.3, Military Objectives, V.

probing attacks now in progress," on the theory of preventing the enemy from shifting reinforcements to the north and with a view to taking advantage of any chance to improve the army's position for future action, Bradley found real encouragement. At headquarters of the Third Army "probing attacks" were popularly known as the "defensive-offensive," which meant, in more widely understood terminology, a major attack. Bradley knew, too, that the Supreme Commander himself well understood General Patton's special lexicon.[27]

Patton's orders, issued on 3 February, scarcely mentioned defense. The Third Army, Patton directed, was to continue to attack on its left to seize Pruem, to drive northeast with its right from the vicinity of Echternach to take Bitburg, and to be prepared to continue to the Rhine.[28]

Since the job of taking Pruem fell naturally to the VIII Corps and thus constituted a continuation of the attack then in progress, though in a different context, the Third Army's drive into the Eifel was barely troubled by the decision of 1 February. The First Army was more severely straitened. While General Patton gave up only two divisions to the Ninth Army, one of which was an inexperienced unit from the army reserve, General Hodges had to surrender the two reserve infantry divisions of the XVIII Airborne Corps and the three divisions of the VII Corps that had been standing by to exploit in the Eifel. Although headquarters of the VII Corps

[27] Ibid.; 12th AGp Ltr of Instrs, 7 Feb 45, confirming previous oral orders; Omar N. Bradley, A Soldier's Story (New York: Henry Holt and Co., 1951), p. 501.

[28] TUSA AAR, 1 Aug 44–9 May 45, vol. I, Opns, p. 255.

was to remain under the First Army, General Collins was to assume responsibility for the southern portion of the Ninth Army's Roer River line, the same front the corps had held before the counteroffensive, and prepare to attack to protect the Ninth Army's flank. In addition, the V Corps had to mount an attack against the Roer dams.

The First Army was to try again to penetrate the West Wall in the Eifel, but under the revised conditions chances of decisive success were meager.

An End to the Offensive

For four more days, through 4 February, the thrusts of the XVIII Airborne Corps and the V Corps continued much as before, particularly in the zone of the airborne corps where the 1st Infantry and 82d Airborne Divisions at last entered the West Wall. While not every pillbox was manned, the cold, the snow, the icy roads hindering support and supply, and the strength lent the defense by concrete shelters still imposed slow going. By 4 February the two divisions had advanced little more than a mile inside the German frontier, although a sufficient distance to insure control of the first tier of villages on a five-mile front within the Losheim Gap. The advance represented a penetration of the densest concentration of pillboxes in this part of the West Wall.

The V Corps meanwhile made substantially greater progress. Indeed, had any authority still existed to turn the Eifel drive into a major offensive, the advances of the V Corps after clearing the Wahlerscheid road junction on 1 February might have been sufficient to justify alerting the forces of exploitation.

On 2 February both the 2d and 9th Divisions pushed almost four miles beyond Wahlerscheid, one in the direction of Schleiden, the other, Gemuend.

Much of their success again could be attributed to the luck of striking astride the boundary between German units. As early as 29 January the northernmost unit of the *LXVII Corps*, the *277th Volks Grenadier Division* around Krinkelt-Rocherath, had lost contact with the southernmost unit of the *LXXIV Corps*, the *62d Infantry Division*, whose southern flank was at Wahlerscheid. Even after the *277th Volks Grenadiers* began to withdraw into the West Wall on the last two days of January, no contact or even communication existed between the two units.[29]

In driving southeast from Monschau, the 9th Division had virtually wiped out the *62d Infantry Division*. As units of both the 2d and 9th Divisions poured northeast through the resulting gap at Wahlerscheid on 2 February, outposts of the *277th Division* on higher ground two miles to the southeast could observe the American columns, but the *277th's* commander, Generalmajor Wilhelm Viebig, had no way of determining what was going on. Although Viebig's artillery could have damaged the U.S. units, so seriously depleted were his ammunition stocks that he decided to fire only if the Americans turned in his direction.

As darkness came on 2 February, Viebig's corps commander, General Hitzfeld, learned of the penetration. Ordering Viebig to extend his flank to the north, he also managed to put hands on small contingents of the *3d Panzer Grenadier Division*, which had been withdrawn from the line for refitting. Yet despite these countermoves, the 9th Division by nightfall of 3 February stood less than two miles from Gemuend, the 2d Division only a few hundred yards from Schleiden.

Had the Americans been intent on exploiting their limited penetration, Hitzfeld would have been hard put to do anything about it, but the hope of major exploitation through the Eifel by the First Army was beyond recall. General Hodges on 4 February made it official with a letter of instructions spelling out various shifts of units for his newly assigned tasks.[30] Not only was the VII Corps to move northward to take over a portion of the Ninth Army's Roer River line but the XVIII Airborne Corps also was to shift to assume responsibility for a part of the Roer line adjoining the VII Corps. The V Corps was to extend its positions southeastward to relieve the airborne corps while at the same time attacking to seize the Roer dams.

Occurring late on 6 February, relief of the airborne corps signaled an end to the offensive in this part of the Eifel. The line as finally established ran along high ground overlooking Gemuend and Schleiden from the west, thence southeastward across the northeastern arm of the Weisserstein to the boundary with the Third Army near Losheim.

Blessed from the first with little more than ambition, the main effort in the Eifel had ground to a predictable halt.

---

[29] German material is from Magna E. Bauer, MS # R-65, The Breakthrough of the West Wall Between Ormont and Monschau.

[30] See First Army Report, 1 Aug 44-22 Feb. 45, pp. 154-55.

CHAPTER IV

The Roer River Dams

In one of the more sharply etched sectors of the Eifel, a few miles northeast of Monschau, German civil engineers over the years had constructed seven dams to impound and regulate the flow of the waters of the Roer River and its tributaries. These were the dams the American soldier had come to know collectively as the Roer River dams, with particular reference to the two largest, the Urft and the Schwammenauel.

Constructed just after the turn of the century on the Urft River downstream from Gemuend, near confluence of the Urft and the Roer, the Urft Dam creates a reservoir (the Urftstausee) capable of impounding approximately 42,000 acre-feet of water. Built in the mid-1930's a few miles to the north on the Roer near Hasenfeld, the Schwammenauel Dam creates a reservoir (the Roerstausee) capable of impounding about 81,000 acre-feet. The Urft Dam is made of concrete; the Schwammenauel of earth with a concrete core. It was these two dams that the Germans might destroy or open the gates of to manipulate the waters of the Roer, flooding a low-lying valley downstream to the north in the vicinity of the towns of Dueren and Juelich, washing out tactical bridges, and isolating any Allied force that had crossed the river.[1]

From September through mid-November, 1944, General Hodges' First Army had launched three separate one-division attacks through an almost trackless Huertgen Forest in the general direction of the dams, though with other objectives in mind. A combination of difficult terrain and unexpectedly sharp German reaction had stopped all three attacks well short of the dams. Realizing at last the importance of the dams to German defense of the Roer River line, the American command had tried to breach them with air strikes, but these too failed. In December a ground attack aimed specifically at seizing the dams had been cut short by the counteroffensive in the Ardennes.[2]

Those attacks launched through the Huertgen Forest had been directed toward commanding ground at the town of Schmidt, two miles north of the Schwammenauel Dam. The short-lived December attack had been planned as a two-pronged thrust with two divisions coming upon the dams from the south while another pushed northeastward from the vicinity of Monschau along the north bank of the Roer to Schmidt. Although the deep cut of the Roer and

---

[1] A more detailed description of the dams is to be found in MacDonald, *The Siegfried Line Campaign.*

[2] MacDonald, *The Siegfried Line Campaign.* Charles B. MacDonald and Sidney T. Mathews, *Three Battles: Arnaville, Altuzzo and Schmidt,* UNITED STATES ARMY IN WORLD WAR II (Washington, 1952), "Objective Schmidt."

the reservoirs themselves would have imposed a tactical divorce on the two thrusts, the best approach to the Urft Dam was from the south and the high ground at Schmidt was essential to gaining and holding the Schwammenauel Dam.

As the new V Corps commander, General Huebner, planned the February attack on the dams, he apparently had the earlier planning in mind. Furthermore, attacks then under way as part of the fading drive into the Eifel fitted in with the two-pronged pattern of the earlier plan. The drives of the 2d and 9th Divisions through Wahlerscheid on Gemuend and Schleiden had the secondary effect of threatening the Roer dams from the south, while a limited objective attack staged by the southernmost division of the Ninth Army to protect the left flank of the First Army had the secondary effect of setting the stage for a thrust northeastward from Monschau toward the Schwammenauel Dam.

This division of the Ninth Army was the 78th (Maj. Gen. Edwin P. Parker, Jr.). Through the Ardennes fighting the division had continued to hold positions near Monschau that had been reached in the December attack toward the dams. It was a foregone conclusion that when the boundary between the First and Ninth Armies was adjusted northward, the 78th would pass to the First Army and become the logical choice for renewing the attack on the Schwammenauel Dam. Begun on 30 January, the division's limited objective attack to protect the First Army's left flank thus was a first step toward capturing the Schwammenauel Dam.

The 78th Division occupied a small

GENERAL HUEBNER

salient about two miles deep into the forward band of the West Wall on a plateau northeast of Monschau. Containing sprawling villages as well as pillboxes, the plateau was one of the few large clearings along the German border between Aachen and St. Vith. As such, it represented a likely avenue for penetrating the West Wall and had been so used, though without signal success, in an attack in October. For want of a better name, the area has been called the Monschau corridor, though it is not a true terrain corridor, since entrance to it from the west is blocked by the high marshland of the Hohe Venn and farther east it is obstructed by dense forest and the cut of the Roer River.

The enemy there was an old foe, having held the sector when the 78th made its first attack in mid-December and having tried in vain to penetrate the 78th lines in early stages of the counteroffensive. This was the *272d Volks Grenadier Division* with a strength of about 6,000 men.[3] The division was a part of Puechler's *LXXIV Corps* of the *Fifteenth Army,* destined to be transferred on 5 February to control of the *Fifth Panzer Army.*[4]

The object of the limited attack was to extend the 78th Division's holdings to the south and southeast to gain the north bank of the Roer River from Monschau to Einruhr, the latter guarding passage of the Roer along a highway leading southeast to Schleiden. The assignment was to be divided between the 311th Infantry on the east and the 310th Infantry on the west, each responsible for taking two of five villages in the target area. Attached to the 78th Division, Combat Command A (CCA) of the 5th Armored Division was to take the fifth village in the center with the help of a battalion of the 311th Infantry. Because the 310th Infantry would be rolling up the West Wall as it advanced, a platoon of British flame-throwing tanks, called Crocodiles, was assigned in support.[5]

The attack began with a good break. Although the division commander, General Parker, had intended a half-hour artillery preparation, General Simpson, with an eye toward building a reserve for the Ninth Army's coming offensive, cut the ammunition allocation so drastically that Parker had to reduce the preparation to five minutes. Accustomed to longer shelling before an American attack, the Germans in the pillboxes in front of the 310th Infantry waited under cover for the fire to continue. They waited too long. In a matter of minutes, men of the 310th Infantry were all around them. In three hours they cleared thirty-two pillboxes and took the village of Konzen. Their final objective, the next village to the south, fell the next morning. So swift was the success that the flame-throwing tanks saw little use.

In the center, the tanks of CCA had trouble with mines concealed by deep snow, but by late afternoon they managed to work their way in the wake of the infantry to the fringe of Eicherscheid. With infantrymen close behind them, they roared into the village and began a systematic mop-up just as darkness came.

Only on the extreme left wing of the 311th Infantry, at Kesternich on the road to Einruhr, was the story basically different. There the 2d Battalion already held a few of the westernmost houses, the sole lasting gain from a bitter fight for the village in December. Yet despite long familiarity with the terrain and the most minute planning, the first companies to enter the main part of the village found control almost impossible. Although the men had studied the location of the houses from a map, they were difficult to recognize. Many were destroyed, some were burning, and the snow hid landmarks. Communications with tankers of the supporting 736th Tank Battalion failed early. Mines ac-

---

[3] 78th Div G–2 Estimate, 26 Jan 45.
[4] See above, ch. III.
[5] A good unit history, *Lightning—The Story of the 78th Infantry Division* (Washington: Infantry Journal Press, 1947), supplements official records.

counted for two tanks, antitank fire two more.[6]

With the Germans doggedly defending each building, it took two full days to clear the last resistance from Kesternich. Capturing the town might have taken even longer had it not been for a squad leader in Company E, S. Sgt. Jonah E. Kelley. Each time Kelley's squad assaulted a building, he was the first to enter. Although wounded twice early in the fighting, he refused evacuation. His left hand useless, he continued to fire his rifle by resting it across his left forearm. Late on the second day, Kelley led an assault on a machine gun position. German fire cut him down as he expended the last three rounds from his rifle and knocked out the machine gun.[7]

In the two-day action, the 311th Infantry lost 224 men, the bulk of them from the 2d Battalion. Just why Kesternich cost so much became clear as artillery observers found they could direct observed fire from the village on all remaining German positions west of the Roerstausee.

Toward Schmidt

In advance of the pending shift of the First Army's boundary to the north, the 78th Division on 2 February passed to operational control of the V Corps. That evening the division commander, General Parker, traveled to headquarters of the V Corps to receive from General Huebner the order for the capture of Schmidt and the Schwammenauel Dam. The task, Huebner told Parker, was the most vital at that time on the entire Western Front; until the dam was in hand, the Ninth Army dared not cross the Roer. Added to this glare of the spotlight was the fact that the 78th Division had had only limited battle experience and the fact that the very name of the town of Schmidt had become a kind of bugaboo among American soldiers after the beating another division had taken there in November. All the ingredients for a bad case of the jitters were present at the start.

As General Parker prepared his plan of attack, it was obvious that terrain would narrowly restrict the force that could be applied against Schmidt and the dam. Schmidt lies spread-eagled on the eastern slopes of a high hill mass, in general an east-west ridge with fingers poking out to north, northeast, and south. Adjacent high ground to the north beyond the little Kall River, which in German hands had contributed to failure at Schmidt in November, was controlled by the neighboring XIX Corps.

It would be hard to get at Schmidt along the route from the southwest that the 78th Division had to take. Except for a narrow woods trail from Woffelsbach, close by the Roerstausee, the only feasible approach from this direction is along a lone main road following the crest of the Schmidt ridge. The road passes from the open ground of the Monschau corridor through more than a mile of dense evergreen forest before emerging again into broad fields several hundred yards west of Schmidt, where it climbs Hill 493 before descending into the town. A narrow but militarily im-

---

[6] Organized and trained to operate amphibious tanks in the invasion of Normandy, the 736th had been converted to a standard tank battalion in November but had received no medium tanks until January. See 736th Tank Bn Hist.

[7] Sergeant Kelley was awarded the Medal of Honor posthumously.

THE URFT DAM

portant feeder road parallels the main road on the north for a few miles before joining the main road at a point where the Germans had constructed a nest of wooden barracks, believed to be strongly fortified.

In addition to normal attachments, the 78th Division was to be reinforced by the reserve combat command of the 7th Armored Division, an engineer combat battalion, fires of V Corps and 7th Armored artillery, and planes of the XIX Tactical Air Command. Jump-off was scheduled for 0300, 5 February.

General Parker intended first to clear the rest of the Monschau corridor and seize a line running inside the woods from the Kall River in the north through the nest of barracks to the Roerstausee. (*Map 2*) From there the attack was to proceed almost due east along the axis of the main road into Schmidt, thence, while subsidiary drives secured villages north and east of the town, southeast to the Schwammenauel Dam. The 309th Infantry, attacking with its 3d Battalion from within the Monschau corridor at Rollesbroich, was to make the main effort in the first phase, seizing the barracks at the juncture of the feeder road

THE SCHWAMMENAUEL DAM

and the main highway. Thereupon the 310th Infantry was to pass through and take Schmidt.

The attack began on a bright note, for late in the afternoon of 4 February a company of the 9th Division reached the Urft Dam after little more than a cross-country march. Although American artillery fire had done some damage to outlet tunnels, the big dam still was intact.

The beginning of the 78th Division's attack went well—unexpectedly well. The 3d Battalion, 309th Infantry (Lt. Col. Floyd C. Call), got off on time at 0300, 5 February, and in rain-drenched darkness moved cross-country through a web of pillboxes. The infantrymen slipped past at least 35 concrete pillboxes and bunkers from which 135 Germans later emerged; but not a shot disturbed them.

As the battalion advanced through successive checkpoints and the word came back over the field telephones, "No enemy contact," commanders prepared the next step. It looked like a penetration, but could it be exploited? Engineers and reconnaissance troops moved out to see if the roads were clear, particularly the feeder road north of the main highway, the main axis of the 309th's

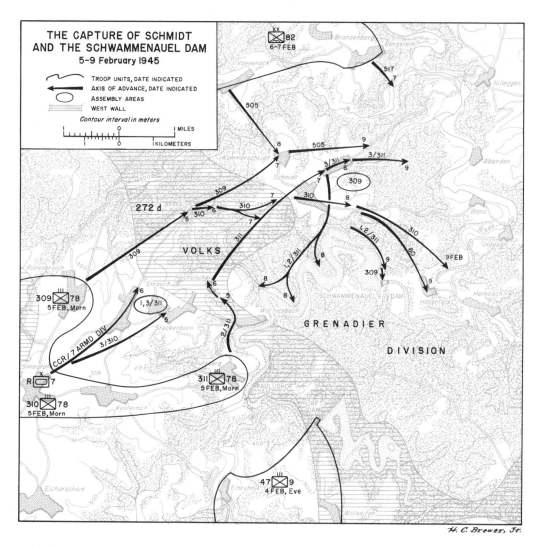

MAP 2

advance. Meanwhile, other troops of the division, including attached tanks of the 7th Armored Division's CCR, prepared to clear the remaining villages in the Monschau corridor.

A little after daylight, General Parker alerted the 310th Infantry for an immediate move through the 309th. Fifteen minutes later Colonel Call reported his

battalion "advancing toward the final objective" and meeting small arms fire for the first time.[8] Shortly thereafter the infantrymen of the 309th overran the German barracks, catching some men sleeping, others eating breakfast. Movement orders for the 310th Infantry,

---

[8] 310th Inf Jnl, 5 Feb 45, entry 0726.

meanwhile, had to await inspection of the road. Inevitably, that took time.

During the wait the commanders considered other possibilities. General Parker thought of sending the 309th out farther than originally planned. General Huebner at V Corps contemplated more drastic changes. Before 0830 he ordered the 78th Division to form a task force built around the 311th Infantry to cross the Roer at Ruhrberg over the Paulushof regulating dam, one of the lesser dams in the Roer system, plow through rough, wooded country between the Urftstausee and the Roerstausee, and come upon the Schwammenauel Dam from the south. At the same time the 9th Division was to send a force across the Urft Dam to block forest roads that the Germans might use to move against the 311th Infantry.[9] These maneuvers were to take place during the night of 6 February. In the meantime the main effort by the 78th Division against Schmidt was to continue.

Shortly before 0900 on the 5th it became clear that mines and craters for the present ruled out use of either the feeder road or the main highway toward Schmidt. The 310th Infantry, General Parker ordered, was to proceed cross-country without supporting weapons. In two hours the infantrymen were on the march.

Men of the 309th Infantry meanwhile had begun to run into resistance as the Germans awoke to their threat. A company on the right received what was reported to be a counterattack, though it apparently was no more than an aggressive defense by a few German squads. A fire fight took place nevertheless, and

in the woods where control is difficult, it checked the advance. The attack, which had flamed so brilliantly, began to show signs of sputtering out.

With so much at stake, commanders grew uneasy. General Parker an hour before noon ordered the 309th Infantry to go as far as possible beyond the barracks and at the same time directed the 310th Infantry not to move into forward assembly areas as planned but to pass immediately through advance units of the 309th Infantry and press the attack. These orders stood less than fifteen minutes; the corps commander, General Huebner, intervened. It seemed to Huebner unsound in the face of seemingly slight resistance to halt the attack while waiting for a new regiment to take over. The 309th, moreover, was the freshest unit in the division. At his instigation, the 309th was to continue to Schmidt, reinforced by its 1st Battalion, heretofore attached to the 310th Infantry. All troops were to advance without supporting weapons until roads could be opened.[10]

The order was difficult to execute. The 1st Battalion of the 309th in order to rejoin its parent regiment had to pass through two battalions of the 310th that had already begun to move forward. It was two hours before men of this battalion began to pass through and late afternoon before they arrived at the forward positions. The 2d Battalion had been clearing pillboxes around the barracks and could not assemble immediately to move on to the east. The 3rd Battalion still was mopping up the pillbox belt that had been negotiated so rapidly before dawn by the 2d Battalion.

As night came, General Parker—ap-

[9] V Corps Ltr of Instrs 051030 Feb 45, as cited in V Corps Opns in ETO, p. 376.

[10] 78th Div AAR, Feb 45.

parently with the concurrence of General Huebner—directed that all units resume their original missions. The 310th Infantry was to pass through the 309th at 0300 the next morning, 6 February.

Both regiments were in low spirits, thoroughly confused by the day of changing orders.[11] Men of at least one battalion of the 309th learned that both division and corps commanders were displeased with their performance. The men of the 310th Infantry were tired, wet, and frustrated, and the regimental commander warned that they would be in poor condition for the next day's attack. The day of 5 February closed on frayed nerves.

While the 311th Infantry had escaped most of the confusion, that regiment's progress, too, was slow. The order to cross the Roer at Ruhrberg General Huebner canceled in the afternoon when reconnaissance revealed that the Germans had blown a great gap in the roadway over the Paulushof Dam and that the swollen Roer was too deep and swift to ford.

The order never had interrupted operations. One battalion continued to push across cruel terrain north of Ruhrberg, the back way to Schmidt. Although resistance was never resolute, the job of clambering through woods, up and down steep hills, and challenging a succession of pillboxes wore the men out. Yet they took the hamlet of Woffelsbach and thus, by nightfall, were roughly on a line with the 309th Infantry in the main attack.

Since all attempts to speed the main attack had failed and one had backfired

in added delays, pressure for quick success increased. General Huebner ordered that the attack on Schmidt itself be made at daylight on 6 February and that the Schwammenauel Dam be taken, if possible, the same day. The First Army commander, General Hodges, was to arrive at the division command post in the morning, which was a military euphemism for "Get cracking, or else!"

At 0300 on 6 February, the 310th Infantry began passing through the lines of the 309th with two battalions in column, but hardly had the men crossed their line of departure when they came under intense grazing fire from automatic weapons. As the men went to ground, commanders temporarily lost control. At daylight, the men rallied, but commanders in the thick woods had no real idea where they were. The day was overcast, and dim light filtering through heavy fir branches scarcely brightened the gloom under the trees. Enemy artillery and mortar fire ranged in. One battalion counted about 200 rounds of mortar fire in half an hour. Apparently unobserved, the shelling caused few casualties, but it was enough to stymie advance. Tanks coming up the road to support the attack drew antitank fire and backed into hull defilade out of contact with the infantry.

In early afternoon the infantry tried a new attack, but it had no punch. Since observers were unable to adjust artillery by sight in the thick woods, artillery preparation was worse than useless, serving only to fell trees and branches in the path of the infantry. Commanders still had only a vague idea of where the men were.

Just before dusk, Company A on the extreme right walked into an ambush.

---

[11] 310th Inf Jnl, 5 Feb 45, entry 1849; Combat interviews with men of 3d Bn, 309th Inf.

The Germans allowed the lead platoon to pass through their positions, then opened heavy small arms fire on the company headquarters and two platoons that followed. The incident disorganized the company and produced wild rumors in the rear. Artillery observers reported that the entire right flank was disintegrating; Company A was "cut to pieces." [12] At division headquarters word was that a substantial counterattack was in progress and had achieved a considerable penetration. Seven men from Company A reported at regimental headquarters that they were the sole survivors.

The truth was that there had been no counterattack and no penetration, but defensive fires from what may have been the enemy's main line of resistance were heavy and damaging. The 310th Infantry commander, Col. Thomas H. Hayes, decided to call off the attack for the night, pulling his advance battalion back to consolidate with another in a nighttime defensive position. Seventy-five men of Company A filtered back to join the defense.

As night came, men of the 310th Infantry had little to console them for the day's sacrifices. Instead of attacking Schmidt, they had barely struggled past the line of departure. Paying the penalty for the confusion and haste of the day before, they had blundered under pressure from higher headquarters into an ill-prepared attack in the darkness through unknown woods against unknown positions and had suffered the consequences that basic training doctrine predicts.

To give the stumbling attack a boost,

General Parker on 7 February committed all three of his regiments. The 310th Infantry was to continue along the axis of the main road and take the crest of the high ground, Hill 493, outside Schmidt. The 309th Infantry on the left was to drive northeast through the woods to Kommerscheidt, just north of Schmidt. The 311th Infantry on the right was to push northeast through the woods from Woffelsbach and take Schmidt itself.

Although a half-hour artillery preparation preceded the new attack, it fell on German positions manned at that point only by a small rear guard. Having managed to use the dense woods and American errors to sufficient advantage to make a stiff fight of it for a while, the *272d Volks Grenadier Division,* lacking depth, had fallen back during the night. The 309th Infantry met little opposition until it reached Kommerscheidt. There a heavy concentration of mortar fire sent the men diving into water-filled shellholes and foxholes, relics of the November fighting. Men of the 310th Infantry, accompanied by tanks of the 744th Tank Battalion, walked and occasionally rode along the main road to occupy Hill 493 by midmorning.

In the rough wooded terrain on the right, the 311th Infantry had slower going, but with considerable finesse men of the leading battalion surrounded and knocked out a succession of pillboxes. At small cost to themselves, they gathered in 117 prisoners during the day. Taking advantage of the 310th Infantry's advance to Hill 493, another battalion of the 311th Infantry with the support of a company of tanks marched down the main road toward Schmidt and arrived at the woods line in time to launch

[12] S–2–S–3 Jnl, 310th Inf, 6 Feb 45.

an attack in early afternoon. With infantrymen riding the tanks, the column prepared to make a dash over the crest of Hill 493 and across a mile of open fields into the town.

Hardly had the lead tank crossed the crest of the hill when armor-piercing shells struck it three times. As the tank burst into flames, the other tanks scurried back to the woods line.

Reorganizing, the infantry set out to do the job alone. Covered by fire from light machine guns, one company plunged across the crest of the hill. Despite persistent German fire, most of the men had by late afternoon gained the westernmost houses in the northern part of the town. Another company tried to come in through a draw south of Schmidt but found the approach covered by fire from automatic weapons. Night was falling as the company gained the first houses. Only at this point did the tanks arrive to help in a house-to-house mop-up of the town.

Toward the Dam

On the same day that the first American troops entered Schmidt, 7 February, a regiment of the 82d Airborne Division began to attack southward across the corps boundary to cross the deep draw of the Kall River and move cross-country to cut the enemy's escape route from Schmidt, the road from Schmidt northeast to the Roer at Nideggen. Terrain imposed such limits on the advance that by the time the 311th Infantry got to Schmidt, little hope remained for a sizable prisoner bag. The next day another regiment of the 82d Airborne crossed the Kall gorge and relieved the 309th Infantry in Kommerscheidt so that the

309th could participate in the final thrust on the Schwammenauel Dam.

General Parker's plan for the final thrust called for the 310th Infantry to pass through Schmidt early on 8 February and drive east and southeast along the highway to Hasenfeld at the foot of the dam. As soon as the 310th had advanced far enough along this road to uncover a line of departure for an attack southward against the dam, the 309th Infantry was to follow and move cross-country to take the dam.

If this plan was to be executed swiftly, Schmidt had to be fully in hand, a condition General Parker believed already met. On 8 February the men of the 310th Infantry discovered otherwise. Many of the houses, particularly those along the road to Hasenfeld, remained to be cleared, and the Germans yielded none without a fight. Noontime came and went, and the 310th still was battling to get past the last houses and into the open.

The First Army commander, General Hodges, made no effort to hide his dissatisfaction with the pace of the attack. The target date for the Ninth Army's offensive across the lower reaches of the Roer, 10 February, was little more than a day away; but not until the 78th took the dam could the Ninth Army move. The First Army artillery commander, Brig. Gen. Charles E. Hart, had seen to it that 40 battalions of artillery (780 guns) could be called upon to help the attack; General Hodges found it hard to understand why with this amount of artillery they could not "blast a road from our present front line positions straight to the dam." [13]

---

[13] Sylvan Diary, entries of 6 and 8 Feb 45.

Shortly before noon on 8 February, General Hodges telephoned the V Corps commander, General Huebner, to express again his dissatisfaction. A few minutes later the commander of the 9th Division, General Craig, walked into the V Corps headquarters on a routine visit. How long, Huebner asked Craig, would it take to shift a combat team of the 9th Division to Schmidt to attack the dam? Craig said he could do it "immediately." Huebner told him to move not only a combat team but also the division headquarters. When Craig arrived in Schmidt, the 78th Division's 309th and 311th Regiments were to be attached to the 9th Division.[14]

Placing a telephone call to his division command post, General Craig urged such speed in the movement that first units of his division already were en route to Schmidt before he himself got back to his command post. Turning over its sector to the 2d Division, the 60th Infantry led the way. A second regiment followed as a reserve, while the third regiment remained behind under attachment to the 2d Division. By midnight men of the 9th were in Schmidt getting set to attack before daybreak the next morning.

General Craig directed the 311th Infantry to clear wooded high ground along the north and northeast banks of the Roerstausee while the 60th Infantry took over the drive to Hasenfeld. The 309th Infantry remained on alert to move against the dam itself.

Despite the introduction of a new

commander and a veteran unit, the going on 9 February again was slow. Not until late afternoon did either the 60th Infantry on the road to Hasenfeld or the 311th Infantry along the northeast bank of the reservoir advance far enough to enable the 309th Infantry to begin its attack against the dam. It was 1800—after nightfall in this period of short winter days—when the leading 1st Battalion, 309th, passed through the 311th Infantry and headed for the dam.

Groping through the darkness, the 1st Battalion upon approaching the dam split into two groups, one to gain the top of the dam and cross over, the other to reach the lower level and take the power house. Those men moving against the lower level were particularly apprehensive lest the Germans at any moment blow the dam, sending tons of concrete, earth, and water cascading down upon them.

With the upper group was a team from the 303d Engineer Battalion, specially briefed on the nature of the big dam. The engineers pressed forward at 2300 to begin a search for demolitions. German fire at first forced them back, but by midnight they were at last able to start.

The engineers intended to cross the dam to the spillway and there descend into an inspection tunnel that intelligence reports stated ran through the dam. Crouched low against continuing German rifle fire, the men raced across but found a portion of the spillway blown and access to the tunnel denied. There was only one other way, to slide down the 200-foot face of the dam and gain the tunnel through its bottom exit.

Although the task was slow and treacherous, the engineers accomplished

---

[14] Capt. Joseph M. Mittelman, *Eight Stars to Victory, A History of the Veteran Ninth U.S. Infantry Division* (Washington: Ninth Division Association, 1948), p. 309; Sylvan Diary, entry of 8 Feb 45.

Damage to the Schwammenauel Dam *causes flooding of the Roer River.*

it. Entering the tunnel, they expected at any moment to be blown to kingdom come. The explosion never came. Subsequent investigation revealed that the Germans already had done all the damage intended. They had destroyed the machinery in the power room and had blown the discharge valves. They had also destroyed the discharge valves on a penstock that carried water from the upper reservoir on the Urft to a point of discharge below the Schwammenauel Dam, which explained why they had allowed the Urft Dam itself to fall into American hands intact. Together the

two demolitions would release no major cascade of water but a steady flow calculated to create a long-lasting flood in the valley of the Roer.[15]

Allied commanders could breathe easily again. The reservoirs that directly and indirectly had cost so many lives at last were in hand. It would have been better, of course, had the Schwammenauel Dam been taken intact, thus

[15] *Lightning,* pp. 118–20, contains a vivid account of the engineer action. In comments on the draft MS for this volume, General von Manteuffel notes that Hitler had specifically ordered that the dams be destroyed but, Manteuffel says, he had forbidden it.

obviating any change in the Ninth Army's plan for crossing the Roer; but it was enough that the Germans had been forced to expend their weapon before any Allied troops had crossed the river downstream.

In the end the success belonged basically to the 78th Division. For all the dissatisfaction with the pace of the attack, this relatively inexperienced division had driven through rugged terrain over a severely canalized approach. Dense forest had nullified much of the artillery's power, as weather did for air support. Too many cooks had appeared from time to time to meddle in the tactical broth, but once the pressure was off and the division's role could be assessed with some perspective, General Huebner could remark to General Hodges that he had "made him another good division." [16]

---

[16] Sylvan Diary, entry of 10 Feb 45.

CHAPTER V

The Drive on Pruem

Since General Eisenhower's order of 1 February ending the 12th Army Group's main effort in the Eifel authorized the Third Army to "continue the probing attacks now in progress," General Middleton's VIII Corps was able to pursue its offensive almost without pause. The Third Army commander, General Patton, nevertheless altered the objective of the attack and provided additional strength. No longer was the Third Army affording flank protection for the First Army but instead was preparing the way for what Patton hoped could be developed eventually into a two-pronged drive to breach the West Wall on a wide front and drive on through the Eifel to the Rhine.

General Patton told Middleton to go beyond the Schnee Eifel ridgeline and take the road center of Pruem. Even before this objective was in hand, he hoped to start General Eddy's XII Corps on a drive northeastward from the vicinity of Echternach to take Bitburg, the other major road center in the western Eifel. Having thus carved out a deep foothold inside the Eifel, he would possess a fulcrum for persuading his superiors to support an offensive the rest of the way to the Rhine.[1]

The VIII Corps zone remained as before, approximately sixteen miles wide from the Loshiem Gap in the north to Luetzkampen, near the northern tip of Luxembourg. Three divisions already were in line, the 87th on the north, the 4th in the center, and the 90th on the south. (*Map IV*)

Commanded now by Brig. Gen. Frank L. Culin, Jr., the 87th Division was to protect the corps north flank, a task of considerable importance since the adjacent divisions of the First Army were no longer advancing abreast. The 87th was to accomplish its mission by penetrating the West Wall and seizing a crossroads astride northern reaches of the Schnee Eifel ridge. In corps reserve, General Kilburn's 11th Armored Division was to be ready to use a part of its strength to protect the south flank of the corps, where the III Corps between Middleton's and Eddy's commands was to remain at first on the defensive.

The 4th and 90th Divisions together were to make the main attack. The 4th was to advance through the West Wall astride the Schnee Eifel north of the West Wall strongpoint of Brandscheid, then wheel against Brandscheid. With the strongpoint taken, the 4th was to turn the town over to the 90th Division and continue eastward to Pruem. The 90th Division was to widen the breach in the West Wall to include Habscheid, two and a half miles southwest of

[1] TUSA AAR, 1 Aug 44–9 May 45, p. 255; TUSA Opnl Dir, 3 Feb 45; Gay Diary, entries of 3–5 Feb 45.

Brandscheid, then go on to take Pronsfeld, another road center on the Pruem
River five miles south of Pruem.[2]

Since no unit of the VIII Corps had
yet entered the main part of the West
Wall, no one could say with any certainty how completely and effectively the
Germans had manned the line. Although
patrols had found some bunkers undefended, it was unreasonable to suppose
that the Germans would abandon the
whole belt of fortifications.[3]

On the basis of identifications made
in the drive up to the West Wall, the
Americans believed that the Germans in
front of the VIII Corps possessed remnants of 7 divisions with a possible total
strength of about 7,000 perhaps supported by as many as 15 artillery battalions. Another 4,500 men of 3 panzer-type
divisions with possibly 70 tanks and
assault guns might be in tactical reserve.[4] Thus in at least the first stages,
the defenders would be pitting something like a reinforced company against
each attacking regiment.

This was, in reality, a generally correct
estimate of the German situation. What
intelligence officers failed to note was
that again the Americans would achieve
an advantage by attacking almost astride
a German interarmy boundary, that

GENERAL MIDDLETON

between the *LXVI Corps* of the *Fifth
Panzer Army* on the north and the *XIII
Corps* of the *Seventh Army* on the south.
As established near the end of January,
the boundary ran generally southeast-
ward between Pronsfeld and Pruem.[5]

In the two German corps, the task of
trying to hold the West Wall had been
detailed to volks grenadier divisions,
none of which exceeded regimental
strength even when reinforced by rear
area security battalions that occupied
some of the West Wall bunkers. All the
more elite formations had left the line
for rehabilitation or to assume reserve

---

[2] Unless otherwise noted, the tactical story is
based on official unit records and combat interviews. See also Hal D. Steward, *Thunderbolt—The
History of the Eleventh Armored Division* (Washington: Infantry Journal Press, 1948); Gerden F.
Johnson, *History of the Twelfth Infantry Regiment in World War II* (Boston: National Fourth
Division Assoc., 1947); Joe I. Abrams, *A History of
the 90th Division in World War II* (Baton Rouge:
Army-Navy Publishing Co., 1946); *A Historical
and Pictorial Record of the 87th Infantry Division
in World War II* (Baton Rouge: Army-Navy Publishing Co., 1946).
[3] VIII Corps G–2 Estimate 19, 4 Feb 45.
[4] *Ibid.*

[5] The German story is based on OKW situation
maps for the period and the following manuscripts: MSS # B–041 (Generalmajor Hans-Kurt
Hoecker, CG *167th Volks Grenadier Division*); #
B–123 (Generalmajor Rudolf Freiherr von Gersdorff, CofS, *Seventh Army*); # B–561 (Generalmajor Karl Wagener, CofS, *Fifth Panzer Army*); #
C–020 (Schramm).

roles. The last troops of the *9th Panzer Division,* for example, had departed the *LXVI Corps* only two days earlier to be rebuilt before shifting to the north against the expected Allied main effort. What was left of the *5th Parachute Division*—little more than a *Kampfgruppe*—still belonged to the *XIII Corps* but was out of the line in a backup position. Remnants of the *2d Panzer Division* with a few tanks also were still around but in a reserve role for the *Seventh Army.* Artillery support averaged about two understrength battalions per front-line division, though additional support could be provided by a volks artillery corps located astride the interarmy boundary. The West Wall, on which German commanders counted strongly to offset the shift of troops to the north, was thinner astride the Schnee Eifel than anywhere else along the frontier. Furthermore, American troops occupying the Schnee Eifel from September until the beginning of the Ardennes counteroffensive had demolished many of the pillboxes.

Into the West Wall

The VIII Corps' 4th Division knew the demolished pillboxes well; it was the same unit that had attacked the Schnee Eifel in September. The division would get a rare opportunity to refight an earlier engagement over the same ground, under similar conditions of enemy strength, against at least one of the earlier opponents. Little would be changed except the weather and stronger support on the division's flanks.

In September two regiments of the 4th Division had caught the Germans unprepared atop the Schnee Eifel and had

peeled off to left and right to clear the thin line of pillboxes, seize Brandscheid, and make room for the division's third regiment in the center. Yet no sooner had the infantrymen emerged from the woods cover of the Schnee Eifel onto relatively open but sharply compartmented ground leading to Pruem than hastily culled German artillery and infantry reserves had appeared. Overextended, tired from a long drive across France and Belgium, lacking the strength to exploit, the 4th had come to a halt.[6]

As in September, the 4th Division's plan in February was to pause one day in the shadow of the Schnee Eifel while patrols probed the West Wall. A delay also would afford time for engineers to clear and repair roads that were rapidly breaking down in an unseasonable thaw. In the very early hours of 4 February, however, a reinforced platoon of the 8th Infantry found the first belt of pillboxes unoccupied, the Germans milling about on foot and in horse-drawn wagons, obviously unprepared for a fight. Just as a previous commander had done in September, the division commander, General Blakeley, ordered immediate attack.

By 0600, 4 February, the 8th Infantry's 1st Battalion was toiling up the slopes of the Schnee Eifel in a snowstorm and utter darkness to lead the attack. An hour later the 22d Infantry's 1st Battalion, a few hundred yards to the south, joined the move. The first objective of both battalions was a road along the crest of the Schnee Eifel, a string beaded with pillboxes. Follow-up battalions of each regiment were to turn left and right to strip off the beads.

---

[6] The action is covered in MacDonald, *The Siegfried Line Campaign.*

MEN OF THE 4TH DIVISION EATING INSIDE CAPTURED PILLBOX

As in September, success the first day was complete. Dazed, disorganized troops of the *326th Volks Grenadier Division* were nowhere near a match for the assaulting force, even with the added strength of the pillboxes. The 8th Infantry took 128 prisoners and incurred only one casualty. After swinging southwest, the 22d Infantry reached a fortified crossroads at the woods line overlooking Brandscheid. Again as in September, seizing the crossroads and Brandscheid itself awaited the second day.

Unfortunately for the Americans, the similarities between the late summer thrust and the winter attack were not to end there. As before, the Germans would be unable to muster sufficient strength to expel the invaders, but they could make every yard of advance increasingly costly.

On the second day, 5 February, German artillery and mortar fire increased considerably. A battalion of the 22d Infantry toiled all morning to clear 11 pillboxes in and around the crossroads above Brandscheid. Thereupon 2 companies poised for a final assault out of the woods across five hundred yards of open ground into the village. With them were 10 medium tanks and 7 tank destroyers equipped with 90-mm. guns.

Shortly after midday, tanks and tank destroyers opened fire against all visible pillboxes along the road into Brandscheid. Heavy machine guns from the woods line chattered support. Infantrymen burst from the forest cover, shooting their rifles and bazookas and tossing white phosphorus grenades as they ran. Although the Germans returned the fire at first, it diminished as the Americans closed in. Within three hours, the 22d Infantry held Brandscheid and a formidable ring of pillboxes. The cost was surprisingly light, a total of 43 casualties, of which 3 were fatalities.

The 8th Infantry for its part continued to roll up the fortified line to the northeast. As the day wore on, the job became increasingly difficult as resistance stiffened like a coil spring under compression.

A few hundred yards to the north, the 87th Division began during the night of 5 February to carry out its mission of cutting the road along the northern end of the Schnee Eifel to protect the corps left flank. Although men of the 87th had little trouble gaining the crest of the ridge, lateral movement the next day northeast and southwest was slowed, chiefly by the increased enemy artillery fire. The division nevertheless accomplished its limited mission in relatively short order.

The 90th Division thus far had participated in the fighting only with a demonstration by fire on 5 February against Habscheid to distract German attention from the 4th Division's attack; a more direct role was in the offing before daylight on the 6th. In performing it, the 90th too was destined to run into the same pattern of easy early success followed quickly by stiffening resistance.

The 90th was to make a two-pronged attack. The 359th Infantry was to take Habscheid in a frontal assault from a starting point just over a mile from the town along the main highway from the Our River through Habscheid to Pronsfeld. Thereupon the 357th Infantry was to pass through for the attack on Pronsfeld itself, not quite five miles away. The 358th Infantry in the meantime was to take over at Brandscheid and drive southeast to seize high ground along the Pruem River between Pronsfeld and Pruem.

At 0400 on 6 February, without artillery preparation, all three battalions of the 359th Infantry jumped off abreast, guiding on the main highway into Habscheid. Despite the general alert occasioned by the previous day's fighting, the regiments took the Germans by surprise. All but two rifle companies were inside Habscheid by daylight. Of about eighty Germans captured, some were taken asleep at their posts.

Then the problems began. On the approach to Habscheid the highway passed through a band of dragon's teeth, the road itself blocked by a heavy gate of logs anchored in concrete. As daylight neared, engineers blew the barrier, only to discover that the infantry passing in the dark had failed to take out enemy machine guns in nearby pillboxes that were sited to cover the gate. Alerted by the explosion, the Germans came to life, drenching the engineers with automatic weapons fire and calling down mortar and *Nebelwerfer* fire on the spot. Along with the engineers, the fires pinned down the two reserve rifle companies that had yet to reach Habscheid. As daylight came, maneuvers to get around the enemy proved impossible.

While the engineers waited, unable to sweep the road ahead for mines, in and beyond Habscheid the bulk of the infantrymen, slowly clearing pillboxes, reported they had gone about as far as they could without tank support. The situation for a moment threatened to become a deadlock, but the Germans had not the numbers close at hand to exploit their temporary advantage. The moment passed. When at length a self-propelled 155-mm. gun arrived to fire directly at the pillboxes covering the approach to Habscheid, the defenders ran. The engineers at last could start sweeping the road. Even so, it was after nightfall before they had cleared it and tanks could get forward.

Meanwhile, it was at Brandscheid that the first of the enemy's adjustments in reaction to the attack became apparent. In the village nobody on either side got much sleep through the night of 5 February.

From the German viewpoint, the 4th Division's penetration at Brandscheid had virtually collapsed the south flank of the *326th Volks Grenadier Division*. Constantly committed since 16 December, the division was a skeleton. Its two regiments had only about 140 men each. Only two 75-mm. guns were in the anti-tank battalion; only eight artillery pieces in support. The division's north flank broken by the surprise penetration of the West Wall on the Schnee Eifel, the division lacked the men even to seal off the thrust at Brandscheid, much less to counterattack. The corps commander, General Lucht, ordered help from the neighboring unit to the south, the *276th Volks Grenadier Division*.[7]

Before daylight on 6 February, an infantry battalion plucked from the vicinity of Habscheid and the *326th*'s engineer battalion, a force totaling about 450 men, counterattacked at Brandscheid. For the Americans, the counterattack could have come at no more inopportune time. A few hours earlier, around midnight, a battalion of the 90th Division's 358th Infantry had moved toward Brandscheid to assume control from the 22d Infantry. It was a memorably miserable night—cold, black, half-raining, half-sleeting. After walking almost four miles, the men arrived in Brandscheid at 0430, thoroughly soaked. The relief of the 22d Infantry was in process when the Germans struck.

Hitting from the south, the Germans quickly stove in the 22d Infantry's line, shattered Company K, and penetrated into the village. While individual riflemen and the crews of the three tank destroyers fought on in the center of the village, Company L, the only unit whose relief had been completed, counterattacked. In a little over two hours the confused fight came to an end. More than 150 Germans surrendered.

Abortive as the Germans thrust proved, it caused substantial casualties. The relieving battalion of the 358th Infantry lost only 9 men, but the 3d Battalion, 22d Infantry, had 12 men killed, 98 wounded, and 38 missing; some of the missing, who had been cut off in pillboxes outside the village, later rejoined their companies.

---

[7] In addition to German sources previously cited, see MS # B–561, *326th Volks Grenadier Division*, 26 January–17 April 1945 (Generalmajor Erwin Kaschner, CG).

After waiting through the morning to make sure Brandscheid was secure, two battalions of the 22d Infantry resumed the attack at noon, moving east from the crossroads above Brandscheid to take the first row of villages beyond the Schnee Eifel. Here in September another battalion of the 4th Division had run into trouble after neglecting to take high ground while advancing down a valley to cross the little Mon Creek. This time strength was at hand to do both jobs at once, and what was left of the *326th Volks Grenadier Division* could have little effect on the outcome. Except for artillery fire, the Germans fought back feebly. The same was true on the Schnee Eifel where the 8th Infantry continued to roll up the pillbox line to the northeast and established contact with the 87th Division.

The 4th Division's success on 6 February boded well for the future, particularly when considered in context with an event of early morning on the south flank of the corps where, southwest of Habscheid, contingents of the 11th Armored Division had attacked the West Wall.

Scheduled to begin before dawn on 6 February, the 11th Armored Division barely struggled into position on time. The thaw and freeze, rain and snow, constant since 1 February, had turned roads into quagmires in some places and in others had glazed them with mud and ice. So great was the traffic congestion during the march that few of the division's tanks could make it forward, thus leaving the first assignment to the armored infantry. The enemy fortunately had no planes in the air to take advantage of the long columns of vehicles

stalled bumper to bumper. Nothing was lost but tempers and sleep.

Even more than the attacks of the other divisions of the VIII Corps, that of the 11th Armored Division would benefit from striking along the enemy's interarmy boundary. From a point just south of Habscheid, the front was the responsibility of the *Seventh Army's XIII Corps,* but the volks grenadier division charged with the defense was so acutely short of men that a portion of the line close to the boundary could be defended only by outposts.

Beginning at 0400, shortly before the German counterthrust at Brandscheid, two dismounted armored infantry battalions moved abreast from Heckhuscheid, southwest of Habscheid, toward Losenseifen Hill (Hill 568), an eminence bristling with pillboxes that had been a key objective of an American division in September. No artillery preparation preceded the move. In the darkness, the Germans in the few pillboxes that were manned hardly knew what hit them. By 0830 the armored infantrymen completely controlled Losenseifen Hill in a penetration a mile and a half deep into the West Wall.

The successes of 6 February meant that the VIII Corps had breached the West Wall on a front of approximately eleven miles, prompting the corps commander, General Middleton, to accelerate and broaden the attack. Urging the 4th and 90th Divisions to increase the tempo of their thrusts, he told the 87th Division and the 11th Armored to disregard previously assigned objectives and "continue on through." [8] The armor was to advance beyond the corps to high

---

[8] 4th Div Jnl, 6 Feb 45.

ground some four miles southwest of Losenseifen Hill, there to help the neighboring III Corps to get across the Our River and into its section of the West Wall.

German Countermeasures

General Middleton's directive actually would have little practical effect. On 7 February the inevitable slowness of clearing pillboxes, combined with the local German countermeasures, provided the Germans an additional twenty-four hours to ready other steps to oppose the attack. Only on the left wing of the 4th Division was the defense still soft. There two battalions of the 8th Infantry descended the slopes of the Schnee Eifel and advanced almost unopposed as much as two miles, crossed the upper reaches of the Mon Creek, and reached the west bank of the Mehlen Creek.

On the north the 87th Division spent the day clearing pillboxes. The 11th Armored Division on the south did the same, postponing any major effort to execute its new mission until the adjacent regiment of the 90th Division came abreast.

It was in the center that the hard fighting took place as the 22d, 357th, and 358th Regiments pushed attacks toward Pruem and Pronsfeld. None could gain more than a mile, and all had to fight off a number of small but determined counterattacks launched by conglomerate units, anything Generals Lucht and Felber could find—remnants of division engineer battalions, local security forces, and the like. In only one case would the counterattacks cause genuine concern, but they would materially delay the advance nonetheless.

Attacking southeast along the Habscheid-Pronsfeld road, the 357th Infantry intended to slip one battalion in the darkness past Hill 510 to take a second height, Hill 511. Another battalion was to follow to seize the bypassed hill.

It failed to work out that way. Control proved difficult in the dark, and the approach march was slow. Daylight and with it enemy fire caught the two battalions strung out along the highway, the point of the leading battalion still short of Hill 511. Fire from the first hill, thick with pillboxes, split the column. The fire isolated most of the leading battalion in an open saddle between the two hills for the entire day. The other battalion finally cleared the pillboxes on Hill 510 but was unable to cross open ground to come to the support of the leading battalion until after dark. Only then were the men able to occupy Hill 511.

The 358th Infantry meanwhile launched a three-pronged attack out of Brandscheid. Moving southeast early on 7 February, the 3d Battalion had little trouble taking Hill 521, a wooded height on the west bank of the Mon Creek. On the other hand, both the 2d Battalion, clearing pillboxes between the other two units, and the 1st came under considerable fire and counted their successes not in yards gained but in pillboxes reduced.

The 1st Battalion proceeded methodically about its task, using tanks and tank destroyers as a base of fire to button up the pillboxes, and by dark had cleared ten and taken about eighty prisoners. The 2d Battalion moved much more slowly, partly because the men found many camouflaged pillboxes not previously reported, partly because the Germans took cover in the concrete forts during preparatory artillery firing, then rushed outside as the shelling stopped to oppose the infantry from foxholes and trenches.

At noon, with the 3d Battalion already on Hill 521 and the 2d still only a few yards out of Brandscheid, the regimental commander, Lt. Col. Jacob W. Bealke, Jr., ordered the 3d Battalion to send a force from Hill 521 westward against the flank of the defenders on Hill 519. Finding no covered route to the hills, the battalion commander asked for a delay until tanks could arrive and night provide concealment.

At dusk Colonel Bealke sent a five-man patrol to search for the best route to the hill, but mortar and small arms fire quickly killed three of the men, prompting the other two to return. A larger patrol from Company I followed with orders to take the hill, if possible, but shortly after emerging from the woods and starting up Hill 519, these men also drew fire and scattered. Not until daylight the next morning was the battalion to try a full-blooded attack.

Through this same day, the 22d Infantry, already in rear of the West Wall, was having its problems too, not with pillboxes but with counterattacks. The 2d Battalion of the 22d took Am Kopf (Hill 554), a piece of dominating ground just east of the Mon Creek, which had been the farthest point of advance in this sector in September. In early afternoon the Germans knocked the battalion off the hill, but the Americans recaptured it just before dark with a reserve company. Another company of the 2d Battalion entered Obermehlen, just over a half mile to the east, but before the end of the day was in "a hell of a fight" there with a company of Germans supported by three tanks.[9]

A few hundred yards to the southwest the 22d Infantry's 1st Battalion also got across the Mon Creek and onto high ground just short of Niedermehlen, but persistent counterattacks denied further advance. The regimental commander sent the 3d Battalion to back up the 2d, prepared to counterattack if necessary to save the beleaguered company in Obermehlen.

The regiment had 62 casualties during the day. Late in the afternoon the commander, Col. Charles T. Lanham, reported: "We are . . . [now] a very serious threat to Pruem. The Germans may be building up a very big thing against us."[10]

The "big thing" was the 2d Panzer Division—which sounded more formidable than it actually was—plus a shift in boundary that would eliminate the problem of divided command that had plagued the Germans since the day the VIII Corps began its attack. Both measures were to take effect the next day, 8 February.

Impressed by the presence of the American Third Army across the Our in Luxembourg, higher German commanders had continued to be concerned lest an American attack hit the Eifel even as the Germans hurried resources northward to meet the expected Allied main effort on the Cologne plain. Yet when the VIII Corps did attack on 4 February, immediate identification of only the 4th Division had led the Germans to ascribe "only local significance" to the strike.[11] By 6 February, when two

---

[9] 22d Inf Jnl, 1 Feb 45.
[10] Ibid.
[11] MS # B–123 (Gersdorff).

more infantry divisions and the 11th Armored had been identified, the danger became obvious.

At this point the army group commander, Field Marshal Model, shifted the *Seventh Army* boundary northward to eliminate the nuisance of responsibility divided with the *Fifth Panzer Army*. He also permitted unrestricted use of the *Seventh Army*'s reserve, the *2d Panzer Division*.

Given a free hand, the *Seventh Army* commander, General Brandenberger, elected to reinforce the threatened sector not only with the panzer division but also with two *Kampfgruppen*—all that that was left—of the two volks grenadier divisions, the *276th* and *340th*. These he shifted into the sector of the *XIII Corps* from the adjoining corps to the south, even though continued identification of a U.S. armored division in Luxembourg indicated that the Third U.S. Army soon might launch another thrust farther south.

Brandenberger also directed northward from the *Seventh Army*'s left wing a *Kampfgruppe* of the *352d Volks Grenadier Division*. Felber's *XIII Corps* thus would contain *Kampfgruppen* of four volks grenadier divisions, the *5th Parachute Division,* and the panzer division. The corps would have in addition a separate armored battalion equipped with Tiger tanks. Counting vehicles of this battalion, of the panzer division, and of occasional guns in the volks grenadier divisions, the *XIII Corps* would have approximately seventy serviceable tanks and assault guns.

For the Americans, the added German strength was all too apparent on 8 February. The only notable advance was in the north where the 87th Division's

345th Infantry, moving before daylight, seized a village on the upper reaches of the Pruem River. On the south flank the 359th Infantry cleared bypassed pillboxes in the 90th Division's zone, but enough of a gap still existed between the 90th Division and the 11th Armored Division to discourage the reluctant armor again from starting its drive to the southeast.

Hard fighting once more was the order of the day in the center where the arrival of the *2d Panzer Division* made a clear impact. The 4th Division's 8th Infantry, which had reached the Mon Creek the day before against little opposition, had to fight all through the 8th and into the 9th to clear the village of Gondenbrett. On the regiment's right, two small counterattacks hit the company of the 22d Infantry in Obermehlen, while another struck Am Kopf Hill, west of the village. These delayed the 22d Infantry's own attack until shortly past noon on the 8th. In the afternoon the 2d and 3d Battalions set out to clear the last houses of Obermehlen and open slopes to the south, whereupon the 2d Battalion tried to cross the Mehlen Creek in order to take high ground between the creek and the settlement of Tafel, whence most of the counterattacks appeared to be coming.

Swollen by the thaw to a width of fifteen feet in some places, the Mehlen Creek proved a major obstacle. A few men of the 2d Battalion found fords; others stepped into deep water and had to swim for it. Except for the weapons platoon, which was cut to pieces by machine gun fire during the crossing, most of Company G nevertheless made the far bank. The platoons advanced halfway up the high ground against a surprising lack of opposition and there prepared to defend in expectation of reinforcement after dark. The stage was unwittingly set for a repetition of a reverse that had happened to another company of the same division five months earlier only a few hundred yards away on the east bank of the Mon Creek.

The men of Company G had no heavy weapons—only their M1's and BAR's. These and their radios as well were soaked. They had salvaged only one bazooka, for which they had only one rocket, and it misfired. Company F, which was to have followed, bogged down under enemy fire west of the creek.

That was the situation when shortly before dark Germans of the *2d Panzer Division* attacked in company strength with three to five tanks in support. The men of Company G had little alternative but to fall back across the creek in a *sauve qui peut.*

The 8th of February was a costly day for the 22d Infantry. Losses exceeded a hundred. Seventeen were known dead.

The story was much the same with the 357th and 358th Regiments of the 90th Division. Although the 358th absorbed relatively little punishment from enemy fire, the regiment still could not solve the problem of the open approaches to Hill 519. The wind was in the wrong direction for using smoke, and artillery could not neutralize the enemy in concrete shelters. By the close of the day the 2d Battalion had cleared a few more pillboxes and had maneuvered into position in the woods on Hill 521, ready to hit Hill 519 in conjunction with the 3d Battalion, but the attack would have to await another day.

The 357th Infantry had no better luck at Hill 511 to the southwest. There, in

early morning, a counterattack by contingents of the *352d Volks Grenadier Division* hit Company K on the hill. Company I, mounted on tanks, hurried forward to help. Thus began a daylong fight in which the 3d Battalion in particular suffered. Driven off Hill 511, the battalion recaptured it before the day was out but was unable to advance beyond. Fire of all kinds beat in on the men from three sides. One supporting tank destroyer was knocked out by direct fire; two tanks were lost.

For the next two days, 9 and 10 February, hard fighting would continue almost everywhere except on the extreme flanks, with the 22d Infantry, the focal unit in the drive, coming in for the bloodiest fighting. Yet for all the difficulties imposed, the Germans clearly would have to muster considerably more strength than that already committed if Pruem and the west bank of the Pruem River were to be denied much longer.

Although what happened to the 4th Division continued to show striking similarities to the division's earlier experience in this same sector, one noteworthy difference between the two engagements was apparent. In September, when a company had fallen back from the high ground just beyond the Mon Creek, the 4th Division's regiments had been spent, all reserves committed. When on 8 February Company G, 22d Infantry, retreated from beyond the Mehlen Creek, both the 8th and 22d Regiments still were strong, the 8th particularly, and the division commander still had a reserve in the uncommitted 12th Infantry.

The day of 9 February opened auspiciously for the 8th Infantry when one battalion moved against only sporadic resistance into a village on the Pruem

River a little over a mile east of Gondenbrett. Yet when another battalion attempted to turn south to take a village on the road to Pruem, the opposition suddenly stiffened. The explanation was to be found in that the regiment had shifted its attack from the relatively undefended left flank of the *Fifth Panzer Army* into the *Seventh Army*'s sector and the domain of the *2d Panzer Division*.

The immediate task still facing the 22d Infantry on 9 February was to recapture the high ground between the Mehlen Creek and Tafel so that the village of Niedermehlen in turn might be taken and the main road to Pruem opened. The regiment's plan was to attack with the 1st Battalion across the creek, then to converge on Niedermehlen from two sides with its other two battalions.

Because road conditions precluded bringing up bridging equipment, the 4th Division's engineers decided to get the 1st Battalion across the creek on an improvised log bridge. By 0930 the bridge was in and two companies began to cross. Both these had made it when, within ten to fifteen minutes of the first man's crossing, an enemy machine gun opened fire up the creek valley from the south. This forced the third company to cover. During the next five hours, fifteen men fell while trying to brave the machine gun fire. Every effort to knock out the German gunner failed.

Companies A and C in the meantime made their way up the high ground and dug in to defend. Although more numerous than the three platoons of Company G the day before, they were little better off. Without tanks and with the only supply road—that through Niedermeh-

len—in enemy hands, they made no attempt to push farther.

At 1300 the enemy again sought a decision on the high ground. With five tanks and two companies of infantry, the Germans struck. In an hour Company A had shot all its bazooka rockets but had two tanks to show for them. Still neither the 1st Battalion's reserve company nor supporting tanks could get across the Mehlen Creek to help. Shells from German tanks plowed into the 2d Battalion in Obermehlen, disorganizing one company there. "Krauts," the 2d Battalion reported, "[are] all over the place." [12] Yet up on the hill Companies A and C with the help of intensive shelling by the 44th Field Artillery Battalion absorbed the shock of the enemy thrust, taking severe casualties but giving no ground.

The 3d Battalion meanwhile had circled west of Niedermehlen, and even before the Germans struck at Companies A and C had attempted with the aid of a platoon of tanks and another of tank destroyers to push into the village. Fire from at least three German tanks or assault guns halted every attempt.

An inconclusive fire fight continued through the afternoon until Companies A and C had defeated the counterattack beyond the creek. At that point, behind a TOT [13] fired by four battalions of artillery, companies of the 2d and 3d Battalions pressed into Niedermehlen. Resistance collapsed, and within two hours the village was clear, a hundred Germans captured. The day's fighting cost the 22d Infantry 121 men, most of

---

[12] 22d Inf Jnl, 9 Feb 45.

[13] TOT stands for time on target, a method of timing the fire of artillery pieces in various locations to fall on a target simultaneously.

them lost on the high ground east of the Mehlen Creek.

Even as these events occurred, the 4th Division commander, General Blakeley, committed his reserve, the 12th Infantry, to take a village off the 22d Infantry's right flank. The regiment accomplished its task with little difficulty and the next day, 10 February, reached the west bank of the Pruem River southwest of Pruem.

The Final Phase

The 22d Infantry's task also was near completion, though remnants of the *2d Panzer Division* with their backs to the Pruem River still fought hard for at least every other yard of ground. On 10 February the 1st Battalion engaged in a bitter house-to-house fight to clear Tafel and again had to repel a tank-supported counterattack. The 3d Battalion moved more easily to occupy high ground directly west of Pruem. During the day another seventy-three men were killed or wounded. Although the 22d Infantry was at the threshold of its objective, the town of Pruem, the regiment would arrive there nearly spent. Reluctant to commit individual replacements during the battle, the regimental commander doubted that his thinned and tired forces would have the strength for another house-to-house struggle the next day.[14]

On 9 and 10 February the 90th Division also advanced, slowly at first, but with a dash on the second day as the enemy in the north of the division's zone fell back behind the Pruem River. When the Germans withdrew from Hill 519 on 9 February, the 358th Infantry followed, then the next day broke free behind the

last of the West Wall pillboxes to take high ground along the west bank of the Pruem. The 357th Infantry at the same time pushed about a mile south of Hill 511 in what was in effect flank protection for the 358th Infantry, while the third regiment, the 359th, cleared the last of the gap between the infantry and the armor on Losenseifen Hill. For the most part, during these two days the Germans were content to sting the attackers with mortar and artillery fire.

Operations at this point entered a new phase, dictated by an uncompromising tyrant called logistics. Not built for heavy military traffic, the roads of Belgium and Luxembourg had literally disintegrated under a combination of alternate freeze and thaw, daily rains and floods, and the coming and going of big tanks, trucks, and guns. The entire engineer strength of the VIII Corps was barely sufficient to keep the most essential supply routes open. In a few days the 22d Infantry was to report that with all roads to the regiment's rear impassable, nothing remained in the forward ammunition supply point. Some units of the VIII Corps had to be supplied by airdrops.

As early as 8 February, General Middleton, as eager as anybody in the Third Army to get on with the attack, felt impelled to suggest to General Patton that he call off the offensive until the road situation improved.[15] The next day, 9 February, Patton agreed that when the corps reached the Pruem River, the attackers might desist and all units dig in for defense.

For the 4th Division this order was qualified by instructions to watch for

---

[14] 22d Inf Jnl, 10 Feb 45.

[15] Patton, *War As I Knew It*, p. 239.

DROPPING SUPPLIES BY PARACHUTE TO THE 4TH DIVISION

any enemy withdrawal, and if one occurred to "jump on it." [16] When prisoners on the 10th reported the Germans evacuating Pruem, General Blakeley took advantage of the qualification to continue the attack into the town. Despite its losses, the 22d Infantry fought into the fringes on the 11th and the next day occupied the rubble that Pruem had become.

It was the condition of the roads that stopped the VIII Corps, but even had the roads held up the attack would have come to a halt on 10 February. The VIII

Corps had run out the period of grace granted with the general standfast orders of 1 February, and a new condition thwarted for the moment any subterfuge Patton might have attempted to change matters. On 10 February General Bradley ordered Patton to give up headquarters of the III Corps to the First Army, which meant that the VIII Corps would have to assume responsibility for General Millikin's sector. Although General Middleton would inherit one of the two divisions of the III Corps, the new responsibility still would involve considerable adjustment and reorganization.

---

[16] 22d Inf Jnl, 10 Feb 45.

The VIII Corps had achieved substantially the objectives set. The corps
had made a clean penetration of the West
Wall, and three out of four divisions had
reached the Pruem River. Pruem itself
was in hand. General Middleton thus
would be free to turn his attention to
the south where other events, under way
since 6 February, invited participation
by the VIII Corps.

For to the south General Patton had
launched another of the probing attacks
authorized by the decision of 1 February.
The objective of the attack was limited—
Bitburg, the other major road center in
the western Eifel, eighteen miles southwest of Pruem; but Patton had more in
mind than Bitburg. He was, he hoped,
kindling a flame that eventually would
become a full-fledged fire carrying the
Third Army all the way to the Rhine.

CHAPTER VI

Bitburg and the Vianden Bulge

When Patton's Third Army drew up to the German frontier at the end of January, the army sector stretched for more than a hundred miles from the Losheim Gap in the north to the northwestern corner of the Saar industrial region, thence southeastward to a point on the Saar River midway between Saarlautern and Saarbruecken. From north to south, the Third Army's order of battle was the VIII Corps (Middleton), III Corps (Millikin), XII Corps (Eddy), and XX Corps (Walker).

Meandering northeastward from Trier, the Moselle River formed a natural division within the Third Army's zone. North of the Moselle lay the Eifel, inhospitable from the standpoint of terrain but inviting nevertheless because it screened the Rhine city of Koblenz and several Rhine bridges. South of the Moselle, the XX Corps faced the considerable obstacle of the Saar River plus the strongest network of concrete fortifications along the entire length of the West Wall. Severely restricted in the forces that might be committed to an offensive, General Patton had chosen the Eifel, for all its drawbacks.

Once the VIII Corps jumped off on 4 February to take Pruem, Patton intended that the XII Corps begin its attack on Bitburg the night of 6 February. Apparently on the assumption that the Germans caught in the middle of these two drives would withdraw when threatened with outflanking on north and south, he directed the III Corps in the center, from Luetzkampen to Vianden, to participate at first only with a series of minor probing attacks designed to prevent the Germans from shifting strength to north and south.

Like the attack of the VIII Corps on Pruem, the maneuver by the XII Corps against Bitburg had been tried once before—in September, by a single armored division, the 5th. At the end of the great pursuit across France and Belgium, the 5th Armored had attempted to take Bitburg by utilizing a semblance of a terrain corridor extending northeast from the village of Wallendorf, about halfway between Vianden and Echternach; but lacking reserves, the armor eventually had fallen back into Luxembourg.[1]

For the February attack General Patton approved a strike along a front of some seven and a half miles from Wallendorf southeast to Echternach. (*Map V*) Although the same semblance of a terrain corridor northeast of Wallendorf still would be used for the final drive to Bitburg, the advance would be attempted only after wooded high ground southeast of Wallendorf, lying between the Sauer and Pruem Rivers at their confluence

---

[1] MacDonald, *The Siegfried Line Campaign.*

near Echternach, had been taken and the corps south flank thus secured.

Before General Eisenhower's decision of 1 February, General Patton had intended that the XII Corps attack on 4 February in order to tie in with the Euskirchen offensive. Having protested the target date on the basis that Patton had no appreciation of "time and space factors," the XII Corps commander, General Eddy, was pleased when Eisenhower's general standfast orders resulted in a two-day postponement.[2] Unfortunately, the postponement virtually coincided with the unseasonable thaw, and the XII Corps would find it difficult to be ready even by the night of 6 February. By the 2d many motor pools and supply depots already were under water, and rapidly rising rivers threatened tactical bridges. By the 4th the level of the Moselle had risen over thirteen feet and ripped away floating bridges uniting the XII and XX Corps. The river that the XII Corps had to cross, the Sauer, was a swollen torrent.

From the German point of view, the raging river was about the strongest deterrent to American success that commanders in this sector could count on. The remnants of two panzer divisions, which the U.S. Third Army G–2, Col. Oscar W. Koch, believed still with the *Seventh Army,* already had moved north; the only remaining armored reserve, the *2d Panzer Division,* would be used to counter the attack on Pruem before the XII Corps operation got underway. The situation in the *Seventh Army*'s center and on its left wing was thus much the same as that confronting the *XIII Corps*

farther north—nothing left but weak volks grenadier divisions. The only exception was the *212th Volks Grenadier Division,* located on the extreme left wing of the army near the confluence of the Sauer with the Moselle, protecting the city of Trier. The *212th* had fallen back to the West Wall ahead of the others and thus had gained time to refit and reorganize.[3]

With the northern boundary just over a mile southeast of Vianden, the *LXXX Corps* under General Beyer was destined to come under attack first. From north to south, Beyer's divisions, all volks grenadier units, were the *79th, 352d,* and the relatively strong *212th.* Before the new American attack began, the *352d* would be lost to the effort to protect Pruem.

Any weakening of the already thin line in the south worried the Germans. Rundstedt himself, the Commander in Chief West, remained for a long time seriously concerned over the possibility of an American advance up the general line of the Moselle on either side of Trier.[4] Yet the Germans there would have the advantage of the West Wall, which was particularly strong on either side of Trier, the early thaw with its rains and swollen rivers, and the terrain. The Our and Sauer Rivers in the sector faced by the XII Corps run through sharp gorges with clifflike sides sometimes 600 feet high. The four-mile stretch from Bollendorf to Echternach, where the U.S. XII Corps would assault, was further protected by large wooded stretches close up to the Sauer.

---

[2] Quotation is from Patton, *War As I Knew It,* p. 234.

[3] The German story is based principally on MS # B–123 (Gersdorff), as confirmed by German situation maps for the period.

[4] MS # C–020 (Maj Percy E. Schramm).

Crossing the Sauer

Available to General Eddy for the Bitburg attack were three infantry divisions
(the veteran 5th and 8oth, the inexperienced 76th) and a veteran armored division (the 4th). To make the main
effort on the right, Eddy chose the 5th
Division (General Irwin), veteran of
many a river crossing. Aided by an
attached regimental combat team (the
417th) of the 76th Division to protect
the right flank, the 5th was to cross between Bollendorf and Echternach to take
the first hill mass, not quite a mile beyond the Sauer. The hill would afford
control of the ground lying in an angle
formed by confluence of the Sauer and
the Pruem Rivers downstream from
Echternach. With one flank secured by
the Pruem River, the 5th Division then
could turn north to gain more open
ground southwest of Bitburg before
jumping the Pruem and advancing on
the main objective. The 8oth Division
(General McBride) meanwhile was to
cross the Sauer from Wallendorf to Bollendorf and advance as far north as
Mettendorf, five miles northeast of Wallendorf, to protect the left flank of the
main effort. Each of the 8oth's assault
regiments received an armored infantry
battalion of the 4th Armored Division as
reinforcement, and each of the five assault regiments in the corps drew the
support of a full engineer battalion.[5]

As engineers and riflemen moved
down to the Sauer on the night of 6

GENERAL EDDY

February, a fitful rain turned to light
snow. Seeking surprise, supporting artillery provided only moderate fire, directed at known enemy positions. Even
this light fire produced some German
response, most of it directed close along
the water line.

From the first the main enemy was the
river itself, swollen to double its normal
90-foot width, its current a turbulent
twelve miles an hour. Salvaged from a
captured Luftwaffe depot, the little in-
flatable rubber boats in which most of
the assault companies were to cross would
fight an unequal battle against the
churning water.

When the first boats pushed out into
the river some capsized almost immediately. Others rampaged out of control far
down the stream or careened crazily back
against the bank. Yet some survived.
These had reached midstream when here
and there lone rifle shots rang out. As if

[5] XII Corps FO 14, 3 Feb 45; 5th Div FO 16 and
8oth Div FO 30, both dated 4 Feb 45. Detailed
combat interviews supplement official records of
both the 5th and 8oth Divisions. See also Fifth
Division Historical Section, *The Fifth Infantry
Division in the ETO* (Atlanta: Albert Love Enter-
prises, 1945).

CROSSING SITE ON THE SAUER RIVER NEAR ECHTERNACH

the shots were signals, the entire east bank of the river appeared to come to life. Brilliant flares lighted the scene. Even those men who survived the treacherous current could scarcely hope to escape the crisscross of fire from automatic weapons.

Only eight men—one boatload—of each assault regiment of the 5th Division reached the far shore. Continuing German fire denied reinforcement.

It was somewhat better at Echternach, where Companies A and B formed the assault wave of the 417th Infantry, protecting the 5th Division's right flank. Yet there too, many of the boats met disaster. A round of mortar or artillery fire hit one boat broadside, sinking it in a flash and sending the occupants with their heavy equipment floundering helplessly downstream. Another boat began to drift directly toward a German machine gun spitting fire from the bank. Frantically, the men in the boat tried to change their course by grabbing at rushes along the water's edge, but in the process, they swamped the frail craft. Shedding as much equipment as they could, the men plunged into the icy water. Some made it to the bank. The current swept others downstream.

In such a melee, squad, platoon, and company organization went for naught. Thrown helter-skelter against the German-held bank, the men tried to reorganize but with little success. A house set afire on the Luxembourg side of the river lit the landscape with an eerie flame that aided German gunners. In the end it would be determined that 56 men and 3 officers of Company A had made it, 52 men and 2 officers of Company B; but no one could have arrived at any figures during the early hours. Before daylight came, most of Company C also got across, but nobody else. Only after nightfall brought concealment were crossings resumed.

In the 80th Division's sector near Wallendorf the attack began at 0300 the morning of 7 February, two hours later than the main assault. With surprise hardly possible in view of the general alert occasioned by the earlier assaults, the men of the 80th smoked likely crossing sites with shells from attached chemical mortars, thereby drawing enemy fire to the smoke, then began to cross the river elsewhere. The stratagem helped considerably and casualties were "not exceptionally heavy";[6] during the first twenty-four hours the bulk of at least six companies gained the far bank.

Of the five attacking regiments, the two of the 5th Division had the worst of it. Although the two little separate eight-man groups hardly represented even a toehold, the division commander, General Irwin, determined to treat them as such. With no further need to withhold

artillery support, he directed all available artillery battalions to mass their fire beyond the crossing site.[7] Tanks and tank destroyers he told to move boldly forward to take German pillboxes under direct observed fire. The corps commander, General Eddy, personally ordered tank destroyers armed with 90-mm. pieces to go to the water's edge. He also told General Irwin to cross his regiments in the 80th Division's or 417th Infantry's sectors should those units establish firm bridgeheads before the 5th Division could get across.[8] Yet as night came on 7 February, the sixteen still were the only men of the 5th Division on the German side of the river.

Contingents of both the 80th Division and the 417th Infantry meanwhile achieved some success against the high ground beyond the river. By nightfall of the first day (7 February), a battalion of the 80th Division held high ground northeast of Wallendorf, a mile and a half beyond the Sauer, and one company was in Wallendorf. With a verve and initiative often displayed by the inexperienced, Companies A and B of the 417th Infantry cleared pillbox after pillbox and occupied a portion of the high ground northeast of Echternach. There, in later afternoon, three German tanks and a small infantry force counterattacked, but Pfc. Lyle Corcoran knocked out one tank with a bozooka, another mired helpless in the mud, and a third withdrew. That ended the threat.

The big problem still was the river. Although all units had plans to put in bridges once the first wave of riflemen

---

[6] 80th Div AAR, Feb 45.

[7] Between 0130 and 0600 divisional and corps artillery in the XII Corps fired 29,000 rounds. See TUSA AAR.

[8] XII Corps msg file, 7 Feb 45.

was across, every effort to span the stream failed. In the 417th Infantry's sector, the 160th Engineer Battalion tried three times to anchor a cable across the river for a footbridge, but the current severed the first two and enemy machine gun fire sank the boat carrying the third. Despairing of success by this method, the engineers constructed a bridge on the near bank and tried to float it into position, but the current soon made quick work of it too.

Dependence on footbridges was one reason the 5th Division's right regiment, the 11th Infantry, failed to get more than eight men across the river. The regiment's assault plan was based on sending only patrols by boat, then constructing footbridges for the bulk of the infantry. Every effort to put in the bridges failed.

The coming of night on 7 February changed the situation but little. A few more men of the 80th Division got across, either in assault boats or by swimming when the boats capsized, but frustration continued generally to be everybody's lot.

Giving up hope of crossing during the night and planning a new attempt the next day, the 5th Division's 10th Infantry sent a boat to rescue its eight men from the far bank, while the eight of the 11th Infantry held fast. After a heavy machine gun section of the 11th Infantry's Company K and six boatloads of Company F got across, contact was at last established with the eight men who still remained on the far bank. Still no one could claim that the 5th Division possessed any kind of workable holding beyond the Sauer.

Some time in the early hours of the 8th, three platoons of Company G, 417th Infantry, and a heavy machine gun platoon of Company H conquered the cur-

rent at Echternach, and before daylight another fifteen boatloads of riflemen made it. Yet as had happened to their predecessors twenty-four hours earlier, German fire and the raging river quickly cut these men off from reinforcement and supply.

The story would continue the same in the XII Corps for three more days, until 11 February when engineers at last succeeded in bridging the river. That the weak and usually isolated units on the far shore could hold their own and even expand their positions was a testament to the courage and tenacity of the men and commanders concerned, plus the excellent support they got from their artillery; but it was a testament, too, to the general ineffectiveness of their enemy. Although the Germans might defend a position doggedly and impose severe casualties on the attacker before giving up, a passive defense augmented by mortar and *Nebelwerfer* fire was about all they could offer. They simply had no reserves for determined counterattacks.

For the Americans it was an incredibly difficult operation. The cliffs on the east bank were no less precipitous whether a man was attacking up them or merely trying to manhandle a case of K rations to hungry comrades at the top. The mud was deep, the weather always wet and cold. Trench foot and respiratory diseases abounded, and evacuation across the swollen Sauer was virtually impossible. German fire and the river greedily consumed assault boats and bridging equipment, and bringing up more over the ruined roads of Luxembourg was a slow process.

In the end it was sheer power mixed with determination and ingenuity that did the job. Although the corps lost at least a dozen bridges to the river, others at last were put in to stay. When two or three engineers were unable to bring back assault boats, six men did the job, limiting the number of infantrymen who could be carried but nevertheless gradually increasing the strength on the far bank. The 5th Division used big searchlights to illuminate the night crossings. Pontons lashed together served as ferries for vital heavy equipment. Moving up close to the river, 155-mm. self-propelled guns poured direct fire on German pillboxes. One battery alone destroyed eight pillboxes in one 24-hour period. To resupply men of the 417th Infantry on the heights above Echternach, fighter-bombers dropped specially loaded belly tanks. When these eluded the infantrymen, artillery liaison planes braved small arms fire to drop supplies with improvised parachutes. Whenever weather permitted, fighter-bombers of the XIX Tactical Air Command roamed far and wide, ready to strike at a moment's notice at any indication that the Germans were reinforcing the sector.

By 11 February, when the first tactical bridges were in, the 5th Division, including the attached 417th Infantry, had forged a bridgehead three miles wide and a mile deep; but several hundred yards of pillbox-studded terrain still separated the bridgehead from the closest regiment of the 80th Division. Nor had the two assault regiments of the 80th Division yet joined their holdings. On the other hand, within the two divisions, thirteen infantry battalions were across the river.

Visiting the sector on 12 February, General Patton was so appalled by the condition of the roads and yet so convinced that the crossings were no longer in danger that he volunteered permission

to halt the attack for a day.[9] General Eddy declined. The unremitting pressure of infantry and artillery was having a slow but inexorable effect; Eddy saw no reason to check the momentum.

Had General Eddy been able to view the situation through his adversary's eyes, he would have been even more convinced that he had chosen the right course. Once the Germans actually occupying the sector were rooted from their pillboxes, little else would stand in the way. Divining that the Echternach thrust was the southern arm of a pincers movement designed eventually to link with the attack of the VIII Corps on Pruem, the Germans gambled that no move would be made against Trier. They shifted the south regiment of the *212th Volks Grenadier Division* from Trier to assist the rest of the division. Although *Army Group B* provided a weak *Kampfgruppe* of the *560th Volks Grenadier Division*—all that was left of that unit—to replace the *212th*'s southern regiment, so critical was the situation around Echternach that this *Kampfgruppe* too had to be committed there. Beyond these two units, no other reinforcements were in prospect.[10]

The only other step the Germans were able to take immediately to help Beyer's *LXXX Corps* was to shift the right boundary of the corps to the south to a point just north of Wallendorf so that the adjacent *LIII Corps* (Rothkirch) could bear some of the burden. Thus once the 80th U.S. Division was across the river and turned north, the opposition came from units of the *LIII Corps*. Yet this corps had already been drained of resources in efforts to shore up the

---

[9] Patton, *War As I Knew It,* p. 240.
[10] MS # B-123 (Gersdorff).

faltering *XIII Corps* in the fight to save Pruem and could provide little more than conglomerate artillery and antitank units hastily converted to infantry roles.[11]

The Germans nevertheless continued to make a telling fight of it. So long as they were able, with the help of the West Wall, weather, terrain, and river, to restrict the size of the bridgehead, they would at the same time restrict the amount of power, including tanks, that the Americans might bring to bear.

Six more days—12 through 17 February—were to pass before the XII Corps could carve a full-fledged bridgehead from the inhospitable terrain. On the morning of the 12th the two assault regiments of the 80th Division finally linked their bridgeheads, and that evening the two divisions also joined. After 11 February, when the 417th Infantry reverted to control of its parent division, units of the 76th Infantry Division (Maj. Gen. William R. Schmidt) began crossing the river to assume defensive positions along the Pruem as the 5th Division turned north, but this was a slow process simply because the 5th's advance was slow.

On 14 February the 5th Division's 11th Infantry finally took Ernzen, southernmost of the villages on the high ground between the Sauer and the Pruem, but only after artillery lined up almost hub-to-hub on the other side of the Sauer joined with fighter-bombers to level the buildings. En route northward, a battalion of the 2d Infantry fought its way out of the woods as night came on the 16th and entered Schankweiler, thereby coming roughly abreast of the 80th Division, but the village was not entirely in hand until the next day.

Although the Germans in most places fought with determination, they could take credit for only part of the delay. The condition of supply roads west of the Sauer and continuing problems of getting men and heavy equipment across the swollen river accounted for much of it. Without the little M29 cargo carrier (Weasel), a kind of full-tracked jeep, vehicular traffic in the mud of the bridgehead would have ground to a halt. Nor did the 80th Division, in particular, launch any large-scale attacks, concentrating instead on mopping up pockets of resistance, jockeying for position on high ground north and northeast of Wallendorf, and building up strength in supporting weapons and supplies before making a major effort to expand and break out of the bridgehead.[12] One unusual item of equipment introduced to both the 5th and 80th Divisions in the bridgehead was the T34 multiple rocket launcher, a 60-tube cluster of 4.5-inch rocket launchers mounted on a Sherman tank.[13]

The Vianden Bulge

The 80th Division was to begin its new advance early on 18 February, but at first it would be directed less toward capture of Bitburg than toward helping eliminate an enemy hold-out position lying between the XII Corps bridgehead and the penetration of the VIII Corps at Pruem. While the VIII Corps drove south and southeast, the 80th Division

---

[11] *Ibid.;* XII Corps G–2 Periodic Rpts.

[12] 80th Div AAR, Feb 45.
[13] For an evaluation of these weapons, see Constance McLaughlin Green, Harry C. Thomson, and Peter C. Roots, *The Ordnance Department: Planning Munitions for War,* UNITED STATES ARMY IN WORLD WAR II (Washington, 1955), pp. 329–30.

was to move north and northeast, the two to join at the village of Mauel, on the Pruem River equidistant from Pruem and Bitburg.

The enemy's hold-out position quickly came to be known on the American side as the Vianden bulge, after a town on the Our. The bulge was some twenty-two miles wide from north to south, from the 90th Division's forward lines near Habscheid to the 80th Division's positions north of Wallendorf. It was eleven to thirteen miles deep, from the German frontier along the Our to the Pruem. It encompassed some of the most rugged terrain in the entire Eifel. A steep, heavily wooded bluff capped by limestone ledges marks the east bank of the Our. Behind the bluff and the pillboxes of the West Wall, the land alternately rises and plunges in a series of high, irregular ridges and deep ravines dotted with thick stands of fir trees and laced with twisting secondary roads.

German commanders responsible for the Vianden bulge wanted to withdraw, to exchange the extended, meandering periphery of the bulge for a considerably shorter line behind the Pruem River. Since they lacked the strength to counterattack the American penetrations to north and south, the bulge had little tactical significance. Nor did the Germans have enough resources even to hold the bulge for any appreciable time.

Once the boundary of the *LIII Corps* was shifted southward to give Rothkirch's troops some of the burden of the bridgehead battle with the XII U.S. Corps, responsibility for the Vianden bulge was split almost in half. Reduced to two weak volks grenadier divisions and a few conglomerate units, the *LIII Corps* held the southern half; General

Felber's *XIII Corps,* severely straitened by the Pruem fighting, the northern half.

For all the desire of the corps commanders to withdraw, "Hitler, like a small child, refused to part with even a small portion of his toy, the West Wall." [14] When General Felber broached the subject of withdrawal to the *Seventh Army* commander, General Brandenberger, the army commander had to refuse even though he personally favored it.[15] Brandenberger himself had recommended the same thing to *Army Group B*, but Field Marshal Model, severely piqued because Brandenberger had failed to repulse the American drives, was in no mood to agree even had Hitler's standfast orders not blocked the way. Model already was contemplating relief of the *Seventh Army* commander.

Strained relations between the army and the army group commander came to a head only two days after the Americans opened their drive to eliminate the bulge. At a meeting at the *Seventh Army*'s forward headquarters on 20 February, Model castigated Brandenberger before his staff and relieved him. He immediately elevated General Felber, who was present, to command of the *Seventh Army*.

If the disgrace of relief hurt Brandenberger's pride, it also may have saved his life. Hardly had he left when an American bomb landed on the headquarters building, killing or severely wounding several staff officers. The chief of staff, stripped of his clothing by the blast, incurred only a superficial head wound; the new commander, General Felber, who had just left the building for a fare-

---

[14] MS # B-123 (Gersdorff).
[15] MS # B-494 (Felber).

well tour of his *XIII Corps,* also incurred a slight wound.[16]

Upon Felber's advancement, General-leutnant Graf Ralph von Oriola assumed command of the *XIII Corps.* After studying the situation in his sector, Oriola made the same recommendation to Felber that Felber had made to Brandenberger—withdraw behind the Pruem. The new *Seventh Army* commander found himself in the uncomfortable position of having to refuse the very request he himself had made a few days before.[17]

Forced to deny a maneuver that he actually endorsed, Felber devised a simple plan that assured him at least a measure of operational control of his army. Working through his chief of staff, General Gersdorff, he told his subordinate commanders they would in the future receive two versions of all orders. One would direct continued defense and was to be filed in official records. The other would give the order Felber actually intended; it was to be destroyed after receipt. To justify withdrawals, operational reports to higher headquarters were to be falsified, all withdrawals officially to be made because of overwhelming American strength.[18]

On the American side, neither the bogging down of the VIII Corps attack because of crumbling supply roads nor General Bradley's order of 10 February removing headquarters of the III Corps from the Third Army was to be allowed to thwart Patton's offensive. Although one division was to depart with the headquarters, the 6th Armored Division and

the 6th Cavalry Group were to remain to be taken over by the VIII Corps. With two armored and three infantry divisions and a cavalry group, the VIII Corps would be strong enough to help eliminate the Vianden bulge, despite an elongated front. Time and almost superhuman engineer efforts eventually would correct the supply situation. The attack was to begin on 18 February at the same time the 80th Division of the XII Corps moved northeastward from Wallendorf.

The VIII Corps commander, General Middleton, planned to use only three of his divisions, plus the cavalry group. Shifting the 90th Division and the 11th Armored westward to enable greater concentration within the 6th Armored Division's sector along the Our, he directed the 90th to drive southeastward from Habscheid. The division was to gain the Pruem River from Pronsfeld all the way to the appointed contact point with the XII Corps at Mauel. Using only one combat command at first, the 11th Armored was to thrust due south to clear a pie-shaped sector between the 6th Armored and 90th Divisions, featured by high ground overlooking the village of Irrhausen on a relatively major east-west road. Two days after the first attacks, the 6th Armored Division was to strike southeastward from a small bridgehead already established across the Our north of the village of Dahnen, west of Irrhausen. The 6th Cavalry Group (Col. Edward M. Fickett) meanwhile was to cross the Our on the right flank of the 6th Armored and clear the southwestern corner of the bulge. Both armored divisions were to be pinched out as the attacks of the cavalry and the 90th Division converged along the south boundary of the corps.

---

[16] Interview, Maj Fred Meyer with Gersdorff, 28 Jul 53; MS # B-123 (Gersdorff).

[17] MS # B-052, *XIII Corps,* 18 February-21 March 1945 (Oriola).

[18] Interview, Meyer with Gersdorff, 26 Jul 53.

Moving before daylight on 18 February without artillery preparation, both the 90th Division and the 11th Armored caught the Germans unprepared.

The more dramatic success was in the center, where the 90th Division's 359th Infantry struck through a thick belt of West Wall pillboxes toward Kesfeld, southwest of Losenseifen Hill, the dominating eminence taken during the Pruem offensive by contingents of the 11th Armored Division. Bypassing pillboxes in the darkness, Company I quickly moved into Kesfeld. It took only a short fire fight to secure the village. Meanwhile, the 2d Batalion and the rest of the 3d cleared forty-eight pillboxes on the approaches to Kesfeld. The regimental commanders and staffs of two regiments of the *167th Volks Grenadier Division* and two battalion commanders and their staffs were captured in their bunks. Almost all of two companies also were captured, and by the end of the day more than 400 Germans were headed for prisoner-of-war cages.[19]

Carrying the burden of the attack for the 11th Armored Division, the reserve combat command had to fight harder but in the end gained more ground than did the 359th Infantry. In CCR's sector just west of Kesfeld, no penetration of the West Wall had yet been made; the attack thus involved passing through concrete dragon's teeth as well as pillboxes. Covered by fire from tanks, armored engineers soon blasted a path through the antitank obstacle, and tanks and armored infantrymen poured through. The advance benefited considerably from the fact that only hours before the attack a regiment of the *276th Volks Grenadier*

Division had relieved contingents of the *340th Volks Grenadier Division,* and the newcomers were unfamiliar with the positions. By nightfall, some seventy-five prisoners were in hand and the 55th Armored Infantry Battalion held Leidenborn, more than one-fourth the distance to the final objective overlooking Irrhausen. The armor spent much of the next day consolidating its penetration.

The going meanwhile had been less encouraging southeast of Habscheid where the 358th Infantry almost a fortnight earlier had learned respect for the kind of opposition the Germans could muster in the pillboxes and on the steep hills along the Habscheid-Pronsfeld highway. Neither the 2d Battalion astride the highway nor the 3d Battalion west of the road gained more than a thousand yards in the face of intense machine gun and artillery fire.

Somewhat inexplicably, the bottom dropped out of the enemy's defense along that road early on the second day, 19 February. Hardly an hour of attack had passed when the battalion west of the road took its objective, the village of Masthorn. An hour later the battalion astride the highway took the last dominating hill short of the Pruem River. Neither battalion incurred a single casualty.

For all practical purposes, the 358th Infantry had reached the Pruem and might begin to pull out the bulk of its forces to participate in a wheeling maneuver that the division commander, General Rooks, set in motion during the afternoon of the 19th. When the 359th Infantry had advanced a mile and a half southeast of Kesfeld, then turned due east toward the Pruem, General Rooks sent his reserve regiment, the 357th In-

---

[19] 90th Div AAR, Feb 45.

WELCOME TO GERMANY FROM THE 6TH ARMORED DIVISION

fantry, swinging southeast around the 359th's right flank. Later he would commit the 358th Infantry around the right flank of the 357th to make a broader, final swing southeast to the Pruem at Mauel.

As this maneuver got underway on 20 February, the 6th Armored Division near Dahnen began to break out of its little bridgehead across the Our. Established originally by CCB as a diversion for the attack of the XII Corps on 6 February, the bridgehead was about two miles wide but less than a mile deep. It nevertheless provided a basis for penetrating the West

Wall without having to attack the pillboxes frontally across the swollen Our and up the east bank escarpment.[20]

CCB made the first assault to break out of the bridgehead, while CCA, west of the Our and farther south opposite Dasburg, staged a mock crossing of the river. Beginning at 0645, artillery laid an in-

---

[20] The 6th Armored Division, under the supervision of its commander, General Grow, published an unusual history. Providing a day-by-day factual account of all units, without embellishment, it is an excellent source. See *Combat Record of the Sixth Armored Division* (Germany, 1945). Action in the 20 February attack also is covered by extensive combat interviews.

tensive preparation across CCB's entire front for twenty minutes, then lifted for ten minutes in hope that the Germans would move from their pillboxes into field fortifications outside. Then for one minute all the artillery switched to a mammoth TOT on the first specific objective, a fortified hill a mile and a half due north of Dahnen.

Close behind the artillery, dismounted armored infantrymen organized into special pillbox assault teams half a platoon strong started up the hill, while others organized as support fire teams took the embrasures of the pillboxes under small arms fire. As an assault team neared a pillbox, a prearranged signal—usually a colored smoke grenade—lifted the support team's fire. Equipped with wire cutters, rocket launchers, and demolition charges, the infantrymen closed in. By 0835 the first pillbox had fallen, and by noon seventeen pillboxes and the crest of the hill were clear. So effective was the method of attack that only one man was lost during the day to small arms fire. Of a total of 5 killed and 66 wounded during 20 February, almost all were lost to mines.

Before daylight the next day, 21 February, CCB struck again. While one force expanded the bridgehead south to take Dahnen, another drove southeast to take the village of Daleiden and thereby cut the major Dasburg-Irrhausen highway. In midmorning at Dahnen, a rifle platoon of the 9th Armored Infantry Battalion mounted a platoon of medium tanks and raced south, bypassing pillboxes, to invest Dasburg and clear a crossing site over the Our for CCA. In a matter of minutes, the tank-mounted infantry gained the village while two infantry companies started south from

Dahnen as reinforcement, clearing pillboxes as they marched. By nightfall Dasburg and the pillboxes standing sentinel over the Our west of the village were secure, but fire from German positions south of Dasburg continued to deny CCA passage over the river.

During these two days, the 90th Division continued to push steadily east and southeast toward the Pruem River. While the 359th Infantry on 21 February approached the last two villages short of the river, the 357th Infantry in its wheeling maneuver overcame stanch resistance on open slopes of towering high ground around a crossroads settlement two miles from the Pruem. An opportune strike by fighter-bombers of the XIX Tactical Air Command provided an assist. In mid-afternoon, with the situation apparently opening up, General Rooks committed the 358th Infantry on its wider wheeling maneuver designed to reach the Pruem at the contact point with the XII Corps at Mauel.

If any doubt remained that the enemy defense was cracking, it rapidly dissipated early the next morning, 22 February, fifth day of the offensive. The 11th Armored Division, for example, heretofore primarily concerned with consolidating its penetration of the West Wall, dashed suddenly southward three miles and occupied its final objective, the high ground overlooking Irrhausen. A battalion of the 358th Infantry on the outer rim of the 90th Division's wheel raced southeast four miles to take a village only three and a half miles from Mauel. One squad of Company A alone took some 100 prisoners, most of them artillerymen frantically trying to hitch their horses to their pieces and escape. Breakthrough everywhere, with the exception of the southwestern corner of the bulge where the light formation of the 6th Cavalry Group still found the going sticky.

Reports of continued rapid advances were coming in the next day, 23 February, when the corps commander, General Middleton, sat down to lunch at his command post in Luxembourg with the commander of the 6th Armored Division, General Grow. "How long will it take you," Middleton asked Grow, "to get a task force on the road to drive across the front of the 6th Cavalry Group and contact XII Corps?" [21] By 1630 a strong force composed of a company each of light and medium tanks, a cavalry troop, an infantry company, a platoon of tank destroyers, and two squads of engineers was on the way. The commander was Lt. Col. Harold C. Davall.

Expanding the XII Corps Bridgehead

The troops that Davall's task force set out to contact had found the opposition stiffer than that facing the VIII Corps but nevertheless had made steady progress. With less ground to cover to reach the intercorps boundary, they would be on hand at the boundary when Davall arrived. These were men of the 80th Division, who on 18 February only a few hours after the VIII Corps jumped off had begun their assignment to help clear the Vianden bulge. At the same time they were expanding the XII Corps bridgehead and preparing the way for a final drive on Bitburg.

Early on 18 February, the 80th Division commander, General McBride, sent two regiments north from the vicin-

ity of Wallendorf toward Mettendorf and Hill 408, the latter the most commanding ground in the second and third tier of hills beyond the German frontier. While protecting the left flank of the 5th Division in the corps main effort, the thrust also would uncover the West Wall pillboxes along the Our River.[22]

The 80th Division's two regiments took three days to reach Hill 408, but before daylight on 21 February a battalion of the 318th Infantry slipped through the darkness to occupy the height after firing only a few shots. In the meantime, a battalion of the 317th Infantry took the enemy by surprise at Enzen, on the little Enz River southeast of Hill 408, seized a bridge intact, and gained a leg on the next fold of high ground lying between the Enz and the Pruem.

The 319th Infantry meanwhile maneuvered against the pillboxes along the Our. Advancing along the west bank of the Gay Creek, the first stream line behind the river and the pillboxes, one battalion during the night of 18 February occupied high ground near Niedersgegen, nestled at the bottom of the creek valley, and soon after daylight took the village itself. The next day, 20 February, the same battalion turned west to the Our, cutting off the Germans in a two and a half mile stretch of the West Wall.

The job of mopping up the pillboxes fell to the 53d Armored Infantry Battalion, attached from the 4th Armored Division. The weather helped. With the ground free of snow and more than a hint of spring in the air, it was no time

[21] Interview, Meyer with Grow, 6 Aug 53.

[22] 80th Div FO 31, 14 Feb 45.

to die. By nightfall of the 21st, when the mop-up was complete, 337 Germans had emerged from the West Wall bunkers, hands high in surrender.

With the West Wall eliminated and Hill 408 taken, time for exploitation appeared at hand. As a first step in commitment of the 4th Armored Division, the corps commander, General Eddy, attached Combat Command B to the 80th Division. On 23 February the armor drove northeast to take Sinspelt and its bridge over the Enz River on a main highway nine miles due west of Bitburg. It was no easy assignment, for in a last-ditch effort to prevent breakout, the Germans rushed the remnants of the 2d *Panzer Division* down from Pruem.[23] Nevertheless, as night fell Sinspelt and a serviceable bridge over the Enz were secure.

Also taken was the settlement of Obergeckler, along the corps boundary just over a mile west and slightly north of Sinspelt. There a battalion of the 319th Infantry kept pace with the armor and as night came was in position to welcome Colonel Davall's task force from the 6th Armored Division, approaching from the north.

Task Force Davall had begun to move at 1630 from the village of Jucken, on a secondary road six miles northwest of Obergeckler. Brushing aside a show of resistance at a crossroads not quite two miles from the starting point, the task force continued southward through the night, gathering in surprised Germans along the way. At 0740 the next morning, 24 February, Task Force Davall made

contact with contingents of the 80th Division just north of Obergeckler.

Before the day was out, the 90th Division too had swept to the corps boundary. At a cost of some 600 casualties, of which approximately 125 were killed, three divisions and a cavalry group had pierced the West Wall in the rough terrain of the Eifel and established a solid front along the Pruem River. In the process, they took more than 3,000 prisoners.[24]

To Bitburg and the Kyll

The Vianden bulge cleared, the XII Corps on 24 February was free to turn full attention to seizing Bitburg. Having assumed command of the corps temporarily when on 22 February General Eddy left for a brief rest, the 4th Armored Division commander, General Gaffey, ordered CCB released from control of the 80th Division and directed the entire armored division to strike northeastward. The armor was to jump the Pruem and Nims Rivers, cut major roads leading north out of Bitburg, and build up along the Kyll River two miles beyond the town. The 5th Infantry Division was to take the town and reach the Kyll to the east and southeast.

In the days since 18 February, while the 80th Division had been expanding the XII Corps bridgehead to north and northeast, the 5th Division had cleared the west bank of the Pruem to a point only six miles southwest of Bitburg. At the same time, the division had regrouped and turned over much of its Pruem River line in the south to the

[23] MS # B-123 (Gersdorff).

[24] Div and cavalry group AAR's, Feb 45.

76th Division.[25] Once the 5th had crossed the Pruem, contingents of the 76th also were to cross and drive southeast to protect the 5th's right flank.

From the first it was apparent that crossing the Pruem River would be considerably easier than crossing the Sauer. There was nothing to equal the clifflike terrain along the Sauer, and the worst of the flood waters resulting from the early thaw had passed. Yet hardly anyone could have anticipated how "unquestionably easy" the crossing would be.[26] Starting at 2300 the night of the 24th, a battalion of the 2d Infantry crossed the river within an hour and took high ground just north of the village of Wettlingen. An hour later a battalion of the 10th Infantry crossed a few miles to the south on the heels of a patrol that found a serviceable vehicular ford. Only scattered mortar and small arms fire opposed either crossing.

As the infantrymen fanned out to the north and northeast, the story was much the same everywhere. "Germans came forward bearing white flags and sickly smiles." [27] By nightfall of 26 February, one battalion of the 2d Infantry stood on the Nims River less than a mile from the western edge of Bitburg. Another bat-

talion of the 2d and two of the 10th Infantry were across the stream farther south and had cut the Echternach-Bitburg highway. The 2d Battalion, 2d Infantry, took a bridge over the Nims intact, and one of the 10th Infantry's battalions crossed over the ruins of a demolished bridge. A regiment of the 76th Division meanwhile crossed the Pruem through the 10th Infantry's bridgehead and also jumped the Nims.

The fate of Bitburg was sealed even had there been no 4th Armored Division racing northeastward along the left flank of the infantry. As early as the evening of 25 February, a day before the infantry crossed the Nims, a task force of the 4th Armored had a bridgehead over the second river a mile and a half northwest of Bitburg. With planes of the XIX Tactical Air Command almost constantly overhead, the bulk of two combat commands got across the Nims on 26 February and spread out to northeast and east. Part of the 80th Division's infantry followed in the wake of the armor to bring in the prisoners, while one regiment moved north and established contact with the VIII Corps at Mauel.

On the German side, the new *Seventh Army* commander, General Felber, appealed to his superiors time after time for help, but to little avail. In the end, *Army Group B* managed to detach a depleted infantry division, the *246th*, from the *Fifth Panzer Army* to the north, but the division began to move toward Bitburg only on 27 February. That was far too late.[28]

As early as 26 February fighter-bomber pilots reported the Germans evacuating

---

[25] On 27 February, as Pfc. Herman C. Wallace of the 76th Division's 301st Engineer Combat Battalion was helping clear mines from a road near the river, he stepped on an S-mine, an antipersonnel device that when activated normally leaps upward to explode in the air. Hearing the sound indicating that his step had activated the mine, Private Wallace spared those around him by holding his foot on the mine and placing his other firmly beside it. This confined the explosion to the ground but inevitably killed him in the process. He was awarded the Medal of Honor posthumously.

[26] *The Fifth Infantry Division in the ETO,* "Across the Sauer Into the Siegfried Line."

[27] *Ibid.*

[28] MS # B-831, *Seventh Army,* 20 February-26 March 1945 (Felber).

Bitburg. Well they might, for by night-fall of the 26th a task force of the 4th Armored Division had reached the west bank of the Kyll two miles northeast of the town, and by nightfall of the 27th a battalion of the 5th Division's 11th Infantry occupied a village a mile southeast of the town while another battalion poised in the southern fringe of Bitburg itself. Before midday on 28 February the 11th Infantry delivered the *coup de grâce* to a town already severely battered by American planes and artillery.

Beginning on 4 February with the start of the VIII Corps offensive aimed at Pruem, two corps of the Third Army in just over three weeks had penetrated the West Wall in some of the most forbidding terrain to be found along the Western Front. At its widest point, the penetration measured more than twenty-five miles. The VIII Corps at the end of February stood on the Pruem while the XII Corps bulged eastward to the Kyll. Although the Rhine still lay some fifty miles away and terrain still might constitute a major obstacle, the enemy's prepared defenses lay behind, and only a miracle could enable the Germans to man another solid front in the Eifel.

The Third Army commander, General Patton, meanwhile had been turning his attention to one more detail that had to be attended to before he could make a final thrust to the Rhine. Striding into the 76th Division's command post early on 26 February, Patton placed a fist on the operations map at the ancient Roman city of Trier on the Moselle.[29]

Almost unnoticed in the bigger picture of the Western Front, an infantry division and an armored division of the Third Army's XX Corps had been nibbling away at the German position south of Trier that had become known as the Saar-Moselle triangle. The XX Corps from the south and the 76th Division from the north, Patton directed, were to envelop Trier.

---

[29] 1st Lt. Joseph J. Hutnik and Tech. 4 Leonard Kobrick, eds., *We Ripened Fast—The Unofficial History of the Seventy-Sixth Infantry Division* (Germany, n.d.), p. 102.

CHAPTER VII

The Saar-Moselle Triangle

During September 1944, the great pursuit across France and Belgium had ended in the north along the German frontier and the West Wall, in the south generally along the line of the Moselle River. In the bitter fighting that followed through the autumn and early winter, the Third Army in the south had breached the Moselle line around Metz, pushed northeast across the German border, and broken the outer crust of the West Wall along the Saar River at Saarlautern, thirty-two miles south of Trier. Although a combination of Third and Seventh Army attacks compromised the Moselle line along most of its length, the Germans had continued to hold the east bank in a triangle formed by confluence of the Saar and the Moselle southwest of Trier. The Third Army had yet to clear the triangle when the call had come in December to move into the Ardennes.

To American troops the uncleared sector was the "Saar-Moselle triangle." From an apex at the meeting of the Saar and the Moselle in the north to a base along an east-west line roughly coterminous with the southern border of Luxembourg, the triangle measured some sixteen and a half miles. The base extended not quite thirteen miles. Although the West Wall in this sector lay behind the Saar, the Germans in 1939 and 1940 had constructed a supple-

mentary fortified line across the base of the triangle from Nennig in the west to Orscholz, at a great northwestward loop of the Saar. The Germans called the position the Orscholz Switch; the Americans knew it as the Siegfried Switch. Assuming the neutrality of Luxembourg, the switch position was designed to protect Trier and the Moselle corridor and to prevent outflanking of the strongest portion of the West Wall, that lying to the southeast across the face of the Saar industrial area.

The Orscholz Switch was similar to the West Wall itself, a defensive position two miles deep, fronted by dragon's teeth or antitank ditches and composed of pillboxes and concrete bunkers reinforced by field fortifications. It sat astride high ground forming a watershed for streams flowing generally northeast to the Saar and west and southwest to the Moselle. The terrain is rolling and sharply compartmented, in many places covered with dense woods. The major roads converge on the town of Saarburg, halfway up the east side of the triangle on the west bank of the Saar River.

In November and December, while striking toward the Saar at Saarlautern, General Walker's XX Corps on the left wing of the Third Army had been able to turn only a scant force against the Orscholz Switch and the triangle. In late November an armored combat command and an infantry regiment had engineered a minor penetration of the left portion of the switch at the villages of Tettingen and Butzdorf; but the XX Corps had had to relinquish the ground in December in the general belt-tightening process to free units for the Ardennes.[1] When in early January a relatively inexperienced infantry division, the 94th under Maj. Gen. Harry J. Malony, arrived in this sector, the forward positions were south of the Orscholz line.

As the 94th Division moved into position on 7 January, the levies imposed by the Ardennes fighting had so severely reduced General Walker's XX Corps that all sectors were thinly manned. Beyond the corps left boundary at the Moselle, a cavalry group of the neighboring XII Corps held the west bank of the Moselle. The 94th Division faced the entire 13-mile stretch of the Orscholz Switch, from Moselle to Saar. The 3d Cavalry Group defended the XX Corps center, approximately nine miles along the Saar River to the confluence of the Saar and the Nied. The 95th Infantry Division held the remainder of the corps front, roughly equal to the distance covered by the cavalry but involving an added responsibility of defending a bridgehead over the Saar at Saarlautern. (The 95th subsequently was replaced by the 26th Division.)

Before arriving in the Saar-Moselle triangle, the 94th Division had fought to contain Germans corralled in the Breton ports of Lorient and St. Nazaire. In part to provide the division offensive combat experience, in part to contain the Germans in the Orscholz Switch and

possibly to draw reserves from other sectors, and in part to gain a foothold in the line for later exploitation, the corps commander, General Walker, told General Malony on 12 January to begin a series of stabs into the line in strengths not to exceed one reinforced battalion.[2]

Probing the Orscholz Switch

As had other units in November, the 94th Division made its first thrusts into the left portion of the Orscholz Switch in an attack designed to hit a sensitive point that might evoke German counterattack, which the Americans might crush with heavy German losses. At dawn on 14 January, the 1st Battalion, 376th Infantry, commanded by Lt. Col. Russell M. Miner, plowed through a foot of snow and in just over an hour overran surprised German outposts to take Tettingen, the first village behind the dragon's teeth on the western slopes of a high hogback ridgeline marked by the trace of a major highway leading northeast to Saarburg. (Map VI) So successful was the assault that the regimental commander ordered Colonel Miner to continue into the adjacent village of Butzdorf. Although fire from an alerted enemy in nearby pillboxes made this task more difficult, Butzdorf too was in hand before noon. The next day, when the 3d Battalion of the 376th Infantry at-

---

[1] Cole, *The Lorraine Campaign*, chs. XI, XIII.

[2] In addition to official records of the 94th Division and a series of combat interviews, see an excellent unit history, Laurence G. Byrnes, ed., *History of the 94th Infantry Division in World War II* (Washington: Infantry Journal Press, 1948). See also XX Corps Association, *The XX Corps: Its History and Service in World War II* (Japan, n.d.) (Hereafter cited as *XX Corps History*), and detailed comments by General Malony on the draft manuscript for this volume.

tacked toward Nennig and two other villages on the Moselle floodplain northwest of Tettingen and Butzdorf, the going was less easy, but as night came on 15 January these three villages forming the western anchor of the Orscholz Switch also were in hand.

The rapidity with which the two thrusts had broken into the switch position was attributable in large measure to the fact that the enemy's *416th Infantry Division,* responsible for the sector since November, was gravely overextended. Only two regiments held the entire Orscholz Switch, while the third defended in the West Wall beyond the Saar. Only the division replacement battalion was available as a reserve.[3]

Before dawn on 15 January, even as the 3d Battalion, 376th Infantry, moved toward Nennig and the other villages on the Moselle floodplain, the *416th Division*'s replacement battalion counterattacked at Butzdorf and Tettingen. Although close-in fighting raged for a time in both villages, the Germans in the end had to fall back. Of some 400 who made the counterattack, scarcely more than a hundred escaped; some died from minor wounds after prolonged exposure in the subfreezing cold.[4]

As General Malony had hoped, the attacks had prompted German counterattack with attendant German losses. What he had not counted on was a coincidence that provided the Germans in the Orscholz Switch a powerful force for another counterattack. While the 94th Division was preparing its two thrusts, the enemy's *11th Panzer Division* had been en route to the very sector General Malony had chosen for his first attacks.

Having been scheduled for the Ardennes counteroffensive but not committed, the *11th Panzer Division* early in January was shifted south across the army group boundary, which bisected the northern corner of the Saar-Moselle triangle. With the shift the panzer division became a reserve for *Army Group G.*

The commander of *Army Group G,* General Blaskowitz, planned a variety of exercises in which he would use the panzer division in concert with other units to complement a faltering Operation *NORDWIND* in Alsace, but for lack of additional units, none of the plans had materialized. In the end, Blaskowitz assigned the panzer division to the *LXXXII Corps* (General der Infanterie Walther Hahm), one of three corps operating directly under the army group without an intervening army headquarters. *The LXXXII Corps* was responsible for a long stretch of the Saar and for the Orscholz Switch. In order to relieve pressure on the embattled *Seventh Army* in the Ardennes, the *11th Panzer Division* was to make a strong armored raid out of the Orscholz Switch, three and a half miles to the southwest to heights on the east bank of the Moselle overlooking the meeting point of the German and Luxembourg frontiers. Target date for the raid was mid-January. The axis of attack was to run directly through Butzdorf and Tettingen.[5]

---

[3] MS # B-573, Battles of the *416th Infantry Division* Between the Moselle and the Saar From 5 October 1944 to 17 February 1945 (Oberleutnant Karl Redmer, after consultation with various officers of the *416th Div, LXXXII Corps,* and adjacent units); MS # B-090, Rhineland Campaign (Generalleutnant Kurt Pflieger, CG *416th Div).*

[4] *Ibid.,* Byrnes, *History of the 94th Infantry Division in World War II,* pp. 95–98.

[5] MSS # B-417, The *11th Panzer Division* in the Rhineland, 20 December 1944–10 February 1945 (Generalleutnant Wend von Wietersheim, CG *11th*

CREW OF A 3-INCH GUN *on the watch for German tanks in the Saar-Moselle triangle.*

For want of fuel and because capacity of bridges over the Saar was limited, some 50 Mark V (Panther) tanks of the *11th Panzer Division* had to remain east of the Saar. The raid would be entrusted to 30 Mark IV (medium) tanks, 20 to 30 assault guns, and 2 relatively full-strength panzer grenadier regiments.[6]

American pilots reported German armor crossing the Saar during the day of 16 January, so that when night came the 94th Division was fully alert. At Butz-dorf, Tettingen, Nennig, and the other

---

Panzer Division); # B-066, Engagements Fought by *LXXXII Army Corps* During the Period 2 December 1944 to 27 March 1945 (Oberst Ludwig Graf von Ingelheim, CofS *LXXXII Corps*); # B-573 (Redmer). See also Magna Bauer, *Army Group G,* January 1945, MS prepared in OCMH to complement this volume.

[6] Unless otherwise noted, sources for *11th Panzer Division* actions are as cited in the footnote above. Note that some of the German officers, having worked without benefit of contemporary records, sometimes erred on dates. Byrnes in his 94th Division history provides a detailed lower-level German account, apparently from prisoner interrogations.

villages, the men worked through 17 January to lay antitank mines and bring up tank destroyers and additional bazookas. (The 94th Division as yet had no attached tank battalion.) Through the night the sound of tracked vehicles emanated from woods and villages to the north and northeast. Then at 0300 on 18 January a patrol returned with two prisoners who confirmed all suspicions: the prisoners were from *11th Panzer Division*.

At dawn on the 18th the storm broke.

For twenty minutes German mortars and artillery worked over Butzdorf and Tettingen, then from the northeast from the nearby village of Sinz emerged a long column of tanks, assault guns, half-tracks bulging with greatcoated Germans, and infantry on foot. Despite heavy concentrations of defensive artillery fire, the Germans kept coming. As half the force struck Butzdorf, the other half swung in a wide arc to hit Tettingen.

For more than an hour confusion reigned in both villages as German tanks and assault guns shot up the landscape and infantrymen of both sides fought at close quarters among the damaged buildings. Mines disabled some of the German vehicles, and a 57-mm. antitank gun caught one tank broadside, but in the main it was a job for intrepid infantrymen stalking with bazookas.

Shortly after 0900 the Germans fell back, but just before noon ten tanks again emerged from Sinz, took up hull defilade positions and persistently pounded the two villages. At 1430 three battalions of German infantry launched a fresh assault, this time directed primarily at Butzdorf. Again the Germans oc-

cupied many of the houses. Again close-in fighting raged.

Throughout the afternoon the lone American company in Butzdorf fought back, but as night approached the survivors controlled only a few buildings. So fire-swept was the open ground between Tettingen and Butzdorf that the Americans could bring neither reinforcements nor supplies forward. As darkness fell General Malony authorized the survivors in Butzdorf to fall back.

The company commander in Butzdorf, 1st Lt. David F. Stafford, already had arrived independently at the conclusion that withdrawal was the only course left to him short of surrender or annihilation. Tearing doors off their hinges to serve as litters for the seriously wounded, what was left of the company slowly pulled back through Stygian darkness and a heavy snowfall while guns of the 284th and 919th Field Artillery Battalions fired covering concentrations.

When the survivors reached Tettingen, they found a fresh battalion of the 376th Infantry in position to defend that village. Although no one could have known it at the time, the high-water mark of the raid through the Orscholz Switch had come and gone. The Germans had taken Butzdorf, and three days later, during the night of 21 January, they succeeded in fighting their way into half the village of Nennig on the Moselle floodplain and into a castle northeast of Nennig, but that was the end. Handicapped by absence of heavy tanks, severely restricted by the snow-covered terrain (one thrust on Nennig bogged down when the tanks foundered in an antitank ditch concealed by snowdrifts), and punished by artillery fire directed from an observation post on heights west

REMOVING GERMAN DEAD AFTER FIGHTING IN NENNIG

of the Moselle, the *11th Panzer Division* could only slow the tempo of the 94th Division's thrusts.[7]

Hardly had the echoes of the fighting with the panzer division died down when General Malony aimed another limited objective attack into the German line. This time he chose to strike at the eastern anchor of the Orscholz Switch, at Orscholz itself, where a regiment of the overextended *416th Infantry Division* still was responsible for the defense. A

[7] For a description of German difficulties, see MSS # B-417 (Wietersheim) and # B-066 (Ingelheim).

penetration at Orscholz, combined with that at Tettingen, might be exploited later into a double envelopment of the center of the switch position.

Orscholz perched atop a ridge with snow-covered open fields gently sloping to the south. The only logical covered approach to the village from the positions held by the 94th Division was through the Saarburg Forest, southwest and west of the village. Through this forest the 301st Infantry commander, Col. Roy N. Hagerty, planned to send his 1st Battalion in a surprise attack just before dawn on 20 January. The battalion was to reach the east-west Oberleu-ken-Orscholz highway running through the woods, then to turn eastward and strike at Orscholz.

As the men of the 1st Battalion moved into position, the night was bitterly cold and a swirling snowstorm made night-time control even more difficult than usual. Daylight had come before the two assault companies were ready to cross the line of departure, a stretch of dragon's teeth in a clearing a few hundred yards south of the Oberleuken-Orscholz high-way. Company B on the left moved si-lently forward, not a shot barring the way. Company A on the right was less fortunate. As the men passed among the projections of the concrete antitank obstacle a drumbeat of explosions filled the air. Mines.

Company B meanwhile continued silently through the forest, reached the highway, and turned east toward Or-scholz. The advance guard overran several German machine gun positions, but in general the move was unopposed. Reaching the edge of the woods over-looking Orscholz, the company com-mander, Capt. Herman C. Straub, halted his men to await the rest of the battalion.

At the line of departure, the battalion commander, Lt. Col. George F. Miller, had tried to shift Company A to the left to follow in the footsteps of Company B, but too late. The explosions in the mine-field had alerted the Germans in pill-boxes and communications trenches overlooking the clearing. Company A came under a withering crossfire from automatic weapons. As the men fell to the ground for protection, mortars and artillery ploughed the clearing with deadly bursts. Among those killed was Colonel Miller.

Although the regimental commander, Colonel Hagerty, sent a company from another battalion to reinforce the attack, every effort to get across the clearing merely increased the casualty toll. One company lost sixty men to antipersonnel mines alone. Tank destroyers tried to help, but the ground in the clearing was marshy and not frozen solidly enough to support the self-propelled guns. Patrols sent out after nightfall in search of a route past the German defenses found no solution.

When daylight came again, the regi-mental executive officer, Lt. Col. Donald C. Hardin, sent to replace Colonel Miller as battalion commander, told Colonel Hagerty it would take an entire regiment to push the attack successfully. Although the corps commander, General Walker, earlier had modified the 1-battalion restriction imposed on the 94th Divi-sion's attacks and had granted approval for using as much as a regiment to ex-ploit a penetration,[8] General Malony saw no reason to reinforce what was in effect a failure at Orscholz. He gave his permis-sion to abandon the effort.

Captain Straub and Company B in the meantime had not long remained un-detected at the woods line overlooking Orscholz. Learning by radio of the mis-fortune that had befallen the rest of the battalion, Captain Straub shifted his men south of the Oberleuken-Orscholz highway to a position adaptable to all-round defense. With the aid of protective fires from the 301st field artillery, the company held, but not without serious losses aggravated by the bitter cold.

With the attack abandoned, word went out to Captain Straub to fight his way

---

[8] 94th Div G–3 Jnl, 18 Jan 45.

out. Straub answered that he "could not comply." Many of the men were seriously wounded; at least one already had frozen to death; and ammunition was almost gone. Although Colonel Hagerty himself talked with Straub by radio, outlining a plan to cover the company's withdrawal with smoke, the captain again said withdrawal was impossible. Every attempt to move, he said, brought heavy enemy fire that pinned the men to their positions.

Company B and attachments, a force of approximately 230 men, raised a white flag.[9]

Expanding the Penetration

For another day after the misfortune at Orscholz, those units of the 94th Division that had penetrated the western end of the switch position at Tettingen and Nennig would be fully occupied fending off the *11th Panzer Division*. Only on 23 January would the division be free to recoup the minor loss of ground incurred and return again to consolidating and expanding the penetration.

Renewed limited objective attacks began early on 23 January when a battalion of the 376th Infantry moved to retake the northern half of Nennig, lost to the Germans the preceding night. It took all day to root a stubborn enemy from the damaged houses and at the same time eliminate five Mark IV tanks.

Two men, T. Sgt. Nathaniel Isaacman, a platoon sergeant, and Pvt. John F. Pietrzah, alone accounted for two of the

tanks and set up a third for the kill. Spotting three tanks advancing up a narrow street, the men climbed to the top of a house, then crept from one rooftop to another to gain a position above the tanks. The first rocket from Pietrzah's bazooka missed, but a second sent the lead tank up in flames. Another rocket put a quick end to the tank in the rear. The third tank, trapped between the other two, fell ready prey to a rifle grenade fired by a man on the ground, Pvt. Albert J. Beardsley.[10]

In the attack at Nennig, the battalion of the 376th Infantry had the assistance of a company of armored infantrymen. This presaged introduction of a new force in the Orscholz Switch, a combat command of the 8th Armored Division. The armored division, yet to see combat, had rushed across France earlier in the month in reaction to Operation *NORD-WIND*. Not used in that fight, the division had been attached temporarily to the Third Army for combat training. The army commander, General Patton, saw in the attachment an opportunity to give the division battle experience while at the same time remedying the 94th Division's lack of attached tanks. He gave General Malony the 8th Armored's Combat Command A (Brig. Gen. Charles F. Colson), but stipulated that the armor

---

[9] 301st Inf and 94th Div AAR's, Jan 45; 94th Div G–3 Jnl, 21–22 Jan 45; Byrnes, *History of the 94th Infantry Division*, p. 138; Combat interview with Hagerty. Direct quotation is from Hagerty.

[10] On the same day, T. Sgt. Nicholas Oresko led his platoon of the 302d Infantry in an attack to clear German-held pillboxes near Tettingen. Sergeant Oresko singlehandedly knocked out a machine gun that was pinning down his men with fire from a bunker. Wounded in the hip, he refused evacuation and again advanced alone to knock out another machine gun firing from a field fortification. Still Oresko refused evacuation until his platoon's mission had been accomplished. He subsequently received the Medal of Honor.

was to be used for only forty-eight hours.[11]

Prodded by General Walker and his staff officers at XX Corps headquarters,[12] Malony was determined to get as much help as possible from the combat command before the time limit expired. He intended to use the armor to help turn the limited penetration of the Orscholz Switch into a genuine breach that might be exploited quickly into breakout.

Malony's plan revolved around capture of Sinz, northeast of Butzdorf and Tettingen, and wooded high ground northwest of Sinz. From there, in a subsequent stage, he planned to take Munzingen, a mile and a half to the east, a village crowning the hogback ridge leading deep into the Saar-Moselle triangle. Holding the high ground northwest of Sinz and at Munzingen, the 94th Division would be all the way through the Orscholz Switch, in a favorable position for exploitation.

The role of the armor in the Sinz attack was to advance northeast from the vicinity of Nennig, clear pillboxes along a road leading into Nennig from the west, then help infantry of the 94th Division take the village. Before committing the armor, General Malony intended his infantry to occupy high ground northeast of Nennig, including the castle occupied earlier by units of the *11th Panzer Division*. That would set up more favorable conditions for using the armor.

As events developed, the battalion of

the 376th Infantry assigned to take the castle was, by the early hours of 25 January, so worn out from the fight at Nennig that the commander urged that some other unit be given the task. The CCA commander, General Colson, volunteered his unit. At dawn on 25 January, half the combat command, organized as a task force under Lt. Col. Arthur D. Poinier, commander of the 7th Armored Infantry Battalion, jumped off, only to discover quickly that the *11th Panzer Division* still had a lot of fight left. So perturbed at the slow pace of the day's advance was the corps commander, General Walker, that he removed all restrictions on the size of the forces the 94th Division might commit. "Go ahead," he said, "and use them all." [13] At the same time, he tacitly agreed to extending the time limit on use of the combat command an extra day—through 27 January.

As finally decided, two regiments and the combat command were to make the attack. On the left, the 302d Infantry (Col. Earle A. Johnson) was to pave the way for the armor; on the right, the 376th Infantry (Col. Harold H. McClune) was to move on Sinz. Avoiding open ground south of Sinz, the regiment was to attack through woods southwest and west of the village and link with the armor along the highway in the woods for the assault on the village itself. A battalion of the 302d, operating directly under division control, meanwhile was to recapture Butzdorf, lost on the first day of German counterattacks.

The most encouraging success on 26 January came on the right. There an antipersonnel minefield hidden by the deep snow stymied one battalion, but

[11] In addition to official 8th Armored Div records, see also 94th Div G–3 Jnl for the period; Capt. Charles R. Leach, *In Tornado's Wake—A History of the 8th Armored Division* (8th Armored Division Association, 1956); Gay Diary, entry of 17 Jan 45.

[12] 94th Div G–3 Jnl, 23–26 Jan 45.

[13] 94th Div G–3 Jnl, 25 Jan 45.

two companies of another battalion slipped past and gained the woods overlooking Sinz from the west. Although three German tanks supported by infantry counterattacked, bazookas accounted for two of the tanks and drove the other away. Artillery fire took care of the German infantry. The two companies dug in for the night, protecting their left and rear with the 376th Infantry's reserve battalion, which got safely past the minefield and into the woods by following the route the two leading companies had taken.

According to the plan, the armor was to have linked with this force along the highway bisecting the forest, but the armor and the 302d Infantry on the left ran into trouble. Intense machine gun fire from the north stopped the infantrymen, while the armor after getting into the western edge of the woods came to a halt before a deep antitank ditch.

The next day, 27 January, as the corps commander, General Walker, warned that the armored combat command would be withdrawn that night, General Malony committed a battalion of his reserve, the 301st Infantry, to help clear a path for the tanks. Although armored engineers during the night had bridged the antitank ditch, the fresh infantry battalion had to spend all morning taking out machine guns and an antitank gun before the armor could cross. Soon after midday CCA's tanks at last started forward and quickly linked with men of the 376th Infantry overlooking Sinz.

Assault on the village itself was delayed, first by a counterattack against the left flank in the woods, then by accurate German tank fire from hills and woods north and east of Sinz. Darkness was falling when a platoon of tanks and

two infantry companies at last gained a toehold in the village against stalwart defenders of the *11th Panzer Division*. In the process, CCA's 18th Tank Battalion knocked out eight German tanks but lost six of its own.

When General Malony asked to keep the combat command to finish taking the village the next day, General Walker declined. The period of indoctrination was over. The 94th Division was to take a rest, then later to resume its limited objective attacks.[14]

Broadening the Effort

Almost coincident with the arrival of a new directive from General Walker to resume the attack but to employ no more than a regiment at a time, the February thaw and the rains came. Beginning on 2 February rain fell for eight days, turning foxholes into frigid dirty bathtubs and roads into oozing ribbons of mud. Yet the attacks began, concentrating on objectives designed to obtain eventual control of the hogback ridge leading into the depths of the Saar-Moselle triangle.

Malony first turned the 302d Infantry against Kampholz Woods, southeast of Tettingen on the western slopes of the ridge. Resistance was stubborn, particularly from a nest of pillboxes on approaches to the woods from the west. The last of the pillboxes held out until 8 February.

Meanwhile, Malony reverted to his original plan of gaining a hold on the hogback ridge at Munzingen by first taking Sinz. Moving just before daylight on 7 February, a battalion of the 301st

---

[14] 94th Div G-3 Jnl, 27 Jan 45.

GENERAL WALKER

Infantry quickly took the first houses and went on to clear the rest of the village during the day; but another battalion, trying to clear Bannholz Woods, a dominating copse north of the village, ran into tanks and panzer grenadiers of the *11th Panzer Division* and had to fall back.

From the German viewpoint, a ready explanation for the differing resistance at Sinz and in the Bannholz Woods was available. Persistent protestations by the *11th Panzer Division* commander, General von Wietersheim, that his reconditioned panzer force was being needlessly bled to death on an inappropriate assignment had begun to pay off two days before. On the 5th the first contingents of the *256th Volks Grenadier Division* had arrived to begin relieving the panzer

division, although a small contingent still was present on the 7th in Bannholz Woods.[15]

Units of the 94th Division made three more tries to take Bannholz Woods during the next few days, but without success. Although the opposition continued to come from the panzer division, bit by bit intelligence information gathered from other parts of the line revealed the gradual withdrawal of the tanks and introduction of the *256th Division*. In light of the condition of the volks grenadiers, badly mauled in Operation *NORDWIND* in Alsace, the shift could only weaken the enemy's hold on the Orscholz Switch. The time clearly was approaching for a full-scale attack to reduce the switch position and open the entire Saar-Moselle triangle to swift reduction. Conferring with Malony on 15 February, the corps commander, General Walker, gave the word to lift all restrictions and launch a major assault.[16]

General Malony developed his plan as a logical extension of the earlier probing attacks, this time aimed at a complete rupture of the Orscholz Switch and early capture of the hogback ridge. Colonel Hagerty's 301st Infantry was to make the main effort from Sinz to reach the crest of the ridge and the highway leading northeast from Munzingen. Colonel Mc-Clune's 376th Infantry was to protect the 301st's left flank, while Colonel Johnson's 302d Infantry on the division's right was to strike almost due east from the Kampholz Woods to the crest of the hogback ridge and then roll up the forward line of pillboxes farther east. An

[15] MSS # B-417 (Wietersheim) and # B-066 (Ingelheim).
[16] Byrnes, *History of the 94th Infantry Division*, p. 239.

elaborate program of corps and division artillery fire was designed to isolate the battlefield but to guard surprise by beginning only as the infantry moved to the attack.[17]

To exploit success, General Walker had no armored force immediately available. The 8th Armored Division early in February had passed to another command. Even though the 10th Armored Division (Maj. Gen. William H. H. Morris, Jr.) had been attached to the XX Corps on 11 February, General Eisenhower had specified that the division be employed only with his approval, a reflection of post-Ardennes insistence on a sturdy reserve. Walker asked Eisenhower, through General Patton, for permission to use the 10th Armored, but received only a promise that the armor would be released once the infantry achieved a clear breakthrough.[18] Walker took the reply as sufficient authority to direct General Morris to reconnoiter zones of advance and prepare for early commitment.

Rain was falling when before daylight on 19 February men of the 301st Infantry moved east from Sinz up the slopes of the hogback ridge in the direction of Munzingen. In less than two hours the pattern the fighting would assume became apparent. An occasional group of Germans would fight back tenaciously, particularly when protected by pillboxes or bunkers, but in the main the opposition bore no comparison to that put up earlier by the panzer division. By daylight the 1st and 3d Battalions held the crest of the ridge, just short of Munzingen.

Antipersonnel mines were the biggest problem. Company B's 1st Platoon, for example, lost all but sixteen men in a minefield before the platoon sergeant, T. Sgt. Henry E. Crandall, managed to blast a path through with primacord. The Germans in a nearby pillbox kept Crandall and his trapped men under vicious machine gun fire until the survivors got past the mines, then surrendered docilely.

A battalion of the 376th Infantry had a similar experience in Bannholz Woods, north of Sinz, the scene of such bitter fighting in the earlier limited objective attacks. Before dawn, men of this battalion pushed past unwary German defenders to gain the far edge of the woods with little difficulty, then later rounded up the prisoners. Totally different from the panzer grenadiers, these Germans had no stomach for the fight.

By this time, the 94th Division's lack of tank support had been remedied with attachment of the 778th Tank Battalion, which participated in the 376th Infantry's attack. Tanks also came to the rescue of men of the 302d Infantry in their drive from Kampholz Woods to the crest of the hogback ridge along the forward line of Orscholz Switch pillboxes. There the infantrymen were taking comparatively severe casualties from pillboxes manned by troops of the *416th Infantry Division* until, with daylight, the tanks arrived.

Only a few hours after dawn on 19 February, the fact was clear that the 94th Division had penetrated the Orscholz Switch, whereupon General Malony urged General Walker to send the 10th Armored Division through. Walker in turn telephoned the Third Army commander, General Patton, for permission. Unable to reach General Bradley at 12th

---

[17] 94th Div FO 11, 16 Feb 45.
[18] Combat Interview with XX Corps G-3, 5 Mar 45; Gay Diary, entry of 18 Feb 45.

Army Group headquarters, Patton telephoned directly to SHAEF, where the operations officer, Maj. Gen. Harold R. Bull, agreed but with the proviso that the armored division be returned to the SHAEF reserve as soon as the Saar-Moselle triangle was clear. Since Patton already was thinking of going beyond the original objectives if all went smoothly, the restriction rankled. He had to accept it nevertheless and notified Walker to turn the armor loose.[19]

The delay in permission to use the armor held up the exploitation until the next day, 20 February, but once committed, the armor was not to be denied. Moving along the west side of the triangle close to the Moselle, the Reserve Combat Command (Col. Wade C. Gatchell), with the 94th Division's 376th Infantry attached, was to advance almost thirteen miles to the northern tip of the triangle while CCA (Brig. Gen. Edwin W. Piburn) drove north up the center of the triangle. When CCR reached the tip, CCA was to swing northeast, hoping to take advantage of enemy confusion to seize bridges across the Saar at Kanzem and Wiltingen, and thereby point a dagger toward Trier.[20]

Except for the problem of herding prisoners, CCR's advance on the 20th was almost a road march, even though the attack was delayed until midday while a battalion of the 376th Infantry

cleared two villages along the line of departure. Not long after midnight the combat command coiled for the night almost halfway up the triangle.

CCA encountered greater difficulties at first. One column, attacking up the highway astride the hogback ridge, ran into mines and fire from assault guns in the first village beyond Munzingen and at each of two succeeding villages, but in all cases the result was more a question of delay than genuine opposition. At one point the column overran a regimental command post.

CCA's left column, hampered by a traffic jam and an unmapped American minefield at the line of departure near Sinz, got moving only after full daylight had come; but by midafternoon it was apparent the column would quickly make up the lost time. Although antitank minefields and craters blown in the roads forced the tanks to move cross-country at the beginning of the thrust, once high ground three miles northeast of Sinz was taken the column returned to the roads. Bypassing opposition, one task force streaked north and then northeast along secondary roads and as darkness came occupied high ground north of Tawern, almost at the tip of the triangle.

The next day, 21 February, CCR renewed its advance and reached the extreme tip of the triangle, while the rest of CCA headed for Tawern, eliminating last remnants of opposition. The 94th Division meanwhile was clearing that part of the triangle southeast of the armored columns and taking the remaining pillboxes of the Orscholz Switch from the rear.

After two days of exploitation the Saar-Moselle triangle was clear at a cost to the Germans in dead and wounded of an

---

[19] Patton, *War As I Knew It*, p. 244; Byrnes, *History of the 94th Infantry Division*, p. 254; Gay Diary, entry of 19 Feb 45. Intentions to go beyond the triangle are clear from XX Corps FO 16, 19 Feb 45.

[20] An excellent account of the 10th Armored Division's action is to be found in Maj. J. Cantey, *et al.*, The 10th U.S. Armored Division in the Saar-Moselle Triangle, a research report prepared at The Armored School, May, 1949.

estimated 3,000 and as many more captured. Only in the 94th Division, where the thick antipersonnel minefields encountered on 19 February raised the division's casualties to over a thousand wounded, were U.S. losses severe.

Crossing the Saar

Despite the speed of the 10th Armored Division's advance, the bridges over the Saar River at Kanzem and Wiltingen were blown before the tanks got there. Operating on the theory of using the armor until SHAEF said stop, General Walker in midafternoon of 21 February ordered General Morris to jump the river. During the night the armor was to cross northeast of Saarburg while the 94th Division crossed southeast of the town. The bridgeheads then were to be joined, whereupon the 94th was to protect the armor's south flank while Morris drove on Trier. The crossings of the Saar then could be linked with the long-held bridgehead to the southeast at Saarlautern.[21]

Influencing General Walker's desire for a quick crossing before the enemy could recover from the debacle in the triangle was the nature of the terrain on the far bank, plus the fortifications of the West Wall. Almost everywhere the east bank dominates the approaches from the west, usually with great wooded, clifflike slopes. West Wall pillboxes arranged in the normal pattern of mutual support covered all the slopes but were in greatest depth, sometimes up to three miles, at those points where the terrain afforded any real possibility for an assault crossing. The river itself was from 120 to

150 feet wide, still swollen from the early February thaw.

Through the night convoys carrying assault boats toiled toward the Saar, but dawn came in the 10th Armored Division's sector with no sign of the boats. Alerted to make the crossing opposite the village of Ockfen, a mile and a half northeast of Saarburg, men of the attached 376th Infantry took cover in houses and cellars.

Southeast of Saarburg, sixty 12-man assault boats and five motorboats were available for the assault battalions of the 301st and the 302d Infantry; the first boat arrived an hour after the planned assault time of 0400 (22 February). Concealed by the darkness and a dense fog, men of both battalions then prepared to cross, one battalion opposite the east bank village of Serrig, the other at the west bank village of Taben.

Carrying a squad of Company C, 302d Infantry, under Staff Sgt. John F. Smith, the first boat pushed out into the river at Taben at 0650. The fog still held, and so difficult was the terrain that the Germans had positioned few defenders at the site.

The road leading down the west bank was steep and winding. Along the far bank ran a 12-foot retaining wall, backed by precipitous wooded slopes leading to Hoecker Hill, an eminence three-fourths of a mile from the river. Finding a ladder in place, Sergeant Smith and his men quickly scaled the retaining wall and captured the startled occupants of a pillbox. Other boatloads of men crossed with little enemy interference, pulled themselves up the clifflike sides of Hoecker Hill, and sent patrols upstream and down to broaden the base of the bridgehead. Before the morning was well along,

---

[21] XX Corps FO 17, 21 Feb 45.

all the 1st Battalion was across and heading north toward Serrig to link with men of the 301st Infantry, while another battalion crossed to defend Hoecker Hill and the south flank.

The crossing went less smoothly opposite Serrig. There the assault boats for the 3d Battalion, 301st Infantry, were even later arriving, and the noise of manhandling them to the water's edge alerted troops of a local defense battalion in the east bank pillboxes. Although German fire was blind in the dark and the fog, it served to scatter the boats of the leading company so that the men touched down with little organization remaining. Since few of the boats survived the swift current on the return journey, through the morning only one company, operating in little isolated groups, was on the east bank. One group under the company commander, Capt. Charles W. Donovan, nevertheless took a few buildings on the northern edge of Serrig and held them until the afternoon when other men of the 3d Battalion crossed in a fresh batch of assault boats equipped with outboard motors. White phosphorus shells fired by the 81st Chemical Battalion and smoke pots emplaced at the crossing site helped make up for loss of the fog cover. As night fell on 22 February, Serrig was secure, the bridgeheads of the 301st and 302d Infantry Regiments joined.

At Ockfen, northeast of Saarburg, the 10th Armored Division's assault boats finally arrived at midday. Under pressure from Patton,[22] General Morris ordered a crossing in late afternoon; but by this time the fog had dissipated and German machine gun fire from West Wall pillboxes so splattered the flats leading to

the crossing site that the 81st Chemical (Smoke Generator) Company could get no smoke generators into position to screen the site. Neither could the assault companies of the attached 376th Infantry get down to the river.

In the brief time between daylight and late afternoon of 22 February, the Germans had managed to supplement the local defense battalions in this part of the West Wall with those remnants of the *256th Volks Grenadier Division* that had escaped across the Saar ahead of the American armor. Although ill-prepared to counter such a quick thrust against the Saar line, the *LXXXII Corps* commander, General Hahm, was helped when his southern boundary was shifted northward to coincide roughly with the east end of the Orscholz Switch, thereby freeing one regiment of the *416th Infantry Division* that had not been involved in the Orscholz fight. He also benefited from the fact that one of the panzer grenadier battalions of the *11th Panzer Division* had yet to leave the area. These forces General Hahm would be able to bring to bear as the bridgehead fight continued.[23]

At Ockfen General Morris had no alternative but to postpone the 376th Infantry's assault again until after nightfall. Beginning an hour before midnight, two battalions, each in column of companies, at last began to cross.

In the northernmost sector, that of the 3d Battalion, the darkness was all that was required. The leading company reached the east side of the river without drawing a single round of enemy fire, quickly cleared the pillboxes guarding

[22] Gay Diary, entry of 22 Feb 45.

[23] MS # B–066 (Ingelheim).

the bank, and opened a way for the rest of the battalion.

Not so at the 1st Battalion's crossing site a few hundred yards upstream. As the boats of Company C touched down on the far bank, the Germans in the pillboxes brought down their final protective fires. Fortunately, visibility was too restricted by darkness and fog for the defenders to spot the attackers, even at distances of only a few feet. Discerning the pattern of enemy fires from tracer bullets, the men of Company C began to advance by small groups in short rushes, gradually forcing their way into the pillbox belt and beginning, one by one, to reduce the fortifications.

German artillery and mortars meanwhile pounded the river itself and the west bank, sinking many of the assault boats and three times wounding the 376th Infantry commander, Colonel McClune. The rest of the 1st Battalion nevertheless crossed to the east bank before daylight, though for lack of assault boats one company had to move downstream and use the 3d Battalion's craft. There, in wake of the 3d Battalion, the 2d Battalion already had crossed. In midafternoon the 2d Battalion moved behind a heavy artillery preparation to take Ockfen; and by nightfall, 23 February, units of the regiment outposted wooded high ground on three sides of the village.

To the XX Corps commander, General Walker, it had occurred earlier in the day that expansion of both his Saar crossings might be speeded by early blocking of the main east-west highway into the sector, a road leading from the enemy's main lateral route behind the Saar at the settlement of Zerf westward to the river at Beurig, across from Saarburg.

Walker ordered a special force, the 5th Ranger Battalion (Lt. Col. Richard P. Sullivan), to cross into the 94th Division's Serrig-Taben bridgehead, then to slip through the woods toward the northeast for some three and a half miles and establish a roadblock on the highway west of Zerf.

Guiding on a compass bearing, the Rangers began to move at midnight, 23 February. They reached their objective just before dawn. Quickly establishing a perimeter defense, they began to collect unwitting Germans as they passed along the road.[24]

Anticipating a determined German reaction against the Rangers' roadblock, Walker arranged a maneuver designed both to relieve the Rangers and to capture the village of Beurig so that tactical bridges could be built across the river from Saarburg to take advantage of the roadnet around the town. As a first step, he ordered General Malony to drive north to Beurig. Since likely bridging sites in the 10th Armored Division's zone still were under observed fire, Walker told General Morris to take his armor south and cross the Saar on a 94th Division bridge that would be ready at Taben in midafternoon on 24 February. The tanks then were to follow units of the 94th Division into Beurig. There they were to pick up their armored infantrymen, who were to cross into the Ockfen bridgehead in assault boats late on 24 February and push south to Beurig. Tanks and armored infantry together were to drive east along the main highway to relieve the Rangers.

The maneuver failed to develop exactly as planned. Although the tanks and

---

[24] 5th Ranger Bn AAR, Feb 45.

half-tracks of Combat Command B (Col. William L. Roberts), leading the 10th Armored's advance, crossed the Taben bridge early on 25 February, the 94th Division's northward drive had been slowed by tenacious resistance from pill-boxes and by heavy mortar fire. Held up on the fringe of Beurig, the infantrymen realized they would be unable to take the village before the armor arrived. They sent guides back down the road to intercept the tanks and lead them along a wooded trail that bypassed Beurig and led to the Beurig-Zerf highway. The only infantry available to assist the tanks were three officers and twenty-four men of the Ranger battalion who had become separated from their unit and had joined CCB's column in Taben.

By midafternoon the lead tank platoon of CCB had emerged from the woods onto the main highway and was headed east into the village of Irsch. Despite a roadblock in the center of the village, Irsch appeared deserted. Two of the platoon's five tanks had passed the roadblock when a Tiger tank, a ground-mount 88-mm. gun, and two *Panzerfausts,* all concealed behind nearby buildings, opened fire. In rapid succession they knocked out the last three U.S. tanks.

Hurrying forward, the little group of Rangers helped the tankers put the Germans to flight, but CCB delayed clearing the village until after nightfall, when a company of armored infantrymen, moving southeast from the Ockfen bridgehead and also bypassing Beurig, arrived to help. The infantrymen took 290 prisoners from the *416th Division.*[25]

The next day, 26 February, while the 301st Infantry cleared Beurig with little

difficulty now that the Germans' escape route had been cut, CCB headed east on the last leg of the drive to relieve the 5th Ranger Battalion. By midmorning, despite long-range fire from the same Tiger tank that had caused trouble in Irsch, contingents of the combat command reached the Rangers. Hard-pressed by shelling and counterattacks during the second day and third morning in their isolated position, the Rangers had not only managed to survive but also had bagged about a hundred Germans.[26]

While these events were taking place beyond the Saar, General Patton had been fighting a rear guard action against return of the 10th Armored Division to the SHAEF reserve. On 23 February all Patton could achieve was a 48-hour respite. When that period expired, he pleaded with the 12th Army Group commander, General Bradley, for help. Bradley himself took responsibility for letting Patton use the armor until nightfall of 27 February for the express purpose of taking Trier.[27]

By dawn of 27 February conditions were good for a quick strike north to Trier. During the preceding afternoon, CCB had advanced beyond the Rangers' roadblock, taking Zerf and gaining a hold on the highway leading north to Trier, eleven miles away. Light ponton bridges were operating both at Taben and Serrig and a heavy ponton bridge was at Saarburg. Only the disturbing fact that prisoner identifications on 26 February revealed the presence of a new German unit, the *2d Mountain Division,* ap-

---

[25] Cantey, The 10th U.S. Armored Division in the Saar-Moselle Triangle, pp. 90–91.

[26] Combat Interview with Lt. Col. J. J. Richardson, CCB, 10th Armored Division.

[27] Patton, *War As I Knew It,* pp. 246–47; Gay Diary, entries of 24 and 25 Feb 45.

peared to stand in the way of a rapid drive to Trier.

Rushed forward by *Army Group G* to bolster the sagging *LXXXII Corps,* the *2d Mountain Division,* like so many other German units, was considerably less impressive than its name might indicate. Its two infantry regiments, for example, had only recently been reconstituted from supply and other noncombatant units, and most of the men were Austrians lacking fervor for a losing cause. Utilizing the sharp defiles, woods, and dense concentrations of pillboxes below Trier, the mountain division nevertheless might have proved an effective delaying force had sizable numbers of men been able to get into position to block a northward drive before CCA started it. As it was, the division, arriving from the southeast, got there too late and could be used only to block to the east and southeast.[28]

Defense of Trier itself remained a responsibility of *Army Group B's Seventh Army,* already sorely pressed by the drive of the U.S. XII Corps on Bitburg. By this time most of the troops of the *Seventh Army's 212th Volks Grenadier Division,* originally charged with defense of the city, already had gone north to oppose the XII Corps and about all that was left to defend Trier were two local defense battalions, the city's police, and the crews of several stationary 88-mm. antiaircraft batteries.[29]

At dawn on 27 February, while the 94th Division and the Ranger battalion sought to expand the Saar bridgehead to east and southeast, General Morris

turned CCA north up the main highway to Trier. As directed by General Patton the preceding day, the 76th Division of the XII Corps turned away from the successful drive on Bitburg to head toward Trier from the north.

For all the lack of solid defensive units, the Germans on 27 February managed to delay CCA's column at several points, usually with isolated tanks or assault guns lying in ambush in terrain that restricted CCA's tanks to one road. The most serious delay occurred in mid-afternoon south of the village of Pellingen where a minefield 300 yards deep disabled two tanks. Armored engineers had to spend painful hours under small arms fire clearing a path, and further advance for the day was stymied.

Since Trier still lay some six miles away and the appointed hour for release of the 10th Armored Division had come, General Patton again had to appeal to General Bradley for continued use of the armor until Trier fell. Having had no word from SHAEF on keeping the division, Bradley told him to keep going until higher authority ordered a halt. And, the 12th Army Group commander added, he would make it a point to stay away from the telephone.[30]

The morning of 1 March, after CCA took Pellingen, General Morris sent the main body of the combat command northwest to the juncture of the Saar and the Moselle to prevent any Germans remaining in West Wall pillboxes along the Saar from falling back on Trier. A task force continued up the main road toward the city while CCB passed through Pellingen and swung to the northeast to come upon the objective

---

[28] MS # B-066 (Ingelheim). See also MS # B-238, Report, 10 February-24 March 1945 (Generalmajor Wolf Hauser, CofS *First Army*).

[29] MS # B-123 (Gersdorff).

---

[30] Patton, *War As I Knew It,* p. 249.

from the east. In late afternoon, as both CCA's task force and CCB continued to run into trouble on the fringes of the city from pillboxes and 88-mm. antiaircraft pieces, Colonel Roberts, CCB's commander, ordered the commander of the 20th Armored Infantry Battalion, Lt. Col. Jack J. Richardson, to enter Trier along a secondary road between the other two attacking forces. Richardson was to head straight for the city's two Moselle bridges.[31]

The night was clear, the moon full, and visibility excellent as Task Force Richardson in early evening started toward Trier. Entering the city before midnight, the task force encountered a German company with four antitank guns, but the surprised Germans surrendered without firing. One of the prisoners revealed that he had been detailed as a runner to notify a demolition team at one of the bridges when the Americans arrived.

Splitting his force, Richardson sent half toward each of the bridges. The northern team found its bridge blown, but the team moving to the ancient Kaiserbruecke, which had stood since the Roman occupation of Trier in the earliest days of the Christian era, reported its bridge intact. Rushing to the bridge himself in a tank, Colonel Richardson found his men under small arms fire from the far bank. Directing .50-caliber machine gun fire from his tank onto the far end of the bridge, Richardson or-

dered a platoon of infantry and a platoon of tanks to dash across. As the infantrymen complied, a German major and five men ran toward the bridge from the far side with detonating caps and an exploder.

They were too late.

It mattered not whether the delay in blowing the bridge was attributable to concern for the historic monument or to the fact that the German officer was drunk. What mattered was that the 10th Armored Division had a bridge across the Moselle.

By morning contingents of Combat Commands A and B had swept into all parts of the city, and the prisoner bag increased as sleepy-eyed Germans awoke to find American tanks all about them. Task Force Richardson alone took 800 prisoners. A day later, early on 3 March, troops of the 76th Division arrived to establish contact with the armor on the north bank of the Moselle.

The Orscholz Switch, the Saar-Moselle triangle, Trier, and the heavily fortified section of the West Wall around Trier —all were taken. With the success of the operation, the Third Army had torn a gaping hole in the West Wall from Pruem to a point below Saarburg.

Studying the operations map, General Patton could see two new inviting prospects before him. Either he could turn to the southeast and envelop the Saar industrial area, or he could head through the Eifel and up the valley of the Moselle to the Rhine at Koblenz.

In either case, the Germans appeared powerless to stop him.

---

[31] The following account is based primarily on combat interviews with Richardson and Maj. C. R. King (10th Armored Division historian).

CHAPTER VIII

Operation GRENADE

While the First Army was focusing on the Roer River dams and the Third Army probing the Eifel and clearing the Saar-Moselle triangle, Field Marshal Montgomery's 21 Army Group was launching the new Allied main effort. Under Montgomery's plan, General Crerar's First Canadian Army was to open the offensive with Operation VERITABLE, a drive southeastward up the left bank of the Rhine from positions gained by the big airborne attack the preceding fall in the vicinity of Nijmegen. A few days later General Simpson's Ninth Army from positions along the Roer River generally northeast of Aachen was to launch Operation GRENADE, an assault crossing of the Roer followed by a northeastward drive to link with the First Canadian Army along the Rhine. From positions along the Maas River in between Americans and Canadians, the Second Army was to be prepared to make a complementary attack if required.

Youngest Allied army then operational on the Continent, the Ninth Army nevertheless had seen considerable fighting—in the conquest of the Brittany peninsula in September and in the drive from the German border to the Roer River in November and early December. The Ninth Army's commander, General Simpson, was an infan-tryman with a distinctive appearance; he stood over six feet tall and kept his head clean shaven. Most of his staff were infantrymen, too, including the chief of staff, Brig. Gen. James E. Moore, and had come to the theater from a training command Simpson earlier had held in the United States. The headquarters already had established a reputation for steady, workmanlike performance. As General Bradley was to put it later, the Ninth Army, "unlike the noisy and bumptious Third and the temperamental First," was "uncommonly normal." [1]

During the Ardennes counteroffensive, the Ninth Army had remained on the defensive, extending its lines north and south in order to free troops to reinforce the First Army. All through January the army had held a 40-mile front extending from the vicinity of Monschau near headwaters of the Roer downstream to Linnich, northeast of Aachen. The command included only five divisions under the XIII Corps (Maj. Gen. Alvan C. Gillem, Jr.) and the XIX Corps (Maj. Gen. Raymond S. McLain).

To prepare for Operation GRENADE, it was necessary both to narrow the army's front and to build the army's strength to at least ten divisions. Reduc-

---

[1] Bradley, *A Soldier's Story*, p. 422.

GENERAL SIMPSON

ing the frontage by shifting the boundary between the First and Ninth Armies northward left the Ninth Army with only its two northernmost divisions, so that during the early days of February eight others were moved in.[2]

With seven of the army's ten divisions in place, boundaries were adjusted on 5 February. The First Army's VII Corps relieved the XIX Corps in place from the vicinity of Monschau to an unfinished autobahn (express highway) running from Aachen to Cologne; General Collins assumed control of the 8th and 104th Divisions and subsequently received the 3d Armored and 99th Divi-

sions. With a zone narrowed to about eight miles from the autobahn north to a point beyond Juelich, the XIX Corps retained the 29th Division on the corps left and received the 30th Division for commitment on the right, plus the 2d Armored and 83d Divisions as reserves. Although the zone of the XIII Corps remained unchanged (from midway between Juelich and Linnich to a point four miles downstream from Linnich) and General Gillem retained control of the 102d Division, the 84th Division moved in on 3 February to take over the northern half of the corps sector and the 5th Armored Division arrived as a reserve.

Through the Ardennes fighting, the Ninth Army's north flank had rested on the little Wurm River a few miles northwest of Linnich. On the other side of the Wurm, a corps of the Second British Army had been containing a German bridgehead west of the Roer, the Heinsberg pocket, which the British cleared during January. The Ninth Army on 6 February then assumed responsibility for eighteen miles of the British line as far as the confluence of the Roer and Maas Rivers at Roermond, thus enabling the British to release forces to the First Canadian Army for Operation VERITABLE. To occupy the new sector, General Simpson attached the 8th Armored and 35th Divisions to a previously uncommitted corps headquarters, the XVI Corps (Maj. Gen. John B. Anderson), and subsequently provided the 79th Division as a reserve.

The Ninth Army thus had ten divisions along the Roer River with the greatest weight in the southernmost XIX Corps. In addition, the army held an infantry division, the 95th, in re-

---

[2] A convenient summary of the moves may be found in *Conquer—The Story of Ninth Army* (Washington: Infantry Journal Press, 1947), one of the most objective of the unofficial unit histories.

serve.[3] The total strength of the army was 303,243 men. Because the First Army's VII Corps, which had four divisions, was to support the Ninth Army's attack, the corps in effect added additional strength to the GRENADE force of approximately 75,000 men.[4]

In direct support of the Ninth Army was the XXIX Tactical Air Command (Brig. Gen. Richard E. Nugent), employing five groups of fighter-bombers (375 planes) and one tactical reconnaissance group. For ground fire support the GRENADE force (the Ninth Army and the VII Corps) had 130 battalions of field artillery and tank destroyers, totaling more than 2,000 guns, one of the heaviest concentrations to be employed on the Western Front. The two corps making the main effort (XIII and XIX) had one artillery piece for each ten yards of front, plus tanks, tank destroyers, antiaircraft guns, and infantry cannon.[5] In armor the GRENADE force had only what had come to be regarded as normal in the theater, but a powerful assembly nonetheless. Each corps had an armored division and each infantry division had an attached tank battalion, a total of 1,394 tanks. More than two-thirds of these were the old Sherman with the 75-mm. gun.[6]

As the target date for GRENADE approached, the Ninth Army's accumulated stocks of supplies rose to huge proportions. In one 5-day period (10–14 February), for example, the army received well over 40,000 long tons, the biggest delivery to any army in the theater in a comparable period. Most of it arrived by rail in more than 6,000 freight cars.[7]

Stocks of gasoline in the army's depots rose to over 3 million gallons, representing over five days of supply with five days' reserve. Augmenting ammunition deliveries with strict rationing, the army amassed 46,000 tons of ammunition, equivalent to at least twenty days' supply at normal rates of expenditure, four times the normal army stockage in the theater. It enabled all artillery units of the XIX Corps to place two units of fire at battery positions in addition to basic loads. The XIII Corps provided two units of fire for artillery of two of its divisions and one unit for that of the other two. The weight of the artillery projectiles that the XIX Corps alone could throw at the enemy in six days of combat on a 2-division front was 8,138 tons.[8]

The Terrain and the Enemy

In attacking across the Roer River in the vicinity of Linnich and Juelich and advancing northeastward to the Rhine,

---

[3] A twelfth division, the 75th, while assigned to the Ninth Army effective 17 February, was placed under operational control of the British. NUSA Sitrep, 18 Feb 45.

[4] NUSA G–1 Daily Sum, 23 Feb 45; VII Corps Estimated Loss Report, 2400, 1 Mar 45, VII Corps G–1 Battle Casualties file.

[5] NUSA Artillery Sec AAR, Feb 45; NUSA FA and TD Info Sum 57, 26 Feb 45; 2d Revised Copy of Appendix 1 to Annex 3, VII Corps FO 15, 22 Feb 45.

[6] NUSA Armored Sec AAR, Feb 45. One of the separate tank battalions had only light tanks.

[7] NUSA G–4 Periodic Rpts and G–4 Jnl for the period.

[8] NUSA Quartermaster and Ordnance AAR's, Feb 45; Annex 2 to XIX Corps FO 30, 6 Feb 45; and Annex 5 to XIII Corps FO 5, 8 Feb 45. Total ammunition allocation for the XIX Corps for the period D-day to D plus 5 included: 202,880 rounds for 105-mm. howitzers; 64,800 rounds for 155-mm. howitzers; 14,400 rounds for 155-mm. guns; 4,500 rounds for 4.5-inch guns; and 9,000 rounds for 8-inch howitzers. XIX Corps G–4 Jnl, 7 Feb 45.

the Ninth Army was to drive diagonally across the Cologne plain. Generally flat, open country traversed by an extensive network of hard-surfaced roads, the Cologne plain stretches from the highlands of the Eifel to the lowlands of northern Germany and the Netherlands. The only high ground worthy of the name in that part of the plain to be crossed by the Ninth Army is an egg-shaped plateau extending eastward from the vicinity of Linnich and rising no higher than 400 feet above sea level. Although this gently sloping plateau was not a critical feature, it drew attention from the Ninth Army's planners because once it was taken, "the remainder of the attack was all downhill." [9] The land throughout the plain is mostly arable and was planted predominantly in grain and stock beets. Observation and fields of fire were excellent.

The only natural military obstacles were two big forests and two rivers, the Roer and the Erft. The larger of the forests was in the north. Beginning on the east bank of the Roer opposite Heinsberg, it extended northward some twenty miles to the Dutch border near Venlo and secreted a portion of the West Wall. Along with the presence of a number of small streams immediately west of the Roer, this obstacle prompted the Ninth Army's planners to forgo Roer crossings in that sector. The other wooded area was the Hambach Forest, east and southeast of Juelich. Although planners originally assigned its capture to the First Army, on the theory that responsibility for a critical terrain feature should not be split, when it became apparent that the Ninth Army needed

a broader base for attack, they assigned the northwestern third of the forest to the Ninth Army.

As planning for the attack began, the Roer River dams were still under German control, making of the Roer River a disturbing question mark. While the Roer is normally a placid stream only some ninety feet wide, the Ninth Army's engineers estimated that a combination of spring thaws and destruction of the Roer dams would convert it into a lake as much as a mile and a half wide. Even after the waters subsided, the Roer valley would be soft and marshy, impassable to vehicles operating off the roads.[10] The planners chose crossing sites at the narrowest points of the river, mostly at the locations of destroyed bridges.

As the Roer was critical in determining the line of departure, so the Erft guided the northeasterly direction of the main attack. Cutting diagonally across the Cologne plain, the Erft splits the 25-mile distance between the Roer and the Rhine almost in half. It enters the Rhine at Neuss, opposite Duesseldorf. Neither the Erft nor the Erft Canal, which parallels the river for much of its course, are major military obstacles, but a boggy valley floor up to a thousand yards wide helps turn the waterways into a good natural defense line. Conversely, the river-canal complex might be utilized as flank protection for northeastward advance to the Rhine in the vicinity of Neuss, the use that the Ninth Army intended to make of it.

Although American intelligence officers assumed the enemy would achieve

---

[9] *Conquer*, p. 147.

[10] XIX Corps G–2, Terrain XIX Corps Front to Rhine, 30 Oct 44, 406th Inf Jnl, Feb 45; 1104th Engineer Combat Gp Rpt, 28 Feb 45, XIX Corps AAR, Sec III, Feb 45.

some defensive advantage from these natural features, particularly the Roer, they looked to the villages, towns, and cities on the plain to provide the core of resistance. The assumption was natural in view of the Ninth Army's experience in November and December in driving from the German border to the Roer, where the Germans had turned villages into mutually supporting strongpoints.

The biggest city in the zone to be crossed by GRENADE forces was Muenchen-Gladbach, a textile center. With suburbs and a contiguous city of Rheydt, Muenchen-Gladbach had a prewar population of 310,000. Considerably smaller but vital as road centers were the towns of Dueren and Juelich on the Roer, both already almost obliterated by Allied bombs, and Elsdorf, Erkelenz, Viersen, Duelken, and Krefeld.

The Germans had augmented the built-up sectors with extensive field fortifications that a large foreign labor force had been constructing since late fall. There were three lines. The first hugged the east bank of the Roer. The other two ran six and eleven miles behind the Roer, the third tying in with the Erft River. In the main these fortifications consisted of entrenchments in a sawtooth pattern with exits into the towns and villages. Antitank obstacles and emplacements for antitank, antiaircraft, and field pieces were located at irregular intervals within and between the lines. Mines and barbed wire were placed rather spottily along the east bank of the Roer.[11]

While American G–2's deemed the defensive network well planned and organized, all indications were that the enemy had far too few troops to man the lines. This strengthened the belief that the defense would be based on strongpoints in towns and villages rather than on a continuous prepared position in depth.[12]

Along the entire Roer front from south of Dueren to Heinsberg, intelligence officers believed, the Germans had about 30,000 men supported by 70 tanks. They estimated six divisions with 23,500 men and 110 tanks to be in reserve near Cologne. Four miscellaneous divisions that had been out of contact for some time were presumed capable of intervention with 17,000 men and 55 tanks.[13]

That was the view on 1 February when General Eisenhower gave the word to mount GRENADE, but from that day on, the Ninth Army noted a steady decrease in German strength. On 6 February, for example, General Simpson observed that the *Fifth Panzer Army* still was committed defensively in the Eifel. Simpson's hopes rose for a speedy penetration of the Roer defenses. "We will have some tough fighting," he said, "but I think we are going right through." [14]

After 8 February, the First Canadian Army's drive southward from the Nijmegen bridgehead (Operation VERI-

---

[11] In addition to intelligence sources previously cited, see: Photo Defense Overprint maps of 30 Jan and 1 Feb 45 in XIII Corps G–2 Jnl, 3 Feb 45; VII Corps Estimate of the Situation, 22 Feb 45; and

30th and 104th Div Estimates of the Situation, 5 and 7 Feb 45, respectively.

[12] XIX Corps G–2 Estimate, 17 Feb, and G–2 Periodic Rpt, 19 Feb 45.

[13] NUSA G–2 Estimate, 2 Feb 45, in XIII Corps G–2 Jnl file, 4 Feb 45.

[14] NUSA Ltr of Instrs 13, 6 Feb 45; Notes on Conf with Officers of 115th Inf, Gen Gerhardt, and Others, 7 Feb 45, in 115th Inf AAR, Feb 45.

TABLE) forced the Germans to commit in the north units from both the general reserve near Cologne and the line of the Maas River opposite the British. Yet in spite of mud and flood, the Canadian attack steadily crushed everything the Germans could throw in the way.

By the end of the first week, the attack had drawn in parts of two parachute divisions, the bulk of an infantry division from the Maas line, and the *15th Panzer Grenadier* and *116th Panzer Divisions*. Most intelligence officers then believed that the *Panzer Lehr Division* was the only armored reserve left to *Army Groups B* and *H* together. During the next week another parachute division also was drawn into the fight, and at the end of the week the *Panzer Lehr* too appeared opposite the Canadians.[15]

The rapid shuttling of German troops confused the intelligence picture. Although commitment of the *Panzer Lehr Division* removed the last known armored division from German reserves, it was hard to believe that the Germans would strip their defense of the Cologne plain completely. Various G–2's tried to guess what divisions the Germans might be able to muster, but the facts remained elusive. The last-minute picture was of an enemy along the Roer totaling some 30,000 men supported by about 85 assault guns and 30 battalions of artillery. Two weak infantry divisions and possibly two armored divisions might be used to bolster the line. On the whole, even if the worst possibilities envisaged by the G–2's materialized, the enemy probably would be outnumbered by at least five to one.

Catch-as-Catch-Can

Having long anticipated that the Allies would strike again toward the Ruhr once they eliminated the Ardennes bulge, Hitler on 22 January, when ordering the *Sixth Panzer Army* to the east, had directed the Commander in Chief West, Field Marshal von Rundstedt, to regroup to the north. To meet the threat, Rundstedt proposed strengthening the southern wing of *Army Group H* opposite the British and Canadians with three divisions culled from various points. Once *Army Group B* had shortened its lines by withdrawing its southern wing from the Ardennes, the forces thus released—about three volks grenadier and three armored or motorized divisions, plus volks artillery and volks werfer brigades—were to be shifted to the army group's northern wing along the Roer.[16]

A major step in readjusting the front involved the exchange of sectors between headquarters of the *Fifth Panzer* and *Fifteenth Armies*. Controlling most of the remaining armored units, Manteuffel's *Fifth Panzer Army* then would be on the north in the most threatened sector and on terrain suited to armor. The *LVIII Panzer Corps* (General der Panzertruppen Walter Krueger) was to be fitted with three armored or motorized divisions and positioned behind the Roer line as an army group reserve.

No one—least of all Rundstedt—could have been sanguine about the situation. No one more than this old

[15] Intelligence Sums issued between 11 and 21 Feb by the 12th AGp, 8 and 12 Corps, and XIII and XIX Corps.

[16] Unless otherwise noted, German material is based on MS # C–020 (Schramm).

soldier appreciated the difficulties of making the various transfers and meeting the new drive once it began. Gasoline shortages, unseasonal February thaws that turned highways previously blocked by ice and snow into quagmires, bomb damage to the limited rail net in the Eifel, responsibility for shipping the *Sixth Panzer Army* to the east, the way Allied aircraft denied almost all daylight movement, personnel and materiel losses in the Ardennes—all combined to project a dismal picture.

"I am not a pessimist," Rundstedt reported on 12 February, "but in view of the decisive nature of the coming battles, I consider it my duty to give a clear report of the situation as I see it." [17]

In all of *Army Group B,* Rundstedt said, infantry strength amounted to the equivalent of forty-five battalions or six and a half full divisions. Within the *Fifth Panzer* and *Seventh Armies,* each battalion faced two-thirds of an enemy division, and within the *Fifteenth Army,* most threatened of all until the shift with the *Fifth Panzer Army* could be made, an entire division. Nor could reserves to improve the balance in the *Fifteenth Army* be assembled and shifted as quickly as additional American forces could be expected to arrive. The proportion of forces on the *Fifteenth Army*'s front was destined to be at least two and a half times less favorable than during the prolonged fighting west of the Roer in November; available artillery ammunition would be less than a third that expended in the earlier fighting.

As Allied intelligence had detected, the American drive from the Ardennes

into the Eifel and the Canadian attack southeastward from Nijmegen seriously interfered with German efforts to strengthen the line behind the Roer. Of particular concern was the necessity to shift the *116th Panzer* and *Panzer Lehr Divisions* to oppose the Canadians. The *116th* still would be engaged there when Operation GRENADE jumped off, and the *Panzer Lehr* would be withdrawn into reserve only on the very eve of Operation GRENADE. General Krueger's *LVIII Panzer Corps* could not be withheld as a reserve but had to be committed in the line in command not of armor but of infantry. Nor would the projected shift of headquarters of the *Fifth Panzer* and *Fifteenth Armies* be completed before the American attack began. Because of the continuing American drive in the Eifel, the exchange would be delayed until the Americans were well beyond the Roer.[18]

As D-day for Operation GRENADE approached, the German lineup in the threatened sector was as follows: From a boundary in the north near Roermond, corresponding to the boundary between British and Americans, *Army Group B*'s *Fifteenth Army* (General von Zangen) was responsible for a front some fifty miles long, extending south to include Dueren. The northern third was held by the *XII SS Corps* (Generalleutnant Eduard Crasemann) with two infantry divisions; the center around Linnich by the *LXXXI Corps* (General der Infanterie Friedrich Koechling) with two infantry divisions bolstered by a volks artillery corps; and the southern third around Dueren by the *LVIII Panzer*

---

[17] As quoted by Schramm.

[18] Magna E. Bauer, Reorganization of the Western Front, MS prepared in OCMH to complement this volume.

Corps (Krueger) with a volks grenadier division and an infantry division, also bolstered by a volks artillery corps.

The *Fifteenth Army* had no reserves. *Army Group B*'s reserves consisted of the *9th Panzer Division,* assembled along the Erft River east of Juelich, and the *11th Panzer Division,* the latter in process of assembling near Muenchen-Gladbach after Hitler personally ordered the division pulled out of the Saar-Moselle triangle. Neither panzer division was anywhere near full strength. Tanks and assault guns in all of *Army Group B* totaled only 276.[19]

Operation GRENADE was destined to strike a front manned and equipped on a catch-as-catch-can basis.

Objectives and Maneuvers

Against this enemy whose numbers were small, whose arms were weak, whose spirit faltered, the GRENADE force planned to deliver a paralyzing blow. So obviously expected, the attack permitted no subtlety; success was staked on power. Although General Simpson decided against air bombardment in favor of starting by night, more than 2,000 big guns were to pound the enemy for forty-five minutes before H-hour. Of the four American corps, three were to cross the river at H-hour, each with two infantry divisions to the fore, on a front from Linnich to Dueren, only seventeen miles long. The remaining corps was to move at H-hour to clear a few enemy nests remaining on the west bank of the Roer while simulating a

GENERAL VON ZANGEN

full-blooded crossing north of Heinsberg.

The objective of the first phase of operations was to place the Ninth Army astride the egg-shaped plateau east of Linnich with the army's right flank anchored on the Erft River. Since this involved a wheel to the north, General McLain's XIX Corps on the outer rim would make the longest advance, while the First Army's VII Corps protected the Ninth Army's right flank by establishing a bridgehead around Dueren and then clearing the bulk of the Hambach Forest and gaining the Erft near Elsdorf.

In the second phase, the Ninth Army was to extend its bridgehead north and northwest, with the main job falling to

---

[19] MS # B-811, *Fifteenth Army,* 15 November 1944–22 February 1945 (General der Infanterie Gustav von Zangen) and *Operationskarte West, Chef WFSt,* 22 and 23 Feb 45.

General Gillem's XIII Corps. By taking the road center of Erkelenz and clearing the east bank of the Roer to a point west of Erkelenz, the XIII Corps was to open the way for an unopposed crossing of the river by General Anderson's XVI Corps.

What happened next depended on whether conditions favored rapid maneuver or forced a plodding infantry advance. Given slackening resistance and firm footing for tanks, General Simpson intended to push immediately with full strength to envelop Muenchen-Gladbach from south and east, then drive on to the Rhine. Should the armor be roadbound or the enemy stubborn, the two corps on the left were to make the main effort, rolling up the West Wall fortifications as far north as Venlo and clearing the big forest lying between Roermond and Muenchen-Gladbach. With supply routes then open from Heinsberg to Roermond, the army was to hit Muechen-Gladbach from west and south and push on to the Rhine.

Both plans conservatively assumed organized resistance throughout the Cologne plain. On the other hand, General Simpson added, "If the violence of our attack should cause disruption of the enemy resistance, each corps will be prepared to conduct relentless pursuit in zone, and phases will be abandoned in favor of taking full advantage of our opportunity." [20]

All plans were complete in expectation of a D-day on 10 February when, on the eve of the attack, the Germans destroyed the discharge valves on the Roer dams. Not for about twelve days would the water in the reservoirs be exhausted. [21]

Upstream from Dueren, where the river's banks are relatively high, the worst effect of the flood was to increase the current sharply, at some points to more than ten miles an hour. Downstream along most of its length, the Roer poured over its banks and inundated the valley floor. Just north of Linnich where the river is normally 25 to 30 yards wide, it spread into a lake more than a mile wide. More common were inundations of 300 to 400 yards. The ground on both sides of the flooded floor was soft and spongy. While engineers watched over the slowly receding river, GRENADE underwent successive postponements. [22]

Acting on advice of the engineers, General Simpson at last set D-day for 23 February, one day before the reservoirs presumably would be drained. Although the river still was in flood, it had receded eight to fourteen inches below the peak, and the current at few places exceeded six miles an hour. By seizing the first practicable moment when the river might be crossed with reasonable chance of success instead of awaiting a return to normal, General Simpson hoped to achieve some measure of surprise. [23]

In making the attack, leading waves were to cross the river in assault boats, while follow-up troops were to use foot-

---

[20] NUSA Ltr of Instrs 10, 28 Jan 45; *Conquer*, pp. 147–51.

[21] See above, ch. V.

[22] For analysis of the flood, see II Corps Engineers, Operations in the European Theater, VI; NUSA G–2 AAR, Feb 45; XIII Corps G–2 AAR, Feb 45; XIX Corps G–2 Spot Rpt, 14 Feb 45; 102d Div G–3 Jnl, 10 Feb 45.

[23] *Conquer*, pp. 165–66; 104th Div G–2 Periodic Rpt 119, 22 Feb 45; 30th Div G–3 Jul, 20 Feb 45; 102d Div G–3 Jul, 22 Feb 45.

BURSTS OF WHITE PHOSPHORUS SHELLS LIGHT UP THE ROER RIVER AT LINNICH

bridges that engineers were to begin constructing at H-hour. In all divisions except the 84th, which was to cross on a one-battalion front, the number of assault boats was insufficient for the first wave, so that units had to plan to shuttle or find other means of crossing. Since shuttling in frail assault boats might break down in the face of a strong current, the 8th Division proposed to make motor-driven double-boat ferries of its assault boats. Some other units planned to rely on cable ferries or LVT's (land vehicles, tracked), amphibious tractors nicknamed alligators.

Each assault division in the Ninth Army planned to screen its crossing sites, either by smoke generators and pots placed on the west bank or by phosphorus shells fired across the river by chemical mortars. A smoke generator company and a chemical mortar battalion were in support of each corps. In the adjacent VII Corps, General Collins delegated the decision on using smoke to the assault division commanders.[24]

Within each division sector, attached corps engineers were to start at H-hour

[24] VII Corps Engineers, Operations in the European Theater, VI.

to build at least three vehicular bridges. Although the threat posed by the Roer dams had passed, each division still was to carry five days' supply of rations and gasoline against the possibility that bridging might be delayed or knocked out. To assure ammunition supply points beyond the Roer soon after the crossings, the XIX Corps attached two truck companies to each of its two assault divisions, while the XIII Corps planned to use three companies under corps control for the same purpose.[25]

In case bridges went out, LVT's and dukws (2½-ton amphibious trucks) were to ferry essential supplies. Although emergency airdrops probably would be unnecessary since the threat from the Roer dams had ended, 500 C–47 transport planes loaded with enough supplies to maintain one division in combat for one day remained on call.[26]

Challenging the Swollen River

On the night of 22 February, the GRENADE force stirred. No sooner was it dark than infantrymen began moving into cellars as close as possible to the river's edge. Engineers started transporting boats and bridging equipment to within easy carrying distance of the water. Artillerymen were careful to fire no more than normal concentrations lest the enemy discern from increased fire what was afoot.[27]

The enemy thus far had given no sign that he knew the long-expected attack was at hand. Although an occasional German plane appeared over the flatlands west of the Roer before dark, all seemed to be on routine reconnaissance or bombing and strafing missions. Incoming artillery and mortar shells were few.

In higher German headquarters, attention still was focused on the Third Army's attacks on Bitburg and Trier and the First Canadian Army's drive in the north. Employing a Canadian corps on the left and a British corps on the right, Operation VERITABLE had carried approximately seventeen miles from jump-off positions along the Dutch frontier near Nijmegen, more than a third of the distance to final objectives along the Rhine upstream from Wesel.[28]

Beginning at 0245 on the 23d, the massed artillery began its thunderous bombardment. Forty-five minutes later, infantrymen of six divisions lowered assault boats into the swollen Roer to do battle from the first with a treacherous current.

Because the river spread into wide inundations both north and south of Linnich, the 84th Division (Maj. Gen. Alexander R. Bolling) of the XIII Corps had to cross at a destroyed highway bridge on a one-battalion front within the town, where, by contrast, the river was still in a narrow channel. (*Map VII*) The first wave got over with relative ease. "I really don't know whether

---

[25] XIX Corps Admin Order 15, 7 Feb 45; XIII Corps Flood Plan, 8 Feb 45; XIII Corps G–4 AAR, Feb 45.

[26] XIII Corps G–4 AAR and Engineer AAR, Feb 45; XIX Corps AAR, Sec IV, Feb 45; NUSA G–4 AAR, Feb 45.

[27] Unless specifically noted, sources for all combat actions are official records and combat interviews of units involved.

[28] For operations of the First Canadian Army, see Col. C. P. Stacey, *The Victory Campaign—Operations in Northwest Europe, 1944–1945,* "Official History of the Canadian Army in the Second World War," vol. III (Ottawa: The Queen's Printer and Controller of Stationery, 1960), pp. 460–526.

ROER RIVER

CROSSING SITES AT LINNICH

the enemy fired any shots at us or not," said 1st Lt. Richard Hawkins of the 334th Infantry's Company A. "Our own guns going off all around us . . . drowned out all other sounds." [29] Although the current hurled two boats far downstream, the bigger problem was a drift of almost all boats some seventy-five yards downstream, making it difficult in the darkness to get them back to the crossing site for the second wave.

Engineers beginning at H-hour to build three footbridges ran into difficulties with all three. One was almost completed when bypassed Germans opened fire with automatic weapons, making it impossible to anchor the bridge on the east bank. Another had no sooner been completed when an assault boat plunged downstream from the neighboring division's sector and knocked it out. A direct hit on a cable by an enemy shell knocked out a third just as it too was almost completed.

The follow-up battalion had to cross by shuttle with the few assault boats that could be retrieved. When one footbridge finally completed just before noon stayed in, the engineers abandoned attempts to build others and concentrated on vehicular bridges. An infantry support bridge was ready for light vehicles by 1730, but a treadway bridge, finished three hours later, had to be closed when a German plane strafed and damaged it. Only after more than four hours were spent on repairs was the treadway again ready for traffic; men of the 84th Division thus spent all of D-day on the east bank without tank or tank destroyer support.

[29] Theodore Draper, *The 84th Infantry Division in the Battle for Germany* (New York: The Viking Press, 1946), p. 145. An excellent unit history.

In the sector of the 102d Division (Maj. Gen. Frank A. Keating) on the right wing of the XIII Corps upstream from Linnich, two regiments made the assault. As in the 84th's sector, fire from the east bank was meager, partly because a patrol had crossed thirty minutes before H-hour and knocked out four machine guns in front of the 407th Infantry. Near misses from mortar fire upset several craft carrying men of the 405th Infantry, but rubber life vests saved the men from drowning.

Again it was the second wave that ran into most difficulty, for the current carried many of the boats used by the first wave far downstream where they impotently sat out successive stages of the assault. When the follow-up battalion of the 405th Infantry reached the river, the men could find at first only two boats. After an intensive search turned up a few more, one company got across. Other men meanwhile tried LVT's, but so muddy was the far bank that these craft could not get far enough up for the men to disembark. As in the 84th Division's sector, an LVT went out of control, crashed into a partially completed infantry support bridge, and sent parts of the bridge careening downstream.

The struggle to build bridges was for the 102d Division also a discouraging task. When engineers completed the first footbridge for the 405th Infantry just before daylight, German artillery promptly knocked it out. They put in another about the same time for the 407th Infantry, but enemy shelling was too intense for the infantry to use it. Spattered by shell fragments, the bridge spanned the river for three hours before a tree fell on it, snapped a cable, and set the pontoons adrift. Shortly after

DERELICT ASSAULT BOATS NEAR LINNICH

midday the engineers at last opened a workable footbridge and a support bridge suitable for light vehicles.

The infantry support bridge had a short life; no sooner had the 407th's antitank company with its towed 57-mm. guns crossed than a shell knocked it out. Getting sufficient antitank support to the far bank became a major concern, for by noon signs of impending counterattack had begun to develop in front of the 102d Division. With the infantry support bridge finally operating again about 2100, General Keating ordered every 57-mm. gun in the division to be towed across immediately.

Although other engineers opened a treadway bridge about the same time, just as a company of tank destroyers started to cross three low-flying German planes knocked out the bridge. Another treadway was completed before midnight, but before tank destroyers could use it trucks loaded with rubble had to cross and build up a soggy exit route on the far bank.[30] It was well after mid-

---

[30] Maj. Allan H. Mick, ed., *With the 102d Infantry Division Through Germany* (Wtshington: Infantry Journal Press, 1947), p. 129.

SMOKE POTS ALONG THE ROER NEAR DUEREN

night before tank destroyers in appreciable numbers began to move beyond the river.

Two miles upstream to the south in the sector of General McLain's XIX Corps the swollen river proved as big an obstacle to successful assault as it had for the XIII Corps. There the 29th Division was to cross around Juelich, the 30th Division three miles farther upstream.

Both assault regiments of the 29th Division (Maj. Gen. Charles H. Gerhardt) faced special crossing problems. North of Juelich, no bridges were to be built for the 115th Infantry because the flooded Roer was more than 400 yards wide. Both the first wave and the follow-up units were to cross in assault boats and LVT's, with additional forces crossing later over bridges to be built at Juelich for the 175th Infantry.

The 175th, on the other hand, was to depend almost entirely on bridges, since the river alongside the east bank town of Juelich flows between high banks. Half an hour before the end of the artillery preparation, two 25-man patrols were to cross in assault boats to stake out small holdings where engi-

CITADEL

ROER RIVER

CROSSING SITES AT JUELICH

neers, working under a smoke screen, could anchor footbridges over which the assault battalions were to cross.

Despite fire from German machine guns, one patrol got across the river. Of two boats carrying the other patrol, one capsized and the current washed the other far downstream.

Working at the site of a destroyed highway bridge, engineers completed a footbridge in less than an hour. Although an assault boat loaded with men crashed into the bridge and knocked it out, engineers had it back in service by 0600. The first infantrymen then crossed on a dead run. Within another hour, two more footbridges were in.

Previously undetected mines on west-bank approaches to the 115th Infantry's crossing site meantime threatened to delay the other assault. A tank maneuvering into a supporting position struck a mine, blocking the road leading to the river, and a tankdozer trying to remove the disabled tank set off another mine. The leading LVT bringing troops to the site also hit a mine, blocking the column of LVT's behind it. Officers on the scene directed the infantry to dismount and join other units crossing by assault boat. The mishap delayed the first wave by twenty minutes, but the LVT's soon found a bypass around the disabled vehicles.

From this point German fire added a new dimension to the problems facing the engineers. Long-range machine gun fire played on one footbridge for much of the morning. A mortar shell struck another while stretcher bearers were crossing with a wounded man.[31] Two

artillery hits on a partially completed treadway bridge prompted engineers to shift the site a few hundred yards upstream where houses in Juelich provided a measure of concealment. Tanks and bulldozers began to cross in late afternoon, the bulldozers to clear paths through the rubble that air and artillery bombardment had made of the town.

Upstream from Juelich, the 30th Division (General Hobbs) faced perhaps the most forbidding stretch of waterline along the entire front. At only two points, both on the division's right wing, was the river considered at all narrow enough for crossings.

Going the 29th Division one better, the 119th Infantry near the village of Schophoven sent a patrol of twenty-five riflemen to the east bank more than an hour before start of the artillery preparation. With the patrol providing a screen, engineers were to begin work on a footbridge at the same time the preliminary shelling began.

At 0215 engineers followed the patrol across in assault boats, dragging behind them prefabricated duckboard bridges to be used to get the infantry across a canal that at this point parallels the Roer. (A patrol had discovered only forty-eight hours before the attack that the canal was too deep for fording.) As the big artillery bombardment began, a battalion of infantry started crossing in assault boats. By the time the last shells fell, a footbridge was in place and the rest of the regiment was racing across.

The 120th Infantry a few hundred yards upstream had no such success. Although the original plan for crossing had

---

[31] Joseph H. Ewing, 29 Let's Go! A History of the 29th Infantry Division in World War II (Washington: Infantry Journal Press, 1948), p. 233. This is an excellent unit history.

FOOTBRIDGE ACROSS THE ROER SERVES MEN OF THE 30TH DIVISION

been much the same, a patrol only the night before had discovered that the current was too swift at that point for assault boats. The engineers quickly made plans for two cable ferries, but they were able to fasten a rope on the far bank for only one. Almost two hours before the artillery preparation began, a company of infantrymen began to pull themselves across in rubber boats, but the current proved too swift even for that method. Only thirty men reached the east bank.

Engineers succeeded finally in fastening an anchor cable for a footbridge just before the preparation fires began. Yet from that moment everything seemed to go wrong. German artillery fire cut the first cable. A second snagged in debris and snapped. A mortar shell cut a third. A fourth held long enough for engineers to construct about fifty feet of bridge before the current snapped the cable and the bridge buckled. Doggedly, the engineers tried again. This time the cable stayed, but the coming of daylight brought such increased German shelling that darkness had fallen on D-day before they got a footbridge in.

The 120th Infantry had resorted to

LVT's to get the bulk of two companies across the Roer not long after the official H-hour of 0330, while the rest of the regiment later in the day crossed on the footbridge constructed for the 119th Infantry. The problem of getting the infantry across at last solved, all hands could turn to a treadway bridge that other engineers already had started. Not until midnight was this bridge completed; men of the 30th Division, like those of the 84th, had spent all of D-day without tank or tank destroyer support.

As costly as German shelling proved to be in the 30th Division's sector and elsewhere, it would have been considerably greater had it not been for the use of smoke. The 29th and 30th Divisions used both smoke pots and chemical smoke generators. The 30th Division began its screen before dawn and kept it up, not for twelve hours as planned, but for thirty-three, in itself testimony to the effectiveness of the screen. The 29th Division discontinued its screen after less than two hours because it interfered with directing artillery fire. The other two divisions, the 84th and 102d, depended primarily on smoke pots emplaced along the west bank, although both used white phosphorus shells fired by chemical mortars to assist the first waves. The 102d Division maintained one smoke screen as a feint at a point where no crossing was contemplated. The smoke drew enemy fire while at the true crossing site nearby, unscreened, scarcely any shells fell.

The First Day on the East Bank

The Roer was unquestionably difficult. In the face of a capable, determined enemy on the east bank, it could have proven far more costly. Fortunately for the eventual outcome of Operation GRENADE, the enemy in general was neither capable nor determined.

Opposite Linnich, the 84th Division had the good fortune to strike almost astride a German corps boundary. The lone unit in the assault, the 334th Infantry's 1st Battalion, hit the extreme north flank of the *59th Infantry Division* of Koechling's *LXXXI Corps*, taking the Germans by surprise and occupying the village of Koerrenzig before daylight. At that point the 1st Battalion turned north in keeping with the mission of clearing enough of the east bank of the Roer for the neighboring XVI Corps to cross unopposed. In the process the battalion began to roll up from the flank defenses of the *183d Infantry Division* of Crasemann's *XII SS Corps*. By nightfall the 1st Battalion was approaching the crossroads village of Baal, three miles from the crossing site, while the 335th Infantry came in to seal the 334th's flank to the east.

Baal was one of only three places where the Germans on D-day mustered counterattacks. As night was approaching, a battalion of the *183d Division* supported by several tanks or assault guns drove south out of Baal at the same time men of the 334th Infantry were trying to break into the village. American artillery and eager Thunderbolts of the XXIX Tactical Air Command broke up the enemy thrust before the opposing forces could actually clash on the ground. Occupying Baal proved relatively simple after that, though just before midnight three understrength German battalions struck with considerable verve. For a while the conflict was intense on the periphery of the village, but by morning small arms and artillery fire had driven the Germans off.[32]

The day's strongest German counter-action developed to the south against the 102d Division. There the 407th Infantry on the north wing had taken the enemy in the village of Gevenich by surprise, seizing 160 prisoners, and in the afternoon occupied an adjacent village to the north. The 405th Infantry on the south wing entered Tetz, southernmost of the day's objectives, against minor opposition; but because of difficulties at the crossing sites, it was midafternoon before the regimental commander, Col. Laurin L. Williams, could send a force northeastward against two other objectives, Boslar, two miles from the Roer, and Hompesch.

Despite a 20-minute artillery preparation fired by fourteen battalions, the men of the 405th Infantry had gotten no farther than Boslar when darkness came. Something had infused new spirit into the defending troops of the *59th Division,* whose performance elsewhere on D-day had been, at best, lackluster. That something was an impending counterattack, signs of which the Americans had been detecting since just before noon.

As the broad outlines of the Ninth Army's attack emerged during the morning of 23 February, the *Army Group B* commander, Field Marshal Model, had acted swiftly to place his reserves, the *9th* and *11th Panzer Divisions,* at the disposal of the *Fifteenth Army.* Although Model had intended to employ the two divisions together under an ad

hoc corps commanded by a tank specialist, Generalleutnant Fritz Bayerlein, not enough of the *11th Panzer Division* had yet arrived from the Saar-Moselle triangle to justify that arrangement. The *Fifteenth Army* commander, General von Zangen, early decided to attach increments of the two divisions as they arrived to Koechling's *LXXXI Corps.* Although Zangen had yet to determine the exact location of the American main effort, he deduced from analysis of crossing sites along the Roer that it probably was directed against the *LXXXI Corps.*[33]

While attachment of the panzer divisions augured well for the future, it would be at least the next day before any part of the divisions could arrive. For immediate counterattack, the *LXXXI Corps* commander, General Koechling, had to depend on his own slender resources. These were two infantry battalions, one each from his two divisions, plus remnants of two separate tank battalions and an understrength assault gun brigade.

Returning the infantry battalions to division control, Koechling gave each division a company of the assault gun brigade with twelve to fourteen 75-mm. guns and smaller portions of the two tank battalions. The *59th Division* then was to strike toward Gevenich, the *363d Infantry Division* toward Boslar and Tetz.

The 102d Division commander, General Keating, meanwhile reacted to the indications of impending counterattack

[32] MS # B–812, *Fifteenth Army,* 23–28 February 1945 (General der Infanterie Gustav von Zangen); Draper, *The 84th Division in the Battle for Germany,* pp. 151–54.

[33] German material from MSS # C–020 (Schramm); # B–812 (Zangen); # B–576, *LXXXI Corps,* 25 January–21 March 1945 (General der Infanterie Friedrich Koechling); # B–053, *Corps Bayerlein,* 11 February–5 March 1945 (Generalleutant Fritz Bayerlein).

by ordering his reserve, the 406th Infantry, into position south and east of Tetz. The 405th and 406th Infantry Regiments then formed a defensive arc extending from high ground between Gevenich and Boslar, through Boslar, and back to the river south of Tetz. The 407th Infantry on the north continued to hold Gevenich and the next village to the north. Confident of his strength in infantry, General Keating felt keenly his lack of antitank support on the east bank. It was this concern that through the afternoon and evening punctuated the engineers' futile efforts to keep bridges functioning across the Roer in hope of getting tanks and tank destroyers across.

As it turned out, the defenders at both Gevenich and Boslar had to rely primarily on artillery fire and bazookas. Although the German thrust at Gevenich proved relatively weak and caused little concern, the Germans at Boslar attacked at least seven times. The first thrust hit just before 2100, employing a mixed force of about 20 assault guns and tanks accompanied by about 150 infantry. While American artillery fire was dispersing tanks and infantry before they reached Boslar, some of the infantry bypassed the village and penetrated the lines of a battalion of the 406th Infantry. A reserve rifle company sealed off that penetration.

In subsequent thrusts, some infantry and tanks got into the streets of Boslar. It was a night, said the commander of the defending battalion, Lt. Col. Eric E. Bischoff, of "indescribable confusion." [34] Infantrymen accounted for four

---

[34] Combat interview with Bischoff.

Mark V tanks with bazookas. Still the Germans persisted.

What the Americans reckoned as the fourth try brought the gravest crisis. Three hours before dawn on 24 February, tanks and infantry swarmed into the village. While the Americans huddled in cellars, forward observers called down artillery fire on their own positions. By daylight the Germans had fallen back, and a count revealed a surprisingly low total of thirty American casualties.

In the sector of the XIX Corps, the Germans launched no counterattacks and in general proffered no stiffer passive resistance than against the XIII Corps. The defending troops were from the same *363d Division* that gave the 102d Division such a hard time at Boslar.

The 115th Infantry, on the north wing of the 29th Division, had no trouble taking the village of Broich, but when the men moved out toward high ground to the northeast on which they intended to anchor the division's bridgehead, they encountered grazing fire from automatic weapons emplaced in farm houses and entrenchments on the reverse slope. Not until darkness came and the men made a stealthy night attack was this position secured.

The 175th Infantry in the meantime had run into less resistance in Juelich than expected, but clearing Germans from the debris of the destroyed town remained a slow process. By nightfall Juelich was in hand except for the Citadel, a medieval fortress surrounded by a moat. According to plan, the assault companies left the Citadel for follow-up troops to clear.

In the adjacent 30th Division, the advance proceeded apace, despite the problems inherent in crossing at a wide part of the flooded Roer. A battalion of the 119th Infantry on the north was in the first village rooting Germans from cellars less than fifteen minutes after the artillery preparation lifted. Soon after dawn the same battalion cleared another village to the north.

Leading companies of the 120th Infantry had harder going because of an extensive antipersonnel minefield in a patch of woods near the village of Krauthausen. The 2d Battalion took at least seventy-five casualties in the woods but still jumped off before dawn against Krauthausen and the neighboring village to the south. One company employing marching fire took the latter village at the cost of one killed and two wounded, while two companies enveloped Krauthausen from south and north.

Both regiments then used follow-up units to push out to slightly higher ground to the east. The 119th Infantry also sent a battalion against a village at the edge of the Hambach Forest and took it by midafternoon.

Since the 30th Division would be on the outside of the Ninth Army's wheel to the north with the farthest to go of the four assault divisions, the commander, General Hobbs, decided to keep going through the night. Reserve battalions of both assault regiments moved northeastward before midnight against Hambach and Niederzier, the only villages remaining in the division's sector short of the Hambach Forest. Distant American searchlights bouncing light off clouds made twilight of the darkness.[35]

Five battalions of artillery fired at maximum rate to help men of the 119th Infantry into Hambach. They timed their concentrations to allow the infantry five minutes to cross on a dead run from the line of departure to the first houses. The village fell with only a few shots fired. Most of a 126-man German garrison had to be routed from cellars where they had retired to sit out the American shelling.

The scheme of maneuver and results in the attack on Niederzier were similar. When shells armed with proximity fuzes exploded over open trenches west of the village the Germans "just got up and left."[36] The 120th Infantry lost not a man.

With some relatively unimportant exceptions, the XIX Corps as dawn came held all its planned D-day bridgehead; yet difficulties could still lie ahead in the Hambach Forest, where the Germans well might elect to stand, or might arise from an open corps right flank. The unprotected right flank had developed because the First Army's VII Corps, charged with protecting the flank, had been having the hardest fight of all to get across the Roer and stay there.

The VII Corps at Dueren

As protection for the Ninth Army's wheel, General Collins's VII Corps of the First Army had to make the deepest penetration of all, to the Erft River beyond Elsdorf, thirteen miles from the Roer at Dueren, and do the job with its

---

[35] Among American units, the Ninth Army had

pioneered in use of battlefield illumination during the drive to the Roer in November. See MacDonald, *The Siegfried Line Campaign.*

[36] Combat interview with Maj. Cris McCullough, ExecO, 1st Bn, 120 Inf.

own right flank exposed for at least two days until another corps to the south joined the attack. The zone of the VII Corps further included two obstacles expected to be strongly contested: ruins of the town of Dueren and most of the Hambach Forest.

As in the corps of the Ninth Army, the VII Corps was to employ two divisions to assault the river line, the 104th (Maj. Gen. Terry de la Mesa Allen) on the left, the 8th (Maj. Gen. William G. Weaver) on the right.[37] Because Dueren was the hub of communications to east and northeast, Collins divided the town between the two divisions. The infantrymen first were to establish a bridgehead anchored on high ground about four miles from the Roer, from the village of Oberzier in the north to Stockheim in the south. At that point Collins intended to send the 4th Cavalry Group to clear the Hambach Forest while the 3d Armored Division passed through the infantry to gain the Erft.

To even a greater degree than the rest of the GRENADE force, the VII Corps would find the swollen Roer the biggest obstacle to achieving D-day objectives. Because the current everywhere might prove too swift for footbridges, all the assault infantry were to cross by boat, each regiment with two battalions abreast. A platoon of engineers with fifteen or sixteen boats was assigned to each rifle company in the first wave, while corps engineers held sixty boats in

reserve. At the last minute, both division commanders decided against using smoke lest it hinder artillery observation and confuse infantrymen moving through built-up urban areas on the east bank.

The bulk of the first waves of the 415th Infantry, on the north wing of the 104th Division, got across with little difficulty, although the current and small arms fire turned one company back. Crossing opposite the northern fringe of Dueren, the 413th Infantry's 1st Battalion had more trouble. After the first company had crossed without opposition, German artillery and machine guns opened fire. Eight boats of Company C stuck on the top of a check dam and then upset. The rest of the 1st Battalion shifted to the 415th Infantry's sector to cross.

By daylight German artillery fire began to make the engineers' job all but impossible. Northwest of the Dueren suburb of Birkesdorf, work began on an infantry support bridge at 0415, but fifteen minutes later artillery and mortar shells destroyed much of the equipment and killed or wounded nineteen men. Although the engineers persisted, their first success came only after nightfall and at a new site.

Upstream opposite Birkesdorf another group of engineers, working under seemingly constant fire, had completed about 160 feet of a support bridge by 1300 when an enemy artillery piece, apparently by indirect fire using long base observation methods, got the range and scored several direct hits. The men hurriedly laid out smoke pots, but through the smoke the German shells still came in on target. Much of the bridge was destroyed.

---

[37] Unofficial histories of these two divisions—Leo A. Hoegh and Howard J. Doyle, *Timberwolf Tracks* (Washington: Infantry Journal Press, 1946), and Lt. Marc F. Griesbach, *Combat History of the Eighth Infantry Division in World War II* (Baton Rouge: Army and Navy Publishing Co., 1945)—are useful more for color than for following the action in detail.

TO MARIAWEILER

ROER RIVER

TO AACHEN

Crossing Sites at Dueren

At three other sites artillery and often rifle and machine gun fire prevented engineers even from starting construction until after nightfall on D-day. All countermeasures failed; counterbattery fire, smoke, direct fire by tanks on machine gun positions, even gradual expansion of the bridgehead—none of these during 23 February checked the deadly accuracy of the enemy fire. The first bridge was not open to traffic until midnight. The 415th Infantry at the only feasible ferry site managed to get three 57-mm. antitank guns across, but those remained during D-day the only supporting weapons east of the river.

Fortunately, the enemy's *12th Volks Grenadier Division* of Krueger's *LVIII Panzer Corps* failed to follow through with determined resistance once the infantry got across. The 415th Infantry took two villages en route to Oberzier without difficulty and by midafternoon had buttoned up along the Dueren-Juelich railroad, the D-day objective line. The 413th Infantry met only light resistance at first in Birkesdorf and Dueren, although enemy machine guns and artillery were increasingly troublesome as the day wore on. The regiment nevertheless cleared most of the northern half of Dueren by dark. In Birkesdorf the men captured an entire battalion of the *27th Volks Grenadier Regiment,* complete with staff. "In comparison with its earlier achievements," the *Fifteenth Army* commander was to note later, "the *12th Volks Grenadier Division* had very much disappointed the command during the initial defensive battle." [38]

More precarious by far through the

day and into the night was the position of the 8th Division upstream to the south. Plagued by an open right flank and daylong observation from foothills of the Eifel highlands, the 8th had the roughest D-day experience of all.

The leading 13th and 28th Infantry Regiments were to cross in assault boats and in double assault boats driven by outboard motors. Cable ferries and footbridges were to be put in as soon as possible for the reserve companies.

Fifty minutes before the scheduled H-hour of 0330, only five minutes after the artillery preparation began, the 28th Infantry's 3d Battalion was to open the assault with the mission of cutting enemy communications to the south and southeast by taking Stockheim. No enemy fire opposed the 3d Battalion's crossing, but the swift river current caused trouble enough. While about three-fifths of the two leading companies got across, the current swept the rest downstream. Even many of those who made it lost their weapons in swamped or capsized boats. Fortunate it was that the crossing took the Germans by surprise; twenty-three rose up from riverside trenches and surrendered. The prisoners' rifles served the men who had lost their own weapons in good stead. Behind a rolling barrage of white phosphorus fired by a company of the 87th Chemical Battalion, the assault companies continued to the edge of woods overlooking Stockheim, there to await the rest of the battalion before seizing the village.

The 3d Battalion's crossing was the only real success the 8th Division could report. Almost without exception the units that began to cross at H-hour found one difficulty piled upon another.

In the cold, damp night air, men of

---

[38] MS # B-814 (Zangen).

the 28th Infantry's other assault battalion, the 1st, could start none of the motors on their six power boats. The two lead companies then secured ten assault boats each and tried to paddle across. In the first company out, five boats made it, landing forty men on the east bank. The other five boats swamped. The next company lost all ten boats, sunk or destroyed by enemy fire. The remainder of the battalion pulled back to reorganize and wait for a footbridge.

The reserve 2d Battalion had scarcely better luck. Company F in the lead was supposed to cross in the boats used by the 3d Battalion, but only half of those returned from the first crossing and they had to transport the 3d Battalion's follow-up company. Eventually the men of Company F rounded up seventeen boats and paddled themselves across. Although most of the men reached the far side, all their boats swamped or overturned. Some 140 men who assembled on the east bank about 0630 had 30 rifles among them. Hardly had they begun moving southward toward their objective, a village close by the river, when heavy shelling from upriver and small arms fire from the village tumbled them into abandoned German trenches, where they remained under fire the rest of the day. They stood alone, for the rest of the 2d Battalion was stranded on the west bank without boats and would not get across until the next morning.

The footbridge for which the 1st Battalion commander waited never got built. A combination of enemy shelling and the swift current compelled the engineers to abandon the project. In the middle of the afternoon the battalion began a shuttle system, ten men pad-

dling over, five bringing the boat back. Two companies crossed in that manner. The rest of the battalion began crossing after dark by a cable ferry. By 2130 that night the 2d Battalion was at last assembled east of the river.

For the 13th Infantry, in the meantime, almost everything went wrong from the first. The two leading battalions were supposed to cross in fourteen double assault boats powered by outboard motors. Near a destroyed highway bridge at Dueren, eighteen men of Company I actually landed in this fashion on the east bank. At the same time, Company K came under intense machine gun fire. One boat overturned. On all the others the motors failed, although the men in one boat succeeded in paddling across. Only thirty-six men of the 3d Battalion made it. Two platoons of Company I arrived by cable ferry later in the day. That was the sum total of the 3d Battalion's assault.

It was even worse for the 13th Infantry's 2d Battalion farther south. Short rounds of white phosphorus shells fired by American artillery knocked out four of company E's boats before the crossing began. Although ten boats were launched, all swamped. The mishaps reduced the three rifle platoons to fifty-six men and thoroughly disorganized the company.

Company F put twelve men over the river under 1st Lt. E. W. Coleman, but when motors on other boats failed and the men found they could not handle assault boats in the current, the rest of the company stayed on the west bank. Lieutenant Coleman's dozen men fought their way into a factory, capturing twelve Germans in the process, but other Germans promptly counterattacked and besieged the small force the rest of the day. Coleman lost the prisoners and half his own men; he and six others managed to hold out, even though all were wounded.

As German fire became more and more intense, the 2d Battalion abandoned all efforts to cross. Although divisional artillery and the 4.2-inch mortars of the 87th Chemical Battalion smoked all known enemy observation points, neither the quantity nor accuracy of German artillery or mortar fire appreciably diminished.

The 3d Battalion continued trying to cross throughout the day but without much success. Ferries, which proved to be the only feasible way of conquering the current, were in operation only a few minutes before artillery or mortar shells severed the cables. By noon all ferries had ceased to operate, and the supporting company of the 12th Engineer Combat Battalion was down to eight men. Only with the coming of darkness did the harassed engineers and infantrymen gain any respite, but by midnight the 13th Infantry still had only four complete companies and elements of two others east of the Roer. These succeeded in pushing only about 400 yards beyond the river into the heaps of rubble that represented the southern half of Dueren.

Thus it was that the 28th Infantry's 3d Battalion, which had reached the woods line overlooking Stockheim, was the only unit of the 8th Division that came near accomplishing its D-day mission. That even this battalion, considerably understrength and inadequately armed, had made any progress had to be credited chiefly to the nature of German resistance. Having all but smashed the

crossing with the aid of a rampaging current and the fire of a supporting volks artillery corps, neither the *12th Volks Grenadier Division* at Dueren nor a weak *353d Infantry Division* south of the town made any move to counterattack the disorganized bridgehead forces.

Through it all, attached corps engineers struggling to construct five vehicular bridges across the Roer had run into the same problem of shelling and current that beset those engineers who tried to build footbridges or cable ferries. At most sites the men worked in vain even to get an anchor cable across. At a site selected for an infantry support bridge for the 13th Infantry, enemy shells came in at an estimated rate of 125 an hour throughout D-day and into the night. The following day as the rate of fire increased to an estimated 200 rounds an hour, the engineers abandoned the site.

Although fire at that particular site was exceptionally severe, it was heavy enough at all bridge sites to deny any successful construction during D-day. The first bridge to be completed in the 8th Division's sector was a Bailey bridge put in on the masonry piers of the destroyed main highway bridge into Dueren. That span was open to traffic on the morning of 24 February. No others opened until the 25th. In constructing nine bridges for the 8th and 104th Divisions, engineers of the VII Corps incurred a total of 154 casualties, of which 8 were killed and 1 was missing.

The experience of the 8th Division revealed strikingly the extent to which the enemy depended on the flooded Roer covered by preregistered artillery and mortar fire to stop the attack. To that kind of opposition the 8th Division was particularly vulnerable. The division's crossings were made at points where steep banks confined the river to its normal course and where the river emerged from a torrential descent through a twisting gorge from the highland reservoirs. The current in consequence was probably at least twice as swift as in the lower and broader reaches downstream from Dueren. The crossings also took place under the shadow of high ground from which the enemy could command the entire river valley around Dueren.

The First Day's Results

Despite the 8th Division's problems, the great hammerblow of GRENADE when viewed as a whole had effectively crushed the enemy. With contingents of six divisions on the east bank, there could be no real doubt henceforth of the outcome. The deep thrust of the 84th Division in the north as far as Baal and the advance of the 30th Division in the center into Hambach and Niederzier, more than two miles east of the Roer, made it particularly evident that GRENADE had irreparably torn the enemy's river line.

On 24 February, barring unforeseen developments on the German side, all the Ninth Army's divisions were to expand their footholds on the east bank and begin the wheel to the north, while the VII Corps strengthened its admittedly weak flank protection. The only major change in plan was made late on 23 February upon the recommendation of General Gillem, commander of the XIII Corps, and General Anderson, commander of the uncommitted XVI Corps. Noting the quick success of the 84th Division, the two commanders agreed that Anderson need not wait to cross the Roer until Gillem had cleared the east bank as far north as Erkelenz; instead the XVI Corps might begin crossing as early as the following day, as soon as the 84th Division had taken the next village downstream from Baal.[39]

If the Roer crossing had proven expensive in terms of bridging equipment and assault craft, it had been relatively economical in what mattered most—men's lives. The entire Ninth Army lost 92 killed, 61 missing, and 913 wounded, a total of just over a thousand. The VII Corps incurred comparatively heavier losses: 66 killed, 35 missing, and 280 wounded, a total of 381.[40]

---

[39] XIII Corps AAR, Feb 45.
[40] 12th AGp, G–1 Daily Sum, Master File, 1 Jan–28 Feb 45.

CHAPTER IX

Ninth Army to the Rhine

On the planning sheets, D plus 1 in Operation GRENADE (24 February) was a day for consolidating the bridgeheads and adding strength beyond the Roer. Despite some interference at bridges by German artillery and ninety-seven futile sorties by German aircraft, including some by the new jets, the plans would be accomplished with relative ease. While antiaircraft gunners were taking advantage of the rare opportunity to do what they were trained for and were knocking down eighteen of the planes, bridgehead strength increased from sixteen to thirty-eight battalions of infantry, and armored support reached all divisions.

In addition, D plus 1 was a day for maneuver. The Ninth Army's General Simpson was anxious to get started on the pivot to the north. This meant that both the XIII and XIX Corps were to thrust forward their right wings. It meant also that in the process each corps would develop an open right flank.

Odds still were that the XIX Corps on the south might have the most trouble both because of the delays experienced on D-day by the First Army's VII Corps and because of the invitation to counterattack inherent in the existence of the Hambach Forest. Yet the concern proved chimerical; the Germans simply had nothing to counterattack with.

Even though almost the entire *9th*

Panzer Division arrived in the *Fifteenth Army*'s sector during the day, the first unit of the division would be able to enter the line only after nightfall. Furthermore, so powerful was the American blow that General von Zangen would have to use the division piecemeal in a futile effort to hold the line rather than to counterattack. In any event, with only twenty-nine tanks and sixteen assault guns the *9th Panzer Division* was something less than the formidable force its name implied.[1]

As events developed, the enemy mustered almost no opposition as the 30th Division drove through the northwestern portion of the Hambach Forest. While sharp local fights developed at two farmhouses and a roadblock along the highway leading from Niederzier to Steinstrass at the northern edge of the forest, they failed to delay the division as a whole. At dark Steinstrass remained in German hands, but the 30th Division's line ran along the north edge of the forest, tying in to the west with the 29th Division astride the Juelich-Cologne highway.[2]

In the 29th Division's sector, only the 175th Infantry advanced during the day,

---

[1] MS # B-812 (Zangen). Strength figures are from Map, *Lage Frankreich, OKW-WFSt Op(H) West Pruef-Nr 1949, Stand: 14.2.45, 2. Lage.*

[2] The tactical story is based primarily on official unit records and combat interviews.

GENERAL McLAIN

and that a short distance to stay abreast of the 30th while a new division was entering the line to bolster the left wing of the XIX Corps. Commitment of another division was with an eye both toward broadening the attack and toward reducing the gap on the left as the XIII Corps swung north. The corps commander, General McLain, introduced a regiment of the 83d Division (General Macon) on the extreme left of the corps, attaching it temporarily to the 29th Division.

The only real difficulty with the pivot maneuver arose within the XIII Corps sector. There the rapid D-day advance of the 84th Division, plus the fact that the left wing of the XIX Corps failed to move, left the 102d Division's right flank open. Expecting continued attack to the east, the Germans were in no po-

sition to halt the 102d's northward move head on, but they could fire directly into the exposed flank.

That fire dealt a crippling blow to two companies of the 701st Tank Battalion supporting the northward advance of the 405th Infantry on the village of Hottorf. Hardly had the tanks started to move when antitank guns to the east opened a deadly fire. They knocked out four tanks from one company, eight from the other. Eight other tanks foundered in German infantry trenches. Two failed mechanically. Only five joined the infantry on the objective.

In the 84th Division, one regiment remained in Baal, the northernmost point reached on D-day, while the 335th Infantry passed through to try to make a swift conquest of the next village, Doveren, and prepare the way for the XVI Corps to cross the Roer unopposed. Yet as men of the 335th moved forward, they ran into one tenacious nest of resistance after another that the swift advance on D-day had failed to clear. Not until mid-afternoon, after tanks of the 771st Tank Battalion arrived to help, did the drive on Doveren pick up momentum, and darkness had fallen before the village was firmly in hand. Anderson's XVI Corps remained on the west bank.

For all the problems in taking Doveren, the hardest fighting on 24 February again fell the lot of the First Army's VII Corps. Not involved in the pivot to the north, the VII Corps still had its work cut out, since the 8th Division had much to do before the division could be said to be firmly established on the east bank of the Roer.

The 13th Infantry with all battalions in line spent 24 February fighting through Dueren. Opposition was intense only at two nests of army barracks, but bomb craters and rubble posed serious obstacles. Not only were streets impassable for vehicles but commanders struggled in vain to relate maps to the field of ruins. The 28th Infantry in the meantime forced additional strength into woods to the south but as night came still was short of the objective of Stockheim, on which General Weaver intended to anchor the division's south flank. Yet for all the limits of the day's advances and continued German shelling of bridge sites, Weaver could breathe more easily as the second day came to an end—his reserve, the 121st Infantry, crossed into Dueren late in the day prepared to attack the next morning through the 13th Infantry.

From the point of view of the corps commander, General Collins, the 8th Division's slow progress was of minor concern so long as the bridgehead remained solid. The job of the VII Corps for the moment was flank protection for the Ninth Army, and continued advance by the 104th Division was what he needed to assure that. Collins was particularly anxious that the 104th gain Oberzier and two other villages facing the Hambach Forest, both to take out German guns that might harass the flank of the neighboring 30th Division and to open the way for the corps cavalry to clear the forest before the Germans could concentrate there for counterattack.[3]

Because the 413th Infantry was occupied mopping up the northern half of Dueren, General Allen assigned all three villages to the 415th Infantry. The 1st Battalion reached one village before daylight but had to fight all day and through the next night to clean out infantry supported by four self-propelled guns. Also making a predawn attack, the 2d Battalion reeled back from Oberzier in the face of heavy German shelling. To prepare the way for a second attack an hour before noon, five battalions of artillery pounded the village for three hours. When the 2d Battalion moved again, the men took Oberzier in the face of only light small arms fire. Because the approach to the third village was exposed to fire from the other two, the 3d Battalion delayed attacking until after dark.

As night fell on the 24th, all conditions for committing the cavalry were yet to be met, nor was there room to commit armor south of the Hambach Forest. Anxious to get his mobile forces into action, Collins ordered both the 8th and 104th Divisions to continue attacking through the night.

Although German commanders had feared an Allied pincers movement west of the Rhine, during this second day they still had not fully fathomed American intentions. While noting with trepidation the northward orientation of the 84th Division, the *Fifteenth Army* commander, General von Zangen, continued to hope that the Ninth Army aimed its attack at the Rhine around Cologne and that the northward thrust was but a secondary effort to secure the road center of Erkelenz. To believe otherwise would be to admit that the entire south wing of *Army Group H* was about

---

[3] General Collins normally issued oral orders to his division commanders, then had them transcribed as written letters of instruction. These are valuable for revealing the reasoning behind the orders. See VII Corps Ltrs of Instrs file, Feb 45.

to be crushed in a vise between convergent Canadian and American drives.[4]

As the only hope for stopping the 84th Division, Zangen sent to Erkelenz advance contingents of a woefully weak infantry division (*the 338th*), which had recently arrived from the Colmar pocket far to the south. Against what Zangen considered the main attack, the eastward thrust, he could do nothing but urge speed in piecemeal commitment of the *9th* and *11th Panzer Divisions*. A panzer grenadier regiment of the *9th* would go into the line during the night of 24 February around Steinstrass in an effort to prevent advance beyond the Hambach Forest. Only the *Reconnaissance Battalion* of the *11th Panzer Division* would be available for commitment during the night and would enter the line a few miles to the north. No matter the harm piecemeal commitments would do to any hope of mounting a major counterattack, Zangen deemed he had no choice.[5]

The Third and Fourth Days

Sensing or at least guessing at German confusion, American commanders on 25 February made every effort to capitalize on it and gain momentum. In a continuing build-up beyond the Roer, at least one combat command of armor arrived during the day to reinforce each corps. Lest the 84th Division be slowed by clearing a crossing site for the XVI

GENERAL ANDERSON

Corps, General Simpson told General Anderson to test the feasibility of crossing on his own.[6]

The position of Anderson's corps was complicated by the existence of several German bridgeheads on the west bank of the Roer, one of which encompassed the town of Hilfarth in a loop of the river southwest of Doveren. If Anderson was to glean advantage from the advance already made on the east bank by the 84th Division, his troops would have to cross at or near Hilfarth, and that meant the town had to be cleared first.

The scheme as General Anderson developed it was for the 79th Division

---

[4] MS # B–812 (Zangen).

[5] *Ibid.* See also MSS # C–020 (Schramm); # B–080, *12th Volks Grenadier Division*, 23 February –March 1945 (Generalmajor Rudolf Langhaeuser, CG); # B–152, *59th Infantry Division*, 2 December 1944–28 February 1945 (Generalleutnant Walter Poppe, CG).

[6] In addition to official sources, see *History of the XVI Corps* (Washington: Infantry Journal Press, 1947), pp. 24–26.

(Maj. Gen. Ira T. Wyche) to stage a feint several miles downstream while the 35th Division took Hilfarth and actually crossed the river. To assist the crossing, the division commander, General Baade, sent his 137th Infantry into the bridgehead of the XIII Corps to take over the assignment of driving north down the east bank. In hope of keeping the Germans from demolishing a highway bridge they had left intact to serve their garrison in Hilfarth, the 692d Field Artillery Battalion early on the 25th began to place harassing fire around the bridge.

A battalion of the 35th Division's 134th Infantry hit Hilfarth before daylight on 26 February. Despite a vicious curtain of fire from automatic weapons, the infantrymen forced their way into the town, only to discover that the Germans had turned it into a lethal nest of mines and booby traps. The bulk of the battalion's casualties came from those.

By midmorning, with the town in hand, infantrymen provided covering fire with their machine guns while engineers erected two footbridges across a narrow stretch of the Roer. As some riflemen began to cross, others turned their attention a few hundred yards downstream. There either thirty-six hours of harassing fire by the 692d Field Artillery or faulty German demolitions had saved the coveted highway bridge. By noon tanks and other vehicles were rolling across.

Giving the XVI Corps responsibility for seizing its own foothold over the Roer had in the meantime freed the 84th Division to concentrate on driving some three miles beyond Baal to take the road center of Erkelenz. Inserting a combat command of the 5th Armored

Division (Maj. Gen. Lunsford E. Oliver) on the right flank of the XIII Corps also released the 102d Division to help. Under General Gillem's plan, the 102d was to attack the town itself while the 84th cut roads to the west.

Although first contingents of the enemy's *338th Infantry Division* had arrived during the night of 25 February at Erkelenz in an effort to bolster the faltering *XII SS Corps,* their efforts were so weak as to be hardly apparent. On the 26th the 102d Division cut through almost without opposition to find Erkelenz practically deserted. After dodging enemy shelling to gain one village, the 84th Division passed on to another to find not only no opposition but, in the village *Gasthaus,* beer on tap.

The resistance had been more challenging to the XIX Corps because of General von Zangen's hurried commitment of portions of the *9th* and *11th Panzer Divisions,* but the challenge was short-lived. Just before dark on the 25th the 30th Division's 117th Infantry broke stubborn resistance by panzer grenadiers at Steinstrass, while the 119th Infantry at the same time bypassed the village to drive almost two miles beyond. Moving fast, shooting as they went, men of the 119th ran a gantlet of heavy flanking fire that knocked out eight supporting tanks, but in the process the men took more than 200 prisoners, including all of a *Nebelwerfer* company that never got a chance to fire. At the end of the day the division commander, General Hobbs, could report to General McLain: "It looks like things are beginning to break a bit." [7]

_____

[7] 30th Div G–3 Jnl, 25–26 Feb 45.

Hobbs was right. Things were beginning to break.

Between them, the 29th and 30th Divisions were rolling up from the flank the enemy's second line of field fortifications and having surprisingly little trouble doing it. The 29th Division on 25 February took five villages and marked up an average advance of about four miles, then the next day gained the southern rim of the egg-shaped plateau that extends from the Roer to the Erft. During those two days, the attached 330th Infantry (83d Division) lost not a man killed and had only fifty-nine wounded. With some men riding attached tanks, a regiment of the 30th Division on the 26th advanced more than three miles. Another bound like that would put even the outside unit of the Ninth Army's wheel onto the egg-shaped plateau.

To the corps commander, General McLain, it was clear that the way to the Rhine was opening. Only antitank fire remained effective; the German infantry appeared confused and drained of all enthusiasm for the fight.

Although the time for exploitation seemed at hand, General McLain was reluctant to turn the drive over to his armor lest the Germans had manned their third and final prepared defense line, which ran five miles to the north through the village of Garzweiler, roughly on an east-west line with Erkelenz. McLain told the 30th Division to continue as far as Garzweiler, whereupon the 2d Armored Division was to take over.

Nor was all the success confined to units of the Ninth Army. While resistance still was stickier opposite the VII Corps, General Collins's divisions had begun to break it by a simple process of continuous, unremitting attack all along the corps front for seventy-two hours. "Contrary to their former customary manner of fighting," the commander of the *12th Volks Grenadier Division* would note, the Americans "continued their fighting day and night. As the enemy could always bring new infantry into the conflict while on our side always the same soldiers had to continue fighting, the over-exertion of our own infantry was extreme." [8]

The hardest fighting occurred on the approaches and within the southern reaches of the Hambach Forest along both sides of an uncompleted Aachen-Cologne autobahn. The explanation became apparent with capture of prisoners from the *9th Panzer Division's 10th Panzer Grenadier Regiment,* but even that once-elite regiment could give only slight pause to a relentless American push. To break up a counterattack at one village, a battalion of the 415th Infantry got nine battalions of artillery to fire for fifteen minutes. Making a night attack along the axis of the Dueren-Cologne railroad, a lone company of the 413th Infantry captured 200 men, all that remained of the *1st Battalion, 10th Panzer Grenadier Regiment.* The bag included the battalion commander.

At the same time, the 8th Division's 13th Infantry was wiping out the last resistance in Dueren with an attack preceded by a 10-minute artillery preparation in which four battalions fired more than 1,500 rounds. In an attack on a village two miles to the east, two battalions of the 121st Infantry fought all day on 25 February without success but per-

---

[8] MS # B–080 (Langhaeuser).

sisted through the night until at last the Germans had enough and pulled out.

On the 25th, the 8th Division commander, General Weaver, suffered the fourth in a series of heart attacks and was evacuated. He was succeeded by Brig. Gen. Bryant E. Moore, former assistant division commander of the 104th Division.

While the two infantry divisions continued to drive through the night, General Collins ordered his cavalry and armor across the Roer bridges. The maneuver he planned for 26 February was simple, flexible, and admirably designed to exploit the full shock of armor.

With the 13th Infantry attached, the 3d Armored Division (General Rose) split into six task forces, one built around the 83d Reconnaissance Battalion, the others each with a nucleus of one battalion of tanks and one of armored infantry, plus increments of engineers, tank destroyers, and artillery. With two task forces, Combat Command A on the right was to attack astride the Dueren-Cologne highway to gain the Erft River while CCB, also with two task forces, was to take the road center of Elsdorf, northeast of the Hambach Forest a few miles short of the Erft. One task force was to remain in division reserve and the 83d Reconnaissance Battalion was to serve as a bridge between the two combat commands. The 24th Cavalry Squadron was to protect the left flank inside the Hambach Forest.

In striking northeastward, the American armor was turning away from the enemy's *LVIII Panzer Corps* into the sector of the *LXXXI Corps*, where the last of the *9th Panzer Division* had arrived to assume a passive defensive role.

Also present was a *Kampfgruppe* of the *3d Panzer Grenadier Division,* rushed northward from the Eifel. Yet neither could do more than impose minor wounds on the full-strength American division. In taking the first village astride the Dueren-Cologne highway, CCA lost eight tanks to concealed German antitank guns, but that was the worst that happened to any part of the 3d Armored Division all day. As night came, contingents of CCB were drawn up before Elsdorf, ready to hit the town the next morning.

For the better part of 27 February the *9th Panzer Division* made a fight of it in Elsdorf, but with fire support from a company of tanks positioned in a neighboring village an infantry battalion broke into the town before noon and began a systematic mop-up. With the tank company was a T26 medium tank armed with a 90-mm. gun, one of the first twenty of this model (the Pershing) sent to the European theater for testing. The tank gave a good account of itself. At a range of a thousand yards, the Pershing hit and destroyed two Mark IV tanks, drilling holes through the thick side armor, and stopped a Mark VI Tiger with a hit at the vulnerable turret joint.

By midafternoon Elsdorf was sufficiently cleared to enable General Rose to commit his division reserve northeastward toward the Erft alongside the 83d Reconnaissance Battalion. As night came the armor held a 3-mile stretch of the Erft's west bank, and after dark infantrymen waded across to establish two small bridgeheads.

On 27 February the VII Corps thus completed its role in Operation GRENADE. In two bounds the armor had cov-

PERSHING TANK T26 WITH 90–MM. GUN

ered ten and a half miles from the original Roer bridgehead line to the Erft to seal the Ninth Army's south flank. Although General Collins would be quick to exploit the crossing of the Erft, the exploitation was logically not part of GRENADE but belonged to another operation General Bradley had been designing to carry his 12th Army Group to the Rhine.[9]

Rundstedt's Appeal

As these events had been occurring

with such swiftness, German commanders who as late as 24 February could hope that the Ninth Army's crushing drive was not designed to converge with the Canadian thrust southeast from Nijmegen were at last impelled to face reality. Operation GRENADE at that point clearly was the hammer aimed at crushing the southern wing of *Army Group H* against the anvil of Operation VERITABLE. Success of the operations meant encirclement or crushing defeat both for *Army Group H's* southern wing, the *First Parachute Army,* and that part of

─────────────
[9] See below, ch. X.

the *Fifteenth Army* that was being forced back to the north.[10]

Admission of that hard fact came at every level of command, from *Fifteenth Army* to *OB WEST*. Although Field Marshal Model at *Army Group B* acknowledged the truth of a grim estimate of the situation made by the *Fifteenth Army,* he could do little to help. He did promise commitment of the *Panzer Lehr Division,* which *OB WEST* accorded him, but the *Panzer Lehr* still was severely bruised from its fight against Operation VERITABLE and in any event could make no appearance in strength for several days.[11]

The Commander in Chief West, Field Marshal von Rundstedt, appealed on 25 February to Hitler for new directives designed to prevent disintegration of the entire Western Front. The situation was bad everywhere, he reported, not only in the north but in the south where attacks by the U.S. Third Army on either side of the Moselle River (Bitburg and Trier) worried Rundstedt most of all. When Hitler made no immediate response, Rundstedt on the 26th begged permission to make at least a minor withdrawal in the north, to pull back the extreme left wing of the *First Parachute Army* out of a salient at the juncture of the Roer and Maas Rivers near Roermond. The withdrawal was designed to ensure contact between the parachute army and the *Fifteenth Army*'s *XII SS Corps* as the latter fell back before the American drive. Yet even such a minor withdrawal Hitler refused to sanction.[12]

Hitler's response on 27 February sought to allay Rundstedt's fears about an attack along the Moselle but offered no palliatives for any of the crises in the west. By redeploying units already present, Hitler directed, the endangered southern wing of *Army Group H* was to hold where it was. Withdrawal behind the Rhine still was unthinkable.

Even as Hitler's message arrived, the crisis along the boundary between *Army Groups B* and *H* was growing more serious. Again Rundstedt appealed for permission to make at least the short withdrawal from the Roermond salient. This time he had the support of the Deputy Chief of the Wehrmacht Operations Staff, who personally briefed Hitler on the crucial situation. Hitler at last agreed—"with a heavy heart."[13]

Pursuit

The Germans had ample reason to be concerned, for on 26 and 27 February both GRENADE and VERITABLE entered new, decisive stages. After a pause for regrouping, the First Canadian Army on the 26th renewed its drive. A British corps on the right (part of the First Canadian Army) aimed at Geldern, nine miles away, where the British intended to meet the Americans; a Canadian corps on the left aimed at sweeping the west bank of the Rhine with a 7-mile jump to Xanten as the first step. It was on the 26th also that the VII Corps began its successful 2-day sweep to the Erft to seal the Ninth Army's right flank.

[10] MS # B–812 (Zangen).

[11] *Ibid.*

[12] Magna E. Bauer, German Top Level Decisions

and Plans, January 1945 to End of War, prepared in OCMH to complement this volume; MS # C–020 (Schramm).

[13] Quotation is from MS # C–020 (Schramm).

The next day, the 27th, the Ninth Army commander, General Simpson, sanctioned commitment of the first of his armored divisions in a major shift to an exploitation phase.

The question in Simpson's mind, as it had been in General McLain's, was whether infantry should continue to lead the way in the zone of the XIX Corps until the advance had passed the German trench system that cut across the front through Garzweiler. There was room already to insert a new unit between the 29th and 30th Divisions, but should this be another infantry division or should it be armor? Gambling that the enemy was no longer capable of an organized defense on any line, Simpson told General McLain to send the armor through to the Rhine at Neuss. As events developed, no real concern was necessary, for before the armor could get going on 28 February, the 30th Division took Garzweiler with no particular trouble.

Elsewhere on the Ninth Army's front no one would even question the immediate use of armor. A combat command of General Oliver's 5th Armored Division already had gone into action in the XIII Corps, originally as flank protection; General Gillem ordered the rest of the division to attack through the 102d Division on 28 February. The 84th Division in the meantime motorized a task force of infantry and tanks. While the 35th Division continued northwestward to gain maneuver room for the XVI Corps, General Anderson alerted a combat command of the 8th Armored Division (Brig. Gen. John M. Devine) to cross the Roer on 27 February and take up the fight to the north.

The weather remained favorable for tanks. Although rain on 26 and 27 February grounded tactical aircraft, it was too light to spoil the footing.

On the last day of February and the first day of March, events proved conclusively that the battlefield belonged to armor. All along the front American units recorded advances of from seven to ten miles, and there was little the Germans could do about it.

By the end of 28 February, the 2d Armored Division (commanded now by Brig. Gen. I. D. White) and an attached regiment of the 83d Division stood only seven miles from the Rhine. The next day, 1 March, a single regiment of the 29th Division took Muenchen-Gladbach almost without a fight. On the same day, a motorized task force of the 35th Division raced to Venlo on the Maas, more than twenty-five miles beyond the bridge at Hilfarth where the division had crossed the Roer. The task force was out of contact with the enemy most of the way, probably because of the German withdrawal from the Roermond salient.

It was all along the front a typical pursuit operation, a return at last to the halcyon days of August and early September. For most of the troops most of the time the tenseness of battle gave way to dull fatigue. The setting no longer looked like a battlefield. In one town electric lights were on, trolleys running. Many a village bore no scar. Returning to the fight after two days of rain, tactical aircraft lent a kind of discordant note with their noisy attacks on fleeing German columns. Almost all firing seemed to have an air of unreality. Giving way to exhaustion, one lieutenant fell asleep in a ditch, later to be awakened by a German woman carrying a child and fleeing from some sense-less machine gun chatter down the road.

Yet the battle had not ceased; it had only been shattered. The bits here and there, meaningless in the larger picture, were grim and bloody for the troops unlucky enough to run into them. The 84th Division, for example, after lung-ing nine miles on 27 February, sud-denly came upon a determined group of Germans of the *8th Parachute Di-vision* at a town west of Muenchen-Gladbach. With a skillfully organized defense that belied the haste with which the paratroopers had had to turn from their British foes in the north to their American enemies at their rear, the Ger-mans brought war back to the 334th In-fantry in a daylong fight as bitter as any in the campaign.

Company G bore the brunt of the ac-tion. It finally required an advance over open ground with marching fire, hand grenades, and in the end bayonets to ex-terminate the enemy. Of an estimated 50 paratroopers, only 2 surrendered. Company G incurred 40 casualties out of a force of about 125 riflemen who took part.

The next day, 1 March, as the 84th Division broke away again, General Simpson shuffled his reserves to make fresh troops available in each attacking corps to maintain pressure. He trans-ferred the 75th Division (commanded now by Maj. Gen. Ray E. Porter), which had been under operational con-trol of the British, to the XVI Corps and shifted the 79th Division (General Wyche) from the XVI Corps to the XIII Corps. His army reserve, the 95th Division (Maj. Gen. Harry L. Twad-dle), he attached to the XIX Corps.

About the only thing of note the Ger-mans accomplished during those two days was an exchange of General von Manteuffel, commander of the *Fifth Panzer Army*, for the *Fifteenth Army* commander, General von Zangen, a step in implementing the long-projected transfer of zones between the two ar-mies. Yet not for another six days would the staffs complete the exchange. Gen-eral von Manteuffel promptly ordered the *Panzer Lehr Division* to counterat-tack southeastward from Muenchen-Gladbach with the aim of linking with a northwestward strike by the *11th Pan-zer Division*, but the *Panzer Lehr* still was assembling when the proposed base of Muenchen-Gladbach fell. The loss prompted Manteuffel to order the feeble *11th Panzer* to desist. The *XII SS Corps* continued to fall back to the north, out of contact with the rest of the army, while the *LXXXI Corps* and the *9th* and *11th Panzer Divisions* (the two op-erating at this point under *Corps Bayer-lein*) withdrew eastward behind the Erft.[14]

Efforts To Seize a Bridge

On the American side, commanders began thinking seriously of the possi-bility of taking intact a bridge across the Rhine. Nobody really counted on succeeding, but all deemed it worth a try. Strong armored punches aimed at the bridges would at least cut up the enemy and possibly trap large numbers even if the armor failed to take a bridge. The Supreme Commander, General Eisenhower, indicated to General Simp-

---

[14] MSS # B–812 (Zangen); B–053 (Bayerlein); # C–020 (Schramm); # B–202, *Fifth Panzer Army*, 1–17 April 1945 (Generalmajor F. von Mellenthin, CofS).

son his intense interest in the Ninth Army's plans for taking a bridge.[15]

On 1 March General McLain of the XIX Corps inserted the 83d Division on the right of the 2d Armored with the mission of capturing Neuss and securing four bridges: a railroad and two highway bridges at Neuss and a highway bridge downstream at Oberkassel. Attacking with two regiments in early afternoon, the 83d continued through the night. One regiment cleared Neuss but found all three bridges there destroyed. The other regiment sent a task force circling wide to the west, bent on taking the bridge at Oberkassel by ruse.

Composed of parts of the 736th Tank Battalion and the 643d Tank Destroyer Battalion, with riflemen from the 330th Infantry, the task force moved by night, its tanks disguised to resemble German tanks. Infantrymen walked beside and behind the tanks to make themselves as inconspicuous as possible while German-speaking soldiers riding on the fronts of the tanks were prepared to do any talking required.

At one point marching down one side of the road while a German foot column moved in the opposite direction down the other, the column reached the outskirts of Oberkassel just at dawn. In the gathering light, a German soldier on a bicycle in a passing column suddenly shouted alarm. Their identity discovered, men of the task force turned their fire on the German column while the Oberkassel town siren blew a warning. Although the task force rushed toward the bridge and some tanks even got on the western end, the Germans demolished it.

North of Neuss at Krefeld-Uerdingen a 1,640-foot bridge named for Adolf Hitler still stood. The bridge lay in the zone of the XIII Corps, with the likeliest candidate to rush it the 5th Armored Division. Another possibility had arisen late on 28 February when the 2d Armored Division of the XIX Corps made sudden gains, though at dark the 2d Armored still was thirteen miles or so from the bridge and separated from it by what could prove a major obstacle, the Nord Canal. Deciding on a wait-and-see policy, General Simpson alerted the XIII Corps to be prepared to shift northward on short notice to make room for the 2d Armored Division should the armor be able to take the Nord Canal in stride.

On 1 March a task force of the 2d Armored's Combat Command A found a bridge intact over the canal and blasted a way across. Combat Command B, which had to put in its own bridges, crossed later in the day. By nightfall Combat Command A had reached the outskirts of Krefeld, only three miles from the Hitler bridge.

Around noon of 1 March, when the Ninth Army's G–3, Col. Armistead D. Mead, had arrived at headquarters of the XIX Corps to check on progress of the attack, he learned that the 2d Armored was rolling. It would be wrong, he believed, to stop the armor at the corps boundary south of Uerdingen. Since General Simpson was away from his command post, Mead issued the necessary orders in his commander's name, changing the boundary between the XIII and XIX Corps. The change would enable the XIX Corps to continue along the west bank of the Rhine beyond Uerdingen while forcing the

---

[15] *Conquer*, p. 184.

XIII Corps to wrench its attack northward.

The commander of the XIII Corps, General Gillem, promptly protested. The terrain near the bridge at Uerdingen, he said, was crisscrossed by canals and road and railway embankments, no fit ground for armor. His own 84th and 102d Infantry Divisions, he insisted, already were well on the way to the Rhine and should be allowed to continue.

Faced with this opposition, Mead and General McLain of the XIX Corps went forward to take a close look at the situation. They learned by their reconnaissance that heavy fighting was holding up the 102d Division in the southern fringes of Krefeld. To Mead, the resistance looked to be stubborn; the best way to break it was to take advantage of the 2d Armored Division's momentum. Although General Gillem continued to debate the issue, he finally gave in near midnight, and the change in boundary stood.

While these discussions were underway, General Simpson and Field Marshal Montgomery were arranging another shift in boundary. Because resistance still was firm in front of the left wing of the First Canadian Army, Simpson proposed to extend his own advance to bring his troops up to the Rhine as far north as a point opposite Wesel, only a few miles short of the Canadian objective of Xanten. Although Montgomery rejected the proposal—possibly because plans he already was formulating for jumping the Rhine involved a British crossing at Wesel—he agreed to shift the boundary as far north as Rheinberg, ten miles short of Xanten.

So late in the day were these changes

GENERAL GILLEM

in boundaries made that they had little effect on the fighting for much of another day. The XIII Corps continued to atack toward Uerdingen with the 5th Armored Division under orders from General Gillem to stop at the new corps boundary only if the 2d Armored Division had arrived. Still unaware of the boundary change, the 84th Division in the meantime was making its own plans. The division commander, General Bolling, ordered the 334th Infantry reinforced by the bulk of the 771st Tank Battalion to bypass Krefeld, rush the Hitler bridge, and, if possible, establish a bridgehead over the Rhine. Neither during the night of 1 March nor through the next morning did any word of the boundary change that would stifle this plan reach the staff of the 334th Infantry.

Men of the 5th Armored Division advanced on 2 March against no effective opposition until, shortly past noon, they met contingents of the 2d Armored just south of Krefeld. There they halted to await further orders. Backing down, General Gillem told his armor to assemble just inside the new corps boundary.

These forward units of the 2d Armored Division belonged to CCA, which had managed only a short northward advance during the day. CCB was coming up on the right, handicapped—as General Gillem had predicted—by ground cut by numerous small streams. At the closest point CCB still was two miles short of the bridge at Uerdingen.

The 84th Division's 334th Infantry meanwhile launched its attack at 1400 from a point almost eight miles from Krefeld, with the intention of veering around the north side of the city to reach the bridge. With attached tanks rolling at top speed, the head of the column got into the suburbs of Krefeld in less than two hours after jump-off, but then the leading tank took a wrong turn heading into the city which the column was supposed to bypass. The tanks quickly became involved in a fire fight with German antitank guns and could disengage only after nightfall. The attack left over from the old orders thus stalled as new orders at last reached the regiment, changing the objective from Uerdingen to a point on the Rhine several miles downstream.

The task of capturing Uerdingen and the still-standing Hitler bridge passed wholly to the XIX Corps. The troops to accomplish it were from the 2d Armored Division's CCB with two attached battalions of the 95th Division's 379th Infantry.

GENERAL BLASKOWITZ

The Germans for their part were hard put to muster a defense on the approaches to the bridge at Uerdingen. The responsibility rested not with *Army Group B,* since in driving rapidly to north and northeast, all columns of the U.S. Ninth Army now had passed into the zone of *Army Group H's First Parachute Army.* For just over a month *Army Group H* had been under General Blaskowitz, former commander of *Army Group G,* a result of command changes late in January when the Nazi party official, Himmler, had left *Army Group Oberrhein* in Alsace for new assignment on the Eastern Front. While Generaloberst der Waffen-SS Paul Hausser assumed command of *Army Group G,* General Blaskowitz had moved to *Army*

Group H to replace General Student, an officer in whom Hitler had little confidence.[16]

General Blaskowitz and the commander of the *First Parachute Army,* General der Fallschirmtruppen Alfred Schlemm, had been up against many of the same problems faced by their colleagues to the south: virtually no reserves and adamant refusal by Hitler to allow any withdrawal to the east bank of the Rhine. In an effort to salvage something in the face of continued pressure from the First Canadian Army and a new threat by U.S. troops from the rear, the German commanders had decided to try to fashion a bridgehead west of the Rhine extending from Uerdingen in the south to Geldern in the west and beyond Xanten in the north. To do the job at Uerdingen, General Schlemm ordered there what was left of the *2d Parachute Division,* some three or four understrength battalions. The paratroopers arrived on 2 March, only a step ahead of the American armor.[17]

Unaware of the arrival of the paratroopers, the 2d Armored Division made plans to attack toward the bridge at 0200, 3 March. In hope of keeping the Germans from demolishing the bridge, the 92d Armored Field Artillery Battalion kept up a continuous harassing fire. Beginning soon after nightfall on 2 March and using shells fixed with proximity fuzes, the artillery fired for more than fifteen hours.

The attack itself ran into trouble from the start. Four tanks knocked out quickly at the head of the column blocked passage of the others. The infantry went on alone to try to clear a new route. When the tanks in early afternoon again attacked, they reached the vicinity of the bridge from the south but ground to a halt under heavy mortar fire punctuated now and then by the sharper sting of an antitank gun or *Panzerfaust.*

The two attached battalions of the 379th Infantry meanwhile fought their way to the highway connecting Krefeld and Uerdingen and tried to turn eastward to the bridge. The paratroopers fought back stubbornly. Tantalizingly close to the bridge, neither infantry nor tanks could push the few remaining yards. A 13-foot hole in the road at the west end of the bridge denied passage for the tanks, and without their help the infantry was unable to pierce a thick curtain of small arms fire.

After dark a six-man engineer patrol led by Capt. George L. Youngblood slipped past the defenders, gained the bridge, and crossed it, cutting all visible demolition wires in the process. The patrol went all the way to the east bank before turning back. Yet the engineers either missed the critical wires or the enemy put in others during the night, for at 0700 the next morning, before a new attack could gain the bridge, the Germans blew the center and west spans.[18]

Fighting to clear Uerdingen continued throughout 4 March and into the morning of the 5th. At the same time

[16] Bauer, *Army Group G,* January 1945.

[17] MSS # B-084, *First Parachute Army,* 20 November 1944–21 March 1945 (General der Fallschirmtruppen Alfred Schlemm); # B-147, *Army Group H,* 10 November 1944–10 March 1945 (Oberst Rolf Geyer, Opns Officer, AGp H).

[18] General Schlemm says: "At Uerdingen the demolition wires were shot out by artillery fire. Their replacement took hours." MS # B-084 (Schlemm).

the corps commander, General McLain, ordered the 95th Division to drive for road and rail bridges at Rheinhausen, not quite six miles downstream from the Adolf Hitler bridge, with the armor attacking northward on the 95th's left. Resistance proved to be light. The reason seemed apparent when during the morning of 5 March pilots of artillery observation planes reported both bridges at Rheinhausen already down. By mid-afternoon the XIX Corps had completed its role in reaching the Rhine but had failed to get a bridge.

There was another reason for the light resistance. In breaking through at Uerdingen, the XIX Corps had compromised the bridgehead line that General Schlemm, the *First Parachute Army* commander, had been trying to hold. With the approval of Blaskowitz at *Army Group H,* Schlemm authorized withdrawal to a second and smaller bridgehead line extending from the confluence of the Ruhr River with the Rhine at Duisburg in the south to the vicinity of Xanten in the north. This was a line of no retreat designated by Hitler personally to enable continued supply of coal by barge to the German Navy along major canals leading to the North Sea ports.

Yet this line also quickly proved too ambitious. As the XIX Corps on 5 March finished clearing its share of the Rhine's west bank, the 5th Armored Division of the XIII Corps dashed into Orsoy, on the Rhine opposite one of the canals the Germans needed for their coal barges. With tanks and half-tracks in high gear and firing as they went, CCR swiftly covered the last two miles into Orsoy, cutting through German infantry and overrunning artillery pieces

before they could fire. The 84th Division meanwhile cleared Moers and Homberg but found road and rail bridges leading across the Rhine into Duisburg already destroyed.

Operation GRENADE as originally conceived was over; but if the Ninth Army's General Simpson had his way, GRENADE would be extended to include a bridgehead over the Rhine and a drive to the northeastern corner of the Ruhr industrial region. Since 1 March Simpson's staff had been considering this stratagem, based in the main on the theory of seizing a bridge intact but, failing that, on a quick surprise crossing.[19]

General Simpson settled on a plan to cross the Rhine between Duesseldorf and Uerdingen, then to turn north to clear the east bank for further crossings and to gain relatively open country along the northern fringe of the Ruhr. It was a stratagem that hardly could have failed, for Hitler's refusal to agree to timely and orderly withdrawal behind the Rhine had left his field commanders little with which to defend the historic moat and in early March totally unprepared to counter a crossing.

Yet Simpson's superior, Field Marshal Montgomery, said no. To a bitter Ninth Army staff, his refusal rested, rightly or wrongly, on the effect an impromptu American crossing might have on the Field Marshal's own plans for staging a grand set-piece assault to cross the Rhine on a broad front.[20]

---

[19] *Conquer,* pp. 189–90.

[20] *Conquer,* p. 190. Speaking with some authority on the British viewpoint, Chester Wilmot in *The Struggle for Europe* (New York: Harper & Brothers, 1952), page 677, wrote that Montgomery refused because a crossing near Duesseldorf would have involved the Ninth Army in the "industrial wilderness" of the Ruhr. In none of his published

The Wesel Pocket

Operation GRENADE as originally conceived was over and would gain no new lease on life beyond the Rhine. Yet it would be extended northward along the west bank, for the Ninth Army still would have a hand in reducing those Germans remaining west of the river. Swinging northeastward after an initial thrust northward from the Roer crossing site, General Anderson's XVI Corps would be thrown into a tough after-fight against remnants of the *First Parachute Army*. The resistance would be stubborn, for never would Hitler actually authorize withdrawal.

From 28 February through 3 March the XVI Corps had been slicing through relatively undefended country. In driving first to Venlo and thence northeastward in the general direction of Rheinberg, midway between Wesel and Duisburg, a motorized task force of the 35th Division and a lone combat command of the 8th Armored Division had led the way, each on a narrow front. For much of the time the armor had to stick to a single road, where its striking power at the head was seldom more than a platoon of tanks and a company of infantry; but neither this nor any other handicap really mattered.

Indications that the road march might be nearing an end emerged on 3 March. The 35th Division's Task Force Byrne (a reinforced 320th Infantry) reached

Sevelen, five miles southeast of Geldern, but there had a stiff fight to take the town. *(Map VIII)* A battalion of the 134th Infantry made contact with the 1st British Corps at Geldern, but resistance there too was determined. Although the 8th Armored Division still had met no real opposition, the armor was about to be pinched out by the change in boundary that sent the neighboring XIII Corps northward. CCB would be attached the next day to the 35th Division, while CCR on the extreme right had to be recalled to make room for units of the XIII Corps.

Contact between the forces of Operations VERITABLE and GRENADE on 3 March at Geldern created a continuous Allied perimeter around those Germans remaining west of the Rhine. Units of the 1st British Corps had reached positions generally on a north-south line between the Xanten Forest, west of Xanten, and Geldern, while the Canadians still were fighting to wrest a ridgeline within the Xanten Forest from German paratroopers.

The perimeter for the moment corresponded roughly to the outer bridgehead line that General Schlemm of the *First Parachute Army* was trying to establish, but not for long. The advances at Geldern and Sevelen meant that in the center as in the south the Germans would have to fall back to the inner bridgehead line, which in this sector ran about six miles east of Geldern along the western edge of the Boenninghardt Forest. The southern edge of the bridgehead would be anchored on Orsoy.

From the vicinity of Xanten to Orsoy, the German bridgehead was some sixteen miles wide. It encompassed the

works did Montgomery himself comment. German commanders almost to a man believed a surprise crossing would have met little resistance, a view reinforced by events in succeeding days elsewhere along the Rhine. See in particular MSS # B–084 (Schlemm); # B–147 (Geyer); # A–965 (Generalmajor Karl Wagener).

only high ground in this generally flat portion of the Rhineland: a boomerang-shaped ridge in the north covered by the Xanten Forest, the wooded Boenninghardt Ridge on a northwest-southeast axis that bisected the Geldern-Wesel highway, and a series of isolated hills south of the Boenninghardt Ridge.

Within the bridgehead General Schlemm still had more than 50,000 men, representing contingents of almost every division that had put up such a determined stand against Operation VERITABLE, including four parachute divisions, the *Panzer Lehr* and *116th Panzer Divisions,* and a panzer grenadier division.[21] Only in the north opposite the Canadians was the bridgehead line solidly organized, for there the Germans had made a grudging withdrawal back to a natural line of defense. Elsewhere hasty withdrawal had left few German units with any real integrity.

Within the bridgehead, two bridges still spanned the Rhine, a road bridge and a rail bridge, both leading to Wesel, the city on the east bank that would lend its name to the pocket of German troops. Those bridges obviously would be a key Allied objective, both because they stood almost exactly in the middle of the bridgehead and because they held out promise for crossing the Rhine with dry feet.

Because of the sparse opposition the Americans had been meeting, Allied commanders believed the best chance of getting the Wesel bridges rested with the XVI Corps. The assignment went to the 35th Division and its attached combat command, which were to drive northeastward to Rheinberg, thence

northward to take the bridges. Although the bridges lay outside the American boundary, the commanders informally eased boundary restrictions.

General Baade's 35th Division attacked on 4 March with two regiments abreast. On the left two battalions of the 320th Infantry came under intense fire from small arms, mortars, and artillery as they approached the Hohe Busch, a small forest not quite half the distance to Rheinberg astride the Sevelen-Rheinberg highway. Fire from neither artillery nor tank destroyers could neutralize the German positions. Although a platoon of riflemen got into a village just west of the wood, the men withdrew when the enemy began closing around them. Under the impression that the platoon held the village, five medium and two light tanks of the 784th Tank Battalion moved in. With *Panzerfausts* the Germans knocked out one of the mediums and both the lights, and only the timely arrival of a reserve rifle company spared the others. Even after the infantry cleared the village, the Germans after dark came back, besieging one American platoon in a hotel with hand grenades thrown through the windows.

It was a touch of the old war again, of the days before anyone talked of German collapse, not only here but to the south where two battalions of the 137th Infantry on the 35th Division's right wing also ran into trouble.

Attacking from a point southeast of Sevelen, a leading company of one battalion encountered heavy fire at the base of one of the isolated hills that afforded a logical extension of any defensive line based to the north on the Boenninghardt Ridge and the Hohe Busch. Two

[21] MS # B-084 (Schlemm).

platoons found some shelter in ditches and behind hedges while the other two ducked into houses. Because the company's artillery observer had lost his radio, the men had no artillery support. As two German tanks rolled down the road, one blast from their guns killed the company commander, Capt. Daniel Filburn, and a platoon leader, 2d Lt. John H. Hartment. With two key leaders lost and the tanks methodically blasting the houses and ditches in which the men sought shelter, all control vanished. The men fled. Reorganized before noon, they went back with tank destroyer support to hold the position, but not until the next day did this battalion mount another attack.[22]

Another battalion of the 137th Infantry also had a day of hard fighting, but with consistent tank and artillery support achieved a noteworthy success. When a patrol came under heavy fire from one of the isolated hills, the battalion commander, Maj. Harry F. Parker, borrowed six half-tracks and several light tanks from the 8th Armored Division's 88th Reconnaissance Battalion, mounted Company G on them, and sent them racing into houses at the foot of the hill. While another company provided supporting fire from the edge of a nearby wood, Company G continued northward to take not only the offending hill but another a few hundred yards to the north. The latter yielded 200 prisoners and prompted Germans on a remaining hill to the north to pull out during the night.

Despite the sudden flare-up of fighting on 4 March, General Baade continued

to anticipate a speedy breakthrough to the Rhine and possibly even across the river by way of one of the bridges at Wesel. To gain a leg on the thrust to the bridges, he ordered Task Force Byrne (the 320th Infantry reinforced) to turn immediately northward to seize a key crossroads on the Geldern-Wesel highway behind the Boenninghardt Ridge. The attached CCB, 8th Armored Division, was to assume the assignment of taking Rheinberg, whereupon the armor and the 137th Infantry together were to turn north toward the bridges.

Task Force Byrne started moving early on 5 March, the men fully expecting to make a rapid advance by bounds. Yet even though the Germans had evacuated most of the Hohe Busch during the night, rear guards held out through the morning. As the 1st Battalion at last passed to the north of the forest, the Germans cut off the leading platoon in a village at the base of the Boenninghardt Ridge. It took the rest of the day to rescue the platoon and clear the enemy from scattered houses nearby. Another battalion that had in the meantime attempted to advance along the main highway toward Rheinberg before turning north met intense fire from automatic weapons and antitank guns. The leading company lost two supporting tanks and its commander.

Even heavier fighting erupted on the approaches to Rheinberg where, under the plan of CCB's commander, Col. Edward A. Kimball, a task force composed largely of infantry was to take the town while another heavy in armor was to be ready to push on to the bridges at Wesel. The plan was based on a premise of negligible resistance; said the commander of the task force of armor, Maj.

---

[22] Extensive combat interviews are available on these actions of the 35th Division.

John H. Van Houten: "We thought it was to be a road march." [23]

The operation started out pretty much that way as the infantry force under Lt. Col. Morgan G. Roseborough marched beyond the isolated hills south of the Hohe Busch and entered the town of Lintfort. The town was secured by 1100, but among the buildings Task Force Roseborough took a wrong turning to end up north instead of east of the town. As the column advanced along a road leading to the main highway into Rheinberg, German antitank guns opened fire, knocking out a half-track and a medium tank. At the same time a rash of small arms fire erupted from nearby houses. The infantry dismounted, deployed, and gave battle.

Anxious to avoid delay in seizing Rheinberg, the CCB commander, Colonel Kimball, called forward Task Force Van Houten. Major Van Houten and his armor, he ordered, were to drive alone on Rheinberg. The infantry of Task Force Roseborough was to follow later in half-tracks.

Major Van Houten split his task force into three columns. One was to bypass the opposition holding up Task Force Roseborough and drive up the main highway into Rheinberg, a second to move along secondary roads to join the first on the main highway a thousand yards out of Rheinberg, and a third to drive east and come into Rheinberg by way of another main highway from the south.

All three columns quickly ran into trouble. Composed mainly of light tanks, the left column on the Rheinberg highway soon lost four tanks to antitank

---

[23] Combat interview with Van Houten.

guns, a *Panzerfaust,* and a mine. The center column never reached the highway as concealed German antitank guns knocked out twelve of fourteen medium tanks. The CCB commander himself, Colonel Kimball, got trapped in a house by mortar and machine gun fire and escaped only after darkness came. The third column meanwhile gained the highway leading into Rheinberg from the south but there encountered a swarm of German infantry and lost two tanks to *Panzerfausts.*

Having no infantry support, the commander of this column, Capt. David B. Kelly, radioed for help; but before infantry could arrive, he decided to risk a quick rush against Rheinberg with tanks alone. While the bulk of his company provided covering fire, three tanks raced forward. German antitank fire got all three of them.

Kelly himself then led a dash by his remaining tanks, but all except Kelly's own tank lagged. Kelly raced into Rheinberg alone, circled the town square, machine-gunned a German who was about to fire a *Panzerfaust,* narrowly escaped hits from German antitank guns five times, then raced back out of the town. On the way back German gunners hit his tank twice but failed to stop it.

Returning to his companions south of the town, Kelly found infantry support at last arriving: two companies of Task Force Roseborough that finally had eliminated the enemy north of Lintfort. In the hour of daylight remaining, the infantry and Kelly's seven remaining tanks mounted a new attack. Kelly himself led it on foot.

Advancing together, infantry and tanks took a hundred prisoners and knocked out three 88's, five 20-mm. antiaircraft guns, and four machine guns. Reaching the southern fringe of Rheinberg as darkness fell, they waited for the 35th Division's 137th Infantry to come up during the night and secure the rest of the town.

The fight for Rheinberg had all but annihilated CCB's armor; of 54 tanks, 39 were lost. For both the 36th Tank Battalion and the 49th Armored Infantry, it had been the first real fight, strikingly sharp action when compared with the skirmishing that had marked the combat command's brief previous experience in battle. Although the men had displayed considerable valor, they had paid dearly with a loss of 92 killed, 31 missing, 220 wounded. In official tones, the 8th Armored Division's staff summarized what had gone wrong: "The employment of the tank elements could have been improved through the provision of closer infantry support, and undoubtedly such support would have materially decreased the tank losses of the Combat Command." [24]

A daylong spectator at the events around Orsoy was the *First Parachute Army* commander, General Schlemm.[25] Fully expecting the Americans to send a column of tanks streaking northward immediately to cut off his remaining troops from the Wesel bridges, Schlemm nevertheless put into effect plans for a new defensive line. Ordering two of his three corps headquarters to retire east of the Rhine, he placed the remaining bridgehead under one corps. The bridgehead still encompassed the town of Xanten and most of the Boenninghardt Ridge.

While the Canadians plugged away at die-hard opposition in Xanten, General Anderson's XVI Corps headed north with two task forces, Task Force Byrne still on the left, Task Force Murray (the 137th Infantry with what remained of the 8th Armored Division's CCB) on the right. Both task forces soon discovered that the hard fighting for Rheinberg on 5 March had been a harbinger of what was to come. Although a British division on the left of Task Force Byrne provided help, the two task forces could do no more through the next three days than inch forward.

Then as suddenly as the determined resistance had formed, it disintegrated. During the night of 9 March the Germans blew both the highway and railway bridges at Wesel, leaving only a few rear guards and stragglers on the west bank. Passing through Task Force Murray, the 134th Infantry the next morning swept to the demolished highway bridge almost unimpeded.

The Beginning of the End

In just over two weeks the Ninth Army had driven approximately 53 miles, from the Roer at Juelich to the Rhine at Wesel, and had cleared some 34 miles of the west bank of the Rhine from Duesseldorf to Wesel. In the process the army had captured about 30,000 Germans and killed an estimated 6,000 more while absorbing less than 7,300 casualties.[26] In the companion drive, the First Canadian Army had driven approximately 40 miles from the Dutch-German border near Nijmegen to

---

[24] 8th Armored Div AAR, Mar 45.
[25] MS # B-084 (Schlemm).

[26] *Conquer*, p. 198.

Wesel. The casualties in VERITABLE were 15,600, prisoners, 22,200.[27]

The First Canadian Army's task had been the more difficult of the two, for the fortune of the delay imposed on Operation GRENADE by the flooded Roer River had shoved the bulk of German strength to the north. The *First Parachute Army* clearly had been superior to the *Fifteenth Army*. In addition, flooded ground over the first few miles of the Canadians' route of attack had imposed serious difficulties.

Although Field Marshal Montgomery had not intended it so, the two operations had developed in a pattern already made familiar in Sicily and again in Normandy, where Montgomery's troops attracted German reserves while American forces achieved a breakthrough and rapid exploitation. In Normandy more favorable terrain had lured the Germans to Montgomery's front; here it was because the Canadian attack had started first. As in Normandy, the Americans with their immense transportation resources were admirably suited for the breakthrough role.

For all the speed of execution, Operation GRENADE was complex, involving the crossing of a flooded, defended river, followed by two major changes in direction of attack and a minor adjustment at the end. A trace along the middle of the Ninth Army's course would resemble a giant S.

The operation also had introduced another complication that all Allied armies now would experience as they thrust deep into the interior of Germany. This was the presence of millions of noncombatants—native civilians, impressed workers from other countries, and liberated prisoners of war.

In some measure the Allies had experienced the problem before in France, Belgium, and the Netherlands, but the populace in those countries had been friendly. In earlier fighting just within the German frontier, many of the civilians had fled the battle zone; but now, as the Allies thrust deeper, there was nowhere for them to go. Literally masses of humanity wandered about, cluttering roads, slowing traffic, sometimes clogging prisoner-of-war channels. Destroyed homes, damaged water, sanitary and electrical facilities, and a complete breakdown of civilian transportation added to the problem. To establish some semblance of order out of the chaos was a mammoth asignment that by 15 March already was occupying more than forty Military Government detachments in the Ninth Army's zone.[28]

Meanwhile, the great build-up for crossing the Rhine began, underscoring the fact that Operations GRENADE and VERITABLE marked the beginning of the end. Not only had these operations put the Ninth Army, the Canadians, and the British into position to cross the Rhine but they had unleashed a flood of offensive operations elsewhere, designed to carry all Allied armies to the river. Indeed, a contingent of one American army already had stolen a march on all others and jumped the big obstacle without pause.

---

[27] Stacey, *The Victory Campaign,* p. 522.

[28] An instructive essay on this subject may be found in *Conquer,* pp. 195–97.

CHAPTER X

Operation LUMBERJACK

Although the American attacks in the Eifel and the Saar-Moselle triangle were unpopular with Field Marshal Montgomery, they were in reality of assistance to him, for they did, in fact, limit the units the Germans could disengage to send north. They also put General Bradley's forces into better positions for gaining the Rhine whenever the signal came and denied hard-pressed German units the respite they desperately needed.

In making plans for going beyond those limited objective attacks, General Bradley had to consider not only the responsibility for protecting the right flank of the Ninth Army as far as the Erft in Operation GRENADE but also an additional task that the Supreme Commander, General Eisenhower, assigned on 20 February. Before Bradley could turn full attention to gaining the west bank of the Rhine, he had to extend his protection of the Ninth Army's right flank by clearing a triangle of land between the Erft and the Rhine extending northward from Cologne to the confluence of the two rivers near Duesseldorf.[1]

Bradley logically gave the assignment to the First Army's General Hodges for execution by Collins's VII Corps. Once the job was completed, the VII Corps was to take Cologne, then head south along the Rhine. As Collins turned south, other contingents of the First Army were to launch a narrow thrust from the vicinity of the road center of Euskirchen southeast to the Ahr River, there to converge with a thrust by the Third Army through the Eifel and create a pocket of trapped Germans in the northern reaches of the Eifel.

Bradley's plan went by the code name, LUMBERJACK.[2]

Despite having relinquished units to flesh out the Ninth Army, the 12th Army Group still was a powerful force. In the First Army, General Hodges had twelve divisions (three of them armored), plus another at reduced strength (the 106th) and two cavalry groups. In the Third Army, General Patton had ten divisions (including three armored) and two cavalry groups. While nondivisional artillery was in no such strength as that which had helped the Ninth Army over the Roer, it was impressive nevertheless. Each corps in the First Army, for example, retained its usual attachments of four battalions of 155-mm. howitzers, two battalions of 155-mm. guns, and a battalion each of 4.5-inch guns and 8-inch howitzers. In deference to the role in GRENADE, the VII Corps had two additional battalions—one light, one medium. The 32d Field Artillery Brigade

[1] Ltr, Eisenhower to Bradley, 20 Feb 45, 12th AGp Military Objectives, 371.2, vol. VI.

[2] Operation LUMBERJACK, Outline Plan, 23 Feb 45, Hq 12th AGp.

with two 8-inch gun and two 240-mm. howitzer battalions, operating under the First Army's control, assumed positions favoring the north wing.[3]

The breakdown of roads under the February thaw was of some concern to all but prompted few special measures except in the First Army where the two assault divisions of the VII Corps were authorized to accumulate five days' supply of ammunition before jumping the Roer. Both armies were relatively close to major railheads—the Third Army to Luxembourg City and Thionville, the First Army to Liège—so that rail transport could handle much of the burden except for the last few miles to the front. Nor was either army so heavily engaged throughout February but that some supplies could be stockpiled. The First Army, for example, built up its Class III (gasoline) reserves from 1.8 days of supply to 6 days. Nevertheless, with the lesson of the 4th Division's supply problems near Pruem in mind, General Bradley directed both armies to instruct division staffs in how to obtain emergency supply by air. He directed also prepackaging of vital supplies at various airfields for prompt loading if needed.[4]

Intelligence officers estimated approximately 40,000 Germans in front of the First Army and some 45,000 facing the Third Army. If the G–2's erred at all, they erred on the side of caution; as noted during the first fortnight in February in the pessimistic report of Field Marshal von Rundstedt, the Germans in all of *Army Group B* amounted to the equivalent of only six and a half full divisions.[5]

During late February, no major changes occurred in the German order of battle opposite the First and Third Armies except those occasioned by Operation GRENADE and by the Third Army's attacks in the Eifel and the Saar-Moselle triangle. Hit by the U.S. VII Corps in GRENADE, the southernmost corps of Zangen's *Fifteenth Army,* Krueger's *LVIII Panzer Corps* (still minus the armor the corps name implied), had been pushed back, in some places behind the Erft River and Canal system. In continuing northeast after crossing the Erft, the VII Corps would strike the remnants of Koechling's *LXXXI Corps* and of *Corps Bayerlein,* the latter composed of what was left of the *9th* and *11th Panzer Divisions* after their piecemeal and futile commitment against GRENADE. From a boundary with the *Fifteenth Army* immediately south of Dueren, Manteuffel's *Fifth Panzer Army* stood with three corps behind the Roer River and its upper tributaries while awaiting the shift in zones with the *Fifteenth Army* that was to come around 1 March beginning with exchange of the two army commanders, Manteuffel and Zangen. Commanded at this point by General Felber, the *Seventh Army* stood behind the Pruem and Kyll Rivers, impotently awaiting continued strikes by the American Third Army.

In reaching the Erft River late on 27 February, General Collins's VII Corps had fulfilled its mission in Operation GRENADE. Yet because of the added assignment of guarding the Ninth Army's flank all the way to the Rhine, the corps

---

[3] FUSA Rpt of Opns, 23 Feb–8 May 45, p. 5; TUSA AAR, Feb–Mar 45.
[4] *Ibid.*

[5] For details, see above, ch. VIII.

would make no pause at the Erft except that necessary to expand the bridgeheads established on the 27th and to put in bridges. By the end of the first day of March, the corps was beyond the Erft complex astride the main highways leading from Juelich and Dueren to Cologne. (*Map IX*) Despite frantic efforts by German planes, usually operating singly, six class 40 bridges were in place across the Erft.

Resistance was at most places light, mainly mortar fire and shells from roving self-propelled guns. Only at Moedrath, lying between the river and the canal, was the defense determined. There, a local defense force, reinforced by stragglers from units of the *LVIII Panzer Corps*, held contingents of the 8th Division's 121st Infantry at bay for two days until a battalion of the 28th Infantry crossed the Erft farther north and came in on the German flank.[6]

The conspicuous feature of the terrain immediately beyond the Erft, west and southwest of Cologne, is a low, plateau-like ridge some twenty-five miles long, the Vorgebirge. The slopes of the ridge are broken by numerous lignite ("brown coal") surface mines with steep, clifflike sides. Abandoned mines have filled with water to create big lakes, often confining passage to the width of the roadways. Factories and heavily urbanized settlements abound. Northwest of Cologne, the country is generally flat and pastoral, dotted with villages and small towns, particularly along the major highways radiating from Cologne.

Because of the basic requirement of protecting the Ninth Army's flank, the VII Corps was to make its main effort

north of Cologne, leaving the city to be taken later. General Collins split responsibility for the assignment between General Rose's 3d Armored Division and the 99th Infantry Division (Maj. Gen. Walter E. Lauer).

The critical assignment went to the armor, beefed up during the opening phase of breaking out of the Erft bridgehead with attachment of the 99th Division's 395th Infantry. Rose was to strike north from the bridgehead to cut the Cologne–Muenchen-Gladbach highway at the town of Stommeln, thereby severing a vital artery leading into the Ninth Army's flank, then was to turn northeast to reach the Rhine at Worringen, eight miles downstream from Cologne. A clear intent was to split the enemy's sector swiftly and forestall reassembly and counterattack by remnants of the panzer divisions of *Corps Bayerlein*. Meanwhile, General Lauer's infantry was to clear the ground between Rose's armor and the Erft with help from the 4th Cavalry Group, while the 8th and 104th Divisions on the corps right wing fought their way through the lignite mining district in the direction of Cologne.[7]

When the armor attacked before daylight on 2 March, all thrusts were successful, but they failed to precipitate immediate breakout. Conglomerate German units, mainly from the *9th Panzer Division*, fought back stubbornly behind antitank ditches and obstacles that made up an extension of the third line of field fortifications the Germans had prepared behind the Roer. The gains here were insufficient to have any effect on the counterattack projected for that day by the· *11th Panzer Division* into the

---

[6] 8th Div AAR, Mar 45.

[7] VII Corps Opns Memo 163, 25 Feb 45; VII Corps FO 16, 1 Mar 45.

Ninth Army's flank; that failed to come off only because the Ninth Army's capture of Muenchen-Gladbach prevented the *Panzer Lehr Division* from launching its converging thrust.[8]

As night fell on 2 March, the armor had expanded the Erft bridgehead to a depth of three miles, which carried it beyond the northern reaches of the Vorgebirge into open country. From that point the Germans would be capable only of delaying actions, almost always in towns and villages since the flat terrain afforded few military features. Although reinforced from time to time by stragglers spilling across the Erft before the steamroller of the Ninth Army, *Corps Bayerlein* had no depth. Conglomerate forces usually including a few tanks or self-propelled guns would have to gauge their defense carefully to keep from being overrun in one village lest there be nothing left to defend the next one.

That fact was demonstrated early on 3 March when two task forces of Combat Command Hickey moved before dawn to take the Germans by surprise in two villages southwest of Stommeln.[9] So complete was the surprise in the first village that the attacking armored infantrymen incurred not a single casualty. At both villages the Germans were annihilated, leaving nobody to a final village still remaining short of Stommeln, the division's intermediate objective.

Combat Command Howze moved against Stommeln from three sides. Despite an extensive antitank minefield covered by a relatively strong concen-

tration of antitank guns, the columns converged on the town in late afternoon. Aided by P–47 air strikes against the antitank defenses, they cleared the last resistance by nightfall. General Rose meanwhile sent a column from his reserve, Combat Command Boudinot, beyond Stommeln to a village just four miles from the Rhine. Only one more town lay between the armor and the final objective of Worringen.

The 99th Division had made comparable progress on the left, cutting the Cologne–Muenchen-Gladbach highway at several points late on 3 March. Nor was success confined to the left wing of the corps. Moving toward Cologne astride the Aachen-Cologne highway and the adjacent right-of-way of the uncompleted Aachen-Cologne autobahn, the 104th Division made relatively short but nevertheless telling gains.[10] So did the 8th Division, advancing astride the Dueren-Cologne highway. Bearing the additional responsibility of protecting the open right flank of the corps, the 8th Division had the slower going but still took the second row of towns beyond the Erft and gained a firm hold on western slopes of the Vorgebirge. The 104th Division cleared a big forest astride the Aachen-Cologne highway and crossed the crest of the Vorgebirge.

Even though the 3d Armored Division still had several miles to go to reach the Rhine, the VII Corps commander, Gen-

---

[8] MS # B-202 (Mellenthin). See above, ch. IX.
[9] The 3d Armored Division usually labeled its combat commands after their commanders.

[10] As the 104th Division prepared to attack before daylight on 2 March, a German shell struck the command post of the 2d Battalion, 414th Infantry, killing the battalion commander, Lt. Col. Joseph M. Cummins, Jr., and two visiting officers, Col. Anthony J. Touart, 414th Infantry commander, and Col. George A. Smith, Jr., assistant division commander. See Hoegh and Doyle, *Timberwolf Tracks*, p. 257.

eral Collins, deemed it time to shift emphasis from the northward thrust to capturing Cologne. The armored division's advance already had split *Corps Bayerlein* from Koechling's *LXXXI Corps,* leaving the remnants of the latter force as the only obstacle to taking Cologne. For two days the Ninth Army's right flank had been anchored on the Rhine at Neuss, so that any threat remaining from the *11th Panzer Division* was minimal. Fighter pilots throughout the day had reported Germans scurrying across the Rhine on ferries and small craft, and more than 1,800 prisoners had entered VII Corps cages.

Late on 3 March Collins told General Rose to continue to the Rhine at Worringen the next day but at the same time to divert a force southeast against Cologne. The attached 395th Infantry was to return to the 99th Division to enable the infantry division with the help of the 4th Cavalry Group to clear all ground northwest of Worringen.[11]

Not waiting for a new day before continuing to the Rhine, patrols of the 3d Armored's 83d Reconnaissance Battalion in early evening of 3 March determined that the one town remaining short of Worringen on the Rhine was stoutly defended. Declining to give battle, the reconnaissance battalion turned north over back roads, bypassed the town, and in the process captured an artillery battery and 300 surprised Germans. Before daylight a 4-man patrol led by 1st Lt. Charles E. Coates reached the Rhine north of Worringen. A task force of Combat Command Boudinot then moved up the main road at dawn, cleared the defended town, repulsed a

counterattack by 200 infantry supported by five tanks, and drove on to Worringen and the river.

The 99th Division had continued to advance on the left in a manner indicating that the threat from what was left of *Corps Bayerlein* was empty. Unknown to the Americans, the splitting of *Corps Bayerlein* and the *LXXXI Corps* had resulted in the paper transfer of the tattered *9th Panzer Division* to the *LXXXI Corps,* leaving only a *Kampfgruppe* of the *11th Panzer Division* and stragglers of the *59th Infantry Division* available to Bayerlein. These had prepared hasty defenses facing northwest toward the Ninth Army, so that the 99th Division was free to come in swiftly from flank and rear. In such a situation, Bayerlein, his staff, and the *11th Panzer Division* were thinking less of fighting than of escaping across the Rhine.[12]

Despite Hitler's refusal of every request to withdraw, most supporting units by evening of 3 March had already crossed the river, and the *11th Panzer Division* held only a small bridgehead on the west bank north of Worringen. Lacking authority to withdraw, General Bayerlein saw the little bridgehead as "the end of the world."[13] On 5 March approval finally came to pull back. Through the day rear guards fought hard to hold open two ferry sites; and as night came, the last contingents of *Corps Bayerlein* pushed out into the stream.

On this same day, 5 March, the attack of the VII Corps against Cologne got going in earnest. The framework upon which the thin fabric of defense of Germany's fourth largest city was hung was

---

[11] VII Corps Opns Memo 167, 3 Mar 45.

[12] MS # B-053 (Bayerlein).
[13] *Ibid.*

THE DEMOLISHED HOHENZOLLERN BRIDGE *at Cologne with cathedral in the background.*

General Koechling's *LXXXI Corps,* now heading the staffs and the few other remains of the *9th Panzer, 363d Volks Grenadier,* and *3d Panzer Grenadier Divisions.* Koechling was to use what was left of those three units—the equivalent of two weak regiments—to defend a so-called outer ring in the city's suburbs, while policemen, firemen, and anybody else who could pull the trigger of a rifle fought from an inner ring deep within the city. Among the defenders of the inner ring were the *Volkssturm,* a levy of old men and youths Hitler had or-

dered to rally to the last-ditch defense of the Reich.[14]

As the 3rd Armored, 104th, and 8th Divisions drove toward Cologne on 5 March, resistance was strongest in the north, where General Rose's armor faced the seemingly ineradicable *9th Panzer Division,* and in the south where the 8th Division at the end of the day still was two miles short of the city limits. The relatively slow progress of the 8th Division reflected not only the

---

[14] MS # B-202 (Mellenthin).

difficulties of attacking through the coal-mining district but also the fact that the division was striking the north flank of the *LVIII Panzer Corps.*

The armor nevertheless broke into Cologne soon after daylight, to be followed two hours later by the 104th Division from the west. In a precursor of what was to come as Allied armies fanned out all across Germany, the stiffest fight developed around an airfield where the Germans turned sixteen stationary 88-mm. antiaircraft guns against the tanks of Combat Command Hickey. The tanks finally eliminated the guns in smoke-screened cavalrylike charge. Almost all resistance by the *9th Panzer Division* collapsed a short while later when the division commander, Generalmajor Harald Freiherr von Elverfeldt, was killed.[15]

As evening approached, the First Army commander, General Hodges, shifted the southern boundary of the VII Corps to the southeast to provide room for the 8th Division to drive to the Rhine south of Cologne and cut the enemy's last landward escape route.[16] The next day, 6 March, the 3d Armored drove quickly through the heart of the city, a wasteland from long years of aerial bombardment, and reached the Hohenzollern bridge, only to find a 1200-foot gap blown in it. Close by amid the sea of ruins stood the stately Cologne cathedral, damaged but basically intact.

By noon of 7 March almost all of Cologne had been cleared, despite curious crowds of civilians jamming the rubble-strewn streets. No road or rail crossing of the Rhine remained. A bat-talion of the 8th Division's 28th Infantry meanwhile reached the river south of Cologne. For the third time in less than a fortnight, the enemy's forces were split. The remnants of the *LVIII Panzer Corps,* along with contingents of the *3d Panzer Grenadier Division,* which had fallen back southward away from Cologne, formed a last-ditch defense across an eastward bend of the Rhine but began to evacuate the position early the next morning.[17]

General Collins and his VII Corps had completed their assigned role in the drive to the Rhine in exactly two weeks, at once a spearhead for the First Army and protection for the flank of the Ninth Army. In operations begun on 25 February, only two days after the VII Corps had assaulted the Roer River line, other parts of the First Army meanwhile had joined the race to the Rhine.

Toward Bonn and Remagen

The operations had begun with limited goals, though with the certainty that they later would be expanded. The plan was to uncover the line of the upper Roer, protect Collins's VII Corps during its added assignment beyond the Erft, and at the same time gain a leg on the drive to the Rhine.

General Hodges directed General Millikin's III Corps, which had joined the First Army in the reorganization that followed halting of the main effort in the Eifel, to cross the Roer south of Dueren and reach the Erft River northward from the road center of Euskirchen. When the VII Corps turned to take

---

[15] *Ibid.*
[16] VII Corps G–3 Jnl, 5 Mar 45.

[17] MSS # B–202 (Mellenthin); # B–080 (Langhaeuser); # B–098, *353d Infantry Division,* 2–22 March 1945 (Oberst Kurt Hummel, CG).

Cologne, the III Corps was to cross the Erft and drive southeast to converge with the Third Army "in the Ahrweiler area," the first basic objective of Bradley's Operation LUMBERJACK. The two corps then were to clear the west bank of the Rhine from the Ahr River to Cologne. General Huebner's V Corps at the same time was to advance its left wing as far as Euskirchen to protect the south flank of the III Corps and to "prepare for further advance to the east." [18]

Confronted with the swollen, closely confined waters of the Roer tumbling headlong through the gorge upstream from Dueren, General Hodges devised a crossing plan that avoided another frontal joust with the river. He directed a division of the III Corps to use bridges of the VII Corps at Dueren, then attack south to clear bridge sites upstream. Each division in the corps in turn was to use the neighboring division's bridges, repeating the attack to the south to clear additional bridge sites. A division of the V Corps finally was to use bridges of the III Corps to get beyond the waters of the Roer reservoirs.[19]

Two battalions of the 1st Division started the maneuver in midmorning of 25 February, a few hours after the 8th Division announced a footbridge and a Bailey bridge available at Dueren. (*See Map IX, inset.*) Crossing in the sector of the adjacent division not only avoided frontal attack across the Roer, it also enabled attached tanks and tank destroyers to cross with the infantry and lend weight to the drive upstream that took the Germans of the *353d Infantry Division* of Krueger's *LVIII Panzer Corps*

GENERAL MILLIKIN

in flank. At noon one of the infantry battalions attacked the Roer town of Kreuzau and made such progress that forty minutes later engineer units that had been waiting impatiently in the wings west of the river began building a footbridge within the 1st Division's sector.

As night came on 25 February, the 1st Division's bridgehead already was firmly established without the loss of a man in the actual crossing of the river. The infantry battalions of two regiments were across, and forward positions were as much as a mile and a half beyond the river.

The next day, 26 February, as the 1st Division expanded its bridgehead with emphasis on gaining more of the east bank of the Roer upstream to the south, engineers put in a Bailey bridge that

---

[18] FUSA Rpt of Opns, 23 Feb–8 May 45, p. 12.
[19] Sylvan Diary, entry of 24 Feb 45.

enabled the 9th Division's 39th Infantry to repeat the river crossing maneuver in late afternoon. Before daylight on 27 February, men of the 9th Division attacked south to clear their own bridge sites at Nideggen, picturesquely located on the rim of the Cologne plain overlooking the gorge of the Roer and the road leading back to Schmidt and the Roer dams. Resistance was firmer than that faced by the 1st Division, mainly because the 9th Division had crossed into the sector of General Puechler's *LXXIV Corps* and encountered a relatively battle-worthy unit, the *3d Parachute Division*. Having undergone a hasty reorganization following the Ardennes counteroffensive, the division contained its full complement of three parachute regiments, though all were understrength.[20]

The 78th Division's 311th Infantry crossed the Roer on the last day of February through the 9th Division's sector and immediately attacked to the south, covering more than a mile against the *272d Volks Grenadier Division*. This completed the river-crossing maneuver in the III Corps, but as the 78th Division created its own bridgehead plans proceeded for the V Corps to follow a similar procedure for getting beyond the Roer reservoirs.

The III Corps commander, General Millikin, had moved quickly to get his armor into the fight as soon as the inhospitable terrain of the Eifel lay behind. CCB of the 9th Armored Division (Maj. Gen. John W. Leonard) was to attack east between the 1st and 9th Divisions to reach the Erft several miles downstream

from Euskirchen, while CCA was to move south and enter the zone of the 78th Division, then turn east, oriented generally toward Euskirchen. CCA was to be joined later by the rest of the armored division operating in a "zone of advance" within the sector of the late-running 78th Division. The 14th Cavalry Group was to follow CCA and protect the south flank of the corps.[21]

Attacking in early afternoon of 28 February, CCB before daylight the next morning came abreast of the most advanced battalions of the 1st Division along the Neffel Creek, half the 15-mile distance from Roer to Erft. Beginning its attack a day later on 1 March, CCA smacked almost immediately into a defensive position lying behind the upper reaches of the Neffel Creek and barring the way to the village of Wollersheim. Manned by troops of the *3d Parachute Division*, the position was reinforced by several tanks and assault guns.[22] When an attack by dismounted armored infantrymen failed to carry it, CCA held up for the night to await arrival the next morning of an infantry battalion from the 78th Division.

On the second day of March genuine exploitation developed all along the front of the III Corps. A double envelopment by CCA's 52d Armored Infantry Battalion and an attached battalion of the 310th Infantry carried the sticky position at Wollersheim, while the 309th Infantry put the 78th Division into the eastward drive and came almost abreast of CCA. Those two advances brought an end to solid defense by the enemy's *3d Parachute Division*. Already the *353d*

---

[20] III Corps AAR, Feb 45; MS # B–118, *LXXIV Corps*, 2 October 1944–23 March 1945 (General der Infanterie Karl Puechler).

[21] III Corps Opnl Dir # 4, 28 Feb 45.
[22] III Corps AAR, Mar 45; MS # B–118 (Puechler).

Infantry Division in the north and the *272d Volks Grenadier Division,* the latter trying to prevent expansion of the 78th Division's bridgehead to the south, were reduced to executing isolated delaying actions.

The commander of the *LXXIV Corps,* General Puechler, had. nothing left to use in the fight except a weak *Kampfgruppe* of the *62d Volks Grenadier Division,* which had been reorganizing behind the line when the American attack began. He sent that force to the north to try to maintain contact with the faltering *LVIII Panzer Corps,* but so weak was the *Kampfgruppe* that the attacking American troops hardly noticed its presence.[23]

The 1st Division on the 2d got within three miles of the Erft, while in the center, the 9th Armored's CCB crossed the river along the Euskirchen-Cologne highway. Following in the wake of CCB, one regiment of the 9th Division approached within two miles of the Erft.

To many a soldier in the III Corps, this day and those immediately following could be summed up in two words: mud and fatigue. As light snow flurries ended in midmorning, a warm sun triggered a latent springtime in the soil and turned roads and fields into clinging mud. The mud and daytime attacks alone would have been enough to produce fatigue, but hardly was there a commander who did not continue to push his men through much of the night in order to overcome the advantage that flat, open fields afforded the enemy in observation.

At command levels, 2 March and the three days following brought preoccupation with boundary changes and juggling of units as General Bradley's original plan for clearing the west bank of the Rhine underwent revision. Prompted by the relative ease with which Millikin's III Corps was advancing, the change limited responsibility of Collins's VII Corps to the city of Cologne while the III Corps was to clear the west bank of the Rhine throughout the rest of the First Army's zone from Cologne to the Ahr River. At the same time the III Corps retained responsibility for crossing the Ahr and establishing contact with the Third Army.[24]

The first shift came on 2 March when General Millikin transferred the 14th Cavalry Group to his north flank for attachment to the 1st Division in anticipation of broadening the 1st Division's sector. The boundary change became effective the next day, 3 March, as the 26th Infantry jumped the Erft and began to climb the Vorgebirge, southwest of Cologne, seven miles from the Rhine. While the 9th Armored's CCB held in place on the Erft, awaiting relief by units of the 1st Division, CCA took the ancient walled town of Zuelpich against little more than a show of resistance. At the end of the day General Millikin assigned the armor a specific zone between the 9th and 78th Divisions.

Despite the importance Bradley and the First Army's General Hodges attached to gaining bridgeheads over the Ahr River for linkup with the Third Army, it was obvious from orders issued by Millikin and his division commanders that the fabled Rhine was the more ir-

---

[23] III Corps AAR, Mar 45; MS # B-118 (Puechler).

[24] 12th AGp Ltr of Instrs 16, 3 Mar 45, 12th AGp Rpt of Opns, vol. V.

resistible attraction.[25] The 1st Division was to reach the river north of Bonn, the 9th Division to take Bonn, and one column of the 9th Armored to come up to the Rhine midway between Bonn and the Ahr. Only one column of the armored division, protected on the south flank by the 78th Division operating in a confined sector, was directed toward the Ahr.

The emphasis on the Rhine around Bonn coincided with expectations of the German army group commander, Field Marshal Model. Believing the main effort of the III Corps to be directed at Bonn, Model began to make ambitious but futile plans to reinforce the city with the *11th Panzer Division* once that division had withdrawn from the triangle between Erft and Rhine north of Cologne, and even to counterattack with the panzer division.[26]

The *Fifteenth Army* commander, General von Zangen, responsible now for this sector, saw it another way. In driving to the Erft, Zangen might note, the III Corps had cleared the cup of a funnel delineated on one side by the Eifel, on the other by the Vorgebirge. The obvious move at this point, Zangen believed, was a drive down the spout of the funnel from Euskirchen southeast of Rheinbach and the Ahr River, thence along the north bank of the Ahr to the Rhine at Sinzig and the nearby town of Remagen.

The town of Remagen was of particular importance because of the location there of a railroad bridge that was being covered with a plank flooring for motor

traffic to provide a vital supply artery for the *Fifteenth Army*. To block the way to Remagen, Zangen asked permission to withdraw his *LXVI* and *LXVII Corps* from the Eifel, where they faced entrapment even if they succeeded in the apparently impossible task of holding their West Wall positions. To this Model said no. The two corps were to continue to hold in conformity with Hitler's longstanding orders to relinquish no portion of the West Wall without a fight. If forced back, Puechler's *LXXIV Corps* was to gravitate toward Bonn.[27]

To Zangen and any other German commander on the scene, probably including Model himself, the absurdity of further attempts to hold west of the Rhine was all too apparent. The only hope was quick withdrawal to save as much as possible to fight another day on the east bank.[28]

Puechler's *LXXIV Corps* provided an obvious case in point. What was left of the corps was incapable of a real fight for even such an important objective as Euskirchen, a road center yielded after only "light resistance" to the 9th Armored Division's CCA on 4 March. Seldom could counterattacks be mounted in greater than company strength and usually they had no artillery support. Furthermore, the corps was split as continued advances by the 78th Division on the south wing of the III Corps forced back the *272d Volks Grenadier Division* onto the neighboring *LXVII Corps*. The split became irreparable when on 3 March the 2d

---

[25] Even though the First Army G–3 had made it clear otherwise. See Memo, sub: Resume of Instructions From General Thorson, G–3 First U.S. Army, 28 Feb 45, III Corps G–3 Jnl file, 28 Feb–1 Mar 45.

[26] MS # B–828 (Zangen).

[27] *Ibid.*

[28] This theme runs through all German manuscripts for the period. Even allowing for postwar extenuation, it can hardly be questioned except in degree.

Infantry Division of the V Corps crossed the 78th Division's Roer bridges and headed south through the Eifel toward Gemuend at the head of the Roer reservoir system.[29]

The boundary adjustments on the American side continued on 5 March when General Hodges made the change that allowed the 8th Division of the VII Corps to drive to the Rhine south of Cologne. Late the same evening Hodges also adjusted the boundary between the III and V Corps, turning it distinctly southeast to a point on the Ahr upstream from Ahrweiler, thereby providing the III Corps over ten miles of frontage on the Ahr.

Those two moves eliminated any lingering misconception about the importance Bradley and Hodges attached to crossing the Ahr River. Early the next day General Millikin shifted all his division objectives to the southeast—the 1st Division to Bonn, the 9th Division to Bad Godesberg, the 9th Armored Division to Remagen and the Ahr from Sinzig to Bad Neuenahr, and the 78th Division to Ahrweiler. When the 9th Armored's G–3, Lt. Col. John S. Growdon, telephoned to ask whether the armor should continue to make its main effort toward the Rhine, the III Corps G–3, Col. Harry C. Mewshaw, replied unequivocally that the Rhine was of secondary importance. The main goal, he said, was "to seize towns and crossings over the Ahr River." [30]

Patton in the Eifel

The force that was to link with troops of the First Army along the Ahr, Patton's

Third Army, had made a start on the assignment in late February and the first days of March with the "probing attacks" that captured Trier and advanced the VIII Corps to the Pruem River and the XII Corps to the Kyll. The decision General Patton faced then—whether to turn southeast and envelop the Saar industrial area or to head through the Eifel to the Rhine—the army group commander, General Bradley, already had made for him. The goal was the Rhine.

On the assumption that this job would be soon done, Patton planned a secondary attack to set the stage for clearing the Saar. To General Walker's XX Corps, he assigned a narrow one-division zone north of the Moselle running from the Kyll to one of the big northward loops of the Moselle, some thirty-six miles downstream from Trier. The zone enclosed a shallow depression lying between the high ground of the Mosel Berge, which parallels the Moselle, and the main Eifel massif. Clearing it would provide access to the transverse valley leading to the Moselle at the picturesque wine center of Bernkastel and thence into the heart of the Saarland.[31]

To General Bradley's protest that the Third Army was spreading its forces too thin and would be unable to make a "power drive" to the Rhine, Patton replied that the terrain and the roadnet in the Eifel permitted a power drive by no more than two divisions in any case.[32] The VIII and XII Corps faced the Hohe Eifel, the high or volcanic Eifel, a region even more rugged in places than the

---

[29] Quotation is from III Corps AAR, Mar 45.
[30] III Corps G–3 Jnl file, 6–7 Mar 45.

[31] TUSA Opnl Dir, 3 Mar 45; XX Corps AAR, Mar 45. For further mention of this attack, see below, ch. XII.
[32] Patton, *War As I Knew It,* p. 252.

western reaches of the Eifel that the corps already had conquered. There, in an effort to overcome the weird convolutions of the land, the limited roads generally follow the low ground along the stream beds, somehow eventually ending up at the Ahr, the Rhine, or the Moselle. If the Third Army in this kind of terrain was to hope to keep pace with the First Army on the open Cologne plain, daring would have to be a major part of of the plan.

When the Third Army's long-term ally, the XIX Tactical Air Command, reported that the enemy already showed evidence of withdrawing and probably would limit his stands to blocking positions along the roads, that was all Patton needed. He ordered that, once the VIII and XII Corps had established bridgeheads over the Kyll, an armored division of each corps was to thrust rapidly northeastward along the better roads without regard to the wooded heights in between. Artillery and fighter-bombers were to take care of the high ground until motorized infantry could follow to secure the gains.[33]

Since General Bradley's plan for Operation LUMBERJACK had put the burden of linking the First and Third Armies along the Ahr River on the First Army, General Patton was free to think primarily in terms of reaching the Rhine. He directed Middleton's VIII Corps to gain the river around Brohl, midway between the Ahr and the ancient Rhine town of Andernach, while the XII Corps (commanded again by General Eddy after return from a brief leave) came up to the river at Andernach.

When Patton's order came, the VIII Corps stood generally along the Pruem River, still some ten miles short of the Kyll. As a corollary to successful clearing of the Vianden bulge, the 6th Cavalry Group and the 6th Armored Division had made substantial advances beyond the Pruem, but they were in the south of the corps zone, relatively far from the main roads leading to the Rhine at Brohl. Besides, the 6th Armored was earmarked for early transfer to the SHAEF reserve, that irritating outgrowth of the Ardennes counteroffensive that seemed constantly to be plaguing some unit of the Third Army. Thus Middleton ordered the 4th Division at the town of Pruem to enlarge its bridgehead over the Pruem River, whereupon the 11th Armored Division was to pass through and strike due east to jump the Kyll, then strike northeast to the Rhine. The 4th Division was to follow to mop up, the 87th Division was to protect the north flank, and the 90th Division, taking the place of the 6th Armored, was to advance on the south wing.[34]

With units of the XII Corps already up to the Kyll, General Eddy gave the job of forging a bridgehead to an infantry division, the 5th; then the 4th Armored Division was to pass through to drive northeast to Andernach. The 5th Division and the 80th were to follow, while the 76th Division protected the right flank.[35]

On the enemy side, it was an understatement to say that German commanders viewed the pending Third Army offensive with anxiety, since the February attacks in the Eifel already had

[33] XIX TAC AAR, Mar 45.

[34] VIII Corps Opnl Memos 26 and 27, 1 and 2 Mar 45; VIII Corps G–3 Jnl file, 1–3 Mar 45.
[35] XII Corps Opns Dirs 83 and 84, 1 and 2 Mar 45.

severely lacerated General Felber's *Seventh Army*. How long the *Seventh Army* could hold in the Eifel depended entirely on how soon and how vigorously the Americans attacked.

A breakthrough across the Kyll could prove fatal, not only to the *Seventh Army* itself but to the two corps (*LXVI* and *LXVII*) forming the center and south wing of the *Fifteenth Army* and to the entire *First Army,* the north wing of Hausser's *Army Group G*. Should the First and Third U.S. Armies quickly join along the west bank of the Rhine, the two corps of the *Fifteenth Army* would be encircled. In the process, the Third Army's clearing of the north bank of the Moselle would expose from the rear the West Wall pillboxes in the Saarland, still held by the *First Army*.

A partial solution, as the *Seventh Army*'s General Felber saw it, was for the *Seventh Army* to withdraw from the Eifel and protect *Army Group G*'s rear by defending the line of the Moselle; but in view of Hitler's continuing stand-fast orders, nobody higher up the ladder of command took the proposal seriously. The only change made was to transfer the faltering *Seventh Army* on 2 March from Model's *Army Group B* to Hausser's *Army Group G*. By vesting control in the army group headquarters that had most to lose should the *Seventh Army* collapse, the change inferred some strengthening of the *Seventh Army* by *Army Group G*. In reality, it merely shifted from one army group headquarters to another the dolorous task of presiding over the *Seventh Army*'s agony.

From confluence of the Kyll and the Moselle near Trier to a point near Pruem, the *Seventh Army*'s zone covered some thirty-five miles. The most seriously

threatened part, General Felber believed, was the center opposite Bitburg, for there stood the U.S. 4th Armored Division, a unit looked upon with considerable respect by German commanders.

With this in mind, Felber shifted to the sector headquarters of the *XIII Corps* on the premise that the corps commander, General von Oriola, having only recently arrived at the front, would be steadier under the coming crisis than would General von Rothkirch, commander of the *LIII Corps,* who for weeks had been watching his command disintegrate. Thus the new lineup of corps from north to south was the *LIII Corps* (Rothkirch) near Pruem, the *XIII Corps* (Oriola) opposite Bitburg, and the *LXXX Corps* (Beyer) between Bitburg and the Moselle.

The *Seventh Army* contained, nominally, ten divisions, but only two—remnants of the *2d Panzer Division* east of Bitburg and the *246th Volks Grenadier Division,* the latter hurried down from what was now the *Fifteenth Army*'s sector too late to save Bitburg—could muster much more than a small *Kampfgruppe*. Both divisions were to remain with the *XIII Corps* in keeping with the theory that Patton's main thrust would be made there with the 4th Armored Division. Because the attack by the U.S. VIII Corps would spill over the *Seventh Army*'s northern boundary against the extreme south wing of the *Fifteenth Army,* another division with some creditable fighting power remaining, the *5th Parachute Division* of the *LXVI Corps* (Lucht), also would be involved. Neither the *Seventh Army* nor the *Fifteenth Army* had any reserves, although the *Seventh* did possess a separate tank battalion with some ten to fifteen Tiger tanks. This battalion General Felber wanted to send to his center opposite Bitburg, but he would still be searching for sufficient gasoline to move the tanks from a field repair shop in the sector of the *LIII Corps* when the American attack began.[36]

Because of the requirement to get from the Pruem River to the Kyll, General Middleton's VIII Corps began to attack first. Indeed, since the south wing of the corps had never stopped attacking after clearing the Vianden bulge and since the XX Corps and the 76th Division of the XII Corps still were giving the *coup de grâce* to Trier as the month of March opened, no real pause developed between the February probing attacks and the March offensive.

For the 4th Infantry Division, enlarging its minuscule bridgehead over the Pruem to enable the 11th Armored Division to pass through, the task was no pushover, primarily because of the presence of the enemy's *5th Parachute Division*. Given some respite since the American drive on Pruem had bogged down on 10 February, the Germans defended from well-organized positions and employed unusually large numbers of machine guns. So determined was the resistance that General Middleton at one point postponed the target date for the armored exploitation twenty-four hours, although subsequent gains prompted him to reinstate it for the original date of 3 March. Nor was stanch resistance confined to the sector of the 4th Division. Protecting the corps left flank by re-

ducing West Wall pillboxes on the Schnee Eifel ridge, the 87th Division found that the fortifications still put considerable starch into the defense.

Passing through the infantry shortly after midday on 3 March, Combat Command B of the 11th Armored Division attacked to seize crossings of the Kyll in a big bend of the river north of Gerolstein, some eleven miles northeast of Pruem. Delayed by confusion in the passage of lines, the armor failed to advance the first afternoon as much as two miles. It was nevertheless apparent that the Germans could muster no real strength short of the Kyll once the tanks got rolling. By late afternoon the next day, 4 March, the combat command overlooked the Kyll from heights a mile southwest of Gerolstein, but patrols sent down to the river drew intense small arms fire from both the east bank and from high ground in the bend of the river. Antitank and artillery fire also rained from the east bank in disturbing volume.

Having followed the path of least resistance, the armor had come up to the Kyll south of its intended crossing site at a point where troops trying to cross would be exposed to fire not only from dominating ground beyond the river but from the big bend as well. Impressed both by the terrain and the amount of German fire and apparently reluctant to risk involving the armor in what could be a time-consuming river-crossing operation, the division commander, General Kilburn, asked for infantry help. While the 4th Division cleared the high ground in the bend of the Kyll, Kilburn suggested, CCB might swing to the north and cross the river north of the bend.

[36] German material comes primarily from MSS # B–831 (Felber); # B–828 (Zangen); # B–123 (Gersdorff); and # B–797, *LIII Corps,* 27 February –10 March 1945 (Oberst Werner Bodenstein, Opns Officer *LIII Corps*).

Although the corps commander, General Middleton, approved, the maneuver took time, particularly when determined Germans, again mainly from the *5th Parachute Division,* kept a regiment of the 4th Division out of the bend in the river through much of 5 March. By 6 March, the fourth day after passing through the 4th Division, CCB did get some troops across the Kyll, but only armored infantry supported by a smattering of tanks and tank destroyers that managed to cross at a ford before the river bed gave way.

Even with a foothold already established on the east bank, General Kilburn remained reluctant to commit his armor to the river crossing operation. Again he prevailed on General Middleton for permission to use infantry of the 4th Division. Only after the infantrymen had expanded CCB's foothold were the tanks and tank destroyers to renew the drive toward the Rhine.

While the armor dallied, less conservative forces elsewhere in the VIII Corps rapidly rewrote the entire script for crossing the Kyll. Assigned to protect the left flank of the corps, the 87th Division went a step further, overtook the armored spearhead, and jumped the Kyll just after midday of the 6th on a bridge captured intact. The 90th Division, commanded now by Brig. Gen. Herbert L. Earnest and committed on 2 March on the corps south wing to relieve the 6th Armored Division, scored an even more striking advance. At the point on the Kyll southwest of Gerolstein that General Kilburn earlier had spurned as a crossing site, a task force organized around the division reconnaissance troop and two attached medium tank companies jumped the river before daylight

on 6 March. At the same time, men of the 359th Infantry crossed a few hundred yards to the south. By late afternoon contingents of the 90th Division had taken Gerolstein and established a bridgehead over a mile and a half deep and some two and a half miles wide.

General Middleton in early evening ordered General Kilburn to alert a second combat command, CCA, to cross the Kyll through the 90th Division's bridgehead. In the end, CCB also would backtrack and use the 90th Division's crossing site.

Just before daylight on 7 March, engineers of the 90th Division—having worked with the aid of searchlights—opened a Bailey bridge over the Kyll. In midmorning, CCA began to cross. The 11th Armored Division at last might get started in earnest on an exploitation that was to have proceeded without interruption beginning five days earlier. Yet Kilburn's men would have to hurry if again they were not to be overtaken by events precipitated by more audacious units, for to the south, opposite Bitburg, General Eddy's XII Corps had struck in a manner not to be denied.

Veterans of many a river-crossing operation, infantrymen of the 5th Division sent patrols across the Kyll before daylight on 3 March, then threw in footbridges to allow the bulk of two battalions to cross near Metterich, due east of Bitburg. Fanning out to the high ground, the infantry cleared Metterich before nightfall, while engineers put in a vehicular bridge before daylight on the 4th. Except against the crossings themselves, the Germans reacted strongly, at one point launching a determined counterattack supported by three tanks, apparently from the *2d Panzer Division,* but to no avail. By dark on 4 March, the bridgehead was ready for exploitation. It was only a question of when General Patton chose to turn the 4th Armored Division loose.

Patton, Eddy, and the armored division commander, General Gaffey, had only one real concern: weather. Days of alternating rain and rapidly melting snow, freeze and thaw, already had wreaked havoc on the generally poor roads of the Eifel, and continued precipitation could severely crimp the plan for the armor to drive boldly forward on the roads, leaving the ground in between to air and artillery. Yet weather alone was hardly sufficient reason to delay the exploitation. The armor got set to move at daylight the next day, 5 March.

General Gaffey's orders were explicit. Passing through the 5th Division's bridgehead, two combat commands were to drive north for some eight miles over parallel roads in rear of the enemy's Kyll River defenses. Having sliced the underpinnings from much of the *XIII Corps* and part of the *LIII Corps,* the armor was to swerve northeast near the village of Oberstadtfeld (five and a half miles southeast of Gerolstein) and head for the Rhine near Andernach, there to seize any bridges that might still stand.[37]

Combat Command B in the lead quickly began to roll. As the tanks approached the first village north of the 5th Division's forward line, artillery and rocket fire ranged near the column; but the tanks roared ahead. A contingent of Germans in the village threw hands high in surrender. Although rain, snow flurries, and overcast denied any tactical air

support, the armor quickly picked up speed. The combat command's reports of the day's advance soon began to read like a bus or railroad timetable—0845: Orsfeld; 1135: Steinborn; 1350: Meisburg; and at the end of the day: Weidenbach, twelve miles northeast of the bridge over which the armor had crossed the Kyll.

In one day CCB's tankers had broken through the north wing of Oriola's *XIII Corps,* plunged deep into the south wing of Rothkirch's *LIII Corps,* and sent over a thousand Germans straggling back to prisoner-of-war compounds. The fighting at day's end at Weidenbach emerged from a desperate effort by General von Rothkirch to delay the advance with the only reserve he could assemble, a *Nebelwerfer* brigade. Draining the last drops of fuel from command cars and other vehicles, Rothkirch managed also to send toward Weidenbach a few of the Tiger tanks that had been languishing in a repair shop, but they failed to arrive during the night and were destined to be shot up individually in the next day's fighting.

Rothkirch also ordered the *340th Volks Grenadier Division,* continuing to hold positions along the Kyll west of the American penetration, to escape during the night along a secondary road still open north of Weidenbach. Counting on the Americans' calling off the war during the night, Rothkirch intended the *340th* to establish a blocking position at Oberstadtfeld, but hours before dawn on the 6th, the American combat command was on the move again. The tanks entered Oberstadtfeld long before the men of the *340th* arrived, forcing the Germans to abandon all vehicles and artillery and to try to escape by infiltrating northeast-

---

[37] XII Corps FO 15, 2 Mar 45; 4th Armored Div FO 12, 3 Mar 45.

ward across the tail of the American column.[38]

Unlike CCB, the 4th Armored's CCA found the going slow on the first day, 5 March, primarily because CCA had been relegated to secondary roads farther east. Boggy from alternate freeze and thaw, the roads and a demolished bridge over a creek at the village of Oberkail held the day's advance to a few miles. Hardly had the tankers warmed their motors the next morning, 6 March, when continuing reports of rapid gains by CCB prompted General Gaffey to order CCA to follow in the other command's wake on the main highway, leaving the secondary roads to the 5th Division.

The infantry division now was experiencing real problems—not so much from the enemy as from the complexities of traffic on narrow, poorly surfaced, winding roads. Until all vehicles of the armored division could clear the bridgehead, the armor had priority; yet the infantrymen also were under orders to move swiftly lest the armor get too far beyond reach of infantry support. With great distances hampering radio communications and the roads too congested for motor messengers, orders to forward units of the 5th Division had to be dropped from liaison planes.

The weather on 6 March again was so bad—rain and fog—that tactical aircraft for the second day could provide no help; but the armor scarcely needed it, for the Germans were in a state of confusion. Even though the tankers actually cleared the enemy from little more than the road and shoulders, preattack concern that the Germans might continue to defend from woods and adjacent high ground failed to materialize. Germans in great bunches, sometime numbering in the hundreds, streamed from hills, woods, and villages to surrender.

At one point, so many surrendering Germans were clustered about a column of tanks of the 37th Tank Battalion that the LIII Corps commander, General von Rothkirch, driving past in his command car, assumed it was a German formation. Too late he saw what was actually happening.

"Where do you think you're going?" asked 1st Lt. Joe Liese of the 37th Tank Battalion's Company B.

"It looks like," Rothkirch replied, not without a touch of irony, "I'm going to the American rear." [39]

Monitoring the American radio net, German intelligence quickly picked up the news of Rothkirch's capture and the extent of CCB's penetration. Apparently with approval of OB WEST, Model at Army Group B tacitly acknowledged the fact that the LIII Corps had been cut off from the rest of the Seventh Army by subordinating the corps to Zangen's Fifteenth Army, whose LXVI and LXVII Corps still held portions of the West Wall opposite the U.S. V Corps. Model also ordered forward a new commander for the LIII Corps, Generalmajor Walther Botsch, who earlier had been charged with preparing defenses for a bridgehead to be held at Bonn and Remagen. Even though troops of the American First Army were fast bearing down on both those towns, so urgent did Model consider the need for a new commander of the LIII Corps that he refused

---

[38] MS # B-797 (Bodenstein); XII Corps G-3 Jnl, 5 Mar 45; 4th Armored Div Periodic Rpt, 6 Mar 45.

[39] George Dyer, XII Corps—Spearhead of Patton's Third Army (XII Corps History Association, 1947) (hereafter cited as Dyer, XII Corps), p. 330.

to allow General Botsch to wait long enough to brief his successor on the situation at Bonn and Remagen.[40]

From that point, no commander on the German side could have entertained any genuine hope for continued defense west of the Rhine either by the *LIII Corps* or by the other two corps of the *Fifteenth Army* still in the Eifel, the *LXVI* (Lucht) and *LXVII* (Hitzfeld). The three corps obviously were in imminent danger of encirclement. It was without question now a matter of trying to save whoever and whatever to help defend the Rhine, but in view of the stranglehold the word of Hitler still exercised at every level, nobody would authorize withdrawal. Botsch, the other corps commanders, Zangen at *Fifteenth Army,* and Model at *Army Group B*—all focused their General Staff-trained minds on issuing defense, assembly, and counterattack orders that looked as pretty as a war game on paper but made no sense in the grim reality of the situation in the Eifel. In the process, each protested to his next higher commander the idiocy of it all.

Model, for his part, ordered the *11th Panzer Division*—or what was left of it after withdrawal from the triangle between the Erft and the Rhine north of Cologne—to recross the Rhine at Bonn and counterattack southwest toward Rheinbach to cut off spearheads of the First U.S. Army's III Corps. That was a patent impossibility. The remnants of the panzer division would be too late even to recross the Rhine, much less counterattack.

Still convinced the main objective of the III Corps was not Bonn but Rema-

gen, General von Zangen ordered General Hitzfeld of the *LXVII Corps* to assume command of the *272d Volks Grenadier Division,* already forced back onto this corps by the south wing of the attack of the U.S. III Corps. He was then to turn over his West Wall obligations to the *LXVI Corps,* and with the *272d* and his own divisions (*89th* and *277th*) to counterattack on 7 March into the flank of the III Corps southeast of Rheinbach to cut the "funnel" leading to the Ahr River and Remagen.[41]

After making the usual protest that the project simply was not feasible, Hitzfeld went through the motions of readying the counterattack. Already the corps was in a somewhat better position to assemble than might have been expected, for as early as 3 March the *89th Infantry* and *277th Volks Grenadier Divisions* had begun limited withdrawals from the West Wall positions in the vicinity of the Roer reservoirs. By 6 March the two divisions were some five miles behind their original lines, almost out of contact with the Americans except on the right wing where the 2d Division of the U.S. V Corps had joined the general offensive.[42]

Even so, assembling for counterattack in the face of continuing advances by the III Corps in the north and the northeastward thrusts of the VIII Corps still was impossible. About all Hitzfeld accomplished in that direction was further to clog roads already choked with withdrawing columns and to expose the north flank of the *LXVI Corps.* Continued bad flying weather was the only thing that prevented Allied aircraft from turning the entire situation to utter chaos.

---

[40] MS # B–828 (Zangen).

[41] MSS # B–101 (Hitzfeld); B–828 (Zangen).
[42] MS # B–828 (Zangen).

The position of General Lucht's *LXVI Corps,* still holding some West Wall positions astride the Weisserstein watershed, was most perilous of all. Already the south wing of the corps had been forced back by the drive of the U.S. VIII Corps to the Kyll River northeast of Pruem. With the north flank exposed also by Hitzfeld's withdrawal, Lucht's divisions now were in serious trouble, a fact underscored early on 6 March when the V Corps commander, General Huebner, began to broaden his thrust—heretofore confined to the 2d Division on his north wing—by sending the 69th Division (Maj. Gen. Emil F. Reinhardt) eastward in the center of his zone. It would be driven home with even greater emphasis the next day when the 28th and 106th Divisions also joined the attack. While a regiment of the 2d Division plunged forward ten miles and took a bridge intact across the Ahr River, a column of the 28th Division (Maj. Gen. Norman D. Cota) overran Lucht's command post, bagging most of the corps headquarters, including the chief of staff. Lucht himself escaped because he was away at the time.[43]

When General Botsch arrived to join the *LIII Corps* with the unenviable assignment of assuming command, he learned he had scarcely any combat troops left. Such as there were—tiny remnants of the *326th* and *340th Volks Grenadier Divisions*—the corps chief of staff had organized into battle groups and given the only realistic mission possible, to harass American columns as best they could.

During the day of 6 March, CCB of the 4th Armored Division gained another

thirteen and a half miles, roughly half the distance between the jump-off on the Kyll and the Rhine near Andernach, then veered northeast off the main highway in the direction of the road center of Mayen. That added another five miles to the day's total before the armor had to stop for the night because of crumbling roads. Other than a growing problem of handling hundreds of prisoners, the combat command had no real difficulty all day except for an undefended roadblock that took about an hour to remove and occasional fire from assault guns or isolated field pieces on the flanks. Although CCA attempted to diverge from CCB's route to force a second passage a few miles to the south, demolished bridges eventually forced that combat command to tie in again on the tail of CCB.

The infantry divisions of the XII Corps in the meantime still found the going slow because of boggy roads, demolished bridges, heavy traffic, and sometimes determined resistance. Having turned north immediately after crossing the Kyll, the armor had left the infantry to deal with the two divisions (*246th Volk Grenadier* and *2d Panzer*) upon which the *Seventh Army*'s General Felber had based his unenthusiastic hopes of stopping the armor. As night came on the 6th, neither the 5th Division nor the 76th, the latter having crossed the Kyll southeast of Bitburg, held bridgeheads more than a few miles deep.

Matters would improve only slightly for the infantry divisions the next day, 7 March. A predawn counterattack, for example, knocked a battalion of the 5th Division from a village on the northeastern periphery of the bridgehead.

---

[43] V Corps Operations in the ETO, p. 394.

Although real and disturbing to the men and commanders who had to overcome it, this resistance when viewed against the backdrop of developments elsewhere in the Eifel on 7 March was negligible and futile. It was on this day that defenses of the *LXVI* and *LXVII Corps* in front of the U.S. V Corps began to fall apart. On 7 March also the 11th Armored Division in Middleton's VIII Corps at last got across the Kyll River in strength at Gerolstein and advanced eleven miles. As night fell, the armor took the important crossroads village of Kelberg, near a famous prewar automobile race course, the Nuerburg Ring. In the process, the tankers forced the newly arrived commander of the *LIII Corps,* General Botsch, and his headquarters troops to flee.

Even more spectacular and—in the end—decisive was the advance on 7 March of the 4th Armored Division's front-running CCB. Backtracking several miles to get on a better highway and avoid the crumbling roads that had stalled advance the evening before, CCB attacked in early morning through rain and fog. Brushing aside halfhearted resistance in the first village, the column paused on the fringe of the second, Kaisersesch, while a German-speaking soldier, using an amplifier, demanded surrender. A heterogeneous collection of German troops meekly complied. Racing on, the tankers drew their next fire five miles farther along at Kehrig. This time a demand for surrender drew more fire from *Panzerfausts* and antitank guns, but an artillery concentration on the town brought a quick end to the defiance.

From that point, the advance was little more than a road march with the tankers signaling German soldiers rearward to be taken prisoner by those who followed. Here and there along the road clusters of impressed laborers of almost every European nationality waved and cheered.

At one point, 1st Lt. Edgar C. Smith, piloting an artillery observation plane, spotted a column of retreating Germans not far ahead, obscured from the tankers by the rolling countryside. At Smith's urging, a company of Sherman tanks speeded up in pursuit.

"They're only 1,500 yards from you now, go faster," radioed Lieutenant Smith.

Later he reported they were only a thousand yards away, still screened by the terrain.

After another pause, the radio crackled again.

"They're around the next curve," Smith said. "Go get 'em!"

The tanks burst upon the rear of the startled Germans and raked the column with 75's and machine guns.[44]

As night fell, the head of CCB's column coiled on the reverse slope of the last high ground before the Rhine, three miles from the river, across from Neuwied. The drive to the Rhine was all but finished in just over two and a half days. The 4th Armored Division had driven forty-four airline miles—much longer by road—from the Kyll to a spot overlooking the Rhine. The division took 5,000 prisoners, captured or destroyed volumes of equipment, including 34 tanks and assault guns, and killed or wounded 700 Germans. The division itself lost 29 men killed, 80 wounded, 2 missing.

---

[44] Dyer, *XII Corps,* pp. 330 and 334.

In the process, the armor had spread havoc through whatever cohesion still remained in the German defense west of the Rhine and north of the Moselle. Everywhere irregular columns of foot troops interspersed with a confusion of motor and horse-drawn vehicles toiled toward the Rhine, hoping to find a barge, a ferry, perhaps a bridge still standing. Other Germans gave themselves up by the hundreds, particularly in front of the V and VIII Corps, while still others—some successfully, most not—tried to slip behind the armored spearheads to escape southward across the Moselle. Abandoned equipment, vehicles, antitank guns, and field pieces, many of them smoldering, dotted the Eifel in macabre disarray.

Yet for all the striking success of the drive, a chance to cap it with an even more spectacular achievement remained. Unknown to commanders and men of the 4th Armored Division, a few miles upstream from CCB's position, midway between Andernach and Koblenz, near the village of Urmitz, a bridge across the Rhine still stood, the Crown Prince Wilhelm Railroad Bridge.

Although the 4th Armored Division was under orders to seize any bridge over the Rhine still standing, nobody entertained any real expectation that a bridge might be taken; and in line with General Eisenhower's plan for a main effort across the Rhine by Montgomery's 21 Army Group, the thoughts of senior commanders in the Third Army were turning from the Rhine to the Moselle, which General Patton hoped to cross in order to trap the Germans in the West Wall in front of the U.S. Seventh Army. Aerial reconnaissance had already confirmed in any case that no bridge still

stood across the Rhine in the Third Army's zone. In keeping with that report and to avoid exposing tanks and other vehicles to antitank fire from the east bank of the Rhine and to the fire of stationary antiaircraft guns ringing nearby Koblenz, the men and vehicles of the 4th Armored Division stopped short of the Rhine itself and remained under cover on the reverse slope of the last high ground short of the river.

The coming of daylight on 8 March provoked something of a mystery. From the high ground observers could see Germans retreating individually and in ragged columns toward what maps showed to be a railroad bridge near Urmitz. Because of haze and generally poor visibility, they were unable to make out a bridge, but presumably the Germans were gravitating there in order somehow to get across the Rhine. As the day wore on, some prisoners and civilians said the Germans had already destroyed several spans of the railroad bridge while others reported that the bridge still stood.

CCA had readied an attack to be launched before daylight on the 9th to drive to the bridge and seize it if it was still intact when word came that General Bradley had approved the Third Army's turn southward across the Moselle. The 4th Armored Division was to change direction and try to seize a bridge over that river.

Soon after daylight on the 9th, after CCA had abandoned its plan to drive for the bridge at Urmitz, the Germans demolished it. Close investigation explained the conflicting reports the Americans had received. The Germans had earlier destroyed two spans of the railroad bridge, but beneath the rails they had hung a tier for vehicular traffic. It was the makeshift bridge that they destroyed early on the 9th.

Whether CCA could have taken the bridge before the Germans blew it was problematical, for by that time the Germans had become exceedingly wary of bridges falling into Allied hands. That was because of a happening a few miles to the north in the zone of the First Army's III Corps. There a 9th Armored Division only recently oriented to make its main effort to seize crossings of the Ahr River had found a Rhine bridge intact at Remagen.

CHAPTER XI

A Rhine Bridge at Remagen

Fortuitous events have a way sometimes of altering the most meticulous of plans. That was what happened as the Allied armies neared the Rhine.

In seeking at the end of January to allay British concern about the future course of Allied strategy, the Supreme Commander had assured the British Chiefs of Staff that a Rhine crossing in the north would not have to be delayed until the entire region west of the river was free of Germans.[1] Field Marshal Montgomery's 21 Army Group, General Eisenhower reiterated in a letter to senior commanders on 20 February, was to launch a massive thrust across the Rhine north of the Ruhr even as the 6th and 12th Army Groups completed their operations to clear the west bank. Those two army groups were to make secondary thrusts across the Rhine later.[2]

While designating the area north of the Ruhr and the Frankfurt-Kassel corridor as the two main avenues of advance deep into Germany, Eisenhower left open the choice of specific Rhine crossing sites to his army group commanders. With an eye toward the Frankfurt-Kassel corridor, the 12th Army Group's planning staff in turn noted, in what eventually was to be the First Army's zone, two acceptable crossing sites. Both were at points where the Rhine valley is relatively broad; one in the north, between Cologne and Bonn, the other between Andernach and Koblenz. From either site access would be fairly rapid to the Ruhr-Frankfurt autobahn and thence to the Lahn River valley leading into the Frankfurt-Kassel corridor.

Both had drawbacks, for both led into the wooded hills and sharply compartmented terrain of a region known as the Westerwald; but both avoided the worst of that region. The most objectionable crossing sites of all were in the vicinity of Remagen; there the Westerwald is at its most rugged, the roadnet is severely limited, and the Rhine flows less through a valley than a gorge.[3]

As the First Army neared the Rhine, General Bradley, the army group commander, like Patton of the Third Army, was looking less toward an immediate Rhine crossing than toward the Third Army's drive south to clear the Saar-Palatinate. The role of Hodges' First Army in the coming operation was to defend the line of the Rhine and mop up pockets of resistance. Hodges also was to be prepared to extend his units to the southernmost of the two acceptable

---

[1] See above, ch. 1; Pogue, *The Supreme Command*, pp. 413-14.

[2] Ltr, Eisenhower to AGp CG's, 20 Feb 45; SCAF 180, 201500 Jan 45. Both in SHAEF SGS Post-OVER-LORD Planning file, 381, III.

[3] 12th AGp Opns Plan, 23 Feb 45; Rhineland Opns Plan (draft), 27 Feb 45.

crossing sites, that between Andernach and Koblenz.[4]

The Germans at Remagen

With Allied troops approaching the Rhine, the order and efficiency normally associated with things German had become submerged in a maelstrom of confused and contradictory command channels. Nowhere was this more apparent than at the railroad bridge on the southern fringe of Remagen. There a small miscellany of troops was operating under a variety of commands. An army officer, Capt. Willi Bratge, was the so-called combat commander of the entire Remagen area, ostensibly with the power of over-all command but only in event of emergency. Capt. Karl Friesenhahn, an engineer officer, was the technical or bridge commander. An antiaircraft officer, responsible to neither, commanded antiaircraft troops in the vicinity. Men of the *Volkssturm* were under Nazi party officials. Furthermore—though no one at Remagen yet knew it—another officer, a major, was destined soon to come to the town to supersede Bratge's command.[5]

This confusion and contradiction was repeated at almost every level of command all along the Rhine front. Much

of it was attributable to the fact that prior to March, responsibility for protecting the Rhine bridges had rested entirely with the *Wehrkreise* (military districts). Troops of the *Wehrkreise* were responsible not to any army command but to the military arm of the Nazi party, the *Waffen-SS,* and jealous rivalry between the two services was more the rule than the exception. As the fighting front in early March fell back from Roer to Rhine, responsibility was supposed to pass from *Wehrkreis* to army group and army, but in practice *Wehrkreis* commanders jealously held on to their command prerogatives. Furthermore, antiaircraft troops answered neither to army headquarters nor *Waffen-SS* but instead to the Luftwaffe; and within the Army itself the Field Army (*Feldheer*) vied for authority with the Replacement Army (*Ersatzheer*).

To complicate matters further, a number of recent command changes had had an inevitable effect. On 1 February, *Wehrkreis VI* had relinquished authority for Remagen to *Wehrkreis XII.* Then, on 1 March, came the shift that took place at the height of Operation GRENADE, exchange of zones between the *Fifth Panzer* and *Fifteenth Armies.* A few days later, as German troops fell back from the Roer, General Puechler's *LXXIV Corps,* gravitating on Bonn, might have been expected to command any bridgehead retained in the vicinity of Bonn and Remagen; but instead, Field Marshal Model at *Army Group B* set up a separate command, the one under General Botsch, commander of a badly depleted volks grenadier division. Botsch was to be responsible directly to Zangen's *Fifteenth Army.*

As General Botsch tried to appraise the

---

[4] 12th AGp Outline Opn UNDERTONE, 7 Mar 45.

[5] The German story is primarily from a study by Ken Hechler, Seizure of the Remagen Bridge, based on postwar German manuscripts and contemporary German records and prepared in OCMH to complement this volume. A U.S. Army historian in Europe during World War 11, Mr. Hechler subsequently wrote a comprehensive and authoritative account of the Remagen action, *The Bridge at Remagen* (New York: Ballantine Books, 1957). The published work includes considerable material developed by Mr. Hechler through postwar interviews in the United States and Germany, and has also been used extensively in the preparation of the first half of this chapter.

situation, he ran head on into the differing views of his two superiors, Zangen and Model, as to the course the Americans presumably would follow—Model with his belief that the main thrust would be made on Bonn, Zangen with the idea that the Americans would exploit the "spout of the funnel" leading to Remagen. To be prepared for either eventuality, Botsch wanted to place his headquarters midway between the two towns, but Model insisted that he locate at or near Bonn. There Botsch ran afoul of Bonn's local defense commander, Generalmajor Richard von Bothmer, who raised questions as to just who was in command at Bonn. Trying to resolve the conflicts, Botsch spent much of the first few days of March driving back and forth between command posts of the *Fifteenth Army* and *Army Group B* and between Bonn and Remagen.

Although tiring and frustrating, these peregrinations probably established General Botsch as the one man who understood how the diverse command complex worked. Driving up the Ahr River valley toward the *Fifteenth Army*'s headquarters early on 6 March, Botsch also got a firsthand view of pandemonium in the making as individuals and depleted units retreated pell-mell toward the Rhine. This personal knowledge of how serious matters really were well might have stood the Germans in good stead at Remagen, but General Botsch had no chance to use it.

For it was General Botsch to whom Field Marshal Model turned in the afternoon of 6 March to replace the captured General von Rothkirch in command of the *LIII Corps*.[6] At 1700 Botsch left on

the futile assignment of trying to resurrect the *LIII Corps* without even being accorded time to brief his successor, his erstwhile disputant at Bonn, General von Bothmer. Thus was lost to the Bonn-Remagen defense the one commander who, because of his knowledge of the complicated command setup and the true nature of German reverses west of the Rhine, might have forestalled what was about to happen at Remagen.

When the *Fifteenth Army* commander, General von Zangen, learned of Botsch's shift, he told General Hitzfeld, commander of the *LXVII Corps,* to send someone to Remagen to check personally on the situation there. A short while later, at 0100 on 7 March, at the same time Zangen ordered the *LXVII Corps* to counterattack the spout of the funnel leading to Remagen, he also told Hitzfeld the Remagen bridgehead was then the responsibility of the *LXVII Corps.*

With the bulk of his troops still thirty-five miles from the Rhine, sorely beset on all sides and under orders to launch a counterattack that on the face of it was impossible, and with American troops no more than ten miles from Remagen, Hitzfeld could do little. Summoning his adjutant, Major Hans Scheller, he told him to take eight men and a radio and proceed to Remagen, there to assume command, assemble as much strength as possible, and establish a small bridgehead. He specifically warned Scheller to check immediately upon arrival as to the technical features of the Remagen railroad bridge and to make sure the bridge was prepared for demolition.

At approximately 0200 (7 March), Major Scheller and his eight men started for Remagen in two vehicles over winding, troop-choked, blacked-out Eifel

---

[6] See above, ch. X.

roads. In the darkness, Scheller's vehicle quickly became separated from the other, the one that carried the radio. Running low on fuel, Scheller ordered his driver to take a long detour to the south to seek out a supply installation where he might get gasoline. Shortly after 1100 on 7 March Major Scheller, still without a radio, finally reached the Remagen bridge. Sounds of battle already were discernible in the distance.

The Hope for a Bridge

As the crucible neared for the Germans at Bonn and Remagen, probably none of the American troops or their commanders, who on 6 March began to make great strides toward the Rhine, entertained any genuine expectation of seizing a bridge across the river intact. (*See Map IX.*) Some units were under formal orders to seize and hold any bridge that still stood, but more as a routine precaution than anything else. Nobody had made any positive plans about what to do should such a windfall occur.

Back in February, as the First Army drive began, some staff officers had toyed with the idea that a Rhine bridge might be taken. So remote appeared the chances nevertheless that they went ahead with a request to Allied air forces to continue to bomb the bridges. Inclement weather rather than plan had provided the bridges respite from air attack during the early days of March.

In the Ninth Army, of course, a flurry of hope for a Rhine bridge had developed on the first day of March, inviting the attention of the Supreme Commander himself.[7] Yet that hope had

_____
[7] *Ibid.*

proved short-lived; and despite the fact that two attempts came heartbreakingly close to success, the failures appeared to confirm the general opinion that the methodical Germans would see to it that nobody got across the Rhine the easy way.

The possibility still continued to intrigue commanders at every level. When General Hodges visited headquarters of the III Corps on 4 March, for example, he and the corps commander, General Millikin, spoke of the possibility of taking the bridge at Remagen; but with troops of the III Corps still a long way from the Rhine, the discussion was brief. The next day, with the 1st Division advancing on Bonn, the division commander asked General Millikin what to do in case the highway bridge at Bonn could be seized. On 6 March Millikin put the question to the First Army G–3, Brig. Gen. Truman C. Thorson. The bridges, Thorson ruled, should be captured wherever possible.

The G–3 of the III Corps, Colonel Mewshaw, and an assistant had mused over the likelihood of taking the Remagen bridge with paratroops or a picked band of Rangers; but so slight appeared the chance that the discussion never went beyond the operations section. In the directive issued to the 9th Armored Division on 6 March, the order in regard to the bridge at Remagen was to "cut by fire"; the order also restricted artillery fire against the bridge to time and proximity fuze. Early in the evening of 6 March the III Corps also asked the air officer at First Army to refrain from bombing both the Bonn and Remagen bridges.

That same evening, 6 March, General Millikin talked by telephone with the

9th Armored Division commander, General Leonard. Among other things, General Leonard recalled later, Millikin had something like this to say about the railroad bridge at Remagen: "Do you see that little black strip of bridge at Remagen? If you happen to get that, your name will go down in glory." [8]

Yet despite all deliberation about the bridge on 6 March, this was the same day that Colonel Mewshaw confirmed for the 9th Armored Division G-3 that the division's main effort should be aimed not at the Rhine but at crossings of the Ahr. Furthermore, neither the 9th Armored Division nor that division's Combat Command B, the unit headed toward Remagen, mentioned in its field order taking the bridge at Remagen, although General Leonard did note the possibility orally as a matter of course to the CCB commander.

For all the talk about getting a bridge over the Rhine, the prospect remained little more than a fancy.

Advance to the Rhine

On 6 March, as General Millikin shifted the objectives of his divisions southeastward to conform with the First Army's emphasis on crossings of the Ahr River, the advance of the III Corps picked up momentum. Despite time lost to a determined German delaying force at the road center of Rheinbach, the 9th Armored Division's Combat Command A gained more than ten miles and stopped at midnight less than two miles from the Ahr. CCB reached Stadt Meckenheim, only eight miles from the Rhine.

A regiment of the 1st Division on the corps north wing got within four miles of the Rhine northwest of Bonn.

The next morning, 7 March, as troops of the neighboring VII Corps eliminated the last resistance around Cologne, General Hodges transferred responsibility for clearing Bonn to General Collins's corps, but with the responsibility went the means, the 1st Division. At the same time, infantry of the 9th Division continued to close in on Bad Godesberg, and the 9th Armored's CCA jumped the Ahr at Bad Neuenahr, even though the Germans fought doggedly to hold open the Ahr valley highway, the main route of withdrawal for General Hitzfeld's *LXVII Corps.* Combat Command B meanwhile sent one column southeastward to cross the Ahr near its confluence with the Rhine and another column toward Remagen.

Built around the 27th Armored Infantry Battalion and the 14th Tank Battalion (minus one company), the task force heading for Remagen was under the tank battalion commander, Lt. Col. Leonard Engeman. To lead the column, Colonel Engeman designated an infantry platoon and a tank platoon, the latter equipped with the new, experimental T26 Pershing tank mounting a 90-mm. gun.

Because bulldozers had to clear rubble from the roads leading out of Stadt Meckenheim before the armored vehicles could pass, Task Force Engeman got a fairly late start on 7 March. The column began to move only at 0820, but the Germans apparently gained nothing from the delay. The first opposition—desultory artillery and small arms fire—developed more than three miles from the starting point. Another mile and a half

---

[8] Combat interview with General Leonard; see also interview with General Millikin and his comments on the draft MS of this volume.

to the east the column turned south, and just before noon entered a big patch of woods west of Remagen. Here and there little clusters of Germans passed, hands behind their heads, anxious to give themselves up to the first Americans who would take the time to deal with them.

A few minutes before 1300, the leading infantry platoon commander, 2d Lt. Emmet J. Burrows, emerged from the woods on a high bluff overlooking Remagen. Below him, the view of the Rhine gorge, even in the haze of 7 March, was spectacular.

The railroad bridge just outside Remagen, Lieutenant Burrows took in at a glance, still stood.

The Crisis at the Bridge

Down at the bridge, confusion reigned, much as it had all morning. Since soon after daylight, frightened and disorganized groups of German troops had been fleeing across the bridge, bringing with them tales of the strength of American forces pouring down the Ahr valley. The wounded and the stragglers—tired, dispirited men with heads bowed—added stark punctuation to the accounts. Lumbering supply vehicles, horse-drawn artillery, quartermaster and other rear echelon service units created mammoth traffic jams. The jams would have been worse had not a 4-day rush job to lay planks across the railroad tracks at last been finished the night before.

Built in 1916, the railroad bridge at Remagen was named for the World War I hero, Erich Ludendorff. Wide enough for two train tracks, plus footpaths on either side, the bridge had three symmetrical arches resting on four stone piers. The over-all length was 1,069 feet.

At each end stood two stone towers, black with grime, giving the bridge a fortress-like appearance. Only a few yards from the east end of the bridge, the railroad tracks entered a tunnel through the black rock of a clifflike hill, the Erpeler Ley.

A year before the start of World War II, the Germans had devised an elaborate demolition scheme for the bridge that included installing an electric fuze connected with explosives by a cable encased in thick steel pipe. Even if the electric fuze failed to work, a primer cord might be lit by hand to set off emergency charges. Later, at the end of 1944, engineers had made plans to blow a big ditch across the Remagen end of the bridge to forestall enemy tanks until the main demolitions could be set off.

Long at his post, the engineer commander at Remagen, Captain Friesenhahn, knew the demolition plan well, but only a few days before 7 March an order had arrived that complicated the task. Because a bridge at Cologne had been destroyed prematurely when an American bomb set off the explosive charges, OKW had ordered that demolitions be put in place only when the fighting front had come within eight kilometers of a bridge; and igniters were not to be attached until "demolition seems to be unavoidable." [9] In addition, both the order to prepare the explosives and the demolition order itself were to be issued in writing by the officer bearing tactical responsibility for the area.

Until just before noon, 7 March, the officer bearing tactical responsibility at Remagen was Captain Bratge. In a growing lather of excitement at the hegira of

[9] A translation of this order appears as Annex 1 to 99th Div G–2 Periodic Rpt, 7 Mar 45.

German units and stragglers, Bratge early in the morning telephoned headquarters of *Army Group B* to ask for instructions, but he was able to get through only to a duty officer. The officer assured him that *Army Group B* was not particularly worried about the situation at Remagen; Bonn appeared to be the most threatened point.

For actual defense of Remagen and the bridge, Captain Bratge had only thirty-six men in his own company, plus Friesenhahn's handful of engineers and a smattering of unreliable *Volkssturm,* the latter technically not even under Bratge's command. The antiaircraft troops that earlier had been set up on the west bank had left in midmorning, joining the retreating hordes crossing the bridge.

General Botsch, Bratge knew, had asked Field Marshal Model at *Army Group B* for an entire division to defend at Bonn and a reinforced regiment at Remagen. That kind of strength, Model had replied, simply was not available. Although Model had promised some reinforcement, none had arrived. During the evening of 6 March, Bratge had tried to reach General Botsch's headquarters to ask for help, but had been unable to get through. He had no way of knowing that Botsch's headquarters had pulled out to go to Botsch's new command, the *LIII Corps.* An officer sent from General von Bothmer's headquarters at Bonn to give Bratge this information had wandered into American positions and been captured.

At one point Captain Bratge managed to corral the remnants of a battalion from the *3d Parachute Division* and persuaded the officers to set up a defense to the southwest to block an expected American advance from the Ahr valley, but a short while later these troops melted into the fleeing columns and disappeared. When an antiaircraft unit stationed atop the Erpeler Ley withdrew, ostensibly under orders to go to Koblenz, even that strategic observation point was left unmanned.

At 1115, Bratge looked up from the unit orders he was checking at the bridge to see a red-eyed major approaching. His name, the major said, was Hans Scheller. General Hitzfeld of the *LXVII Corps,* he continued, had sent him to take command at Remagen.

Once Captain Bratge had assured himself that the major was, in fact, from the *LXVII Corps* and that his orders were legitimate, he was pleased to relinquish command. Together the two officers went to check with the engineers on progress of the demolitions. Although reports began to arrive that Americans had reached the bluffs overlooking Remagen, Scheller was reluctant to order the bridge destroyed. An artillery captain, arriving at the bridge, had insisted that his battalion and its guns were following to cross the bridge, and Major Scheller felt keenly that combat units should not be penalized by having the bridge blown in their faces, particularly when they were bringing with them precious items such as artillery pieces.

On the hill above Remagen, Lieutenant Burrows's excitement at discovering the bridge intact had brought his company commander, 1st Lt. Karl H. Timmerman, hurrying to the vantage point at the edge of the woods. Timmerman in turn called for the task force commander, Colonel Engeman.

The task force commander's first reac-

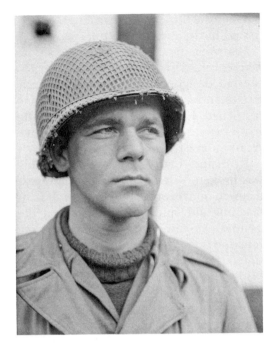

LIEUTENANT TIMMERMAN, *first officer to cross the Remagen Bridge.*

tion was much like that of Burrows and Timmerman, awe and surprise tempered by a sharp desire to get artillery time fire on the bridge immediately to hamper the German retreat. Supporting artillery nevertheless declined to fire, citing reports, actually erroneous, that friendly troops already were too close to the bridge.

As Colonel Engeman directed Lieutenant Timmerman to start his infantry company moving cross-country into Remagen with the platoon of Pershing tanks to follow down the winding little road from the bluff, CCB's operations officer, Maj. Ben Cothran, arrived on the scene. Like the others before him, he got a tingling shock of excitement as he emerged from the woods and saw the Rhine below him, the Remagen bridge still standing.

"My God!" Cothran exclaimed. "I've got to get the Old Man." [10]

He was referring to Brig. Gen. William M. Hoge, the CCB commander. In keeping with the theory that the other column of the combat command heading for the Ahr was making the main effort, Hoge had followed closely behind that thrust. In response to Cothran's radio report, he tore cross-country to the scene.

He might lose a battalion, General Hoge mused, if his men crossed the bridge before the Germans blew it. If they destroyed it while his men were in the act of crossing, he probably would lose a platoon. On the other hand . . . .

Turning to Colonel Engeman, Hoge said, "I want you to get to that bridge as soon as possible."

A short while later, at 1515, a message arrived from CCB's other column, which earlier had found a bridge across the Ahr River at Sinzig and had fought its way across. In Sinzig the men had discovered a civilian who insisted that the Germans at Remagen intended to blow the Ludendorff railroad bridge precisely at 1600. Although the Germans in fact had no specific time schedule, the civilian's report nevertheless spurred General Hoge to urge Task Force Engeman to greater speed in seizing the bridge at Remagen.

Having fought through the town of Remagen against an occasional die-hard German defender, Lieutenant Timmerman, his infantrymen, and the supporting platoon of tanks neared the bridge around 1600. As they approached, dodging occasional small arms and 20-

---

[10] Direct quotations in this section are from Hechler, *The Bridge at Remagen.*

mm. fire from the towers, a volcano of rocks, dirt, and noise erupted. Captain Friesenhahn on his own initiative, when he saw the Americans appear, had exploded the charge designed to prevent tanks from reaching the bridge. Timmerman and his men could see the Germans on the other side of the river scurrying to and fro, apparently getting ready to blow the bridge itself.

Major Scheller and Captain Bratge had already crossed the bridge to the railroad tunnel. Friesenhahn hurried to join them to get the order to destroy the bridge, but concussion from a tank shell knocked him to the floor of the bridge, unconscious. Fifteen precious minutes passed before he came to his senses. Still dazed, he resumed his trek toward the tunnel.

In the railroad tunnel, pandemonium. Terrified civilians cowering against the walls, children wailing. Reluctant *Volkssturm* awaiting only a chance to surrender. Clusters of apprehensive soldiers, some foreign workers, even some animals. White phosphorus shells from the American tanks across the river creating a heavy, eye-stinging smoke screen. Some soldiers caught outside the tunnel screaming as the phosphorus burned into their flesh.

As Captain Bratge rushed outside to survey the situation, he came upon Captain Friesenhahn and yelled at him to get the order from Major Scheller to blow the bridge. When Scheller gave his approval, Bratge insisted on waiting while a lieutenant wrote down the exact timing and wording of the order. Going ouside again, he shouted to Friesenhahn to blow the bridge. True to his instructions from OKW, Friesenhahn insisted at first on having the order in writing, then relented in the interest of time.

Warning the civilians and soldiers to take cover, Captain Friesenhahn turned the key designed to activate the electric circuit and set off the explosives. Nothing happened. He turned it again. Still nothing happened. He turned it a third time. Again, no response.

Realizing that the circuit probably was broken, Friesenhahn sought a repair team to move onto the bridge; but as machine gun and tank fire riddled the ground, he saw that not enough time remained to do the job that way. He called for a volunteer to go onto the bridge and ignite the primer cord by hand. When a sergeant responded, Friesenhahn himself went with him as far as the edge of the bridge and there waited anxiously while the sergeant, crouching to avoid shells and bullets, dashed onto the bridge.

After what seemed an eternity, the sergeant started back toward the east bank at a run. Seemingly endless moments passed. Had the sergeant failed? Would the primer cord ignite the charge?

At last, a sudden booming roar. Timbers flew wildly into the air. The bridge lifted as if to rise from its foundations.

Cowering against the explosion, Friesenhahn breathed a sigh of relief. The job was done.

Yet when he looked up again, the bridge was still there.

Lieutenant Timmerman had barely finished the order to his men of Company A, 27th Armored Infantry Battalion, to storm across the railroad bridge when the explosion came. Some men flung themselves to the ground for protection. Others watched in awe as the

SERGEANT DRABIK, *first American across the Rhine.*

big span lifted and a giant cloud of dust and thick black smoke rose. Moments later, like Friesenhahn and the Germans on the east bank, they saw in incredible surprise that the bridge still stood.

As the smoke and dust cleared, Timmerman could discern that even though the explosion had torn big holes in the planking over the railroad tracks, the footpaths on either side were intact. Signaling his platoon leaders, he again ordered attack.

Bobbing and weaving, dashing from the cover of one metal girder to another, the men made their way onto the bridge. Machine gun fire from the towers near the east bank spattered among them, but return fire from the riflemen themselves and from the big tanks on the Remagen side kept the German fire down. With a

few well-placed rounds, the Pershings silenced German riflemen firing from a half-submerged barge in the river.

Close behind the first riflemen went two sergeants and a lieutenant from the engineer detachment operating with Task Force Engeman. Working swiftly, the engineers cut every wire they could find that might possibly lead to additional demolitions. They shot apart heavy cables with their carbines.

Nearing the far end, several men digressed to clean out the machine gunners from the towers, while others continued to the east bank. The first man to set foot beyond the Rhine was an assistant squad leader, Sgt. Alex Drabik. (*Map 3*) Others were only moments behind, including the first officer to cross, the Company A commander, Lieutenant Timmerman.

As Timmerman's men spread out on the east bank and one platoon began the onerous task of climbing the precipitous Erpeler Ley, Major Scheller in the railroad tunnel tried time after time to contact his higher headquarters to report that the bridge still stood. Failing that, he mounted a bicycle and rode off to report in person. As American troops appeared at both ends of the tunnel, Captain Bratge and the other Germans inside, including the engineer officer, Captain Friesenhahn, surrendered.

Reaction to the Coup

Hardly had the first of Timmerman's men crossed the Rhine when Colonel Engeman radioed the news to the CCB commander, General Hoge. Because Hoge in the meantime had received word to divert as much strength as possible from Remagen to reinforce the

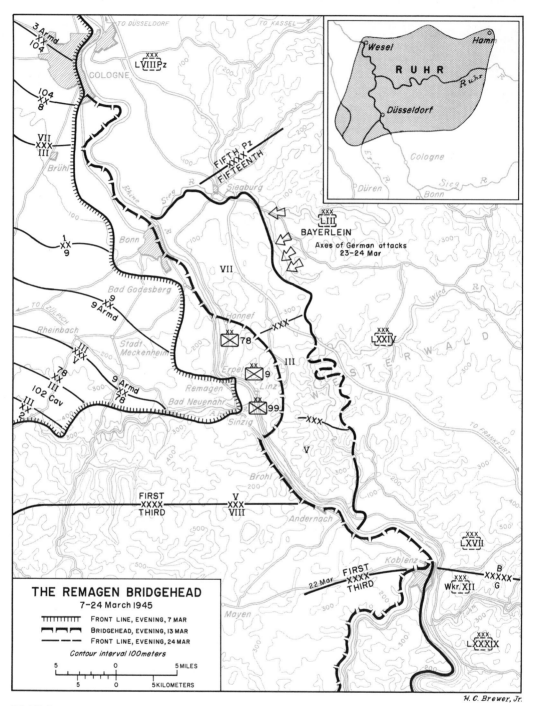

THE REMAGEN BRIDGEHEAD
7–24 March 1945

	FRONT LINE, EVENING, 7 MAR
	BRIDGEHEAD, EVENING, 13 MAR
	FRONT LINE, EVENING, 24 MAR

Contour interval 100 meters

5   5 MILES

5   0   5 KILOMETERS

Axes of German attacks
23–24 Mar

H. C. Brewer, Jr.

MAP 3

bridgehead over the Ahr River at Sinzig, he would be acting contrary to an order still in effect if, instead, he reinforced the Rhine crossing. He hesitated only momentarily. Send the rest of the armored infantry battalion across immediately, he told Engeman; then he drove to his own command post for a meeting with his division commander, General Leonard.

General Leonard's first reaction to the news was mock concern against Hoge's upset of the plans. "But let's push it," he added, "and then put it up to Corps." [11]

At 1630 the 9th Armored Division chief of staff telephoned the command post of the III Corps.

"Hot damn!" cried a little sergeant as he transferred the call to the chief of staff and threw down the telephone. "We got a bridge over the Rhine and we're crossing over!" [12]

Although the corps commander, General Millikin, was away from the command post, his chief of staff, Col. James H. Phillips, believed he knew how his commander would react. Even before trying to contact Millikin, he told the 9th Armored Division to exploit the crossing.

When Phillips relayed the news to headquarters of the First Army, General Hodges ordered engineers and boats to Remagen even before calling General Bradley at 12th Army Group for approval.

"Hot dog, Courtney"—General Bradley later recalled his own reaction—

"This will bust him wide open . . . . Shove everything you can across it." [13]

General Eisenhower's reaction was much the same. Only the planners appeared to question in any degree the advisability of exploiting the coup. The SHAEF G-3, General Bull, who happened to be at Bradley's headquarters when the news arrived, remarked that a crossing at Remagen led no place and that a diversion of strength to Remagen would interfere with General Eisenhower's plan to make the main effort north of the Ruhr.[14] Yet Bradley would have none of it, and Eisenhower confirmed that view.

"Well, Brad," Eisenhower said, "we expected to have . . . [four] divisions tied up around Cologne and now those are free. Go ahead and shove over at least five divisions instantly, and anything else that is necessary to make certain of our hold." [15]

Confirmed approval to exploit the crossing reached the III Corps at 1845 on 7 March, and an hour and a half later General Hodges relieved the corps of the assignment of driving south across the Ahr. General Millikin in the meantime had been making plans to motorize the reserve regiments of his two infantry divisions and rush them to the bridge. Engineers, artillery, antiaircraft—units of all types stirred in the early darkness and headed for Remagen. All roads lead-

---

[11] Hechler, *The Bridge at Remagen*, p. 155.
[12] *Ibid.*, p. viii.

[13] Bradley, *A Soldier's Story*, p. 510.
[14] *Ibid.* For General Bull's view of this event, see John Toland, *The Last 100 Days* (New York: Random House, 1966), pp. 214–15.
[15] Dwight D. Eisenhower, *Crusade in Europe* (New York: Doubleday and Company, 1948), p. 380; Capt. Harry C. Butcher, USNR, *My Three Years with Eisenhower* (New York: Simon and Schuster, 1946), p. 768. Bradley, *A Soldier's Story*, page 514, says four divisions.

ing toward the little Rhine town soon were thick with traffic. Before midnight three heavy caliber artillery battalions already were in position to fire in support of the little band of infantrymen east of the Rhine.

At the bridge, the handful of engineers from Task Force Engeman worked unceasingly to repair the damage the demolition had done to the flooring of the bridge. Although considerable work remained, the engineers shortly before midnight signaled that tanks might try to cross.

Nine Sherman tanks of the 14th Tank Battalion crossed without incident, but the first tank destroyer to try it foundered in an unrepaired hole in the planking. The vehicle appeared to teeter precariously over the swirling waters far below, but for almost five hours every effort either to right the destroyer or to dump it into the river failed. At 0530 (8 March) the vehicle was at last removed.

In the 27th Armored Infantry Battalion's minuscule bridgehead, the infantrymen and their limited tank support spent a troubled night fighting off platoon-size counterattacks along their undermanned perimeter and expecting the Germans at any moment to strike in force. At dawn, when the disabled tank destroyer was removed from the bridge, the arrival of a battalion of the 78th Division's 310th Infantry relieved the pressure. As the first vestiges of daylight appeared, a battalion of the 9th Division's 47th Infantry also crossed into the bridgehead.

In the twenty-four hours following seizure of the bridge, almost 8,000 men crossed the Rhine, including two armored infantry battalions, a tank battal-

ion, a tank destroyer company, and a platoon of armored engineers of the 9th Armored Division; a regiment and two additional battalions of the 78th Division; a regiment and one additional battalion of the 9th Division; and one and a half batteries of antiaircraft artillery.

During that twenty-four hours and into the next day, 9 March, General Eisenhower's initial jubilation over capture of the Ludendorff Bridge cooled under the impact of admonitions from his staff. Committed to a main effort north of the Ruhr with the 21 Army Group, he actually had few reserves to spare for Remagen. Late on 9 March his G-3, General Bull, informed General Bradley that while the Supreme Commander wanted the brideghead held firmly and developed for an early advance southeastward, he did not want it enlarged to a size greater than five divisions could defend. Bradley in turn told General Hodges to limit advances to a thousand yards a day, just enough to keep the enemy off balance and prevent him from mining extensively around the periphery. Once the troops reached the autobahn, seven miles beyond the Rhine, they were to hold in place until General Eisenhower ordered expansion. Thus, almost from the start, the forces in the Remagen bridgehead were to operate under wraps that would not be removed for more than a fortnight.

On the German Side

Like the Americans, the Germans had no plan ready to cope with the situation at Remagen. Indeed, the fact that the U.S. Ninth Army had made no immediate move to jump the Rhine had lulled many German commanders into the belief that the Allies would pause to mop up and regroup before trying to cross; and that had engendered a measure of apathy in regard to the possibility of losing a bridge.

Nor did the Germans have any reserves close at hand to throw quickly against the little Remagen bridgehead. Most combat units near Remagen were still on the west bank, struggling to escape American pincers and get back somehow across the Rhine. Most of the service troops in the Remagen area were busy ferrying the depleted combat forces.

As the news about the Ludendorff Bridge spread slowly through a disorganized German command, officers near Remagen assembled about a hundred engineers and antiaircraft troops and fought through the night of the 7th, but to little avail. One group of Germans did reach the bridge itself with explosives in hand, but men of the 78th Division captured them before they could do any damage.

Because of the fluid tactical situation, many higher German commanders were on the move during the night of 7 March and failed for hours to learn about loss of the bridge. Field Marshal von Rundstedt's headquarters got the word earlier than most through a chance conversation between the operations officer and local commanders. Nobody could find the *Army Group B* commander, Field Marshal Model, in whose sector the debacle had occurred. Model himself was at "the front," his headquarters on the move.

When *OB WEST* finally did establish contact with *Army Group B,* Model still was away. So preoccupied was the army group staff with trying to save divisions of the *LXVI* and *LXVII Corps,* threatened with entrapment by the 4th Ar-

mored Division's sweep to the Rhine above Andernach, that the headquarters at first reacted apathetically. When Model returned during the morning of 8 March, he ordered the *11th Panzer Division,* which by that time was preparing to recross the Rhine at Bonn to make the projected counterattack southwest toward Rheinbach, to sweep the Americans into the river and blow the Ludendorff Bridge.

The *11th Panzer Division* had about 4,000 men, 25 tanks, and 18 artillery pieces, a force that well might have struck a telling blow had it been available soon after the first Americans crossed the Rhine. Yet the panzer division, assembled near Duesseldorf, had somehow to obtain gasoline for its vehicles and thread a way along roads already jammed with traffic and under attack from Allied planes. Not until two days later, 10 March, were even the first contingents of the division to get into action against the bridgehead.[16] Field Marshal Model meanwhile designated a single commander to co-ordinate all counteraction at Remagen, General Bayerlein, erstwhile commander of *Corps Bayerlein,* who had fallen back before the drive of the VII Corps on Cologne. Bayerlein on 9 March took command of a heterogeneous collection of service troops opposite Remagen with the promise of the incoming *11th Panzer Division,* some 300 men and 15 tanks masquerading under the name of the once-great *Panzer Lehr Division,* another 600 men and 15 tanks under the seemingly imperishable *9th Panzer Division,* and a company-size remnant of the *106th Panzer Brigade* with 5 tanks. Once all troops

---

[16] MS # B-590, *11th Panzer Division,* 6–21 March 1945 (Generalleutnant Wend von Wietersheim).

arrived, including relatively strong artillery units, Bayerlein was to have approximately 10,000 men grouped under the headquarters staff of the *LIII Corps.*

When Model visited Bayerlein's new headquarters on 9 March, Bayerlein outlined a plan to attack at dusk on 10 March against the center of the bridgehead, then roll up the flanks. The main component was to be the *Kampfgruppe* of the *Panzer Lehr Division;* but when the bulk of that force failed to arrive on time, Model vetoed the entire plan.[17] Model's first concern was to draw some kind of cordon around the bridgehead, but in the process he let pass the possibility of counterattacking before the Americans became too strong to be evicted. As American attacks continued, the incoming *11th Panzer Division* also became drawn into the defensive cordon and could launch only small, localized counterattacks.

As for the Commander in Chief West, Field Marshal von Rundstedt, the loss of the Remagen bridge was the excuse Hitler needed to relieve the old soldier of his command. Already upset by Rundstedt's failure to hold west of the Rhine, Hitler on 8 March summoned from Italy Generalfeldmarschall Albert Kesselring, longtime Commander in Chief South (*OB SUED*). The next day Hitler told Kesselring to take charge in the west. In the process he emphasized that the Remagen bridgehead had to be wiped out in order to gain time for refitting and reorganizing the exhausted German units behind the moat of the Rhine. Kesselring left Berlin for his unenviable

FIELD MARSHAL KESSELRING

assignment the night of 9 March, the relief to be effective the next day.[18]

Build-up and Command Problems

The First Army commander, General Hodges, had made various organizational shifts to enable the III Corps to exploit the Rhine crossing. During the night of 7 March, he attached a second armored division, the 7th, to Millikin's corps, along with an antiaircraft battalion, an engineer treadway bridge company, and an amphibious truck company. He also relieved the 78th Division of its offensive mission with the V Corps south of the Ahr River and ordered the division to join its reserve regiment at Remagen.

---

[17] MSS # A–970, Remagen Bridgehead—*LIII Corps* (Generalleutnant Fritz Bayerlein) and # B–590 (Wietersheim).

[18] Kesselring's personal account of his stewardship may be found in his memoirs, *A Soldier's Record* (New York: William Morrow and Company, 1954), pp. 283ff.

Finding troops to send to Remagen was easier than expected because resistance west of the Rhine collapsed so rapidly. A final surge by the Third Army's late-running 11th Armored Division to reach the Rhine at Brohl on 8 March took all semblance of organization out of the defense south of the Ahr, and the next day the 2d Division of the V Corps swept to the Rhine to link with the armor. On those two days and the next, resistance was so indifferent that the corps artillery could find no targets. It was much the same in the sector of the VII Corps, where on 9 March the 1st Division eliminated the last defenders from the university city of Bonn, there to discover the Rhine bridge destroyed. The German commander in Bonn, General von Bothmer, escaped to the east bank of the Rhine, only to be called before a court-martial that stripped him of his rank, whereupon Bothmer shot himself.[19]

For all the speed of the American thrusts, thousands of Germans made their way across the Rhine, mostly on ferries on in small river craft. In terms of prisoners taken, the pincers movement south of the Ahr was disappointing—the V Corps, for example, in its drive to the Rhine, captured just over 5,000 Germans, while the VII Corps between the Erft and the Rhine had been taking over 13,000.[20] Yet those Germans who escaped did so in disarray, unit integrity in most cases gone; and behind them they left small mountains of equipment, ammunition, weapons, and vehicles. While most ranking commanders got across the Rhine, two—

Generalleutnant Richard Schimpf, commander of the *3d Parachute Division,* and Generalmajor Ludwig Heilmann, commander of the *5th Parachute Division*—failed to make it. Both were captured, as was General Rothkirch earlier.

At Remagen and on the roads leading to the town, congestion was a serious problem. The ancient wall-encircled town of Zuelpich and bomb-devastated Euskirchen particularly were bottlenecks, but the worst difficulty was at the Ludendorff Bridge itself. Although moderately heavy German artillery fire fell almost constantly around the bridge, it failed to halt traffic for any period longer than a quarter-hour. The slow pace imposed on vehicles by the condition of the bridge and by congestion on the east bank still served to back up traffic for several miles outside Remagen.

Almost from the start, the First Army's General Hodges was dissatisfied with the way his corps commander, General Millikin, handled the problems both at the bridge and in the bridgehead. Hodges and some members of his staff complained long and vocally that control was poor on both sides of the river and that accurate information on troop dispositions beyond the Rhine was lacking. Even after the order passed down from General Eisenhower on 9 March to limit advances within the bridgehead, Hodges continued to chafe at what he considered slow, uninspired attacks that failed to push far enough east to relieve the bridge site of observed artillery fire.

General Millikin on 9 March placed the commander of the 9th Armored Division, General Leonard, in specific control of all activity in the vicinity of the bridge and put all troops east of the

[19] MS # C–020 (Schramm).
[20] V Corps Operations in the ETO, p. 401; VII Corps AAR, Mar 45.

LUDENDORFF RAILROAD BRIDGE AT REMAGEN

river under the 9th Infantry Division commander, General Craig; but Hodges continued to complain. Unaccustomed to working with Millikin, whose III Corps in months past had served under the Third Army, Hodges and his staff made no attempt "to hide the fact that everybody here wishes the bridgehead command had fallen to General Collins." [21]

Millikin's problems, on the other hand, were myriad. Although he himself

was frequently at the bridge, getting accurate, timely information from the east bank was a frustrating chore. In the first days of an impromptu operation of this sort, there were bound to be shortages of matériel and of specialized troops. One of these was in Signal Corps units. So frequently did vehicles and artillery cut telephone lines laid across the railroad bridge and so often did debris and a swift current break wires strung in the river that telephone communications with the east bank were out about as much as they were in. Neither liaison officers, who often were delayed in threading their way back across the congested bridge, nor radio communications could solve the problem entirely.

Committing incoming infantry units on the far bank was a piecemeal proposition, geared both to when units arrived and to where the most pressing need existed at the time. Not even the various components of all regiments were able to stay together, and splitting the parts of divisions was the rule. This heightened problems of control that haste, improvisation, and the sharply compartmented terrain had already made bad enough.

To General Millikin, the way to overcome his problems was not to make bold thrusts here and there but to expand the entire periphery of the bridgehead systematically. On 8 March he ordered a controlled advance to three successive phase lines: the first—two and a half miles north and south of the Ludendorff Bridge and about two miles deep—designed to free the bridge site from small arms fire; the second designed to eliminate observed artillery fire; and the third—extending as far north as Bonn, as far south as Andernach, and east well beyond the autobahn—designed to free the bridge site of all shelling.[22]

As night fell on 10 March, the 78th Division's 311th Infantry had advanced beyond the first phase line and taken Honnef, almost five miles north of the bridge. Progress was marked too in the south, where the 27th Armored Infantry Battalion captured a village beyond the

town of Linz, not quite three miles southeast of the bridge.

In the high wooded hills east of the bridge progress was slower. There the 9th Division's 60th Infantry had been able to go less than a mile from the river. German tenacity there could be explained in part by the rugged terrain but owed much also to relatively strong artillery support. Since artillery units had retreated across the Rhine ahead of the infantry and tanks, a number of them had reached the east bank in fair shape, particularly those a little farther north where advance of the VII Corps had shoved them across the Rhine before the III Corps came up to the river at Remagen. A volks artillery corps from the north was committed early to the fighting east of Remagen, and other artillery units were on the way. Soon the Germans would be employing against the bridgehead some fifty 105-mm. barrels, another fifty 150-mm. howitzers, and close to a dozen 210-mm. pieces. The shortage of ammunition rather than guns was the more serious problem.[23]

Although the extent of progress belied it, General Millikin intended the eastward and southeastward thrusts to be his main effort, in keeping with the theory —advanced by both Bradley and Eisenhower—that the troops in the bridgehead could best serve the over-all scheme by driving toward the Lahn River valley and the Frankfurt-Kassel corridor. At the same time, Millikin reasoned, such thrusts would also more quickly eliminate German observation on the bridge. General Hodges for his part wanted the III Corps first to push north-

---

[22] III Corps Opnl Dir 10, 8 Mar 45; General Millikin's comments on the draft MS of this volume.

[23] MS # B–547 (Generalleutnant Eduard Metz).

ward in order to clear crossing sites for General Collins's VII Corps. Yet he failed to make this clear to Millikin until the fourth day, 11 March, when for the first time he crossed the Rhine into the bridgehead. Even then he issued no specific order, although he did make several allusions to the north and strongly suggested that the main effort be made in that direction.[24]

The suggestion was enough for Millikin. He promptly put emphasis behind the 78th Division's thrust by narrowing the division's sector and shifting the bulk of the 9th Division to the northeast. On the following day, 12 March, with the arrival of most of the 99th Infantry Division in the bridgehead to take over the southern and southeastern portions of the periphery, he ordered all units shifted back to their parent divisions; but by that time, the chance for a really spectacular drive northward had passed.

Indications that the going might become more difficult developed as early as 11 March, when contingents of the *11th Panzer Division* counterattacked at Honnef, temporarily regaining the town.[25] On the same day a second volks artillery corps reached the front. On 13 March, as remnants of the *340th Volks Grenadier Division* arrived, the German commander, General Bayerlein, put them into the line east of Honnef. Later in the day the *130th Infantry Regiment,* a well-equipped and comparatively fresh separate unit of 2,000 men, arrived from the Netherlands. Although Bayerlein wanted to counterattack immediately

with the *130th Infantry* reinforced by tanks, Field Marshal Model ordered that the regiment be used to bring the *340th Volks Grenadier Division* back to reasonable strength. Thus, the *130th* too went into the defensive line.[26]

Unlike Bayerlein, Model believed that no decisive counterattack could be launched until sufficient infantry reinforcement arrived to release the armored units from the line. In this he was supported by General von Zangen, under whose *Fifteenth Army* Bayerlein's forces opposing the bridgehead operated. Yet in disagreement with Zangen, Model insisted that the strongest line be built in the north to thwart what he remained convinced would be the Americans' major thrust. At a meeting on 11 March with Model and the new Commander in Chief West, Field Marshal Kesselring, Zangen protested this line of thought. Field Marshal Kesselring for his part apparently sanctioned it, for Model's view prevailed.[27]

With disapproval of the plan to use the *130th Infantry* offensively, General Bayerlein saw his last hope for an effective counterattack pass. To Bayerlein, there was no chance of assembling sufficient forces to drive the Americans into the Rhine once they had gained additional time to reinforce their bridgehead.[28] On the other hand, Model's decision did serve to slow operations in the sector where the American commander, General Millikin, now planned, temporarily, his main effort. Thus General Hodges' dissatisfaction with Milli-

---

[24] Combat interview with Col Phillips, CofS III Corps; Sylvan Diary, entry of 11 Mar 45; Gen Millikin's comments on the draft MS of this volume.

[25] MSS # A-970 (Bayerlein) and # B-590 (Wietersheim).

[26] See criticisms in MS # B-829 (General der Infanterie Gustav von Zangen).

[27] MSS # B-829 (Zangen) and # B-101 (General der Infanterie Otto Hitzfeld).

[28] MS # A-970 (Bayerlein).

kin's handling of the bridgehead fight continued.

At the bridge site, concentrated efforts were made from the start toward supplementing the Ludendorff railroad bridge. One of the first units to arrive for the purpose was Naval Unit No. 1, a U.S. Navy force with twenty-four LCVP's (landing craft, vehicle and personnel) that had been attached to the First Army for some months in anticipation of the Rhine crossings.[29] Also quick to arrive was an engineer unit of the III Corps, the 86th Engineer Heavy Ponton Battalion, with orders to operate three ferries, one well north of the Ludendorff Bridge, one close to the bridge at Remagen, and the third well south of the bridge. As assembled by the engineers, the rafts were made of five pontons covered with wooden flooring. Used as free ferries propelled by 22-hp. outboard motors, the craft began to operate as early as the morning of 9 March. The ferries and LCVP's were augmented on 14 March by dukws (2½-ton amphibious trucks) of the 819th Amphibious Truck Company.[30]

Survey teams of the 1111th and 1159th Engineer Combat Groups, scheduled to build tactical bridges across the Rhine, reached Remagen during the morning of 8 March. Because of road priorities granted at first to infantry units and engineers who were to operate ferries, the bridging units themselves began to move to the river only during the night of 9 March. Construction of the first bridge, a treadway from Remagen to Erpel, began early on 10 March.

Although jammed roads leading to Remagen continued to hamper bridge construction, the most serious delays derived from German artillery fire and air attacks. During 8 and 9 March, the Germans maintained an average rate of one shell every two minutes in the vicinity of the bridge sites, but by 10 March, their fire had fallen off to four or five rounds per hour.[31] Artillery fire during the course of construction of the Remagen treadway bridge destroyed four cranes, two Brockway trucks, two air compressors, three dump trucks, and thirty-two floats. The treadway, nevertheless, was opened for limited traffic at 0700, 11 March, and for full use in late afternoon. A heavy ponton upstream at Linz was opened at midnight on the 11th. On the 13th engineers closed the Ludendorff Bridge in order to repair damage caused by Captain Friesenhahn's emergency demolition.

Unlike the artillery fire, German air attacks were more annoying than destructive. A strong cordon of defenses around the bridge manned by the 16th Antiaircraft Artillery Group, antiaircraft battalions borrowed from the divisions of the III Corps, and additional units transferred from the V Corps sharply interfered with German accuracy. On 12 March, at the height of air attacks against the bridge, sixteen 90-mm. gun batteries were emplaced on the west bank of the Rhine and twenty-five batteries of automatic antiaircraft weapons were almost equally divided between the two banks,

---

[29] LCVP's could carry thirty-six soldiers with full combat equipment, vehicles up to the size of ¾-ton ambulances or trucks, or four tons of cargo. See Samuel Eliot Morison, *The Invasion of France and Germany* (Boston: Little, Brown and Company, 1957), pp. 317–23.

[30] For the engineer story, see AAR's of the engineer units, III Corps Engineer War Diary, and combat interviews with engineer officers.

[31] Sylvan Diary, entries of 8–10 Mar 45; III Corps AAR, Mar 45.

probably the most intensive tactical grouping of antiaircraft weapons in the European theater during the course of the war.[32]

The Luftwaffe first struck at the railroad bridge on the morning after Lieutenant Timmerman and his intrepid little band had crossed. Although low overcast interfered with flight, the Germans made ten sweeps with a total of ten planes, most of them Stuka dive bombers. None inflicted any damage on the bridge, and antiaircraft units claimed eight destroyed.[33]

Exhortation to the Luftwaffe to strike and strike again was one of the few immediate steps Field Marshal Kesselring could take toward eliminating the Ludendorff Bridge after he assumed command in the west on 10 March. He conferred that day with senior Luftwaffe commanders, urging them to knock out the bridge and any auxiliary bridges the Americans might construct.

From 8 through 16 March, the Luftwaffe tried. The German planes struck at the railroad bridge, at the ferries, and at the tactical bridges, but with no success. Whenever the weather allowed, American planes flying cover over the bridgehead interfered; even when the German pilots got through the fighter screen, they ran into a dense curtain of antiaircraft fire. When they tried a stratagem of sending slow bombers in the lead to draw the antiaircraft fire, then following with speedy jet fighters, the Americans countered by withholding part of their fire until the jets appeared.

American antiaircraft units estimated that during the nine days they destroyed 109 planes and probably eliminated 36 others out of a total of 367 that attacked.

By three other means the Germans tried to destroy the railroad bridge. Soon after losing the bridge, they brought up a tank-mounted 540-mm. piece called the Karl Howitzer. The weapon itself weighed 132 tons and fired a projectile of 4,400 pounds, but after only a few rounds that did no damage except to random houses, the weapon had to be evacuated for repairs. From 12 through 17 March a rocket unit with weapons emplaced in the Netherlands fired eleven supersonic V–2's in the direction of the bridge, the first and only tactical use of either of the so-called German V-weapons (*Vergeltungswaffen,* for vengeance) during World War II. One rocket hit a house 300 yards east of the bridge, killing three American soldiers and wounding fifteen. That was the only damage. Three landed in the river not far from the bridge, five others west of the bridge, and one near Cologne; one was never located.[34]

The night of 16 March, the Germans tried a third method—seven underwater swimmers in special rubber suits and carrying packages of plastic explosive compound—but from the first the Americans had anticipated such a gambit. During the first few days of the bridgehead, before nets could be strung across the river, they dropped demolition charges to discourage enemy swimmers

---

[32] A convenient summary of the antiaircraft defense may be found in 16th AAA Gp AAR, Antiaircraft Artillery Defense of Rhine Bridges, 17 Mar 45.

[33] III Corps AAR, Mar 45.

[34] SHAEF Air Defense Division, Summary of Casualties and Damage from V-Weapon Attack, Report for the Week Ending 19 March 1945; British War Office, The German Long-Range Rocket Programme, 1930–1945, MIA4/14, 30 Oct 45, copy in OCMH; Royce L. Thompson, Military Impact of the German V-Weapons, MS in OCMH.

and stationed riflemen at intervals along the railroad bridge to fire at suspicious objects. Later, with nets in place, they stationed tanks equipped with searchlights along the river.

When the German swimmers first tried to reach the bridge, American artillery fire discouraged them from entering the water. On the next night, the 17th, they moved not against the railroad bridge but against tactical ponton bridges, only to be spotted by the American searchlights. Blinded by the lights, the seven Germans, one by one, surrendered.

While these events occurred along the Rhine, gains in the bridgehead continued to be steady but unspectacular, and General Hodges remained displeased with General Millikin's conduct of the battle. On 15 March Hodges discussed with the 12th Army Group commander, General Bradley, the possibility of relieving Millikin. "Mind you," Hodges remarked, "I have only the greatest admiration and respect for the GIs doing the fighting out there, but I think they have had bad leadership in this bridgehead battle." [35] Bradley left Hodges' headquarters agreeing to look for a replacement for the III Corps commander.

Two days later General Van Fleet, former commander of the 90th Division, arrived at Hodges' headquarters to take Millikin's place. Shortly before 1500, Hodges telephoned Millikin.

"I have some bad news for you," Hodges said, then went on to inform him of his relief.

The III Corps commander waited until Hodges had finished.

"Sir," he said finally, "I have some bad

GENERAL VAN FLEET. (*Photograph taken in 1951.*)

news for you too. The railroad bridge has just collapsed." [36]

The End of the Bridge

It happened during a period of relative quiet. No German planes were around, and German artillery was silent. About 200 American engineers with their equipment were working on the bridge.

The first indication that anything was wrong was a sharp report like the crack of a rifle. Then another. The deck of the bridge began to tremble. The entire deck vibrated and swayed. Dust rose from the planking. It was every man for himself.

---

[35] Sylvan Diary, entry of 15 Mar 45.

[36] *Ibid.*, entry of 17 Mar 45.

With a grinding roar of tearing steel, the Ludendorff railroad bridge slipped, sagged, and with a convulsive twist plunged into the Rhine. Of those working on the bridge at the time, 93 were injured, 28 killed.

The collapse of the bridge could be attributed to no one specific factor but rather to a combination of things, some even antedating the emergency demolition. As far back as 1940 Allied planes had launched sporadic attacks against the bridge, and in late 1944 had damaged it to such an extent that it was unserviceable for fifteen days. Then came the heavy planking to convert the bridge for vehicles; the assault by the 27th Armored Infantry Battalion's Company A and the fire of the big Pershing tanks that accompanied it; Friesenhahn's emergency demolition; the drumbeat of hundreds of infantry feet; the heavy tread of tanks and other vehicles; the pounding of German artillery; the vibrations from German bombs, from American antiaircraft pieces and big 8-inch howitzers emplaced nearby, from the near misses of the V–2's; and then the weight of heavy engineer equipment as the Americans tried to repair the bridge. All had to be borne by the downstream truss alone after Friesenhahn's demolition so damaged the upstream truss that it was useless. In the end, it was too much for one weakened truss.[37]

More speculative is the explanation of why the German demolitions failed, in the first place, to destroy the Ludendorff Bridge. Sabotage, for example, either by a German soldier or a foreign laborer,

hardly could be ruled out.[38] Since the electric circuit designed to set off the main demolitions had been tested shortly before it was to be used and was in order, something happened to the circuit shortly before Friesenhahn turned the key. Most Germans familiar with the events believed that a lucky hit from an American shell—probably fired by a tank—severed the main cable leading to the demolitions. The Americans themselves conducted no immediate postmortem, and once the bridge had fallen into the Rhine, the evidence was gone.

Whether the reason could be ascertained or not, Hitler at the time was determined to find scapegoats to pay for the debacle. He convened a special 3-man military tribunal that acted with little regard for legal niceties.[39] The tribunal condemned to death two majors who had commanded engineer troops in the vicinity of the bridge, Herbert Strobel and August Kraft; a lieutenant of *Flakartillerie*, Karl Heinz Peters; the major sent by General Hitzfeld of the *LXVII Corps* to assume tactical command at the bridge, Hans Scheller; and the previous tactical commander, Captain Bratge. The engineer in charge of demolitions, Captain Friesenhahn, who had been captured by the Americans, was acquitted in absentia. Because Bratge too was an American prisoner, he survived. The other four died before firing squads.

Expansion of the Bridgehead

The loss of the Ludendorff Bridge had no effect on operations in the Remagen bridgehead. The bridge had been closed

---

[37] Combat interview with Lt Col Clayton A. Rust, CO 276th Engineer Combat Bn.

[38] Hechler, in *The Bridge at Remagen*, pages 212–20, analyzes the various speculations in detail.
[39] *Ibid.*, pp. 192–212.

THE RHINE AT THE REMAGEN BRIDGE SITE. (*Photograph taken in 1948.*)

for repairs since 13 March, and the forces in the bridgehead already were accustomed to working without it. General Hodges nevertheless quickly authorized construction of a floating Bailey bridge about a mile downstream from Remagen. In a remarkable engineering feat, the Bailey bridge was completed in just under forty-eight hours and opened for traffic on 20 March.[40]

One reason for a new bridge was the presence of a new force in the Remagen

bridgehead. Beginning early on 15 March, the 1st Division of General Collins's VII Corps had crossed the Rhine over the III Corps bridges and on ferries, and at noon the next day, Collins assumed responsibility for the northern portion of the bridgehead. In the process, Collins's corps absorbed the 78th Division.

The specific role the Supreme Commander, General Eisenhower, intended the Remagen bridgehead to play in future operations meanwhile had been made clear on 13 March. The bridge-

---

[40] III Corps Engineer War Diary, 120600 Mar 45.

head, Eisenhower directed, was to be used to draw enemy units from the Ruhr area opposite the 21 Army Group and from the 6th Army Group's Rhine crossing sites in the south. Although an exploitation eventually might be made in the direction of Frankfurt, a minimum of ten First Army divisions had to be reserved for the time being as a possible "follow-up force" for the 21 Army Group, still designated to make the Allied main effort.[41]

From this restriction, it was obvious that Eisenhower had no wish to see the bridgehead expanded appreciably. General Bradley in turn told the First Army to advance no farther than a line approximately twenty-five miles wide at the base along the Rhine and ten miles deep, in effect, a slight expansion of the third phase line that the III Corps commander, General Millikin, earlier had imposed.[42]

The First Army's General Hodges disagreed, though to no avail. Like almost everybody at First Army headquarters, Hodges was piqued about the elaborate preparations Field Marshal Montgomery was making for his 21 Army Group's crossing of the Rhine and the emphasis General Eisenhower continued to place on that crossing when, in Hodges' view, a breakout from the Remagen bridgehead could have been staged at will. With evident amusement he listened to the story—probably apocryphal—of how the 21 Army Group on 7 March had asked Supreme Headquarters to stage a diversion before Montgomery jumped the Rhine and how, five minutes later, SHAEF passed the word that the First

Army had already staged a diversion; the First Army had crossed the Rhine.[43]

While advances in the Remagen bridgehead continued to average only about a thousand yards a day, Hodges was convinced this was less a reflection of German strength than of timidity in American attacks. By 17 March the German order of battle opposite the bridgehead sounded impressive on paper—in addition to those units early committed, the Germans had brought in contingents of the *26th, 62d, 272d, 277th,* and *326th Volks Grenadier Divisions;* the *3d* and *5th Parachute Divisions;* and the *3d Panzer Grenadier Division*—but in no case were these real divisions. All were battalion-size *Kampfgruppen* or else had been fleshed out to something more than regimental strength with inexperienced replacements culled from various *Wehrkreise* up and down the Rhine.[44] In most cases the Americans characterized the resistance as "moderate to light." Although the German defense appeared to be "orderly," the more serious problem was difficult terrain.[45]

By 16 March, when troops of the 78th Division made the first cut of the Ruhr-Frankfurt autobahn northeast of Honnef, expansion of the bridgehead had proceeded to the point where artillery no longer was able to support the attacks properly from the west bank of the Rhine. As artillery units began to cross the river, engineers supporting the VII Corps began construction of three more tactical bridges to care for the increased logistical burden. Keyed to the northward advance of the infantry east of the

[41] SCAF 232, SHAEF to Bradley, 13 Mar 45, in 12th AGp Military Objectives, 371.3, vol. VI. Quote is from Bradley, *A Soldier's Story,* p. 517.

[42] 12th AGp Ltr of Instrs No. 17, 13 Mar 45.

[43] Sylvan Diary, entry of 15 Mar 45, and *passim.*

[44] III Corps and VII Corps AAR's Mar 45, and pertinent German MSS.

[45] III Corps AAR, Mar 45.

Rhine, the first of the bridges was completed late on 17 March, another on 19 March, and a third, located at the southern fringe of Bonn, on 21 March. Screened by smoke from chemical generators, the engineers incurred only one casualty during the course of construction.[46]

Of all the American attacks, those to the north and northeast by the 1st and 78th Divisions continued to bother the German army group commander most. More than ever convinced that the Americans intended to make their main effort northward toward the Ruhr, Field Marshal Model recognized that a strong counterattack had to be staged soon or the Americans would breach the natural defensive line in the north, the Sieg River, which enters the Rhine just downstream from Bonn, and then be ready for exploitation.

On 19 March Model began to strip all armored units from the eastern and southern portions of the line to assemble them in the north for counterattack. In the process, he introduced the *LXXIV Corps* to command the northern sector, then ordered the commander, General Puechler, to exchange places with the tank expert, General Bayerlein of the *LIII Corps,* thereby reversing the two corps headquarters. As finally constituted, the ring around the Remagen bridgehead involved the *LIII Corps* under Bayerlein in the north, the *LXXIV Corps* under Peuchler in the center, and the *LXVII Corps* under General Hitzfeld in the south.[47]

Unfortunately for Model's plan, the

Americans afforded no pause in their attacks. Once relieved from the line, the depleted German armored units had to be committed piecemeal again to try to block the continuing thrusts. Although this produced occasional intense combat, particularly at towns or villages blocking main highways, nowhere was it sufficient to stall or throw back the infantry of the two American divisions. Operating with only normal tank and tank destroyer attachments, the 78th Division on 21 March gained the Sieg River, the northern limit of the bridgehead as authorized by General Bradley. At that point the corps commander, General Collins, attached to the 78th Division a combat command of the 3d Armored Division to attack east along the south bank of the Sieg. By 22 March the divisions of the VII Corps had reached the final bridgehead line, both at the Sieg River and along the west bank of the little Hanf Creek that empties into the Sieg just over nine miles east of the Rhine.

The 9th and 99th Divisions of the III Corps, commanded now by General Van Fleet, profited from the shift of German armor to the north. On 18 March the 9th Division at last cut the autobahn, while patrols from the 99th Division reached the meandering Wied River almost due east of Remagen. Other contingents of the 99th Division drove swiftly southward close along the Rhine almost to a point opposite Andernach. By 20 March the III Corps had reached the prescribed bridgehead line.

As both corps neared the planned line, General Hodges at the First Army's headquarters fretted at the restrictions still binding his troops. Watching with admiration far-reaching drives west of

<hr>

[46] VII Corps Engineer Office, Rhine Crossings of VII Corps; VII Corps AAR, Mar 45.

[47] MSS # A–970 (Bayerlein); # B–829 (Zangen); # B–101 (Hitzfeld).

the Rhine by the Third Army, Hodges was convinced the end for Germany was near. "The war is over, I tell you," he kept repeating to his colleagues; "the war is over." [48]

The next day, 19 March, as pleasant but unfounded rumors swept the First Army of an impending armistice, Hodges flew, at the 12th Army Group commander's behest, to meet General Bradley in Luxembourg City. During the morning, Hodges learned, Bradley had conferred with General Eisenhower. In anticipation of an early attack by Montgomery's 21 Army Group to cross the Rhine, Hodges was authorized to send a maximum of nine divisions into the Remagen bridgehead. From 23 March on, he was to be prepared to break out to the southeast, the main objective to be Limburg and the Lahn River valley and linkup with Third Army troops once Patton's forces crossed the Rhine. [49]

The wraps thus were about to be removed from the First Army, though the final unveiling was predicated on Montgomery's crossing the Rhine. The date for the First Army's big push later would be set for 25 March.

In preparation for the attack, Hodges on the 21st sent General Huebner's V Corps into the bridgehead to take over the southern periphery from the 99th Division. When the attack date came, nine divisions, including three armored divisions, would be ready for the exploitation.

It remained for the Germans to write a final, futile postscript to the Remagen bridgehead fighting. On 24 March, still imbued with the idea that the Americans

were aiming directly for the Ruhr, Field Marshal Model managed to assemble the bulk of the German armor for his long-delayed counterattack under the direction of General Bayerlein. Yet when the Germans struck the divisions of the VII Corps, their efforts were poorly co-ordinated and far too weak for the job. It was, in effect, not one counterattack but several small ones that brought intense fighting at various points but, in the end, gained nothing. The Germans merely frittered away irreplaceable troops that would be needed desperately the next day elsewhere along the periphery of the Remagen bridgehead and already were needed at other points on the elongated Rhine front, where on 23 March portentous events had begun to occur.

The capture of the Ludendorff railroad bridge and its subsequent exploitation was one of those *coups de théâtre* that sometimes happen in warfare and never fail to capture the imagination. Just how much it speeded the end of the war is another question. The bridgehead dealt a serious blow to German morale that may well have been partly responsible for lackluster resistance at other points, and it served as a magnet to draw a measure of fighting strength from other sites. On the other hand, the German Army clearly would have been beaten without it, perhaps just as quickly. [50]

From 7 through 24 March, the Remagen bridgehead fighting cost the III Corps approximately 5,500 casualties, including almost 700 killed and 600 missing. the VII Corps, from 16 through 24 March, incurred not quite 1,900 casualties, including 163 killed and 240

---

[48] Sylvan Diary, entry of 18 Mar 45.
[49] *Ibid.*, entries of 19–20 Mar 45.

[50] For a German view, see Wagener, MS # A–965.

missing. In the same time span, the Germans lost more than 11,700 men as prisoners alone.

When the First Army attacked again on 25 March, a new war of movement even more spectacular than that displayed in the drive to the Rhine was to open. A precursor of what it would be like was to be seen in a drive already underway by the Third Army into the Saar-Palatinate.

CHAPTER XII

The Saar-Palatinate

General Patton of the Third Army was "just a little envious" of the First Army's Rhine crossing at Remagen.[1] Yet there was little he could do immediately—once the 4th Armored Division had turned away from the Rhine—to emulate it. The Third Army was obligated to assist in a pending drive to eliminate the last German position west of the Rhine, and Patton himself was eager to expand his army's part in that operation from support to major effort.

The position to be erased had become known to American planners and commanders, after the political entity that made up the bulk of the area, as the Saar-Palatinate. Lying south of the Moselle, the area embraced more than 3,000 square miles and included the Saar industrial region, the old Bavarian Palatinate, part of the provinces of Rhineland and Hessen, and a belt of French territory along the Franco-German border in the northeastern corner of Alsace. Near the southern base of the region stood the West Wall, there stronger than anywhere else. On the western edge, General Walker's XX Corps, having cleared the Saar-Moselle triangle and captured Trier, had already pierced the West Wall; the rest of the Third Army, having conquered the Eifel, was in behind the German defenders.

To the Allies, the Saar-Palatinate had been an important goal since preinvasion planning days. The Saar was second only to the Ruhr as a source of Germany's war-making muscle, and the region screened feasible Rhine crossing sites lying between Mainz and Mannheim. Both the Third Army and General Devers's 6th Army Group needed access to those crossing sites to assure their logical roles in the final broadfront advance into the heart of Germany.

From the German viewpoint, the Saar-Palatinate was important both for its economic significance and for the military obstacle it posed to Allied armies. Based on the nearby iron ore of Lorraine and on extensive coal fields in the Saar River basin around Saarbruecken, the heavy industry of the Saar contributed 10 percent of Germany's iron and steel capacity. Coal production totaled 7,000,000 tons annually. Despite the proximity of Allied troops and almost daily raids by Allied planes, the Germans in early March still were shipping twelve trainloads of coal daily to plants east of the Rhine, and the foundries of the Saar continued to operate. At Homburg, northeast of Saarbruecken, stood one of the comparatively few synthetic oil plants still producing in the Reich; and at Ludwigshafen, across the Rhine from Mannheim, some

---

[1] Patton, *War As I Knew It*, p. 254.

40 to 50 percent of the nation's entire output of chemicals was centered in an I. G. Farben plant. The industry of small cities such as Kaiserslautern, Speyer, and Worms also was important.[2]

As a miiltary obstacle, the Saar-Palatinate drew strength not only from the West Wall but also from the built-up industrial region, from deep stream valleys, and from mountainous terrain. Along the northern boundary twists the deep valley of the Moselle, backed by the Hunsrueck Mountains, higher than the Eifel. Along the western and southern boundaries, the Saar and the Lauter Rivers pose similar barriers, the former also backed by the Hunsrueck Mountains, the latter by the densely forested Haardt or Lower Vosges Mountains, rising as high as 2,300 feet. Between the Hunsrueck and the Haardt lies the Pfaelzer Bergland, or Palatinate Highland.

The watershed between the Pfaelzer Bergland and the Haardt Mountains is high and narrow but also relatively flat and traversed by a good highway leading from Saarbruecken through Kaiserslautern to the Rhine in the vicinity of Worms, thus constituting a small corridor with considerable military utility. This corridor has become known as the Kaiserslautern Gap. A northeastward extension of the Metz Gap in Lorraine, it is one of only two logical passages through the Saar-Palatinate for sizable

military forces. The other, the Wissembourg Gap, whence the Prussians debouched against France in 1870, opens a way from the northeastern corner of France into the valley of the Rhine.

The man responsible for defending the Saar-Palatinate was General Hausser, who had assumed command of *Army Group G* near the end of January after recovering from a wound incurred while commanding an army in France the preceding summer. In addition to the *First Army,* which long had held the Saar front, Hausser's command at first had included the *Nineteenth Army,* formerly a part of that anomaly called *Army Group Oberrhein;* but as the *Nineteenth Army* in early February withdrew under pressure from the Colmar pocket to the east bank of the Rhine, one by one its combat divisions had been commandeered for more active fronts. In early March, as the drive by Patton's Third Army threatened to riddle the Eifel and expose the long line of the Moselle, thereby prompting *OB WEST* to shift the *Seventh Army* in the Eifel to Hausser's command, the *Nineteenth Army* passed to direct control of the Commander in Chief West.

In most ways, the shift was a case of *plus ça change, plus c'est la même chose.* Yet Hausser's responsibility for the *Seventh Army* meant that his point of main danger shifted from the Kaiserslautern and Wissembourg Gaps to the winding trench of the Moselle facing the Eifel.

Unless additional units could be sent to bolster the *Seventh Army,* Hausser notified *OB WEST,* successive withdrawals back to the Rhine was the best *Army Group G* could hope to accomplish. "Otherwise," Hausser warned, "envelop-

---

[2] The Seventh United States Army Report of Operations, France and Germany, 1944–1945, vol. III, p. 695, a comprehensive three-volume work prepared with the assistance of historical officers attached to the Seventh Army (hereafter cited as Seventh Army Report). See also MS # B-600, *Army Group G,* Report of the Commander (Generaloberst Paul Hausser).

ment and annihilation of *First Army* will be imminent." [3]

The answer from Field Marshal von Rundstedt, acting out his last days as Commander in Chief West, was succinct, uncompromising.

Hold the Saar-Palatinate.

American Plans

For the Americans, clearing the Saar-Palatinate would be a return to unfinished business that the Third and Seventh Armies had been conducting in December when forced to retrench to help defeat the Ardennes counteroffensive and Operation *NORDWIND,* the secondary counteroffensive in Alsace. Both armies had reached the West Wall guarding the Saar-Palatinate in December. The Third Army had forged two bridgeheads into the fortified line, one of which, at Saarlautern, remained intact. The Seventh Army had cleared northeastern Alsace and jumped the Lauter River at two points to confront the West Wall, but the necessity to spread out in order to free Third Army units for the Ardennes and to recoil before Operation *NORDWIND* had forced withdrawals, in some places as much as nineteen miles. Through most of February the Seventh Army had staged limited objective attacks to straighten lines and gain favorable ground for a major offensive against the Saar-Palatinate. Nevertheless, by the end of the first week in March, most of the northeastern corner of Alsace still was in German hands. The front departed from the Saar River near Sarreguemines and extended almost di-

rectly southeast through Hagenau to the Rhine.[4] (*Map X*)

Anticipating early completion of operations to clear the west bank of the Rhine north of the Moselle, General Eisenhower on 13 February had told his two American army group commanders, Bradley and Devers, to begin planning for a joint drive to sweep the Saar-Palatinate. Assigned a target date of 15 March, the offensive was to begin only after the 21 Army Group had reached the Rhine. It was to be designed both to draw enemy units from the north and to provide an alternate line of attack across the Rhine should the principal Allied drive in the north fail. The main effort, SHAEF planners contemplated, was to be made by the 6th Army Group's Seventh Army, which was to be augmented by transferring one armored and three infantry divisions from the Third Army.[5]

During the first week of March, General Devers at 6th Army Group approved a plan (Operation UNDERTONE) prepared by General Patch's Seventh Army. Three corps were to attack abreast from Saarbruecken to a point southeast of Hagenau. A narrow strip along the Rhine leading to the extreme northeastern corner of Alsace at Lauterbourg was to be cleared by a division of the First French Army under operational control of the Seventh Army. The Seventh Army's main effort was to be made in the center up the Kaiserslautern corridor.[6]

---

[3] MS # B-600 (Hausser).

[4] These actions are covered in Robert Ross Smith, The Riviera to the Rhine, a forthcoming volume in the UNITED STATES ARMY IN WORLD WAR II series.

[5] SHAEF GCT/37057/Plans, Note on Early Concentration for Saar Offensives, 14 Feb 45, SHAEF files.

[6] Seventh Army Report, pp. 698–99.

GENERAL DEVERS. (*Photograph taken in late 1945.*)

Approving the plan in turn, General Eisenhower noted that the objective was not only to clear the Saar-Palatinate but also to establish bridgeheads with forces of the 6th Army Group over the Rhine between Mainz and Mannheim. The 12th Army Group (i.e., the Third Army), he also noted, was to be limited to diversionary attacks across the Moselle to protect the 6th Army Group's left flank.[7]

Eisenhower approved on 8 March, the same day that General Patton obtained approval from General Bradley for the plan prepared by the Third Army staff for a major attack across the Moselle.[8]

The 12th Army Group commander in turn promoted the plan with General Eisenhower.[9] Noting that the Germans had given no indication of withdrawing from the West Wall in front of the Seventh Army and that General Patch thus might be in for a long, costly campaign, Bradley suggested that the Third Army jump the Moselle near Koblenz, sweep south along the west bank of the Rhine to cut the enemy's supply lines, and at the same time press from its previously established Saar-Moselle bridgehead near Trier to come at the West Wall fortifications from the rear. General Eisenhower approved the plan without qualification.[10]

While the proposal to employ the Third Army in the Saar-Palatinate was based on sound tactical considerations, Bradley and Patton both also saw it as a way of getting the Third Army involved, thereby obviating loss of divisions either to Montgomery's 21 Army Group or to Devers's 6th Army Group.[11] Yet the stratagem proved unnecessary as far as the 21 Army Group was concerned, since General Eisenhower told Field Marshal Montgomery that if ten U.S. divisions went north to help the 21 Army Group, Bradley's 12th Army Group headquarters would also move north to command the First and Ninth Armies. That may have played a part in silencing Montgomery on the subject of

---

[7] FWD 17655, SHAEF to Devers and Bradley, 081650 Mar 45, SHAEF SGS Post-OVERLORD Planning file, 381, III.

[8] See above, ch. X; Gay Diary, entry of 8 Mar 45.

[9] Bradley, *A Soldier's Story*, p. 516.

[10] *Ibid.* A plan for a combined Third-Seventh Army thrust to clear the Saar-Palatinate had been prepared at 12th Army Group as early as February, when flooding of the Roer River appeared likely to delay Operation GRENADE indefinitely. See Col. Harrison H. D. Heiberg, Study of Future Operations, 12th AGp Miscellaneous Log 214.

[11] Bradley, *A Soldier's Story*, p. 255.

additional American divisions to exploit his Rhine crossing.[12]

The stratagem only partially succeeded with the 6th Army Group; Bradley at last felt compelled to relinquish two divisions, the 4th Infantry and 6th Armored, the latter already designated as SHAEF reserve. Although he agreed to part with a third, impending arrival of the last serials of a new division from the United States made it unnecessary. As the target date for the Saar-Palatinate campaign neared, the 6th Army Group had eleven infantry and three armored divisions in the Seventh Army, plus the First French Army. The Third Army retained twelve divisions, four of them armored.

Although General Devers was briefly reluctant to endorse Third Army operations south of the Moselle lest the two forces become entangled with their converging thrusts, he too in the end approved the plan. He and Bradley agreed on a new boundary that afforded the Third Army a good road leading northeast from Saarlautern to headwaters of the Nahe River, some thirty-five miles northeast of Saarlautern, thence along the valley of the Nahe to the Rhine at Bingen. This boundary gave the Third Army responsibility for clearing the northwestern third of the Saar-Palatinate. Bradley and Devers also authorized the commanders of the two armies, Third and Seventh, to deal directly with each other rather than through their respective army group headquarters. Patton and the Seventh Army commander, General Patch, agreed in turn that once operations were

GENERAL PATCH

under way, Patton's right corps and Patch's left might also deal directly.[13]

Facing the undented fortifications of the West Wall, the Seventh Army commander planned a set-piece attack, preceded by an extensive program of aerial bombardment. Before the attack could begin, supplies had to be accumulated, division and corps boundaries adjusted, some units shuffled, and new divisions joining the army fed into jump-off positions.[14] This meant to General Patch

---

[12] *Ibid.*, pp. 517–18.

[13] Msg, 6th AGp to SHAEF, 081708 Mar 45, SHAEF SGS file, 381, III; 12th AGp Ltr of Instrs 17, 13 Mar 45.

[14] In a local attack on 13 March to better positions for start of the offensive, T. Sgt. Morris E. Crain of the 36th Division's 141st Infantry provided exemplary leadership without regard for his own safety through much' of the day, then

that the Seventh Army could not attack before the target date, 15 March.

General Patton, on the other hand, based his entire plan for participation in the Saar-Palatinate on exploiting disorganization in German ranks resulting from his Eifel drive. The sooner he could start the better his chances for far-reaching results. He saw no point in waiting for the Seventh Army.

That was part of the reasoning behind Patton's preoccupation with bridges over the Moselle which resulted in shifting the 4th Armored Division away from the Rhine on 9 March.[15] When the attempt to capture a bridge intact across the Moselle failed, Patton turned to a deliberate attack to be opened with a strike by the XX Corps on 12 March.

While the 76th Division, transferred from the XII Corps, took over an earlier assignment given the XX Corps to clear a narrow sector along the north bank of the Moselle, the rest of the XX Corps was to drive east from the Saar River bridgehead south of Trier, the bridgehead established as a corollary of the operations to clear the Saar-Moselle triangle. As soon as regrouping was complete, General Eddy's XII Corps was to jump the lower Moselle near Koblenz and head for Bingen, at the juncture of the Nahe and the Rhine, and for Bad Kreuznach, a few miles upstream on the Nahe. Walker and Eddy thus were, in effect, to make converging attacks that, if unaltered later, would join along the

Nahe River. General Middleton's VIII Corps, meanwhile, was to hold the west bank of the Rhine above Koblenz, finish the mop-up in the Eifel, and eventually reduce Koblenz. If, in the process of its watch on the Rhine, the VIII Corps saw a chance to jump the river, Middleton was to allow it to do so.[16]

Those were the written orders. While they conformed to the established boundary with the Seventh Army along the Nahe River, General Patton from the first intended that the boundary impose no restrictions on his maneuver. Orally, he told his corps commanders that the objective was to establish bridgeheads over the Rhine in the vicinity of Mainz, Oppenheim, and Worms—the same sites he had picked the preceding summer, long before the detour to Bastogne and through the Eifel.[17] All three sites lay in what was then the Seventh Army zone. Patton clearly anticipated a swift breakthrough and rapid exploitation that would impel further boundary adjustment.

The Defenders

As indicated by the warnings of the *Army Group G* commander, General Hausser, that his forces could hope to accomplish no more than a fighting withdrawal from the Saar-Palatinate, the German situation conformed to Patton's expectations. Even had the problem remained merely to defend the old *First Army* front from Trier to the Rhine, most of it bolstered by West Wall fortifications, Hausser's units would have been hard put to hold. As it was, Hausser had to thin already dangerously stretched

---

stayed behind as a one-man covering force when a tank-supported counterattack forced his platoon to withdraw. Sergeant Crain died when German fire demolished the building from which he was fighting. He was awarded the Medal of Honor posthumously.

[15] See above, ch. X.

[16] TUSA Opnl Dir, 10 Mar 45.

[17] Patton, *War As I Knew It,* p. 254.

First Army units in an effort to strengthen his new charge, the *Seventh Army,* along the Moselle.[18]

In the retreat from the Eifel, General Felber's *Seventh Army* lost not only thousands of soldiers but a corps headquarters, the *LIII Corps.* Split away from the rest of the army by the U.S. 4th Armored Division's plunge to the Rhine, the corps commander, General Botsch, and some of his staff had escaped across the Rhine, while the bulk of those in the *Seventh Army* who got away were falling back behind the Moselle. To take the place of this corps, the *Army Group G* commander, General Hausser, called on the *LXXXIX Corps* under General der Infanterie Gustav Hoehne from the extreme left wing of the *First Army.* Leaving behind its assigned divisions to be absorbed by the neighboring corps, the headquarters of the *LXXXIX Corps* arrived at the Moselle on 9 March.

To General Hoehne went the task of defending some twenty-five miles of the Moselle from Koblenz to a point upstream from Cochem. As everywhere along the Moselle, the snakelike convolutions of the river added to the actual length of the front and created dangerous re-entrants. To defend such a serpentine obstacle with any real hope of success would have required either enough troops on the north bank to stop the re-entrants or sufficient reserves to hit any crossing quickly. The *LXXXIX Corps* and the *Seventh Army* had neither.

As the *LXXXIX Corps* moved into position, General Hoehne assumed command of *Kampfgruppe Koblenz,* a 1,800-man local defense force whose only fire support was from stationary antiaircraft guns, mostly east of the Rhine, and the *276th Infantry Division,* which had escaped from the Eifel with the equivalent of two infantry, two engineer, and two light field artillery battalions. Withdrawn from the *First Army* as a first step in providing a reserve for the *Seventh Army,* a third unit, the *159th Infantry Division,* had to be used instead to augment Hoehne's corps. A force of fairly presentable strength, the *159th* took over the left wing.[19]

By further stretching the *First Army* defenses, the *Army Group G* commander had freed another unit, also scheduled originally for the *Seventh Army* reserve —the *6th SS Mountain Division,* perhaps the most combat-worthy division remaining in *Army Group G.* Yet on 5 March, in a belated reaction to the U.S. 10th Armored Division's capture of Trier, *OB WEST* had ordered that division to counterattack across the Ruwer River south of Trier to sever the American armored division's line of communications. Striking the U.S. 94th Division, the mountain division the next day had cut the main highway into Trier from the south.[20]

It was a Pyrrhic victory. In the attack and against the American counterattacks that followed, the flower of the *6th SS Mountain Division*'s manpower fell. Two days later, as *OB WEST* finally gave in to *Army Group G*'s protestations, the remainder of the division began to withdraw, but for lack of gasoline one

---

[18] Unless otherwise noted, the German story is based on the following MSS: # B–238 (Hauser); # B–123 (Gersdorff); # B–831 (Felber); # B–600 (Hausser); and # C–020 (Schramm).

[19] MSS # B–377, Fighting of the *LXXXIX Corps* From 10 to 16 March (General der Infanterie Gustav Hoehne); # B–831 (Felber).
[20] 94th Div AAR, Mar 45.

regiment had to stay behind. Although General Hausser decided, reluctantly, to give the division to the *LXXXIX Corps* rather than hold it in reserve, only the reconnaissance battalion would reach the corps before the Moselle front erupted.

Hausser had only one other hope for a reserve. For more than a week he had sought to withdraw the *559th Volks Grenadier Division* from a salient extending beyond the West Wall south of Saarbruecken; but since that would involve abandoning some West Wall positions, authority had to come from Hitler himself. The permission finally arrived but, as events were to prove, too late. The first contingents of the division became available to assist the *Seventh Army* only on 15 March.

On the left of the *LXXXIX Corps,* responsible for another twenty-five miles of steep, rocky, vine-clad river bank, stood General von Oriola's *XIII Corps,* consisting of remnants of three volks grenadier divisions and the *2d Panzer Division.* None of the divisions could be classed as more than a *Kampfgruppe* and the panzer division, though somewhat stronger in numbers than the others, had only a few tanks. The rest of the Moselle front to the vicinity of Trier, thence southeast along the Ruwer River to a point of contact with the *First Army* three miles south of the Moselle, belonged to General Beyer's *LXXX Corps.* Beyer commanded remnants of three volks grenadier divisions.[21]

Despite the withdrawals to aid the *Seventh Army, Army Group G*'s other major component, the *First Army* under General der Infanterie Hermann Foertsch, remained the considerably stronger force. Having benefited by transfer of a number of the *Nineteenth Army*'s divisions following withdrawal from the Colmar pocket, the *First Army* had seen little major fighting in recent weeks except that in the Saar-Moselle triangle and the limited objective attacks in Alsace launched by the American Seventh Army in February. Yet the weakest point of the *First Army* front was at the same time the most threatened, and the necessity of giving up divisions to the *Seventh Army* meant that General Foertsch could do little about it.

The point in question was the bridgehead beyond the Saar River and the West Wall south of Trier established by the U.S. XX Corps. There stood the *LXXXII Corps* under General Hahm, part of which earlier had been driven from the Saar-Moselle triangle. Until 10 March, the corps still had only three divisions, two of which had been roughly treated in the triangle. The third, the *2d Mountain Division,* was also seriously understrength following its futile, piecemeal counterattacks against the bridgehead over the Saar. On 10 March command of the remnants of another division passed from the *Seventh Army*'s *LXXX Corps* to the *LXXXII Corps,* but with it came responsibility for defending an additional three miles of front close to Trier. With this addition, General Hahm's line ran from a point east of Trier southeast to the other American bridgehead over the Saar at Saarlautern. Somewhat less than one-half of this line

---

[21] MSS # B-052, *XIII Corps,* 18 February–21 March 1945 (Generalleutnant Ralph von Oriola); # B-082, *The Final Fighting of the LXXX Army Corps From the Marne to the Danube* (General der Infanterie Franz Beyer), p. 3.

benefited from West Wall fortifications.[22]

Containing the Saarlautern bridgehead was one of the responsibilities of the *LXXXV Corps,* commanded by General der Infanterie Baptist Kniess. The corps had three divisions, all nearly at full strength; but one, the *559th Volks Grenadier,* was destined for transfer to the *Seventh Army.*[23] Unlike the commander of the adjoining *LXXXII Corps* and those defending the Moselle, General Kniess was confident his troops could hold against frontal attack, for the West Wall in his sector was in considerable depth. It was concern about American breakthrough from the rear that plagued both Kniess and the commanders of two other corps that extended the *First Army* line southeast to the Rhine. Although these two corps, the *XIII SS* and the *XC,* would no doubt be driven back from their advanced positions in Alsace, they would gain strength by retiring into the West Wall.

When the new Commander in Chief West, Field Marshal Kesselring, paid his first visit to *First* and *Seventh Army* headquarters on 13 March, the army group commander, General Hausser, and the two army commanders used the occasion to emphasize how sterile and potentially disastrous they considered the policy of all-out defense west of the Rhine. It could only result, they insisted, in wholesale losses, perhaps annihilation. The latter, General Felber of the *Seventh Army* pointed out, seemed highly likely, because the U.S. 4th Armored Division was apparently concentrating along the

lower Moselle near Cochem for a quick thrust that could cut the entire army group off from the Rhine.

Yet Kesselring, true to his charge from his Fuehrer—whether he believed in it or not—refused to sanction either withdrawal or a deliberate delaying action. "The positions," Kesselring said, "have to be held."[24]

Through the Hunsrueck

General Patton's plan of attack was admirably designed to capitalize on German weaknesses. Striking first, Walker's XX Corps might attract any available reserve, whereupon Eddy's XII Corps was to jump the Moselle at one of the defenders' weakest points, the sector of Hoehne's *LXXXIX Corps.* Quick convergence of the two drives well might trap the other two corps of the *Seventh Army,* and a logical extension of Eddy's thrust southward alongside the Rhine could, as the German General Felber feared, trap all of *Army Group G.*

For the opening attack, General Walker had an outsize corps of four infantry divisions, two cavalry groups, and an armored division. One cavalry group, the 3d, started the fighting during the afternoon of 12 March with a diversionary attack in a loop of the Moselle near the confluence of the Moselle and the Ruwer. After nightfall, as a drizzling rain showed signs of diminishing, troops of three infantry divisions moved toward lines of departure along the periphery of the Saar bridgehead south of Trier. At 0245 on 13 March an impressive total of thirty-one divisional and corps field

---

[22] MS # B-066 (Ingelheim).

[23] MS # B-121, *LXXXV Corps,* 25 January-23 March 1945, Operations in the Saar (General der Infanterie Baptist Kniess).

[24] Quotation is from MS # B-600 (Paul Hausser). See also MSS # B-123 (Gersdorff); # B-831 (Felber); # B-238 (Wolf Hauser).

artillery battalions opened fire. Fifteen minutes later, the infantry moved through the darkness to the attack.

The 94th Division (General Malony) on the left headed east toward the cross-roads town of Hermeskeil, ten miles beyond the Ruwer; the 80th Division (General McBride) in the center drove southeast toward Weiskirchen and Losheim, approximately seven miles away. Capture of these objectives would put the XX Corps through the most densely wooded portions of the Hunsrueck and open the way for armor. The 26th Division (General Paul) meanwhile attacked almost due south in a narrow zone close to the Saar to roll up the West Wall. After daylight, a regiment of the 65th Division (Maj. Gen. Stanley E. Reinhart), new to combat, staged a diversionary, limited objective attack in the Saarlautern bridgehead.[25]

Nowhere was the going easy. The terrain—high, fir-covered hills, deep draws and ravines, and a secondary roadnet already churned into mud by German vehicles—was enough in itself to see to that; but the German regiments, seriously depleted in numbers, could take advantage of the difficult ground only at isolated points rather than along a continuous line. In the darkness, the attacking battalions stumbled onto some enemy positions, ran into minefields, and drew heavy small arms and mortar fire, but more often than not, a sideslipping to left or right brought quick relief and continued advance. The action was more an infiltration than an attack, with reserve companies and reserve battalions

taking out the strongpoints after daylight came.

By early evening of 13 March, the 94th and 80th Divisions both had firm holds on the first ridgeline beyond the original bridgehead, as much as two miles from the jump-off points, and bridges were in place across both the Ruwer and a feeder stream that cut the 80th Division's zone.[26] Unlike the other two units, the 26th Division in the pillbox belt near the Saar came in for frequent local counterattacks, but that division also advanced as much as two miles.

The next day, 14 March, the drive slowed down. The Germans, wherever encountered, fought back defiantly, giving no indication of general withdrawal. This was particularly true among the pillboxes faced by the 26th Division, where a combination of concrete-reinforced resistance and rough terrain brought advances that had to be measured in yards rather than miles. A counterattack by the regiment of the *6th SS Mountain Division* that had been left behind by its parent division for want of gasoline slowed the advance of the 80th Division.[27] When the weather cleared in the afternoon, planes of the XIX Tactical Air Command got into the fray in strength, but because it was hard to pinpoint advance positions in the thick fir

[25] For assignments, see XX Corps FO 18, 10 Mar 45. Unless otherwise noted, this account is based on official records of the XX Corps and its divisions.

[26] Part of the success achieved by the 80th Division's 318th Infantry was directly attributable to the actions of one officer, 2d Lt. Harry J. Michael. He singlehandedly captured two machine guns and their crews, then led his platoon in a charge that carried an artillery position and seized three guns. A few hours later he individually captured 13 Germans, wounded 4, and killed 2, then again led a successful charge against German pillboxes. The next morning a shot from ambush cut Lieutenant Michael down. He was awarded the Medal of Honor posthumously.

[27] MS # B–066 (Ingelheim).

forests, the strikes had to be confined to targets well in front of the infantry.

Visiting all three division command posts during the day, the Third Army commander was disturbed at the slow pace. General Patch's Seventh Army, General Patton knew, was to begin its offensive the next morning. Patton was concerned lest Patch beat him to the Rhine.[28]

Patton need not have worried. On the third day, 15 March, no general German collapse developed, but the signs were there. The 94th Division's 302d Infantry plunged forward four miles and reached a point less than three miles from the division objective of Hermeskeil. A battalion of the 80th Division's 318th Infantry fought its way into Weiskirchen, one of that division's objectives, there encountering a veritable hornet's nest of opposition. The battalion nonetheless achieved a sizable gain and was on the edge of more open country. Another battalion made an even deeper thrust farther south. Although the 26th Division had the usual hard time with pillboxes, the 26th's attack was a subsidiary operation that nobody looked on as the bellwether of the drive.

To the XX Corps commander, General Walker, the time for exploitation seemed at hand. Although air reconnaissance found no evidence of wholesale German withdrawal, this report merely reinforced Walker's determination to commit his armor. A swift strike by tanks might trap the Germans before they had a chance to escape.

Just after midnight Walker told the 10th Armored Division, already on one-hour alert, to jump off before daylight

on the 16th to pass through the 94th and 80th Divisions. The goal was the Nahe River, some twenty-five miles away.

Across the Lower Moselle

Playing a large part in Walker's decision was the situation in the zone of General Eddy's XII Corps on the lower Moselle. There, before dawn on 14 March, two infantry divisions had set out to cross the river.

The terrain along the lower Moselle is forbidding at the river line itself—precipitous, forested slopes rising to a thousand feet, with egress from the river bottom by steep twisting roads—but only a mile or two from the river most of the roads emerge onto open, relatively flat-surfaced ridgelines broad enough for military maneuver. Thus the XII Corps commander, General Eddy, anticipated that once his infantry had reached the crest of the ridgelines, armor could quickly take over and drive the remaining thirty miles to the Nahe River. Although he ordered his infantry divisions to attack toward the Nahe as soon as they had established bridgeheads over the Moselle, he alerted the 4th Armored Division for rapid commitment and urged corps engineers to begin building bridges capable of handling tanks even as the infantrymen were crossing the river in assault boats.[29]

Concealed by darkness and a heavy fog, two regiments of the 90th Division (General Earnest) and one of the 5th (General Irwin) began to cross the Moselle at 0200, 14 March, behind a 30-minute artillery preparation. A second regiment

---

[28] Patton, *War As I Knew It*, p. 259.

[29] See XII Corps FO 16, 11 Mar 45. Unless otherwise noted, the tactical story is from official records of the corps and divisions.

of the 5th Division—arrival of its assault boats delayed by traffic-jammed roads—crossed two hours later. Only an occasional inaccurate burst of fire from restless German machine gunners interfered with any of the crossings.

On the far bank, the infantrymen found resistance centered almost exclusively in the towns and villages. In Treis, riverside nexus of several good roads leading southeast and six miles downstream from Cochem, contingents of the enemy's *159th Division* held a battalion of the 5th Division's 2d Infantry at bay until after nightfall when opening of a treadway bridge across the Moselle enabled tanks to help mop up. It took a battalion of the 90th Division's 357th Infantry until noon to clear other troops of the *159th Division* from the town of Brodenbach, while in another town just over a mile downstream the *6th SS Mountain Division*'s reconnaissance battalion held out until midafternoon.

In the meantime, the other battalions of both the 5th and 90th Divisions had been occupying the high ground between and behind the villages. By nightfall some units had pushed more than two miles beyond the river; casualties in the two divisions together totaled less than a hundred. At first concealed by fog, then by smoke, and hampered only by a swift current and sporadic, ineffective German shelling, engineers soon after nightfall opened treadway bridges to serve both divisions.

The comparative ease of the crossing early prompted the 5th Division commander, General Irwin, to alert a regiment for a fast motorized advance the next morning, 15 March, aimed at the corps objective along the Nahe River. The corps commander, General Eddy,

was similarly impressed. When Irwin asked for trucks to transport his infantry, Eddy cautioned that he intended to commit the 4th Armored Division (General Gaffey) early the next day. To Irwin's protest that his infantry could reach the objective while the armored division was sorting itself out after crossing the river, Eddy insisted that the exploitation was a job for armor.[30]

To the German *LXXXIX Corps* commander, General Hoehne, it was equally apparent that the American bridgehead was firmly established and soon would explode. While he knew that the main body of the *6th SS Mountain Division* probably would arrive the next day, he also recognized that the division was too depleted from the futile counterattack south of Trier and the loss of a regiment to General Hahm's *LXXXII Corps* even to postpone the inevitable. As the division began to arrive piecemeal early on the 15th, Hoehne committed it against the left flank of the U.S. 90th Division, hoping thereby at least to hold open an escape route eastward to the Rhine.[31]

General Hoehne's preoccupation with the American left flank became manifest on 15 March in the pattern of American advance. On the left, in the relatively narrow triangle of land between the Moselle and the Rhine, the 90th Division's 357th Infantry absorbed two sharp counterattacks, one supported by two tanks, another launched by newly arrived troops of the *6th SS Mountain Division*. At the forest-cloaked village of Pfaffenheck, midway between the Moselle and the Rhine, a hundred SS troopers

---

[30] The 5th Division telephone journals are a valuable source for this period.

[31] MS # B-377 (Hoehne). See also MSS # B-123 (Gersdorff); # B-831 (Felber).

supported by a lone tank fought furiously and successfully against the 357th Infantry's 2d Battalion to hold a road leading to the Rhine. Although a platoon of Company E forced its way into the village in early morning, the Germans cut off and captured the riflemen before reinforcements could arrive.

Attacking down parallel roads to the southeast, the 90th Division's other two regiments expanded the bridgehead line six miles beyond the Moselle before the 4th Armored Division's Combat Command A passed through in the afternoon. The armor almost immediately ran into stubborn resistance built around four antitank guns and extended the line only a little more than an additional mile before coiling for the night.

On the right wing of the XII Corps, where the enemy corps commander soon lost all communications with his *159th Division* and presumed the unit doomed, similar resistance failed to develop.[32] The advance was spectacular. Passing through troops of the 5th Division at noon, the 4th Armored's Combat Command B quickly picked up momentum. Roadblocks at the entrance of each town, usually defended by no more than a cluster of riflemen and machine gunners, were about all that stood in the way. White sheets fluttered from upper-story windows, a now familiar sign that German civilians had divined the approaching end. Enjoying a bright, sunlit day, fighter-bombers of the XIX Tactical Air Command worked in close co-ordination with the armor and before night fell had flown 643 sorties to claim a new record for five groups in one day.[33] In just over five hours, CCB moved sixteen miles beyond the Moselle, more than half the distance to the Nahe River. The tankers stopped for the night in Simmern, only a few miles from the Soonwald, the last big terrain obstacle short of the Nahe.

Convinced beyond doubt that CCB's deep thrust presaged a quick end to organized resistance, General Eddy attached motorized regimental combat teams from the 90th and 5th Divisions to CCA and CCB, respectively. In order to broaden the front and prevent other German units from turning against the penetration, he ordered the 89th Division (Maj. Gen. Thomas D. Finley), experiencing its first combat, to cross the Moselle beside the 5th Division early the next morning, 15 March. Shifted by General Patton from the VIII Corps, the 11th Armored Division was to follow on the 17th.[34]

With General Hoehne's *LXXXIX Corps* split by Combat Command B's thrust, the *Seventh Army* commander, General Felber, made the usual cry for help to his *Army Group G* superior, General Hausser. Noting that the first contingents (two infantry battalions) of the *559th Volks Grenadier Division* had arrived in the army's sector during the afternoon, Hausser promised to do what he could to speed the rest of the division. He also ordered the *First Army* to release another volks grenadier division, but in view of the canopy of American fighter planes that spanned the Saar-Palatinate during daylight, neither division probably would be able to arrive in time to help.

For his own part, General Felber ordered General Hoehne to conduct a fighting withdrawal using those forces of

[32] MS # B–377 (Hoehne).
[33] XII Corps Opnl Dir 88, 16 Mar 45.

[34] *Ibid.*

the *LXXXIX Corps* that were east of the American penetration. If compelled, Hoehne was to fall back across the Rhine. What was left of the *159th Division* was to be attached to the *XIII Corps* (General von Oriola) and was to assume a bridgehead defense north of the Nahe River. The bridgehead was to be used as a reception station for the *XIII Corps* once approval for the corps to withdraw could be wrung from higher command.[35]

The German commanders had every reason to ask for withdrawal; two corps of the *Seventh Army,* the *XIII* and *LXXX Corps,* both still holding along the Moselle, were in danger of encirclement. The 4th Armored Division breakthrough was but one aspect of that danger. The German commanders also had to cast wary glances over their left shoulders at the attack of the U.S. XX Corps.

Plunge to the Nahe and Fall of Koblenz

In General Walker's XX Corps, combat commands of the 10th Armored Division (General Morris) began passing through infantry of the 80th and 94th Divisions before daylight on 16 March. Although the Germans of General Hahm's *LXXXII Corps* during the night had formed a new crust of resistance sufficient to deny genuine armored exploitation for another twenty-four hours, no doubt remained among either American or German commanders as the day ended that a deep armored thrust was in the offing.

When it came, the exploitation would possess added power as a result of a visit the Supreme Commander paid the Third Army commander in late morning of the 16th. Patton asked General Eisenhower for another armored division, the 12th, then in Seventh Army reserve, and Eisenhower agreed. Like General Eddy's XII Corps, Walker's XX Corps was to have six divisions.[36]

In the XII Corps, meanwhile, the exploitation involved no delay. Renewing the drive from Simmern, the 4th Armored's CCB took the obstacle of the Soonwald in stride and plunged almost unimpeded another fourteen miles. The head of the column reached the Nahe River at noon near Bad Muenster, two miles upstream from the corps objective of Bad Kreuznach, seized a railroad bridge intact, and quickly established a bridgehead.

Fighter-bombers of the XIX Tactical Air Command again were out in force, bombing and strafing anything German that moved on the roads. Ironically, it was the fighter-bombers that saved the German *Seventh Army* commander, General Felber, and his chief of staff, General von Gersdorff, from capture. In the process of moving their command post, the two officers had to take to the woods to escape strafing American planes. Minutes later tanks of the 4th Armored Division passed nearby, unaware of the prey the planes had forced into hiding. For an hour Felber and Gersdorff had to hide in the woods before they were able to escape over a back road.

It was but a short-lived respite for the two German officers. Even as they rejoined the rest of the *Seventh Army* staff in Gensingen, midway between Bad Kreuznach and the Rhine, the 4th Armored's other attacking combat com-

---

[35] MSS # B–831 (Felber); # B–123 (Gersdorff).

[36] Patton, *War As I Knew It,* pp. 259–62.

mand was fast bearing down on them. Having run into stanch resistance near the north edge of the Soonwald from the *6th SS Mountain Division*'s reconnaissance battalion, Combat Command A again had found the going slower than had CCB; but once air and artillery support had helped overcome the opposition, CCA too began to roll. The head of CCA's column reached the Nahe opposite Gensingen before dark. Although all bridges over the river had been demolished, fire from the tankers' guns forced the *Seventh Army* staff again to flee.[37]

At the Moselle River, German miseries were compounded on 16 March in two places. Upstream from Cochem and the 5th Division crossing sites, General Finley's 89th Division before daylight sent two regiments across the river in assault boats against a modicum of resistance. As with the earlier crossings, fighting was restricted almost entirely to the riverside villages, and there the weak task forces of General von Oriola's *XIII Corps* could hope to hold only briefly. By the end of the day, the inexperienced 89th Division held a substantial bridgehead and was ready to receive the tanks of the 11th Armored Division.

German troubles also increased downstream near the confluence of the Moselle with the Rhine. There General Middleton, his VIII Corps reduced to but one division and cavalry group, sent his lone division, the 87th, across the Moselle to capture the city of Koblenz.[38]

The 87th Division commander, General Culin, planned to do the job with two regiments. The 347th Infantry was to cross the river before daylight on 16

March about five miles upstream from Koblenz. Through a narrow clearing in the high woodlands that feature most of the narrow triangle between the Moselle and the Rhine, the regiment was to drive southeast about seven miles to the Rhine, thus cutting off the defenders of Koblenz from any possible aid from the south. A second regiment, crossing the Moselle opposite Koblenz itself, was to reduce the city.

Aware from intelligence reports that the enemy's *LXXXIX Corps* had few troops for defending the little triangle other than weak contingents of the *276th Volks Grenadier Division* and local Koblenz defense forces, General Culin anticipated no major fight. The utter ease of the 347th Infantry's crossing nonetheless came as a surprise. Not a shot, not a round of shellfire, indeed, not a sign of the enemy met the two assault battalions. Dawn was fast approaching when the first opposition developed, a scattering of small arms fire in a village several hundred yards from the river.

The first really troublesome resistance came in the afternoon at Waldesch, midway between the Moselle and the Rhine. There recently arrived contingents of the *6th SS Mountain Division* effectively blocked a little corridor of cleared land leading to the Rhine.

Noting the ease of the 347th Infantry's crossing, General Culin saw no need to repeat the process opposite Koblenz. Instead, he ordered a second regiment to cross in the 347th's sector, then swing northeast against the city. By the end of the day, 16 March, two battalions were in the southern fringes of the city and had cleared a new Moselle crossing site for the rest of the regiment.

To the German *Seventh Army* com-

---

[37] MSS # B–831 (Felber); # B–123 (Gersdorff).
[38] VIII Corps FO 15, 14 Mar 45.

ENGINEERS OF THE 87TH DIVISION *ferry a tank across the Moselle.*

mander, General Felber, advent of the new American force removed any rationalization that might have existed for the *LXXXIX Corps* to attempt to hold longer west of the Rhine. At noon on the 16th he told the corps commander, General Hoehne, to begin his withdrawal, though in Koblenz itself *Kampfgruppe Koblenz* was to fight to the last. As night came, a heavy fog favored the evacuation. Some 1,700 men, all that remained of Hoehne's *LXXXIX Corps*, made it to the east bank.[39]

Aided by deadly airbursts from high-velocity antiaircraft guns firing from beyond the Rhine, the 1,800-man *Kampfgruppe Koblenz* put up a stout defense the next day, 17 March, even though the outcome of the fight was inevitable. The last resistance was destined to fade early on 19 March with no more than half a hundred survivors escaping across the Rhine.[40]

---

[39] MSS # B-377 (Hoehne); # B-123 (Gersdorff); # B-831 (Felber). See also MS # B-124, *276th*

Volks Grenadier Division (Col. Werner Wagner, Actg Comdr.)
[40] MS # B-377 (Hoehne).

Seventh Army's Deliberate Attack

All along the Moselle, from Koblenz to Trier, the German *Seventh Army* on 17 March was in peril, if not from direct attack, then from the flanking thrust against the right wing of the *First Army* by General Walker's XX Corps. Collapse of the *Seventh Army* clearly was but a question of time. Soon the German *First Army,* too, would be in dire straits, for the American Seventh Army two days earlier, on 15 March, had launched a power drive against General Foertsch's army along a 70-mile front from the vicinity of Saarlautern southeastward to the Rhine. Even if that offensive failed to penetrate the West Wall, it might tie the *First Army* troops to the fortifications while Patton's forces took them from the rear.

The U.S. Seventh Army traced its origin back to Sicily where General Patton had first led it into battle. An infantryman who had seen combat many months before on Guadalcanal, "Sandy" Patch, had assumed command for the invasion of southern France and a swift advance northward. Patch's chief of staff was an artilleryman, Maj. Gen. Arthur A. White, who had held a similar post under Patch on Guadalcanal.

The Seventh Army numbered among its ranks several relatively inexperienced units but retained a flavoring of long-term veterans. The VI Corps (Maj. Gen. Edward H. Brooks), for example, and three divisions—the 3d, 36th, and 45th—had fought at length in the Mediterranean theater, including the Anzio beachhead. The XV Corps (Maj. Gen. Wade H. Haislip) had joined the Seventh Army after fighting across France with the Third Army. A third corps, the

XXI (Maj. Gen. Frank W. Milburn), was relatively new, having joined the army in January.

As the Seventh Army offensive began, the basic question was how stubbornly the Germans would defend before falling back on the West Wall. Only General Milburn's XXI Corps, on the Seventh Army left wing near Saarbruecken, was fairly close to the West Wall, while other units were as much as twenty miles away. Making the army's main effort in the center, General Haislip's XV Corps faced what looked like a particularly troublesome obstacle in the town of Bitche. Surrounded by fortresses of the French Maginot Line, Bitche had been taken from the Germans in December after a hard struggle, only to be relinquished in the withdrawal forced by the German counteroffensive. On the army's right wing General Brooks's VI Corps, farthest of all from the West Wall, had first to get across the Moder River, and one of Brooks's divisions faced the added difficulty of attacking astride the rugged Lower Vosges Mountains.

Two German corps and part of a third were in the path of the impending American drive. At Saarbruecken, the left wing of General Kniess's *LXXXV Corps* would receive a glancing blow from Milburn's XXI Corps. Having recently given up the *559th Volks Grenadier Division* to the *Seventh Army,* Kniess had only two divisions, one of which was tied down holding West Wall positions northwest of Saarbruecken. Southeast of the town, with boundaries roughly coterminous with those of Haislip's XV Corps, stood the *XIII SS Corps* (SS Gruppenfuehrer and Generalleutnant der Waffen-SS Max Simon) with three divisions. Extending the line to the

Rhine was the *XC Corps* (General der Infanterie Erich Petersen) with two volks grenadier divisions and remnants of an infantry training division.

Although the Germans worried most about a breakthrough in the sector of Petersen's *XC Corps* into the Wissembourg Gap rather than through Simon's *XIII SS Corps* into the Kaiserslautern corridor, the shifts and countershifts made in preceding weeks to salvage reinforcements for the *Seventh Army* actually had left the *XIII SS Corps* the stronger. In addition to two volks grenadier divisions, Simon's corps had the *17th SS Panzer Grenadier Division,* at this point not much more than a proud name, but a unit possessing considerably more tanks and other armored vehicles than were to be found in the entire adjacent corps. The American main effort thus aimed at the stronger German units, though at this stage of the war strength in regard to German divisions was but a relative term.[41]

As General Patch's Seventh Army attacked before daylight on 15 March, the apparent answer on German intentions was quick to come. Only in two places could the resistance be called determined. One was on the left wing, where the 63d Infantry Division (Maj. Gen. Louis E. Hibbs) sought to bypass Saarbruecken on the east and cut German escape routes from the city. The fact that the 63d Division early hit the West Wall provided ready explanation for the

stanch opposition there. The other was on the extreme right wing where an attached 3d Algerian Infantry Division (3e Division d'Infanterie d'Algerie) was to clear the expanse of flatland between Hagenau and the Rhine. There an urban area closely backing the Moder River defensive line and flat ground affording superb fields of fire for dug-in automatic weapons accounted in large measure for the more difficult fighting.[42]

Elsewhere local engagements sometimes were vicious and costly but usually were short-lived. Antipersonnel and antitank mines abounded. German artillery fire seldom was more than moderate and in most cases could better be classified as light or sporadic. That was attributable in part to a campaign of interdiction for several days preceding the attack by planes of the XII Tactical Air Command (Brig. Gen. Glenn O. Barcus) and by D-day strikes by both the fighter-bombers and the mediums and heavies of the Eighth Air Force. The latter hit West Wall fortifications and industrial targets in cities such as Zweibruecken and Kaiserslautern. The weather was beautifully clear, enabling the aircraft to strike at a variety of targets, limited only by range and bomb-carrying capacity. Among the German casualties were the operations officers of two of the three *XC Corps* divisions.[43]

Of the units of the outsized (six divisions) XV Corps, only a regiment of the 45th Division (Maj. Gen. Robert T. Frederick) faced a water obstacle at the start. That regiment had to cross the Blies River at a site upstream from where

[41] For the German story, see MSS # B–071, *XC Infantry Corps* December 1944–23 March 1945 (General der Infanterie Erich Petersen); # B–711, Engagements of the *XIII SS AK* West of the Rhine (Waffen-SS Oberst:urmbannfuehrer Ekkehard Albert, CofS, *XIII SS Corps*); # B–121 (Kniess); # B–238 (Wolf Hauser); and # B–600 (Paul Hausser).

[42] Unless otherwise noted, the account of Seventh Army action is based on official records of Seventh Army and subordinate units.

[43] MS # B–071 (Petersen).

the Blies turns northeast to meander up the Kaiserslautern corridor. Yet even before dawn men of the regiment had penetrated the enemy's main line of defense beyond the river. Aided by searchlights, they bypassed strongpoints, leaving them for reserves to take out later. As night came the 45th Division had driven almost three miles beyond the Blies to match a rate of advance that was general everywhere except in the pillbox belt near Saarbruecken and on the flatlands near the Rhine.

On the right wing of the XV Corps, men of the 100th Infantry Division (Maj. Gen. Withers A. Burress) drove quickly to the outskirts of the fortress town of Bitche. Perhaps aided by the fact that they had done the same job before in December, they gained dominating positions on the fortified hills around the town, leaving no doubt that they would clear the entire objective in short order the next day, 16 March.

The only counterattack to cause appreciable concern hit a battalion of the 3d Division's 7th Infantry. Veterans of combat from the North African campaign onward, the regiments of the 3d Division (Maj. Gen. John W. O'Daniel) were making the main effort in the center of the XV Corps in the direction of Zweibruecken and the Kaiserslautern corridor. Although a company of supporting tanks ran into a dense minefield, disabling four tanks and stopping the others, a battalion of the 7th Infantry fought its way into the village of Uttweiler, just across the German frontier. Then an infantry battalion from the *17th SS Panzer Grenadier Division,* supported by nine assault guns, struck back. The Germans quickly isolated the American infantrymen but could not

force them from the village. Supported by a platoon of tank destroyers and the regimental antitank company organized as a bazooka brigade, another of the 7th Infantry's battalions counterattacked. The men knocked out four multiple-barrel 20-mm. flakwagons and seven assault guns and freed the besieged battalion.

On the Seventh Army's right wing, pointed toward the Wissembourg Gap, divisions of General Brooks's VI Corps experienced, with the exception of the 3d Algerian Division, much the same type of opposition. Although all four attacking divisions had to overcome the initial obstacle of a river, either the Moder or a tributary, they accomplished the job quickly with predawn assaults. The Germans were too thinly stretched to do more than man a series of strongpoints. On the corps left wing, the 42d Infantry Division (Maj. Gen. Harry J. Collins) overcame the added obstacle of attacking along the spine of the Lower Vosges by avoiding the roads and villages in the valleys and following the crests of the high ground. Pack mules, already proved in earlier fighting in the High Vosges, provided the means of supply.

As with the 3d Division, a battalion of the 103d Infantry Division (Maj. Gen. Anthony C. McAuliffe) ran into a counterattack, but the reaction it prompted was more precautionary than forced. Having entered Uttenhofen, northwest of Hagenau, the battalion encountered such intense small arms fire and shelling from self-propelled guns that the regimental commander authorized withdrawal. When German infantry soon after nightfall counterattacked with support from four self-propelled pieces, the battalion pulled back another few

TROOPS OF THE 63D DIVISION *cross dragon's teeth of the West Wall.*

hundred yards to better positions on the edge of a copse.

In the sector of the 36th Infantry Division (Maj. Gen. John E. Dahlquist), the day's fighting produced a heroic performance by a rifleman of the 142d Infantry, Pfc. Silvestre S. Herrera. After making a one-man charge that carried a German strongpoint and bagged eight prisoners, Herrera and his platoon were pinned down by fire from a second position protected by a minefield. Disregarding the mines, Herrera also charged this position but stepped on a mine and lost both feet. Even that failed to check him.

He brought the enemy under such accurate rifle fire that others of his platoon were able to bypass the minefield and take the Germans in flank.[44]

The 3d Algerian Division meanwhile got across the Moder with little enough trouble but then encountered intense house-to-house fighting. Despite good artillery support made possible by the unlimited visibility of a clear day, grazing fire from automatic weapons prevented the Algerians from crossing a stretch of open ground facing the buildings of a

[44] Private Herrera was awarded the Medal of Honor.

former French Army frontier post. A welter of mines and two counterattacks, the latter repulsed in both cases by artillery fire, added to the problems. As night fell, no Algerian unit had advanced more than a mile.

On the second day, 16 March, indications that the Germans were fighting no more than a delaying action increased everywhere except, again, on the two flanks. It seemed particularly apparent in the zone of the XV Corps, where all three attacking divisions improved on their first day's gains. Mines, demolitions, and strongpoints usually protected by a tank or an assault gun were the main obstacles. By nightfall both the 3d and 45th Divisions were well across the German frontier, scarcely more than a stone's throw from the outposts of the West Wall, and the 100th Division, relieved at Bitche by a follow-up infantry division, had begun to come abreast. Fighter-bombers of the XII Tactical Air Command again were out in force.

Even though the Germans appeared to be falling back by design, in reality they intended a deliberate defense. Although corps commanders had begged to be allowed to withdraw into the West Wall even before the American offensive began, General Foertsch at *First Army* and General Hausser at *Army Group G* had been impelled to deny the entreaties. The new Commander in Chief West, Field Marshal Kesselring, remained as faithful as his predecessor to the Hitler-imposed maxim of no withdrawal anywhere unless forced.[45]

As events developed, no formal order to pull back into the fortifications ever emerged above corps level. Beginning the

night of 16 March, commanders facing the U.S. XV Corps simply did the obvious, ordering their units to seek refuge in the West Wall whenever American pressure grew so great that withdrawal or annihilation became the only alternatives. The next day commanders facing the U.S. VI Corps adopted the same procedure.

It became at that point as much a matter of logistics as of actual fighting before all divisions of the Seventh Army would be battling to break the concrete barrier into the Saar-Palatinate; but as more than one German commander noted with genuine concern, whether any real fight would develop for the West Wall was not necessarily his to determine. That responsibility fell to those units, decimated and increasingly demoralized, which were opposing the onrush of American Third Army troops from west and northwest into the German rear.

Breakthrough

Along the Nahe River units of the *Seventh Army*'s hard-pressed *LXXXIX Corps* got a measure of respite on 17 March as General Gaffey's front-running 4th Armored Division paused to regroup. Having established a bridgehead over the Nahe late on 16 March, Gaffey wanted time to service his tanks and to enable his reserve combat command and the infantry divisions of the XII Corps to come up. The ensuing delay in American attacks aided the *LXXXIX Corps* in its withdrawal, authorized the day before, to the east bank of the Rhine.[46]

Elsewhere in the German *Seventh Army* and on the right wing of the *First*

---

[45] See, in particular, MS # B–711 (Albert).

[46] Msg, CG 4th Armored Div to CG 5th Inf Div, 161820 Mar 45, 5th Div G–3 Jnl file, 16 Mar 45.

Army, there was no respite. As the recently transferred 12th Armored Division moved to reinforce General Walker's XX Corps early on 17 March, the 10th Armored Division drove eight miles and seized a bridge intact over the little Prims River, last water obstacle short of the Nahe. Bringing searchlights forward to provide illumination, the armor prepared to continue the drive through the night toward the Nahe itself at St. Wendel, eleven miles away. On the right wing of the XII Corps, the 89th Division expanded its Moselle bridgehead while the 11th Armored Division moved in behind the infantry as prelude to another thrust toward the Nahe at Kirn, twenty miles beyond the Moselle.[47]

Before daylight on the 17th, the *Seventh Army* commander, General Felber, sent two divisions of the *XIII Corps* to counterattack what appeared to be the most pressing of the converging American threats, the breakthrough of the 4th Armored Division. The effort proved futile. One division lacked sufficient transport even to assemble in time to counterattack, and the other, the *2d Panzer Division* (reduced to 4 tanks, 3 assault guns, about 200 panzer grenadiers, and 2 artillery battalions), found its route

blocked by antitank barriers prematurely closed by panicky German villagers.[48]

Both Felber and the *Army Group G* commander, General Hausser, had for several days been pleading with *OB WEST* for authority to withdraw the entire *Seventh Army* behind the Rhine. All requests drew the usual negative reply. With the collapse of Felber's two-division counterattack, it became obvious to those on the scene that in a few days, if not in hours, both the *XIII Corps* and the *LXXX Corps* would be encircled.

That was the prospect when on 17 March Field Marshal Kesselring issued an ambiguous order. While directing "the retention of present positions," the new Commander in Chief West added a qualification. "An encirclement and with it the annihilation of the main body of the troops," the order stated, "is to be avoided." Hausser seized on this as sufficient authority to pull back at least behind the Nahe.[49]

In the meantime, the swift Third Army advances had stirred higher commanders on the American side. Impressed by Patton's gains, the Supreme Commander on 17 March met at Lunéville, in Lorraine, with the 6th Army Group commander, General Devers, and the two Army commanders concerned, Patton and Patch. Noting the Third Army's gains and the obstacle of the West Wall still opposing the Seventh Army, General Eisenhower asked Patch if he objected to Patton's attacking across the northern portion of the Seventh Army's zone perpendicular to the Seventh Army's axis of attack. General Patch said no; the objective was to de-

---

[47] As an extension of an assignment to sweep the north bank of the Moselle downstream from Trier, the 76th Division the night of the 18th launched a limited objective attack across the Moselle alongside the 89th Division. In this attack, made by the 304th Infantry without active German opposition, a medical aidman, Pvt. William D. McGee, entered an antipersonnel minefield to rescue two men wounded by exploding mines. He carried one to safety but in returning for the other, he himself set off, a mine and was seriously wounded. Refusing to allow others to risk their lives by coming to his rescue, he died of his wounds. Private McGee was awarded the Medal of Honor posthumously.

[48] MS # B-052 (Oriola).
[49] Quotation is from MS# B-600 (Paul Hausser). See also MS # B-123 (Gersdorff).

stroy the German forces. "We are all," he added, "in the same army." [50]

As worked out in detail by Patch and Patton, the two armies split the area between the Nahe River and the Rhine almost equally, with a new boundary running just north of Kaiserslautern and reaching the Rhine south of Worms. Patton nevertheless intended to take Kaiserslautern himself and then turn one infantry and one armored division southeast, deeper into Patch's zone, to link with the Seventh Army's VI Corps along the Rhine. Thereby he hoped to trap any Germans who might remain in front of the Seventh Army in the West Wall. That accomplished, Patton "would clear out of [Patch's] area." [51] The plan presumed, of course, that the Seventh Army at that point would still be involved in the West Wall, but in any event, Patch apparently accepted the agreement with the same good grace earlier accorded the Supreme Commander's proposal.

To General Patton's subordinates, the authority gained at Lunéville meant pressure and more pressure. Why, Patton railed to his XII Corps commander, General Eddy, had the 11th Armored Division failed to push through the 89th Division's Moselle bridgehead on the 17th? Nor was there any excuse for the 4th Armored Division to pause for any time at all at the Nahe River. "The heat is on," General Eddy told his own subordinates, "like I never saw before." [52]

It took another day before the effects generated by the heat began to show up on headquarters situation maps, but by 19 March a graphic representation of the Third Army's gains looked, in the words of Patton's colleague, General Hodges of the First Army, "like an intestinal tract." [53] With the added weight of the 12th Armored Division (Maj. Gen. Roderick R. Allen), General Walker's XX Corps made the more spectacular gains. By midnight of the 19th, the 12th Armored was across the upper reaches of the Nahe and had gone on to jump a little tributary of the Nahe, more than twenty-three miles from the armor's line of departure of the day before. The 10th Armored Division stood no more than six miles from Kaiserslautern. Two of the infantry divisions of the XX Corps, their regiments motorized on organic transport supplemented by trucks from supporting units, mopped up behind the armor, while the 26th Division completed its onerous task of rolling up West Wall fortifications, then turned eastward in a drive that converged with a northeastward thrust from Saarlautern by the 65th Division.[54]

In the XII Corps, the 4th Armored Division on 18 and 19 March failed to regain its earlier momentum, partly because the division had to divert forces to clear Bad Kreuznach and partly because the Germans with their backs not far from the Rhine stiffened. In the two

---

[50] Seventh Army Report, p. 720. See also General Devers's personal diary, lent to OCMH (hereafter cited as Devers Diary); Patton, *War As I Knew It*, pp. 262 and 265.

[51] Patton, *War As I Knew It*, p. 265.

[52] Msg, XIII Corps to 5th Div, and Telecon, CG XII Corps to CG 5th Div, both in 5th Div G–3 Jnl, 17 Mar 45; Patton, *War As I Knew It*, p. 264.

[53] Sylvan Diary, entry of 9 Mar. 45.

[54] During the 65th Division's attack on 18 March, an aidman in the 259th Infantry, Pfc. Frederick C. Murphy, continued to minister to his comarades although wounded in one shoulder. Even after setting off a mine that severed one of his feet, he crawled about to help other wounded around him until at last he set off a second mine that killed him. He was awarded the Medal of Honor posthumously.

days, the 4th Armored advanced just over ten miles beyond the Nahe.

It remained for the newly committed 11th Armored Division on the XII Corps right wing to register the more spectacular gains. Following its disappointing showing in the Eifel, the 11th Armored had a new commander, Brig. Gen. Holmes E. Dager. Under Dager's command, the division on 18 March raced twenty miles to the Nahe River at Kirn. The next day the armor streaked another nineteen miles to the southeast, reaching a point as far east as Kaiserslautern.[55]

When combined with the drive of the 12th Armored Division on the north wing of the XX Corps, the 11th Armored's rapid thrusts tied a noose around what remained of the enemy's *XIII* and *LXXX Corps*. As the efforts of those two corps to withdraw across the Nahe and form a new defensive line went for naught, the infantry divisions following the American armor mopped up the remnants of the *2d Panzer Division* and three volks grenadier divisions. Little more than the headquarters of the two corps escaped.

From all indications, the Germans in the *Seventh Army* and on the right wing of the *First Army* (Hahm's *LXXXII Corps*) were destined for annihilation. As American armored spearheads appeared without warning, seemingly over every hill and around every curve, and as American planes wreaked havoc from the air, hardly any semblance of organization remained in German ranks. It was less withdrawal than it was *sauve qui peut*. Camouflage, antiaircraft security, dispersal—those were fancy terms from some other war, without meaning in this maelstrom of flight. Highways were littered with wrecked and burning vehicles and the corpses of men and animals. Roadblocks at defiles and on the edges of towns and villages might halt the inexorable onflow of tanks and half-tracks temporarily, but the pauses were brief and in the long run meaningless. Improvised white flags flying from almost every house and building along the way added a final note of dejection to the scene.

Yet German commanders, still denied the authority they begged to withdraw behind the Rhine, continued to build up new lines and to shift units here and there—mainly on paper. As night came on the 19th, the *Seventh Army's* General Felber might point to a new line running southwest from Mainz in front of the cities of Alzey and Kaiserslautern, but Felber himself would have been among the first to admit that it was less a line than a proliferation of improvisations.[56]

To the most optimistic German, the end was near. Events on 20 March underscored the fact. In late afternoon contingents of the 90th Division, on the left wing of the XII Corps, arrived on high ground overlooking Mainz and the Rhine. A short while later troops of the 4th Armored Division fought their way into Worms and began to clear a path through the city to the Rhine. Both the 10th and 12th Armored Divisions of the XX Corps still had to emerge from the

---

[55] When a rocket from a *Panzerfaust* hit a tank of the 41st Tank Battalion, wounding the platoon sergeant and prompting others of the crew to abandon the vehicle, the bow gunner, Pfc. Herbert H. Burr, stayed inside and drove the tank into the town of Doermoschel. Rounding a turn, he encountered an enemy 88. Alone, unable to fire while driving, Burr headed directly toward the muzzle of the 88, forcing the crew to flee and overrunning the piece. He was awarded the Medal of Honor.

[56] See MS # B-082 (Beyer) and other manuscripts previously cited for this chapter.

wooded hills of the Pfaelzer Bergland onto the Rhine plain, but they would be on the plain by nightfall of the 20th.

Tacit admission from the Germans that the campaign for the Saar-Palatinate was almost over came late in the day with long-delayed approval for the *Seventh Army* withdrawal. That night on ferries, rafts, small boats, almost anything that floated, General Felber, his headquarters, and headquarters of Oriola's *XIII Corps* began to make their way across the Rhine. General Beyer's *LXXX Corps* stayed behind, taking over all combat troops and being transferred to the *First Army* in an effort to forestall further American advances directly into the rear of the *First Army.*[57]

Thrust to the Rhine

As the breakthrough of General Walker's XX Corps developed in the direction of Kaiserslautern, concern had mounted in the *First Army* lest those units in the West Wall around Saarbruecken and Zweibruecken be trapped. Once Kaiserslautern fell, the only routes of withdrawal left to those troops led through the Haardt Mountains south of Kaiserslautern. Covered by a dense wood, the Pfaelzer Forest, the region was crossed laterally by only one main highway, by a secondary highway close behind the West Wall, and by a few minor roads and trails. The natural difficulties posed by these twisting, poorly surfaced routes already had been heightened by a mass of wrecked vehicles as American fighter pilots relentlessly preyed on hapless targets.

Using the authority granted by Kessel-

ring on 17 March to pull back units threatened with encirclement, the *First Army*'s General Foertsch authorized withdrawal by stages of his westernmost troops, those of General Kniess's *LXXXV Corps.* Over a period of three days, units of the corps were to peel back from west to east, redeploying to block the main highway leading northeast through the Kaiserslautern Gap.

Unfortunately for Foertsch's plan, the principal threat to the Kaiserslautern Gap came not from west or southwest but from northwest where Walker's XX Corps was pouring unchecked through General Hahm's *LXXXII Corps.* The 10th Armored Division's arrival at Kaiserslautern itself on 20 March meant not only that the gap was compromised by a force well in the rear of Kniess's formations but also that the only way out for both Kniess's troops and those of the adjacent *XIII SS Corps* was through the Pfaelzer Forest.

As Kniess's withdrawal progressed, it had the effect of opening a path through the West Wall for the left wing of the American Seventh Army. Despite a stubborn rear guard, the 63d Division of General Milburn's XXI Corps broke through the main belt of fortifications near St. Ingbert late on 19 March. Had events moved according to plan, Milburn then would have sent an armored column northward to link with Walker's XX Corps near St. Wendel; but so swift had been the advance of Walker's troops that all worthwhile objectives in Milburn's sector beyond the West Wall already had fallen. Milburn and his XXI Corps had achieved a penetration but had no place to go.

The Seventh Army commander, General Patch, seized on the situation to pro-

---

[57] MSS # B-831 (Felber); # B-123 (Gersdorff); # B-600 (Paul Hausser).

vide a boost for his army's main effort, the attack of the XV Corps through Zweibruecken toward the Kaiserslautern Gap. In two days of hammering at General Simon's *XIII SS Corps,* the divisions of the XV Corps still had opened no hole through the West Wall for armored exploitation.[58] Send a combat command, Patch directed the XV Corps commander, General Haislip, to move through the 63d Division's gap and come in on the rear of the West Wall defenders facing the XV Corps.

That the Americans would exploit the withdrawal was too obvious to escape the *First Army* commander, General Foertsch. During the night of the 19th, he extended the authority to withdraw to the west wing of the *XIII SS Corps.* Thus, hardly had the American combat command begun to move early on 20 March to exploit the 63d Division's penetration when the 45th Division of the XV Corps also advanced past the last pillboxes of the West Wall near Zweibruecken. During the night of the 20th, the rest of the SS corps also began to pull back, and the momentum of the 3d

Division's advance picked up accordingly.[59]

The German problem was to get the survivors of both the *LXXXV Corps* and the *XIII SS Corps* through the Pfaelzer Forest despite three dire threats: one from the closely following troops of the American Seventh Army; another from the 10th Armored Division of Walker's XX Corps, which at Kaiserslautern was in a position to swing south and southeast through the Pfaelzer Forest and cut the escape routes; and a third from the Argus-eyed fighter bombers of the XII Tactical Air Command.

It was the last that was most apparent to the rank and file of the retreating Germans. Since speed was imperative, the men had to move by day as well as by night, virtually inviting attack from the air. Since almost everybody, including the troops of the motorized *17th SS Panzer Grenadier Division,* had to use either the main east-west highway through the forest or the secondary road close behind the West Wall, American fighter pilots had only to aim their bombs, their cannon, and their machine guns in the general direction of those roads to be assured of hitting some target. An acute gasoline shortage added to the German difficulties. Almost every foot of the two roads soon became clogged with abandoned, damaged, or wrecked vehicles, guns, and equipment.[60]

The destruction in the Pfaelzer Forest was in keeping with the pattern almost everywhere. So long a target of both artillery and aircraft, the drab towns and cities in and close to the West Wall were

---

[58] For no lack of effort, as exemplified by heroic actions of two members of the 45th Division. On 18 March when eight men of the 180th Infantry were wounded while attacking a troublesome pillbox, the company commander, Capt. Jack L. Treadwell, went forward alone. Armed with a submachine gun and hand grenades, he charged the pillbox, captured 4 Germans in it, and went on to reduce singlehandedly five other pillboxes and to capture 14 more prisoners. In three days, culminating on the 18th, Cpl. Edward G. Wilkin, 157th Infantry, did much the same for his company. He too reduced six pillboxes singlehandedly, killed at least 9 Germans, wounded 13, and took 13 prisoner. Captain Treadwell received the Medal of Honor. Corporal Wilkin was awarded the Medal of Honor posthumously; he was killed in a subsequent action before his special act of valor could be officially recognized.

[59] For the German story, see MS # B-238 (Wolf Hauser).

[60] MSS # B-507 (Petersen); # B-238 (Wolf Hauser).

a shambles. "It is difficult to describe the destruction," wrote the 45th Division commander, General Frederick. "Scarcely a man-made thing exists in our wake; it is even difficult to find buildings suitable for CP's: this is the scorched earth." [61] In Zweibruecken, with the entire business district razed, only about 5,000 people of a normal population of 37,000 remained, and they were hiding in cellars and caves. Fires burned uncontrolled, neither water nor fire-fighting equipment available to quench them. No local government existed. Thousands of released slave laborers and German soldiers who had changed into civilian clothes complicated the issue for military government officials. In more than one city, particularly Homburg, looting and pillage were rampant.

Running the gantlet of American fighter aircraft through the Pfaelzer Forest, the amorphous mass of retreating Germans faced still a fourth American threat—General Brooks's VI Corps, which had followed closely the German withdrawal from northeastern Alsace and on 19 March had begun to assault the West Wall on either side of Wissembourg. There General Petersen's XC Corps was charged with holding the fortifications and denying access to the flatlands along the Rhine.

In the Seventh Army's original plan, the attached 3d Algerian Division on the right wing of the VI Corps along the Rhine was to have been pinched out after it reached the Lauter River at the German frontier. The planners had not reckoned with the aspirations of the French and their First Army commander, General de Lattre. Assured of support from the provisional head of the French state, General Charles de Gaulle, de Lattre was determined to acquire a zone along the Rhine north of the Lauter in order to assure a Rhine crossing site for the final drive into Germany.[62]

As the Algerians matched and sometimes exceeded the strides of the American units of the VI Corps and reached the Lauter along a ten-mile front, de Lattre had no difficulty pressing his ambition on the 6th Army Group commander, General Devers. Using the 3d Algerian Division and a combat group from the 5th French Armored Division, again to be attached to the VI Corps, the French were to continue northward some twelve miles beyond the Lauter River, thereby gaining limited Rhine River frontage inside Germany.[63]

The adjustment meant that the West Wall assault by the four American divisions of the VI Corps was to be concentrated in a zone less than twenty miles wide. Since the German XC Corps had only the remnants of two volks grenadier divisions and an infantry training division to defend against both Americans and French, a breakthrough of the fortifications was but a matter of time. Yet just as had been the case in the zones of the XXI Corps and the XV Corps, it was less the hard fighting of the VI Corps that would determine when the West Wall would be pierced than it was the

---

[61] Seventh Army Report, p. 738.

[62] De Lattre discussed the matter with de Gaulle in Paris shortly before the Seventh Army's offensive began. See Marshal Jean de Lattre de Tassigny, *Histoire de la Première Armée Française* (Paris: Librarie Plon, 1949), pp. 407–14.

[63] *Ibid.;* Devers Diary, entry of 18 Mar 45; Ltr, CG 6th AGp to CG's SUSA and First French Army, sub: Creation of *Groupement Monsabert* and Modification of Letter of Instructions Number 11, SUSA Oral Instructions file, 19 Mar 45.

rampaging thrusts of the Third Army's XX Corps in the German rear.

The divisions of the VI Corps had been probing the pillbox belt less than twenty-four hours when General Walker, leaving the task of gaining the Rhine to the 12th Armored Division and of actually capturing Kaiserslautern to an infantry unit, turned the 10th Armored Division south and southeast into the Pfaelzer Forest. By nightfall of 20 March, two of the 10th Armored's columns stood only a few hundred yards from the main highway through the forest, one almost at the city of Pirmasens on the western edge, the other not far from the eastern edge. A third was nearing Neustadt, farther north beyond the fringe of the forest. The 12th Armored meanwhile was approaching the Rhine near Ludwigshafen. Not only were the withdrawal routes through the Pfaelzer Forest about to be compromised but a swift strike down the Rhine plain from Neustadt and Ludwigshafen against the last escape sites for crossing the Rhine appeared in the offing.

In desperation the Luftwaffe during 20 March sent approximately 300 planes of various types, including jet-propelled Messerschmitt 262's, to attack the Third Army's columns, but to little avail. Casualties on the American side were minor. Antiaircraft units, getting a rare opportunity to do the job for which they were trained, shot down twenty-five German planes. Pilots of the XIX Tactical Air Command claimed another eight.[64]

In the face of the 10th Armored Division's drive, the word to the westernmost units of the *XC Corps* to begin falling back went out late on the 20th,

and when the 42d Division, in the mountains on the left wing of the VI Corps, launched a full-scale assault against the West Wall late the next day, the attack struck a vacuum. Soon after dawn the next morning, 22 March, a regiment of the 42d cut the secondary highway through the Pfaelzer Forest. A column of the 10th Armored had moved astride the main highway through the woods and emerged on the Rhine flatlands at Landau. Any Germans who got out of the forest would have to do so by threading a way off the roads individually or in small groups.

By nightfall of 22 March the Germans west of the Rhine could measure the time left to them in hours. In the West Wall on either side of Wissembourg, Germans of Petersen's *XC Corps* continued to fight in the pillboxes in a manner that belied the futility of their mission. A breakthrough by the 14th Armored Division (Maj. Gen. Albert C. Smith) would nevertheless come soon. Both at Neustadt and at Landau, remnants of two divisions of the *XIII SS Corps,* including the *17th Panzer Grenadier Division,* had held through the day, but early in the evening the defense collapsed. General Beyer's *LXXX Corps,* transferred from the *Seventh Army* to plug the hole from the north alongside the Rhine, had hardly anything left to prevent the 12th Armored Division from driving southward from Ludwigshafen toward Speyer. By nightfall of the 22d, a column of the 12th Armored stood only six miles from Speyer.

To forestall a second Remagen, the Germans by 19 March had blown all Rhine bridges from Ludwigshafen northward. Of three that remained upstream, the southernmost, at Maximiliansau, was

---

[64] Figures are from TUSA AAR.

destroyed on 21 March when a round of American artillery fire struck a detonator, setting off prepared demolitions.[65] A second, at Speyer, was too immediately threatened and too far removed from the main body of German troops to be of much use to any but the defenders of Speyer itself. It would be blown late on the 23d.[66]

Over the remaining bridge, at Germersheim, roughly east of Landau, as many vehicles and field pieces as could be salvaged began to pass during the night of the 22d. Still no orders for final withdrawal beyond the Rhine came from the Commander in Chief West. Headquarters of both the *First Army* and *Army Group G* still were west of the river.[67]

Some German officers were beginning to wonder if every last increment of the *First Army* was to be sacrificed when at last, on 23 March, authority came to cross the Rhine.[68] While the bridge at Germersheim continued to serve artillery and vehicles, foot troops began to evacuate the west bank at three ferry sites south of the town. A smattering of infantrymen, an occasional tank or assault gun, and a regiment of antiaircraft guns operating against ground targets formed rear guard perimeters west of the ferry sites.

Although all divisions of the U.S. VI Corps achieved clear breakthroughs during 23 March, they came in contact only with rear guards and failed to affect the German evacuation materially. Because a German force in Speyer fought doggedly, contact between the 12th and 14th

Armored Divisions was delayed. Both armored divisions early on 24 March sent task forces in quest of the lone remaining Rhine bridge, the one at Germersheim, but neither had reached the fringes of the town when at 1020 the Germans blew up the prize.[69] Formal German evacuation of the west bank ended during the night of the 24th, while American units continued to mop up rear guards and stragglers through the 25th.

It is impossible to ascertain how many Germans escaped from the Saar-Palatinate to fight again on the Rhine's east bank, or how much equipment and matériel they managed to take with them. Yet German losses clearly were severe. "Tremendous losses in both men and matériel," noted the chief of staff of the *First Army*.[70] The staff of the American Seventh Army estimated that the two German armies had lost 75 to 80 percent of their infantry in the Saar-Palatinate fight. The Seventh Army and its attached French units captured 22,000 Germans during the campaign, and the Third Army imprisoned more than 68,000.[71] The Third Army estimated that the German units opposing its advance lost approximately 113,000 men, including prisoners, while the Third Army casualties totaled 5,220, including 681 killed. The Seventh Army, much of its fighting centered in the West Wall, probably incurred about 12,000 casualties, including almost a thousand killed.[72]

For all the inevitability of German

---

[65] MSS # B–507 (Petersen); # B–711 (Albert).

[66] 12th Armored Div AAR, Mar 45.

[67] See MSS # B–507 (Petersen); # B–238 (Wolf Hauser); # B–600 (Paul Hausser); # B–082 (Beyer).

[68] MS # B–238 (Hauser).

[69] VI Corps AAR, Mar 45.

[70] MS # B–238 (Wolf Hauser).

[71] The Third Army's figure is from 18 through 22 March only. See TUSA AAR, p. 315.

[72] Seventh U.S. Army casualties are an estimate based on detailed figures found for the VI Corps only.

defeat, the Saar-Palatinate campaign had provided a remarkable example of offensive maneuver, particularly by the Third Army. It was also a striking demonstration of co-operation and co-ordination among units and their commanders at various levels, including air commands. There had been moments of confusion—in the XII Corps, for example, ambitious 5th Division units got astride the routes of attack of the 4th Armored Division, and on 21 March a column of the Seventh Army's 6th Armored Division got entangled with the Third Army's 26th Division—but in view of the number of units and the speed and extent of the maneuver, those moments were few. This was despite the fact that four of the American corps contained an unwieldy six divisions, which, in the words of the XII Corps commander, General Eddy, was "like driving six horses abreast while standing astraddle on the center pair." [73]

In view of the success of the campaign,

---

[73] Dyer, *XII Corps* p. 344.

criticism of it would be difficult to sustain. Yet it was a fact nonetheless that the German *First Army*—and to some extent the *Seventh Army*—for all the losses, conducted a skillful delaying action to the end in the face of overwhelming strength on the ground and in the air and never succumbed to wholesale encirclement, despite a higher command reluctant to sanction any withdrawal. In the process the Germans had withstood the clear threat of a rapid drive by some unit of the Third Army or the Seventh Army along the west bank of the Rhine to trap the German *First Army*.

Those contingents of both German armies that did escape would have to be met again on the east bank of the Rhine. To assure that the Germans would be at the utmost disadvantage in that meeting, the commander of the Third Army and, to a somewhat lesser extent, the commander of the Seventh Army had been thinking for several days in terms of quick crossings of the Rhine.

And already Patton had done something about it.

CHAPTER XIII

The Rhine Crossings in the South

From the first, General Patton had hoped to exploit his Third Army's part in the Saar-Palatinate campaign into a crossing of the Rhine. He wanted a quick, spectacular crossing that would produce newspaper headlines in the manner of the First Army's seizure of the Remagen bridge. He wanted it for a variety of reasons, no doubt including the glory it would bring to American arms, to the Third Army, and possibly to himself, but most of all he wanted it in order to beat Field Marshal Montgomery across the river. Despite General Eisenhower's earlier indications to the contrary, Patton remained concerned lest the Supreme Commander put the First and Third Armies on the defensive while farming out ten American divisions to the 21 Army Group.[1]

It was this concern, shared by Generals Bradley and Hodges, that hovered specterlike over the meeting of the three American commanders at Bradley's headquarters in Luxembourg City on 19 March. Having received Eisenhower's permission earlier in the day to increase the First Army's strength in the Remagen bridgehead and an alert to be ready to break out from 23 March onward, General Bradley told Patton to do the very thing the Third Army commander wanted to do—take the Rhine on the

run.[2] Once the Third Army had jumped the river in the vicinity of Mainz, the First and Third Armies were to converge in the Lahn River valley, then continue close together to the northeast, generally up the Frankfurt-Kassel corridor. The object—in Patton's mind, at least—was to get such a major force committed in a far-reaching campaign that the 12th Army Group rather than Montgomery's 21 Army Group "could carry the ball."[3]

To avoid a second crossing operation at the Main River, which joins the Rhine at Mainz, the most logical Rhine crossing site for the Third Army was at some point downstream from Mainz. To General Patton and his staff, determined resistance in the outskirts of Mainz seemed to indicate that the Germans appreciated this fact and would be watching for a crossing near the city. Why not, Patton reasoned, accept the handicap of a crossing of the Main in exchange for surprise at the Rhine? Patton told General Eddy of the XII Corps to make a feint near Mainz while actually crossing the Rhine ten miles upstream at Oppenheim.[4] (*Map XI*)

As the troops of the XII Corps drew

---

[1] Patton, *War As I Knew It,* p. 264.

[2] Bradley, *A Soldier's Story,* p. 519.
[3] *Ibid.*
[4] Dyer, *XII Corps,* p. 360; Patton, *War As I Knew It,* pp. 266–67. Patton later wrote that he considered it a "great mistake" not to have made this first crossing downstream from Mainz in order to avoid an assault crossing of the Main.

up to the Rhine, General Eddy had intended to put the 5th Division in corps reserve. With that in mind, the division commander, General Irwin, called a conference of his unit commanders, but before the meeting could begin early on 21 March, Irwin himself received a summons to appear at corps headquarters. When he returned, his manner and opening remarks alerted his commanders to startling news. Conqueror of twenty-two rivers in France, Belgium, and Germany, the 5th Division was to challenge the mightiest of them all—the Rhine.[5]

While the 90th Division made a feint behind a smoke screen at Mainz, General Irwin explained, the 5th Division was to launch a surprise night crossing at Oppenheim. Perhaps the most startling news of all was the timing. Although Irwin personally believed Patton would not order the crossing before the 23d, the division was to be prepared to go within a few hours that same night, 21 March.

The magnitude of the task of bringing assault boats, bridging, and other engineer equipment from depots far in the rear was argument enough for delaying the crossing at least until the 23d. Yet hardly had General Bradley on the 19th told Patton to cross when convoys started forward with this equipment from stocks carefully maintained in Lorraine since the preceding fall. Although another day would pass before tactical advances in the Saar-Palatinate opened direct routes for the convoys, the Third Army commander would listen to no voices cautioning delay. Each day, even each hour,

gave the Germans additional time to recover from the debacle in the Saar-Palatinate and prepare a Rhine defense. Furthermore, Field Marshal Montgomery's Rhine crossing was scheduled to begin during the night of 23 March. If Patton was to beat Montgomery across, he had to move by the night of the 22d.

When General Eddy in midmorning of 22 March told General Irwin that Patton insisted on a crossing that night, Irwin protested that it would be impossible to make a "well-planned and ordered crossing" by that time. On the other hand, Irwin added, he would be able "to get some sort of bridgehead." [6] Some sort of bridgehead was all General Patton was after.

During late morning of the 22d the commander of the 5th Division's 11th Infantry, Col. Paul J. Black, was at his 3d Battalion's command post in the town of Nierstein, a mile downstream from Oppenheim, when word came from General Irwin. The 11th Infantry was to cross the Rhine that night at 2200.

Allotted about 500 boats manned by the 204th Engineer Battalion, the 11th Infantry was to employ two battalions in the assault wave, the 3d crossing at Nierstein, the 1st at Oppenheim. Although an impressive artillery groupment of thirteen battalions stood ready to fire on call, they were to eschew preparatory concentrations in quest of surprise. Observation for the artillery was excellent: hills on the west bank of the Rhine overlook an expanse of generally flat ground stretching more than ten miles beyond the river. The ground is crisscrossed by small canals and drainage

---

[5] Irwin Diary, 20–21 Mar 45, as cited in Dyer, *XII Corps*, p. 364; Conf Notes, 5th Div G–3 Jnl file, 21 Mar 45; XII Corps AAR, Mar 45; XII Corps Opnl Dir 92, 21 Mar 45.

[6] Quotations are from Irwin Diary, as cited in Dyer, *XII Corps*, p. 364.

ditches. The width of the Rhine at this point ranges from 800 to 1,200 feet.

Once the 11th Infantry and its sister regiments had secured a bridgehead, the 4th Armored Division was to exploit to the northeast, bypassing Frankfurt-am-Main and gaining a bridgehead over the Main River east of Frankfurt at Hanau. From that point the XII Corps was to drive northward toward a juncture with the First Army in the Lahn River valley. The 6th Armored, 89th, and 90th Divisions also were available.[7]

Despite the haste involved in the timing of the assault, a force of 7,500 engineers made elaborate preparations for supporting the infantry and bridging the Rhine. Early assault waves were to transport bulldozers and air compressors so that work could begin immediately on cutting ramps for dukws and preparing bridge and ferry sites. Although first waves were to paddle across in assault boats, reinforcements were to cross in dukws and—as at Remagen—LCVP's manned by Naval Unit 2 of the U.S. Navy. With the aid of searchlights mounted on tanks, bridge building was to begin soon after the first infantrymen reached the far shore.[8]

As the troops prepared for the crossing, the Third Army commander entertained a suggestion from his chief of artillery, Brig. Gen. Edward T. Williams, to speed build-up of reinforcements by a novel method. Williams urged assembling approximately a hundred artillery liaison planes to carry one soldier each to landing fields on the east bank.

With each plane making two flights each half hour, a battalion could be airlifted every two hours. Although the 5th Division commander, General Irwin, protested, fearing heavy losses from antiaircraft fire, General Patton went so far as to order a practice flight. Appearance of German planes over the crossing sites eventually would prompt cancellation, but Patton remained convinced the idea was "extremely good." [9]

Troops of the 11th Infantry could discern few indications that the Germans would seriously contest the assault. An occasional cluster of shells from artillery and mortars fell in the streets of Nierstein and Oppenheim, reminder enough that an enemy with the power to kill still peopled the far bank, but neither American artillery observers nor aircraft pilots could find lucrative targets.

Only two days had passed since Field Marshal Kesselring had given his blessing to withdrawal of the *Seventh Army* behind the Rhine, and German commanders were as intent at the moment on re-establishing some semblance of organization in their fleeing remnants as on actually manning a defensive line. Charged with holding more than fifty miles of the Rhine from Wiesbaden, opposite Mainz, to Mannheim, the *Seventh Army* commander, General Felber, had only one regular corps headquarters, the *XIII Corps* (General von Oriola), and headquarters of the local military district, *Wehrkreis XII*. Heretofore engaged solely in recruiting, training, and rear area defense, the *Wehrkreis* headquarters was summarily upgraded to become the *XII Corps*, though Felber had no divisions to go with the advancement. In

[7] TUSA Opnl Dir, 22 Mar 45; XX Corps FO 17, 22 Mar 45.

[8] Conf Notes, 5th Div G–3 Jnl file, 21 Mar 45; P. H. Timothy, The Rhine Crossing, student thesis prepared at the Engineer School, Fort Belvoir, Va., 1946; AAR's of engineer units.

[9] Patton, *War As I Knew It*, p. 267; XII Corps G–3 to 5th Div G–3, 5th Div G–3 Jnl, Mar 45.

the entire *Seventh Army* he possessed only four divisions still organized as such.

Two of those divisions were little more than remnants grouped around their surviving staffs. A third, the *559th Volks Grenadier Division,* still had about 60 percent of its normal strength, since some battalions had arrived too late for active commitment in the counterattack role planned west of the Rhine. All three divisions were under the *XIII Corps,* the *559th* near Mannheim, the other two extending the line to the north. The fourth division, the *159th Volks Grenadier,* though severely depleted and disorganized, Felber had earmarked as an army reserve.

Thus the provisional *XII Corps,* charged with the Wiesbaden-Oppenheim sector, had no divisional unit, only rear echelon security detachments, hastily equipped students and cadres from nearby training schools, and convalescent companies. Neither headquarters of the *XII Corps* nor Felber himself knew much about the numerical strength of these conglomerate forces, but their fighting abilities clearly were limited. Although efforts were under way to rally the residue of other divisions, including the *2d Panzer,* and organize them under division staffs as small task forces, it would be some days before those efforts produced results.[10]

While Felber and other German commanders might hope the Americans would pause for a systematic build-up before jumping the Rhine, the experience at Remagen and all previous dealings with General Patton indicated otherwise. An immediate attack held particular concern for General Felber, since of three sites along the upper Rhine the Germans considered most suitable for crossing attempts, one was in the *Seventh Army* sector—at Oppenheim. Yet because of the accidental site where fleeing troops had reassembled after crossing the Rhine, the bulk of the *Seventh Army's* formations, the three so-called divisions under the *XIII Corps,* were well south of Oppenheim.

Despite a promise from the army group commander to bring up more trainees, convalescents, stragglers, anybody to swell the ranks, Felber knew that the only hope of thwarting an immediate crossing at Oppenheim lay with his own reserve, the *159th Volks Grenadier Division.* A visit to that command revealed only two weak infantry regiments of two battalions each and two light artillery batteries, plus a few odds and ends.

To complicate matters further, General Felber had lost all communication and contact with the *First Army* to the south, some of whose units still were fighting on the west bank. To the north contact existed with the *LXXXIX Corps,* which had withdrawn several days earlier behind the Rhine. On the theory that this corps, holding the sector opposite Koblenz, would be drawn into the fighting against American units breaking out of the Remagen bridgehead, *OB WEST* had transferred it to *Army Group B.*

The chances of repelling a blow at Oppenheim, should it come right away, were pathetically meager.

The moon shone with disturbing brightness as men of the 11th Infantry's

---

[10] For the German story, see MSS # B–831 (Felber); # A–893, The Final Phase of the War, (Generalmajor Freiherr von Gersdorff); and # B–392, Historical Report on the Campaign "Central Germany" From 22 Until 31 March 1945 (Generalleutnant Graf Ralph von Oriola).

3d Battalion crept down to the Rhine at Nierstein a few minutes before 2200 the night of 22 March. Half an hour behind schedule, the leading assault boats carrying men of Company K pushed out into the stream. Not a sign of protest arose from the opposite shore.

First to touch down on the east bank was an assault boat carrying a platoon leader, eight men, and Company K's commander, 1st Lt. Irven Jacobs. The rest of the company arrived safely moments later. Seven surprised Germans promptly surrendered and obligingly paddled themselves across the river without escort.[11]

Leading the 1st Battalion's assault a few hundred years upstream at Oppenheim, men of Companies A and B were less fortunate. The assault boats were in midstream when German machine gunners opened fire. The infantrymen and their engineer colleagues had no choice but to paddle straight into the teeth of the fire. Most of them made it, but a fierce skirmish went on for half an hour before the last German defender gave in. For all the noise and apparent ferocity of the defense, the German gunners imposed few losses on the attackers. In the assault crossing of the Rhine, the entire 11th Infantry incurred only twenty casualties.

By midnight all troops of the 11th Infantry were across and ready to drive on the first tier of villages beyond the river, and men of a second regiment had begun their trek to the assault boats. Only at that point did the first hostile artillery fire—a smattering of what might

have been expected—begin to fall. Some fifty rounds, for example, including occasional shells from self-propelled guns, fell before daylight on Oppenheim.

Soon after dawn twelve German planes strafed and bombed the crossing sites, the first of a series of aerial raids, usually by only one or two planes, that were to persist throughout the day of 23 March. Damage was negligible. Two men in a battalion command post in Oppenheim were wounded and an ammunition truck was set ablaze, but otherwise the only casualty of the German strikes was General Patton's scheme to transport infantry reinforcements across the river in artillery liaison planes. American pilots who flew cover most of the day claimed nineteen German planes destroyed.

Success of the assault crossing assured, American commanders concentrated on quick and heavy reinforcement and on putting as much distance as possible between the forward troops and the river. A deep bridgehead was important because of a lack of dominating high ground on which to anchor defense of the bridgehead and because of the absence of a reasonably good road network short of the town of Grossgerau, six and a half miles beyond the river.[12]

By daylight (23 March) the second of the 5th Division's regiments was across, and by early afternoon the third. A fourth regiment attached from the 90th Division then followed. During the morning attached tanks and tank destroyers began to move across by ferry and LCVP. A class 40 treadway bridge opened in late afternoon. Engineers speeded traffic to the crossing sites by tearing down fences bordering the main

---

[11] Unless otherwise noted, the tactical story is from official unit records, combat interviews, and the unofficial 5th Division history. Although few, the combat interviews are particularly valuable.

[12] Combat interview with Lt Col Randolph C. Dickens, 5th Div G–3.

REINFORCEMENTS OF THE 5TH DIVISION *cross the Rhine in an LCVP.*

highway and widening the road to accommodate three lanes of one-way traffic.

The leading infantry battalions fanned out from the crossing sites against varying degrees of resistance. Advancing northeast along the main road toward Grossgerau, the 11th Infantry's 1st Battalion was pinned down in flare-illuminated open fields short of the first village until platoon leaders and squad sergeants rallied the men and led them forward, employing intense marching fire. "Walking death," the men called it. At the same time the 3d Battalion, attacking more directly north, raised scarcely a

shot until it reached a small airstrip. There almost a hundred Germans counterattacked with fury, but when the coming of daylight exposed their positions to American riflemen and machine gunners, they began surrendering en masse.

Seldom did the Germans employ weapons heavier than rifles, machine guns, machine pistols, and *Panzerfausts,* except for occasional mortars and one or two self-propelled guns. With those they staged demonstrations sometimes disturbingly noisy but seldom inflicting casualties. A battalion of the 10th Infantry, for example, engaged in an almost continuous fire fight while advancing southeast from the crossing sites, took no casualties, and found it unnecessary to call for supporting artillery fire until after midday.

The German units were a veritable hodgepodge: here an engineer replacement battalion, there a *Landesschuetzen* replacement battalion, elsewhere a *Kampfgruppe* of SS troops.[13] Most were youths or old men. Having once exhibited a furious spurt of resistance or delivered a reckless counterattack, they were quick to capitulate. The *Volkssturm* among them often hid out in cellars, awaiting an opportunity to surrender.

By the end of the first full twenty-four hours of attack beyond the Rhine, the radius of the 5th Division's bridgehead measured more than five miles, and Grossgerau and its essential network of roads lay little more than a mile away. So obvious was the success of the surprise crossing that in late afternoon of 23 March the corps commander, General Eddy, ordered the 4th Armored Division to start across early on the 24th, the first step toward exploitation.

Anticipating quick commitment of American armor and with it loss of any hope, however faint, of annihilating the bridgehead, the *Seventh Army*'s General Felber struggled through the day of the 23d to mount a counterattack. Although Felber believed the Americans intended to drive east against Darmstadt rather than northeast toward Frankfurt, he chose to make his main effort against the northern shoulder of the bridgehead where he believed the Americans to be

---

[13] Unit identifications are from 5th Division G–2 records.

weakest. Also, a regimental-size unit formed from students of an officer candidate school in Wiesbaden had become available for commitment there. Augmented by a few tanks and assault guns, this force was potentially stronger than the army reserve, the depleted *159th Volks Grenadier Division*.

Still disorganized from the flight across the Rhine and harassed all day by American fighter-bombers, the volks grenadiers were far from ready to launch a projected subsidiary thrust against the eastern tip of the bridgehead when at midnight, 23 March, General Felber decided he could delay no longer. Not only did the thought of the pending advent of American armor disturb him, but Felber also had to endure the critical eyes of his superiors, the Commander in Chief, Field Marshal Kesselring, and the *Army Group G* commander, General Hausser, both of whom watched the preparations anxiously from the *XII Corps* command post in Grossgerau. The officer candidates, Felber directed, would have to go it alone.

Only moments after midnight the student officers struck three villages along the northern and northeastern periphery of the bridgehead. Although the Germans displayed a creditable elan, the presence of two battalions of American infantry in each village made the outcome in all three inevitable. Infiltrating Germans caused considerable confusion through the hours of darkness, particularly when they took three of the battalion command posts under fire; but the coming of day enabled 5th Division infantrymen to ferret them out quickly. Although other Germans outside the villages remained close, fire from some of the seventeen artillery battalions that already had moved into the bridgehead and from sharpshooting riflemen and machine gunners soon either dispersed the enemy or induced surrender.

The *159th Volks Grenadier Division* apparently never got into the fight in strength. A subsidiary thrust against a village on the southeast edge of the bridgehead caused some concern when it struck moments after a battalion of the 90th Division had relieved a battalion of the 10th Infantry, but nothing more developed. A battalion of the 10th Infantry, moving up for a dawn attack, bumped into a German column moving down a road and may have been responsible. The Germans fled in disorder.

Even before the defeat of the counterattacks put a final seal on success of the Rhine crossing, the 12th Army Group commander, General Bradley, released news of the feat to the press and radio. American forces, Bradley announced, were capable of crossing the Rhine at practically any point without aerial bombardment and without airborne troops. In fact, he went on, the Third Army had crossed the night of 22 March without even so much as an artillery preparation.[14]

Both the nature and the timing of Bradley's announcement were aimed at needling Field Marshal Montgomery, whose 21 Army Group was then crossing the Rhine after an extensive aerial and artillery bombardment and with the help of two airborne divisions. Although General Patton had informed Bradley of his coup at the Rhine early on the 23d, he had asked him to keep the news secret; shortly before midnight he telephoned again, this time enjoining Bradley to re-

veal the event to the world. Thus the announcement came at a time calculated to take some of the luster from news of Montgomery's crossing.

Some officers of the Third Army's staff drew added delight from the fact that the British Broadcasting Corporation the next day played without change a prerecorded speech by Prime Minister Churchill, praising the British for the first assault crossing of the Rhine in modern history. That distinction everybody knew by this time belonged not to the 21 Army Group but to the Third Army.[15]

The VIII Corps in the Rhine Gorge

As if to furnish incontrovertible proof for General Bradley's boast that American troops could cross the Rhine at will, the Third Army was readying two more assault crossings of the river even as Montgomery's 21 Army Group jumped the lower Rhine. Ordered on 21 March, shortly after Patton approved plans of the XII Corps for crossing at Oppenheim, the new crossings actually reflected a concern for success of the Oppenheim maneuver and of the subsequent crossing of the Main River that was intrinsic in the original decision to go at Oppenheim.[16]

Responsibility for both new Rhine crossings fell to General Middleton's VIII Corps, its boundaries adjusted and its forces augmented following capture of Koblenz. Before daylight on 25 March, the 87th Division was to cross near Bop-

---

[14] Gay Diary, entry of 23 Mar 45.

[15] Gay Diary, entry of 24 Mar 45; Bradley, *A Soldier's Story*, pp. 521–22; Patton, *War As I Knew It*, p. 273.

[16] For date of the order, see Gay Diary, entry of 21 Mar 45.

pard, a few miles upstream from Koblenz. Slightly more than twenty-four hours later, in the early hours of 26 March, the 89th Division—transferred from the XII Corps—was to cross near St. Goar, eight miles farther upstream.[17]

After establishing a firm hold on the east bank in the angle formed by confluence of the Lahn River with the Rhine, the 87th Division on the left was to be prepared to exploit to the east, northeast (toward juncture with First Army troops from the Remagen bridgehead), or southeast (toward the rear of any enemy that might be defending the Main River). The 89th Division was earmarked for driving in only one direction, southeast. The two divisions were, in effect, to begin clearing a pocket that was expected to develop between the First Army and the XII Corps.

Terrain, everybody recognized, posed a special challenge. The sector assigned to the VIII Corps, from Koblenz upstream to Bingen, embraced the storied Rhine gorge. There the river has sheared a deep canyon between the Hunsrueck Mountains on the west and the Taunus on the east. Rising 300 to 400 feet, the sides of the canyon are clifflike, sometimes with rock face exposed, other times with terraced vineyards clinging to the slopes. Between river and cliff there usually is room only for a highway and railroad, though here and there industrious German hands through the years have foraged enough space to erect pic-

turesque towns and villages. These usually stand at the mouths of sinuous cross-valleys where narrow, twisting roads provide the only way out of the gorge for vehicles.

So sharply constricted, the Rhine itself is swift and treacherous, its banks in many places revetted aginst erosion with stone walls fifteen feet high. Here, just upstream from St. Goar, stands the Lorelei, the big rock atop which sits the legendary siren who lures river pilots to their deaths on outcroppings below. Here in feudal times lived the river barons who exacted toll from shippers forced to pass beneath their castles on the heights. Here still stood the fabled castles on the Rhine.

A more unlikely spot for an assault crossing no one could have chosen. This very fact, General Patton claimed later, aided the crossings.[18] Whether infantrymen who braved the tricky currents and the precipitous cliffs would agree is another matter.

Certainly General Hoehne's *LXXXIX Corps*, defending the Rhine gorge, was relatively better prepared for its job than were those Germans on the low ground opposite Oppenheim; that preparation was attributable less to expected attack than to the simple fact that the *LXXXIX Corps* had had almost a week behind the Rhine. Hoehne's corps would have been considerably better prepared had not Field Marshal Kesselring ordered transfer on the eve of the American assault of the *6th SS Mountain Division*, still a fairly creditable unit with the equivalent of two infantry regiments and two light artillery battalions. Kesselring sent the divisions to the south-

---

[17] Unless otherwise noted, the story of these crossings is from official unit records and combat interviews. The interviews for both divisions are sketchy. The unofficial history of the 87th Division is noted in Chapter V; for the 89th, see the 89th Infantry Division Historical Board, *The 89th Division 1942–1945* (Washington: Infantry Journal Press, 1947).

[18] Patton, *War As I Knew It*, p. 275.

east toward Wiesbaden, probably in reaction to the Oppenheim crossing, not from any sense of complacency about the Rhine gorge.

Transfer of the SS mountain division left General Hoehne with what remained of the *276th Volks Grenadier Division* (some 400 infantrymen and 10 light howitzers), a few corps headquarters troops, a conglomerate collection of *Volkssturm,* two companies of police, and an antiaircraft brigade. The antiaircraft troops were armed mainly with multiple-barrel 20-mm. pieces, most of them lacking prime movers.[19]

On the 87th Division's left (north) wing, it would have been hard to convince anybody in the 347th Infantry that the Rhine gorge afforded advantages of any kind for an assault crossing. At one battalion's crossing site at Rhens, "all hell broke loose" from the German-held east bank at five minutes before midnight, 24 March, six minutes before the first wave of assault boats was to have pushed into the stream.[20] Fire from machine guns, mortars, 20-mm. antiaircraft guns, and some artillery punished the launching site. Almost an hour passed before the companies could reorganize sufficiently for a second try. Possibly because few of the defenders had the stomach for a sustained fight, the second try at an assault proceeded with little reaction from the Germans. Once on the

east bank, the men "let loose a little hell of their own."

A few hundred yards downstream leading companies of another battalion moved out on time, apparently undetected, but hardly had they touched down when German flares flooded the river with light. Men of the follow-up company drew heavy fire, and at both this site and the one at Rhens the swift current snatched assault boats downstream before they could return for subsequent waves. Reluctance of engineers to leave cover on the east bank to paddle another load of infantrymen across the exposed river added to the problem. All attempts at organized crossing by waves broke down; men simply crossed whenever they found an empty boat. After daylight an attempt to obscure German observation by smoke failed when damp air in the gorge prevented the smoke from rising much above the surface of the water. In early afternoon the 347th Infantry's reserve battalion still had been unable to cross when the assistant division commander, Brig. Gen. John L. McKee, acting in the temporary absence of the division commander, ordered further attempts at the site abandoned.

Upstream at Boppard, two battalions of the 345th Infantry had experiences more in keeping with Patton's theory that crossing in the inhospitable Rhine gorge eased the burden of the assault. Although patrols sent in advance of the main crossings to take out enemy strongpoints drew heavy fire, the assault itself provoked little reaction. The leading companies made it in twelve minutes, and engineers were back with most of the assault boats in eight more. In contrast to 7 men killed and 110 wounded in the battalion of the 347th Infantry

---

[19] MS # B–584, Defensive Actions Fought by the *LXXXIX Infantry Corps* on the Rhine Front Between 18 March 1945 and 29 March 1945 (General der Infanterie Gustav Hoehne). Hoehne's recollection of dates should be reconciled with dates and events as established from American records.

[20] This and subsequent quotations are from combat interview with Maj H. J. Withors, ExecO 1st Bn, 347th Inf, *et al.*

that crossed at Rhens, one of the battalions at Boppard lost 1 man killed and 17 wounded. In midafternoon General McKee made up for the lack of a reserve with the 347th Infantry opposite Rhens by sending a battalion of his reserve regiment to cross at Boppard and advance downstream to help the other regiment.

For neither assault regiment was the going easy once the men got ashore, but both made steady progress nevertheless. Machine guns and 20-mm. antiaircraft guns were the main obstacles, particularly the antiaircraft pieces, which were strikingly effective against ground troops. Although plunging fire is seldom so deadly as grazing fire, the spewing of these guns was painful even when it came from positions high up the cliffs.

By late afternoon the 345th Infantry had a firm hold on high ground lying inside a deep curve of the Rhine opposite Boppard, and the 347th had a similar grasp on high ground and the town of Oberlahnstein at the juncture of the Lahn and the Rhine. Probably reflecting the presence of the 276th Infantry Division around Oberlahnstein, the only counterattack of the day—and that of little concern—struck a battalion of the 347th Infantry. The worst obviously over with the assault crossing itself, General McKee readied his reserve regiment to extend the attack to the east early the next morning.

Throughout the morning of 25 March the 89th Division commander, General Finley, watched progress of the 87th's attack with the hope that part of his division might use the Boppard crossing site and sideslip back into its own zone, thereby obviating another direct amphibious assault. As the day wore on, he reluctantly concluded that congestion

and continued enemy fire at Boppard meant he had to go it alone.

The experiences of both assault regiments of the 89th Division turned out to be similar to those of the 347th Infantry. Time and places were different (0200, 26 March, at St. Goar and Oberwesel), and the details varied, but early discovery by the Germans, the flares, erratic smoke screens, and the seemingly omnipresent 20-mm. antiaircraft guns were the same.

As at Rhens, for example, a battalion of the 354th Infantry at St. Goar came under intense German fire even before launching its assault boats. Flares and flame from a gasoline-soaked barge set afire in midstream by German tracers lit the entire gorge. Into the very maw of the resistance men of the leading companies paddled their frail craft. Many boats sank, sometimes carrying men to their deaths. Others, their occupants wounded, careened downstream, helpless in the swift current. A round from an antiaircraft gun exploded in Company E's command boat, killing both the company commander, Capt. Paul O. Wofford, and his first sergeant.

Although their ranks were riddled, the two leading companies reached the east bank and systematically set about clearing the town of St. Goarshausen. Most of the 89th Division's casualties (29 killed, 146 missing, 102 wounded) were sustained by the 354th Infantry.

Perhaps the most unusual feature of the 353d Infantry's crossing upstream at Oberwesel was the use of dukws for ferrying reinforcements even before the crossing sites were free of small arms fire. Word had it that an anxious, determined, division commander, General Finley, personally prevailed upon engi-

CROSSING THE RHINE UNDER ENEMY FIRE AT ST. GOAR

neers at the river to put the "ducks" of the 453d Amphibious Truck Company to early use. Capable of carrying eighteen infantrymen at once, the dukws speeded reinforcement. They also made less noise than power-propelled assault boats, and when noise more often than not invited enemy shelling, that made a difference.

Having organized two light task forces for exploiting the crossings, General Finley was eager to get them into the fight. When by noon he determined that both regimental bridgeheads still were too confined for exploitation, he arranged to fall back on his earlier hope of using the 87th Division's site at Boppard. There a bridge was already in place.

In midafternoon the first of the two task forces began to cross at Boppard. Almost coincidentally, resistance opposite both St. Goar and Oberwesel beban to crumble, revealing how brittle and shallow was the defense. In late afternoon, following a strike by a squadron of P–51 Mustangs, riflemen of the 354th Infantry carried rocky heights near the Lorelei, eliminating the last direct fire from the St. ·Goar crossing site. A few minutes later they raised an American flag atop the Lorelei.

RAISING THE AMERICAN FLAG ATOP THE LORELEI *overlooking the Rhine gorge.*

As night fell on 26 March, report after report reaching the VIII Corps commander, General Middleton, indicated that the enemy's Rhine defense everywhere was collapsing. Fighter pilots told of German vehicles trying to withdraw bumper-to-bumper down roads clogged with soldiers retreating on foot. Shortly before dark the 87th Division's 345th Infantry broke away from the Rhine cliffs for a five-mile gain. Even more encouraging news came from other units to the north and south. From the north an armored column emerging from the First Army's Remagen bridgehead down the Ruhr-Frankfurt autobahn seized Limburg on the Lahn River and was pointed across the VIII Corps front toward Wiesbaden. To the south the Oppenheim bridgehead too exploded. Reacting to the obvious implications of these developments but lacking an armored division to exploit them, General Middleton told the 6th Cavalry Group to divide into light armored task forces and head east the next day.

What might well become the last big pursuit of the war appeared to be starting.

To the Main River and Frankfurt

The first explosion from the Oppenheim bridgehead came during the afternoon of 24 March soon after Combat Command A arrived as vanguard of the 4th Armored Division. The armor headed southeast to swing around the city of Darmstadt before setting out on the main axis of attack to the northeast. Once started, CCA's tankers and armored infantrymen appeared loath to halt. Taking advantage of a bright moonlit night, the combat command finally stopped after midnight only after half encircling Darmstadt and reaching a point more than fifteen miles from the Oppenheim crossing site.[21]

The spectacular start of the armor prompted the German *Seventh Army's* General Felber to abandon defense of Darmstadt. "In order to avoid the unnecessary annihilation of the few forces committed for the defense of the city," Felber rationalized later.[22] Felber's action enabled the 4th Armored Division's reserve combat command to move in with little difficulty the next day.

On 25 March the explosion became a general eruption. Leaving the jobs of mopping up and expanding the base of the bridgehead to infantry divisions, the XII Corps commander, General Eddy, ordered the 6th Armored Division into the bridgehead to strike directly northeast for a crossing of the Main River between Frankfurt and Hanau. Combat Commands A and B of the 4th Armored Division also headed for the Main, one at Hanau, the other fifteen miles upstream at Aschaffenburg.

Having earlier missed an opportunity at the Moselle, men and commanders in both combat commands seemed obsessed with one thought: get a bridge. In both cases the obsession paid off. Held up along a main highway by 20-mm. flak guns, CCA left a platoon each of tanks and infantry to deal with the opposition, then continued the advance over back roads and trails. A mile upstream from Hanau, the combat command found a railway bridge to which an appendage had been added for vehicular traffic. At

---

[21] In addition to official records, see a series of helpful combat interviews on the 4th Armored Division.

[22] MS # B–381 (Felber).

the last moment the Germans set off demolitions. Although they effectively blocked the railway portion of the bridge, the appendage, though damaged, still hung in place. While supporting artillery placed time fire over the bridge to deny the Germans a second chance, a company of armored infantry got ready to cross. Despite mines and booby traps that killed six men and wounded more than ten, the infantry made it. About the same time, Combat Command B at Aschaffenburg took a railway bridge intact.

German efforts to dislodge the attackers were relatively feeble at Aschaffenburg but caused considerable concern near Hanau, where only two companies of armored infantry were yet across the river and where the damaged bridge had so deteriorated that neither tanks nor additional foot troops could cross. Not long before dark a train bearing German troops and four 150-mm. railway guns arrived in the town opposite the bridge. Although the troops apparently were surprised to find Americans in the town, they quickly set out to drive them into the river. Men of both sides soon were so intermingled that for a while American artillery dared not risk firing on the German guns. Fighting raged at close quarters until well after dark when American engineers completed a treadway bridge and a third company of armored infantrymen joined the fray. By midnight the Americans were in firm control of the town.

Early the next morning, 26 March, the 6th Armored Division's Combat Command A dashed through a large forest south of Frankfurt, bypassing the sprawling Rhine-Main Airport, which infantry of the 5th Division would clear later in the day. In early afternoon the combat command reached the Main at Frankfurt's southern suburb of Sachsenhausen. There General Grow's armor also found a bridge still standing, although too damaged by demolitions for vehicles to use. A company of armored infantry crossed quickly to secure a few buildings at the north end of the bridge.

What the demolitions had failed to accomplish, German self-propelled guns inside Frankfurt and big stationary antiaircraft pieces on the periphery of the city tried to redeem. Almost any movement in the vicinity of the bridge was sufficient to bring down a rain of deadly shelling, much of it airbursts from the antiaircraft pieces. A battalion of the 5th Division's 11th Infantry nevertheless dashed across the bridge soon after nightfall and began to expand the slim holdings of the armored infantrymen on the north bank.

All through the next day the German shelling continued to be so intense that engineers had no success trying to repair the bridge to enable tanks and tank destroyers to cross. During lulls in the enemy fire, more infantrymen of the 5th Division nevertheless managed to reach the north bank and get on with the task of clearing the rubble-strewn city, where police and some civilians along with a hodgepodge of military defenders tried in vain to deny the inevitable.

The Hammelburg Mission

News of the crossing of the Main at Aschaffenburg had in the meantime excited the Third Army commander. General Patton saw in it an opportunity for a foray deep into German territory to liberate hundreds of American prisoners of war from an enclosure near Hammelburg, some thirty-five miles to the northeast. A successful thrust to Hammelburg would outdo a similar raid executed a month earlier by General Douglas MacArthur's forces in the Philippine Islands, while possibly concealing from the Germans the Third Army's pending change of direction to the north.

The man whose troops would have to carry out the foray was the 4th Armored Division commander, General Hoge, one of the heroes of Remagen who only a few days earlier had assumed command of the division when General Gaffey moved up to a corps. Both Hoge and the XII Corps commander, General Eddy, deplored Patton's scheme. When they failed to talk him out of it, General Eddy insisted on sending a small armored task force instead of diverting an entire combat command as Patton suggested. The change further upset Hoge, as it did the commander of CCB, Lt. Col. Creighton W. Abrams, whose command received the assignment. Both Hoge and Abrams believed a small task force would be destroyed, but they failed to convince Eddy.

To make the thrust, Colonel Abrams created a task force built around a company each of CCB's 10th Armored Infantry and 37th Tank Battalions. Because of the illness of the infantry battalion commander, the infantry S–3, Capt. Abraham J. Baum, took command. Basic armament consisted of 10 medium and 6 light tanks, 27 half-tracks, and 3 self-propelled 105-mm. assault guns.

Strength totaled 293 officers and men, and Maj. Alexander Stiller, one of Patton's aides, as well. Although Stiller outranked Baum, the understanding was clear that Baum was in full command.

Stiller told both General Hoge and Colonel Abrams that he wanted to go along "only because General Patton's son-in-law [Lt.] Colonel [John K.] Waters, was in the prison camp." [23]

Captain Baum's mission was to proceed as rapidly as possible to the prisoner-of-war camp two miles south of Hammelburg. (*Map 4*) He was to load all vehicles to capacity with liberated prisoners for the return trip and to give the remaining prisoners a choice either of accompanying the task force on foot or making their way on their own to American lines.

As Baum's little task force began to move shortly after midnight, 25 March, small arms fire in the first few towns inflicted a number of casualties; but in general the Germans along the route were too surprised to fight back. It was still dark when at Lohr, just past the midpoint of the journey, the task force stumbled on a column of German ve-

[23] Quotation is from a letter from Abrams to OCMH, 13 Sep 67; see also comments by General Hoge on the draft MS for this volume. General Patton later denied to newsmen that he had known his son-in-law was at Hammelburg and told Waters the same thing. See letter, Waters to Editor, *Army Magazine*, 25 June 1965, commenting on an article in the magazine by Martin Blumenson, "The Hammelburg Affair." See also letter, Waters to OCMH, 9 June 1967. Patton unquestionably knew that Waters had been shifted westward from a prisoner-of-war camp in Poland just over a month before, for the word had come to him from Moscow by way of SHAEF. (See Gay Diary, entry of 9 February 1945.) Other sources for this account of the Hammelburg action are as follows: Combat interview with Baum; 4th Armored Division, Notes on Task Force Baum, 10 April 1945 (loaned by Brig. Gen. Hal C. Pattison, formerly Executive Officer, Combat Command A); Patton, *War As I Knew It*, pages 275, 280–81; Capt. Kenneth Koyen, *The Fourth Armored Division from the Beach to Bavaria* (Munich, Germany, 1946), pages 117–42 in the first edition, pages 181–206 in the second; Dyer, *XII Corps*, page 388; the article by Blumenson; and Toland, *The Last 100 days*, pages 287–99.

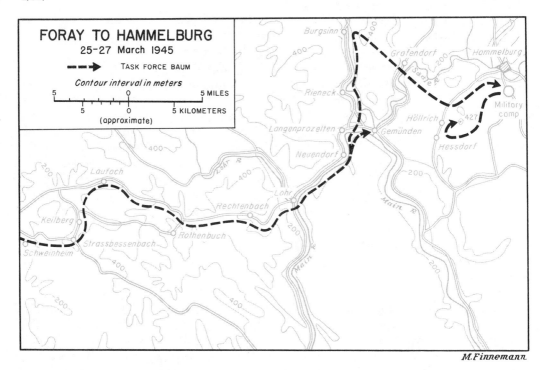

FORAY TO HAMMELBURG
25–27 March 1945

➤ TASK FORCE BAUM

Contour interval in meters

5   0   5 MILES
5   0   5 KILOMETERS
(approximate)

M.Finnemann

MAP 4

hicles heading west. Not even pausing in the advance, the American tankers opened fire, destroying twelve German vehicles with a loss of one medium tank. Outside Lohr they destroyed a German locomotive, and just before dawn at Gemuenden, three-fourths of the way to Hammelburg, they shot up seven more.

On the outskirts of Gemuenden, defending Germans destroyed two more of Baum's tanks and blew up a bridge over a small stream, forcing a detour to the north. It was well into the day of 26 March when, a few miles from Hammelburg, the task force liberated about 700 Russian soldiers, to whom they entrusted some 200 Germans captured in the course of the journey. A short while later

the men spotted a German liaison plane hovering near the column.

To Baum and his men the plane spelled trouble—an airborne Paul Revere alerting the German command against the thrust—but it actually mattered little, for the alarm already had been sounded. In advancing toward Lohr, Task Force Baum had passed within two miles of headquarters of the *Seventh Army,* which had escaped from Darmstadt and Aschaffenburg only steps ahead of the 4th Armored Division columns. For want of anything better, the staff quickly alerted headquarters of the local *Wehrkreis.*[24]

---

[24] MS # A–893 (Gersdorff).

It was not this alert but mere chance that actually was responsible for the troubles that began to beset Task Force Baum. In midafternoon, as the task force sought to bypass the town of Hammelburg, a German assault gun battalion that had arrived only minutes before opened fire.[25] It took two hours of hard fighting and the loss of three more medium tanks, three jeeps, and seven half-tracks, including one loaded with precious gasoline, for the American column to force a way through. The Germans' loss of three assault guns and three ammunition carriers was small consolation for the American losses and the delay.

When at last Task Force Baum approached the prisoner-of-war enclosure, the tankers mistook Yugoslav prisoners for Germans and opened fire. At the request of the camp commandant, three U.S. officers volunteered to go with a German officer under a makeshift American flag to have the fire lifted. One of the Americans was Colonel Waters, Patton's son-in-law, captured two years earlier in North Africa. As the group marched beyond the enclosure, a German soldier in a nearby barnyard fired one round from a rifle, wounding Colonel Waters.

While the other officers were taking Colonel Waters back to the compound, the tanks of Task Force Baum broke the wire enclosure. The pandemonium of liberation took over. The number of prisoners far exceeded any previous estimate: 4,700, of whom 1,400 were American officers. While as many as possible climbed aboard the remaining tanks and half-tracks, others formed to march alongside.

Well after dark Task Force Baum—reduced to about 110 men and only four of its medium tanks—started the return journey. By that time Germans rallied by an unidentified major home on leave in Hammelburg were ready. A round from a *Panzerfaust* knocked out Baum's leading tank a scant fifty yards from the prisoner-of-war enclosure. All hope of the physically unfit's accompanying the task force faded. They returned under a white flag to the enclosure.

Seeking to avoid the apparent German strength near Hammelburg, Captain Baum turned the task force to the southwest; but at the village of Hessdorf, five miles away, another contingent of Germans equipped with *Panzerfausts* lay in wait. There Baum lost two light tanks and one more medium.[26]

Retiring to a nearby hill to reorganize, Baum found the gasoline in his remaining vehicles dangerously low. He directed the men to siphon the fuel from eight of the half-tracks, then to destroy them. He placed the seriously wounded men in a building marked with a red cross, then readied the rest of the force, which included some sixty-five of the liberated prisoners, for another try at the return journey.

They had yet to move out when, just before daylight (27 March), a dozen German tanks supplemented by assault guns opened fire. Under cover of this fire, two companies of German infantry attacked. In rapid succession, one after another of Baum's tanks and other ve-

---

[25] *Ibid.*

[26] One of the American prisoners who started the return journey with Task Force Baum, Lyle J. Bouck, Jr., has provided considerable detail on these events in a letter to OCMH, 8 March 1968.

GENERAL HAISLIP

hicles went up in flames. His position apparently hopeless, Baum called a council of war. His instructions were brief. The survivors were to form in groups of three or four and attempt to infiltrate through the converging Germans and make their way to American lines.

Baum himself tried to escape in company with an unidentified lieutenant and Major Stiller. For most of the day they successfully kept under cover, while in the distance they could hear the baying of bloodhounds as the Germans methodically tracked down the survivors. Just before dark a German sergeant spotted the three officers. He fired, striking Captain Baum in a leg (his third wound of the operation). There seemed little choice but to surrender.

Over the next few days, fifteen men from Task Force Baum made their way back to American lines. Nine were estab-

lished as killed, 16 missing, 32 wounded, the others captured. There remained only for the Germans to make propaganda of the ill-starred raid. An entire American armored division attacking Hammelburg, the Germans claimed, had been destroyed.[27]

The Seventh Army Crossing at Worms

As disappointing and tragic as was the outcome of the raid on Hammelburg, it was a relatively minor incident in an otherwise uninterrupted surge of Allied power against and beyond the Rhine defenses. General Patch's Seventh Army, its West Wall breakthrough and mop-up in the Saar-Palatinate completed, added its strength to that surge before daylight on 26 March, even as Task Force Baum began its ill-fated drive.

Before the ease and extent of the victory in the Saar-Palatinate had become apparent, the Supreme Commander, General Eisenhower, had offered an airborne division (the 13th) to help the Seventh Army across the Rhine. Primarily because of the advantages the hills and forests of the Odenwald, east of Worms, would afford as a barrier to hostile movement against an airhead, General Eisenhower's planners focused their attention on a crossing near Worms. From the viewpoint of advance beyond the bridgehead, the Seventh Army would have preferred a crossing about twenty miles to the south near Speyer, for there a plateau between the Odenwald and the Black Forest provides egress to the east. On the other hand, the help inherent in

---

[27] Patton, *War As I Knew It*, p. 279; MS # C–020 (Schramm). Casualty figures are from Koyen, *The Fourth Armored Division* (first edition) p. 142.

an airborne attack was a compelling argument.[28]

After the unexpectedly rapid and deep intrusion of the Third Army into the Saar-Palatinate sharply narrowed the Seventh Army's Rhine frontage, Worms lost some of its attraction as a crossing site because it then lay on the extreme left of the Seventh Army's zone. News that preparations for the airborne assault could be completed only near the end of March took away still more of the lure. Then the Third Army's successful crossing of the Rhine at Oppenheim made Worms attractive again, even while making it obvious that an airborne assist would be unnecessary. The advantages of making the assault close to the Third Army's already established bridgehead, General Patch decided, outweighed other factors. Ordering his VI and XXI Corps to make contingent plans for subsidiary crossings near Speyer, he told General Haislip's XV Corps to make the main thrust at Worms.[29]

Mop-up of German pockets on the west bank, relief of Third Army divisions that had violated the interarmy boundary, and the time-consuming trek of convoys bearing boats and bridging equipment from far in the rear imposed inevitable delay on the assault. Not for the Seventh Army a running broad-jump like that of the Third Army's 5th Division. General Haislip's XV Corps was to make a deliberate two-division assault, the 45th Division just north of Worms, the 3d Division just south of town, with two more infantry divisions and a cavalry group scheduled for quick follow-up.

The attack was to begin at 0230, 26 March.[30]

The mechanics of getting ready rather than concern for enemy strength dictated the timing of the Seventh Army assault. Although intelligence officers estimated that remnants of twenty-two divisions had escaped across the Rhine in the general area, they could not believe, in view of the confusion accompanying their flight, that the German units represented any formidable strength. The Third Army's experience at Oppenheim corroborated the view, as did the experience of several reconnaissance patrols. One patrol, led by a battalion commander of the 45th Division's 180th Infantry, reconnoitering on the east bank for half an hour the night of 24 March, found no mines, barbed wire, or emplacements. Although the men saw a few Germans and believed the Germans saw them, they drew no fire.[31]

Based on the actual German situation, General Patch's reasoning in deciding to cross the Rhine near Worms was justified. Those Germans manning the east bank were part of the same *Seventh Army* that had already been rent asunder by the Third Army crossing. The sector came under General von Oriola's *XIII Corps,* already affected by the American attack at Oppenheim.

This was the corps that had one fairly respectable divisional unit, the *559th Volks Grenadier Division,* located at

---

[28] Seventh Army Report, III, 741.

[29] SUSA Opns Instrs 103, 104, and 107, dated 22, 23, and 24 Mar 45.

[30] XV Corps FO 23, 2400 24 Mar 45; SUSA Opns Instrs 111, 25 Mar 45.

[31] Seventh Army Report, III, 747. Unless otherwise indicated, the account that follows is based on this source, on official records of the Seventh Army, its corps and divisions, and on Donald G. Taggart, ed., *History of the Third Infantry Division in World War II* (Washington: Infantry Journal Press, 1947).

Mannheim. Two other units that went by the names of the *246th* and *352d Volks Grenadier Divisions*, extending the line northward, were *Kampfgruppen* of about 400 men each. When the U.S. 4th Armored Division had broken out from the Oppenheim bridgehead on 24 March, the northernmost *352d Division* had had to fall back.[32]

Like almost all German commanders in the vicinity, General von Oriola expected the American armor to turn southeast to cut in behind the Odenwald and trap the adjacent *First Army* or at least to expand the Oppenheim bridgehead southward as far as Mannheim and the Neckar River. Two major north-south highways, the Darmstadt-Mannheim autobahn on the Rhine flats and the Bergstrasse, the latter forming a dividing line between the Odenwald hills and the Rhine lowlands, invited a turn to the south. In a feeble effort to forestall such a move. Oriola turned the retreating remnants of the *352d Division* to face northward astride the highways.

Defense of the Rhine itself north and south of Worms was left to the *246th* and *559th Volks Grenadier Divisions*, whose numbers permitted only "very sparse" occupation of the east bank and no depth at all.[33] The lack of depth was particularly disturbing because of the exposed nature of the defensive positions on the Rhine flats. The only corps reserve of any kind was an assault gun brigade that still had five guns. Artillery consisted of six understrength battalions, plus some

ninety stationary antiaircraft pieces around Mannheim.

The new American assault against the Rhine would begin before any major realignment of German forces in response to the Oppenheim breakout occurred; but before the first day of the new attack came to an end, Oriola's *XIII Corps* was destined to be transferred to the *First Army*. That was a logical move since the American breakout had effectively split the *Seventh Army* and since the *First Army* appeared seriously threatened should the Americans turn southeast or south.

General Foertsch's *First Army* had escaped across the Rhine in slightly better shape than had the *Seventh Army*, but still was in no condition to pose any real challenge. It had three corps headquarters and the skeletons of twelve divisions, though two of the latter were en route to the *Seventh Army* the night of 25 March and three others were in such a condition that General Foertsch had sent them to the rear in hope somehow of reconstituting them. That left seven, few of which were anything more than regimental-size *Kampfgruppen*. To provide an army reserve, Foertsch counted on the *17th SS Panzer Grenadier Division*, whose troops got behind the Rhine only late on the 25th and would require at least a day or two to reorganize.[34]

To know the status and locations of the major units in the German *XIII Corps* is to possess the basic ingredients of the story of the Rhine crossing by the Seventh Army XV Corps. In the zone of the 45th Division, north of Worms, where the weak *Kampfgruppe* called

---

[32] The German account is drawn primarily from MS # B–392 (Oriola). See also MSS # A–893 (Gersdorff) and # B–348, Report on the Combat Engagements Within the Framework of the *First Army* During the Period from 24 March to 8 May 1945 (Generalmajor Wolf Hauser).

[33] MS # B–392 (Oriola).

[34] The *First Army* story is from MS # B–348 (Hauser).

246th Volks Grenadier Division barred the way, it was a case of fierce initial opposition from small arms, machine guns, mortars, and small caliber antiaircraft pieces, then a collapse. In the zone of the 3d Division, where the *559th Volks Grenadier Division* had 60 percent of normal strength and where the big (up to 128-mm.) antiaircraft guns protecting Mannheim were in effective range, it was different.

Vigilant German pickets opposite the 3d Division, perhaps alerted by feigned crossing attempts to the south near Speyer, detected movement on the American-held west bank well before the H-hour of 0230. The Germans opened fire, primarily with mortars and antiaircraft guns, seriously hampering American engineers who were trying to move assault boats to the water's edge and to shave the steep revetted banks for the amphibious vehicles that were to come later. Surprise compromised, American artillery opened a drumbeat of fire. In thirty-eight minutes the artillery expended more than 10,000 rounds, "painting the skyline a lurid red." [35]

Despite the light from a burning barn that illuminated the crossing site, little German fire fell as the first wave of infantrymen pushed into the stream. The artillery support had done its job well. The first wave of "storm boats" (metal pontons propelled by 50-hp. outboard motors) took less than a minute to cross the thousand feet of water. Only then, as the artillery desisted, did enemy fire begin to fall in disturbing volume.

In the 45th Division sector, supporting artillery held its fire, for the hope was that the crossing preparations had gone

undetected. The hope proved vain. Although the first wave got almost across before the Germans came to life, the far bank at that point seemed to erupt with fire. The infantrymen had to come ashore with rifles and submachine guns blazing. For the better part of an hour a fight raged, while succeeding waves of boats took a fierce pounding. In the 180th Infantry's sector more than half the assault boats in the second and third waves were lost, but once the first flush of resistance was over, men of the 45th Division began to push rapidly eastward.

About the only opposition that developed from then on came in the villages. Planes that kept a constant vigil over the battlefield all day helped eliminate this resistance, by nightfall contact had been established with contingents of the Third Army on the left, and forward troops were across the Darmstadt-Mannheim autobahn, a good eight miles beyond the Rhine.

The 3d Division, the effect of its artillery preparation dissipated, lagged behind. One problem was an incessant chatter of machine gun and antiaircraft fire from an island in an offshoot of the Rhine southeast of Worms. Despite a smoke screen laid at the crossing sites, the fire hampered follow-up operations until well after midday when a battalion of the 15th Infantry cleared the island after an amphibious assault against the enemy's rear. Elsewhere the main resistance centered in the villages and in every cluster of houses. At two of the villages the Germans of the *559th Volks Grenadier Division* crowned their opposition with counterattacks supported by self-propelled guns and mobile 20-mm. flakwagons.

---

[35] Taggart, ed., *History of the Third Division*, p. 339.

INFANTRY OF THE 3D DIVISION *climb the east bank of the Rhine.*

Here and in the 45th Division sector amphibious tanks that crossed the Rhine close behind the infantry assault waves were put to good use. These were "DD" (duplex drive) tanks, M4 mediums equipped with twin propellers for propulsion in the water and with a normal track drive for overland. An accordion-like canvas skirt enabled the tank to float. Of twenty-one DD tanks supporting the 3d Division, fifteen made it across the river. Of the six that failed, one was destroyed by shellfire before crossing, one stuck in the mud at the water's edge, the canvas on two was badly torn by shell fragments before the crossing, and two others sank after fragments punctured their canvas during the crossing. All fourteen DD tanks assigned to the 45th Division crossed safely.

As night came, troops of the 3d Division still had to pick their way through some two miles of thick forest before reaching the autobahn, and on the south flank heavy fire from the antiaircraft guns ringing Mannheim still proved troublesome. Indications nevertheless were developing that the *559th Volks Grenadier Division* at last was giving up and that the XV Corps would be ready early the next morning, 27 March, to make the most of it. Already both a treadway bridge and a heavy ponton bridge were supplementing dukws, rafts, and ferries serving the 3d Division, and bridges were nearing completion behind the 45th Division. All artillery normally supporting the four assault regiments was across, and the Seventh Army commander, General Patch, had ordered transfer of the 12th Armored Division to the XV Corps for exploitation. During the crossing operations more than 2,500 Germans had surrendered, while XV Corps casualties reflected more noise than effect in the day's German fire. Losses totaled 42 killed and 151 wounded.[36]

The XX Corps in the Rhine-Main Arc

By nightfall of 26 March General Bradley's 12th Army Group had established four solid bridgeheads across the Rhine—the First Army's at Remagen, the Third Army's VIII Corps along the Rhine gorge and XII Corps at Oppenheim, and the Seventh Army's XV Corps at Worms. A fifth was pending, for the Third Army's General Patton still had one corps on the Rhine's west bank that he chose to send across by assault rather than by staging through either of his already established bridgeheads. He wanted General Walker's XX Corps to cross between his other two corps at Mainz.

Just why Patton chose to make another

assault crossing at this stage is mainly conjectural. He probably disdained any thought that the Germans could seriously interfere with a new crossing. Patton also wanted to get on with the task of building permanent rail and highway bridges across the Rhine to speed his army's advance. Mainz with its network of roads and railways and its central location in relation to the army boundaries was the logical spot for the bridges; and an assault crossing appeared the quickest way to free the east bank of Germans.[37]

Patton's original plan was to send a regiment from the already established VIII Corps bridgehead southeastward along the Rhine's east bank to support the new assault crossing by seizing high ground overlooking the crossing site. The 80th Division of the XX Corps then was to cross at Mainz. Eddy's XII Corps was to continue its drive to cross the Main River east of Frankfurt, whereupon all three corps were to head for the same objective, the town of Giessen and juncture with the First Army. "I told each Corps Commander that I expected him to get there first," Patton recalled later, "so as to produce a proper feeling of rivalry." [38]

Somewhere along the line, Patton did away with the preliminary thrust to take the high ground overlooking the 80th Division crossing site. The reason went unrecorded, but it may have been because of the explosive dash of an armored

---

[36] The 3d Division lost 29 killed, 131 wounded; the 45th, 13 killed, 20 wounded. Casualty figures are from XV Corps G–1 Report, 26 March 1945. Some of the day's casualties, particularly men listed as missing, may not have been reflected until the next day's report, but in any case XV Corps losses probably were less than 250.

[37] Patton, *War As I Knew It*, p. 274; Gay Diary, entry of 26 Mar 45. See also XX Corps, *The Assault Crossing of the Rhine and Into Germany* (a printed operational report), p. 3, and The XX Corps Association, *XX Corps—Its History and Service in World War II* (no date), an unofficial unit history.
[38] Patton, *War As I Knew It*, p. 274.

DUPLEX-DRIVE TANK WITH SKIRT FOLDED

division from the First Army bridgehead that looked for awhile as if it would carry to Wiesbaden, across the Rhine from Mainz. In late afternoon of 26 March, the 12th Army Group chief of staff, Maj. Gen. Leven C. Allen, telephoned the news that the armor had seized a bridge intact over the Lahn River at Limburg, less than twenty miles from Wiesbaden. If the Third Army approved, a combat command was prepared to cut across the front of the VIII Corps and capture Wiesbaden.[39]

[39] Gay Diary, entry of 26 Mar 45; Patton, *War As I Knew It,* pp. 276–77.

Patton did approve, but it was well into the next day, 27 March, before the armored force could start its drive; although a bridge had been captured, the Germans had blown it after only four tanks had crossed. When units of Middleton's VIII Corps broke out of their bridgehead early on the 27th, their columns quickly became entangled in those of the combat command. The objective soon ceased to be getting the armor to Wiesbaden; it became instead getting it out of Middleton's way. With the XX Corps scheduled to launch its crossing of the Rhine before daylight the next morn-

DUPLEX-DRIVE TANK ENTERS THE WATER

ing, chances were the attackers would find no friendly forces either in Wiesbaden or along the Rhine opposite Mainz.

Details of the XX Corps plan were worked out not by Patton but by his chief of staff, General Gay, while Patton was in the XII Corps bridgehead setting up Task Force Baum.[40] The 80th Division (General McBride) was to send one regiment across the Rhine at Mainz while another regiment, having crossed into the XII Corps bridgehead, was to jump the Main River three miles upstream from the Rhine opposite Hochheim. Forces from the two bridgeheads then were to converge to clear the angle or arc formed by the confluence of the Main and the Rhine. Aside from the obvious advantages of dividing the opposition with two crossings, the decision to jump the Main as well as the Rhine hinged on a desire to make full use of existing stocks of bridging equipment; the stocks were insufficient for two Rhine bridges but would suffice for one over

---

[40] Gay Diary, entry of 26 Mar 45.

the Rhine and another over the narrower Main.[41]

The Germans remaining in the Rhine-Main arc would give the XX Corps commander, General Walker, and his staff little pause. Even a cautious G–2 could find reason to believe that but one divisional unit and a hodgepodge of lesser forces defended there, and the estimate of even one divisional unit was actually in error. To the Germans it was quite apparent that Wiesbaden and the surrounding sector were soon to be either captured or encircled; the Americans in the bridgeheads both north and south of the city would see to that. With this in prospect, no one on the scene would have been willing to leave sizable forces in the threatened arc—even had they been available.

The same provisional *XII Corps* that had come to grief in the Oppenheim bridgehead had borne responsibility for this part of the front as well until midday 25 March, when General Kniess and the staff of his *LXXXV Corps* arrived. Theirs was a thankless, hopeless task; indeed, part of the staff had trouble even getting to the scene. Having been sent northward by *Army Group G,* the staff found American armor pouring out of the Oppenheim bridgehead and had to make a long detour to the east to avoid it, not to mention having the usual difficulty with ubiquitous American fighter-bombers that circumscribed almost all movement in daylight.[42]

When General Kniess took over from

the provisional *XII Corps* on 25 March, he inherited only one divisional unit, the weak, almost ineffectual *159th Infantry Division,* which was still south of the Main River. He had promise of three others, of which only one, the skeleton of an infantry division sent from the *First Army,* actually arrived. The other two were the *11th Panzer Division,* fast becoming the fire horse of the front now that the *9th Panzer Division* had virtually expired at Cologne, and the *6th SS Mountain Division,* the latter ordered out of the lines of the *LXXXIX Corps* just before the U.S. VIII Corps established a bridgehead across the Rhine gorge; but both would become involved with units breaking out of the VIII Corps bridgehead before they could reach General Kniess's sector.

Responsible for defending the Main River around Frankfurt and Hanau as well as the Rhine opposite Mainz, General Kniess had to focus his attention on the Main River cities, since American armor was already racing toward them from the Oppenheim bridgehead. When a request to *OB WEST* for permission to withdraw from the Rhine-Main arc drew the usual blunt refusal, Kniess and the *Seventh Army* commander, General Felber, resorted to what Felber's chief of staff termed "the well tested method" of withdrawing most of the troops from the arc, leaving a weak shell in place to maintain a semblance of defense.[43]

By that move Felber and Kniess wrote off the Rhine-Main arc and laid plans for a new defensive line extending north from Frankfurt. Just what troops were left in the arc by nightfall of 27 March neither of them probably knew for sure;

---

[41] XX Corps, *The Assault Crossing of the Rhine,* p. 3.

[42] For the German story, see MSS # A–893 (Gersdorff), # B–831 (Felber), and # B–324, Rhine-Main (Maj. Hans H. Krueger of the *LXXXV Corps* staff, with comments by Gen Kniess).

[43] MS # A–893 (Gersdorff).

but as of two days before, there had been available to defend almost twenty-five miles of Rhine-Main frontage only three infantry replacement battalions with some engineer support, two artillery battalions, and scattered antiaircraft detachments.

The connivance with Kniess to abandon the Rhine-Main arc was one of General Felber's last acts as commander of the *Seventh Army*. Somebody had to pay for the failure—however inevitable —to prevent the American crossing of the Rhine at Oppenheim. That somebody was the army commander. Late on 26 March, Felber relinquished his command to General der Infanterie Hans von Obstfelder, a former interim commander of the *First Army*. General Kneiss, the *LXXXV Corps* commander, unable to do anything about either the armored spearheads spreading from Oppenheim or American crossings into the Rhine-Main arc, would follow Felber into Hitler's doghouse only three days later.

It was a noisy little war the 80th Division staged at Mainz and a few miles away on the Main River before daylight on 28 March, but few, on the American side at least, were hurt. Following a half-hour artillery preparation, men of the 317th Infantry pushed out in assault boats at 0100 from slips and docks of the Mainz waterfront, despite a blaze of German fireworks, mainly small arms and 20-mm. antiaircraft fire. Once the troops were ashore, the Germans mounted two small counterattacks, which like the fire on the river produced more tumult than effect. By the end of the day contingents of a follow-up regiment had cleared Wiesbaden and more than 900 Germans had thrown up their hands; the 317th Infantry had lost not a man killed and only five wounded. One of the more noteworthy events of the day was capture of a warehouse with 4,000 cases of champagne.

The 319th Infantry meanwhile encountered less clamor along the Main opposite Hochheim but took a few more losses—3 men killed, 3 missing, 16 wounded; there too it looked more like theatrics staged by *condottierei* than genuine battle. By early afternoon the 319th had linked its bridgehead solidly with that of the 317th, and bridge construction was proceeding apace with scarcely a round of German shellfire to interfere.[44]

The Third Army's third major Rhine bridgehead came easy. Even those who believed their audacious army commander might have spared his troops a third assault crossing by using one of the bridgeheads previously established could find little quarrel with the outcome.

---

[44] This account is based primarily on official records of the 80th Division and its regiments.

CHAPTER XIV

The Rhine Crossings in the North

Source of weird and romantic legends, the Rhine River has long held a peculiar fascination for the German people, a historic moat guarding them against the traditional enemies to the west. As the German armies in the summer of 1944 fell back from defeat in France, their commanders appealed for authority to withdraw behind that moat, the only hope, they believed, for stopping the Allied armies and recovering from the debacle in France. Yet Hitler said no and continued to say no all through the fall and winter, so that with the coming of spring the military force that might have hoped to defend successfully at the Rhine had ceased to exist, destroyed in the fighting west of the river.

That American armies had already jumped the Rhine before Field Marshal Montgomery was ready for an assault had no effect on General Eisenhower's plan to make the main Allied effort with the 21 Army Group in the north, for the prize at which the main effort was aimed remained to be taken. This was the vast complex, fifty miles wide at its base along the Rhine, sixty miles deep, prewar producer of 65 percent of Germany's crude steel, 56 percent of its coal, the only major source of power left to the Germans after the Russians had overrun Silesia and the Americans the Saar: the *Ruhrgebiet,* or Ruhr industrial area.

In the planning days that preceded the invasion, the Allies had held that the Ruhr was the vital economic objective whose capture would precipitate German collapse. Since before D-day the Supreme Allied Commander and the senior British commander, Montgomery, had held with single-minded determination to the view that the way to get the Ruhr was to make the main effort in the north.

Long an exponent of the deliberate, set-piece attack, Field Marshal Montgomery had been looking ahead to the crossing of the Rhine since September of the preceding year when a daring *coup de main* involving three airborne divisions had failed to get the British across a downstream branch of the Rhine in the Netherlands.[1] So had the planners at SHAEF and at the First Canadian, Second British, and Ninth U.S. Armies.

Planning conferences, particularly among engineer and ordnance specialists, had begun as early as October 1944.[2] By November a broad outline sufficiently detailed for general planning was at hand. A number of engineer units behind the lines were designated to train

---

[1] For background on Operation MARKET-GARDEN, see MacDonald, *The Siegfried Line Campaign.*

[2] For Ninth Army planning, see *Conquer: The Story of Ninth Army,* pp. 199–242; for British planning, Field Marshal Bernard L. Montgomery, *Normandy to the Baltic* (Germany: Printing and Stationery Service, British Army of the Rhine, 1946), pp. 247–54; and for Canadian, Stacey, *The Victory Campaign,* pp. 527–34.

and experiment with amphibious equipment and river-crossing techniques. To an engineer group given that mission in the Ninth Army was attached Naval Unit Number 3, largest of three naval contingents supporting U.S. armies, equipped with twenty-four LCVP's and twenty-four LCM's (landing craft, medium). A harbor craft company of the Transportation Corps later was attached to the engineer group to instruct in operating Seamules, 38-foot tugs powered by two 143-hp. engines.[3] A contingent of the Royal Navy also equipped with LCVP's and LCM's provided amphibious support for the British.[4]

When planning resumed early in 1945 after a lapse during the Ardennes counteroffensive, the question of adequate numbers of assault and landing craft and of sufficient bridging equipment came into consideration. Since the plan was that the other two Allied army groups were to cross the Rhine soon after the major effort in the north, there had to be enough for all three. Following a theaterwide survey, including Great Britain, General Eisenhower asked for hurry-up shipments from the United States. Also in January the Supreme Commander called a three-day meeting at SHAEF where river-crossing specialists from all three army groups pooled their knowledge. The SHAEF G–4 meanwhile estimated supply requirements for a Rhine bridgehead at 540 tons per day per division, and Field Marshal Montgomery made plans to forestall a supply bottleneck behind the lines by ordering

construction of eight more bridges to supplement existing tactical bridges over the Maas River.[5]

In late January when the Ninth Army chief of staff, General Moore, attended a planning conference at headquarters of the 21 Army Group, it became apparent that little additional work could be done without at least a preliminary assignment of zones. Both the Second Army and the Ninth Army, for example, had been counting on using bridge sites at Wesel. In a directive issued on 21 January, Field Marshal Montgomery moved to clarify the situation, only to create, in the process, considerable concern among the Ninth Army staff.

The Second Army, Montgomery directed, was to prepare to cross the Rhine at three places, near Rees (twenty-five miles upstream from Arnhem), east of Xanten (another seven miles upstream near Wesel), and in the vicinity of Rheinberg (some ten miles farther upstream at the northwestern corner of the Ruhr). Although an American corps of two infantry divisions was to be attached to the British for the crossing, the Ninth Army was not to participate in the assault. The American army was to be committed only for the exploitation phase.[6]

The Ninth Army, its historian has noted, was "flabbergasted!"[7] That only an American corps, submerged within a British army, was to participate in the great assault was to the Ninth Army staff inconceivable; but aside from that appar-

---

[3] The Seamules could be disassembled into four sections for transport overland. LCM's were 50-foot tank lighters, able to carry one medium tank, sixty men, or comparable cargo. For a description of LCVP's see above, Chapter XI.

[4] Stacey, The Victory Campaign, p. 535.

[5] 21 AGp, Planning Dir for Opn PLUNDER, 17 Feb 45, 12th AGp file, 37.13, V; Min, conf held at SHAEF to discuss problems connected with the crossing of the Rhine, SHAEF file, 370–47, I.

[6] M–548, Opnl Dir, 21 AGp, 21 Jan 45, SHAEF SGS file, 381, III.

[7] Conquer: The Story of Ninth Army, p. 209.

FIELD MARSHAL MONTGOMERY

They proposed narrowing the British sector, splitting the area around Xanten between the two armies, and making room for a two-corps assault by the Ninth Army from Xanten to Rheinberg. They proposed further that the assault be extended to the northwest to make room for the First Canadian Army on the left of the British.

Although Montgomery turned down the proposal, he appeared to comprehend the American position. On 4 February he issued new instructions assigning the Rheinberg area to a one-corps assault under the Ninth Army. Acknowledging the Ninth Army's requirements for additional bridge sites near Xanten at Wesel, he registered his intent to transfer Wesel to American use once the bridgehead was secure. Because of floodplains, poor approaches, and high ground commanding likely crossing sites downstream from Rees, he vetoed a Canadian assault but planned to attach a Canadian brigade to the British and subsequently commit additional Canadian forces in the bridgehead at Rees to drive downstream and clear a crossing site for the First Canadian Army. Although this plan was little different from the first one, it assuaged American feelings by giving the Ninth Army control of the participating U.S. corps.[8]

ent affront, what of the supply and evacuation problems arising from employment of American units with the British? What of the mass of assault and bridging equipment already accumulated in the Ninth Army? Why waste in inaction the Ninth Army's formidable strength of twelve divisions? And what of the logistical problems of passing the entire Ninth Army through the British bridgehead?

Fortunately, staffs and commanders of the Second British and Ninth U.S. Armies had through long experience in operating side by side achieved considerable rapport. After several discussions the Ninth Army commander, General Simpson, and his British opposite, General Dempsey, submitted a revised plan calling for fuller American participation.

The Big Build-up

It was a staggering force of more than a million and a quarter men that Montgomery summoned to the assault in his final order issued on 9 March, two days after Remagen and the same day that the last Germans abandoned the west bank

---

[8] *Ibid.*, p. 210; Stacey, *The Victory Campaign*, pp. 529–31.

of the Rhine in the 21 Army Group zone. The Second Army had 11 divisions (3 of them armored, 2 airborne) and 6 brigades (including 4 armored and 1 Commando). The Ninth Army also had 11 divisions (3 of them armored). The First Canadian Army had 8 divisions.[9]

Given a target date of 24 March and the code name PLUNDER, the 21 Army Group's crossing of the Rhine was to rival D-day in Normandy in terms not only of number of troops involved but also in build-up of supplies, transport, and special equipment, in amount of supporting firepower, in complexity of deception plans, and in general elaboration. A sampling of statistics provides a ready index to the immensity of what probably was the most elaborate assault river crossing operation of all time. The British alone marshaled 60,000 tons of ammunition, 30,000 tons of engineer stores, and 28,000 tons of other commodities, all in addition to normal daily requirements. The Ninth Army built up another 138,000 tons of supplies. More than 37,000 British engineers were to participate, and 22,000 American. Including attached Canadian units, the British had 3,411 artillery pieces, antitank and antiaircraft guns, and rocket projectors; the American, 2,070. The Ninth Army alone issued over 800,000 maps.

Both armies made extensive efforts to conceal their build-up, devising elaborate schemes of camouflage, creating dummy installations and equipment, intensifying patrolling and artillery fire in sectors not scheduled for assault, and

maintaining a chemical smoke screen for ten days along a 20-mile front. Hardly any detail went unnoticed. To make room for mammoth trucks bringing the big landing craft to the water, bulldozers shoved buildings aside. Railheads were pushed forward, new roads constructed. Civilians for several miles west of the Rhine were evacuated. In the Ninth Army, engineers went so far as to borrow chemical heating pads from hospital units to wrap around outboard motors of assault craft to assure a ready start in the early spring chill.[10]

Along the 21 Army Group's front, the width of the Rhine varied from 900 to 1,500 feet. In March, the current seldom exceeds five miles per hour and the depth is never less than nine feet, thus meeting conditions for employing both small and medium-size assault and landing craft. Banks of mixed sand and gravel are suitable for launching assault craft, but dikes rising twelve to fifteen feet above the surrounding ground and standing as much as two miles from the main channel of the river pose an engineering obstacle and provide a ready line of defense.

The land on both sides of the Rhine is low and flat, creased by numerous creeks, canals, and drainage ditches. Running on an east-west course and emptying into the Rhine just south of Wesel, the Lippe River and the generally parallel Lippe-Seiten Canal split the zone that Montgomery had chosen for the assault. The river would serve along part of its course as a boundary between American and British forces. One to four miles beyond the Rhine runs the Ruhr-Wesel-

---

[9] The 21 Army Group in mid-March contained 1,703 Dutch, 5,982 Czechs, 6,696 Belgians, 14,915 Poles, 182,136 Canadians, 328,919 Americans, and 744,361 British, for a total strength of 1,284,712.

[10] *Conquer: The Story of Ninth Army,* pp. 199–245; Montgomery, *Normandy to the Baltic,* pp. 248–55; Stacey, *The Victory Campaign,* p. 533.

Arnhem rail line, along the most of its length built on fill, with highways passing through culverts underneath. In the sector assigned the Ninth Army, the railroad becomes two lines, not quite a mile apart. Like the dikes, the railroads might serve a defender well, as might numerous towns, hamlets, settlements, and scattered buildings dotting the landscape. This is not the urban complex that is the Ruhr a few miles away—indeed, extensive fields and hundreds of patches of deciduous woods ranging from small woodlots to forests four to seven miles across provide a rural atmosphere —but the man-made structures are sufficient to afford a determined defender many a solid strongpoint. In winter and at the beginning of spring it was a drab, dull landscape, a study in shades of grey in which the technicolor of exploding shells looked out of place.

Extending eleven miles south from the Lippe River, the Ninth Army's assault zone contained good roads leading east and northeast only on either flank, but that of the British afforded a spider web of highways leading northwest, north, and northeast. The concentration of roads made readily apparent why the Second Army's attack constituted Field Marshal Montgomery's main effort. While the Ninth Army with its assault corps blocked to the southeast to seal off the Ruhr, the British were to expand the center of the bridgehead and prepare for a deep strike northeastward across the north German plain. Once crossing sites were available downstream from Rees, the Canadians were to drive swiftly northward to trap any German forces remaining in the Netherlands. The Ninth Army was to send a corps through the British sector, taking advantage of

the roadnet there to get into position for a thrust eastward to come in behind the Ruhr from the north. The Ninth Army was to move once Montgomery deemed the bridgehead secure enough for bridges at Wesel and for a main road north of the Lippe to be turned over permanently to the Ninth Army.[11]

As of 9 March, when Montgomery issued his basic order, plans for using the two airborne divisions that were attached to the Second Army and headquarters of the XVIII Airborne Corps that controlled them still were indefinite. Montgomery directed only that they make an airborne attack in support of the Second Army's assault, that they be called on to conduct independent operations for no longer than ten days, and that as soon as possible one of the airborne divisions— British—was to pass to control of the Second Army, the other—American—to the Ninth Army.[12]

Despite the vagueness, Allied commanders had long planned to augment the major crossing of the Rhine with an airborne attack designed to eliminate enemy artillery and to block movement against the bridgehead. The Supreme Commander himself had expressed personal interest in it. Since August of the preceding year planning had proceeded off and on, and in February the First Allied Airborne Army (General Brereton) had published a broad outline plan. Called Operation VARSITY, the plan involved participation by three airborne divisions, but when a survey revealed insufficient airport facilities and transport aircraft for such a force, it was scaled down to a two-division effort. It

[11] 21 AGp, M–579, 9 Mar 45, Orders for the Battle of the Rhine, SHAEF SGS file, 381—PLUNDER, I.
[12] Ibid.

was to be made by the XVIII Airborne Corps under General Ridgway, employing the British 6th Airborne Division and the U.S. 17th.[13]

The job of transporting the airborne troops went to the U.S. IX Troop Carrier Command (Maj. Gen. Paul L. Williams), with the 38 and 46 Groups of the Royal Air Force attached, all old hands at that sort of task. The Royal Air Force 2d Tactical Air Force (Air Chief Marshal Sir Arthur Coningham) was to provide air cover, escort, and tactical support.

As with the ground assault, preparation for the airborne attack involved a prodigious amount of planning and work. While detailed planning proceeded, hundreds of construction engineers and civilian workers began expanding runways of Continental airfields that normally accommodated only tactical aircraft. Having seen no combat since the Normandy invasion, the British 6th Airborne Division was at full strength, while the U.S. 17th Airborne Division had fought hard in the Ardennes and required intensive training to integrate individual replacements. A new table of organization and equipment for airborne divisions, which the U.S. War Department had ordered to go into effect on 1 March, complicated the task. Since the new table allowed only one glider infantry regiment, the division had to inactivate one regiment and absorb the men from it in other units. Converting the glider field artillery battalions from two firing batteries to three left the division short one battalion, for which a replacement was to arrive only ten days before the target date.

Men of the 17th Airborne Division also had to learn to operate two previously untried weapons—the 57-mm. and 75-mm. recoilless rifles. Only recently brought to the European theater by ordnance specialists from Washington, a hundred of the rifles were distributed among the four U.S. airborne divisions in the theater. Not only in lack of recoil were the weapons revolutionary but also in weight. The 57-mm. rifle weighed only 45 pounds and could be fired from the shoulder. The 75-mm. rifle weighed 114 pounds (as compared to 3,400 pounds for the standard 75-mm. gun and carriage) and was fired from a machine gun tripod. In the 17th Airborne Division, the 57-mm. rifles were distributed directly to the parachute battalions, with special crews trained to man them, while the 75-mm. pieces went to the antitank battalion.[14]

Even a hasty glance at a map of the 21 Army Group's zone would reveal that the focus for any major attempt to cross the

---

[13] Unless otherwise noted, material on airborne planning is from Lewis H. Brereton, *The Brereton Diaries* (New York: William Morrow and Company, 1946), Part VI; Matthew B. Ridgway, Summary of Ground Forces Participation in Operation VARSITY, 25 April 1945, XVIII Corps Operation VARSITY Report; First Allied Airborne Army, Operation VARSITY, 19 May 1945; "Mission Accomplished," A Summary of Military Operations of the XVIII Corps (Airborne) in the European Theatre of Operations, 1944–1945, published in Schwerin, Germany (no date) by the XVIII Corps (Airborne); Operation VARSITY, the Historical Report of the 17th Airborne Division; and other official records of the First Allied Airborne Army and the XVIII Airborne Corps. See also Historical Division, Research Studies Institute, Air University, USAF Historical Study No. 97, Dr. John C. Warren, Airborne Operations in World War II, European Theater, published at Maxwell Air Force Base, Alabama, September 1956.

[14] For technical data on recoilless rifles, see TM 9–314; for development, see Green, Thomson, and Roots, *The Ordnance Department: Planning Munitions for War*, pp. 330–31.

Rhine would be the city of Wesel (population, 24,000) with its roads and rail network. Thus the assignment given to the XVIII Airborne Corps was logical: to seize high ground crowned by the Diersfordter Forst northwest of Wesel, thereby denying the enemy dominant observation on both the Wesel and Xanten crossing sites and blocking major highways leading both north and northwest from Wesel.

The objective was concentrated, admirably suited to capture and retention by two airborne divisions. At the same time, it was little over a mile from the projected Rhine crossing sites. Although the distance augured well for early linkup with the ground forces, it also dictated that if the airborne troops dropped before or coincident with the ground assault, which was normal practice, the ground troops would have to forgo all but the shallowest artillery support. Further, the ground troops needed to begin their attack in darkness, whereas experience had shown daylight best for an airborne attack.

The Second British Army commander, General Dempsey, suggested the solution. The paratroopers and glidermen were to delay their assault until British infantry had gained a footing beyond the river. It seemed a simple solution, but nobody had ever done it that way before.

Interdiction From the Air

Not as an integral part of Operation PLUNDER but as a general preliminary to assault across the Rhine, Allied air forces since mid-February had been conducting a heavy bombing program called "Interdiction of Northwest Germany." [15]

---

[15] Craven and Cate, *AAF III*, 771–73.

The object was to seal off the Ruhr from the rest of Germany by destroying rail bridges and viaducts and attacking canal traffic along a broad arc extending from Bremen near the North Sea south and southwest around the periphery of the Ruhr to the Rhine south of the industrial region. West of this line attacks were directed at communications centers, rail yards, industry, and similar targets.

From mid-February to 21 March Allied air forces concentrated on this task whenever any planes could be spared from other operations. Against the transportation system within the Ruhr alone, Allied bombardiers directed 31,635 tons of bombs. Heavy and medium bombers made 1,792 sorties against 17 rail bridges and viaducts along the arc encompassing the Ruhr. By 21 March, according to aerial reports, 10 of the bridges were destroyed and 5 others too damaged to use. After completing the job of helping the Canadian First Army and the U.S. Ninth Army to reach the Rhine, fighters and fighter-bombers of the British 2d Tactical Air Force and the U.S. XXIX Tactical Air Command (General Nugent) joined the Ruhr campaign. Most of the 7,311 sorties flown by these pilots between 11 and 21 March were directed against the rail and road systems of the Ruhr.

In the last three days before the 21 Army Group's assault, the heavy bombers of the Eighth Air Force concentrated on enemy airfields and barracks, with particular attention to fields known to harbor jet aircraft. The heavies flew 3,859 sorties. During the same period 2,000 medium bombers of the U.S. 9th Bombardment Division hit communications centers, rail yards, and flak positions. Heavies of the Royal Air Force

Bomber Command carried out a similar program, while the Allied tactical aircraft hit a variety of targets—airfields, flak positions, and troop concentrations. The total air effort during those three days, which the airmen called "processing of the terrain," amounted to some 11,000 sorties. For such a restricted area and against targets that already had been blasted from time to time over at least the preceding three years, the blow was devastating.

The View From the East Bank

Already mortally wounded in the late winter fighting west of the Rhine, stabbed anew at Remagen, the Germans dutifully went about preparing to defend the lower reaches of the river against a major attack that was but a question of time and specific location. This "shadow of an army," one German army group chief of staff called it; morale of the troops varying "from suspicion to callous resignation," an officer corps that "lacked confidence and wondered just what were the demands of duty"; this army, he said, "could only pretend to resist." [16]

Given not quite two weeks' respite following the last withdrawal of troops to the east bank, German commanders deployed their surviving formations in accord with their estimate that the main Allied attack would hit between Emmerich and Dinslaken (the latter seven miles southeast of Wesel). The commander of *Army Group H*, General Blaskowitz, thus gave this sector to the stronger of his two weak forces, General Schlemm's *First Parachute Army*, while assigning the sector downstream from

Emmerich to the *Twenty-fifth Army* (General der Infanterie Guenther Blumentritt). Blaskowitz and other German commanders also anticipated an airborne operation in conjunction with the river crossing, expecting that it would be launched ten miles or so northeast of Wesel to facilitate exploitation of the Allied bridgehead in that direction.[17]

Field Marshal Montgomery's intelligence staff estimated total German strength, including *Volkssturm* troops, opposite the entire 22-mile zone of assault at approximately 85,000, or some 35,000 less than the strength of the one American corps involved in the assault. Yet even that figure probably was high. The *First Parachute Army,* whose positions were basically contiguous to the zone of assault, had three corps, two of which had three makeshift divisions each and the third, two divisional formations. The strongest of the three, the *II Parachute Corps,* located opposite the British near Rees, had only about 12,000 men, less than the normal strength of an Allied division. The parachute army's only reserve was a replacement training division. *Army Group H*'s reserve was the *XLVII Panzer Corps*, which had remnants of a panzer grenadier division and a panzer division; between them, the two divisions had only 35 tanks. In all the army group there were no more than 200 tanks and assault guns.[18]

On the plus side, *Army Group H* still

---

[16] MS # A–965 (Wagener).

[17] MSS # B–414, *Army Group H (OB NORDWEST)*, 10 March–9 May 1945 (Col. Rolf Geyer, G–3, *AGp H* and later of *OB NORDWEST*); # B–593, The Battles of *Army Group B* on the Rhine up to Its Dissolution, 22 March–17 April 1945 (Generalmajor Karl Wagener).

[18] MSS # B–414 (Geyer); # B–198, *XLVII Panzer Corps*, 8 March–16 April 1945 (General der Panzertruppen Heinrich von Luettwitz).

contained a reasonable complement of
artillery, including a volks artillery corps
and a volks werfer brigade to support the
army group reserve. Firepower was increased by withdrawing almost all
mobile antiaircraft units from the Netherlands and using them to supplement
the fixed batteries in the vicinity of
Wesel with an eye toward possible Allied
airborne attack. (Allied commanders
reckoned the Germans had 81 heavy and
252 light antiaircraft pieces in this sector.) Although all fortifications were of
the hasty field variety, during the fortnight after the withdrawal behind the
Rhine the Germans had prepared a fairly
solid forward line along the river and
the railroad that parallels the river,
though there was little time for creating
positions in depth. The new Commander
in Chief West, Field Marshal Kesselring,
reviewed and approved the defensive
measures on 14 March.[19]

Despite the approval, Kesselring could
have entertained no genuine optimism
that his forces could hold successfully,
for he had no reserves to send to *Army
Group H*'s assistance. Such optimism as
there was received a sharp blow a week
later, on 21 March, as Allied aircraft
stepped up their bombardment. On that
date, a bomb demolished a building
housing headquarters of the *First Parachute Army*. The commander, General
Schlemm, was seriously wounded. Although Schlemm would remain on the
scene until General Blumentritt could
be released from the *Twenty-fifth Army*
to assume command on the 28th, he ran
a high fever and was in no condition to
exert real influence on the battle.[20]

"*Two if by sea*"

To the British and Americans it was
clear that the Germans knew the assault
was coming soon. Even if the spectacular
smoke screen maintained on the west
bank actually concealed all the preparations, which it did not, the very presence
of the screen would indicate impending
assault. On 20 March the *Army Group H*
commander, General Blaskowitz, ordered
"an increased state of alert." [21]

Nervousness betrayed German concern to the waiting assault force. As the
target date of 24 March neared, har-
rassing artillery fire from the east bank
increased markedly; patrol after patrol
probed the west bank in quest of information, as often as not ending up in
Allied prison camps. Taking advantage
of periods when Allied aircraft were ab-
sent, German planes individually or in
small groups strafed the Allied concentrations of men and equipment, though
without appreciable effect. Some German
pilots concentrated on knocking American artillery observation planes from the
skies and succeeded in destroying eight.[22]
Almost every Allied patrol that sought
to cross the river triggered nervous German fire.

By midafternoon of 23 March, all on
the Allied side was ready. In deference
to the projected airborne assault, there
remained only a last-minute consultation
with the weather prophets before Field
Marshal Montgomery at 1530 made the
decision that set the vast machine the 21
Army Group had become into motion.

---

[19] MS # B-414 (Geyer).
[20] *Ibid.*; MS # B-674 (General der Infanterie

Guenther Blumentritt); Stacey, *The Victory Campaign*, p. 535n.
[21] MS # B-414 (Geyer).
[22] *Conquer: The Story of Ninth Army*, pp. 235-
36.

To hundreds of waiting units went the code words, "Two if by sea," which meant the British were coming.

Around 1800 on the same day, normal British harassing artillery fires against German positions near Rees began to build in intensity. By 2100 the shelling had reached a crescendo as assault waves of a division of the Second British Army's 30 Corps (Lt. Gen. Brian G. Horrocks) entered the river southeast of Rees. (*Map XII*) In less than seven minutes the British assault craft touched down on the far bank against no more than sporadic opposition. Paratroopers of the *II Parachute Corps* (General der Fallschirmtruppen Eugen Meindl) were on hand, but the artillery had kept them down. In a matter of a few hours a column of British infantry had reached the outskirts of Rees.

While recognizing that this probably was not the main assault, the German army group commander, General Blaskowitz, directed the *15th Panzer Grenadier Division* from his reserve to counterattack at Rees in hope of throwing back the first group before the main assault could begin.[23] Since the British attack was designed primarily to draw German attention away from the Wesel sector, the German reaction demonstrated that the first phase of the Rhine crossing was a success.

An hour after the first troops began to cross, a British Commando brigade paddled stealthily across the river at a point about two miles west of Wesel.

The commandos had little trouble touching down, then moving quietly overland toward the city. Halting less than a mile outside, they waited while some 200 planes of the Royal Air Force Bomber Command pounded their objective for fifteen minutes with more than a thousand tons of bombs. When the commandos moved in after midnight, the city was a mound of rubble, though German defenders were still much in evidence. Here stood a conglomerate force, the *Wesel Division,* organized around a nucleus of antiaircraft artillery units. The tenacity of the resistance belied the division's heterogeneity and loose organization. It would be well into the day of 24 March before the commandos could deem Wesel secure and dawn the next day before all resistance collapsed. Among the German casualties was the division commander, Generalmajor Friedrich Deutsch, killed in the fighting.

At 0100 (24 March) a mammoth artillery preparation for the main assault had begun. A division of the British 12 Corps (Lt. Gen. Sir Neil M. Ritchie) prepared to cross the river an hour later northwest of Xanten. A division of the U.S. Ninth Army was to make a simultaneous assault across the Rhine north of Rheinberg, to be followed an hour later by another division east and southeast of Rheinberg.

Operation Flashpoint

To General Anderson's XVI Corps, a fledgling among American corps with combat experience only in the drive from the Roer to the Rhine, fell the assignment of directing the Ninth Army's assault crossing, called Operation FLASHPOINT. The two divisions selected to

---

[23] German material is from MSS # B–414 (Geyer) and # B–198 (Luettwitz). Unless otherwise noted, the account of British and Canadian operations is from Montgomery, *Normandy to the Baltic;* Stacey, *The Victory Campaign;* and Headquarters, British Army of the Rhine, Battlefield Tour, Operation PLUNDER.

make the crossing were, on the other hand, veterans of combat in the European theater since the preceding June— the 30th and 79th Divisions. Backing them up were the 8th Armored and the 35th and 75th Divisions. The Ninth Army in addition still contained the XIII and XIX Corps with a total of six divisions. The army commander, General Simpson, directed the XIII Corps to continue to defend along the Rhine south of the crossing sites while the XIX Corps assembled for early commitment in the bridgehead.

With five divisions, Anderson's XVI Corps already was considerably larger than a normal corps and was beefed up further with supporting units. In addition to regular XVI Corps artillery (Brig. Gen. Charles C. Brown), attached in general support were the 34th Field Artillery Brigade (Brig. Gen. John F. Uncles) with 13 battalions of medium, heavy, and superheavy pieces and the XIX Corps artillery headquarters (Brig. Gen. George D. Shea) with 11 battalions. Also attached were a tank destroyer group with 6 battalions, 6 separate tank battalions, 3 engineer combat groups, 2 antiaircraft artillery groups, a smoke generator battalion, a chemical (4.2-inch mortar) battalion, and a host of smaller units, including the assigned naval contingent. These raised the strength of the corps to 120,000 men, more an army than a corps, supported by an impressive 54 field artillery battalions. Artillery units of the XIII Corps and of one infantry division of that corps were to participate in the preparation fires and to answer calls for supporting fire as needed.[24]

The Ninth Army's usual ally in the sky, General Nugent's XXIX Tactical Air Command, joined other Allied air units in the pre-D-day interdiction program and was to expend part of its effort on 24 March in support of the big airborne attack, Operation VARSITY. Yet enough planes were left over to provide armed reconnaissance in support of the Ninth Army and to assign a fighter-bomber group to work directly with each of the two assault infantry divisions.

East of the Rhine, German defense of the approximately eight miles of front destined for assault by the XVI Corps was split between two corps of the *First Parachute Army*. The *LXXXVI Corps* under General der Infanterie Erich Straube had a primary task of holding Wesel but was also responsible for the sector from the Lippe River to a point on the Rhine southwest of Dinslaken. The *180th Division* of this corps would face the American 30th Division and part of the 79th. The parachute army's weakest command, the *LXIII Corps*, under General der Infanterie Erich Abraham, bore responsibility for the remaining two miles plus additional frontage as far south as the army group boundary in line with the Ruhr River south of Duisburg. The northernmost unit of Abraham's corps, a makeshift formation called the *Hamburg Division*, would face part of the 79th Division, while the *2d Parachute Division* held the southern portion of the corps zone.[25]

---

[24] Unless otherwise noted, the Ninth Army's story is from official records of the XVI Corps and its divisions, from extensive combat interviews, and from three unofficial unit histories: Hewitt, *Workhorse of the Western Front; History of the XVI Corps;* and *Conquer: The Story of the Ninth Army.*

[25] MS # B–414 (Geyer); XVI Corps intelligence reports.

A three-quarter moon dimly lit the landscape and a providential west wind was blowing the long-maintained smoke screen toward the enemy as engineers and infantrymen began to move storm and assault boats to the river's edge soon after midnight on 24 March. Accompanied by General Simpson, the Supreme Commander himself mingled and talked with the troops. The men were, General Eisenhower wrote later, "remarkably eager to finish the job." [26]

At 0100 as General Eisenhower and General Simpson moved to an observation post in a church tower, the 2,070 artillery pieces supporting the XVI Corps opened fire in a thunderstorm of sound. The earth trembled as one deafening explosion after another merged into a constant, ear-pounding cacophony. Every minute for sixty minutes, more than a thousand shells ranging in weight from 25 to 325 pounds crashed to earth beyond the Rhine. During the hour-long preparation, the artillerymen fired a total of 65,261 rounds.[27] At the same time 1,500 heavy bombers were attacking a dozen airfields within range of the crossing sites. Against the backdrop of violence, infantrymen and engineers took their places in storm and double assault boats, while other engineers hoisted big pontons close to the water to begin their job of building bridges the moment the west bank was free of the first assault waves.

All three regiments of the 30th Division participated in the assault—the 119th Infantry on the left, just southeast of the village of Buederich, near the confluence of the Lippe with the Rhine; the 117th Infantry in the center at the village of Wallach; and the 120th Infantry two miles to the southeast near a big bend in the river just northeast of Rheinberg. Each regiment used one battalion in the assault. Each assault battalion was organized into four waves with two-minute intervals between waves. Each battalion had 54 storm boats (7 men and a crew of 2) powered by 55-hp. motors and 30 double assault boats (14 men and a crew of 3) driven by 22-hp. motors. Machine guns firing tracer bullets guided the first wave, while colored aircraft landing lights would show the way for those who followed.

As the men awaited the signal to push into the stream, occasional German mortar fire fell, though with little effect. Only after the boats raced out onto the water and disappeared in swirls of gray smoke did any German shells find a target. They knocked out two of the 119th Infantry's storm boats, killing one man and wounding three. That was all.

In a matter of minutes, the bottoms of the boats in the first wave were scraping on the far bank, the men leaping from the craft and running toward the big dike. Only at one point, where men of Company G, 120th Infantry, landed a few hundred yards from their planned crossing site, was there fire from dug-in Germans on the dike, and Company G quickly silenced that without loss. Everywhere else the Germans were mute. Although the artillery had scored few hits on the dike, the German defenders were blinded by the smoke and thoroughly cowed by the shelling.

"There was no real fight to it," noted 1st Lt. Whitney O. Refvem, commander

---

[26] Eisenhower, *Crusade in Europe*, p. 389; *History of the XVI Corps*, p. 40.

[27] In the next four hours, they doubled this figure for a total of 131,450 rounds. See *Conquer: The Story of the Ninth Army*, p. 243.

of the 117th Infantry's Company B. "The artillery had done the job for us." [28] The artillery was timed perfectly, the lieutenant observed, lifting only moments before the assault boats reached the east bank. Two rounds of white phosphorus served as the signal that the artillery was passing on to more distant targets.

Nor was there appreciable opposition to the crossing of succeeding waves, which normally could have been expected to attract heavier shelling. The answer again was to be found in the mammoth artillery preparation, which had silenced at least some German guns and apparently had cut all telephone wires; since few forward observers had radios, they had no way to call for fire. Daylight was at hand before the first German shelling in appreciable amounts struck the crossing sites.

There could be no question from the first that the 30th Division had staged a strikingly successful crossing of the sprawling Rhine. Within two hours of the jump-off, the first line of settlements east of the river was in hand, all three regiments had at least two battalions across, and a platoon of DD tanks had arrived to help the center regiment. In the assault crossing total casualties among all three regiments were even less than for the one regiment that had made the Third Army's surprise crossing twenty-eight hours earlier at Oppenheim.

The British had crossed with similar ease near Xanten and had quickly pushed a thousand yards beyond the Rhine. It remained for the 79th Division to execute the last amphibious phase of the big assault, to cross the Rhine at

0300 at points east and southeast of Rheinberg.

It was because of the southeastward curvature of the Rhine that the 79th Division's attack came an hour later than that of the 30th Division, thus affording men of the 30th a chance to overcome the handicap and also avoiding the risk of exposed inner flanks for both divisions.[29] For the Germans opposite the 79th Division, it meant two hours of artillery punishment instead of one.

The 79th Division commander, General Wyche, chose to make his crossing with two regiments side-by-side, each regiment using one battalion in the assault. Unlike the 30th Division, which used only storm boats for the first wave, reserving the slower assault boats for subsequent crossings, the assault units of the 79th Division mixed the two. They overcame the difference in speed by giving the assault boats a head start.[30]

Although the hour's delay afforded the 79th Division additional artillery preparation, it also added an element of confusion, for by 0300 the west wind had decreased, allowing nature's fog and man's smoke to cling closely to the water and to both banks of the river. Except for a smattering of small arms fire, the Germans opposed the crossing no more effectively than they had that of the 30th Division; but the difficulty of holding course in the fog and smoke scattered and intermingled the units on the east bank. The men in some boats lost direction altogether and returned to the west bank. Thinking they had landed on the enemy

---

[28] Combat interview with Lieutenant Refvem.

[29] Combat interview with General Wyche, CG 79th Division.

[30] In addition to the usual records and combat interviews, the 79th Division prepared a special report, Rhine Crossing by the 79th Infantry Division.

side of the river, men in one boat raced
ashore in a skirmish line, only to meet
other Americans coming down to the
water to load.

Yet in the absence of serious enemy
reaction, the confusion was short-lived.
Within forty-five minutes both assault
battalions had assembled and begun their
drives to the east. Like the men of the
30th Division, those of the 79th attributed much of their easy success to
the artillery preparation. The fire lifted
only after the first boats were three-
fourths of the way across the river.
Prisoners said "they had never encountered anything like it, and it completely
stunned, scared, and shook them." [31]

Well before daylight, two battalions
were ashore in each regimental sector,
and again there could be no question of
the extent of the success. For both divisions of the XVI Corps, detailed planning, rehearsal on sand tables and on
rear area rivers, careful attention to deception, and intimate co-ordination with
a powerful artillery arm had produced
remarkable results. Together the two divisions had crossed one of the most imposing water obstacles in western Europe
at a cost of thirty-one casualties.

The Drive to the Railroads

Success continued to crown the attack
as the men drove eastward. Even before
the second battalion of the 79th Division's 315th Infantry had begun to
cross the river, the leading battalion
swept past the first railroad to the outskirts of Dinslaken, a city of 25,000 almost two miles from the crossing site.
The leading battalion of the 313th In-

fantry, on the south, also reached the
first rail line quickly, then swung southeast to build up a flank defense along a
canal that leads eastward from a man-
made inlet forming the harbor of the
Rhine town of Walsum.

Seldom did the Germans offer more
than perfunctory defense. One explanation was that the 79th Division had
struck on the seam between the *180th
Division* and the *Hamburg Division*,
which was also the boundary between
Straube's *LXXXVI Corps* and Abraham's *LXIII Corps*. Another was the
limited number of trained men available
to the Germans. Still another, obviously,
was the weight of the Allied artillery
bombardment. In those cases where the
Germans did stand to fight, the American regiments brought to bear a weapon
they had borrowed from their enemy—
the *Panzerfaust*. Both regiments had
equipped their assault battalions with
200 of these one-shot German antitank
rockets. The blast effect of the weapons
against buildings more often than not
convinced even die-hard occupants to
surrender.

So irresolute and spotty was resistance
in front of the 79th Division that not
once during the day of 24 March did
the division call on the fighter-bomber
group that was assigned in support. Nor
was the weight of armor—often crucial
in a bridgehead battle—necessary; the
fact that medium tanks and tank destroyers did not arrive in the bridgehead
until midafternoon mattered little. By
nightfall the 79th Division held a bridgehead more than three miles wide and
deep, securely anchored on canal lines
on both north and south, embracing
Dinslaken, and in the north extending
well beyond the second railroad. The di-

[31] Combat interview with Lt Col Norman King,
Asst G-2, XVI Corps.

vision reserve, the 314th Infantry, was on hand, along with supporting tank and tank destroyer battalions. More than 700 prisoners were on their way to the rear, and American casualties were few. The 313th Infantry, for example, lost 1 man killed and 11 wounded.[32]

For the 30th Division, striking into the center of the enemy's *180th Division*, most gains were harder to come by, but they came nevertheless. The 119th Infantry, on the north, ran into its first real trouble in midmorning at a highway underpass at the first railroad. It took the help of light tanks, ferried across the Rhine in LCM's, to force a way past. The 117th Infantry had similar trouble at another underpass farther to the south, where an antitank piece blocked efforts to fill a crater that barred the road; supporting artillery eventually eliminated the German gun. By the end of the day both regiments had passed beyond the second railroad, while a two-company task force had cleared troublesome antiaircraft pieces from a spit of land north of the Lippe-Seiten Canal and had reached the Lippe River across from Wesel.

In the zone of the third regiment, the 120th Infantry, on the south, the most exciting development occurred. There, when the 3d Battalion under Maj. Chris McCullough soon after midday took the village of Moellen, astride the first railroad, patrols ranging eastward reported they found almost no Germans. Although the battalion already was considerably ahead of the rest of the regiment, the regimental commander, Col. Branner

P. Purdue, determined to attempt a deep probe past the second railroad into open farm country beyond. By midafternoon a company of medium tanks, brought across the Rhine on Bailey rafts, and a platoon of tank destroyers, transported to the east bank by LCM's, were on their way to join the battalion.

One rifle company was loading on the tanks to start the drive when, without warning, a heavy concentration of artillery fire began to fall. The men scrambled for cover, then realized in consternation that the fire had come from the west. It was "friendly" fire. A quick check revealed no error on the part of artillery units supporting the 30th Division. The fault lay with the neighboring 79th whose troops had spotted the 3d Battalion's assembly and thought it a German force preparing to counterattack.

The 30th Division commander, General Hobbs, was quick on the telephone to his counterpart in the 79th Division, General Wyche. Since the interdivision boundary was a readily recognizable canal line, Hobbs could see no excuse for the error. He needed no artillery assistance, he said caustically. "We have battalions to spare to fire into anything in our zone."[33]

The fire fortunately caused only minor casualties. Quickly re-forming, Major McCullough's battalion and his attached tanks and tank destroyers soon found the patrol reports were accurate. The column swept swiftly eastward, picking up forty docile Germans on the way, and halted for the night in open country a mile beyond the Dinslaken-Wesel highway. Although this position was only

---

[32] No total figure is available for the 315th Infantry, though losses were considerably higher, since one battalion incurred 38 casualties and another 30.

[33] Telecon, Hobbs to Wyche, 30th Div G–3 Jnl file, 23–25 Mar 45.

three miles beyond the easternmost curve of the Rhine and generally on line with advance contingents of the 79th Division, it was well forward of other units of the 30th Division and six miles beyond the Rhine as it ran through the division's sector. McCullough's battalion thus had reached the limit of effective direct support artillery fire.

Although thus forced to halt, Major McCullough and his superiors were convinced they had achieved a breakthrough of the German positions. A 105-mm. artillery battalion, General Hobbs promised, would be on hand to support a swift advance the next day.

As a result of ingenious advance preparations by supporting engineers and of a continuing smoke screen that hampered German observation, a treadway bridge was opened to traffic at 1600. The bridge later was damaged when a Bailey raft loaded with a tank crashed into it, but not before the 118th Field Artillery Battalion had crossed. The bridge was back in service soon after midnight.

This bridge and the quick advance of Major McCullough's battalion made the 30th Division's position as night fell on the first day even more promising than that of the 79th Division. In the latter's sector, artillery fire and airbursts from big antiaircraft pieces delayed bridge construction and, though resistance was light, no indication of a clear breakthrough had developed. The 30th Division had taken 1,500 prisoners, more than double the number taken by the 79th.

Operation Varsity

Troops of the 30th Division were fighting at the first railroad and those of the 79th were clearing Dinslaken when shortly before 1000 on 24 March the steady drone of hundreds of aircraft motors began to emerge from the west. For two hours and thirty-two minutes the deep, throbbing hum of the motors was to continue. Since no pathfinder planes came in advance, even the first glimpse of planes gave the impression of the coming of a vast air armada. The great train was composed of 889 escorting fighters, 1,696 transport planes, and 1,348 gliders, bringing to the battlefield 21,680 paratroopers and glidermen, followed closely by 240 four-engine Liberator bombers of the U.S. Eighth Air Force dropping 582 tons of supplies.[34] Another 2,153 fighter aircraft either maintained a protective umbrella over the target area or ranged far over Germany in quest of any German plane that might seek to interfere. None did. In addition, 2,596 heavy bombers (660 of them from the Fifteenth Air Force in Italy) and 821 medium bombers attacked airfields, bridges, marshaling areas, and other targets throughout Germany.

---

[34] Statistics from *Report by the Supreme Commander to the Combined Chiefs of Staff on the Operations in Europe of the Allied Expeditionary Force, 6 June 1944 to 8 May 1945* (Washington, 1946) (hereafter cited as Eisenhower, *Report*), p. 100, and John C. Warren, Airborne Operations in World War II, European Theater, pp. 228–29. The total number of troops, aircraft, and gliders exceeded the total for the first day in Operation MARKET (about 20,000 troops, 1,545 transport planes, and 478 gliders), though additional troops landing after D-day made MARKET the larger operation. Unless otherwise noted, the account of VARSITY is based on the two sources cited and on the following: First Allied Airborne Army, Operation VARSITY; 17th Airborne Division, Operation VARSITY; journals and other official records of the division; XVIII Airborne Corps, Operation VARSITY; and two combat interviews with officers of the division. The unit history of the XVIII Airborne Corps, "Mission Accomplished," is sketchy.

The men of the U.S. 17th Airborne
Division (General Miley) had risen
from twelve airfields north and south of
Paris, those of the British 6th Airborne
Division from airfields in England. In an
intricately timed maneuver, they had
rendezvoused near Brussels. Tails of both
divisions, including 2,005 motor vehicles
belonging to the American unit, had
earlier headed for the target area by
land. In anticipation of early linkup of
airborne and ground troops, the commander, General Ridgway, and staff of
the XVIII Airborne Corps did not participate in the airborne assault but were
already in position on the west bank of
the Rhine. The commander of the First
Allied Airborne Army, General Brereton, also took up post on the west bank.
The Supreme Commander and British
Prime Minister Churchill, the latter in
company with the Chief of the Imperial
General Staff, Field Marshal Sir Alan
Brooke, watched the airborne attack
from vantage points on separate hills.[35]

There was much to see even before
the aerial train approached. Executing
the climax to operations begun three
days earlier, medium bombers and
fighter-bombers of the Ninth Air Force
and British Second Tactical Air Force,
for half an hour preceding arrival of the
first transports, rained fragmentation
bombs on antiaircraft batteries in the
vicinity of the drop and landing zones.[36]

AMERICAN PARATROOPER CAUGHT IN A
TREE

At the same time, artillery of the British
Second Army pounded antiaircraft gun
positions short of a predesignated bomb
line.

The sky was clear and bright in midmorning of 24 March, but a ground haze
aggravated by drifting smoke from the
screen along the Rhine lowered visibility
close to the ground. Slightly ahead of
schedule, the first flight of transport
planes appeared over the target area at
0953. Carrying a battalion of the 507th
Parachute Infantry, the planes missed the
designated drop zone, a spot of cleared
land just northwest of Wesel on the
southern skirt of the Diersfordter Forst,
the closest planned drop zone to the
Rhine. The paratroopers came to earth
instead a mile and three-quarters to the

[35] Eisenhower, *Crusade in Europe*, p. 390; Winston
S. Churchill, "The Second World War," vol. VI,
Triumph and Tragedy (Boston: Houghton Mifflin
Company, 1953), p. 413. The next day, D plus 1,
Churchill, Brooke, Montgomery, and Generals
Simpson and Anderson made a round trip across
the Rhine in an LCM in the sector of the XVI
Corps.

[36] Craven and Cate, *AAF III*, 774.

northwest on the other side of the wood in a field near the town of Diersfordt.[37]

Because this flight arrived close behind the air and artillery antiflak program, it received little antiaircraft fire, but the drop pattern was widely dispersed nonetheless. The paratroopers coalesced into two relatively equal groups, one under the regimental commander, Col. Edson D. Raff, the other under the battalion commander, Maj. Paul F. Smith.

While Major Smith's group was destroying several antiaircraft positions, Colonel Raff's men disposed of a nest of machine guns and dug-in infantry and began to work southward through the forest toward the assigned regimental objective, relatively high ground along the fringe of the wood near Diersfordt. Spotting a battery of five 150-mm. artillery pieces firing from a clearing, Raff and his force detoured to eliminate it. They captured both the German artillerymen and the guns and spiked the guns with thermite grenades. By the time Raff's paratroopers reached the vicinity of Diersfordt, they had killed about 55 Germans, wounded 40, and captured 300, including a colonel.

The other two battalions of the 507th Parachute Infantry had in the meantime landed successfully on the assigned drop zone. As one of these, the 3d, got ready to attack Diersfordt and a castle that

dominates it, two German tanks emerged from the castle and headed down a narrow forest road toward the waiting paratroopers. An aptly placed antitank grenade induced the crew of the lead tank to surrender, whereupon a tank hunter team armed with a 57-mm. recoilless rifle set the second afire with a direct hit, the first instance of successful combat use of the new weapon.

Resistance in Diersfordt, it soon developed, meant the castle. While two companies laid down a base of fire from the edge of the forest against turrets and upper windows, Company G entered and began to clean out the castle, room by room. Two hours later, at 1500, those Germans who remained capitulated. Among the 300 prisoners were several senior officers of General Straube's *LXXXVI Corps* and of the *84th Infantry Division.*

By nightfall the 507th Parachute Infantry had consolidated along the woods line near Diersfordt and patrols had established contact with the 1st Commando Brigade in Wesel. Ten 75-mm. pack howitzers of the 464th Parachute Field Artillery Battalion were tied in to the position.

Second of the 17th Airborne Division's regiments to drop, the 513th Parachute Infantry incurred intense antiaircraft fire from an enemy no longer deterred by the Allied bombardment. All three battalions of the regiment landed more than a mile from their assigned drop zones inside the sector of the 6th Airborne Division north of Wesel near the town of Hamminkeln. Heavy small arms fire followed the paratroopers to the ground. After a short but sharp fire fight, they were able to assemble by battalions and fight their way southward to their as-

---

[37] A stick of paratroopers landing together in a field came under sharp fire from German riflemen and a machine gunner even as the paratroopers struggled to free themselves from their harnesses. One man, Pvt. George J. Peters, charged the machine gun, seventy-five yards away. Halfway to the gun, German fire knocked him down, but he struggled to his feet to continue the charge. Knocked down again, he crawled close enough to the gun to eliminate it with hand grenades before dying from his wounds. Private Peters was awarded the Medal of Honor posthumously.

GLIDER TROOPS AFTER LANDING NEAR WESEL

signed zones. In the process the paratroopers destroyed two German tanks, a self-propelled gun, and two batteries of 88's. While one battalion dug in on the landing zone, another cleared the woods north of Diersfordt and a third moved to the little Issel River, which marked the eastern extremity of the planned D-day objective line.[38]

Although the 513th's supporting artillery, the 466th Parachute Field Artillery Battalion, landed on the correct drop zone southwest of Hamminkeln, enemy fire there was even heavier than that encountered by the infantry. A number of key men, including all the officers of one battery, were killed or wounded on the drop zone. The artillerymen nevertheless managed to assemble some

---

[38] As Company E was advancing, Germans in a complex of buildings opened fire with automatic weapons, rifles, and four field pieces. The lead platoon was pinned to the ground until a runner, Pfc. Stuart S. Stryker, rose in full view of the enemy, rallied the men, and led a charge on the buildings. German fire cut Stryker down as he

---

neared the buildings, but the others went on to overrun the position. They captured more than 200 Germans and rescued three captive American airmen. Private Stryker was awarded the Medal of Honor posthumously.

of their howitzers within half an hour, enabling them to place direct fire on the Germans and gradually to eliminate the opposition. By noon they had captured ten German 76-mm. pieces and were in position to provide supporting fire for the 513th Parachute Infantry.

It remained for the glider echelons, including service elements of the division, to better the record for accuracy in landing. At least 90 percent of the gliders descended on the proper landing zones north and northeast of Wesel in an eastward-oriented angle formed by the Issel River and the Issel Canal. Although German fire was in some cases intense, destroying some of the gliders even after they had landed safely, men of the 194th Glider Infantry within two hours of landing had swept to the river and the canal and most of the howitzers of the division's two glider field artillery battalions were in position to support them. One of the infantry battalions knocked out two German tanks en route to its objective along the river, then accounted for two more in repulsing small counterattacks after the men had dug in.

The British 6th Airborne Division encountered similar difficulty with flak and enemy ground fire but also moved swiftly to seize D-day objectives. By 1300 the town of Hamminkeln was in British hands along with several bridges over the Issel River east and northeast of the town.

Operation VARSITY, the airborne phase of the big Rhine assault, was an impressive success. All airborne troops were on the ground by 1230, along with 109 tons of ammunition, 695 vehicles, and 113 artillery pieces; and in a matter of hours, both Americans and British had seized all objectives assigned for the first

day. In the process they had virtually eliminated the artillery and service elements of the enemy's *84th Infantry Division*. Except for a surrounded pocket north of Diersfordt made up mainly of remnants of the *1053d Infantry*, the enemy division had ceased to function as a tactical organization.[39] The 17th Airborne Division claimed 2,000 prisoners, the 6th Airborne Division, another 1,500.

Linkup with British ground troops was firm by nightfall, and as early as midafternoon the XVIII Airborne Corps commander, General Ridgway, joined the 17th Airborne Division commander, General Miley, beyond the Rhine. By late afternoon supplies were moving across the Rhine in dukws in such volume as to eliminate the need for additional supply by air.

Yet for all the success of Operation VARSITY, the question remained whether under the prevailing circumstances an airborne attack had been necessary or was even justified. It unquestionably aided British ground troops, but at a cost to the 17th Airborne Division alone during the first day's operations of 159 men killed, 522 wounded, and 840 missing (though 600 of the missing subsequently turned up to fight again). The IX Troop Carrier Command alone lost 41 killed, 153 wounded, 163 missing.[40] The airborne assault also cost over 50 gliders and 44 transport aircraft destroyed, 332

[39] Intelligence Sum for period 241800 to 242359, XVIII Airborne Corps, and Sitrep 4, 24 Mar 45, XVIII Airborne Corps.

[40] Figures are from 17th Airborne Division History, 15 April 1943–16 September 1945, and Warren, Airborne Operations in World War II, p. 229. First-day losses of the two U.S. infantry divisions that crossed the Rhine on 24 March by amphibious assault were 41 killed, 450 wounded, 7 missing. See *Conquer: The Story of the Ninth Army,* p. 247.

damaged. In the low-level supply mission flown directly after the assault by 240 Liberators of the Eighth Air Force, 15 aircraft were lost.[41]

In view of the weak condition of German units east of the Rhine and the particular vulnerability of airborne troops in and immediately following the descent, some overbearing need for the special capability of airborne divisions would be required to justify their use. Although the objectives assigned the divisions were legitimate, they were objectives that ground troops alone under existing circumstances should have been able to take without undue difficulty and probably with considerably fewer casualties. Participation by paratroopers and glidermen gave appreciably no more depth to the bridgehead at Wesel than that achieved by infantrymen of the 30th Division. Nor did the airborne attack speed bridge construction (as the XVIII Airborne Corps commander subsequently claimed),[42] for not until 0915 the next day, 25 March, did engineers start work on bridges at Wesel. A treadway bridge had been opened to traffic behind the 30th Division seventeen hours before that.

At the End of D-Day

As night fell on 24 March, only on the extreme left of the forces involved in the 21 Army Group's Rhine crossing was there concern for Allied success. There, near Rees, twelve British and Canadian battalions supported by thirty DD tanks

had crossed the river. Contingents of the *7th Parachute Division* of General Meindl's *II Parachute Corps* still held onto high ground commanding the crossing sites, thereby preventing bridge construction and hindering all reinforcement. German paratroopers also clung tenaciously to a town northwest of Rees, cutting off and surrounding small groups of British troops that had gotten into the buildings. It would be well into the morning of the 25th before a relief force of Canadian infantry could set the situation right.

Despite this tenacity, the condition of the *II Parachute Corps* at nightfall on 24 March actually was precarious. The collapse of the *84th Division* of the neighboring *LXXXVI Corps* under the impact of the Allied airborne attack exposed the left flank of the corps. When the counterattack by the *15th Panzer Grenadier Division* failed to shake the British around Rees, General Meindl would have no choice but to pull back the paratroopers forming his left wing along the Rhine and face them to the east. The German situation at Rees, Meindl concluded, was "hopeless." [43]

The Germans thus faced likely disaster at three points: Rees, Wesel, and south of the Lippe River where the U.S. XVI Corps was close to a clean breakthrough. All that was available to ward off all three threats was the *XLVII Panzer Corps* with its lone remaining unit, the *116th Panzer Division*. Although the *Army Group H* commander, General Blaskowitz, earlier had considered using the panzer corps to oppose any Allied airborne attack, he believed now that the greatest danger, despite the psycho-

---

[41] Statistics on glider and aircraft losses vary slightly. See Eisenhower, *Report*, p. 100; Montgomery, *Normandy to the Baltic*, p. 257; Brereton, *The Brereton Diaries*, pp. 406–07; and Warren, Airborne Operations in World War II, pp. 228–29.

[42] XVIII Airborne Corps, Operation VARSITY.

[43] MS # B–674 (Meindl); MS # B–198 (Leuttwitz); Stacey, *The Victory Campaign*, pp. 537–38.

logical impact of the airborne assault, was posed by the Americans south of the Lippe. Already, early in the day, in a local measure the commander of the *LXIII Corps,* General Abraham, had ordered his *2d Parachute Division* on his south wing, untouched by the American crossings, to move against the U.S. 79th Division. At 1400, Blaskowitz released the *XLVII Panzer Corps* from army group reserve and ordered the commander, General von Luettwitz, to send the *116th Panzer Division* south of the Lippe to halt the U.S. 30th Division.[44]

Located near the Dutch-German border, the *116th Panzer Division* would have to make a long, circuitous march to avoid the area of Allied airborne landings. This meant that additional fuel would have to be found before the division could depart; it meant also, in view of Allied fighter-bombers, a move by night. To General Luettwitz it was apparent that the main body of the panzer division could get started only after nightfall the next day, 25 March. Would this be in time to stop a breakout from the American bridgehead?

The Try for a Breakout

On 25 March the idea of breakout was strong in the mind of the 30th Division commander, General Hobbs. Delaying the morning's attack to allow the last of his divisional artillery to take position east of the Rhine, Hobbs at 0900 sent two regiments two miles to the east to seize high ground marked by an incomplete section of autobahn. When little opposition developed except dispirited remnants of the *180th Infantry Division,*

he ordered both regiments to form mobile task forces built around an attached tank destroyer battalion and two tank battalions and strike for deep objectives. A task force from the 117th Infantry on the left was to drive nine miles to Dorsten, a road and rail center on the south bank of the Lippe-Seiten Canal; another from the 120th Infantry was to seize Kirchhellen, six miles to the east on a main highway leading from Dorsten into the Ruhr.

Although General Hobbs had in mind sharp, rapid thrusts designed to shake loose from the opposition and break into the clear, he was reckoning without the problems of terrain and limited roadnet the two task forces would encounter. For approximately five miles the attacking columns would have to pass through dense stretches of woods crossed only by narrow dirt roads and trails. In that kind of country a few strategically placed roadblocks manned by a handful of resolute defenders could impose telling delays.

Slowed by the inevitable problems of assembling diverse units, the first of the task forces, that of the 120th Infantry, began to attack only at 1600. Almost from the outset the tankers and infantrymen had to fight for every little gain. The Germans suffered—they lost four half-tracks armed with multiple-barrel 20-mm. antiaircraft guns, two 75-mm. guns, three 105-mm. pieces, and several motor vehicles, including an ammunition truck that caught fire and set a patch of the forest ablaze—but they imposed the delay they wanted. Night was falling when interrogation of prisoners revealed the story: the task force was no longer fighting *Volkssturm* nor even disconsolate survivors of the *180th Division;* the prisoners were from the *60th Panzer*

---

[44] MS # B-198 (Luettwitz); 79th Division combat interviews.

Grenadier Regiment, 116th Panzer Division.

The 117th Infantry's task force, delayed when trucks hauling the infantry bogged down on trails churned to mud by tank treads, had not even reached its line of departure when word came of the portentous prisoner identifications. The news was not to be taken lightly, for men of the 30th Division had learned respect for the *116th Panzer Division* long ago in the hedgerows of Normandy. Not until well after dark did the division commander, General Hobbs, decide to proceed with the attack; and the objective he assigned for the night was designed merely to bring the second task force abreast of the positions gained by the first. When the men dug in shortly after midnight, they were still seven miles short of Dorsten, those of the other task force still more than four miles from Kirchhellen. Furthermore, before daylight another battalion of the 117th Infantry, providing flank protection for the task forces by attacking the town of Huenxe on the Lippe-Seiten Canal, brought in a new batch of prisoners. These, it turned out, were from the panzer division's second grenadier regiment.

Although the evidence pointed to impending commitment of the entire *116th Panzer Division,* General Hobbs determined to try again for his breakout before the enemy armor could make its full weight felt. Since the mission of the 79th Division was to wheel south and southeast to the Rhein-Herne Canal to block toward the Ruhr industrial area, all hope of early breakout rested with the 30th Division. Merely to accomplish the relatively limited flank protection mission was causing the 79th some difficulty; during the day, arrival of reinforcements from the *2d Parachute Division,* albeit a depleted force, had introduced a touch of serious combat. Although a regiment of the 35th Division (General Baade) had entered the line during the day between the 79th and 30th Divisions, presaging arrival of the rest of the division the next day, the 35th Division too was scheduled to peel off to the southeast to block toward the Ruhr.

The 30th Division on the third day, 26 March, made some impressive gains, despite continuing problems with narrow, muddy forest trails and despite an enemy bearing no resemblance to the one who first had opposed the Rhine crossing. One battalion of the 119th Infantry reached Gahlen, another canal town midway between Huenxe and Dorsten, but there became so involved in a fight that a second battalion had to come to its aid. The 117th Infantry reached open ground just over three and a half miles from Dorsten but had trouble holding the position because of fire from tanks in a nearby town and woodlot and from 128-mm. antiaircraft guns emplaced in concrete near an airfield.

The 120th Infantry had the roughest going of all at first, but in the end crowned the day with a strikingly successful maneuver. Continuing through the woods toward Kirchhellen, the regiment's 2d Battalion first had to disperse a counterattack by a company of the *116th Panzer Division*'s grenadiers supported by five tanks. From that point it was a slow, yard-by-yard advance until just before nightfall when the men reached the edge of the woods to look down on the airfield from which antiaircraft guns were harassing the neighboring 117th Infantry. Waiting for darkness, the regimental commander, Colonel Purdue, committed a fresh battalion. As soon as preliminary artillery fire began to fall the assault companies rushed forward, vacating the foxholes at the line of departure, while the reserve company remained well back of the line. When the enemy's counterbarrage began, it fell on empty foxholes. The assault companies dashed downhill to clear the airfield in less than an hour. Not a man was lost.

These were impressive gains, but they were not breakout. By nightfall of 26 March the enemy's *116th Panzer Division* had clearly thwarted immediate breakout and, though incapable of decisive counterattack, was strong enough to hold an attacker to limited gains. Only a small advance guard of the panzer division had been on hand to cause trouble for the 120th Infantry the night of 25 March, but the bulk of the division's infantry and some tanks had arrived by daylight of the 26th. The remainder of the division entered the line that evening, whereupon responsibility for the sector south of the Lippe passed to the *XLVII Panzer Corps.* With the responsibility came a second divisional unit, the *190th Infantry Division,* rushed from the Netherlands to take up positions south of the panzer division. It was a makeshift division equipped with little heavy fire support, including only one artillery battalion and few antitank weapons.[45]

Faced with this situation, the 30th Division's General Hobbs would have been content with more leisurely attacks that would afford his tired infantry battalions a chance to rest, but pressure for breakout had begun to build from the Ninth

Army commander, General Simpson. Behind the lines, Simpson held not only two more divisions belonging to General Anderson's XVI Corps but also the entire XIX Corps and, potentially, the XIII Corps, with no place to commit them. Late on the 26th General Anderson ordered the 8th Armored Division to move through Hobbs's infantry in search of the maneuver room the Ninth Army needed.[46]

How To Bring the Ninth Army's Power To Bear

The inability of the 30th Division to break into the open was but one aspect of the problem facing the Ninth Army, the decision to commit the 8th Armored Division but one possibility for solving it. The core of the problem lay in the way operations had developed in the British bridgehead and its effect on use of bridges at Wesel and on maneuver room to be made available to the Ninth Army north of the Lippe River and canal complex.

Pressed back to the north and the northwest, the paratroopers of Meindl's *II Parachute Corps,* reinforced by the *15th Panzer Grenadier Division,* sharply restricted British and Canadian gains and by their opposition also slowed bridge construction near Xanten and Rees. In the British sector, by nightfall of 26 March, only the XVIII Airborne Corps, driving eastward along the north bank of the Lippe, had made progress comparable to that of the American troops to the south.

Lacking adequate bridges downstream,

⁴⁵ MS # B-198 (Luettwitz).

⁴⁶ 30th Div G-3 Jnl file, 26-28 Mar 45.

the British transferred the bulk of their cross-river traffic to Wesel, where a treadway bridge and a 25-ton ponton bridge had been completed by Ninth Army engineers and where a floating Bailey bridge was nearing completion. Although the Ninth Army had running rights on these bridges for five out of each twenty-four hours, the time was insufficient for a major build-up; and once beyond the Rhine at Wesel, there was no place to go. Under Field Marshal Montgomery's plan of operations, the XVIII Airborne Corps was to sideslip to the north to make room for the Ninth Army's XIX Corps, but because of lack of progress by British units to the northeast, the airborne troops could not yet make the shift.

To the Ninth Army's General Simpson it was frustrating to have to fight doggedly forward in frontal attacks against opposition that could be dealt with summarily if only he could bring additional power to bear. Ninth Army engineers had by this time put in enough bridges—one 25-ton ponton and three treadway bridges were carrying traffic and two floating Bailey bridges were almost finished—to support considerably larger forces than the three infantry divisions already in the XVI Corps bridgehead, but so constricted was the bridgehead—eleven miles wide and nowhere more than thirteen miles deep—that to commit even the 8th Armored Division was to invite congestion. Nor was there any possibility for maneuver unless the armored division could achieve a really deep penetration.

The makeshift solution General Simpson proposed, as revealed to his assembled corps commanders during the afternoon of 27 March, was to take the risk of overcrowding and concentrate the XIX Corps in the bridgehead. Once bridges could be built over the Lippe the XIX Corps was to cross, thereby bypassing the bottleneck of Wesel, and launch a drive alongside the XVIII Airborne Corps to cut in behind those Germans holding up the 30th Division.

Attending the meeting at Simpson's request, the XVIII Airborne Corps commander, General Ridgway, promptly discouraged the plan. While acknowledging that to avoid Wesel would be helpful, Ridgway still doubted that the crowded roads north of the Lippe could yet support any contingent of the Ninth Army. He held out hope nevertheless that if the XVIII Airborne Corps continued to advance at its current pace for about two more days, there then might be room for some portion of the Ninth Army.

In the end, General Simpson deferred a decision while couching an appeal in strong terms to the Second British Army commander, General Dempsey, and to Field Marshal Montgomery for exclusive use at the earliest possible date of the Wesel bridges and the main highway leading east out of Wesel along the north bank of the Lippe. If he could have these facilities, Simpson said, he could utilize both the XIX Corps and the XIII Corps.[47]

That commitment of the 8th Armored Division (General Devine) in quest of a breakthrough south of the Lippe was no solution to Simpson's problem was demonstrated early on 28 March. Although the fatigued infantrymen of the 30th Division had fought through the night of the 26th and the day of the 27th to open

---

[47] The account of the meeting is from *Conquer: The Story of the Ninth Army*, pp. 260–61.

a route for the armor, they failed to do more than dent the positions of the enemy's *116th Panzer Division*. Dense forest and poor roads, when combined with determined resistance from German tanks and antiaircraft guns, prevented the armor from gaining more than three miles. When the fighting died down with the coming of night on 28 March, the Germans still held Dorsten. Prospects of a breakout faded.

It was a different story north of the Lippe. There, in fulfillment of the promise foreseen by General Ridgway, paratroopers of the 17th Airborne Division's 513th Parachute Infantry in mid-afternoon of 28 March mounted Churchill tanks of the British 6th Guards Armoured Brigade.[48] With scarcely a pause, they raced seventeen miles beyond Dorsten. As the commander of the enemy's *XLVII Panzer Corps,* General Luettwitz, was quick to note, the spectacular advance outflanked the positions of his corps, including those of the *116th Panzer Division*.[49]

On this same date, 28 March, Field Marshal Montgomery issued a new directive to govern operations across the north German plain to the Elbe River, deep inside Germany. In the process, he spelled out a new policy for use of the Rhine bridges at Wesel and provided an

expanding corridor for employment of portions of the Ninth Army north of the Lippe River. Beginning early on the morning of 30 March, the routes leading east from Wesel were to pass to the Ninth Army, thus enabling General Simpson to begin moving forces north of the Lippe even before gaining full control of the Wesel bridges. Those bridges were to pass to the Ninth Army early the next morning, 31 March, though with running rights to the British for five hours out of each twenty-four.

Operation PLUNDER was over. Four Allied armies were across the last great barrier to the heartland of Germany and had either begun to exploit or were poised to begin the last deep thrusts. Only the First Canadian Army on the north flank and the First French Army on the south had yet to establish their own bridgeheads. The Canadians already were building up through the British bridgehead, and the French were preparing to cross in their own right before the month of March was out.

Whether at this stage of the war elaborate preparation and support on the scale marshaled by the 21 Army Group was necessary or even justified for forcing the Rhine would forever remain conjecture. The entire production might have been avoided, for example, had Montgomery allowed Simpson's Ninth Army to jump the Rhine in a surprise assault back in the first week of March. Yet in the jubilation of the success that accompanied Operation PLUNDER, few but the most carping critics would continue to belabor the point.

"My dear General," Prime Minister Churchill had said to the Supreme Commander as he watched Allied power unleashed against the Rhine on 24 March,

---

[48] Culminating a series of gallant acts, T. Sgt. Clinton M. Hedrick, 194th Glider Infantry, entered a castle at Lembeck, seven miles north of Dorsten, on 28 March to accept surrender of the German garrison. The Germans instead opened fire with a self-propelled gun. Mortally wounded, Sergeant Hedrick rained such a fire on the Germans that his colleagues were able to escape. He was awarded the Medal of Honor posthumously.

[49] MS # B-198 (Luettwitz).

"the German is whipped. We've got him. He is all through." [50]

To a man and to a nation that almost five long years before had known the nadir of Dunkerque, the pyrotechnics of 23 and 24 March were sweet and just and good and right.

---

[50] Eisenhower, *Crusade in Europe,* p. 390.

CHAPTER XV

At the End of March

"My dear General," telegraphed Charles de Gaulle to the commander of the First French Army on 29 March, "you must cross the Rhine, even if the Americans do not agree and even if you have to cross it in rowboats. It is a matter of the greatest national interest." [1]

To de Gaulle, the Allied governments' failure yet to designate any portion of Germany for occupation by France indicated an unwillingness to recognize French claims. To circumvent any attempt to freeze out the French, he was determined to seize a sector beyond the Rhine.[2]

The French field commander, General de Lattre, actually was a step ahead of his chief of state. Conscious that the French had been assigned no frontage along the Rhine not covered from the east bank by West Wall fortifications (the twelve miles obtained earlier north of the Lauter River faced an east-bank spur of the West Wall designed to protect the city of Karlsruhe), de Lattre two days before, on 27 March, had visited General Devers at headquarters of the 6th Army Group. Having noted that the American Seventh Army's Rhine crossing before daylight on the 26th had occurred

at Worms, on the extreme northern edge of the Seventh Army's zone, de Lattre believed that the Americans would happily relinquish part of their zone in order to free units for the attack in the north. His talk with Devers confirmed it.

De Lattre left Devers's headquarters not only with expanded frontage along the Rhine—all the way north to Speyer, more than half the distance from Karlsruhe to Mannheim and well beyond the spur of the West Wall—but also with orders to prepare to cross the Rhine, seize Karlsruhe, and drive deep to the southeast to take Stuttgart.[3] Yet Devers gave him no target date for the crossing. Concerned lest American columns driving south from the Worms bridgehead might overrun the French sites before Devers approved a crossing date, de Lattre told the commander of his II Corps, Maj. Gen. A. J. de Monsabert, to begin crossing before daylight on 31 March.

After receiving de Gaulle's telegram, de Lattre reiterated his order to de Monsabert. It was not a question, he said, of whether de Monsabert could be ready to cross on the 31st, it was a question of beating the Americans into the new sector beyond the Rhine. French national honor was at stake.

When General Devers on the 30th asked when the French could start cross-

---

[1] De Lattre, *Histoire de la Première Armée Française*, pp. 487–90. Unless otherwise noted, the story of the French crossings of the Rhine is from this source, pp. 485–99.
[2] Pogue, *The Supreme Command*, p. 432.

[3] 6th AGp Ltr of Instrs 12, 27 Mar 45, 6th AGp AAR, Mar 45.

ing, de Lattre proudly answered that he would begin before daylight the next morning. Devers promptly approved.

By 0230 on 31 March, infantrymen of the 3d Algerian Division at Speyer had found only a single rubber assault boat. Undaunted, the Algerians began to shuttle silently across the Rhine, ten men at a time. Shortly before daybreak when they had located four more rubber boats to speed the shuttle, the Germans awoke to the crossing and began to shell the site. The enemy was too late; already an entire infantry company was across. Having made even Patton's surprise crossing at Oppenheim look like a deliberate, set-piece assault, the French were on the east bank to stay.

A few miles upstream at Germersheim, a more conventional crossing fared less well. Because of confusion at hastily chosen embarkation points, the first wave of the 2d Moroccan Division pushed into the river only after daylight had come and the first impact of an artillery preparation had dissipated. In that wave, only three of some twenty storm boats equipped with outboard motors survived German small arms and mortar fire and made it to the east bank. While thirty men from the three boats hung on grimly, French artillery encased the minuscule bridgehead in fire until subsequent waves, still taking heavy losses, could build up. By nightfall the bulk of two battalions was across and a foothold assured.

The next day, 1 April—Easter Sunday—General Brooks of the neighboring VI Corps gave permission for French vehicles to cross an American bridge at Mannheim. Before the day was out, French reconnaissance units had pushed eighteen miles beyond the Rhine, in the

process coming upon a column of the 10th U.S. Armored Division deep within the assigned French zone. It was an error on the part of the American armor—American commanders had entertained no idea of depriving the French of their opportunity for an assault crossing of the Rhine—but to General de Lattre the presence of the U.S. unit justified the haste of the French crossing. A 24-hour delay, he reckoned, would have condemned the French to a passive role in the invasion of Germany.[4]

To speed the taking of Karlsruhe, de Lattre would make a third Rhine crossing on 2 April midway between Germersheim and Karlsruhe and even a fourth some days later,[5] but the main crossings at Germersheim and Speyer in effect marked the end of the passage of all three Allied army groups to the east bank of the Rhine.

An Awesome Power

By the end of March the great river barrier was a challenge only to bridge-building engineers. A tatterdemalion German Army on the brink of total defeat lay exposed to a mighty Allied force of almost four and a half million men, including ninety divisions, twenty-five of which were armored, five airborne.[6] As

---

[4] De Lattre, *Histoire de la Première Armée Française*, p. 449. See also below, ch. XVIII.

[5] The third crossing was at Leimersheim, the fourth at Strasbourg. For details of the fourth crossing, see below, ch. XVIII.

[6] Of the divisions, 61 were American, 12 British, 11 French, 5 Canadian, and 1 Polish. One British division would arrive from Italy before V–E Day to bring the total force under General Eisenhower to 91 divisions, plus several independent brigades. See SHAEF G–3 War Room Daily Sums, 2 Apr and 9 May 45.

the multiple drives beyond the Rhine began, Montgomery's 21 Army Group controlled thirty divisions. Included were twelve U.S. divisions in the Ninth Army and a new Canadian corps with two Canadian divisions and an armored brigade. The Canadian corps had arrived during the month of March from Italy as a result of a decision made at the Malta Conference to reinforce British forces for the final thrust into Germany.[7]

Bradley's 12th Army Group had thirty-four divisions, including six in its new army, the Fifteenth, under General Gerow. Although the Fifteenth Army had become operational in early January, the headquarters heretofore had handled only rear echelon assignments, including control of the 66th Infantry Division, which was containing German holdouts in Brittany ports. The Fifteenth Army now was to move forward to assume a holding mission along the Rhine, facing the Ruhr, then later was to relieve the other armies of the 12th Army Group of occupation duties as they drove deep into Germany.

Devers's 6th Army Group had twelve U.S. and eleven French divisions, although two of the latter were unavailable for the drive beyond the Rhine, since one was holding the Alpine front facing Italy and another was containing Germans along the Gironde estuary in southwestern France. The remaining three divisions of the total of ninety were U.S. airborne divisions under control of the First Allied Airborne Army.

Allied air power, its declining losses readily replaceable, remained everywhere overwhelmingly dominant, men-

GENERAL GEROW

aced only occasionally by the sporadic activity of German jet fighters. Antiaircraft fire from the flak-heavy Ruhr noticeably decreased, apparently indicating German ammunition shortages. Continuing a long-range program against oil supplies, American strategic bombers of the Eighth Air Force during March directed 36,000 tons of bombs against refineries and storage depots. Communications centers, railroads, factories, jet aircraft plants, and submarine pens also continued to take a pounding. Raids almost always involved more than a thousand bombers, with losses seldom exceeding five aircraft, though on 18 March, in one of the largest daylight raids of the war on Berlin, German jet planes shot down 24 bombers and 5 fighters, while flak damaged more than

---

[7] Stacey, *The Victory Campaign*, p. 529; Montgomery, *Normandy to the Baltic*, p. 247.

half the 1,200 bombers, 16 of which had to crash-land behind Russian lines.

Heavies of the Royal Air Force also continued their destructive campaign; at one point, on 12 March, they established a new record for tonnage in a single strategic attack by dropping 4,899 tons from 1,107 aircraft on Dortmund. Close co-ordination was often achieved with heavy bombers of the Fifteenth Air Force in Italy. Despite occasional bad weather, the campaign in the air was so successful that by the end of March the strategic air forces were almost out of targets.[8]

The big raid on Berlin on 18 March was part of a program begun the preceding month after the Combined Chiefs of Staff at Malta decided to send the strategic air forces of Britain and the United States against major transportation centers in eastern Germany through which the Germans might funnel reinforcements for the Russian front. "There was also a hope that heavy air raids would increase the panic and confusion already prevalent in those cities, which were thoroughly frightened by the sudden Russian advance and full of refugees."[9]

The raids quickly produced charges, particularly in the American press, of terror bombing. Although American air officers pointed out that they were not bombing cities indiscriminately but attacking transportation facilities inside the cities, severe criticism would persist even into the postwar period. Of particular horror was a Royal Air Force raid on Dresden the night of 13 February, followed on the next two days by U.S. attacks. These raids created a firestorm like that which had gutted Hamburg in 1943, and may have caused as many as 135,000 civilian deaths.[10]

During the first two weeks of April, the Luftwaffe would make feeble efforts with thin remnants of conventional and jet fighter forces but would succeed in bringing down only eighteen American bombers. At the same time Allied air commanders would consider the strategic air war at an end. As early as 7 April the British would discontinue area strikes against German cities, and on 16 April the chief of the United States Strategic Air Forces in Europe, General Carl Spaatz, would declare the strategic air war won. The big bombers would still make a few raids aimed at rail junctions, marshaling yards, or other targets of direct concern to the ground armies.[11]

The Logistical Backbone

On the ground, as the prospect of unqualified pursuit warfare loomed, there stood behind the awesome power of Allied armies a logistical establishment geared to demands that, had they been made during the pursuit across France the preceding summer, would have been preposterous. For example, no longer did the Allied armies have to depend on makeshift facilities at the invasion beaches or on minor ports far behind the fighting lines. Antwerp, one of Europe's great ports, lying only a little over a hundred miles behind the front, alone handled 558,000 tons of supplies in March. In the south, Marseille and sub-

---

[8] Craven and Cate, *AAF III*, 736-55.
[9] *Ibid.*, p. 725.

[10] This figure is higher than that of the combined total of deaths (110,000) in the atomic bombings of Hiroshima and Nagasaki. Craven and Cate, *AAF III*, 724-31; David Irving, *The Destruction of Dresden* (London: William Kimber, 1963).
[11] Craven and Cate, *AAF III*, 753-54.

sidiary ports handled 575,500 tons in March, making the 6th Army Group virtually independent of the lines of communication serving the other Allied forces.[12]

While there were occasional delays in discharging ships in all the ports, moving the supplies to inland depots was the major problem, attributable in part to a perennial shortage of transportation but in the main to an inadequate system of depots echeloned in depth. The problem would be intensified as the pursuit east of the Rhine increased demands for transport close behind the front.

An extensive program of pipeline construction helped ease the burden on transport. By the end of March a line from Antwerp was operating as far as Wesel on the Rhine, another from Cherbourg as far as Thionville in Lorraine, and a third from Marseille almost to the Saar River. To relieve congestion on the Rhine bridges, pipelines were laid across the river at four points soon after the crossings, and gasoline delivered by railway tank cars was pumped across. Three of the pipelines were later tied in with the main arteries from the ports. At the time of the Rhine crossings, gasoline stocks in both the Communications Zone and the armies themselves were the highest they had ever been. Only in the last days of April would deliveries fall short of daily consumption, and never would gasoline exercise the tyranny over operations that it had in France and Belgium in 1944.

Rail reconstruction also proceeded swiftly. By the end of March a line was open to the Rhine at Wesel and another

at Koblenz, while on the 1st of April engineers opened another as far as Mainz. On 7 April the 1056th Port Construction and Repair Group, having worked around the clock for ten days, would open a 1,753-foot rail bridge over the Rhine near Wesel. A second rail bridge over the Rhine at Mainz was opened six days later and others, at Mannheim and Karlsruhe, before the month of April was out. All single-tracked, the bridges were inevitable bottlenecks; their existence nevertheless would enable the railways by mid-April to equal the tonnage carried beyond the Rhine by truck transport and by the end of the war to handle three-fourths of the total tonnage. This record was accomplished despite shortages of locomotives and rolling stock and frustrating delays in unloading freight cars at their destinations.

Taking a cue from the Red Ball Express truck route that had sped highway traffic behind the armies the preceding year, the Transportation Corps in January had inaugurated an express rail service for high priority freight. A train of twenty cars, labeled the "Toot Sweet Express" (a play on the French phrase *tout de suite*), left Cherbourg each day, picked up additional cars and split into two sections at Paris, then ran to Verdun and Namur and later as far as Bad Kreuznach and Liège. Beginning in March a similar service, originating in Liège, delivered perishable foods to railheads close behind the First and Ninth Armies—the "Meat Ball Express."

Motor transport meanwhile increased to an unprecedented tempo. In contrast to the improvisation of the Red Ball and other express routes the preceding summer, the Communications Zone had prepared detailed plans to marshal three-

---

[12] The section on logistics is based on Ruppenthal, *Logistical Support of the Armies II* .

THE RHINE RAILROAD BRIDGE AT WESEL

fourths of the motor transport under its control for direct support of the pursuit beyond the Rhine. Under a three-phase plan called "XYZ," more than 4,000 trucks, most of them either 10-ton tractor-semitrailer combinations or 10-ton diesels, eventually were to deliver up to 15,000 tons a day to forward depots. Trucks received detailed maintenance before every run, and some of the convoys carried their own mechanics and packets of most commonly needed spare parts. On one route serving the Seventh Army, drivers could pause at rest stops called "GI Diners," where they might exchange cold rations for hot. In addition to these trucks, the armies themselves had about forty truck companies each, supplemented by provisional companies made up of the organic transportation from field artillery and antiaircraft units.

Building roads and bridges occupied thousands of engineers, whose numbers were augmented by civilians and prisoners of war and sometimes by men from uncommitted combat units. Engineers assigned to the armies did most of the work, constructing, for example, 52 of the 57 highway bridges built over the Rhine. Just over half of the bridges were

FRANKLIN D. ROOSEVELT MEMORIAL BRIDGE AT MAINZ. *Construction proceeded
day and night.*

fixed wooden pile; of 26 treadway and
heavy ponton bridges, most would be
phased out by early May.

Air transport also contributed far
more than it had the preceding summer,
both because airfields were plentiful and
because few planes were withdrawn for
airborne training or operations. During
the second week of April, more than
6,200 sorties were flown—a peak—and
more than 15,000 tons of supplies (mostly gasoline) set down on forward fields.
On return flights the big transport craft
evacuated casualties or liberated prison-

ers of war. During April approximately
40,000 casualties were removed from the
combat zone by air, and in the closing
days of the war one sky train after another carried Recovered Allied Military
Personnel (RAMPS) westward. The
Third Army alone evacuated 135,000
men in the last month by air.

All these efforts added up to a supply situation in which the Communications Zone and the support services in
the armies could take justifiable pride,
and this done with a theaterwide division
slice of only about 26,000 men, a figure

PONTON BRIDGE ACROSS THE RHINE SERVING SEVENTH ARMY

usually considered minimal. Some shortages persisted, particularly in spare parts for vehicles and weapons, and forward supply officers were sometimes reduced to nervous fretting and fuming, but minor shortages were fairly characteristic of supply in a highly mobile situation and rarely affected operations. Although fewer combat losses of tanks, vehicles, and equipment and reduced expenditure of ammunition—both features of pursuit warfare—helped, the credit in general belonged to a sound logistical apparatus expertly administered. The infantryman or the tanker might complain of a mo-

notonous diet of emergency rations, but so fast was he moving that he would have had little time for more substantial fare in any case. What was more important, he always ate, and many a time he could relieve the monotony with "liberated" eggs or other produce from a farmyard.

Decisions at the Top

Meanwhile, a variety of decisions had been or were being made at both theater and intergovernmental levels that, while not affecting the actual conduct of tactical operations, nevertheless produced an

LIBERATED PRISONERS OF WAR *waiting to board C-47 transport planes.*

impact on the armies and the fighting men in them. These decisions ranged from President Franklin D. Roosevelt's "unconditional surrender" formula, enunciated long months before at the Casablanca Conference, to a so-called nonfraternization policy and SHAEF's definition of the difference between loot and legitimate booty, almost as difficult as the nonfraternization policy to administer.

The policy of unconditional surrender, some thought at the time and after, prolonged the war because it afforded the Germans no out. In view of the control over the armed forces and the populace exercised by the Nazi apparatus and of clarifying statements issued from time to time by the Allied governments, the opinion would appear to be more speculative than conclusive. It clearly was no barrier to the surrender of German soldiers, individually or sometimes en masse, nor to the nation as a whole when the Hitler mystique ceased to exist. More likely it was, as Winston Churchill, among others, once put it, that the German people continued to fight not out of fear of Allied victory but out of fear of conquest by the Soviet Army.[13]

Imposed at the intergovernmental level, the nonfraternization policy had been proclaimed the previous September, the day after the first American patrols crossed the German frontier, but only with the rapid sweep through the Rhineland had it come to affect more than a few U.S. units. Under the terms of General Eisenhower's directive, all fraternization with the German population was forbidden. There was to be no "mingling with Germans upon terms of friendliness, familiarity, or intimacy, individually or in groups in official or unofficial dealings." [14] It was, in the words of an official British historian, an attempt "to send the whole German people to Coventry largely in order to express disgust for the bestialities of Nazism." [15]

The policy soon broke down, perhaps inevitably, though it would remain officially in force for several months after the fighting ended. Given the generally friendly disposition of the young, healthy American—and Allied—soldier, strict enforcement of such a rule, particularly in regard to children and women, proved impossible.[16] Nor was it practical when

seeking to govern a conquered population by indirect means to carry out prohibitions against soldiers accompanying Germans in the street, conversing with them in public, or even shaking hands with them. Few Germans could have been unaware of the policy, but when it was enforced it probably caused more resentment than remorse.

The nonfraternization program may have served other objectives—security and protecting the lives of individual Allied soldiers, though the German population in any case provoked few major incidents. While some civilians on occasion took up arms beside their soldiers and in isolated instances sniped or engaged in other acts of violence against individual soldiers, the people for the most part were "passive, lethargic, negative, disciplined, docile, deferential, cooperative, obedient." [17] They hung out white sheets from upper windows of their homes as the troops approached, then in general conformed to the dictates of the tactical commanders and later of the military government officials. German children quickly learned the trade that had long been an art in the liberated countries of begging for chewing gum and candy, and "frauleins" reacted to the shouts from passing columns—"*schlafen mit?*" either with haughty disdain or with a European woman's sly appreciation at masculine approval. There was one notable exception. The night of 24 March Nazis or Nazi sympathizers murdered the man appointed by the Allies to be burgomaster of Aachen.

On the first of April, Hitler issued a

---

[13] For a detailed discussion of the subject as it related to SHAEF, see Pogue, *The Supreme Command*, pp. 339–43.

[14] Ltr, SHAEF, 12 Sep 44, sub: Policy, Relationship Between Allied Occupation Troops and Inhabitants of Germany.

[15] F. S. V. Donnison, C.B.E., *Civil Affairs and Military Government, North-West Europe 1944–1946* (London: Her Majesty's Stationery Office, 1961), p. 374.

[16] Oliver J. Fredericksen, *The American Military Occupation of Germany 1945–1953* (Germany: The Stars and Stripes, 1953), for the Historical Division, Headquarters, U.S. Army, Europe; Historical Division, European Command, Fraternization with the Germans in World War II, in a multivolume **MS series, Occupation Forces in Europe, 1945–46.**

[17] Historical Division, European Command, Operations From Late March to Mid-July 1945, in a multivolume MS series, United States Military Government in Germany, p. 20.

proclamation calling on all Germans to become "werewolves" to prey on Allied troops, Jews, and those Germans who co-operated with Allied forces.[18] Some incidents involving German youth could be traced to this appeal, but it attracted no broad support. The mass of the people continued to react with resigned relief that the war was nearing an end.

More a problem to security and discipline was the presence in Germany of several million displaced persons, usually impressed workers from countries earlier conquered by the Germans. Only some 50,000 of these were encountered in the Rhineland; but before the sweep across Germany was over, the American armies alone had liberated more than 2,300,000 displaced persons.[19] The exuberance of these people upon liberation and sometimes their desire to wreak immediate vengeance on their oppressors led on occasion to violent, tragic excesses, which the soldiers were reluctant to deal with.[20] That they did not fall under the nonfraternization policy contributed to the problem. Many a case of venereal disease incurred by an Allied soldier could be traced to a cantonment for displaced persons. Looting by these people, sometimes in organized bands, continued to be a problem until well after the German surrender when repatriation at last reduced their numbers to more manageable proportions. All armies had to detail at least small service and tactical units to assist military government officials with displaced persons, and the

Ninth Army in mid-April assigned one division and later the entire XVI Corps to military government duties.

Looting by American soldiers was also a problem. To many a soldier this nation that had plunged the world into war seemed fair game. The plundering ranged from simple pilferage—appropriating china or glassware as a substitute for mess kits or taking some trinket as a souvenir (as likely as not to be discarded another day when something more appealing caught the eye)—to outright theft of objects of genuine value. Entire sets of silver and fine china, typewriters, cameras, or valuable *objets d'art* were packaged and sent home by way of the Army postal service. How much of this went on depended in large measure at first on the attitude of company, battalion, and regimental commanders; but the practice became so widespread that General Eisenhower's headquarters attempted to set up strict rules as to what constituted legitimate booty.

Under terms of Eisenhower's directive, issued in April, the only booty that might be mailed home consisted of objects that were Nazi in origin—Nazi flags, armbands with swastika emblems, batons encrested with Nazi symbols—or those belonging to the German armed forces—uniforms, rifles, or other items found in military installations. A set of china, for example, might be legitimate booty if found in a German officers' mess. Before a package could be mailed, it had to bear an affidavit from an officer of the soldier's unit attesting to its legitimacy.

While the system sharply curtailed looting, it did nothing to ameliorate an old dispute over booty that long had raged between men in combat units and

---

[18] For a summary of the proclamation, see XIII Corps G–2 Periodic Rpt 146, 3 Apr 45.

[19] Fredericksen, *The American Military Occupation,* p. 73.

[20] See, for example, Toland, *The Last 100 Days,* pp. 443–46.

those in support and service echelons. Combat soldiers complained that they moved too fast and had to travel too light to have any opportunity for mailing booty home, while soldiers behind the front protested that the combat troops had purloined the valuable prizes before others could get to them. Except for pistols (Lugers and P-38 Walthers, particularly, were premium prizes), which were more readily come upon by the infantryman or tank crewman, one argument probably canceled out the other.

Wine and schnapps in reasonable amounts continued to be ready prizes for anybody wherever found. They could be made to disappear, with not unpleasant results, before any overly conscientious investigating officer could check to see where they came from. German vehicles also continued to find their way into American hands, though some division commanders prohibited them or else insisted on rigid inspection of their serviceability lest they delay the columns. And there were few platoons that did not soon have a handsome civilian radio set, one that might be "traded up" as new towns were taken.

To locate and then prevent looting and destruction of important industrial facilities, research establishments, banks, museums, galleries, and German records, each Allied army carried special intelligence teams. In American armies, these included teams from the technical services, plus special groups known as "T-forces" designated to search for items of scientific value. The latter were especially alert for materials related to German research in rockets, which had led to the 'second of Hitler's V-weapons, the V–2 supersonic rocket that had begun to bombard England the preceding Sep-

tember. Another special force known as the ALsos mission, seeking information on German developments in nuclear fission, had determined the preceding November from German scientists and documents taken in Strasbourg that the Germans still were a long way from producing an atomic bomb.[21]

As with looting, some American soldiers achieved personal gain in black market currency. Although the official exchange for all Allied troops was the Allied military mark, soldiers presumably could get regular German marks in legitimate dealings as change (though how this was possible under the nonfraternization policy, no one bothered to explain), and finance officers even made some official disbursements in German marks. Thus there was at first no regulation prohibiting a soldier from exchanging German marks for military marks of or below the 100-mark denomination (the largest bill disbursed in military marks) or from transmitting these or large amounts of military marks to his credit back home.

Only after it became obvious that black market dealings were imposing a heavy drain both on Army funds and on goods—food, cigarettes, PX rations, and other items—did the European theater's fiscal director, in April, order finance officers neither to receive nor to disburse German marks. By that time substantial amounts of Allied military marks had found their way into the economy, and this move alone would be insufficient to eliminate the black market.

---

[21] Boris T. Pash, *The Alsos Mission* (New York: Award House, 1969); Samuel A. Goudsmit, *ALSOS* (New York: William Morrow & Co., 1964); *Conquer: The Story of the Ninth Army*, pp. 284–85.

Although another regulation prohibited a soldier from transmitting to the United States more than his normal pay and allowances unless the excess was certified by his personnel officer as legitimately obtained, that too would not halt all dealings. Since gambling was allowed, what personnel officer could question, unless the sum to be transmitted were extraordinarily high, that it came from lucky dice? The problem remained to be settled after the end of the fighting, and then only after the Russians had flooded the economy with Allied military marks, making the situation worse.[22]

The more serious crimes—desertion, misbehavior before the enemy, murder, rape, and assault with intent to commit rape—sharply increased in March and would continue to do so through the rapid drive across Germany. The upswing in cases of rape was particularly marked; 32 men were brought to trial in January and February, 128 in March, and 259 in April. The pattern duplicated the experience of the previous year during the race across France. In great measure it could be attributed to the larger number of troops in Germany, to lessened control and supervision by officers in mobile warfare, and possibly to the soldier's knowledge that he would be moving on rapidly and thus was less likely to be apprehended for the crime. Then too, the soldiers came as arms-bearing conquerors of a population that long had been propagandized to believe that Allied troops would rape, pillage, and kill. Although many Americans suspected that crying rape was a German woman's way of getting back at the conqueror and although some soldiers undoubtedly interpreted lack of resistance as seduction, the military courts generally held that even where physical force was not proved, the victim had submitted through fear.[23]

Although any incidence of crimes of violence or misbehavior before the enemy was serious, the total for the entire war in Europe represented only .53 of 1 percent of the total number of Americans who served in the theater. Seventy soldiers were executed, one for desertion, the others for murder, rape, or rape associated with murder.[24]

As March came to an end, the war was in many ways unrecognizable as the same war of those grim days of frozen, snow-drenched foxholes and yard-by-yard advances along the German frontier. Spring was finally more than a promise, while more often than not, the war revolved about villages, towns, or cities, so that most men had a roof over their heads at night. Companies vied with battalion and regimental headquarters for a town's choicest villa for a command post, whereupon interpreters might dispatch the inhabitants with an unceremonious *"Alle Einwohner, 'raus!"* Sometimes electricity and water still functioned, and many a grimy infantryman luxuriated in a tub of hot, soapy water while his comrades impa-

---

[22] Walter Rundell, Jr., *Black Market Money* (Baton Rouge: Louisiana State University Press, 1964), provides an authoritative account of these activities, based on official Army records.

[23] Fraternization with the Germans in World War II, pp. 80–82.

[24] Office of the Judge Advocate General, U.S. Forces, European Theater, History Branch Office of the Judge Advocate General With the United States Forces European Theater 18 July 1942–1 November 1945, MS in OCMH.

tiently awaited their turn. Farther to the rear, units had time to renovate shower facilities in clubs, schools, or factories. Short passes to Paris or the Riviera, begun the preceding fall, continued for a fortunate few, while for a magic smattering, those longest in combat, there was leave in the United States that would not end before the war did.

As in the old days, copies of the soldier newspaper, *Stars & Stripes,* and the weekly magazine, *Yank,* continued to reach the front, though often several days late, along with pocket-sized editions of U.S. magazines and paperback books. Blue-uniformed American girls who had smiled their way indefatigably through Britain, France, and Belgium, continued to dispense doughnuts and coffee from Red Cross clubmobiles. Reflecting the improvement in the logistical situation over the preceding summer, the supply of cigarettes—still issued free to front-line soldiers—was usually ample, though other post exchange rations reaching the combat troops were meager. The combat soldier would continue to complain, not without considerable justification, that successive echelons to the rear shortstopped the choicer items.

Some higher staff levels were already planning for redeployment to the United States or to the Pacific theater, while others continued to work on plans to be used in the event of German surrender. Begun before D-day in France and originally given the code name TALISMAN, these plans now were known, following a presumed compromise of security, as Operation ECLIPSE. Constantly altered and adjusted, the plans at first had been oriented toward the possibility of sudden German collapse, but more and

more as the final campaign unfolded, they evolved primarily into guidelines for the occupation. While some dramatic features, such as a possible air-landing in Berlin, remained to the end, ECLIPSE dealt mainly with more prosaic matters such as armistice terms, disarmament, displaced persons, prisoners of war, and German courts.[25] In conformity with the nature of the advance into Germany and the likelihood that final surrender would come only after the entire country was occupied, SHAEF decreed in April that no formal transition to ECLIPSE was to take place, but that ECLIPSE conditions were presumed to be in effect in those areas progressively overrun.

Another factor no longer disturbing the staffs and commanders was a formerly critical shortage of infantry replacements, or reinforcements, as by decree for morale purposes they had come to be known. Various methods adopted during the preceding winter when the problem had become acute during the Ardennes fighting had by March produced creditable results, including an extensive retraining program for troops culled from U.S. Army Air Forces and service units, though the Air Forces, in particular, was accused of channeling into this program only its misfits.

One aspect of the program was the appearance in March of fifty-three platoons of Negro troops, men who had volunteered, often taking reductions in grade in the process, to leave their service units for the front. In the 12th Army Group the platoons were attached to a number of veteran divisions, usually one to a regiment, to serve under a white

---

[25] For details, see the SHAEF file on Operation ECLIPSE. For a convenient summary see Fredericksen, *The American Military Occupation,* pp. 2–5.

lieutenant and platoon sergeant as a fifth platoon in a rifle company. In the 6th Army Group they were employed as provisional companies. In both cases, particularly when used as platoons, the men performed so creditably that eventually the experience had an impact on the Army's traditional policy of employing Negroes only in segregated units.[26] This and the other retraining measures, as well as the sharp decline in casualties in mobile warfare against a disintegrating foe, had by mid-March spelled an end to the replacement problem.[27]

The matter of occupation zones in Germany, still troubling France's provisional head of state in late March, had already been fairly well settled before the Yalta Conference in February. Except for Berlin, which was to be administered on a tripartite basis, the Russians were to occupy the region from the Oder River westward to the Weser, the British that part of northern Germany west of the Weser and north of a line from Koblenz through Kassel, and the Americans the rest of the Rhineland and southern Germany. It was at Yalta that the question of French participation had arisen. Although the conferees had agreed to create a French zone from parts of the British and U.S. zones, the actual boundaries would not be finally assigned until 2 May. Drawn mostly from the U.S. zone, the French zone resembled an hourglass, the top encompassing the Saar-Palatinate and the bottom a portion of southern Germany next to the Rhine.[28]

The Plight of the Germans

By the end of March, Germany was as nearly prostrate as any nation in history had ever been while still continuing to fight. As early as the end of January, the Reich Minister for Armament and War Production, Albert Speer, had reached the conclusion that the war was lost; at that time he could supply only a quarter of the coal and a sixth of the steel that Germany had been using in 1944.[29] By the 1st of April some small cities were as much as 90 percent destroyed, the capital 75 percent; the housing situation was nearly desperate, the food supply only relatively less so. As Russian armies drove deep into eastern Germany, an already acute refugee problem became ever more serious with ten million refugees on the move. In the west the Rhineland was completely lost and the Rhine as a line of defense irretrievably compromised. In the east Russian armies had overrun almost all of East Prussia and Poland, had reached the Baltic coast east of Danzig, had conquered part of Czechoslovakia, all of Rumania and Bulgaria, and much of Yugoslavia and Hungary, and had crossed the Oder River to reach a point some thirty miles from Berlin.

Yet the war went on.

There were many Germans, some in high places, who, like Speer, accepted the futility of fighting longer, yet in their ideas of how to end the war persisted in trying to bargain at a time when Germany had nothing left to barter. As early as mid-January the Reich Foreign Minister, Joachim von Ribbentrop, with-

[26] Ulysses Lee, *The Employment of Negro Troops,* UNITED STATES ARMY IN WORLD WAR II (Washington, 1966). ch. XXI.

[27] Ruppenthal, *Logistical Support of the Armies II,* ch. XVII.

[28] Pogue, *The Supreme Command,* pp. 463–65.

[29] William L. Shirer, *The Rise and Fall of the Third Reich* (New York: Simon & Schuster, 1960), p. 1097.

DESTRUCTION IN THE HEART OF WUERZBURG

out Hitler's knowledge had sent emissaries to Sweden and Switzerland to make contact with Allied representatives and discuss a negotiated peace, but neither had been able to establish fruitful connections. On 25 January the Chief of the Army General Staff, Generaloberst Heinz Guderian, had urged peace in the west so that what was left of the German armies could be concentrated against the Russians; it earned him only an accusation of "high treason" from his Fuehrer.[30] In early April representatives

of the German command in Italy made contact with Allied agents in Switzerland, but negotiations led nowhere until the last week of the war.[31]

Either in the bomb-damaged Reich Chancellery or, increasingly, in the *Fuehrerbunker* fifty feet under the garden of the chancellery, Adolf Hitler trod a narrow path between acknowledging defeat and believing in a miracle, between sanity and insanity. In February only with difficulty had subordinates

---

[30] Heinz Guderian, *Panzer Leader* (New York: E. P. Dutton & Co., Inc. 1952), pp. 401–02, 404–05.

[31] For this story, see Ernest F. Fisher, Cassino to the Alps, a volume in preparation for the series UNITED STATES ARMY IN WORLD WAR II.

talked him out of denouncing the Geneva Convention, ordering all captured airmen shot, and resorting to gas warfare. While his nation fell apart, he spent long, tedious hours arguing trivial details (promotion policy for officers, whether to cut down trees in the Tiergarten to make an aircraft landing strip) or, without regard for realities, lecturing and raging at the presumed perversities of his underlings ("I am lied to on all sides. I can rely on no one. They all betray me.") On 19 March, seeming at last to accept the inevitability of defeat and having determined to bring the entire temple crashing down with him, he directed a scorched earth policy designed to turn Germany into a wasteland, an order circumvented only by the subterfuge of Albert Speer. Yet in the curious little world of delusion he had constructed about himself, the Fuehrer only a few days. later could share the enthusiastic belief of his propaganda chief, Josef Goebbels, that in the same way the death of the Czarina had saved Frederick the Great in 1762, some miracle would happen to set the tenpins of the Third Reich upright again. Somehow the Grand Alliance between east and west was going to fall apart and the Western Allies would come obsequiously begging to long-suffering Germany to be allowed to join the holy war against bolshevism.[32]

The fighting in the west was now almost devoid of central direction from Berlin. The old order to stand fast, nowhere to give any ground even in quest of reinforcements for other sectors, was still in effect—the only "strategy." Such decisions as Hitler did make were usually based on colored daily briefings by Generaloberst Alfred Jodl, chief of the Armed Forces Operations Staff (*Wehrmachtfuehrungsstab*), who by this time had learned how to phrase his remarks to avoid inciting the Fuehrer to rage. In any case, the once powerful high command was reduced to the spectacle of pondering tactical and administrative trivialities—when, for example, five tank destroyers, the only available reserve, might be readied for commitment against the Oppenheim bridgehead, or whether to send liaison officers to some part of the front or another to get the facts on the situation.

Nor was there much more direction at the level of the Commander in Chief West, Field Marshal Kesselring, for what could he do? New to his post, the field marshal "felt like a concert pianist who is asked to play a Beethoven sonata . . . on an ancient, rickety, and out-of-tune instrument."[33] Kesselring, who four times during the first six weeks of his command spoke frankly with Hitler about the situation in the west, apparently was one of the few military men who retained the Fuehrer's trust. Each time he found Hitler "understanding," appreciative of the fact "that the situation in the west had deteriorated too far to be effectively remedied." At a meeting on 15 March Hitler promised an infantry division to be transferred from Denmark, but that was all except for a nebulous

---

[32] Hitler's last days have been adequately documented in a number of works, all of which have drawn on the surviving fragments of the Fuehrer Conferences. See, for example, Pogue, *The Supreme Command;* Shirer, *The Rise and Fall of the Third Reich;* Alan Bullock, *Hitler: A Study in Tyranny* (New York: The Macmillan Company, 1947); and Felix Gilbert, *Hitler Directs His War* (New York: Oxford University Press, 1950). See also Toland, *The Last 100 Days,* and Cornelius Ryan, *The Last Battle* (New York: Simon & Schuster, 1966).

---

[33] Kesselring, *A Soldier's Record,* p. 305.

plan to find enough men somehow to create new units. Kesselring's lasting impression was that Hitler "was literally obsessed with the idea of some miraculous salvation, that he clung to it like a drowning man to a straw." [34]

Probably not even Kesselring knew the true strength of the German forces remaining in the west, but something of their condition could be gleaned from the fact that the Allied armies, since the February beginning of the battle for the Rhineland, had taken more than 250,000 prisoners. These, together with killed and wounded, the SHAEF intelligence staff estimated, amounted to the strength of more than 20 full divisions. Although the German order of battle showed over 60 divisions in the west, some were little more than divisional staffs, others only *Kampfgruppen,* and probably none at anywhere near full strength. They represented, according to Allied estimates, the equivalent of only 26 complete divisions, in marked contrast to Eisenhower's 90 full-strength divisions. [35]

Partly because German units in the north had been afforded a brief respite behind the Rhine before the Allies crossed and partly because the *Twenty-fifth Army* in the Netherlands had yet to be directly engaged, *Army Group H* under General Blaskowitz was in better shape than the other two army groups. Yet Blaskowitz saw no hope of stemming the 21 Army Group's drive from the bridgeheads. Noting developments opposite Remagen in the adjacent sector of Field Marshal Model's *Army Group B,* Blaskowitz thought it only a matter of a day or so before American forces from

that bridgehead would be east of the Ruhr, in a position to swing against his rear. Goaded by General Blumentritt, who on 28 March arrived from the *Twenty-fifth Army* to take the badly wounded General Schlemm's place in command of the *First Parachute Army,* Blaskowitz went over Field Marshal Kesselring's head with what the Commander in Chief West called a "supererogatory account" of the situation.

As a result of *Army Group B*'s problems, Blaskowitz indicated, the situation in *Army Group H* would soon become critical. He wanted authority to withdraw his entire force behind the Weser River, some 125 miles east of the Rhine. Abandoning his two southernmost corps (Luettwitz's *XLVII Panzer Corps* and Abraham's *LXIII Corps*) to fight on in the Ruhr with *Army Group B,* Blumentritt would withdraw the rest of the *First Parachute Army* across some fifty miles of generally flat terrain to the first logical delaying position, the Teutoburger Wald, a range of low hills extending northwest from the eastern fringe of the Ruhr, there to cover withdrawal of the *Twenty-fifth Army* from the Netherlands. [36]

This report and request angered both Hitler and Kesselring, the former not only because of its inherent defeatism but because it contained none of the psychological niceties to which he had become accustomed. Although Kesselring wanted Blaskowitz replaced, Hitler settled instead for sending a former commander of *Army Group H,* General

[34] *Ibid.,* pp. 311–12.
[35] SHAEF Intelligence Sum 53, week ending 25 Mar 45.

[36] Kesselring, *A Soldier's Record,* pp. 302–03; MSS # B–414 (Geyer); # B–354, Battles Fought by the *First Parachute Army* Between 28 March and 9 April 1945 (General der Infanterie Guenther Blumentritt).

Student, to "assist" Blaskowitz, a calculated rebuke to an officer of Blaskowitz's high standing in the command structure. Blaskowitz was to hold firm while giving Student command of a provisional army to counterattack southward into the developing British-American breakthrough in the sector of the *First Parachute Army*.

As Kesselring himself recognized, that assignment was impossible. Under the continuing attacks of the British Second and U.S. Ninth Armies, the degeneration in *Army Group H* had progressed too far to be reversed with the means at hand. Disapproved or not, the withdrawal to the Teutoburger Wald was soon to get under way.[37]

Field Marshal Model's *Army Group B* was, as Blaskowitz noted, in grievous trouble. Its *Fifth Panzer Army*, commanded now by Generaloberst Josef Harpe (General von Manteuffel left on 8 March for an emergency assignment on the Eastern Front), was tied down with the task of defending the east bank of the Rhine along the face of the Ruhr; the stronger elements of Zangen's *Fifteenth Army* had been grouped along the northern periphery of the Remagen bridgehead to counter an anticipated American drive north from the bridgehead. Thus Field Marshal Model would have little with which to oppose the actual American breakout when it came, not to the north but to the east and southeast. Nor did he have any forces with which to strengthen the connection between his *Army Group B* and General Hausser's *Army Group G* to the south, a tenuous link that would be quickly severed by a combination of the U.S.

First Army's breakout from Remagen and a rapid expansion of the U.S. Third Army's Rhine bridgeheads. *Army Group G* was in the worst condition of all. Rent asunder by the U.S. Third Army's multiple Rhine crossings, the German *Seventh Army* had been hurt anew by the American Seventh Army's crossing, which also virtually isolated the German *First Army* on the army group's south wing.

It was a somber picture, one in which few other than a megalomaniac like Adolf Hitler could have seen any hint of light. Yet see it Hitler did—or so he professed. The battle then developing in the east against the Russians along the line of the Oder and Neisse Rivers, the Germans would win, Hitler insisted, if only the Allied armies from the west could be held at arm's length for a few more weeks. If Kesselring's forces could delay long enough, Hitler could form a reserve, mustered from all able-bodied manpower still uncommitted to the fight, to be assembled in the Harz Mountains of central Germany. That force, to be known as the *Twelfth Army*, then was to come to Kesselring's rescue by counterattacking through *Army Group B*'s sector to split the Allied armies.[38]

A Decision on Berlin

In the Allied camp, a number of events occurring during the month of March prompted the Supreme Commander, General Eisenhower, to revise his plan

---

[37] *Ibid.*

[38] Kesselring, *A Soldier's Record*, p. 314; MS # B–606, The Last Rally—Battles Fought by the German *Twelfth Army* in the Heart of Germany, Between East and West, 13 April–7 May 1945 (Oberst Guenther Reichhelm).

for the *coup de grâce* against Germany. For the more immediate task, encircling the Ruhr, the long-approved stratagem of cutting off the industrial region by converging thrusts of the First and Ninth Armies remained unchanged; but for the final thrust beyond the Ruhr, Eisenhower signaled a major change in plan that for a time ruffled British-American command relations and raised the issue of the extent that military decision should be influenced by political considerations.[39]

As early as September 1944, General Eisenhower had outlined his intention to proceed from the Ruhr to the German capital, Berlin, long considered—perhaps theoretically or symbolically—the final objective in the war against Germany. The 21 Army Group, assisted by an American army, was to make the main effort. Yet at the same time, General Eisenhower introduced a reservation. Recognizing that the Russians might already have taken Berlin by the time Allied armies fanned out across Germany, he suggested that the 21 Army Group might take Hannover and the north German ports, the 12th Army Group the Leipzig-Dresden industrial complex of central Germany, and the 6th Army Group the industrial cities of southern Germany.

By late March 1945 the Red Army had yet to reach Berlin. In the bridgehead across the Oder River some thirty miles from the capital, the Russians had paused, presumably to regroup and bring up supplies. There seemed little doubt that they would renew the drive momentarily and take the city. Since the closest Allied troops were still 275 miles from Berlin, the Red Army apparently would get there first.

Once Berlin ceased to be an objective, it was relatively easy to find justification for shifting the Allied main effort from the north to the center, from Montgomery's 21 Army Group to Bradley's 12th. With the addition of the Fifteenth Army to handle mop-up and occupation duties, the 12th Army Group was the stronger force and could be strengthened even more by transferring the Ninth Army back to Bradley's command once the Ruhr was encircled. The 12th Army Group was also in a position to capitalize quickly on the surprise bonus of the Rhine crossings at Remagen and Oppenheim, and, by its location in the center, was the logical candidate both for linking with the Russians to split Germany in two and for seizing the Leipzig-Dresden area, one of the last major industrial complexes that would be left to the Germans after loss of the Ruhr and Silesia.

As further justification for a shift in main effort, some members of the SHAEF staff pointed to the possibility of a last-ditch Nazi hold-out position rumored to be under construction in the Alps—a National Redoubt. The rumors had gained substance the preceding fall and of late had been fed by planted information from the Nazi propaganda chief, Dr. Goebbels. Although some influential Germans had earnestly espoused the idea of a redoubt, it did not, in fact, exist; and although many in Allied—particularly British—command and intelligence circles discounted it entirely, the possibility of some form of last-ditch resistance in the Alps was a factor—though

---

[39] This section is based on the annotated account of these events in Pogue, *The Supreme Command*, pp. 434-36, 441-47.

in no sense decisive—in Eisenhower's decision to shift his main effort.[40]

General Eisenhower announced his new plan on 28 March. Once the Ruhr was encircled, Eisenhower stipulated, the Ninth Army was to revert to the 12th Army Group, whereupon Bradley's armies were to make the main offensive eastward to link with the Russians. If he needed it, Montgomery might have the Ninth Army once Bradley reached the Elbe; but until that time Montgomery's basic assignment was to protect Bradley's northern flank while Devers's 6th Army Group guarded the southern flank.

Undoubtedly disappointed, Field Marshal Montgomery asked permission to use the Ninth Army up to the Elbe rather than beyond. Eisenhower refused, pointing out that Bradley needed control of the Ninth Army to complete operations in the Ruhr and accomplish relief by the Fifteenth Army. There the matter might have rested had the issue been nothing more than a shift in main effort, but it was more. The real issue was Berlin.

Learning of Eisenhower's decision and the fact that the Supreme Commander had asked the Allied military missions in Moscow to tell the Soviet head of state, Marshal Josef Stalin, of the change in plan, the British Chiefs of Staff protested both the decision and Eisenhower's communicating directly with the Soviet chief. They asked that Eisenhower's message be withheld from Stalin until the Combined Chiefs of Staff could discuss the matter.

The U.S. Chiefs replied that to hold up General Eisenhower's message would be to discredit or at least to lower the prestige of a highly successful field commander. The Supreme Commander was, after all, they would rationalize later, within his rights in communicating with Stalin since the Soviet head of state was also the head of the Soviet armed forces. As for the decision on Berlin, they would be willing to ask General Eisenhower for amplification of his plan, but the battle for Germany, they believed, had reached a point "where the commander in the field is the best judge of the measures which offer the earliest prospects of destroying the German armies or their power to resist." [41]

Dismayed at this reaction, Prime Minister Churchill appealed to both Eisenhower and President Roosevelt to reconsider. Aside from what he felt was an affront to the British forces, he deplored the decision not to go to Berlin:

I say quite frankly that Berlin remains of high strategic importance. Nothing will exert a psychological effect of despair upon all German forces of resistance equal to that of the fall of Berlin. It will be the supreme signal of defeat to the German people.

The Russians, Churchill continued, were about to overrun the capital of Austria; if they also could claim credit for capturing Berlin, might they not gain an undue impression of the extent of their contribution to victory, leading them into a mood that would raise "grave and formidable difficulties" for the future? [42]

Both Mr. Roosevelt and General Eisenhower assured Mr. Churchill that

---

[40] On this subject, see a detailed survey by Rodney G. Minott, *The Fortress That Never Was* (New York: Holt, Rinehart and Winston, 1964) See also below, ch. XVIII.

[41] Memo by JCS, CCS 805/2, 30 Mar 45, cited in Pogue, *The Supreme Command*, p. 442.

[42] Msg, Churchill to Roosevelt, 931, 1 Apr 45, cited in Pogue, *The Supreme Command*, p. 443.

they had no intent to disparage British contributions to the campaign against Germany. Eisenhower went on to explain that once Allied forces reached the Elbe, he thought it probable that U.S. forces would be shifted to the 21 Army Group for a drive beyond the Elbe at least far enough to seal off the Jutland peninsula; but until the nature of the opposition in central Germany fully unfolded, he deemed it important to keep his forces concentrated near the center. As for Berlin, if it could be captured, he intended to share honors equally between British and U.S. forces; but to him Berlin had lost too much of its importance as a strictly military objective to warrant mounting a major effort to seize it.

Disturbed by the alacrity with which Marshal Stalin agreed to General Eisenhower's decision to drive for Leipzig instead of Berlin, the British Chiefs of Staff a few days later again asked that the decision on Berlin be reconsidered. Again the U.S. Chiefs declined. At a time when it appeared that Allied troops could not possibly beat the Russians to the capital, when it was known that any ground taken beyond the Elbe would have to be relinquished to the Russians for the occupation, and when the Allies still apparently faced a strong fight in the Pacific for which they desired Russian assistance, the U.S. Chiefs showed no disposition to insist on taking Berlin. Clearly brushing aside the political implications, they noted that "Only Eisenhower is in a position to know how to fight this battle, and to exploit to the full the changing situation." [43]

To the Combined Chiefs of Staff Eisenhower explained that he considered it much more important to divide the Germans by a thrust to Leipzig than to concentrate against an objective like Berlin, which had lost so much of its military importance. "But," he added,

. . . I am the first to admit that a war is waged in pursuance of political aims, and if the Combined Chiefs of Staff should decide that the Allied effort to take Berlin outweighs purely military considerations in this theater, I would cheerfully readjust my plans and my thinking so as to carry out such an operation. [44]

Although seemingly settled, the issue arose again. On 8 April Field Marshal Montgomery asked to borrow ten U.S. divisions for a major thrust by the 21 Army Group to cut off the Jutland peninsula by driving to the Baltic coast near Luebeck and to take Berlin. In one of his sharper ripostes as Supreme Commander, Eisenhower responded: "You must not lose sight of the fact that during the advance to Leipzig you have the role of protecting Bradley's northern flank. It is not his role to protect your southern flank." As for Berlin, he went on, "I am quite ready to admit that it has political and psychological significance but of far greater importance will be the location of the remaining German forces in relation to Berlin. It is on them that I am going to concentrate my attention. Naturally, if I get an opportunity to capture Berlin cheaply, I will take it." [45]

The change in plan, as enunciated on 28 March, would stand. It was under this plan—to encircle the Ruhr and then

---

[43] Memo by JCS, CCS 805/5, 6 Apr 45, cited in Pogue, *The Supreme Command*, p. 444.

[44] Eisenhower to Marshall, FWD 18710, 7 Apr 45, cited in Pogue, *The Supreme Command*, p. 446.

[45] Eisenhower to Montgomery, 8 Apr 45, cited in Pogue, *The Supreme Command*, p. 446.

make a main effort with the 12th Army Group through central Germany to link with the Russians—that the Allied armies, in the meantime, had launched the breakout drives from their bridgeheads over the Rhine.

CHAPTER XVI

Reducing the Ruhr

In the Remagen bridgehead, commanders and troops of the First U.S. Army had known since 19 March that they would be permitted to break out of their bridgehead soon after the 21 Army Group had staged its Rhine crossing. Since 22 March they had known that the breakout attack was to be made on the 25th.[1] While tolerating accusations of timidity from news correspondents, the First Army commander, General Hodges, used the wait to advantage by launching limited objective attacks to secure key roads and terrain designed to speed the breakout when the time came.

The 12th Army Group's orders for the breakout reflected the employment both General Bradley and General Eisenhower had planned almost from the first for the forces in the Remagen bridgehead. Between them, Hodges' First Army and Patton's Third were to create a bridgehead ninety-two miles wide, extending from the Sieg River in the north to the Main in the south. From that lodgment the two armies were to drive astride the Lahn River northeast up the Frankfurt-Kassel corridor to Kassel; the First Army was then to turn northward to form the right pincers of a double envelopment of the Ruhr. Since the plan was originally formulated before Patton had achieved any crossing of the Rhine,

the orders included provision for part of the First Army to cross the Lahn to help clear the Third Army's half of the bridgehead.[2]

Holding the northern rim of the Remagen bridgehead, where the Germans had concentrated their greatest strength in the belief a breakout would be aimed northward toward the Ruhr, General Collins's VII Corps was occupied through the 24th in turning back the piecemeal armored counterattacks that represented the best that the German tank expert, General Bayerlein, could muster. The corps nevertheless had gained the scheduled line of departure beyond the Ruhr-Frankfurt autobahn whence General Collins was to send his own armor eastward, with the Sieg River affording left flank protection. General Van Fleet's III Corps in the center of the bridgehead meanwhile juggled its units after relinquishing the southern periphery of the bridgehead to the incoming V Corps, then secured its line of departure east of the autobahn with a night attack that met only crumbling opposition.

General Huebner's V Corps began its limited objective attacks on 22 March. Aware that the bulk of German armor had shifted to the north, nobody expected resistance in the south to be reso-

---

[1] See above, ch. XI.

[2] 12th AGp Ltr of Instrs 18, 25 Mar 45.

lute; neither was anybody prepared for an impending German collapse. Close by the Rhine a combat command of the 9th Armored Division crossed the Wied River with little difficulty and advanced four miles, while the 2d Division's 38th Infantry, alongside the armor, covered more than eight miles in three days to establish a second bridgehead over the Wied four miles deep. Both armor and infantry could readily have advanced even farther with little more effort. Huebner's V Corps quite clearly could break out at will.

Having anticipated fairly firm resistance at the start of the breakout, General Hodges had planned the First Army's main effort to be made by Van Fleet's III Corps, directed southeastward toward the Lahn at Limburg; the V Corps would mop up the east bank of the Rhine down to the Lahn, and there be pinched out by Van Fleet's advance and shifted into army reserve. The experience of the V Corps in its limited objective attacks changed the plan. To take advantage of the apparent soft spot, Hodges shifted the intercorps boundary to swing the III Corps northeastward short of Limburg, aim Huebner's V Corps at Limburg, and provide General Huebner with a zone of advance to the northeast for what seemed to be a fast-developing breakout operation.[3]

The soft spot represented all that was left of General Hitzfeld's *LXVII Corps,* southernmost of the three corps under General von Zangen's *Fifteenth Army.* That Hitzfeld was down to tattered remains of some five or six infantry divisions and had no armor was known to his superiors, but they could provide no reinforcement without stripping General Bayerlein's *LIII Corps* in the north. This Field Marshal Model at *Army Group B* refused to sanction because of his persisting belief that the breakout attack would be directed northward. Nor would the *Fifteenth Army* commander approve a shift to the south. Even though Zangen disagreed with Model's estimate of the direction the breakout would take, he thought it would be directed not to the southeast but east-northeast generally from the center of the bridgehead. Furthermore, as of 24 March, the north wing had already been weakened by orders from Field Marshal Kesselring at *OB WEST.* In response to General Patton's surprise crossing of the Rhine at Oppenheim, Kesselring had ordered *Army Group B* to release the *Fifteenth Army's* strongest unit, the *11th Panzer Division,* to go to the aid of *Army Group G* at Oppenheim.[4]

With the loss of the *11th Panzer Division,* there were few reinforcements that either Zangen or Model might have sent in any case. Already Model had drained the *Fifth Panzer Army,* which was holding the east bank of the Rhine along the face of the Ruhr, to a dangerously low level, and in all of *Army Group B* there remained only some sixty-five tanks, fifty of which already were fighting along the northern periphery of the bridgehead. Otherwise there was available behind the front only "a confused army of stragglers," and even though commanders constantly gathered and

---

[3] See FUSA Report of Operations, 23 February–8 March 1945, pp. 38–41.

[4] The German story is based primarily on MS # B–593 (Wagener) and MS # B–848, *Fifteenth Army,* 23 November 1944–30 March 1945 (Zangen). See also MS # B–409, *LIII Infantry Corps 23–29 March 1945* (Bayerlein).

committed these men, they did so only
to see them "slip away again." [5]

Obsessed with the idea that the Americans would strike north, Field Marshal
Model based his only hope of preventing
a breakout on a strong defense along the
natural barrier of the Sieg River and
subsequent counterattack into the flank
of any northward penetration. General
von Zangen counted instead on a hope
that when the Americans struck eastward, as he expected, against Puechler's
LXXIV Corps in the center, Bayerlein's
LIII Corps and Hitzfeld's *LXVII Corps*
could maintain contact with Puechler's
flanks to present a cohesive front long
enough to enable Bayerlein's armor to
mount a counterattack from the north.

Somehow managing to ignore bigger
American gains southward across the
Wied River, Zangen took the limited
objective attacks of the U.S. VII and III
Corps as proof of his theory that the
breakout would be directed east-northeast. When he pressed *Army Group B*
with that presumed evidence, he detected
a weakening in Model's position. The
army group commander nevertheless
continued to believe that the location of
his greatest strength in the north was
advisable, since he might counterattack
from the north into the flank of either
a northward or an eastward drive.

The Breakout Offensive

Even if Model and Zangen were not
actually aware of it at the time, they were
soon to realize that they were balancing
one vain hope against another. Indeed,
so weak were the Germans everywhere
and so powerful all three corps of the
American First Army that neither commander would discern, even after the
assault began, that the Allied main thrust
was directed not to the east or even
northeast but to the southeast toward
the Lahn.[6] ·

Five infantry and two armored divisions opened the First Army breakout
drive before daylight on 25 March. Aiming first for the road center of Altenkirchen, then for crossings of the Dill
River more than forty-five miles east of
the Rhine, General Collins's VII Corps
used an infantry division, the 78th, to
hold that part of the Sieg River line
already captured while another, the 1st,
protected the corps north flank by attacking eastward along the river. (*Map XIII*)
At the same time, the 3d Armored Division attacked through positions of a
third infantry division, the 104th, due
east toward Altenkirchen, while the infantry mopped up bypassed resistance.

The Germans at many points made a
real fight of it that morning. Reflecting
the German concentration near the
northern periphery of the bridgehead,
the 1st Division and the two northern
columns of the armor had the worst of it.
There a newly arrived *Kampfgruppe* of
the *Panzer Lehr Division*—all that was
left of the division—and contingents of
the *11th Panzer Division* that had not
yet departed for the *Army Group G* sector fought with old-time fury; German
artillery fire from north of the Sieg was
so heavy at some places that it reminded
veterans of hectic days in the Siegfried
Line. Steep, wooded hills and gorgelike
draws and valleys added to the difficulty,
but in the end, American power was

---

[5] Quotations are from MS # B–593 (Wagener).

[6] In MS # B–858, Zangen justifies his prediction
of a threat to east-northeast on his reading of how
the American attack actually developed.

simply too overwhelming. In sparkling clear skies, fighter-bombers of the XIX Tactical Air Command time after time struck German formations with particular attention to tanks and assault guns. Supporting artillery fired 632 missions. One Tiger tank and a self-propelled gun fell victim to an American T26 (Pershing), one of the experimental tanks in the 3d Armored Division. By midday the armor was through the enemy's main line, and when night came stood twelve miles beyond its line of departure, half the distance to Altenkirchen.[7]

General Van Fleet's III Corps in the center, also driving toward eventual crossings of the Dill River but with a southeastward orientation at first in order to help the advance of the V Corps, withheld its armor on the first day. There too resistance was strongest in the north, where the 9th Division brushed against the remnants of the resurrected *9th Panzer Division,* the only force of any appreciable power left to General Puechler's *LXXIV Corps.* The 9th gained almost four miles through densely wooded, sharply convoluted terrain, while the 99th Division on the right picked up more than five miles. An order from the army commander, General Hodges, to get the 7th Armored Division into the fore the next day arrived moments after General Van Fleet himself had made the same decision and alerted the armor for the move.

In the V Corps, headed for Limburg on the Lahn, the 9th Armored Division continued its thrust down the east bank of the Rhine, coming to a halt only after an advance of over eight miles to the Rhine town of Vallendar, a few miles

short of Koblenz. From there good roads led almost due east to Limburg. The 2d Division's 23d Infantry meanwhile carried the advance on the armor's left, losing two men killed and fifteen wounded in exchange for gains of more than five miles. The promise of the earlier limited objective attacks in this sector clearly was to be fulfilled.

During the course of this advance, soon after midday, the 23d Infantry's Company G gained a crossing of the little Sayn River, only to face a clifflike stretch of wooded high ground beyond. Tired from the morning's fight, hot in a wool uniform baked by a brilliant spring sun, the company commander deplored the thought of walking with heavy equipment up the winding road ahead. "Climb on the tanks," he ordered his men. They responded by enthusiastically clambering aboard two platoons of attached medium tanks. You did not ride, the men knew, until the resistance had begun to collapse.

Events the next morning, 26 March, proved the men and their company commander right, to the immense pleasure of the army commander, General Hodges, and his guests of the day, Generals Eisenhower and Bradley.[8] The day before, the Third Army's 4th Armored Division had broken out of the Oppenheim bridgehead and seized bridges over the Main River at Hanau and Aschaffenburg, and the VIII Corps had begun jumping the Rhine gorge at Boppard. Before daylight on the 26th, the Seventh Army had begun to cross the Rhine near Worms, and British and American units north of the Ruhr were straining to achieve a breakout. With those develop-

---

[7] Unless otherwise noted, the tactical story is from official unit records and combat interviews.

[8] Sylvan Diary, entry of 26 Mar 45.

ments as a backdrop, Hodges was elated when news of his three-pronged armored advance began to come in.

Despite an early morning counterattack by infantry supported by assault guns, apparently designed to allow remnants of the *Panzer Lehr Division* to pull back behind the Sieg River, the 3d Armored Division in General Collins's VII Corps raced eastward in great bounds. With a motorized combat team of the 104th Division attached, the armor bypassed Altenkirchen, leaving that road center for reserves to clear. After taking high ground outside Hachenburg, half the distance from the original bridgehead to the objectives on the Dill River, it coiled for the night. At those points where the Germans elected to make a stand, mainly along the north flank, planes of the 48th Fighter-Bomber Group in close co-ordination with the armor swooped down to take out tanks and self-propelled guns. In late afternoon such organized units as still opposed the advance began to peel back across the Sieg.

In the III Corps the time proved fully propitious for committing armor. After an early delay caused by craters blown in the roads and by mines, demolished bridges, and a mix-up with the V Corps over running rights on the autobahn, the 7th Armored Division broke loose to roam almost at will southeastward toward Weilburg on the Lahn River. By road measurement some units of the division advanced over thirty miles. When night came the 7th Armored Division held high ground overlooking Weilburg, while infantry of the 9th and 99th Divisions, advancing on attached tanks and tank destroyers and by shuttle in trucks borrowed from artillery antiaircraft

units, struggled to keep up. The III Corps on 26 March captured 17,482 Germans, more than 12,500 taken by the armored division. Several hundred of these prisoners represented the rear echelon of the *11th Panzer Division,* caught as they moved diagonally across the front en route to commitment with *Army Group G.*

The story was much the same with the 9th Armored Division of the V Corps. Once calls to higher headquarters straightened out the brief run-in with the 7th Armored Division on the autobahn, the 9th Armored drove eastward toward Limburg against almost no opposition. Although remnants of General Hitzfeld's *LXVII Corps* fled ahead of the armor, in most cases their flight served merely to augment the prisoners of the adjacent III Corps.

In midafternoon Combat Command B found a bridge intact over the Lahn River and got four tanks across before the Germans could ignite the prepared demolition and blow the span. Dismounted armored infantrymen then made their way across on the rubble and systematically began to clear Limburg of scattered small arms resistance, augmented occasionally by fire from *Panzerfausts.* Although most of the town was in hand soon after dark, the division commander, General Leonard, postponed a continuation of the drive beyond the river to cut in behind those Germans opposing the Third Army's VIII Corps until he could get a treadway bridge built across the Lahn.

Collapse of the LXXXIX Corps

On 27 March, as General Leonard prepared to send his reserve combat command southeastward along the autobahn, the German *LXXXIX Corps,* having fought vainly to prevent crossings of the Rhine gorge, had fallen back from the Rhine to a line not quite midway between the river and the autobahn. This was the corps, commanded by General Hoehne, that only shortly before the American VIII Corps attacked had been transferred to *Army Group B's Fifteenth Army;* in the confusion of events, no contact had ever been established with the army headquarters and little with headquarters of the army group. This was the corps, too, that had lost the *6th SS Mountain Division* at the order of Field Marshal Kesselring only hours before the VIII Corps attacked. Like the incoming *11th Panzer Division,* the mountain division, its 6,000 men representing a still creditable fighting unit, was supposed to be used to counterattack Patton's crossing at Oppenheim.[9]

Receiving the news of American armor racing toward the Lahn, Kesselring had quickly reconsidered and reassigned the mountain division to the *LXXXIX Corps* to be committed to hold the line of the Lahn around Limburg. Because the division had no gasoline, the men had to march on foot, arriving at the southern edge of Limburg late on the 26th only after American armor had already entered. With additional units of the division that arrived during the night, the commander, Generalmajor Karl Brenner, built up a line facing north astride the autobahn.[10]

It was too little too late. In an attack that started shortly after midday on 27 March, the 9th Armored Division's CCR sliced quickly through the hasty defenses on the autobahn and reached its objective of Idstein, fifteen miles to the southeast, before dark.

Pressed hard from the west by the oncoming VIII Corps and faced with this sizable American force to his rear, the commander of the *LXXXIX Corps,* General Hoehne, finally managed in late afternoon to establish radio contact with Field Marshal Kesselring at *OB WEST.* To Hoehne's request that he be allowed to withdraw east of the autobahn, Kesselring gave a decisive no.

It made little difference. Having already lost communications with whatever remained of the *6th SS Mountain Division,* Hoehne during the morning learned from his one surviving division, the *276th Infantry Division,* that collapse was imminent. Hoehne took it upon himself to order withdrawal. His own headquarters was under hostile fire from reconnaissance cars and infantry when, with a group of some thirty of his staff, he headed east. "Corps HQ," he was to note later in something of an understatement, "was no longer in a position to exercise effective command."[11]

What was left of General Brenner's *6th SS Mountain Division*—some 2,000 men—meanwhile continued to hold out west of the autobahn and from time to time during the next two days set up roadblocks on the autobahn, even after forward units of the VIII Corps had moved well to the east and the 9th Armored's CCR had gone back north of the Lahn. During the night of 30 March

---

[9] See above, ch. XIII.

[10] MSS # B–584 (Hoehne) and # B–715, *6 SS Geb Div "Nord,"* During the Defensive Combat in the Area Koblenz-Eltville and Limburg-Diez, East of the Rhine, 19 March–3 April 1945 (General der Waffen SS Karl Brenner).

[11] MS # B–584 (Hoehne).

Brenner and his force would begin an attempt to infiltrate back to German lines, an odyssey destined to end three days later, on 2 April, when the remnants, including General Brenner, were finally rounded up.

During the course of their peregrinations, the SS troops captured an American field hospital, where they obtained critically needed gasoline and transportation. Although they treated the hospital personnel correctly, a rumor that they had murdered the staff and raped the nurses accounted, General Patton reported later, for the fervor with which American troops hunted them down. Some 500 were killed before a last 800 surrendered.[12]

The collapse of the *LXXXIX Corps* severed the last tenuous link between *Army Groups B* and *G,* and there was nothing the Germans could do about it. The only reserve even remotely available, the remains of the *11th Panzer Division,* would be swept up in the general American advance and ripped to pieces with no chance of mounting a counterattack. Only the division commander and the reconnaissance battalion even reached their destination with *Army Group G.*[13]

A Turn to the North

Even without that collapse, the two army groups soon would have been separated, for the American First Army's breakthrough of the positions of the *Fifteenth Army* opposite the Remagen bridgehead on 26 March was total. In the process the army commander, General von Zangen, lost contact with almost everybody but his own staff and the headquarters of one of his corps, General Puechler's *LXXIV Corps,* which had been utterly crushed by the breakout offensive. Unable to reach the *Fifteenth Army* headquarters by radio or telephone, Field Marshal Model at *Army Group B* was fast coming to the conclusion that Zangen had been captured.[14]

Since he was unable to contact Zangen, Model dealt directly with the commander of the *LIII Corps,* General Bayerlein, ordering him to pull back behind the Sieg, relinquish the line of the Sieg to contingents of the *Fifth Panzer Army,* and prepare for a counterattack into the American flank in the direction of Limburg. To Bayerlein, knowing how weak were the remnants of his corps, a counterattack seemed "impossible and entirely hopeless . . . insane," but he dutifully began preparations.[15]

The pace of the American drive on this same day, 27 March, supplied any affirmation Bayerlein might have needed that counterattack would be in vain. While occupied with the thrust south of the Lahn River, the 9th Armored Division of the V Corps made no further eastward advance. In the VII Corps, on the north wing of the First Army, the 3d Armored Division gained an impressive twenty-two miles to jump the Dill River in two places. At the same time, the 7th Armored Division of the III Corps also crossed the Dill, seizing four bridges intact. Fog in morning and afternoon and a low overcast the rest of the day pre-

---

[12] Patton, *War As I Knew It,* p. 282. Patton errs in naming the unit as the *2d Mountain Division.*

[13] MS # A–893 (Gersdorff).

[14] See MSS # B–848 (Zangen); # B–593 (Wagener); # B–409, *LIII Corps,* 23–29 March 1945 (Generalleutnant Fritz Bayerlein).

[15] MS # B–409 (Bayerlein).

vented air support, but the armored columns had little need of it. They were roaming the enemy's rear areas, everywhere catching the Germans by surprise, and finding them unprepared to defend with more than an occasional roadblock covered by a smattering of small arms fire or perhaps a *Panzerfaust* or a lone self-propelled gun that could be quickly put to flight. Only on the First Army left flank, where the 1st Division continued to sweep up to the south bank of the Sieg, was there any real resistance, and it was more a reminder that there were sizable German forces beyond the Sieg covering the Ruhr than it was an immediate problem.

The next day, 28 March, the armor of the VII Corps again set the pace, driving another twenty-one miles and seizing the little cultural center of Marburg on the upper reaches of the Lahn. The town's thirteenth century cathedral and its university, founded in 1527, showed no scar from twentieth century battle. En route, the 3d Armored Division overran several German hospitals with more than 5,600 soldier patients, took another 10,000 prisoners, so many they could not all be processed during the day, and sent scores of liberated foreign laborers coursing happily toward the west. The V Corps meanwhile took a day to reorganize, while the armor of the III Corps kept almost abreast, advancing thirteen miles, capturing Giessen, and dispersing a fairly persistent delaying force before seizing crossings over the Lahn.

To the 12th Army Group commander, General Bradley, the time had arrived to begin the great wheel to the north designed to join with the Ninth Army to encircle the Ruhr. Redrawing army boundaries, Bradley turned the First Army northward toward Paderborn, leaving the Third Army oriented northeast on Kassel to protect the First Army right flank; anticipating a rapid drive, he rejected a proposal from the First Allied Airborne Army for an airborne attack to sieze Kassel. (*Map XIV*) The new Fifteenth Army was to take over defense of the Rhine's west bank so that all the First Army divisions could cross the river to man the ever-lengthening front facing the Ruhr.[16]

Within the First Army, General Collins's VII Corps from its position on the inside of the wheel was the obvious choice for making the main thrust to Paderborn, despite the continuing sensitive reaction of the Germans on the left flank. The other two corps were to continue northeastward to protect Collins's right flank.

A task force, commanded by Lt. Col. Walter B. Richardson and built around a medium tank battalion that included three of the new Pershing tanks, led the 3d Armored Division advance on 29 March. The orders: "Just go like hell!"[17] Although the objective—Paderborn— lay more than sixty miles away, Richardson was determined to make it before calling a halt.

Crashing through some roadblocks, bypassing others, occasionally shooting up the landscape, everywhere encountering dismayed Germans who obviously had no inkling that American troops were near, Task Force Richardson plunged rapidly forward, hardly missing the tactical air support that a hazy, overcast day denied. Follow-up units, supply troops, liaison

---

[16] 12th AGp Ltr of Instrs 19, 28 Mar 45.
[17] Toland in *The Last 100 Days*, pages 309–11, provides a vivid account of this day's action.

officers, and messengers probably did more actual fighting than did the leading force, since German stragglers and bypassed groups often recovered from their first bewilderment to fight back. The longest delay for Richardson's column developed in Brilon, twenty-five miles short of Paderborn, where, as Richardson and an advance guard pushed on, someone among the tank crews discovered a warehouse filled with champagne. When the tanks finally caught up with their commander, the actions of many of of the crewmen provided disconcerting evidence of their find.

Task Force Richardson at last halted around midnight fifteen miles short of Paderborn. The decision to stop was based on about equal parts of concern for exhausted troops and a report that tanks from an SS panzer replacement training center were in the Sennelager maneuver area near Paderborn. Although still short of the objective, Richardson and his men had covered forty-five miles at a cost of no casualty more severe than the headaches some men suffered from too much champagne.

The next day, 30 March, the complexion of the battle abruptly changed. Hardly had Task Force Richardson resumed the advance when the point bumped into a defensive line hastily manned during the night by students from an SS panzer reconnaissance training battalion and an SS tank training and replacement regiment, banded together with support from an SS tank replacement battalion of approximately sixty Tiger and Panther tanks into a unit named *SS Ersatzbrigade Westfalen.* By midafternoon Richardson's men had forced their way into a town only six

miles short of Paderborn. There they fought the rest of the day and much of the night against at least two tanks and more than 200 Germans, most of whom employed *Panzerfaust* antitank weapons with suicidal fervor.

Coming up on Richardson's right, another task force commanded by Col. John C. Welborn tried to bypass the town by a secondary road. Dusk was approaching when small arms fire from either side of the road and round after round from tanks and self-propelled guns cut the column. One of those who dived for cover in a ditch was the 3d Armored Division commander, General Rose, on his way forward to supervise the final assault on Paderborn with his aide and a small party traveling in jeeps and an armored car.

Hardly had Rose finished sending a radio message to his command post to dispatch another task force to take out this nest of opposition when four German tanks appeared, coming up the road from the rear. In the early evening darkness, Rose and his party tried to escape by racing past the tanks, but one of the tanks suddenly swerved, pinning Rose's jeep against a tree. A German standing in the turret motioned with a burp gun. Rose, his aide, Maj. Robert Bellinger, and his driver, Tech. 5 Glen H. Shaunce, dismounted. They had no choice but to surrender.

Standing in front of the tank, Bellinger and Shaunce unbuckled their pistol belts and let them drop. Rose started either to do the same or to remove his pistol from its holster. The German in the turret quickly swung his burp gun, and a spout of flame split the darkness. Rose pitched forward. Bellinger and Shaunce dived for a ditch and, in the confusion, got away. Maurice Rose, esteemed by his superiors as one of the best division commanders in the theater, was dead.[18]

As the cordon designed to encircle all of *Army Group B* rapidly took shape, the army group commander, Field Marshal Model, had no stomach for a last-ditch stand among the bomb-shattered factories, mines, and cities of the Ruhr. Summarizing the situation for *OB WEST* on the 29th, Model noted that he had lost contact with headquarters of the *Fifteenth Army* and that his only reserve consisted of headquarters of the *LIII Corps* (Bayerlein), two mobile *Kampfgruppen* (the *Panzer Lehr* and *3d Panzer Grenadier Divisions*), and a partially rebuilt infantry division, the *176th*. With the forces and supplies remaining, Model reckoned, he might be able to hold out in the Ruhr, even though encircled, until mid-April at the latest; but if a decisive attack were not mounted from the outside by that time, the army group likely would be destroyed.[19]

Model clearly wanted to withdraw immediately from the Ruhr, saving his army group to fight again in central Germany. To assist a withdrawal, he urged an immediate attack by Bayerlein's *LIII Corps* from the vicinity of Winterberg, in densely wooded hill country fourteen miles south of Brilon, eastward to the Eder-See, a reservoir approximately midway between Winterberg and Kassel. To complement the thrust, he hoped for a converging attack from

Kassel to be launched by troops of the *Fifteenth Army*, which he presumed had fallen back on Kassel. The two attacks, Model hoped, might cut off the American armored columns even then closing in on Paderborn and prevent encirclement long enough for *Army Group B* to pull out.

Kesselring's reply came that night. Attack, yes; withdraw, no. Only the day before, Hitler had reiterated his long-standing order to authorize no withdrawal on pain of death. *Army Group B* would have to stand in the Ruhr and—Model well might have predicted—die there as well.

Having already alerted General Bayerlein and subordinate units to the possibility of an attack east from Winterberg, Model dutifully continued with the arguments. In the absence of the *Fifteenth Army* commander, he designated the army group artillery commander, General der Artillerie Karl Thoholte, to command the attack and to create a defensive line from Siegen to Brilon, the line to be manned by Luftwaffe units, alarm and construction troops, and *Volkssturm*. Recognizing that the only chance of success lay in striking before the Americans could consolidate behind their armor, Model ordered that the attack begin with whatever units had arrived by the evening of 30 March.

The *Fifteenth Army* commander, General von Zangen, though out of contact with headquarters of the army group, had in the meantime been trying to erect some kind of defensive barrier across the Frankfurt-Kassel corridor. He still had communications with remnants of Puechler's *LXXIV Corps* and had established liaison with a corps headquarters that had been attached to the *Fifteenth*

---

[18] Accounts of this episode vary in details. The author has relied primarily on the 3d Armored Division after action report for March 1945 and on the unit history, *Spearhead in the West*.

[19] The German story is based primarily on MS # B–593 (Wagener) and MS # B–396, *LIII Corps, 29 March–7 April 1945* (Bayerlein).

Army sans combat troops soon after the American breakthrough, the *LXVI Corps* under Generalleutnant Hermann Floerke.[20]

Zangen ordered both corps to collect stragglers (the roads were jammed with them), security troops, ambulatory hospital patients, whatever, to build a line across the corridor near Giessen; when American armor overran that position before any barrier could be raised, he ordered the line built south of Marburg. Again the American columns overran the position.

Hardly had Zangen dutifully designated a third line, this time along the Lahn River north of Marburg, when word reached him that American armor already had jumped the Lahn and by-passed his headquarters town of Biedenkopf on both east and west. (This was on 29 March, the day of the 3d Armored Division's explosive advance toward Paderborn behind Task Force Richardson.) The third line obviously had been compromised even before Zangen designated it, and his headquarters was cut off not only from the army group but also from the two remaining corps commands.

Only a step ahead of American tanks, Zangen herded his headquarters staff and attached units out of Biedenkopf into a nearby forest. There, as night came, he and his men hid, warily eyeing tanks and vehicles of the 3d Armored Division driving past.

When sentries reported large gaps in the American column, Zangen seized

upon a daring scheme to escape and make his way back into the Ruhr. Organizing his men and more than a hundred remaining vehicles into small groups, he ordered them to thread their way in the darkness into the gaps, march with the Americans for several miles to a road junction, then turn to the west as the Americans continued northward. Zangen and almost his entire force escaped. Only one truckload of troops and a motorcyclist failed. They made the mistake of calling out in their native tongue to the lead vehicle in an American serial that came up behind them.

The Thrust From Winterberg

In pinning much of their hope for a successful attack from Winterberg on striking before American infantry could consolidate behind the armored spearheads, German commanders failed to give proper consideration to the speed of the infantry units. Conscious of insufficient infantry strength in the old-style "heavy" armored divisions, of which the 3d Armored was one, General Rose and the VII Corps commander, General Collins, had long practiced attaching an entire infantry regiment to the armor in breakthrough situations. As the 3d Armored had rolled toward Paderborn, the 104th Division's 414th Infantry had gone along, some men mounted on the armored division's tanks, tank destroyers, and half-tracks, others in the regiment's own vehicles. These "doughs" (short for doughboys), as the tank crewmen called them, were not to mop up resistance but to help the tankers if the going got sticky.

Close behind the armor and its attached infantry came the rest of the

---

[20] The *Fifteenth Army* story is from MSS # B–848 (Zangen) and # B–382, Report Covering the Activities of the Staff of the *LXVI Armeekorps* During March and April 1945 (Generalleutnant Hermann Floerke).

104th Division, mounted on its own vehicles, those of its artillery and attached antiaircraft battalion, trucks furnished by the First Army quartermaster, and the battalions of tanks and tank destroyers that by that stage of the war had for so long been constantly attached that the division looked upon them almost as permanent fixtures. Motorized and supported in this manner, an infantry division could move almost with the speed of an armored division, particularly when following in the wake of armor. Thus the infantry was quickly available to mop up and to provide depth to the armored spearheads.

To the Germans at Winterberg, chances of success appeared brighter because a distance of only about fifteen miles separated Winterberg from their objective, the elongated Eder-See, a narrow corridor through which apparently only forward elements of one armored division had passed. They were reckoning without the 104th Division. They were reckoning, too, without the speed of the other two corps of the First Army.

By nightfall of 30 March, the 7th Armored Division of General Van Fleet's III Corps had come up close along the right flank of the VII Corps to seize a dam at the east end of the Eder-See and several bridges over lower reaches of the reservoir and of the river downstream from the dam.[21] This the troops of the III Corps had accomplished despite meeting a fresh German unit, the *166th*

Infantry Division, moved from Denmark in accord with Hitler's earlier promise. Meanwhile, the 9th Armored Division of General Huebner's V Corps also reached the Eder River downstream from the dam and forced a crossing. Infantry divisions followed the armor closely in both corps, providing strength close at hand either to knife into the flank of any complementing German thrust that might be launched toward the Eder-See from Kassel or to furnish reinforcement for the VII Corps.

In their hope for a complementary thrust from Kassel, the Germans were doomed to disappointment. There simply was no German unit at Kassel strong enough to launch an attack. For lack of co-ordination, the incoming *166th Infantry Division,* which might have formed the nucleus for an attack, had already been committed futilely two days earlier and cut up in an engagement with the U.S. III Corps. Although Field Marshal Model had counted on the *SS Ersatzbrigade Westfalen* to assist a drive from Kassel, he had not known how locked in combat this makeshift force was with the 3d Armored Division spearheads just outside Paderborn.

For the Americans, rumor after rumor passed on by German stragglers and civilians during the 30th had pointed to a concentration of German tanks and infantry at Winterberg, massing for a breakout attempt that night. To guard against it, the 104th Division commander, General Allen, ordered his regiments to occupy key towns and road junctions along the corps left flank facing Winterberg. He also sent a mobile task force racing through the night over roads bypassing Winterberg to defend Brilon, which, aside from having provided

---

[21] In the course of the 7th Armored Division's advance on 29 March, S. Sgt. Robert H. Dietz, 38th Armored Infantry Battalion, charged alone against defenders of two bridges at the town of Kirchhain. He had secured one bridge and disconnected demolition charges from the second when German fire cut him down. He was awarded the Medal of Honor posthumously.

champagne for Task Force Richardson, afforded a blocking position astride a major highway leading from the Ruhr across the 3d Armored Division's rear to Kassel. The First Army commander, General Hodges, ordered Van Fleet's III Corps to release its leading infantry division, the 9th, to go to the VII Corps the next day.

For the start of the attack from Winterberg on the night of 30 March, only two *Kampfgruppen* had yet arrived, each representing a mixed battalion of infantry and combat engineers, plus twelve tanks of the *Panzer Lehr Division,* a few assault guns, but no artillery. The *LIII Corps* commander, General Bayerlein, sent these battalions with guides from the local forestry service down forest trails leading southeast to cut a highway connecting the towns of Hallenberg and Medebach. From this highway, westernmost of three routes serving the 3d Armored Division, Bayerlein intended to continue the attack to the Eder-See once the rest of his troops, including the *176th Infantry Division,* arrived.[22]

The columns on the forest trails got moving at midnight. As dawn approached, both columns cut the Hallenberg–Medebach highway with no difficulty, but a battalion of the 415th Infantry posted in each of the two towns rapidly restored the route. The hottest fight, meanwhile, developed at a village midway between the two towns, where sixteen men from Company A, 414th Infantry, had bedded down for the night while crews of two 3d Armored Division tanks they had been riding awaited a

maintenance vehicle. Also on hand, awaiting maintenance, was a crippled self-propelled artillery piece.

One of the infantrymen, S. Sgt. Cris Cullen, recalled the start of the fight:

The first thing I heard that morning was one of the Polish slave laborers running around yelling, 'Panzer! Panzer!' Then as I started to go back to sleep, mumbling to myself about that 'damn crazy Polack,' I heard the unmistakable sound of a German machine gun. That fixed the sleep.

While I was cramming on my boots, one of our men came in for ammo and I asked him what was going on. 'Plenty,' he said. 'There's a Kraut tank coming down the street.' People exaggerate when they are excited. I would go look for myself before I got excited.

I got excited. About forty yards away and coming slowly forward was a German tank with a gun on it that looked as large as a telephone pole.[23]

Before Sergeant Cullen and the others could bring rifle and bazooka fire to bear from the houses, the German tank knocked out the unmanned artillery piece; but as the tank commander raised his head from his turret to survey his victim, one of the riflemen cut him down. A fusillade of small arms fire from the houses drove the accompanying German infantry to flight. The tank followed.

Through the rest of the day, the Germans made occasional forays against some points along the highway, but they had not the strength to take the 415th Infantry's sally ports of Hallenberg and Medebach, which would have to be occupied if any cut of the highway was to be sustained. The *Fifteenth Army* commander, General von Zangen, who assumed over-all command following his

[22] See MSS # B–396 (Bayerlein); # B–593 (Wagener); # B–849, *Fifteenth Army* in the Ruhr Pocket, 31 March to 15 April 1945 (General der Infanterie Gustav von Zangen).

[23] Hoegh and Doyle, *Timberwolf Tracks,* p. 307.

escape from encirclement, opted to delay hitting the two towns until additional troops arrived.

The thrust from Winterberg had thus far been little more than a nuisance raid.

Breakthrough North of the Ruhr

Even as the Germans in the Ruhr first prepared to launch the weak beginning of their attempt to force a corridor to the outside, their plight was about to be compounded by developments along the northern edge of the Ruhr. There, on 28 March, troops of the XVIII Airborne Corps had scored a rapid gain to Haltern, on the north bank of the Lippe River more than twenty-five miles east of the Rhine, opening the way for the breakthrough that the 30th Division and the 8th Armored Division of General Anderson's XVI Corps had sought in vain south of the Lippe. On the same date Field Marshal Montgomery had announced his new policy, to be put into effect on the 31st, for use of the Rhine bridges at Wesel and the roadnet north of the Lippe that insured a way for General Simpson to bring more of his powerful Ninth Army to bear.

On the 29th Simpson published his plan for the breakout drive to the east. While Anderson's XVI Corps swung southeastward to build up along the Rhein–Herne Canal on the northern fringe of the Ruhr, General McLain's XIX Corps, moving north of the Lippe River, was to take over the main effort. With two armored and three infantry divisions, McLain's corps was to drive first to Hamm, at the northeastern tip of the Ruhr, then go on to link with the First Army at Paderborn. General Gillem's XIII Corps, meanwhile, as maneuver

room developed and as the Wesel bridges passed to the Ninth Army, also was to move north of the Lippe and drive northeastward on Muenster, twenty miles north of Hamm. In the process, the XVIII Airborne Corps was to be relieved, British units within the corps passing to the British Second Army and General Gillem assuming control of the U.S. 17th Airborne Division.[24]

Alerted in advance to the orders, a combat command of the 2d Armored Division, reinforced by an attached infantry regiment, began to cross the Rhine into the crowded rear areas of the XVI Corps early on 28 March. From there the armor was to cross the Lippe, bypassing the bottleneck of Wesel, and start its eastward thrust even before the Wesel bridges passed to the Ninth Army's control.

Although the rapid advance of the XVIII Airborne Corps and pending commitment of the XIX Corps north of the Lippe at this point obviated the necessity of a breakthrough south of the river, the division that earlier had been assigned the goal, the 8th Armored, continued to attack. The armor was to take the long-sought objective alongside the Lippe, the town of Dorsten, needed as a bridge site to serve the XIX Corps, then was to continue eastward to cross upper reaches of the Lippe. Both the 8th Armored and the 30th Divisions then were to pass from control of the XVI Corps to that of the XIX Corps.

Renewing the attack on 29 March, the 8th Armored Division found the enemy's *116th Panzer Division*, which as part of General Luettwitz's *XLVII Panzer Corps*

---

[24] *Conquer: The Story of the Ninth Army*, pages 264–66, provides a convenient summary of these orders.

had thwarted a breakout from the Rhine bridgehead, still making a fight of it. By nightfall the American armor claimed Dorsten, but it had been a plodding fight against an enemy helped by marshy ground, woods, and deadly nests of big antiaircraft guns in concrete emplacements. Given the wooded nature of the terrain east of Dorsten, there was no evidence but that the same kind of slow, dogged advance might be in the offing for days.

The story was far different north of the Lippe. There reconnaissance forces of the 2d Armored Division had moved out of Haltern before midnight on the 29th with every indication of a swift sweep eastward. Not long after daylight the next morning, 30 March, the main columns reached the Dortmund–Ems Canal, paused while engineers built bridges, then resumed the advance in late afternoon. All through the night of the 30th and the next day the armor rolled, while the 83d Division, mounted on trucks belonging to the corps artillery, followed closely. In the process the tanks cut two major rail lines leading north and northeast from Hamm, leaving only one railroad open to the Germans in the Ruhr. In late afternoon of the 31st the armor also cut the Ruhr–Berlin autobahn near Beckum, northeast of Hamm, just under forty miles beyond the original line of departure.

To the top German commanders north of the Ruhr—Blaskowitz of *Army Group H* and Blumentritt, the new commander of the *First Parachute Army* —the American breakthrough north of the Lippe mocked the standfast orders that Hitler and Kesselring had so recently issued when denying Blaskowitz's appeal to withdraw, first to the Teuto-

burger Wald, then behind the Weser River.[25] So swift and deep was the American thrust, irreparably splitting the *First Parachute Army* down the middle, that the end result was bound to be much the same as the withdrawal Blaskowitz and Blumentritt had recommended.

With the means at hand, no hope existed of counterattacking southward into the American flank, as Hitler's emissary, General Student, would himself discover upon his arrival. Those contingents of the parachute army north of the breakthrough had no choice but to fall back toward the Teutoburger Wald—indeed, they would be hard put to keep ahead of American and British troops. All communications with the *First Parachute Army* and *Army Group H* having been severed, Luettwitz's *XLVII Panzer Corps* and Abraham's *LXIII Corps* south of the breakthrough appealed for orders to Field Marshal Model at *Army Group B.* Just as Blaskowitz earlier had urged, Model told both corps to form a new line facing north behind the Rhein–Herne Canal and, farther east, behind the Lippe River. These two corps, brigaded under Luettwitz's headquarters as *Gruppe von Luettwitz,* then would comprise the defense for the northern face of the Ruhr.[26]

For a day or so Field Marshal Kesselring would fuss and fret over Model's presumption in absorbing the two corps, though he would inevitably be forced to accept it. Thus, by the first day of April, the lineup of units around the

[25] See above, ch. XV.
[26] MS # B-354 (Blumentritt); MS # B-593 (Wagener).

perimeter of the Ruhr was basically complete: in the north and turning the northeastern corner short of Lippstadt, some twenty miles up the Lippe from Hamm, *Gruppe von Luettwitz;* beginning at the Moehne Reservoir on the upper reaches of the Ruhr River, Zangen's *Fifteenth Army,* which faced east and southeast, to a point on the Sieg River near Siegen; facing south along the Sieg and west along the Rhine, Harpe's *Fifth Panzer Army.* As this lineup took shape, the time left before the Germans in the Ruhr would be fully encircled could be measured in hours.

Late on 31 March, as the Ninth Army's 2d Armored Division was cutting the autobahn near Beckum, the army commander, General Simpson, received a troubled telephone call. It was from Joe Collins, commander of the First Army's VII Corps. His 3d Armored Division, Collins said, had stirred up a fury of opposition from fanatic SS troops near Paderborn. It might take days to eliminate the resistance and continue north to the army group boundary to establish contact with the Ninth Army, thereby sealing the circle around the Ruhr. Furthermore, he went on, the Germans inside the pocket already had begun to strike at the rear of the 3d Armored Division in what prisoners reported was the beginning of a major effort to break out of the Ruhr.

Collins asked Simpson to turn a combat command of his 2d Armored Division southeast toward Lippstadt, midway between Beckum and Paderborn. Collins, for his part, would divert a force from the 3d Armored to meet the combat command halfway.

General Simpson promptly ordered a combat command of the 2d Armored Division to turn southeast toward Lippstadt. Before daylight the next morning, 1 April—Easter Sunday—a task force commanded by Lt. Col. Matthew W. Kane, including a battalion of 3d Armored tanks transporting "doughs" from the 414th Infantry, turned from the fight at Paderborn toward Lippstadt. Neither force encountered serious opposition; fire came mainly from small arms, though there were a few rounds from flak guns, whose dispirited crews quickly fled or surrendered. By noon pilots of artillery liaison planes from the 2d and 3d Armored Divisions could see leading ground troops of both divisions. About 1300 the two columns came together, amid cheers and ribald jokes, on the eastern fringe of Lippstadt.

The Ruhr industrial area was encompassed. Trapped in a pocket measuring some 30 miles by 75 miles were the headquarters and supporting troops of *Army Group B,* all of the *Fifth Panzer Army,* the bulk of the *Fifteenth Army,* and two corps of the *First Parachute Army,* a total of 7 corps and 19 divisions. American intelligence officers estimated that the force consisted of some 150,000 men. They were, events soon would disclose, far too conservative.

Making Motions at Breakout

Although the trap was closed the German command, with commendable bravado but little else, was making bellicose but empty motions and issuing pretty but illusory orders aimed at opening a corridor into the Ruhr Pocket. While General von Zangen's *Fifteenth Army,* using Bayerlein's *LIII Corps,* renewed its attack from Winterberg, Field Marshal Kesselring tried to mobilize a force near

Kassel strong enough to push a way through from the east.[27]

To command the attack, Hitler sanctioned using headquarters of the *Eleventh Army,* a staff that in happier times had compiled a good record on the Russian front. Only recently reconstituted, the staff was to be subordinated directly to *OB WEST.* The commander was to be General Hitzfeld, heretofore commander of the *Fifteenth Army's LXVII Corps,* which had escaped entrapment in the Ruhr.

General Hitzfeld was to have his own *LXVII Corps,* General Floerke's *LXVI Corps,* and a provisional corps headquarters created from the staff of the local *Wehrkreis.* This force looked solid enough on paper; in reality, it signified little. Its strongest component was to be the *SS Ersatzbrigade Westfalen,* which late on 1 April finally relinquished Paderborn to the American 3d Armored Division and fell back with possibly as many as forty tanks and assault guns still fit to fight. There were in addition two surviving battalions of the ill-starred *166th Infantry Division,* stragglers, *Volkssturm,* hospital returnees, and about twenty tanks from a factory at Kassel. With those odds and ends Hitzfeld was not only to break into the Ruhr but was also to build a solid line against further eastward advance along the Weser River.

Hitzfeld's force was only beginning to assemble when, before daylight on 1 April, the Germans at Winterberg renewed their heretofore feeble attempts to push eastward to the Eder-See.[28] Although the *176th Infantry Division* still

had not arrived, enough troops and artillery and a few tanks of the *3d Panzer Grenadier* and *Panzer Lehr Divisions* were on hand to send a column against each of the two key towns, Medebach and Hallenberg.

About 150 panzer grenadiers with four tanks struck Medebach before dawn on 1 April. In the first flush of the attack, they gained a toehold in the western fringes of the town, but a battalion of the 104th Division's 415th Infantry held fast. Organic 57-mm. antitank guns knocked out one German tank; a bazooka accounted for another. The other two and those panzer grenadiers not killed or captured hastily retreated.

At Hallenberg the *Panzer Lehr* attack never got going; it ran head on into an attack by the 9th Division, hurriedly transferred from the adjacent III Corps to strike the supected base of the German breakout offensive. Men of the 39th Infantry, attacking up the road from Hallenberg toward Winterberg, never even knew a German attack was in progress. The drive, the regiment reported, encountered "moderate resistance." "Here," the *LIII Corps* commander, Bayerlein, was to note later, "the enemy seemed to form a point of main effort."[29]

With arrival of part of the *176th Division* later in the day, the Germans at Winterberg launched another thrust early on 2 April. While the *Panzer Lehr* to the southeast and the *176th* to the northeast held the shoulders, the *3d Panzer Grenadier Division* was to make the main effort, again through Medebach.

Medebach was not to be had. Although the panzer grenadiers this time

---

[27] See MS # B–581, *Eleventh Army,* 1–23 April 1945 (Oberst Fritz Estor).

[28] MS # B–593 (Wagener); MS # B–396 (Bayerlein).

[29] Quotations are from VII Corps AAR, Apr 45; MS # B–396 (Bayerlein).

infiltrated around the town in the darkness to hit from both east and west, the men of the 415th Infantry again held fast, killing 30 Germans and capturing 61. The defending battalion itself lost 2 dead and 2 wounded. Part of the force infiltrating around the town machine gunned an artillery battery supporting the 415th but melted away when the artillerymen hastily formed a skirmish line and returned the fire.

The German attack beaten back by midmorning, the 104th Division commander, General Allen, ordered the 415th Infantry to make a counterthrust, driving from Medebach and along another road from the northeast toward Winterberg. When night came, men of the 415th were locked in close combat with remnants of the German force in woods several miles west of Medebach.

The *Panzer Lehr Division,* meanwhile, had failed to do its job of holding the southern shoulder of the German attack. Despite steep hillsides and dense woods, a battalion of the 9th Division's 39th Infantry pushed into Winterberg just as day was breaking. In the town itself, the Germans offered no fight in deference to several hospitals in the town and to hordes of refugees seeking cover there.[30] The most severe fighting occurred in midmorning at a village southwest of Winterberg where infantry of the *Panzer Lehr* supported by a few self-propelled guns launched what men of the 9th Division's 60th Infantry took to be a counterattack. The Germans held the village briefly until a battalion of the 39th Infantry came in on their rear from Winterberg.

Farther north, General Collins had moved the 1st Division to clean out woods and villages close behind the positions of the 3d Armored Division.[31] With three infantry divisions thus in place to hold that part of the corps left flank, any danger that a thrust in no greater strength than that launched by Bayerlein's *LIII Corps* might succeed had passed. Bayerlein's weak force would be hard put even to hold defensive positions on wooded hills west of Winterberg.

As for the *Eleventh Army* and the proposed strike from the vicinity of Kassel, it had become apparent early to the army commander, General Hitzfeld, that the entire scheme had been from the first no more than a fantasy. The Americans were already exerting pressure toward the east and obviously soon would break into the open and jump the Weser. Hitzfeld had scarcely enough men to irritate such a thrust when it came, let alone launch an attack.[32]

By radio Hitzfeld appealed on 3 April to Field Marshal Kesselring to cancel the attack. Kesselring waited to reply until the next day when he could visit Hitzfeld's headquarters. A firsthand look then made the situation all too clear. Kesselring canceled the order but, probably for the record, directed a sub-

---

[30] MS # B–396 (Bayerlein).

[31] In an attack on 30 March near the town of Eisern, S. Sgt. George Peterson and 1st Lt. Walter J. Will, both of Company K of the 1st Division's 18th Infantry, displayed extraordinary heroism. Although wounded, Sergeant Peterson singlehandedly knocked out three German machine gun positions, then fell before enemy fire as he tried to rescue a wounded comrade. Lieutenant Will rescued three of his wounded men from exposed positions, incurring a painful wound himself in the process, then led his platoon in an attack in which he personally eliminated three machine gun positions before receiving mortal wounds. Both were awarded the Medal of Honor posthumously.

[32] MS # B–581 (Estor).

stitute thrust southward into spearheads of the U.S. Third Army. Like the thrust to relieve the Ruhr Pocket, that one too, Kesselring and Hitzfeld both must have known, would never come off in any appreciable strength.

The Ruhr Pocket

Upon the collapse of Bayerlein's counterattack from Winterberg, Field Marshal Model and his staff inside the Ruhr Pocket retained little hope of assistance from the outside.[33] *The Eleventh Army* they deemed too weak to break through. Because the *Twelfth Army* was not even to be activated until 2 April, they saw no chance of help from that quarter, no matter what faith Hitler still might have in it. Their only possibility of escape, most believed, was to break out southward, where the Americans seemed to be weakest. Even that depended on gaining a respite from the fighting, which would come only if the Americans, while concentrating their power in the continuing drive to the east, should try to contain the pocket rather than to erase it.

Under this condition, plans for another try at breakout never passed the talking stage. Even while completing the encirclement of the Ruhr, American commanders, rich in resources, had been adjusting their units in order to move on to the east and at the same time reduce the Ruhr.

By 1 April when the pincers around the pocket snapped shut, Simpson's Ninth Army had one corps already engaged, in effect, in reducing the pocket. Having wheeled southeastward against

the Ruhr after establishing a Rhine bridgehead for the Ninth Army, Anderson's XVI Corps had three infantry divisions in the line. Two were fighting among the houses, apartments, shops, and factories on the fringe of the Ruhr along the north bank of the Rhein–Herne Canal.

On 2 April, after representatives of the First and Ninth Armies established the Ruhr River as the dividing line between them, General Simpson also gave General McLain's XIX Corps a role in the reduction of the Ruhr, but coupled it with a continuing drive to the east. Along with General Gillem's XIII Corps, a portion of the XIX Corps was to drive east, while two divisions attacked southwest from the vicinity of Hamm and Lippstadt toward the Ruhr River.

In the First Army, General Hodges gave the job of renewing the drive east to Collins's VII Corps and Huebner's V Corps. Van Fleet's III Corps, pinched out of a lineup at the Eder reservoir, was to take over from Collins along that part of the periphery of the Ruhr Pocket facing generally west, while headquarters of Ridgway's XVIII Airborne Corps, its job in Operation VARSITY over, shifted to the First Army and assumed command of those units facing northward along the Sieg River. The attack to clear the pocket thus was to be, in essence, a converging attack by the equivalent of four corps.[34]

Splitting the pocket at the Ruhr River gave almost all the heavily built up industrial district to the Ninth Army. There the landscape is so urbanized that one city, grimy from the smoke of steel mill and blast furnace, blends

---

[33] MS # B–593 (Wagener).

[34] For General Bradley's orders, see 12th AGp Ltr of Instrs 20, 4 Apr 45.

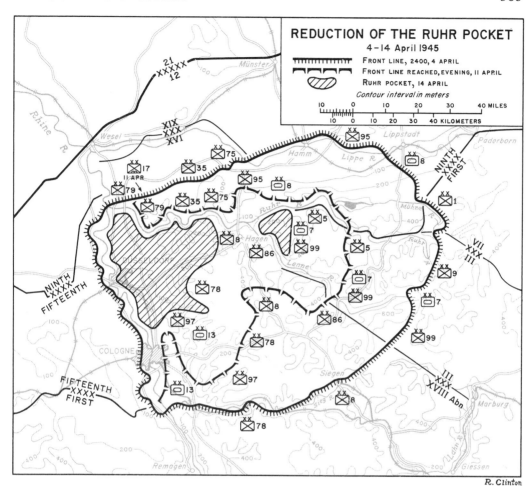

REDUCTION OF THE RUHR POCKET
4-14 April 1945

FRONT LINE, 2400, 4 APRIL
FRONT LINE REACHED, EVENING, 11 APRIL
RUHR POCKET, 14 APRIL
Contour interval in meters

R. Clinton

MAP 5

almost imperceptibly into another—Duisburg, Essen, Gelsenkirchen, Bochum, Dortmund. If the Germans had had sufficient strength, the fighting there could have become a plodding, block-by-block campaign.

South of the Ruhr River, the First Army sector had no such concentration of industrial districts, though there were major cities—Duesseldorf, Wuppertal, the eastern suburbs of Cologne—but it was about three times the size of that of the Ninth Army. It was a sector of rugged terrain—steep hills and gorge-like valleys—at least 80 percent forested —a region known as the Sauerland.

The two corps of the Ninth Army began to attack in earnest on 4 April, the day the Ninth Army passed to control of the 12th Army Group. (*Map 5*) As the drive to clear the pocket began, no pattern emerged in the German defense north of the Ruhr River. As might have been expected the Germans made a con-

INFANTRYMEN OF THE 79TH DIVISION CROSS THE RHEIN-HERNE CANAL

test of it behind the water obstacle of the Rhein–Herne Canal, but once that established position was broken, one city or town might be stoutly defended, another abandoned without a fight.

It took a regiment of the 95th Division four days to clear Hamm, while contingents of the 17th Airborne Division, given a sector alongside the Rhine, walked into Duisburg almost without firing a shot. The 79th Division and other units of the 17th Airborne found no resistance in Essen, site of the great Krupp steel works, while at Dortmund, for no apparent reason, the Germans op-

posed the 75th and 95th Divisions stiffly, sometimes counterattacking with a fervor belying their lost cause. A combat command of the 8th Armored Division forestalled a sharp fight for Soest by making a quick 25-mile end run around the city, so threatening contingents of the *116th Panzer Division* with encirclement that the Germans withdrew. At many small towns the burgomaster came out with a white flag; at others, the Germans fought until overwhelmed. The presence of SS troops more often than not made the difference.

South of the Ruhr River, where the

inhospitable terrain—laced by a limited roadnet passing through dense woods and narrow defiles and dotted with seemingly countless bridges over deep-cut streams—lent itself admirably to defense, resistance followed more conventional delaying tactics. The III Corps began to attack on 5 April, the XVIII Airborne Corps the next day. During the first few days, the Germans defended in some degree almost every town and village and most ridge and stream lines, particularly in the vicinity of Siegen, where several tank-supported counterattacks were apparently designed to keep the 8th Division from breaking into a fairly open corridor leading through the Sauerland, and near Winterberg, where the Germans had concentrated for their attempt at breakout; but as they were pushed back some four to six miles each day, their numbers and their resolution decreased.[35]

By 11 April the Germans were seldom defending ridges or wooded areas; resistance centered only in towns and villages along main roads. Sometimes bridges were left intact even when prepared for demolition. At Wuppertal, an S-2 of the 78th Division used the civilian telephone system to try to talk the mayor into surrender, but in vain. At other places both the 78th and 99th Divisions had greater success by using tank-mounted public address systems to demand surrender. In those later days op-

position almost always centered around a roadblock covered by infantry supported either by a few tanks and assault guns or by antiaircraft pieces, usually 20-mm. "flakwagons." At one point the Germans delayed the 7th Armored Division by blanketing a valley with a dense smoke screen.[36]

Beginning on 7 April days of overcast and light rain gave way to warm sunny weather, enabling planes of the IX and XXIX Tactical Air Commands to aid the mop-up. North of the Ruhr River, the aircraft could make few contributions other than those against isolated strongpoints, both because that part of the pocket shrank fairly rapidly and because pilots now were forbidden to hit a usual primary target, railroad rolling stock (the Allies soon would need all boxcars they could get). Although the ban also applied to planes of the IX Tactical Air Command south of the Ruhr River, the area there was vast enough to provide other targets, particularly columns of foot troops and horse-drawn and motor vehicles retreating or shifting positions.

In the Ninth Army's sector, notably in the zone of the XVI Corps, artillery operating for the first time with unrationed ammunition supplies more than made up for the restrictions on aircraft. Artillery in support of the XVI Corps alone fired 259,061 rounds in fourteen days. Both artillery and air units had to observe the Ruhr River scrupulously as

---

[35] Helping a platoon of the 8th Division's 13th Infantry defend a house in the town of Birken against a local German spoiling attack on 3 April, Pfc. Walter C. Wetzel threw himself on two grenades that the Germans heaved through a window. Taking the full force of the explosions, he died while saving his comrades from injury. He was awarded the Medal of Honor posthumously.

[36] On the first day of the 7th Armored Division's attack, 5 April, Cpl. Thomas J. Kelly, a medical aidman in the 48th Armored Infantry Battalion, made ten trips across ground exposed to heavy German fire to rescue and evacuate casualties of the company to which he was attached. Corporal Kelly was awarded the Medal of Honor.

a "no fire" line lest, in the converging attack, they hit friendly troops.

In the course of the advance almost every division overran a number of military hospitals, and several units liberated prisoner-of-war camps. At Waldbroel, not far north of the Sieg River, the 78th Division freed 71 hospitalized American soldiers, only 2 of whom were able to walk. At Hemer the 7th Armored Division rescued 23,302 prisoners of war, most of them Russians, living under appalling conditions of filth, disease, and hunger. The only Americans, a group of 99, were in fair condition, having been assigned to the camp only a few days. Among the others, deaths were averaging more than a hundred a day.[37]

The advance also freed thousands of forced laborers. In Hagen alone, 16,000; in Wuppertal, 30,000. Almost everywhere the sudden release of these people on the countryside produced incidents of looting and terrorizing. In the III Corps liberated slave laborers so congested the roads that the corps commander ordered them restricted to their compounds. Finding food and transportation for them and for thousands of German prisoners harried quartermasters and transportation officers alike.

In the cities, block after block of rubble attested to the destructive proficiency of Allied bombers, although the effect on German production had been less real than apparent. Machines and facilities were in many cases intact or could be put into operation after relatively minor repairs. Many plants had been moved to protected locations or their operations decentralized into scores of small, isolated buildings often untouched by bombs.

During the course of the attack, command adjustments took place in both the First and Ninth Armies. The 5th Division joined the attack of the III Corps on 9 April, releasing the 9th Division for a rest; arrival of the 13th Armored Division (Maj. Gen. John B. Wogan) on 9 April provided an armored component for the XVIII Airborne Corps. North of the Ruhr, the 194th Glider Infantry Regiment of the 17th Airborne Division reinforced the XIX Corps, while the remainder of the division went to the XVI Corps. To control the glider infantry, the 15th Cavalry Group, the 8th Armored Division, and the 95th Division, while the rest of the XIX Corps participated in the Ninth Army's continuing drive to the east, the corps commander, General McLain, grouped them on 7 April into a task force under the 95th Division commander, General Twaddle. As the two divergent attacks put the two contingents of the XIX Corps ever farther apart—180 miles by 8 April—General Simpson transferred operational control of Task Force Twaddle to Anderson's XVI Corps.[38]

In the First Army, the commanders of both corps tried hard to speed the advance by shaking loose their armored divisions, but it was 12 April before the 7th Armored Division of the III Corps could move out in front of neighboring infantry divisions, and the 13th Armored Division of the XVIII Airborne Corps never did achieve a lightning advance. Committed on 10 April to pass through troops of the 97th Division (Brig. Gen.

---

[37] See 7th Armd and 78th Div AAR's, Apr 45.

[38] See NUSA Ltr of Instrs, 8 Apr 45.

Milton B. Halsey), the 13th Armored was to drive rapidly along relatively flat terrain close by the Rhine to a point east of Cologne, then turn northeast to get in behind those Germans fighting against the 8th, 78th, and 86th (Maj. Gen. Harris M. Melasky) Divisions, deep in the Sauerland. This was the armored division's baptism of fire; only two of its combat commands and little of the division trains had arrived by jump-off time early on 10 April, and both men and equipment were worn out from two road marches totaling more than 260 miles with no time between for rest or servicing equipment. One combat command was down to 50 percent of normal strength in medium tanks.

Pressed by General Hodges to speed the mop-up in order to release units to reinforce the drive to the east, the corps commander, General Ridgway, would approve no pause before the attack; but Ridgway himself, in effect, slowed the attack in advance by ordering the division to "destroy" German forces encountered.[39] Although the order ran contrary to armored doctrine, the division commander, General Wogan, and his subordinates took it literally.

Hardly had the advance begun when communications among various components of the division broke down and some units lost their way. A stream held up the columns as tanks and infantry deployed to "destroy" the enemy. (General Ridgway specifically changed the order on the 12th.) Not until late on 13 April did leading troops reach the point east of Cologne where the division was to change direction to the northeast. By that time the infantry divisions that the armor was to have assisted by trapping the enemy in front of them were already practically on top of the armor's final objectives.[40]

Early on the 14th General Ridgway changed his instructions, telling the armor to continue north generally along the Rhine. Even then bad luck continued to plague the division as the commander, General Wogan, having gone forward to speed removal of a roadblock, was seriously wounded by rifle fire. The former commander of the III Corps, General Millikin, took his place.

Driving past what had been the armored division's objectives and going another ten miles to the north, a battalion of the 8th Division's 13th Infantry late on 14 April reached the Ruhr River at Hattingen, southeast of Essen. Jubilantly, the men shouted across the river to men of the 79th Division's 313th Infantry. On the north bank the last of the Ninth Army's forces had closed to the river, signaling elimination of that part of the Ruhr Pocket. The 13th Infantry's thrust meant that the pocket south of the river was split into two enclaves, the larger to the west embracing the cities of Duesseldorf and Wuppertal.

For the next two days there would still be an occasional sharp engagement in the Ruhr Pocket, but for the most

---

[39] XVIII Airborne Corps Opnl Instrs 7, 091600 Apr 45, found in 8th Div G–3 Jnl file, 9–11 Apr 45.

[40] In an attack by the 97th Division's 386th Infantry on 12 April, Pfc. Joe R. Hastings time after time braved heavy German fire to put his light machine gun in a position to support his company's riflemen. At one point he advanced directly against an enemy position, firing his machine gun from the hip. Killed four days later, Private Hastings was awarded the Medal of Honor posthumously.

RUSSIAN PRISONERS LIBERATED BY THE NINTH ARMY

part a new phase of the battle had begun. It was a time for mass surrenders, a full and final collapse.

"The predominant color was white."

The question of when and how to surrender had been before German staffs and commanders in the Ruhr since the American pincers closed on Easter Sunday, particularly so since failure of the breakout attempts at Winterberg. Yet the belief among most of the staff of *Army Group B* was that the fight was worthwhile because it was holding up the

drive to the east by pinning down eighteen American divisions (four were west of the Rhine).[41]

When news of continuing American advances to the east came on 7 April, this rationale was no longer valid. Field Marshal Model's chief of staff, Generalmajor Karl Wagener, urged Model to spare his troops and the civilians in the Ruhr further fighting by asking Hitler's approval to surrender. This Model declined to do. In the first place, permission hardly would be granted. Further-

[41] MS # B-593 (Wagener). For this period, see also MS # B-614 (Zangen).

GERMAN SOLDIERS ON THE WAY TO A PRISONER-OF-WAR CAMP WITHOUT GUARD

more, Model himself could not reconcile surrender with the demands he had put on his officers and troops through the years. Yet news both within and without the Ruhr Pocket was so utterly devoid of hope that Model continued to struggle with his conscience for a solution. Every life saved was another life capable of taking up the struggle to rebuild Germany. He at last decided, in effect, simply to dissolve *Army Group B* by order. There could be no formal surrender of a command that had ceased to exist.

All youths and older men, Model decreed on 15 April, were to be discharged from the army immediately, provided with discharge papers, and allowed to go home (the order, thousands were to discover, lacked American concurrence). As of two days later, 17 April, when ammunition and supplies presumably would be exhausted, all remaining noncombatant troops were to be free to surrender, while combat soldiers were to be afforded a choice either of fighting in organized goups in an attempt to get out of the pocket or of trying to make their way, either in uniform or civilian clothes but in any case without arms, back to their homes. The latter was a veiled authority to surrender.

Even before this order was issued, sharply increasing numbers of German troops had begun to capitulate. American divisions that in the first few days of April were taking 300, 500, or even 1,000 prisoners a day, by 11 April and the days following were capturing in almost all cases 2,000 and sometimes as many as 5,000. Many a German walked mile after mile before finding an American not too occupied with other duties to bother to accept his surrender. A man from the 78th Division's 310th Infantry started out of Wuppertal with 68 prisoners and discovered, upon arrival at the regimental stockade, that he had 1,200.

The most famous individual to emerge from the Ruhr was taken early. On 10 April, a patrol from the 194th Glider Infantry found Franz von Papen, the German chancellor before Hitler's rise to power, at his estate near Hirschberg, not far from the eastern periphery of the Ruhr Pocket.

On the 13th, having lost all control over subordinate units, the commander of the *Fifteenth Army,* General von Zangen, surrendered along with his staff to the 7th Armored Division, as did General Koechling of the *LXXXI Corps.* The commander and all that remained of the once mighty *Panzer Lehr Division* surrendered on 15 April to the 99th Division.

On 16 April an all-out rush to give up began. People displayed handkerchiefs, bed sheets, table linen, shirts, anything to show intent to surrender. "The predominant color," noted the 78th Division's historian, "was white." [42] While

liberated slave laborers milled about, cheering, laughing, and shouting, glum German civilians, incredulity stamped on their faces, watched silently or sought to ingratiate themselves with the conquerors by insisting that they had never been Nazis, that they were happy the Americans had come. There were no Nazis, no ex-Nazis, not even any Nazi sympathizers any more.

The prisoner-of-war list read like an order of battle, and with the commanders usually came their staffs and remaining troops: Bayerlein of the *LIII Corps,* Luettwitz of the *XLVII Panzer Corps,* Waldenburg of the *116th Panzer Division,* Denkert of the *3d Panzer Grenadier,* Lange of the *183d Volks Grenadier,* commanders of the *180th, 190th,* and *338th Infantry Divisions,* and the final remnants of the *9th Panzer Division.* Paratroopers of the 17th Airborne Division apprehended the commander of the *Fifth Panzer Army,* General Harpe, as he tried to cross a bridge over the Ruhr River in an effort to make his way to German positions in the Netherlands. The commander of the XVIII Airborne Corps, General Ridgway, sent his aide under a white flag to headquarters of *Army Group B* to try to persuade Field Marshal Model to surrender himself and the entire command. Model refused.

The flow of prisoners continued on the 17th—young men, old men, arrogant SS troops, dejected infantrymen, paunchy reservists, female nurses and technicians, teen-age members of the Hitler Youth, stiffly correct, monocled Prussians, enough to gladden the heart of a Hollywood casting director. In every conceivable manner, too, they presented themselves to their captors: most plodding wearily on foot; some in civil-

---

[42] *Lightning,* p. 227.

PRISONERS OF WAR IN THE RUHR POCKET

ian automobiles, assorted military vehicles, or on horseback; some pushing perambulators; one group riding bicycles in precise military formation; a horse-drawn artillery unit with reins taut, horses under faultless control; some carrying black bread and wine; others with musical instruments—accordions, guitars; a few bringing along wives or girl friends in a mistaken hope they might share their captivity. With tears streaming down his face, the officer in charge of a garrison in one town surrendered his command in a formal, parade-ground ceremony.

Prisoner-of-war cages were nothing more than open fields hurriedly fenced with a few strands of barbed wire. Here teeming masses of humanity lolled in the sun, sang sad soldier songs, stared at their captors, picked at lice. Those among them who spoke English offered their services profusely as translators. Some were in high spirits, others bedraggled, downcast. There was nothing triumphant about it; it was instead a gigantic wake watching over the pitiable demise of a once-proud military force.

"Have we done everything to justify our actions in the light of history?"

Field Marshal Model asked his chief of staff on one of those last days. "What is there left to a commander in defeat?"

Model paused, then answered his own question.

"In ancient times," he said, "they took poison." [43]

On 18 April all but a few stragglers gave up, all resistance at an end. Some 317,000 Germans were captured—more than the Russians took at Stalingrad, more even than the total of Germans and Italians taken at the end of the campaign in North Africa. Thousands more, of whom there was no record, had perished in the fighting.

The mop-up cost units of the Ninth Army 341 killed, 121 missing, and not quite 2,000 wounded. The First Army losses probably were about three times as high. [44]

As the battle ended, one of the stragglers was the commanding general of *Army Group B,* Field Marshal Model. Having ordered his staff to disperse, Model himself repaired with his aide and two other officers to a forest north of Duesseldorf.

To those who knew the field marshal intimately, it was a certainty that he would never surrender. He had long been critical of Field Marshal Friedrich Paulus for capitulating at Stalingrad. "A field marshal," he had said then, "does not become a prisoner. Such a thing is just not possible."

During the afternoon of 21 April, Model asked his aide to accompany him and walked deeper into the forest, away from the other two officers. There he shot himself. [45]

---

[43] MS # B–593 (Wagener).

[44] Ninth Army casualty statistics are from *Conquer: The Story of the Ninth Army,* p. 283. The First Army records provide no breakdown of casualties for this particular phase, but a tabulation from various after action reports reveals that the divisions of the III Corps alone had 291 killed, 88 missing, and 1,356 wounded, while a single division of the XVIII Airborne Corps, the 8th, lost 198 killed, 101 missing, and 1,238 wounded.

---

[45] Ltr, Maj Hansgeorg Model to U.S. Army Historical Office, Europe, 29 Mar 66, filed in OCMH. Model's aide buried the field marshal, marked the grave, and after the war identified it for the field marshal's son, who later had the body reinterred in a soldier's cemetery in the Huertgen Forest, among the graves of men the field marshal had commanded.

CHAPTER XVII

Sweep to the Elbe

As the First Army had swung northward to close the pincers around the Ruhr, General Hodges was secure in the knowledge that his right flank and rear would be adequately screened by Patton's Third Army. Having sent the XX Corps across the Rhine at Mainz on 28 March in the last of three major Rhine crossings, Patton by nightfall of the same day had already gained a leg on the assignment of protecting the First Army by driving on Kassel.

Through 28 March, the Third Army's success story could be told pretty much in terms of General Eddy's outsized XII Corps. At the same time, the sudden swing of that corps from the Oppenheim bridgehead almost due north across the Main River had created one of those situations seemingly peculiar to the Third Army that would require some legerdemain to straighten out.

Even as Task Force Baum was fighting for its life at Hammelburg, the rest of the 4th Armored Division on 26 March had begun to exploit the little bridgehead over the Main near Hanau and by nightfall of the 28th had plunged more than thirty miles northward to a point near Giessen. Also under the XII Corps, the 6th Armored Division on the 28th had crossed the Main into a bridgehead won by the 90th Division west of Hanau and by nightfall was

fifteen miles north of the river. Continued advances along these lines by the two armored divisions soon would pinch out both Walker's XX Corps and Middleton's VIII Corps.

As General Bradley adjusted army boundaries on the 28th to turn the First Army north on Paderborn, General Patton solved his problem by juggling units. The 6th Armored Division and the 5th Division, the latter having finished the job of clearing Frankfurt, went to the XX Corps. That move had the effect of splitting the zone that the XII Corps had taken over, giving the left half and the divisions there to the XX Corps. The two corps now could drive side by side on Kassel. Although Middleton's VIII Corps still would be pinched out, Patton could deal with that situation later.

The swift advance by the two U.S. armored divisions reflected the general disruption of the north wing of the enemy's *Seventh Army* that the Third Army's multiple Rhine crossings had produced. By driving north, the armor had cut in behind the *LXXXV Corps* (Kniess), only recently committed to hold the Rhine–Main arc, and the *LXXXIX Corps* (Hoehne), which had turned too late to flee before the Rhine crossings of the VIII Corps and the drive down the autobahn from Limburg by a combat command of the First

Army. The *LXXXIX Corps,* headquarters included, simply disintegrated. Although the staff of the *LXXXV Corps* eventually would make its way to safety, neither the headquarters nor any of its subordinate units would be able to do anything to stop the American armor's headlong dash toward Kassel. As did Hodges' First Army, Patton's Third Army would profit from the great gap created between *Army Groups B* and *G.*[1]

Under terms of the shift to the northeast, the 6th Armored Division of the XX Corps was to head for Kassel while the 4th Armored Division of the XII Corps passed through the northern reaches of the Fulda Gap, a narrow divide between two clusters of wooded hills known as the Vogels Berg and the Hohe Rhoen, and then turned eastward. The 11th Armored Division, committed 29 March on the right wing of the XII Corps, headed directly for the Fulda Gap. In all three cases infantry divisions were to follow closely for the usual mop-up.

For both the 4th and 6th Armored Divisions, the attacks on the next two days, 29 and 30 March, were little more than road marches. For the 11th Armored Division, committed through the Main bridgehead at Hanau, it was much the same, but not until the armor, with the help of infantrymen of the 26th Division, had expanded the bridgehead through great stretches of woods to the east and northeast. This newly created wing of the XII Corps was brushing

against the northern flank of the one fairly cohesive defensive force left to the new commander of the *Seventh Army,* General von Obstfelder. There stood the *LXXXII Corps* (Hahm) with remnants of three divisional formations, charged with holding the line of the Main and containing the bridgeheads at Hanau and Aschaffenburg.[2]

During those two days, General von Obstfelder was trying to piece together an armored force to counterattack into the 4th Armored Division flank. As a nucleus he had a new unit, *Panzer Brigade Thueringen,* a training group with a tank battalion, an assault gun battalion, and a panzer grenadier regiment. He hoped to join that force with the reconnaissance battalion of the *11th Panzer Division,* the only part of the division to reach the *Seventh Army* after leaving *Army Group B.* He counted too on some forty new tanks scheduled to arrive momentarily by rail.

He would never see the tanks. On the 29th they reached an unloading point near Bad Hersfeld, some thirty miles south of Kassel, at about the same time as a column of the 4th Armored Division. The American tanks opened fire. Less than a dozen of the German tanks got away.[3]

When news of this debacle reached Obstfelder, he used it as an excuse to call off his embryonic plan for counterattack. It would be futile in any case, he reasoned, now that the 4th Armored Division flank was protected by an infantry and another armored division. Besides, Obstfelder was sharply conscious of the necessity for sending some force northward to build a line behind

---

[1] See MSS # A–893 (Gersdorff) and # B–703, The Fighting of *Heeresgruppe G* in the West—The Final Battle in Central and Southern Germany Until Capitulation, 22 March 1945–6 May 1945 (Oberst Horst Wilutzky, Opns Officer, *Army Group G*).

[2] MS # A–893 (Gersdorff).
[3] *Ibid.* See also 4th Armd Div AAR, Mar 45.

the Werra River, a tributary of the We-ser, and making some effort, as the high command in Berlin insisted, to establish contact with the *Eleventh Army,* there-by sealing the great gap that had opened between *Army Groups B* and *G.*

Relieving General Kniess from com-mand of the *LXXXV Corps* for his fail-ure to hold the Rhine–Main arc, Obst-felder gave the command—for what it was worth—to General der Panzertrup-pen Smilo Freiherr von Luettwitz and sent the corps to positions behind the Werra in front of the city of Eisenach.[4] The only appreciable strength available to the new commander was the recon-naissance battalion of the *11th Panzer Division,* beefed up with odd collections of artillery, troops with five tanks from an armored training center, and strag-glers. General von Luettwitz did succeed in establishing tenuous contact with contingents of the *Eleventh Army* at Kassel, but it lasted only briefly.

In the center of the *Seventh Army*'s zone, Obstfelder had to use the *XII Corps,* the upgraded *Wehrkreis* head-quarters that had been called to oppose the Oppenheim crossing. Led by Gen-eraloberst Herbert Osterkamp, the corps had little other than *Panzer Bri-gade Thueringen,* which was to absorb stragglers from the *2d Panzer Division* and assume that once-proud division's name. Recognizing that Osterkamp had insufficient strength to do more along his 35-mile front than delay the Ameri-cans temporarily, Obstfelder designated a "combat commander" (*Kampfkom-*

mandant) for the city of Fulda, a grow-ing practice when a city was about to be bypassed or surrounded. All these combat commanders usually had for a city's defense were stragglers, *Volks-sturm,* and any fixed antiaircraft instal-lations that might exist.

To the south of the zone was General Hahm's *LXXXII Corps* with its three makeshift divisions. General Hahm would face not only the right wing of the Third Army but also the left wing of General Patch's U.S. Seventh Army.

Throughout the *Seventh Army* zone, signal and supply services had broken down. For communications, command-ers frequently used the civilian tele-phone network; for supplies, they scrounged from army, Luftwaffe, or SS installations. The troops were sometimes shocked at what they found in those depots—in one, 95,000 pairs of fur-lined boots, something the men had been beg-ging for the preceding winter in the mud and snow of the West Wall. To meet gasoline needs, the units appropri-ated the hoarded stocks of Nazi party officials. "Flight fuel," the troops bitterly called it.

As German commanders made their arrangements, dutifully drawing tidy boundary lines and spotting units on operations maps as if it all had some meaning, the armor of the XX Corps and the XII Corps drove relentlessly toward the northeast. So heavy was the collection of American armor that Gen-eral von Obstfelder reckoned the drive to be either a race to beat the Russians to Berlin or an Allied main effort to link with the Russians and split Ger-many in two.[5]

---

[4] Not to be confused with the commander of the *XLVII Panzer Corps.* For the *LXXXV Corps,* see MS # B–617, Combat Report of the *LXXXV Corps* (General der Panzertruppen Smilo Freiherr von Luettwitz).

[5] MS # A–893 (Gersdorff).

During midafternoon of 30 March, in a roadside meeting, the XX Corps commander, General Walker, told the 6th Armored Division's General Grow to make a dash for Kassel. If resistance proved firm, Walker said, Grow was to leave the city to the infantry, jump the Fulda River, and continue to the east.

By nightfall of that day Grow's division was only six miles short of Kassel, holding a bridge captured intact across the Eder River. The next day, the 31st, the leading combat command began to meet organized resistance. It came from part of the *166th Infantry Division,* the unit Hitler had sent from Denmark, and various makeshift units available to the combat commander of Kassel. While continuing the attack through the day and into the night, General Grow prepared for a shift to the east by sending another combat command toward the Fulda River. Armored infantrymen after nightfall forced a crossing of the river under machine gun fire.

The 4th Armored Division of the XII Corps by nightfall of the 31st was only a few miles from the Werra River southwest of Eisenach. The 11th Armored Division meanwhile gained high ground overlooking the city of Fulda.

Leading units having reached those positions, the Third Army had come abreast of the easternmost positions held by the First Army. If Patton's columns continued eastward with the same momentum, they soon would outdistance a First Army that would have to regroup after encircling the Ruhr before turning part of its strength to the east.

Although General Bradley saw a need to halt the Third Army until the First was ready to drive alongside, he had received vague but enticing information

from a German officer deserter, apprehended west of the Rhine by the 4th Armored Division, that a high-level German headquarters or communications center was to be found some thirty miles beyond the Werra River in the town of Ohrdruf, a few miles south of Gotha. Told by planners of the First Allied Airborne Army that they would be unable to mount an airborne assault on the town on short notice, both Bradley and General Eisenhower agreed to give Patton free rein for another twenty-four hours in hope of seizing Ohrdruf.[6]

The next day, Easter Sunday, the urge for Ohrdruf and whatever mystery its capture might reveal proved stronger than the urge to hold back the Third Army to await a new drive by the First. Although the 4th Armored Division seized a bridgehead across the Werra River and the 11th Armored Division came almost abreast farther south, both divisions still were about twenty miles from Ohrdruf when in late afternoon General Bradley telephoned the news that the armor could keep going until Ohrdruf was in hand.

Against resistance that now could be considered normal—roadblocks manned by motley contingents of infantrymen, antiaircraft artillerymen, *Volkssturm,* whatever; an occasional tank or self-propelled gun; sometimes a quick strafing run by one or two Me 109's; blown bridges—one combat command of the 4th Armored Division headed for Gotha, the other for Ohrdruf. The head of CAA's column at one point ran into an ambush; in rapid succession two bat-

---

[6] Gay Diary, entry of 31 Mar 45. See also Dyer, *XII Corps,* p. 398; Koyen, *The Fourth Armored Division,* p. 115; and combat interview with Lt Col Hal C. Pattison, ExecO CCA, 4th Armd Div.

WHITE FLAGS HANG ABOVE A DESERTED STREET

teries of 88's knocked out seven tanks and four half-tracks. Yet civilian authorities surrendered Gotha without a fight on the morning of 4 April (men of a small military garrison were discovered later masquerading as patients in the city hospitals), and CCA moved on in the afternoon to take Ohrdruf. (*Map XV*)

They found at least part of what they had been expecting in Ohrdruf—an immense underground communications center set in deep concrete tunnels, with radio facilities, cables, and telephone switchboards large enough to serve a small city.[7] It had been constructed as a headquarters for the Armed Forces High Command (OKW) during tense days preceding the Czechoslovakian crisis in 1938, but never used. In recent weeks the Reichsfuehrer SS, Heinrich Himmler, had ordered the facilities expanded as a possible retreat for Hitler and his entire entourage, to be presented to the Fuehrer for his birthday on 20

[7] Koyen, *The Fourth Armored Division*, p. 115; CCA, 4th Armd Div, AAR, Apr 45.

April; but work had hardly begun before the Americans arrived.[8]

The men of the 4th Armored Division unknowingly had missed by hours a chance to capture important live prey at Ohrdruf. Less than twenty-four hours earlier, Field Marshal Kesselring and headquarters of *OB WEST* had fled the town.[9]

The 4th Armored found something else at Ohrdruf. On the fringe of the town, the soldiers came upon the first of the notorious concentration camps to be uncovered by the advancing Allied armies. Small by the standards of others to be discovered later, the camp nevertheless contained enough horror to make the American soldier and even his Supreme Commander, General Eisenhower, pale. Patton, when he saw it, vomited. Forced by the XX Corps commander, General Walker, to tour the camp, the burgomaster of Ohrdruf and his wife went home and hanged themselves.[10]

Elsewhere in the Third Army during those first days of April there were sometimes fierce engagements with die-hard defenders, other times unopposed advances sweeping up docile Germans left behind in the rapid thrusts of the armor. In most cases the nature of the defense depended not so much on the number of troops available as on the character of the local commander. If a true Nazi, thoroughly indoctrinated, he saw to it

that the men under him fought back; otherwise there might be only token opposition or none at all, a weary acceptance of the inevitable.

During the last day of March and the first two of April, General Brenner and the survivors of his *6th SS Mountain Division,* bypassed in the swift American drive, tried to fight their way out to the east, in the process capturing an American field hospital.[11] On 2 April one battalion of the 26th Division was sufficient to clear Fulda; at Kassel, the entire 80th Division had to fight fiercely for the better part of four days before a defiant German garrison surrendered on 4 April. On several occasions at Kassel the Germans counterattacked sharply with infantry supported by as many as ten tanks, apparently drawn from the big Henschel tank works in the city. As at other industrial cities, fixed antiaircraft batteries firing deadly flak bolstered the defense.

On the south flank of the XII Corps, the 2d Cavalry Group on 2 April entered Bad Orb, liberating 6,500 Allied prisoners of war, half of them Americans. Farther east, a battalion of the 11th Armored Division overran a Walther small arms factory, finding enough pistols—including many of one of the war's most prized souvenirs, the P38—to equip almost every man in the division.

As the Third Army paused, General Patton inserted Middleton's VIII Corps back into the lineup between the XX Corps on the left and the XII Corps on the right, again juggling divisions in the process. While some units completed mop-up of rear areas, others made local

[8] General Bruce C. Clarke (USA, Ret.), *The Command, Control and Communications National System of Germany During World War II* (Menlo Park, Calif.: Stanford Research Institute, 1963), pp. 11, 18.

[9] MS # C–020 (Schramm).

[10] See Koyen, pp. 115–16; Patton, *War As I Knew It*, pp. 292–94; see also Toland, *The Last 100 Days*, p. 371.

[11] See above, ch. XVI.

advances to secure better positions for the new jump-off once the order came.

In one of these local operations, a battalion of the 90th Division's 358th Infantry occupied the village of Merkers, west of the Werra River, southwest of Eisenach, and made one of the war's more sensational finds. By chance the men discovered that in a nearby salt mine the Germans had hidden almost all the nation's gold reserve, great stores of German and foreign currency, and hundreds of priceless works of art. At Meiningen on the Werra, other troops of the XII Corps captured the central records depository for all prisoners of war in Germany. Far to the rear, a Quartermaster detachment accepted the surrender of the commander of the *LXXXIX Corps,* General Hoehne, whose command had disintegrated before the Rhine crossing of the VIII Corps.[12]

A New Allied Main Effort

The pause in the Third Army's operations coincided with the Supreme Commander's return of General Simpson's Ninth Army to the 12th Army Group. With this transfer on 4 April, General Bradley had under his command 4 field armies, 12 corps, and 48 divisions—more than 1,300,000 troops, the largest exclusively American field command in U.S. history.[13] Using this powerful force, Bradley was, while reducing the Ruhr, to cut a wide swath across the center of

Germany in the general direction of Leipzig and Dresden in a new Allied main effort aimed at splitting Germany in two by linking with the Russians.

The main role in the new drive fell to Hodges' First Army in the center, a thrust directly east on Leipzig, to be followed by a crossing of the Elbe east of Leipzig. The Third Army also was to drive eastward, aiming for Chemnitz, but was to be prepared to turn later to the southeast. Unaware of General Eisenhower's decision to forgo a drive on Berlin, the Ninth Army commander, Simpson, and many of his subordinates deduced that the Ninth Army had drawn the choice objective, the grand prize, Berlin. General Bradley's formal order, issued on 4 April, inferred as much. Once the Ninth Army had seized a bridgehead over the Elbe, Simpson was to "be prepared to continue the advance on Berlin or to the northeast." [14]

In conjunction with the new main effort, the Second British Army on the Ninth Army's left was to strike for that part of the Elbe extending from the coast to Wittenberge, eighty miles upstream from the great port of Hamburg. The First Canadian Army meanwhile was to aim for the coast from the mouth of the Weser westward. With its left wing, the Canadian army was to drive north from the vicinity of Arnhem some thirty miles to the IJsselmeer (Zuider Zee), thereby cutting off any Germans left in the western part of the Netherlands.[15]

As the Ninth Army passed to the 12th Army Group's control before daylight on 4 April, both the 5th Armored and

---

[12] Dyer, *XII Corps,* p. 406; Patton, *War As I Knew It,* pp. 287, 291–92; Eisenhower, *Crusade in Europe,* pp. 407–08. See also Toland, *The Last 100 Days,* p. 364.

[13] Bradley's command included the Fifteenth Army west of the Rhine with two corps and six divisions.

[14] 12th AGp Ltr of Instrs 20, 4 Apr 45.

[15] Montgomery, *Normandy to the Baltic,* pp. 261–63; Stacey, *The Victory Campaign,* pp. 539, 546.

84th Divisions of General Gillem's XIII Corps, forming the army's left wing, reached a great westward loop of the Weser River near Minden, almost due west of the metropolis of Hannover. The 2d Armored Division of General Mc-Lain's XIX Corps, having run into delaying action by remnants of the *First Parachute Army* in the Teutoburger Wald, would arrive at the Weser later in the day near Hameln (Hamelin), the town which the Pied Piper reputedly rid of rats and children. Mopping up resistance in the Teutoburger Wald, the 30th Division was soon to press forward behind the armor. Even though part of the Ninth Army was helping to reduce the Ruhr Pocket, General Simpson still could provide for the eastward drive these four divisions plus the 102d, which had begun to cross the Rhine, and the 83d, recently relieved from the fight for the Ruhr.

The forces of General Hodges' First Army that would be available for the eastward thrust once regrouping had been completed consisted of the 3d Armored, 1st, and 104th Divisions in Collins's VII Corps on the left and the 9th Armored, 2d, and 69th Divisions in Huebner's V Corps on the right. The First Army was to take over Kassel from the Third Army once the city was clear, broadening the frontage for the First Army's main effort to approximately thirty miles.

As the Third Army paused, its forward line formed an east-facing arc from Muehlhausen in the north, through Gotha and Ohrdruf, back to Meiningen in the south. Following the shuffle of divisions to bring headquarters of the VIII Corps back into action, Walker's XX Corps on the left had both the 4th

and 6th Armored Divisions, plus the 76th and 80th Infantry Divisions; Middleton's VIII Corps in the center, the 65th, 87th, and 89th Divisions; and Eddy's XII Corps, the 11th Armored, 26th, and 90th Divisions, plus a newcomer to the front, the 71st (Maj. Gen. Willard G. Wyman). Another new division, the 70th (Maj. Gen. Allison J. Barnett), was mopping up rear areas and providing security for bridges over the Rhine.

That portion of central Germany facing the 12th Army Group provided two ready avenues leading eastward, one on either side of the storied Harz Mountains. Once a stronghold of paganism, in more modern times a tourist retreat, the Harz, rising higher than 3,000 feet, served as anchor for the boundary between the First and Ninth Armies. The Ninth Army on the north could advance across low, rolling country providing ready access to Magdeburg on the Elbe, while south of the Harz the First Army and the north wing of the Third could utilize the wide Thueringen Plain for their drives on Leipzig and Chemnitz. The Third Army's right wing would find the terrain less hospitable; here, extending southeastward from the vicinity of Eisenach, stands the Thueringer Wald, a spinelike range of forested mountains with many heights above 3,000 feet.

Having already jumped the Fulda and Werra Rivers, the Third Army faced no more formidable water obstacles. Both the First and Ninth Armies still had to get across the Weser, which, like the Rhine and Elbe, is a sprawling waterway, and the First Army's right wing would have to cross lower reaches of the Werra River as well.

Except for Leipzig—then Germany's fifth city—and an intermediate objective, Halle, the bigger cities lay in the zone of the Ninth Army—Hannover, ancient seat of the Hannoverian kings, Braunschweig (Brunswick), and Magdeburg. The Third Army faced smaller cities—Erfurt, Weimar, Jena.

From the standpoint of German units available for the defense, the shift of Allied main effort from the north wing to the center was unquestionably well advised. Almost all of *Army Group B,* plus the south wing of the *First Parachute Army,* having been encircled in the Ruhr, and the north wing of *Army Group G* having been pushed back rudely by the Third Army's swift crossings of the Rhine, the armies of the 12th Army Group faced a vast gap with nothing but the hastily constituted *Eleventh Army* (Hitzfield) to plug it. Although Hitler had issued his fanciful order to form a new army, the *Twelfth,* to assemble in the Harz Mountains and drive to the relief of *Army Group B,* most of the troops designated to fill the new divisions were in officer training schools and replacement training centers east of the Elbe and had yet to head for the Harz. Not until 6 April would Hitler even settle on a commander for the new army, General der Panzertruppen Walter Wenck, who was recuperating in a Bavarian resort from injuries incurred in an automobile accident.[16]

The Role of the Third Army

As the Third Army paused, General Patton shifted his infantry divisions to the fore to be prepared if a new crust of resistance should form. He also sent the 11th Armored Division of the XII Corps in a one-day advance to the southeast to get out of the worst of the mountainous terrain of the Thueringer Wald into the southwestern foothills whence the division would later continue the drive to the southeast. This shift was in keeping with the plan to turn the entire Third Army eventually to the southeast.

On the Third Army's north wing, the 76th and 80th Divisions, as well as the 6th Armored, which had paused at Muehlhausen, absorbed a series of small counterattacks, in one case involving close to a thousand infantry supported by more than a dozen tanks. The stabs represented a feeble attempt by General Hitzfeld's *Eleventh Army* to carry out Field Marshal Kesselring's dictum to counterattack into the north flank of the Third Army in exchange for permission to abandon the drive from Kassel to reach *Army Group B* in the Ruhr.[17] Although the Americans had to relinquish one village temporarily, the darting thrusts required no realignment of forces.

At last free on 10 April to get on with the offensive, Patton turned the 11th Armored Division loose for its drive along the southwestern slopes of the Thueringer Wald and gave the infantry divisions a day to break a band of resistance protecting the city of Erfurt. On the 11th as the 80th Division drove into Erfurt, the 4th Armored Division pushed eight miles beyond the infantry's lines along the autobahn south of Erfurt, while the 6th Armored Division exploited the gap between the enemy's

---

[16] MSS # B-606 (Reichhelm); # B-581 (Estor). Ryan in *The Last Battle,* pages 274-76, tells of Wenck's appointment.

[17] See above, ch. XVI; MS # B-581 (Estor).

GERMAN PRISONERS HEAD FOR THE REAR *as American armor advances.*

Eleventh Army and *Army Group G's Seventh Army* for the day's most noteworthy advance. In rapid strides, General Grow's armor drove fifty miles, halting for the night only after seizing bridges intact across the Saale River north of Jena.

The next day the 6th Armored Division advanced another fifteen miles and crossed the Weisse Elster River near the city of Zeitz. This time the advance was markedly difficult; the armor was brushing against the southern end of a broad belt of fixed antiaircraft defenses forming a semicircle before Leipzig.

At the same time the 4th Armored Division, bypassing Jena and the battlefield where Napoleon had defeated the Prussians in 1806, picked up momentum to reach points flanking the autobahn more than five miles beyond Jena. While the 80th Division's 318th Infantry cleared stubborn defenders from Erfurt, the city of Weimar, capital of the shortlived Weimar Republic, capitulated as a flight of fighter-bombers hovered overhead to give weight to a surrender ultimatum. The defenders of Jena, other men of the 80th Division discovered as night fell, would elect to fight. The city

GERMAN CIVILIANS, *forced to disinter victims of a concentration camp from a mass grave, carry them through the streets for reburial.*

would be in hand nevertheless before another day had passed.

In the course of the day's advance, the 4th Armored Division's CCB uncovered one of Nazi Germany's largest concentration camps northwest of Weimar at Buchenwald. Aside from the horror that was common to all the camps, this one merited special notoriety because the commandant's wife, Ilse Koch, collected the tattooed skin of prisoners to make ornaments and lamp shades.

Also on 12 April Patton's superiors, Eisenhower and Bradley, visited the Third Army commander. After touring the treasure cave at Merkers and the concentration camp at Ohrdruf, they retired in the evening to Patton's command trailer, where General Eisenhower confided that Patton was to stop his victorious armor short of the objective of Chemnitz. Pending detailed arrangements for meeting the Russians, the Third Army was to halt at the Mulde River, ten miles west of Chemnitz, roughly on a north-south line with that part of the Elbe River to be reached by the Ninth Army. The First Army, too, was to halt at the Mulde. Eisenhower had made up his mind to make no attempt to take Berlin.[18]

Before the three commanders went to sleep, they learned the news that during the day had shocked their nation and the world. The Commander in Chief, Mr. Roosevelt, was dead.[19]

It took General Walker's XX Corps, with the 4th Armored Division moving into the lead, only one more day to reach the Mulde. By nightfall of the 13th General Hoge's combat commands had seized four bridges intact across the river and carved out holdings large enough to protect the bridges. Middleton's VIII Corps, with no armor to spearhead the advance, would make it to the Mulde on the 17th. Eddy's XII Corps meanwhile had taken the city of Coburg on the 11th after a night of unceasing artillery fire and a hovering aerial threat similar to that at Weimar, and on the 14th entered Bayreuth at the southeastern tip of the Thueringer Wald. There the XII Corps too paused to await a new order turning the entire Third Army to the southeast.

A Bridgehead to Nowhere

On the other flank of the 12th Army Group's new drive, in the meantime, General Simpson's Ninth Army was under no obligation to pause until its divisions had crossed the Weser River and reached a point as far to the east as the Third Army's starting line east of Ohrdruf. Imbued with a sense of urgency because the army group's orders indicated that the eventual goal was Berlin, units of both the XIII Corps on the left and the XIX Corps attacked with a special fervor.[20]

Despite unusual efforts to seize a bridge intact across the 255-foot width of the Weser, nobody succeeded. With the assistance of the attached 119th Infantry of the 30th Division, a combat command of the 2d Armored Divi-

---

[18] See Toland, *The Last 100 Days*, p. 371.
[19] Eisenhower, *Crusade in Europe*, p. 409; Bradley, *A Soldier's Story*, p. 541; Patton, *War As I Knew It*, pp. 294–95.

---

[20] This attitude is clearly evident in official records of the period.

sion nevertheless quickly established a bridgehead near Hameln early on 5 April against only a smattering of small arms fire. The rest of the 30th Division followed quickly to clear knots of suicidal resistance from the picturesque river town.[21]

The adjacent 84th Division of the XIII Corps also tried a crossing on the 5th but abandoned it in the face of shelling directed on exposed approach routes to the river from a high east-west ridgeline, the Wesergebirge, that split the division's sector. Moving before dawn on the 6th to another site, a battalion of 84th Division infantrymen paddled across without a sound from the enemy other than erratic firing by a 20-mm. antiaircraft gunner apparently trying to calm his own nerves with noise. A second battalion crossing a few minutes later drew fire in the fading dark, but not a man was hit.

Like most of the 12th Army Group, the men of the Ninth Army were striking into a vacuum. The *XLVII Panzer Corps* that might have been expected to defend the Weser in this sector had been trapped with *Army Group B* in the Ruhr. The rest of General Blumentritt's *First Parachute Army* was falling back to the northeast in front of the British. The only troops immediately available to hold the Weser's east bank were in makeshift formations belonging to *Wehrkreis VI*, which technically was under command of Hitzfeld's feeble *Eleventh Army*.[22]

Seeing that the American thrust had virtually severed communications between General Blaskowitz's *Army Group H*, which included the *First Parachute Army*, and Field Marshal Kesselring at *OB WEST*, OKW on the same day that the 84th Division crossed the Weser, 6 April, removed the northern army group from Kesselring's control. Henceforth, *Army Group H* was to be known as *Oberbefehlshaber Nordwest (OB NORDWEST)*, directly subordinate to OKW. The commander was to be Field Marshal Ernst Busch, a veteran of the Russian front who most recently had handled defense of Germany's north coast. Blaskowitz was shifted to become *Oberbefehlshaber* of the Netherlands, subordinate to Field Marshal Busch, an indication of Hitler's continuing disenchantment with Blaskowitz, which had been demonstrated earlier when he sent General Student to lead a counterattack by Blaskowitz's troops.[23]

While Kesselring retained authority over the rest of the Western Front, Busch was to command everything in the north, including men of the Navy and the Luftwaffe, an unusual procedure. For defending the Weser from Hameln to the coast (a line already breached), Busch was to have a hastily created special force called *Army Blumentritt*. The commander, General Blumentritt, was to assume control of units

---

[21] In the advance on Hameln, a platoon leader in the 30th Division's 119th Infantry, 1st Lt. Raymond O. Beaudoin, was killed while making a one-man charge to eliminate German fire that was raking his platoon. Lieutenant Beaudoin was awarded the Medal of Honor posthumously.

[22] MS # B-354 (Blumentritt); MS # B-217, Central Germany From 22.3.1944 to 11.5.1945 (General der Infanterie Mattenklott, Comdr, *Wehrkreis VI*).

[23] See above, ch. XV; MS # B-354 (Blumentritt); MS # B-414 *A GP H (OB NW)*, 10 Mar-9 May 45 (Oberst Rolf Geyer); Kesselring, *A Soldier's Record*, p. 315.

and staffs of *Wehkreise VI* and *XI,* plus some naval troops in the downstream sector near Bremen.[24]

While the Germans thus played at shuffling essentially paper commands, the 2d Armored Division of the XIX Corps dealt in tangibles called power and speed. Long anxious to be turned loose toward Berlin, the division commander, General White, had directed his operations officer to prepare a plan even before the division crossed the Rhine. His army commander, General Simpson, was equally enthusiastic. Judging from the eager way the men in the tanks and the half-tracks took off from the Weser, the zeal of their commanders had passed down the line without diminution.

It took the armor just one day (6 April) to traverse the eighteen miles from the Weser to the little Leine River. The Leine was a phase line established by General Bradley as a means of control to release his three horses—the First, Third, and Ninth Armies—from the starting gate at the same time. Although obligated to pause along the Leine until given the starting signal, the eager 2d Armored made a point of seizing bridges intact across both the Leine and another river ten miles farther east before coming to a full halt the next day, 7 April.

The two infantry divisions of the XIX Corps—the 30th and 83d—meanwhile made their way to the Leine. To the north the 84th Division of the XIII Corps, having completed a bridge over

the Weser late on the 7th, reached the Leine on the 8th. There the infantry crossed on a bridge seized intact by the 11th Cavalry Group northwest of Hannover. In the process the division captured a German soldier who was carrying a map of Hannover's defenses. These, the map revealed, were concentrated in the southwest and south. Before daylight on 10 April, the men of the 84th moved against the city from the northwest and north, clearing it by midafternoon. Acres of rubble from Allied bombing and thousands of foreign laborers made overly exuberant by looted liquor posed more problems than did the Germans.

As with the Third Army, the word to resume the eastward drive reached units of the Ninth Army on the 9th. General White's armor in the center of the XIX Corps the next day made about twenty miles, despite a brief but violent encounter with sixty-seven big antiaircraft guns arrayed to protect the Hermann Goering Steel Works southwest of Braunschweig. While the 83d Division continued eastward on the right wing of the corps, dropping off a regiment to deal with that part of the Harz Mountains in the Ninth Army's zone, the 2d Armored Division's Combat Command B on 11 April broke free.

The men of CCB and their commander, Brig. Gen. Sidney R. Hinds, were imbued with one thought: get a bridge across the Elbe. Overtaking fleeing German columns, sweeping aside the defenders of roadblocks with blasts from the cannon of their tanks, surprising *Volkssturm* defenders who could but gape in bewilderment and then throw down their newly acquired arms, the tanks and half-tracks of CCB drove relentlessly eastward.

---

[24] This force was first commanded by General Student and called *Army Student,* but four days later Student and Blumentritt exchanged commands. MSS # B–354 (Blumentritt) and # B–414 (Geyer).

In late afternoon an attached contingent of the division's reconnaissance squadron raced into a western suburb of Magdeburg, startling civilian shoppers. After dark a column of tanks commanded by Maj. James F. Hollingsworth made a run for a bridge across the Elbe southeast of Magdeburg at Schoenebeck, but the Germans who had been fleeing suddenly turned to fight. Although Hollingsworth's tanks got within a few feet of the bridge, they at last had to fall back in the face of determined German fire. Before a new attack with infantry could reach the bridge, the Germans demolished it.

The first news of CCB's exploits to reach headquarters in the rear arrived shortly after 2000 the evening of 11 April. The message was laconic, but it said all that needed to be said: "We're on the Elbe." During the day, CCB had traveled fifty-seven airline miles, seventy-three when measured by road.

Making such extensive use of captured German vehicles, military and civilian, that news correspondents nicknamed them the "Rag Tag Circus," men of General Macon's 83d Division were only a step behind the armor. Late on the 12th, men who themselves preferred another nickname, the "83d Armored Division," reached the Elbe a few miles upstream from Schoenebeck at Barby. About the same time, the armor of the XIII Corps, General Oliver's 5th Armored Division, having pushed past the 84th Division at Hannover, rolled up to the Elbe fifty miles downstream from Magdeburg at Tangermuende, only fifty-three miles from Berlin. As tankers and armored infantrymen swarmed toward a bridge that still stood, the Germans destroyed it.

The 30th Division meanwhile cleared Braunschweig after a fight with flak guns on the western approaches, and the 84th and 102d Divisions advanced in the wake of the armor of the XIII Corps. But the most important news after night fell on the 12th again came from the 2d Armored Division. Using dukws hastily brought forward, two battalions of armored infantry slipped quietly across the sprawling Elbe at Westerhausen, just south of Magdeburg. Not a shot sounded from the far shore.

Not to be outdone, men of the 83d Division, the Rag Tag Circus, fought hard through the 12th to clear a stubborn contingent of Germans from Barby on the Elbe (the 329th Infantry lost 24 men killed, 5 missing, 35 wounded), then in early afternoon of 13 April sent two battalions of infantrymen across the river in assault boats behind a heavy smoke screen. It was "just like a Sunday afternoon picnic with no fire of any kind." [25] The regimental commander, Col. Edwin B. Crabill, went up and down the west bank, exhorting the men to get going. "Don't waste the opportunity of a lifetime," he shouted. "You are on your way to Berlin." [26]

Colonel Crabill did not know it, nor did even the Ninth Army commander, General Simpson, but he and his men were not on their way to Berlin. Their Supreme Commander had already made and would soon reaffirm the decision that was to turn their holdings into a bridgehead to nowhere.

---

[25] Combat interview with 1st Lt William Stout. Several interviews deal with this action.

[26] Combat interview with Crabill.

INFANTRYMEN RIDE AN ARMORED CAR IN THE RACE TO THE ELBE

A Flak-Infested Route to the Mulde

The role of the First Army in the 12th Army Group's eastward drive meanwhile had developed according to the location of the divisions of the V and VII Corps when the attack to seal off the Ruhr came to an end. In General Collins's VII Corps on the left, the 3d Armored Division took the lead. Starting to drive eastward on 5 April, the division encountered stubborn resistance at numerous roadblocks the next day from remnants of the *Ersatzbrigade Westfalen,* which had proved such a persistent foe near Paderborn, and reached the Weser on 7 April only to find all bridges destroyed.

In General Huebner's V Corps, the 2d and 69th Infantry Divisions headed the advance. Ordered first to relieve troops of the Third Army in Kassel, the 69th Division began its eastward drive as darkness was approaching on the 5th. In a region of wooded hills in an angle formed by confluence of the Fulda and Werra Rivers, which meet at the town of Hann-Muenden to form the Weser, the division almost immediately ran into those Germans that constituted the best of General Hitzfeld's *Eleventh Army,* the *LXVII Corps.* Nowhere did they give in without a fight. Not until late on the 7th was Hann-Muenden cleared and were crossings gained over the Werra there and upstream.

It was the happy chance of the 2d Division in the meantime to strike the weakest part of the *Eleventh Army* defense before the Weser. Little more than the garrison of a training center at Hofgeismar, ten miles from the river, barred the way. There the Germans on 5 April fought tenaciously, but the next day the division's 23d Infantry reached the Weser. Crossing unopposed in assault boats moments after darkness fell, rifle companies pushed quickly to a towering wooded ridgeline a mile to the east. The First Army had gained a bridgehead only a day behind the Ninth Army.

On the 7th, a battalion of the 104th Division used the 2d Division's bridge to provide a first crossing of the Weser for the VII Corps, followed later by assault crossings by other contingents of the 104th and by units of the 1st Division on the north wing of the corps. Only intermittent and generally ineffective machine gun fire posed any threat to the crossings. The 2d Division meanwhile extended its bridgehead to a depth of six miles against resistance no more formidable than that posed by a hastily formed battalion including men impressed from mental hospitals. By nightfall of the 7th, concern that the enemy might have formed a solid position anywhere along the Weser had been dispelled.

The fact was just as apparent to the German commander, General Hitzfeld, as to his adversaries. Without bothering to seek approval from *OB WEST,* Hitzfeld told his units to begin a step-by-step withdrawal to the Leine River, thirteen miles east of the Weser, there to try again to make a stand. He then compromised that position immediately by declaring the east-bank university town of Goettingen an open city because of thousands of hospitalized soldiers there.

Hardly were his orders disseminated when Hitzfeld relinquished command of the *Eleventh Army* to General Lucht, who as commander of the *LXVI Corps* had narrowly escaped capture in March

CROSSING OF THE WESER RIVER BY MEN OF THE 1ST INFANTRY DIVISION

when his command post west of the Rhine had been overrun.[27] This was no prejudicial relief of Hitzfeld; Lucht had been earmarked all along to command the *Eleventh Army* but had been unavailable earlier. General Hitzfeld returned to command of the *LXVII Corps.*[28]

General Lucht had been in his post only a few hours on 8 April when new orders arrived from his commander in chief, Field Marshal Kesselring. In keeping with Hitler's grandiose scheme for a counteroffensive from the Harz Mountains to relieve *Army Group B* in the Ruhr, all available troops were to withdraw into the Harz, where they were to turn the wooded region into a fortress to be held until General Wenck's hastily forming *Twelfth Army* could arrive to start the counteroffensive. To gain time to prepare the Harz for defense, the *Eleventh Army* was to defend the Leine River "under all circumstances." [29]

---

[27] See above, ch. X.
[28] MS # B-581 (Estor).

[29] *Ibid.* See also MS # B-606 (Reichhelm).

How impossible to execute was the latter, if not the first, part of the order was amply demonstrated within the day as men of the 2d Division seized a bridge intact across the Leine outside Goettingen and pushed rapidly beyond the undefended university town. The 69th Division too crossed the Leine, though without benefit of a bridge. On the 9th both divisions drove more than ten miles to the east. The 2d Division occupied Duderstadt, east of Goettingen, liberating 600 Allied prisoners of war, including a hundred Americans (another 44 had died within the last month from malnutrition); the 69th captured Heiligenstadt, a few miles to the southwest.

A day behind the V Corps in crossing the Weser, General Collins of the VII Corps made up the time by committing his armor early on 9 April. Resistance in rolling wooded country along the left wing was occasionally strong; at one point a dozen Mark V and Tiger Royal tanks knocked out five of the 3d Armored Division's Shermans, but as night came the armor held a bridgehead over the Leine at Northeim.

For the First Army, there was to be no pause at the Leine, because the arrival of its divisions there coincided with General Bradley's release of all restrictions on eastward movement, effective on the 10th. In the VII Corps, the 3d Armored Division continued to pace the drive, while General Huebner committed the 9th Armored Division to take the lead in the V Corps.

For the Germans, the object was to try to get as many men as possible into the Harz Mountains, to hold there in keeping with the myth that the *Twelfth Army* soon would arrive to set every-thing right again. All contingents of Lucht's *Eleventh Army* except Hitzfeld's *LXVII Corps* tried to reach the mountains on the 10th. Hitzfeld's corps drew an equally impossible assignment of building a line from the Harz eastward to Halle, in order to keep the American forces from turning north-eastward behind the Harz and thereby denying the *Twelfth Army* its destination. Although the German generals involved admitted to themselves the futility of it all, they somehow were able to close their minds to reality and try to bring it off.[30]

As General Collins set the 1st Division to sweeping the mountains systematically from the west, to be joined a few days later by the 9th Division, the 3d Armored Division and infantrymen of the 104th continued eastward. Seldom was there more opposition than occasional delaying actions except when some column turned north toward the Harz. In those instances, the Germans reacted with determination, sometimes employing small coveys of tanks or self-propelled guns.

On the 11th the armor swept into Nordhausen, uncovering more grisly, almost unbelievable evidence of Nazi bestiality in another concentration camp. Here is how a sergeant from the 329th Medical Battalion saw it:

Rows upon rows of skin-covered skeletons met our eyes. Men lay as they had starved, discolored, and lying in indescribable human filth. Their striped coats and prison numbers hung to their frames as a last token or symbol of those who enslaved and killed them . . . One girl in particular I noticed; I would say she was about seventeen years old. She lay there where she had

---

[30] MS # B–581 (Estor).

fallen, gangrened and naked. In my own thoughts I choked up—couldn't quite understand how and why war could do these things . . . We went downstairs into a filth indescribable, accompanied by a horrible dead-rot stench. There in beds of crude wood I saw men too weak to move dead comrades from their side. One hunched-down French boy was huddled up against a dead comrade, as if to keep warm . . . There were others, in dark cellar rooms, lying in disease and filth, being eaten away by diarrhea and malnutrition. It was like stepping into the Dark Ages to walk into one of these cellar-cells and seek out the living.[31]

Outside Nordhausen men of the 104th Division found large underground factories, one for manufacturing V–2 rockets. Scientific teams later shipped a hundred of the rockets to the United States for study, along with scientific data found buried in an abandoned mine a few miles away.[32]

Near the V-weapon factory was a slave labor camp with a capacity of 30,000. Indisputable evidence showed that no workers ever left camp and factory alive; if they became too weak to work, they were simply left to die and their remains disposed of in crematory ovens. Suvivors testified that 150 bodies a day were cremated.[33]

Pausing briefly at Nordhausen to await arrival of gasoline and oil, the tankers of the 3d Armored Division resumed their advance early on 12 April, entering Sangerhausen, twenty-two miles to the east, by midday. From that point the armor turned northeast, heading for the Elbe at Dessau, while the 104th Division began a march on Halle. Although the men in the tanks noted increased resistance on 13 April, particularly in volume of antitank fire, they advanced another twenty-three miles and established bridgeheads over the Saale River a few miles northwest of Halle. Another day would pass before the portent of the increased resistance would be revealed.

During the first two days after the 9th Armored Division was committed on 10 April, the V Corps made similar progress. On the third day, 12 April, the armor got a rude shock. Just over five miles from the Saale River, a task force forming the division's north column suddenly came under heavy fire from fixed antiaircraft guns. The guns were as deadly against tanks as against the airplanes they had been designed to combat. Only after losing nine tanks did the task force succeed in knocking out the big pieces.

Like the Third Army's 6th Armored Division, which on this same day at Zeitz had bumped into a nest of the fixed antiaircraft pieces, the 9th Armored Division had come up against one of the most concentrated belts of flak guns in all Germany. The belt formed a great arc extending from Bitterfeld, northeast of Halle, southwestward to encompass Halle, Merseburg, and Weissenfels on the Saale River, then southeastward to Zeitz. Although Leipzig stood behind the center of the arc, the Germans had not created the ring of steel to protect the city but to defend a number of synthetic oil refineries and industrial plants related to them: nitrogen, explosives, hydrogen, and synthetic

---

[31] Sgt. Ragene Farris, as quoted in Hoegh and Doyle, *Timberwolf Tracks*, pp. 330–31.
[32] See McGovern, *CROSSBOW and OVERCAST*.
[33] 104th Div AAR, Apr 45.

rubber.[34] Near Merseburg, for example, was Germany's largest synthetic rubber plant, second largest synthetic oil refinery, and a big hydrogen plant.[35]

The build-up in antiaircraft defenses had begun in May 1944, with assignment to the area of a flak division with headquarters in Leipzig. Beginning with 374 guns ranging in caliber from 75-mm. to 128-mm., the defenses had been increased by the spring of 1945 to possibly a thousand pieces.[36] Grouped in batteries varying from 12 to 36 guns, the weapons were particularly effective against ground targets in the Leipzig area because relatively flat terrain afforded excellent observation and fields of fire.

Although the concentrated belt of flak was well known to Allied airmen as a notorious "flak alley," nobody had reported the concentration to the ground troops that now had to face the guns. Allied air forces had detailed plottings of the locations of the batteries, but it took three days for the 9th Armored Division's urgent requests for information to produce results. Slave laborers and occasionally a German civilian sometimes helped the troops to spot the guns before they opened fire, but too often the first warning was the sharp crack of shells exploding in a rain of deadly fragments.

Since the flak guns appeared to represent the outer defenses of Leipzig, the V Corps commander, General Huebner, directed the 9th Armored Division to shift southeast to bypass Leipzig and gain the Mulde River, thirteen miles beyond the city. While the 2d Division took over the drive on Leipzig from the west, the 69th was to follow the armor, then come in on the city from south and southeast.

Having stirred up a fury of resistance at Weissenfels on the Saale, the armor on 13 April backed away, crossed the river on a bridge taken intact southwest of the town, then before the day was out crossed the Weisse Elster River near Zeitz. Two days later CCR on the south wing broke free of the flak belt and dashed all the way to the Mulde, twenty miles southeast of Leipzig. Having seized two bridges intact, CCR the next day, 16 April, crossed, captured Colditz, and released 1,800 Allied prisoners of war, including several ranking British officers.

The 69th Division's 271st Infantry meanwhile cleared a determined garrison of 1,500 from Weissenfels on the 13th and 14th, in the process crossing the Saale in assault boats. The 2d Division on the 15th took Merseburg and neighboring industrial towns with their large synthetic oil and rubber plants. To avoid observed fire from antiaircraft batteries, one regiment that night crossed the Saale over a damaged railroad bridge, the start of a series of night attacks designed to circumvent the big flak guns. Advancing by night, the men could get close enough to the guns to bring accurate artillery fire on them. Since the gun crews were unaccustomed to ground combat, the stratagem was usually sufficient to prompt them to flee.

---

[34] British Air Ministry, *The Rise and Fall of the German Air Force (1933 to 1945)* (London, 1948), p. 355.

[35] V Corps Operations in the ETO, p. 430.

[36] This figure is an estimate based on reports of American units involved and on a letter from Dr. Arenz, *Militaergeschichtliches Forschungsamt*, Freiburg, Germany, to USAREUR Historical Division, 31 October 1966, in response to a query by the author. Copy in OCMH.

A 12.8–CM. "FLAK" GUN, *as deadly against American ground troops as against planes.*

Within Leipzig itself as American troops closed in, a contest of will had developed between the head of the city's 3,400-man police force, General-major der Polizei Wilhelm von Grolman, and the "combat commander" of the city, Col. Hans von Poncet. Poncet expected the Hitler Youth, *Volkssturm,* odds and ends of regular troops, and the police to wage a fight to the death. To General von Grolman, that plan was folly, assuring nothing but destruction of the city. Imploring Colonel von Poncet not to fight, Grolman asked par-

ticularly that he avoid demolishing the bridges over the Weisse Elster River in order to save water, gas, and electric lines running under the bridges to western sectors of the city. When Poncet insisted on fighting, Grolman determined to maintain control of the police himself and withhold them from the struggle.[37]

Hoping to keep casualties to a minimum in view of the impending end of

[37] MS # B–478, The Collapse of the German Reich as Seen From Leipzig (Generalmajor der Polizei Wilhelm von Grolman).

the war, both the 2d and 69th Divisions made measured advances toward Leipzig. Only on the 18th did the two divisions break into the city. In the south and southeast, the 69th Division found resistance at times determined, particularly around the city hall and Napoleon Platz, the site of a monument (*Voelkerschlachtsdenkmal*—Battle of the Nations Memorial) commemorating Napoleon's defeat in 1813 in the Battle of Leipzig. Approaching from the west, men of the 2d Division encountered their first real fight at the bridges over the Weisse Elster, which were defended by *Volkssturm* and a sprinkling of regulars who were behind overturned trolley cars filled with stones. Whether on order of Poncet, Grolman, or otherwise, the bridges stood.

As men of the 2d Division settled down for the night on the east bank of the Weisse Elster, a police major approached with word that General von Grolman wanted to surrender the city. A rifle company commander accompanied him to police headquarters, but there discovered that Grolman, still begging Poncet in vain by telephone to surrender, controlled only the police.[38]

Although General von Grolman returned with the U.S. officer to American lines to confer further with higher commanders, the negotiations had no effect on Colonel von Poncet and the Germans at Napoleon Platz. As resistance in the city hall collapsed early on the 19th (inside, the mayor, his deputy, and their families were suicides), Colonel von Poncet and about 150 men holed up

in a sturdy stone base of the Battle of the Nations monument. Through much of 19 April, tanks, tank destroyers, and artillery employing direct fire pounded Poncet's position. Because the Germans held seventeen American prisoners, the 69th Division commander, General Reinhardt, declined to use flame throwers.

In midafternoon, a German-born American captain went under a white flag to the monument where for nine hours he argued to convince Poncet to surrender. At long last, past midnight, Poncet finally agreed.[39]

By this time a special control force formed from artillery battalions of the V Corps already was arriving to administer Leipzig, and first contingents of the 2d and 69th Divisions were on their way to join the corps armor at the Mulde River. In keeping with General Eisenhower's decision not to go to Berlin, the pending assignment for these troops was to await contact with the Russians.

A Short New War

While this kind of fairly typical pursuit warfare took place in the First Army's V Corps and throughout the Third Army, what seemed by contrast to be almost a new war had suddenly erupted a few miles to the north. In the Harz Mountains, at Halle, on the roads to Dessau, and in the bridgeheads over the Elbe, men of the First and Ninth Armies who had been engaged in what appeared to be an end-the-war pursuit suddenly found themselves fighting a determined though ill-equipped foe. The combat was as senseless as it was

---

[38] Details of this episode are in Charles B. MacDonald, *Company Commander* (Washington: Infantry Journal Press, 1947), pp. 241–55. See also MS # B–478 (Grolman).

[39] Toland, *The Last 100 Days,* pages 394–96, provides details.

unexpected. The Germans could hope to accomplish nothing other than to insure a warrior's death for more men on both sides and, by slowing the American drive, expose more of their people and their land to the mercy of the Russians, whom they all feared.

The new war in all cases could be laid directly or indirectly to a new force, the inchoate *Twelfth Army*, which Hitler absurdly counted on to sweep to the Harz, then to the Ruhr, thus gaining time in the west while some nebulous something happened to wrench victory from defeat in the east. The *Twelfth Army* made its presence felt first against the 2d Armored Division's little bridgehead on the east bank of the Elbe.

Hardly had the army commander-designate, General Wenck, reached his command post on 12 April in a panzer training school at Rosslau, across the Elbe from Dessau, when word arrived from the combat commander of Magdeburg that Americans had crossed the river nearby. While the artillery under the combat commander, including Magdeburg's fixed antiaircraft pieces, opened fire on the American crossing site, Wenck tried to discover what force he could send to attack the bridgehead.

His new command, Wenck found, was to consist of four corps headquarters, to be withdrawn from the east, and nine divisions. In most cases named after heroic figures from German history, the divisions were formed primarily of young men from army schools, particularly officer training schools, and from the Reich labor service. They were in varying stages of mobilization. Although food and ammunition were ample, most of the divisions would have no tanks; all would have little transport, only a few assault guns per division, and little artillery. Filled with spirited young men led by experienced officers who had been instructors at the schools, the divisions would make up in *esprit* something of what they lacked in training and equipment.[40]

One unit, *Division Potsdam*, was lost to General Wenck from the first. While being formed from army schools in the vicinity of the Harz Mountains, it had been trapped by the rapid American drive. Three other divisions would be insufficiently organized for commitment for more than a week. Two more, along with one of the corps headquarters, were under orders from OKW to assemble west of the Elbe north of the American zone of attack with the aim of driving south by way of Braunschweig to the Harz while the main body of the *Twelfth Army* drove west. General Wenck thus had immediately available at the Elbe only three divisions plus some small miscellaneous units.

Under orders from OKW before Wenck's arival, the commanders of two divisions, *Scharnhorst* and *Ulrich von Hutten,* had committed their units as they became available to hold a bridgehead west of the Elbe around Dessau whence the *Twelfth Army* might start its drive to the Harz. The third division was holding the east bank of the Elbe far to the north of Magdeburg.

To counter the 2d Armored Division's bridgehead south of Magdeburg, Wenck had to depend for the moment on *Volkssturm* and a miscellany with-

---

[40] Information on the *Twelfth Army* is from MS # B-606 (Reichhelm) and MS # B-394, Report on the *12th Army*, compiled for Historical Division, U.S. Army (General der Panzertruppen Walter Wenck).

drawn from the local defense force of Magdeburg. To supplement these, he ordered *Division Scharnhorst* to ready one regiment to counterattack the bridgehead in conjunction with a mixed force of assault guns drawn from an assault gun training school, and a few tanks.[41]

Before daylight on 13 April, a battalion of the 30th Division's 119th Infantry crossed into the 2d Armored Division's bridgehead, bringing the strength there to three battalions; but no antitank guns, tanks, or tank destroyers made it across. *(See Map XV, inset.)* So shallow was the water near both banks of the river that supporting engineers despaired of operating vehicular ferries and concentrated instead on bridging the river. Construction was slow in the dark, and sporadic German shelling interfered. With the coming of daylight the shelling increased, much of it deadly air bursts from big antiaircraft pieces at Magdeburg. Although supporting artillery tried constantly to neutralize the fire and engineers laid out smoke pots to screen the site, neither effort had apparent effect. Call after call went back for fighter-bombers to strike the artillery positions, but so far behind had airfields fallen in the race across Germany that the Elbe was almost beyond range of tactical aircraft. None showed up.

Despite the shelling, engineers by midday of the 13th had advanced their pontons and treadway tracking to within twenty-five yards of the far shore. Then came a deluge of shells that wrecked everything.

Giving up on that site, the 2d Armored Division commander, General White, directed the three infantry battalions to move after nightfall—in effect, to attack —upstream approximately three miles to a point opposite the bridge earlier demolished by the Germans at Schoenebeck. As daylight approached, Company L, 119th Infantry, and portions of a battalion of the 41st Armored Infantry were inside Elbenau, not quite two miles from the river, while the other battalion of armored infantry had cleared some 250 Germans from the riverside village of Gruenewalde. Other units were digging in on open ground to form the wings of a bridgehead. That was the situation when, in the dissipating darkness, a regiment of *Division Scharnhorst* supported by *Assault Gun Training School Burg* with approximately eight tanks and assault guns began to attack.

Catching the American infantrymen in the process of establishing their bridgehead and still without antitank defense other than bazookas, the Germans rapidly cut off the 119th Infantry's Company L in Elbenau and began systematically to reduce the defenders in the open, foxhole by foxhole. In the confusion, a score of Americans surrendered. The Germans put them in front of their tanks, forcing them at gunpoint to shield their continuing advance. The bridgehead began to go to pieces.

Five miles upstream, out of range of the enemy's artillery and antiaircraft guns at Magdeburg, men of the 83d Division were having little difficulty in their bridgehead opposite Barby. No sooner had two battalions of the 329th Infantry crossed in midafternoon of the

---

[41] The German sources make no mention of tanks but in the extensive combat interviews available on the ensuing action, so many American witnesses speak of tanks that their presence can hardly be doubted.

13th than engineers began to ferry supporting vehicles across, while other engineers went to work on a treadway bridge that was completed by nightfall. They named the bridge after their new Commander in Chief, President Harry S. Truman, and called it the "Gateway to Berlin." Although four small counterattacks struck the bridgehead during the day of the 14th, the presence of attached tanks and tank destroyers enabled the infantrymen to disperse them readily.

Remarking the contrast between the fortunes of the two bridgeheads, General White early on the 14th ordered his reserve combat command into the 83d's bridgehead to attack down the river's right bank and relieve the beleaguered men at Gruenewalde and Elbenau. CCR moved out early in the afternoon, but hardly had the attack begun when word came to call it off.

So desperate had matters become in CCB's little bridgehead that one of the armored infantry battalion commanders in midmorning returned to the west bank to report his battalion lost. He had seen his companies overrun, many men surrendering. The CCB commander, General Hinds, himself went into the bridgehead to survey the situation.

Engineers at the river had in the meantime been constructing a ferry and anchoring a guide cable for it to the east bank. Although the water at this site also was shallow close to the west bank, they coped with it by hauling rubble into the river to create a loading ramp. At noon a ferry carrying a bulldozer to be used to shave the east bank began to cross, but as the ferry neared the far shore a concentration of German antiaircraft artillery fire severed the cable.

Set free in a swift current, the ferry careened downstream.

To General Hinds, this was the end. Aware of the 83d Division's successful crossing and the plan to send CCR into that bridgehead and acutely conscious of the crisis in his own bridgehead, the failure to get tanks across, and the lack of air support, General Hinds gave the order to withdraw.

Returning to the west bank, Hinds reported his decision to his division headquarters where, in the absence of General White, he talked with the chief of staff. General White later concurred in the order, as did the corps commander, General McLain.

By late afternoon, most of the surviving infantrymen had made their way back to safety except for the men of Company L, cut off and hiding in cellars in Elbenau. These men finally learned of the withdrawal when their artillery forward observer established radio contact with an artillery observation plane. The forward observer called for a blanket of artillery fire on Elbenau to catch the Germans in the open. When the fire lifted, some sixty men made a break for the river. As tanks and tank destroyers fired from the west bank to cover their withdrawal, fighter-bombers of the XXIX Tactical Air Command with auxiliary fuel tanks in place of bombs finally arrived to strafe German positions. Most of the sixty men returned safely.

Through the night and the next day other survivors trickled back from the east bank, including one group of 30. Final losses totaled 330; of those only 4 were known dead and 20 wounded, an indication that many had been captured. Although the fighting in the bridgehead obviously had been severe, reports of eyewitnesses revealed that the confusion caused when the Germans struck before the defenders were organized had as much to do with the loss of the bridgehead as did anything else.

Word of the 83d Division's success at the Elbe had in the meantime flashed up the chain of command to General Eisenhower. When General Bradley gave him the news by telephone, the Supreme Commander was moved by the turn of events to reconsider his decision not to go to Berlin. How many casualties, he asked Bradley, might it cost to drive through and capture Berlin? Bradley estimated 100,000.[42]

The men inside the Elbe bridgehead were confident the drive on Berlin would be resumed momentarily. While the infantry with help of the 2d Armored's CCR extended the bridgehead to a depth of about five miles, the 320th Infantry (attached from the 35th Division to make up for a regiment of the 83d left behind in the Harz) attacked southeast across the Saale River to clear Germans from the angle formed by confluence of the Saale and the Elbe so that a second bridge could be constructed over the Elbe nearby. Although an occasional German plane harassed the bridgehead, American fighter-bombers extending their range with auxiliary fuel tanks in place of bombs were active much of the day, artillery and armored support were plentiful, and nobody doubted the 83d Division's ability to break out of the bridgehead at will.

The Ninth Army staff already had a plan for driving to Berlin, couched behind the euphemistic phrase, "to enlarge

the Elbe River bridgehead to include Potsdam [a suburb of Berlin]." On the 15th General Simpson flew to General Bradley's headquarters to present it. Although Bradley listened closely as General Simpson's G–3, Colonel Mead, disclosed the plan, he said he would have to telephone General Eisenhower for a decision. Overhearing Bradley's end of the conversation, Simpson soon had his answer.

"All right, Ike," Bradley said, "that's what I thought. I'll tell him. Goodbye."

There was to be no drive on Berlin.[43]

Two more combat assignments remained for the Ninth Army. One was to reduce Magdeburg, where the combat commander refused an ultimatum to surrender. After a strike by 350 medium bombers of the 9th Bombardment Division during the afternoon of 17 April, the 30th Division and parts of the 2d Armored began a systematic reduction of the city. The next day, as the last resistance faded, at least one American commander, General Bradley, was pleased that the Germans demolished the last bridge over the Elbe, for it spared him from putting men across to create another bridgehead to nowhere.[44]

The second assignment was to defeat an incursion into the zone of the XIII Corps from the north and to clear a newly assigned sector along the Elbe that originally had been a British responsibility, a two-faceted task which the XIII Corps aptly named Operation KAPUT.

According to orders of OKW, two of the newly formed divisions of Wenck's *Twelfth Army* were to have attacked

---

[42] Bradley, *A Soldier's Story,* p. 535.

[43] Quotations are from comments on the draft MS of this volume by Mead.

[44] Bradley, *A Soldier's Story,* p. 539.

southward into the Ninth Army's flank to gain the Harz Mountains, but because one division got tied down in a fight with the British, only the other showed up. That was *Panzer Division von Clausewitz,* formed from staff and students of a panzer training school off the Ninth Army's flank near Uelzen. At full strength in men, the division had at least fifty tanks and additional armor that included experimental and antiquated equipment found at the school.[45]

Conditions favoring employment of German forces against the Ninth Army's flank had begun to develop around 15 April when the 8 Corps of the adjacent British Second Army swung north at Uelzen in keeping with a British main effort toward Hamburg. A 60-mile stretch of the Ninth Army's north flank from Uelzen to the Elbe was thus left exposed except for British cavalry patrols and a screen maintained by the 11th Cavalry Group.

The XIII Corps already had been having trouble in its rear areas as a result of bypassed Germans who holed up in some of the vast expanses of woodland in the corps zone and refused to give up. Astride the Wesergebirge on the east bank of the Weser, the 102d Division fought for two days against more than 2,000 Germans who had coalesced in the wooded highland. Farther east on 13 and 14 April contingents of both the 84th and 102d Divisions fought to eliminate two other pockets of resistance, one of which encompassed eight tanks.

The first indication of the presence of *Panzer Division von Clausewitz* emerged

on 15 April when the British identified a portion of the division in a counter-attack at Uelzen. Before daylight the next day, a force estimated at a thousand men and thirty tanks cut the main supply route of the XIII Corps near General Gillem's command post at Kloetze, 36 miles southeast of Uelzen. For four more days, contingents of the new panzer division turned up at various points in the rear of the corps, involving at one time or another in the fight to erase them contingents of all three divisions in the corps, including the 5th Armored Division and a newly assigned division, the 29th. Telephone communications and motor messenger service between the XIII Corps and the Ninth Army were disrupted for two days. Half in jest, half in earnest, service troops complained that it was safer on the front line at the Elbe than in the rear echelon.

In most cases the German thrusts were stopped well short of the corps south boundary, although portions of one column did get into the zone of the XIX Corps, where contingents of the 2d Armored Division wiped them out. The most persistent of all the enemy groups hid in a forest near Kloetze. A chemical mortar battalion tried in vain to burn the Germans out with white phosphorus shells. A regiment of the 29th Division supported by 155-mm. and 8-inch pieces was required to "give Kloetze Forest a real hair cut" and eliminate the force.[46]

Although more troublesome than serious, the German forays delayed for a day a start on a new assignment handed the XIII Corps to assume responsibility for the vast triangle of uncleared territory north of the Ninth Army's boundary

---

[45] MS # B–606 (Reichhelm). Tank strength is based on prisoner-of-war statements in XIII Corps G–2 Periodic Reports and on numbers destroyed in ensuing actions.

[46] Quotation is from XIII Corps G–2 Periodic Rpt, 20 Apr 45.

between Uelzen and the Elbe. When the attack finally began on the 21st, the 5th Armored Division encountered and destroyed the last of *Panzer Division von Clausewitz*. All together, American forces had knocked out forty-seven tanks and more than a dozen assault guns.

The sweep north of the former army boundary gained rapidly on the 22d. By 24 April the new assignment was completed, with the Ninth Army holding the line of the Elbe to a point near Dannenberg, thirty miles downstream from Wittenberge.

The brush of the First Army's VII Corps with General Wenck's *Twelfth Army* began in earnest on 14 April, the day after the 3d Armored Division had seized bridgeheads over the Saale River northwest of Halle. Heading for Dessau, where the Mulde River flows into the Elbe, the 3d Armored hit positions of *Division Scharnhorst* and *Division Ulrich von Hutten,* which were striving to hold a bridgehead west of the Elbe as a base for the *Twelfth Army* drive to the Harz.

Roadblocks now were more numerous, more stoutly defended, and the larger towns, such as Koethen, eleven miles from Dessau, could be taken only after slow house-to-house fighting. One combat command reached Koethen at nightfall on the 14th; it was nightfall the next day before tanks and half-tracks could move on. Although planes of the IX Tactical Air Command were overhead much of the time, their help generally was limited to strafing because, like planes of the XXIX Tactical Air Command in support of the Ninth Army, they had to carry auxiliary fuel tanks in place of bombs.

Except for a task force on the extreme south wing of the division, which came within range of fixed antiaircraft guns near Bitterfeld at the northeastern tip of the flak belt encompassing Leipzig, seldom did the columns encounter enemy shelling. The main obstacles were towed antitank guns and *Panzerfausts*. Sometimes the Germans turned *Panzerfausts* against deployed armored infantrymen, firing them in batteries like mortars. The going posed problems for rear echelons of the division too; no infantry division of the VII Corps was available for mop-up, and these youthful Germans revealed no inclination to surrender simply because armored columns had passed them by. After Koethen was cleared in a fight that lasted twenty-four hours, so many Germans infiltrated back into the city that another twelve hours of fighting ensued before Koethen was finally secure. As the armor drew up to Dessau, a wide swath of forest south of the city served as a base for German raids and counterattacks.

Bypassing defended towns, one task force fought through a portion of the forest to reach the Mulde River at a demolished autobahn bridge just two miles southeast of Dessau on 15 April. Although infantrymen scrambled across the wreckage to form a small bridgehead, difficult approaches and occasional shelling delayed building a bridge until, on 16 April, the same stop order that had halted the Ninth Army the day before at the Elbe prompted the division commander, General Hickey, to pull back the bridgehead.

As part of the armored division swept the west bank of the Mulde southward in the direction of the First Army's V Corps, the attack on Dessau began early on 21 April. It took two days of house-to-house fighting to clear the city and another day to erase a hold-out position along a railroad leading across the Elbe to Rosslau. Although the ultimate fate of two divisions, *Scharnhorst* and *Ulrich von Hutten,* had been inevitable from the first, the two hastily formed units had forced upon the armor of the VII Corps ten days of unpleasant anticlimax to the war.

The 104th Division, in the meantime, also had a hard fight. At Halle a die-hard combat commander, Generalleutnant Anton Rathke, was determined to hold out as long as possible with about 4,000 men, including troops from a communications school, a sprinkling of SS, and antiaircraft gunners who were part of the Leipzig defense belt.[47] An aerial bombardment of leaflets demanding surrender and urging civilians to convince the troops to spare the city brought no immediate response.

All bridges over the Saale on the city's western boundary having been destroyed, General Allen sent his units to cross the 3d Armored Division's tactical bridges and strike the city from the north. A house-to-house fight was well under way when on 16 April Count Felix von Luckner, who had gained renown as a sea-raider in World War I, came into American lines to negotiate. While General Rathke refused to surrender, Luckner said, he did agree, in order to spare civilians and Allied and German patients in the city's hospitals, to confine his defense to the southern third of the city.

For three more days, through the 19th, the 104th Division's 414th Infantry fought for Halle, killing or capturing unorganized three- to five-man groups in almost every building, while the division's other regiments turned east to conquer Bitterfeld and reach the Mulde River.

The other German holdout was in the Harz Mountains, unattainable goal of General Wenck's *Twelfth Army.* As many as 70,000 Germans had congregated there for a last stand under the aegis of General Lucht's *Eleventh Army.* It was with some surprise that those Germans found themselves under immediate attack, since they had hoped the Americans might merely contain them and drive on to the east. The Germans were reckoning without the plethora of power available to American commanders.[48]

The 1st Division pierced the western fringe of the Harz as early as 11 April. *(Map 6)* On the same day the 330th Infantry, left behind when the 83d Division drove for the Elbe as part of the Ninth Army, began to attack along the northern fringe, and later was supported by a combat command of the 8th Armored Division. On 13 April the 9th Division joined the VII Corps to sweep the eastern end of the Harz from a starting position northeast of Nordhausen.

Many of the ingredients for a grim stuggle to the death were present in the Harz—a trapped enemy, harsh, sharply etched terrain cloaked by dense woods,

---

[47] MS # B-219, Activity of the German *XLVIII Panzerkorps* in the American Campaign Against Central Germany (General der Panzertruppen Max Freiherr von Edelsheim). Halle came under Edelsheim's command as his headquarters moved from the Eastern Front to become part of the *Twelfth Army* only a few days before the 104th Division's attack.

[48] Kesselring, in *A Soldier's Record,* pages 314-15, gives undue credit to the holdout in the Harz for delaying American advance eastward.

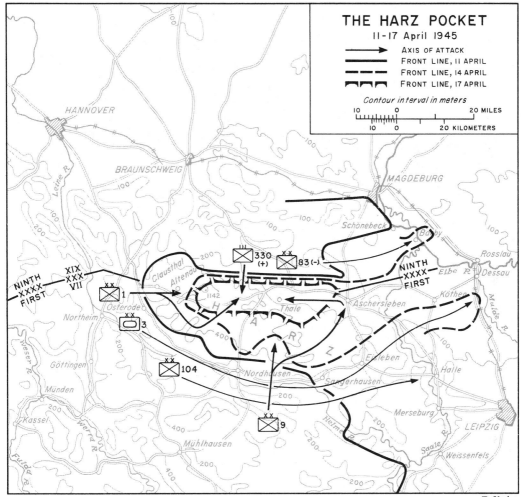

MAP 6

caves, mines, and winding roads that could be readily blocked at defiles, stream crossings, and almost anywhere else within the woods. Some of the fighting conformed to the inhospitable setting, but most of it failed to follow the form. Since the Germans lacked appreciable strength in mortars and artillery, the lethal tree bursts that often characterize forest fighting were missing. Nor

was there the steadfast determination to fight to the end usually associated with a trapped foe. Theirs was a lost cause; the end of the war was at hand; the men represented less an army than a conglomeration; and few other than the young newcomers of *Division Potsdam* saw much point in dying at that stage of the denouement.

Further, the *Eleventh Army* commander, General Lucht, doubted his assignment. The Harz had no prepared defenses, no stockpiled supplies, and he had no faith in the fancy that the hastily created *Twelfth Army* could break through the powerful American units that had flowed around the Harz. Lucht refused to consider a scorched earth policy to prolong a hopeless defense. As a soldier, he deemed it a matter of honor to follow his orders and fight, but he determined in the process to spare his troops and the civilian population as much as he could.[49]

The Harz was above all a network of roadblocks, the barriers limited in size only by the energy of those who constructed them, for on every hand there were trees enough and more. On the most logical routes for American advance —those from the west taken by the 1st Division—the Germans backed up the roadblocks with the few tanks they possessed (judging from the numbers ultimately knocked out, probably fewer than twenty-five). So long as a chance to hold the position existed, the tanks remained, but when American infantrymen flanked the defenses through the woods or advanced under cover of artillery fire or of their own tanks, the Germans at the last moment usually withdrew. It was 15 April, fifth day of the fight, before men of the 1st Division caught up with more than one or two German tanks. On that date they knocked out four, plus three self-propelled guns. Two days later they accounted for ten more. In a small counterattack at the town of Altenau, the Germans employed a captured U.S. light tank.

During the first few days German infantrymen sometimes used the concealment of the woods to infiltrate back into towns and villages. In some cases they laid mines or erected log barriers behind American columns, and occasionally they counterattacked with perhaps as many as a hundred men; but in general they carried on a delaying action on a large scale. When pressed, the Germans either withdrew or surrendered.

Some 200 men holding the Brocken, at 3,747 feet the highest point in the Harz, proved an exception. Here stood a radio station, the *Eleventh Army*'s only means of communication with *OB WEST*. Here the Germans held on 18 April against an assault by the 330th Infantry that followed a bombardment by planes of the IX Tactical Air Command's 365th and 404th Groups, but the resistance collapsed the next day when pressed from the other side of the hill by a company of the 1st Division's 26th Infantry.

Reflecting the nature of the fighting, the 1st Division during the first few days took about 200 prisoners a day, while the 9th Division, which was in effect cutting across the enemy's rear, averaged a thousand. On the 16th, the 1st Division's prisoner total rose to a thousand; the 9th Division took 2,000. Those figures almost doubled on the 18th as many Germans took to the mountain roads for a flight to nowhere and as American fighter planes made one strafing run after another.

Some idea of the quandary of German units seeking to avoid capture was apparent in the peregrinations of the *Eleventh Army* command post: one day in the town of Braunlage, the next in a limestone quarry, another in a forester's

---

[49] MS # B-581 (Estor).

cottage, then a cave, a monastery, and, at last, a wooded hill just beyond the northern fringe of the Harz near Blankenburg.

On 20 April the end drew near as German units began to surrender en masse. Some drove their vehicles under a white flag into American lines. By the close of the day, the 9th Division had taken over 8,000 prisoners, the 1st Division, 10,000. In the mop-up that followed, stragglers surrendered passively. Finally, on 23 April, a patrol found the *Eleventh Army* command post near Blankenburg and captured the staff, including General Lucht.

The fight was over in the Harz, at Halle, Dessau, and Magdeburg, the infiltrators north of the Ninth Army's old boundary had been cleared, and the Germans of Wenck's *Twelfth Army* were wondering why the Americans made no move toward Berlin from the 83d Division's successful bridgehead at Barby when, on 23 April, the *Twelfth Army* began to turn its back on the Americans.

Seven days earlier, on 16 April, the Russians had begun their attack across the Oder River toward Berlin, thirty miles away. By the 22d, two Russian army groups were closing on the city. Tank spearheads had bypassed the city on the north, forces approaching the city from the east had at one point penetrated the inner defense ring, and others approaching from the southeast were close to surrounding the German army defending there. All else having failed, Hitler decreed that the *Twelfth Army* turn and come to the rescue of Berlin.[50]

Having learned on 31 March through General Eisenhower's message that the new Allied plan was to drive to the Leipzig-Dresden area rather than to Berlin, Marshal Stalin had moved swiftly to speed a Soviet thrust on the German capital. While professing to agree with Eisenhower that Berlin had lost strategic significance and indicating that a new Russian offensive would begin only in the second half of May, Stalin on the first day of April had called in the commanders of the two army groups closest to Berlin to determine how quickly they might attack. The Allies, said Stalin, were trying to beat the Red Army to Berlin.[51]

Whether Stalin believed Eisenhower's message a ruse designed to lull the Russians while the Allies captured the capital or whether he merely used it to spur his field commanders, the effect was the same. In the first two weeks of April, the Soviet armies executed "their fastest major redeployment of the war." [52]

In approximately nine of the fifteen days when the Russians were making their preparations, roughly from 5 through 13 April, the First, Third, and Ninth U.S. Armies had driven some 150 miles across central Germany, not, as Marshal Stalin accused in a letter to President Roosevelt on 3 April, through some deal with the Germans to open the front to the Allies, but because the

---

[50] For the Russian offensive, see Earl F. Ziemke, *Stalingrad to Berlin: The German Defeat in the East,* in the ARMY HISTORICAL SERIES (Washington, 1968), ch. XXI.

[51] Ziemke, *Stalingrad to Berlin,* pp. 467–69; Herbert Feis, *Churchill, Roosevelt, Stalin* (Princeton: Princeton University Press, 1957), pp. 604ff; and John Ehrman, *Grand Strategy* (London, 1957), vol. VI in the official British history of World War II, pp. 132, 142. Ryan, *The Last Battle,* pages 243–52, provides an account of the Stalin conference based on interviews conducted in the Soviet Union well after the war.

[52] Ziemke, *Stalingrad to Berlin,* p. 470.

Germans who might have defended central Germany were trapped in the Ruhr.

Although American supply lines at the conclusion of the drive were taut, they were nowhere near a breaking point. The essentials—food, gasoline, ammunition—were ample. Only forward airfields were lacking, and captured German fields could have been put into shape quickly had close air support been essential. While the *Twelfth Army* had given a new complexion to the fighting for a few days, Wenck's troops in the long run were no more than a nuisance. Even though the *Twelfth Army* imposed some hurt (having averaged 80 casualties a day in early stages of the drive, the VII Corps in five days of increased resistance averaged 260 casualties a day), its commitment in no sense threatened to halt or even seriously delay the offensive. Nor did the Germans have other than Wenck's troops to pit against the American drive.

The American armies, the Ninth in particular, could have continued their offensive some fifty more miles at least to the fringe of Berlin. The decision of the Supreme Allied Commander and

nothing else halted the Americans at the Elbe and the Mulde.[53]

What taking Berlin might have accomplished to speed the end of a war already tumbling to a conclusion or to insure a postwar world more favorable for Allied policies was another matter; but it would probably have been little, since prestige was about all that was at stake. A question remained, too, of what the Russians might have done upon arriving at the prize of the German capital to find an American force already there, contrary to Eisenhower's word to Stalin. That General Eisenhower halted his troops at a time when they were capable of continuing, in the process sparing them casualties not worth additional prestige which the powerful Allied force had no need of, made his decision to halt all the more judicious.[54]

---

[53] On this point, see General Simpson's letter to the editor in *The New York Times Book Review*, 12 June 1966.

[54] In addition to sources previously cited dealing with this decision, see General Walter Bedell Smith, *Eisenhower's Six Great Decisions* (New York: Longmans, Green and Co., 1956), pp. 181–86, and Stephen E. Ambrose, *Eisenhower and Berlin, 1945—The Decision to Halt at the Elbe* (New York: W. W. Norton & Co., Inc., 1967).

CHAPTER XVIII

The Myth of the Redoubt

Under General Eisenhower's plan to break out of the Rhine bridgeheads and encircle the Ruhr—the plan that had served as blueprint for the spectacular dash to the Elbe—the role assigned General Devers's 6th Army Group was to protect the 12th Army Group's right flank. With the Third Army swinging almost due north toward Kassel, General Patch's Seventh Army from its Rhine bridgehead near Worms would have to drive northeast with a left boundary anchored on the Hohe Rhoen, the wooded hills forming the southeastern wall of the Fulda Gap.

Despite the northeastward orientation, General Devers was aware that as the southernmost Allied force, his 6th Army Group also would be responsible eventually for clearing southern Germany and dealing with an alleged last-ditch hold-out position the Nazis might be planning in the Alpine region of southern Germany and western Austria. It was called variously the Alpine Redoubt or National Redoubt.

Most Allied intelligence officers discounted the likelihood of any formidable, self-contained fortress in the Alps, mainly because of limited agricultural and industrial resources in the region. Yet they did see the possibility of remnants of the German Army retiring to the Alps for a final suicidal stand. Future generations then might claim,

noted General Eisenhower's chief of intelligence, Maj. Gen. Kenneth W. D. Strong, that National Socialism and the German nation had never surrendered.[1]

In late March the Seventh Army G–2, Col. William W. Quinn, gave some substance to various reports of German defense preparations in the Alps. Although Colonel Quinn thought many of the reports fanciful and exaggerated, enough hard evidence existed, he concluded, to indicate that Hitler was consciously planning a final stand there.[2]

Only six days later, on the last day of March, so rapidly did the Western Front crumble that the 6th Army Group G–2, Brig. Gen. Eugene L. Harrison, foresaw an end to any German hopes of a genuine redoubt. Denied any respite after falling back behind the Rhine in the wake of the staggering defeat in the Saar-Palatinate, General Hausser's *Army Group G* had proved incapable of containing any Allied bridgehead and had failed to close the corridor leading northeast to Kassel, thereby sealing the fate of neighboring *Army Group B* in the Ruhr. Since the greatest threat to German integrity was the thrust to en-

---

[1] JIC (Joint Intelligence Committee) Report, Ability of the German Army in the West to Continue the War, 10 Mar 45, SHAEF JIC Rpts.
[2] SUSA G–2 Rpt, Study of the German National Redoubt, 25 Mar 45.

circle the Ruhr, *Army Group G* could count on no priority for reinforcement.

Army Group G's foundering *Seventh Army,* General Harrison noted, had not enough strength to re-establish contact with *Army Group B.* In dire need of a thorough rebuilding, a *First Army* already threatened by Rhine crossings of the Seventh U.S. Army and First French Army had to take on the job of preventing further expansion of the Oppenheim bridgehead. Reduced almost to a training command after withdrawing from the Colmar pocket, the *Nineteenth Army* (responsible directly to *OB WEST* rather than to *Army Group G*) was holding some 100 miles of front along the Rhine covering the Black Forest and could only withdraw or await envelopment from flank or rear. The present commander of the *Nineteenth Army* was a former head of the *Seventh Army,* General Brandenberger, who had been summarily relieved in February for failing to hold in the Eifel.[3]

"The turn of military events," General Harrison concluded, "is effectively destroying the 'National Redoubt' for want of both territory and personnel. Any retreat into the mountains of southeastern Germany will hardly be voluntary on the part of the German leaders."[4]

Even though a formal National Redoubt might not exist, the Alps represented such a natural fortress that it would be well to launch an attack as soon as possible to prevent major German forces from retiring into the region. General Eisenhower held that view, though he accorded no immediate pri-

ority to the operation. Once the Ruhr was encircled, the 12th Army Group's drive toward Leipzig was to have full priority, and any operations of the 6th Army Group toward the southeast would be mounted only if they were possible without jeopardizing protection of the 12th Army Group's south flank. On the other hand, so near an end was the enemy's ability to resist that the Supreme Commander intended soon to expand operations everywhere, perhaps to include reinforcing the 6th Army Group with a southeastward drive by the Third Army "to prevent Nazi occupation of a mountain citadel."[5]

Looking ahead to the day when approval would be granted, General Devers contemplated a preliminary attack by the Seventh Army's right wing generally to the south and southeast to cut behind the bulk of the enemy's *First Army* and the entire *Nineteenth Army* in the Black Forest. Once the First French Army had enough troops on the east bank of the Rhine, the French were to drive south to eliminate the trapped enemy. Most of the Germans facing the army group thus dispatched, Devers presumed he could drive swiftly to the southeast to link with the Russians, possibly somewhere along the northwest frontier of Austria.[6]

Sending his G–3, Brig. Gen. Reuben E. Jenkins, to confer with SHAEF planners on 31 March, Devers learned that

---

[3] See above, ch. VI.

[4] 6th AGp Weekly Intell Sum No. 28, 31 Mar 45.

[5] Eisenhower to AGp CG's, SCAF 224, 8 Mar 45, and SCAF 247, 25 Mar 45, in SHAEF SGS Post-OVERLORD Planning file, III; Ltr, SHAEF to AGp CG's in GCT/370-62/Plans, 18 Mar 45; Eisenhower to CCS, SCAF 224, 24 Mar 45, and SCAF 260, 31 Mar 45, in SHAEF SCAF Cable files. Quotation from last source.

[6] See Hq, 6th AGp, History, ch IX.

SHAEF was thinking instead of a broad arclike sweep by the Seventh Army's left wing deep inside Germany to the vicinity of Nuremberg and Bayreuth, thereby continuing to protect the 12th Army Group's flank, thence southeast down the valley of the Danube to Linz in Austria. Two days later General Eisenhower directed General Devers to begin the thrust as soon as troops and supplies were available.[7]

The next day, 3 April, the SHAEF G–3, General Bull, read the special report on the redoubt prepared by the Seventh Army's Colonel Quinn. While referring it to the SHAEF G–2 for comment, Bull suggested expanding the 6th Army Group operations into the Alps of western Austria. When the commander of Allied forces approaching the Alps from the Italian side, Field Marshal Sir Harold R.L.G. Alexander, indicated he would welcome such a drive, General Eisenhower approved it.[8]

Although SHAEF intelligence a few days later concluded that no positive evidence existed of German strategy based on a National Redoubt, the possibility that the German armed forces would continue to resist unless Hitler died or was overthrown was real, in which case the Alps appeared the logical place for a final stand. Since troops from the Eastern, Western, and Italian fronts might converge there, the contemplated thrust into the Alps still might be needed.[9]

The First Phase Beyond the Rhine

As these plans gradually took shape, General Patch's Seventh Army was continuing the assignment of protecting the 12th Army Group flank. Having crossed the Rhine at Worms and established breakout conditions in the bridgehead by nightfall of 27 March, General Haislip's XV Corps was the logical choice for the main role on the left. (*Map XVI*) The corps was to drive some fifty miles from the Main River northeast through the Spessart Mountains to the Hohe Rhoen. To protect Haislip's flank and to prepare a way for the expected turn to the southeast, General Patch planned to commit General Milburn's XXI Corps in the center to drive east through the Odenwald, General Brooks's VI Corps on the right to attack southeast across a plateau known as the Kraichgau Gate between the Odenwald and the Black Forest. With ten infantry and three armored divisions, the Seventh Army had enough strength for all three thrusts.

While the 3d and 45th Divisions passed through rear elements of the Third Army in the Oppenheim bridgehead to reach jump-off positions being vacated by Third Army units along the Main near Aschaffenburg, the 12th Armored Division on 28 March pushed into the Odenwald as a vanguard of the XXI Corps. To open a route for the VI Corps, the 44th Division drove south from the Worms bridgehead to reduce Mannheim. Although surrender negotia-

---

[7] *Ibid.* See also, Eisenhower to AGp CG's, SCAF 261, 2 Apr 45, in SHAEF SCAF Cable files.

[8] Memo, Operations in Austria, 4 Apr 45, GCT/370-68/Plans, SHAEF SGS Post-OVERLORD Planning, IV; Memo re Evaluation of SUSA Study of German National Redoubt, 3 Apr 45, SHAEF G–3, Ops file 175; Eisenhower to SACMED, SCAF 267, 6 Apr 45, in SHAEF SCAF Cable files; SACMED to Eisenhower, NAF 915, 9 Apr 45, OPD IN files, 1–30 Apr 45.

[9] See JIC SHAEF (45) 13 (Final), The National Redoubt, 10 Apr 45, in SHAEF JIC Rpts.

tions conducted with the city's acting burgomaster went awry when German troops shelled American parliamentaries with mortars, the Germans pulled out during the night of 28 March, and men of the 44th Division moved in the next day. Since Mannheim lies on both banks of the Neckar River, occupying the city provided a bonus of a bridgehead over the Neckar.

In the main thrust by the XV Corps, the 45th Division crossed the Main River on 28 March on the railroad bridge, just south of Aschaffenburg, that had been taken earlier by the 4th Armored Division—the place where Task Force Baum had begun its ill-fated foray to Hammelburg. In the three days since Task Force Baum had passed, General Hahm had sent one of the three divisions constituting his *LXXXII Corps* to contain the little bridgehead. The 45th Division thus had to fight hard to break out.

The firmest resistance was on the left, from the fringes of Aschaffenburg, where a combat commander took seriously orders from OKW to fight to the end. There occurred one of the few instances in Germany where civilians in large numbers joined actively in the fighting, sometimes lining rooftops to drop grenades on U.S. troops below. German ranks also were heavy with Hitler Youth, boys who had hardly begun to shave.

To spare his own men, the 45th Division commander, General Frederick, directed his 157th Infantry to clear Aschaffenburg systematically, making maximum use of artillery and aerial bombardment. For six days men of the 157th fought from house to house until at last, on the morning of 3 April, the combat

commander, who had hanged several German soldiers and civilians for advocating surrender, gave himself up.

The rest of the 45th Division meanwhile had advanced twenty-five miles to the northeast of Aschaffenburg. The 3d Division, having crossed the Main upstream from Aschaffenburg early on 30 March without opposition, traversed the wooded ground lying in a great southward loop of the Main to reach the river a second time twenty miles to the northeast. Against neither division was resistance determined. Most delays were attributable to the densely wooded hill country and its winding roads, sometimes a defended town, and occasionally a roadblock. "Sixty-one minute roadblocks," some German civilians called them derisively—the American soldiers would laugh at them for sixty minutes, then tear them down in one.[10]

Committed on the 2d of April, generally along the boundary between the two infantry divisions, the 14th Armored Division also reached the Main for the second time, and on the 3d seized Lohr, where Task Force Baum earlier had shot up a column of German vehicles. The Germans fought all night in Lohr, but as elsewhere, it was no more than a last-ditch stand by conglomerate units often lacking communications with higher command.

As the gap between *Army Group B* and *Army Group G* facilitated the Third Army's drive on Kassel and the subsequent thrust across central Germany by the First and Third Armies, so it also markedly influenced the campaign of the American Seventh Army. Constant efforts to close the gap to the north had

---

[10] Taggert, *History of the Third Infantry Division*, p. 346.

"SIXTY-ONE MINUTE ROADBLOCK," *typical of obstacles erected before many German towns.*

the effect of pulling *Army Group G's Seventh Army,* including Hahm's *LXXXII Corps* on the south wing, gradually northward, in the process creating a gap within *Army Group G* between the *First* and *Seventh Armies.*[11]

To OKW's continuing insistence that the *Seventh Army* close the gap to the north, the army group commander, General Hausser, replied with a counterproposal. The only hope for establishing a cohesive defense, Hausser believed, was to relinquish control of the area north of the Main River, turning the *Seventh Army* over to direct control of the Commander in Chief West, with whom Hausser himself had lost communications; *Army Group G* with the *First* and *Nineteenth Armies* might then withdraw into southern Germany. For his trouble in arriving at this solution, Hausser paid with his job. On 2 April his replacement, General der Infanterie Friedrich Schulz, reported from the

[11] See MS # B–703, The Final Battle in Central and Southern Germany Until Capitulation, 22 Mar 45–6 May 45 (Oberst Horst Wilutzky, CofS, *AGp G*).

Eastern Front to the Reich Chancellery for a personal briefing by Hitler.

It was imperative, Hitler told Schulz, to hold out another three or four weeks in the west, whereupon so many new jet-propelled aircraft would join the fight that the Germans would obtain "equilibrium, if not superiority" in the air. "This would at the same time," Hitler said, "entirely change the situation on the ground as well." [12]

The impact that German efforts to close the gap to *Army Group B* was having on the *First* and *Seventh Armies* had become strikingly apparent in the Odenwald, thickly wooded hill country lying between the great southward loop of the Main River and a northward hook of the Neckar River twenty miles to the south. Obviously gambling that the Germans had little for defending the Odenwald, General Patch had sent armor rather than infantry to lead the way through the rugged terrain.

Defending the Odenwald was the responsibility of General von Oriola's *XIII Corps,* which had absorbed a one-two punch from the Third Army's crossing of the Rhine at Oppenheim and the Seventh Army's crossing at Worms. Separated from its parent *Seventh Army* by the Third Army thrust, the *XIII Corps* had passed to control of the *First Army* even as U.S. troops began to exploit the bridgehead opposite Worms. Two divisions having been nearly annihilated in opposing the Rhine crossing and a third still committed farther south, General von Oriola had only a hodgepodge for holding the Odenwald and little

GENERAL MILBURN

enough of that. To his knowledge he had not a single antitank gun, assault gun, or tank. Compounding an already desperate situation, Oriola's right flank was anchored on air.[13]

As a vanguard of General Milburn's XXI Corps, the 12th Armored Division went through the briar patch of the Odenwald as if its tanks were rabbits. An effort by Oriola's *XIII Corps* to build a new position along creek beds in the twenty-mile gap between the loops of the Main and the Neckar attracted scarcely any notice. Although the *First Army* commander, General Foertsch, committed the *17th SS Panzer Grenadier Division,* which he had hoped to rehabilitate to form an army reserve, the panzer grenadiers hardly managed to get north of the Neckar before U.S. infantry

---

[12] MS # B-583, Report on the Position, Mission, and General Measures of *Heeresgruppe 'G'* in April 1945 (General der Infanterie Friedrich Schulz).

[13] For German operations in this period, see MSS # B-173, *XIII Corps,* 21 March-2 May 1945 (Major W. Gaebelin); # B-392 (Oriola); # B-348 (Wolf Hauser).

following close behind the armor forced them onto the defensive. By 30 March the armor had emerged from the Odenwald into relatively open country.

The next day, as General von Oriola visited the command post of one of his makeshift divisions, a staff officer rushed in with news that American tanks were approaching. They closed in before Oriola could get away. The general surrendered.

By nightfall of the 31st, the 12th Armored Division had reached the Tauber River, a tributary of the Main almost sixty miles beyond the Rhine and little more than a day's run at the pace the tanks had been traveling from the corps objective of Wuerzburg on a second big southward loop of the Main. Although some indications of stiffening resistance were apparent along the Tauber, they were nothing to excite concern.

The resistance reflected efforts by *Army Group G* to bring the headlong retreat of the *First Army*'s right wing to an end, peg the front on fairly defensible river lines, and shore up the widening gap between the *First* and *Seventh Armies*. Assuming command of *Wehrkreis XIII* and its replacement and training troops, General Hausser in one of his last acts before his relief put them under command of headquarters of the *XIII SS Corps,* pulled that headquarters from the *First Army*'s south wing, and charged the commander, General Simon, with building a new line along the Tauber and across a narrow land bridge between the Tauber and the Jagst River. Commanded now by Generalleutnant Max Bork, the troops that had comprised the south wing of the *XIII Corps* and thus had escaped the thrust of the 12th Armored Division were to extend the line southwest along the Jagst and south along the Neckar River to Heilbronn.[14]

With American armor on the east bank of the Tauber by nightfall of 31 March, the northern part of the new line was under immediate threat. Indeed, except at Koenigshofen, where 400 years earlier the Peasants' War had come to a bloody end, both the 12th Armored Division and the infantry of the XXI Corps (the 4th and 42d Divisions) took the Tauber in stride. At Koenigshofen an SS antiaircraft replacement regiment that included a battalion of mobile 88-mm. guns fought for the better part of two days against a contingent of the 12th Armored Division and two battalions of the 4th Division's 22d Infantry, but late on 2 April the town was cleared.

On the same day the bulk of all three divisions of the XXI Corps drew up to the Main River along the big loop embracing Wuerzburg, and a battalion of the 4th Division's 8th Infantry crossed the river nine miles southeast of Wuerzburg at the southern end of the loop. General Simon and the *XIII SS Corps* now tried desperately to establish a new line from Koenigshofen to the Main, but the odds against building a firm position were high. In addition to the shortages of troops and transport, so numerous and persistent were American planes that no German unit could move with impunity during daylight.

General Simon had, too, that continually nagging problem of an open flank. Although responsibility for defending the Main River lay with the *Seventh*

---

[14] In addition to sources previously cited, see MS # B-737, Employment of the *XIII SS Army Corps* Between the Rhine and the Alps (SS Obersturmbannfuehrer Ekkehard Albert, CofS, *XIII SS Corps).*

GENERAL BROOKS. (*Photograph taken in 1949.*)

Army to the north, so wide was the gap between the *First* and *Seventh Armies* that Simon had to figure on defending the river at least as far north as Wuerzburg. The next day, 3 April, as the 42d Division began to cross the Main at Wuerzburg, *Army Group G* formally handed responsibility for the city and the river line south of it to the *First Army*.

By 3 April both the south wing of the *Seventh Army* and the north wing of the *First* were in unmitigated trouble from the rampaging divisions of the U.S. XV and XXI Corps. At the same time similar problems had been building up for the other wing of the *First Army* as the U.S. VI Corps pressed its role in the breakout.

As with the XXI Corps, armor took the lead in General Brooks's VI Corps,

in this case, the 10th Armored Division, while the 63d and 100th Infantry Divisions followed to mop up. Charged with maintaining contact with the XXI Corps to the north, one column of the armor had to advance through the southern reaches of the Odenwald, generally astride the snakelike Neckar River; but the main body of the armored division attacked southeastward toward Heilbronn over relatively open ground of the Kraichgau Gate.

Had it not been for the presence of the *17th SS Panzer Grenadier Division,* which had remained in the southern fringe of the Odenwald following the unsuccessful effort to halt the XXI Corps, the men of the VI Corps probably would have advanced with the same ease as their neighbors to the north. Facing makeshift formations of the *LXXX Corps* (Beyer), the center and right columns of the 10th Armored Division roamed almost at will in the Kraichgau Gate. One overeager task force on 2 April penetrated several miles across the army boundary, an event that convinced General de Lattre that he had been wise to hurry his Rhine crossings lest the Americans deny the French the honor of a crossing.[15]

On the first day, 1 April, the American armor on the left also moved swiftly, more than two-thirds the distance from Heidelberg to confluence of the Jagst with the Neckar, but on the second day the panzer grenadiers barred the way. Conducting a fighting withdrawal, these troops on several occasions provoked sharp skirmishes. As the armor neared the Jagst River, the Germans called down occasionally heavy fire from assault guns

---

[15] See above, ch. XV.

on the heights to the east. The center column too had to push back determined delaying detachments of panzer grenadiers when on 3 April its tanks drew up to the Neckar north of Heilbronn.

By nightfall of 3 April the Neckar from Heilbronn back to the Rhine nevertheless was clear, and just above the confluence with the Jagst armored infantrymen of the 10th Armored's left column forged a small bridgehead across the Jagst. Although the bridgehead appeared to afford a ready opportunity for getting on with the pursuit the next day, the Germans' failure to melt away before it and the volume of shelling emanating from various points along the crescent formed by the Jagst and the Neckar gave many in the VI Corps pause.

The Americans could not yet know that they had come up against the new line planned by General Foertsch's *First Army*. The panzer grenadiers now were a part of that line under the *XIII Corps*, while all that remained of the *LXXX Corps* extended the line behind the Neckar south beyond Heilbronn. Pushed southward by the French, the *First Army*'s southernmost force, the *XC Corps* (Petersen), would be unable to extend the line farther, and would relinquish its units instead to the *Nineteenth Army* in the Black Forest; but by one stratagem or another, frantic German efforts had produced enough strength along the Jagst-Neckar crescent to give the war a brief, troublesome turn.[16]

---

[16] German material is from MS # B-320, The Final Combat of the *LXXX Army Corps* From the Marne to the Danube (General der Infanterie Dr. Franz Beyer), and MS # B-507, The Fighting From 20 March–6 May 1945 (General der Infanterie Erich Petersen).

The Struggle for Heilbronn and Crailsheim

Presence of the *First Army*'s only remaining battleworthy division, the *17th SS Panzer Grenadier,* plus imposing river obstacles, gave real substance to that part of the new German line along the Jagst-Neckar crescent. In addition, General Foertsch had managed through prodigious efforts to accumulate a sizable conglomeration of other troops—two battalions of an engineer school, several regular engineer battalions, replacement artillery and antiaircraft units, *Volkssturm,* a few tanks and assault guns, and a miscellany, including several hundred Hitler Youth, belonging to the combat commander of Heilbronn. These troops and remnants of four divisions, plus the panzer grenadiers, were all subordinated to General Bork's *XIII Corps.* Loose ends of two other divisions, including the *2d Mountain Division,* were positioned on the north wing of Beyer's *LXXX Corps* and thus might be used to help defend Heilbronn.

Before daylight on 4 April, a battalion of the 100th Division's 398th Infantry slipped silently across the Neckar in assault boats a mile or so north of Heilbronn. As the men turned south toward the city after daybreak, a German battalion counterattacked sharply. The ensuing fight forced the American infantrymen back to within a few hundred feet of the river. There they held, but not until another battalion crossed under fire in late afternoon were they able to resume their advance. Even then they could penetrate no deeper than a thousand yards, scarcely enough to rid the crossing site of small arms fire. Until the bridgehead could be expanded, engineers had no hope of building a bridge.

Impressed by the resistance there and against the minuscule bridgehead established the day before over the Jagst by armored infantrymen of the 10th Armored Division, the commander of the VI Corps, General Brooks, decided to employ a wide enveloping maneuver to erase the enemy's new position. Sending Combat Command B south along the Neckar in search of an intact bridge, he directed the rest of the armored division to move northeast to the land bridge between the Jagst and Tauber Rivers. While CCR blocked there to the east, CCA was to drive southeast twenty-five miles to the road center of Crailsheim. Leaving a task force behind to hold Crailsheim, the rest of CCA was to drive west and northwest and in conjunction with CCB, which was to cross the Neckar south of Heilbronn, take the enemy along the Jagst-Neckar crescent in rear.

It was a daring, imaginative maneuver, one apparently justified by the grand sweeps underway elsewhere in the U.S. Seventh Army. While CCB sought a way across the Neckar, the rest of the armored division moved swiftly across the Jagst-Tauber land bridge (already pierced by a regiment of the 63d Division) . As darkness fell on 5 April, CCA had a leg on the drive to Crailsheim. Resistance was no more than that normally encountered in a breakthrough operation—demolished bridges, occasional roadblocks, small arms fire, antitank rockets. Before dark on the second day, 6 April, CCA had plunged all the way into Crailsheim.

On the third day, 7 April, trouble started. Although the bulk of CCA advanced twelve miles westward from Crailsheim to begin the second phase of

enveloping the Jagst-Neckar crescent, resistance occasionally included fire from 88-mm. pieces and dug-in, determined infantry. At the same time a small task force of CCR, driving southeast toward Crailsheim to keep open CCA's line of communications, encountered stubborn clumps of German infantry supported by antitank guns. On occasion through the day German planes strafed the armored column and at Crailsheim subjected American troops to a rare bombing raid. The task force of CCR laagered for the night without getting through to Crailsheim.

To the Germans, CCA's deep penetration threatened to erase all hope of *Army Group G's* preventing an American drive into southern Germany to roll up the *First* and *Nineteenth Armies*. Almost in desperation, the *First Army* commander, General Foertsch, strove to accumulate troops to throw against it. He directed small contingents pulled from the line of the Jagst to move against CCA's communications while a battalion from an SS training school counterattacked at Crailsheim. As luck would have it, a so-called Alpine regiment, recently formed by a neighboring *Wehrkreis,* was on the way northward for commitment against the U.S. XXI Corps and had reached a point north of Crailsheim. Foertsch committed the Alpine regiment too against CCA's communications.

At Crailsheim the SS troops penetrated deep into thinly held American positions on 8 April, while northwest of the little city the Alpine regiment blocked roads so effectively that the task force of CCR got no place in its efforts to break through. Before the day was out, the 10th Armored Division commander, General Morris, called on CCB, which had failed to find a bridge over the Neckar, to trace CCA's path to Crailsheim, while the Seventh Army commander, General Patch, released a regiment of the 44th Division (Maj. Gen. William F. Dean) from his reserve to help. The commander of the VI Corps, General Brooks, canceled the plan to drive west on Heilbronn, substituting a shallower envelopment to the northwest against the Jagst line.

A contingent of CCB finally got through with a few supply trucks early on the 9th, but to travel the road to Crailsheim remained a task for the fearless and the strong. Before night fell on the 9th, sixty C–47's of the IX Troop Carrier Command flew to a captured airfield just outside the city to deliver supplies and remove a growing number of wounded. While the C–47's were on the field, German planes bombed and strafed them, though with little effect. The strikes were part of some 100 sorties flown against the VI Corps on 9 April, most in the vicinity of Crailsheim. Only those few veterans of the corps who had fought long months ago in Italy could recall a day when German air had been so active.

On the 10th, as C–47's flew another resupply mission to Crailsheim, that part of CCA defending the city repulsed one more counterattack by a second Alpine regiment. Demolished bridges meanwhile frustrated the bulk of CCA in the effort to make a limited envelopment of the enemy's Jagst line. The armor had to settle for a route northwestward that before the end of the day provided contact with the 63d Division along upper reaches of the Jagst but no envelopment of enemy positions.

To American commanders, the embattled salient at Crailsheim was not worth the effort to hold it. As night fell on 11 April and as German commanders watched in relieved incredulity, the last of the armor pulled back.

Bitter from the first, the fighting for Heilbronn had continued heavy. Although three of the 100th Division's battalions eventually crossed into the little bridgehead north of the city to push south into a melange of factories on the northern outskirts, the going always was slow. Since the crossing site remained under German fire, engineers still had no hope of putting in a bridge. Without close fire support, the infantrymen depended upon artillery on the west bank of the Neckar, but fire was difficult to adjust in the confined factory district. Protected from shelling by sturdy buildings, the Germans seldom surrendered except at the point of a rifle, though many of the Hitler Youth had had enough after only a brief flurry of fanatic resistance. At one point, in response to intense mortar fire, a platoon of Hitler Youth soldiers ran screaming into American lines to surrender while their officers shot at them to make them stop.

During the night of 5 April, a battalion of the 397th Infantry crossed the Neckar south of Heilbronn and found resistance at that point just as determined. There engineers had nearly completed a bridge during the afternoon of the 7th when German artillery found the range. Although the engineers at last succeeded early the next morning, less than a company of tanks and two platoons of tank destroyers had crossed before German shells again knocked out the bridge. Two days later much the same thing happened to a heavy ponton ferry after it had transported only a few more tanks and destroyers across.

Not until 12 April was the rubble of Heilbronn cleared of Germans and a bridge built across the Neckar. In nine days of fighting, the 100th Division lost 85 men killed and probably three times that number wounded. In the process, men of the 100th captured 1,500 Germans.[17]

The 63d Division, aided in later stages by tanks of the 10th Armored Division, had in the meantime kept up constant pressure against the enemy's line along the Jagst River, driving southwestward from the vicinity of the Jagst-Tauber land bridge in hope of trapping the *17th SS Panzer Grenadier Division* near the confluence of the Jagst and the Neckar.[18]

_____

[17] Within a company of the 100th Division's 398th Infantry, sent north to reinforce the little bridgehead established by contingents of the 10th Armored Division near the juncture of the Jagst and Neckar, Pfc. Mike Colalillo on 7 April displayed extraordinary courage in the face of heavy German fire. His company pinned down, Colalillo climbed on a supporting tank and opened fire with a machine gun mounted on the turret; when ammunition was exhausted, he grabbed a submachine gun and continued forward on foot. He alone killed or wounded twenty-five Germans. He was awarded the Medal of Honor.

[18] In fighting along the Jagst River on 6 April, a forward observer of the 63d Division's 861st Field Artillery Battalion, 1st Lt. James E. Robinson, Jr., took charge when the commander of the infantry company he was supporting was killed. Despite a serious wound in the throat from a shell fragment, he led twenty-three surviving members of the company to capture a defended town. Only then, when the wound had so weakened him that he could no longer speak, did Lieutenant Robinson turn from the attack and walk almost two miles to an aid station; there he collapsed and died from his wound. On the same day, S. Sgt. John R. Crews of the same division's 253d Infantry charged alone against a German machine gun that poured flanking fire on his company. In hand-to-hand fighting, he eliminated the machine gun and a supporting automatic rifle. Both Sergeant Crews

Although a contingent of armor at last established contact with the 100th Division near Heilbronn on 14 April, the panzer grenadiers had left.

General Foertsch's hasty but surprisingly strong position along the Jagst-Neckar crescent had required eleven days of often heavy fighting to reduce. In view of the determined resistance, American casualties were relatively light, a daily average for the VI Corps of approximately 230. Yet that number was almost double the number of casualties the corps suffered in the pursuit up to the two rivers.

To the Hohe Rhoen and Schweinfurt

On the right wing of the *First Army* and the left of the *Seventh Army,* the Germans had been able to achieve no such reprieve from slashing strokes of other portions of the U.S. Seventh Army. General Hahm's *LXXXII Corps* was powerless to do more than delay General Haislip's XV Corps briefly at occasional towns and roadblocks as Haislip's armor and infantry marched side by side to clear the Hohe Rhoen and protect the 12th Army Group's south flank. Having come too late on the scene to build a firm position behind the Tauber River, General Simon's *XIII SS Corps* was also powerless to stop General Milburn's XXI Corps at the Main River near Wuerzburg.

In the XV Corps, CCB experienced the 14th Armored Division's only major fight, at Gemuenden, at the confluence of the Fraenkische Saale River and the Main. With the help of fighter-bombers

_____

and Lieutenant Robinson were awarded the Medal of Honor, the latter posthumously.

A Tank of the 14th Armored Division *enters the prisoner-of-war camp at Hammelburg.*

of the XII Tactical Air Command, which set many of the houses aflame, the armor cleared the town in an overnight attack. The next day, 6 April, CCB's tanks liberated some 4,000 Allied prisoners of war at Hammelburg. Only 75 Americans, most of them wounded—including General Patton's son-in-law, Colonel Waters—remained in the camp, the rest having been marched to the east as an aftermath of the raid by Task Force Baum.

"I have this?" asked an ecstatic Serb, clutching a shoulder patch of the armored division; "I frame it, for my children and grandchildren." [19]

On 7 April, the 14th Armored's CCA in conjunction with a regiment of the 3d Division took Bad Neustadt on the Fraenkische Saale only a few miles from the Thueringer Wald and the boundary with the Third Army, while the rest of the 3d Division and the 45th advanced almost unimpeded over narrow, winding

[19] Capt. Joseph Carter, *The History of the 14th Armored Division* (privately printed, no pagination).

mountain roads to sweep the Hohe Rhoen. The next day the armor established contact with the Third Army.

In the XXI Corps, brief delays occurred. Although a battalion of the 4th Division on 2 April crossed into the last big southward loop of the Main River, a counterattack and then a stubborn defense by a *Kampfgruppe* built around a company of tanks of the *XIII SS Corps* delayed clearing the southern end of the Main loop. Only on 5 April did infantry of the 4th Division and tanks of the 12th Armored cross the ground lying within the loop and make another crossing of the meandering Main at Kitzingen, southeast of Wuerzburg.

At Wuerzburg men of the 42d Division gained their first foothold over the Main by using two canoes found along the bank. By the 4th, two regiments were inside the city. Because engineers quickly spanned a 100-foot gap in a highway bridge, no problems developed in getting tanks and tank destroyers into the fight, but clearing the city, which had been heavily bombed, was slow. A heterogeneous force under a combat commander, including police and firemen and some civilians, holed up in the rubble, and it took most of three days to root them out. The climax came on the 5th with defeat of a last-gasp company-size counterattack aimed at the bridge over the Main.

With the 42d Division delayed at Wuerzburg, the XXI Corps commander, General Milburn, sent the 12th Armored Division's CCA on toward the next objective, Schweinfurt, twenty-two miles to the northeast, oft-bombed hub of the German ball-bearing industry. Hardly had the armor begun to advance on 5 April when the tanks ran into a defensive position erected across the main highway

to Schweinfurt by a regiment formed from students and staff of an infantry school. Attached to General Hahm's *LXXXII Corps*, these troops had hurriedly gone into position only the night before as impending collapse of the defense at Wuerzburg threatened to expose further Hahm's south flank.[20]

The German infantry was still holding CCA's tanks at bay when on 7 April men of the 42d Division arrived to help. As the Germans at last fell back, the 42d Division commander, General Collins, sent one regiment to seize high ground north of Schweinfurt, cutting escape routes in that direction, while CCA crossed the Main River and on 10 April cut a remaining major road to the southeast of the city. Medium bombers of the 9th Bombardment Division at the same time were giving the city a final working over. Infantry in one day, 11 April, cleared the bulk of resistance from the rubble that Schweinfurt had become.

A Shift to South and Southeast

These drives of the XV and XXI Corps to the northeast and the Third Army's change of direction to the east and southeast as it approached Kassel had created a converging attack. Both the XV Corps and the north wing of the XXI Corps were only a few miles from positions of the 11th Armored Division, right wing unit of the Third Army, which was driving along the southwestern slopes of the Thueringer Wald. Caught in the squeeze was Hahm's *LXXXII Corps.*

Soon after the new *Army Group G* commander, General Schulz, had reached the front, he had come to the same con-

---

[20] MS # B–183 (Ingelheim).

clusion for which his predecessor had been relieved—the army group should relinquish the *Seventh Army* to direct control of the Commander in Chief West and fall back to the south and southeast. Devoid of communications to Field Marshal Kesselring, Schulz recommended this step directly to OKW but received no reaction until 9 April, after the U.S. XV Corps had established contact with the Third Army, thus cutting off the *LXXXII Corps* from the rest of the *Seventh Army*. Ordering Schulz to make Hahm's corps a part of Foertsch's *First Army*, *OKW* tacitly approved *Army Group G's* relinquishing the *Seventh Army*.

Although OKW still granted no authority for *Army Group G* to withdraw to the south and southeast, the American thrusts already had forced the bulk of the *First Army* in those directions. Only Hahm's *LXXXII Corps* had a choice, and that was either to conform or be trapped against the Thueringer Wald.

Both General Haislip's XV Corps and General Milburn's XXI Corps had to turn south and southeast at this point or be pinched out at the Thueringer Wald by the Third Army's southeastward drive. They began their turns on 11 April, the XV Corps aiming toward Bamberg and Nuremberg, the XXI Corps toward Ansbach, southwest of Nuremberg. Two days later, the enemy's defense at Heilbronn and along the Jagst River having been broken, General Brooks's VI Corps turned south into the Loewenstein Hills southeast of Heilbronn.

Although these moves marked the end of the Seventh Army's northeastward thrust to protect the flank of the 12th Army Group, they represented no unrestricted shift to the drive into southern

Germany. As early as 4 April, General Devers had placed broad though definite restrictions on any advances except for the northeastward drive of the XV and XXI Corps. Faced with increasing responsibilities for securing rear areas and performing occupation functions, Devers considered his strength too limited for an all-out thrust. The First French Army was particularly weak, still having to keep some troops on the west bank of the Rhine facing the Black Forest and others to contain the enemy along the French-Italian frontier and in ports along the French coast. This left to Patch's Seventh Army a disproportionate share of the 6th Army Group front, some 120 miles, more than double the width of army sectors in the 12th Army Group. The scattered but nonetheless troublesome resistance the Germans continued to muster, in contrast to a virtual collapse in front of parts of the 12th Army Group, gave substance to Devers's concern.[21]

Only with arrival of the Ninth Army at the Elbe and unqualified success of the 12th Army Group's drive assured did General Eisenhower act to bolster the 6th Army Group and reduce the width of its zone. On 15 April he issued a directive to govern remaining operations for the defeat of Germany. While Montgomery's 21 Army Group drove northeast to the Baltic Sea near Luebeck and cleared the German littoral and the Netherlands, the 12th Army Group was to hold with two armies along the Elbe-Mulde line and send the Third Army southeast down the valley of the Danube River into Austria to Salzburg for eventual linkup with the Russians. The

---

[21] See entries in Devers and Seventh Army Diaries for this period.

6th Army Group was to drive south and southeast into western Austria, making its main effort at first on the right wing of the Seventh Army to trap the enemy *Nineteenth Army* in the Black Forest.[22]

For the offensive into southern Germany and Austria, General Eisenhower shifted the boundary between the 6th and 12th Army Groups west to Wuerzburg. From there the boundary ran southeast, splitting the Austrian frontier midway between Munich and Salzburg and reducing by about fifty miles the width of the 6th Army Group zone. While the Third Army was to be brought up to 15 divisions, the 6th Army Group was to be afforded unrestricted use of 2 divisions that had been assigned for some weeks but had been earmarked as a SHAEF reserve. French and American divisions to be employed in southern Germany were to total 34. In addition Eisenhower offered use of the First Allied Airborne Army should Devers want it, and specifically reserved a new airborne division, the 13th, for a possible airborne assault to speed the main effort south of Stuttgart.

Flying to headquarters of the 12th Army Group on 16 April, General Devers conferred with Generals Bradley and Patton. Rather than effect a time-consuming relief of those Seventh Army divisions already engaged in what was to become the Third Army zone, Devers and Patton agreed that they should continue to attack but should shift their axes of advance to the southeast. The shift would carry them in time into the Seventh Army's altered zone. They later agreed that the 14th Armored Division, which was committed close to the former

Third Army boundary, should become a part of the Third Army and that General Patch should receive a new armored division.

The Supreme Commander's instructions for the offensive were in line with General Devers's original plan, which the 6th Army Group commander had had to forgo in order to protect the 12th Army Group flank. The right wing of the Seventh Army (General Brooks's VI Corps) was to make the main effort up the valley of the Neckar River past Stuttgart to Huebingen, thence south to Lake Constance (Bodensee) and the Swiss frontier. The German *Nineteenth Army* thus trapped in the Black Forest, the VI Corps was to assist the First French Army in clearing the forest while the other two corps of the Seventh Army continued south and southeast across the Danube and into Austria.[23]

Nuremberg and the Drive to the Danube

Even as these plans and orders were being formulated, General Haislip's XV Corps had been making its turn from northeast to southeast, heading first for Bamberg at the meeting of the Main and Regnitz Rivers, then for Nuremberg, scene of annual rallies of the Nazi party and thus a shrine of National Socialism. Because what remained of General Hahm's *LXXXII Corps* was retreating precipitately to avoid entrapment, the first of the objectives, Bamberg, fell on 13 April to contingents of the 3d and 45th Divisions after only a day of fighting against local defense forces.

German commanders were acutely conscious of their lack of troops in this

---

[22] SCAF 281, FWD 19226, in SHAEF SGS Post-OVERLORD Planning file, 381, IV.

[23] 6th AGp Ltr of Instrs 14, 16 Apr 45, in SHAEF SGS Post-OVERLORD Planning file, 381, IV.

sector.[24] What was in effect a transfer of little more than a corps headquarters from *Seventh Army* to *First* would hardly eliminate a gap that the U.S. Third Army's right wing astride the Thueringer Wald and now the U.S. Seventh Army's left wing marching alongside were constantly recreating. Although Field Marshal Kesselring with headquarters of *OB WEST* arrived in the south on 10 April and ordered General Schulz to bring the German *Seventh Army* back under the aegis of *Army Group G,* that by itself would accomplish little more than to pin the onus for the whole problem on one man, Schulz.

General Schulz tried a desperate solution. Since an Allied breakthrough on the right soon would sever all communications, however roundabout, with German forces east of the Elbe River and with Berlin, Schulz decided to bolster his right even at the expense of a breakthrough on his left on the seam between the *First* and *Nineteenth Armies,* since those armies could withdraw in the face of heavy attack without dire results. Although aware that strong Allied attacks soon would hit that seam, Schulz pulled out the remains of the *2d Mountain* and *17th SS Panzer Grenadier Divisions* for transfer to the gap between the *First* and *Seventh Armies.* He would rob Peter to pay Paul, then face the consequences of the theft as best he could when the day of reckoning came.

Lack of gasoline delayed the transfer. After making a strong case for his needs, General Schulz finally obtained some gasoline from a Luftwaffe depot, but before he could bring much of it forward, the head of OKW, Field Marshal Wilhelm Keitel, forbade its use. Such was the dream world in which Hitler and OKW were living that Keitel was saving the fuel for the future strategic employment of jet fighters that presumably were to save the dying Third Reich.[25]

Because of this delay, the remnants of the two divisions arrived too late for fighting at Bamberg. They contributed instead to a stanch defense of Nuremberg, already almost obliterated by Allied bombs.

Like all major German cities, Nuremberg had a ring of fixed antiaircraft guns. These and their crews constituted the core of the defense. The commander and staff of an otherwise defunct *9th Volks Grenadier Division,* operating under General Simon's *XIII SS Corps,* were in charge. To the northwest, blocking the U.S. XXI Corps, whence the Germans expected the main blow on Nuremberg to come, was the *2d Mountain Division.* To the east of the city, trying to shore up the faltering *LXXXII Corps,* went the *17th SS Panzer Grenadiers,* minus one regiment, which was committed inside the city. Within Nuremberg in addition were several Luftwaffe and *Volkssturm* battalions and a regiment provided by *Wehrkreis XIII.* Available a few miles northeast of the city was *Gruppe Grafenwoehr,* composed of two battalions of infantry and thirty-five tanks of various types gleaned from factories in Nuremberg and from a panzer training center whence the force drew its name.[26]

Under a buzzing canopy of aircraft of the XII Tactical Air Command, the 3d

[24] See MS # B-703 (Wilutzky).

[25] MS # B-703 (Wilutzky).

[26] German material is from MSS # B-703 (Wilutzky); # B-348 (Wolf Hauser) and # B-737 (Albert).

A Patrol of the 3d Division Makes Its Way Through the Rubble of Nuremberg

and 45th Divisions in two days spanned the thirty miles from Bamberg to the outskirts of Nuremberg and began an assault on the city on 16 April. The 3d Division moved in from the north, the 45th from east and southeast. The 106th Cavalry Group at the same time swept around the city to block exits to the south, while the 42d Division of the neighboring XXI Corps advanced on the western suburb of Fuerth.

The Germans wasted their few available tanks on the 14th Armored Division northeast of Nuremberg. In a counter-attack on the 15th, *Gruppe Grafenwoehr* struck the 94th Cavalry Reconnaissance Squadron, but reinforcements rushed from the reserve combat command helped bring the strike to a standstill. Within two days *Gruppe Grafenwoehr* had ceased to exit.

It was a grueling fight for Nuremberg, made all the more difficult by deadly antiaircraft fire directed against the men on the ground. Once the ring of flak guns was broken, the fight developed into the slow, often costly, business of clearing one crumbling building after another, one more heap of rubble, one more cellar, defeating one more futile though dangerous counterattack launched by a few men, a squad, a platoon.[27] All the while fighter-bombers and artillery kept pounding an already ruined metropolis.

Late on 19 April the 3d Division's 30th Infantry penetrated medieval walls to enter the old town in the heart of the city. Before daylight the next morning, the Nazi gauleiter, who had vowed in a message to Hitler to fight to the death, directed a final, fanatic counterattack. Except for a few Germans who had to be rooted from the rubble, that ended the fight. The gauleiter himself was found dead in a cellar. The shrine of nazism fell, ironically, on 20 April, Hitler's birthday.

With the collapse of the defenses at Nuremberg, the *First Army* right wing gave way. In the same manner that one pushing against a closed door hurtles forward when the door suddenly opens, both Haislip's XV Corps and Milburn's XXI Corps plunged some fifty miles to the Danube. Launching a drive from Feuchtwangen, southwest of Nuremberg, on 20 April, the 12th Armored Division of the XXI Corps got there first, crossing

the river two days later on a bridge seized intact at Dillingen. General Milburn's infantry divisions, the 4th and 63d, made it on the 25th. Relinquishing the 14th Armored Division to the Third Army, Haislip's XV Corps used two infantry divisions, the 42d (transferred from the XXI Corps during the fight for Nuremberg) and the 45th, also to reach the Danube on the 25th. In the process the two divisions moved southwestward from Nuremberg to get out of the zone that was to be transferred to the Third Army.

The Third Army too benefited from the collapse of the German *First Army* right wing; the collapse reopened a gap between the *First* and *Seventh Armies* into which the Third Army in its new drive to the southeast could plunge. Because of the regrouping maneuver that left the VIII Corps and five divisions in place along the Mulde River for transfer to the First Army and brought the III Corps and six divisions from completed assignments in the Ruhr, the Third Army was ready to exploit the gap with full force on 23 April, though the drive actually began as early as the 19th.

Before the new drive started the XII Corps commander, General Eddy, because of high blood pressure, relinquished command to the former commander of the 5th Division, General Irwin. Under the new leader, the XII Corps began on 19 April to edge southeastward from an earlier stopping point at Bayreuth, while the III and XX Corps continued shifting zones. Contingents of General Walker's XX Corps from new positions in the center of the Third Army began to advance the next day. Although General Van Fleet's III Corps was not to assume control of the 14th

---

[27] For gallantry in singlehandedly defeating one of these counterattacks on 17 April, 1st Lt. Frank Burke of the 3d Division's 15th Infantry received the Medal of Honor. The next day, 18 April, Capt. Michael J. Daly of the same regiment fought alone in four separate engagements, killing fifteen Germans, knocking out three machine guns, and inspiring his company to advance. He also was awarded the Medal of Honor. On the same day, Pvt. Joseph F. Merrell of the same regiment launched a one-man assault against two German machine gun positions, eliminated them despite a serious wound in the stomach, then fell before a burst from a German machine pistol. Private Merrell was awarded the Medal of Honor posthumously.

Armored Division until 23 April, the fact that the division was continuing to attack as a part of the Seventh Army meant that the front on what would become the Third Army's right wing was also moving forward.

By the time the III Corps officially took over on the right wing the night of 22 April, forward troops of the III and XX Corps were south and southeast of Nuremberg, only forty miles from the Danube, while contingents of the XII Corps were well south of a highway that leads east from Nuremberg to Pilsen, Czechoslovakia. Although resistance to the heretofore measured advance had at some points been stanch, no question existed that all three corps could advance almost at will as they threw full strength into the fight.

When the attack began in earnest on 24 April, many of the units General Patton had received in exchange for the VIII Corps were relative newcomers to battle—the 13th Armored, 65th, 71st, 86th, and 97th Divisions—but in the pursuit warfare that the times demanded, their inexperience scarcely showed. As in the battle-tested divisions, infantrymen clung precariously to anything that moved by motor—tanks, tank destroyers, trailers, ready at the first sound of enemy fire to jump from their perches and assume the age-old mode of infantry attack. Corps artillery often was left far behind, its trucks mobilized to shuttle infantrymen forward. Everywhere captured German vehicles dotted the columns.

The countryside of the Fraenkische Highland was strikingly beautiful with spring. Here a cluster of daffodils, there a farmer turning a damp furrow, cows grazing in green fields. Only in the towns

and cities did war seem to have any place. There the streets were dead, sometimes block after block of rubble, or else owed their survival to great white flags of surrender hanging from every building. Almost everywhere during late April, front lines had ceased to exist, so that nobody knew when or where the fighting might erupt—at the next hill, ridge, village, stream, wherever a group of Germans with a will to fight took a stand. Sometimes the Germans would let infantry and tanks pass unmolested, then turn sudden, unanticipated wrath on artillery and supply units bringing up the rear. Other times men who had dug in to fight would for some inexplicable reason throw away their weapons to raise hands high in surrender. Everybody knew that the war was over, yet somehow, at one isolated spot or another, the war still went on, real enough for the moment and sometimes deadly for those involved.

While awaiting arrival of an assigned armored division, General Walker's XX Corps in the Third Army center used the 3d Cavalry Group to reach the Danube first. Gaining the river southwest of Regensburg early in the afternoon of 24 April, the cavalry opened the way for assault crossings by the 65th and 71st Divisions the following night. On the army's right wing around Ingolstadt, three divisions of the III Corps—14th Armored, 86th, and 99th—reached the Danube in early afternoon on 26 April. Paced by the 11th Armored Division, the XII Corps meanwhile advanced down a narrow corridor between the Danube and the Czechoslovakian frontier. Guarding the corps right flank, the 26th Division reached the Danube on the 26th.

The Drive on Stuttgart

For the Allied main effort—a sweep by the VI Corps up the valley of the Neckar River, thence across the Danube to the Austrian frontier—General Patch in the meantime had been employing three infantry divisions and the 10th Armored Division in an attack that was supposed to be co-ordinated closely with a subsidiary thrust by the First French Army against Stuttgart. Under the 6th Army Group's plan, the French attack had to be timed carefully lest a premature advance prompt the German *Nineteenth Army* to pull out before the VI Corps could bypass Stuttgart and block major highways south of the city leading out of the Black Forest. Although the French were to capture Stuttgart, they were then to afford Seventh Army troops running rights on the main highways through the city to help speed the Seventh Army's continuing advance across the Danube into Austria. The 13th Airborne Division (Maj. Gen. Elbridge G. Chapman) was tentatively scheduled for an airdrop thirty miles south of Stuttgart to seize an airfield and create an airhead to block German escape routes.[28]

Another reason Devers wanted to put American forces east and south of Stuttgart before the French attacked was the presence in the 6th Army Group at the time of the special ALSOS intelligence mission, which sought data on German developments in nuclear fission. The ALSOS group was to accompany the VI Corps in the drive to cut roads south of Stuttgart and then make a dash for the town of Hechingen, fifty miles southwest of the city, where German scientists reportedly were conducting nuclear experiments. The ALSOS mission wanted to capture the scientists and their research data before they fell into French hands.[29]

As General Devers issued his instructions formally on 16 April, the VI Corps had completed a reorientation to the south following the unexpectedly sharp fight for Heilbronn and the Jagst-Neckar crescent. Although the Germans had pulled out the *2d Mountain* and *17th SS Panzer Grenadier Divisions* from this sector, a general collapse of remaining troops in Beyer's *LXXX Corps* and Bork's *XIII Corps* was yet to develop.

The French meanwhile had been making gains that to their commander, General de Lattre, appeared to warrant unilaterally superseding General Devers's instructions. Having quickly captured Karlsruhe (4 April) and Pforzheim (8 April) and having cleared a crescent formed by confluence of the Enz River with the Neckar just over 10 miles from Stuttgart, de Lattre had staged a dramatic maneuver. Once an armored division had swept quickly up the east bank of the Rhine to a point opposite Strasbourg, de Lattre on 15 April sent a corps across the Rhine there and launched an advance eastward along a highway splitting the Black Forest. Other French troops were at the same time driving south along roads in the eastern fringe of the forest. As General Devers issued his directive on 16 April, the citizens of Strasbourg were ringing their church bells to celebrate the city's relief from German artillery fire, and

---

[28] See 6th AGp Ltr of Instrs 14, 16 Apr 45, and Warren, *Airborne Operations in World War II, European Theater*, p. 201.

[29] Pash, *The ALSOS Mission*, ch. XXI.

the two French forces were within a few miles of linking up, thus writing off the northern half of the Black Forest and gaining the upper reaches of the Neckar close to the network of roads south of Stuttgart that constituted the Seventh Army's first objective.

To conform to General Devers's orders in the wake of these developments was, to de Lattre, to abandon all benefits accruing from the maneuvers. To delay further French advances while the Americans still were some twenty to twenty-five miles north and northwest of Stuttgart was to invite the Germans to escape from the city and the southern half of the Black Forest. Despite an explicit explanation of General Devers's plan, presented on 17 April, de Lattre ignored Devers's directive and ordered one corps to launch a double envelopment of the southern half of the Black Forest, the other to begin immediately to envelop Stuttgart from the south and east.[30]

The maneuver to envelop Stuttgart opened with signal success on 18 April. Crossing the interarmy boundary into the zone assigned the Seventh Army, the French seized the road center of Tuebingen, on the Neckar almost due south of Stuttgart. If they could repeat that success as they turned north toward Stuttgart the next day, they sood a chance of trapping sizable German forces. Although the thrust to Tuebingen had split the enemy's *LXIV Corps* (General der Artillerie Max Grimmeiss), the bulk of the corps, including commander and staff, were north of the penetration. In

GENERAL DE LATTRE. (*Photograph taken in 1951.*)

addition, the *LXXX Corps* (Beyer), recently transferred to the *Nineteenth Army,* was defending astride the Neckar north of Stuttgart and also might be trapped should the French envelop the city.[31]

Faced with encirclement, the Germans on 19 April stiffened, while the remnants of two divisions of the *LXIV Corps* tried to muster a counterattack southward to cut off the French penetration to Tuebingen. Although the counterattack never got under way, the Germans held their French adversaries to relatively minor gains all through the 19th and 20th.

---

[30] De Lattre, *Histoire de la Première Armée Française*, pp. 529–31; for French operations in early April, pp. 506–28. See also Hq, 6th AGp, History, p. 273.

[31] See MS # B-598, The Combat Actions of the *LXIV Corps* East of the Rhine, Part II, 4–22 Apr 45 (General der Artillerie Max Grimmeiss) and MS # B-320, The Final Combat of the *LXXX Army Corps* From the Marne to the Danube, Part III, 8 Feb–30 Apr 45 (Beyer).

A greater threat to the two German corps then arose from the Americans. After three days of short advances by the 63d and 100th Divisions through minefields and roadblocks in the Loewenstein Hills southeast of Heilbronn and at Schwaebisch Hall to the east, the 10th Armored Division on the 19th suddenly broke free. In rapid strides the armor swept southward more than thirty miles, passing to the east of Stuttgart, while men of the 44th Division followed closely to mop up and protect the flanks of the penetration. The next day the tank columns continued to Kirchheim, in the hill country of the Swabian Highland fourteen miles southeast of Stuttgart, there cutting the autobahn leading from Stuttgart to Ulm. Because of that thrust and the earlier drive by the French, the projected airborne assault south of Stuttgart was canceled.[32]

By this time the French had reached a point only ten miles southwest of Kirchheim, leaving to the Germans in and around Stuttgart only one main road as a route of escape. Although the commander of the *LXXX Corps,* General Beyer, tried to arrange with his opposite in the *LXIV Corps,* General Grimmeiss, for a combined breakout attempt, Grimmeiss's troops were too closely engaged. The bulk of Beyer's *LXXX Corps* the night of the 20th pulled out alone through the narrow gap, while General Grimmeiss and remnants of his *LXIV Corps* the next day tried to infiltrate southward through French positions. Few made it. After wandering for twelve days and nights,

Grimmeiss himself at last fell captive to the French near the Swiss border.[33]

Faced with a *fait accompli,* General Devers on the 20th legitimatized the French foray into the Seventh Army's zone by a change in the interarmy boundary, whereupon a French column the next day pushed down the valley of the Neckar by way of Esslingen, enveloped Stuttgart, and broke into the northeastern fringe of the city early in the afternoon. Other columns entered a few hours later from south, west, and northwest. The following day, 22 April, Stuttgart was clear.

In an imaginative, aggressive maneuver, de Lattre's First French Army in twelve days had swept the northern half of the Black Forest, trapped the bulk of the *LXIV Corps,* and seized Stuttgart, in the process taking some 28,000 prisoners at a cost of 175 French troops killed, 510 wounded. Whether more Germans might have been captured had de Lattre conformed to General Dever's plan could only be surmised. Devers and his staff believed the bag would have been bigger.[34]

At the same time the French had seriously jeopardized the ALSOS mission's intended foray to seize German scientists and nuclear research data at Hechingen, southwest of Stuttgart. This the Americans had circumvented by directing the ALSOS group and an escort of motorized combat engineers to circle back to the northwest of Stuttgart and drive south into the French sector to Freudenstadt in order to come on Hechingen from the

---

[32] SUSA Diary, entry of 20 Apr 45; Warren, Airborne Operations in World War II, p. 201.

[33] MS # B-598 (Grimmeiss); MS # B-320 (Beyer). See also de Lattre, *Histoire de la Première Armée Française,* p. 557n.

[34] De Lattre, *Histoire de la Première Armée Française,* p. 539; Hq, 6th AGp, Hisotry, p. 273.

west. With the ALSOS military commander, Col. Boris T. Pash, employing
considerable bluff, the group made its
way successfully through the French sector, then on 22 April pushed beyond
forward French positions and moved
swiftly to Hechingen, where it found the
German research center hidden in a cave
and captured the scientists in the town.[35]

A French Incursion to Ulm

Aside from Stuttgart, two other specific
objectives in that part of Germany held
special attraction for General de Lattre
and the French. One was the town of
Sigmaringen, on the Danube River not
quite fifty miles south of Stuttgart. There
Marshal Henri Philippe Pétain, Pierre
Laval, and others of the collaborationist
Vichy government had come after fleeing
France the preceding August and had
set up a government-in-exile. The other
was the imperial city of Ulm, also on the
Danube roughly the same distance southeast of Stuttgart, scene of Napoleon's
triumph over the Austrians in 1805.

As General Devers had drawn the interarmy boundary in his original instructions for the offensive, neither of those
objectives had fallen in the French zone.
Running southwestward from the vicinity of Stuttgart to Rottweil on upper
reaches of the Neckar, thence almost due
south to the Swiss frontier west of Lake
Constance, the boundary reflected Devers's view that the first task for the
French was to dispense with the German
Nineteenth Army in Stuttgart and the
Black Forest. That accomplished, Devers's order made clear, the boundary was
to be adjusted to swing to the southeast

and give the French a role in entering
Austria.[36]

General de Lattre also saw Stuttgart
and the Black Forest as primary goals,
as demonstrated on 17 April when he
sent half his force against Stuttgart, half
to clear the southern part of the Black
Forest. Yet all along de Lattre had his
eyes on a third goal: Ulm, and, in the
process, Sigmaringen.

"The true maneuver," de Lattre had
told one of his subordinates as early as
15 April, "is to march at full speed [*tam-
bour battant*] in order to be in Ulm by
25 April." [37]

In terms of the original interarmy
boundary, Ulm lay forty-four miles east
of the French zone. While the 10th Armored Division bypassed the city to the
west, the 44th Division was to capture it.
Although the change in boundary ordered on the 20th extended the French
zone southeastward from Rottweil to Sigmaringen, and by any logical extension
provided the French some forty miles
of the Austrian frontier east of Lake
Constance, the adjustment still left Ulm
fully forty miles outside the French zone.

De Lattre refused to be deterred. Late
on 20 April he directed the commander
of the corps that was attacking Stuttgart
to divert an armored division southeastward toward Rottweil and the Danube
with the aim of eventually swinging back
to the northeast astride the Danube
through Sigmaringen to Ulm.

General de Lattre would note later
that there were other reasons for the
French to drive on Ulm than reawak-
ening the memory of past glory. The
drive was, he would argue, a logical ex-

---

[35] Pash, *The ALSOS Mission*, ch. XXI.

[36] See 6th AGp Ltr of Instrs No. 14, 16 Apr 45.
[37] De Lattre, *Histoire de la Première Armée Française*, p. 544.

tension of the envelopment of Stuttgart to trap those Germans who had escaped the encirclement there and thus deny them access to the National Redoubt. He also looked on the drive as a step in establishing French forces along the length of the Iller River, extending generally south from Ulm to the Austrian frontier, a line lying almost entirely within the Seventh Army's zone. That move, he believed, would force the American command to provide the French a zone for entering Austria rather than leave them impotently facing the Swiss border.[38]

These were less reasons than rationalizations. By the night of 20 April when de Lattre ordered the start of the thrust on Ulm, the U.S. 10th Armored Division was at Kirchheim, less than thirty miles from the Danube, and was fully capable of handling any German force that had escaped from Stuttgart. Similarly, the boundary adjustment that General Devers ordered on the 20th already had assured the French a forty-mile zone of entry into Austria.

On 21 April the French drive southward to clear the southern half of the Black Forest picked up momentum. French forces advancing along the eastern fringe of the forest crossed the Danube and gained the northwestern tip of Lake Constance, thereby sealing off the *Nineteenth Army's XVIII SS Panzer Corps* in the Black Forest. Another column attacking up the east bank of the Rhine turned to seize the city of Freiburg. An armored division achieved the first goal in the roundabout thrust on Ulm, reaching the Danube a few miles upstream from Sigmaringen.

De Lattre was ecstatic. "Bravo!" he cheered, then ordered the division to push *"pleins gaz"* via Sigmaringen to Ulm. "The Americans will perhaps dislodge us from it," he continued. "But the French flag will have flown there." [39]

Too late to catch Pétain and Laval at Sigmaringen, the French armor nevertheless made rapid strides along the Danube. So did the U.S. 10th Armored Division in its drive to the Danube. By nightfall of the 22d the Americans had reached the river at Ehingen and had seized a bridgehead. The French would thus have to pass directly through the American positions, raising the specter of a clash with American troops who were unaware of the French presence.

Fortunately, when the French armor encountered outposts of the 10th Armored Division near Ehingen early on 23 April, the Americans for all their surprise quickly identified the intruders. As de Lattre recalled it, the 10th Armored Division commander, General Morris, raised no objections, remarking that, "Among tankers, we always understand each other." [40]

When word of the incident reached General Devers at the 6th Army Group that afternoon, he was considerably less amenable. He sent a liaison officer to de Lattre's headquarters with orders to withdraw immediately.[41] De Lattre paid him no heed.

The leading French platoon drew up outside Ulm at dusk on 23 April. Soon after the 44th Division's 324th Infantry arrived at dawn the next day, that regiment, the 10th Armored Division's CCR, and two French battalions attacked

---

[38] *Ibid.,* pp. 558–60.

[39] *Ibid.,* p. 560.
[40] *Ibid.,* p. 563.
[41] Hq, 6th AGp, History, pp. 281–82.

the city from the southwest along the north bank of the Danube. By nightfall most resistance was at an end, and the French were free to unfurl their tricolor, as Napoleon had done, above the city's old fort.

Mission accomplished, General de Lattre at last promised to take his troops inside the French boundary.[42]

The "Stuttgart Incident"

In Stuttgart, in the meantime, General Devers's patience with the French had been undergoing an even more severe test. While according the French the honor of capturing Stuttgart, General Devers had planned from the first to use main roads through the city to support the Seventh Army. Disturbed by the presence of thousands of liberated, deliriously happy foreign laborers in Stuttgart, including 20,000 French deportees, he decided on 22 April that the Seventh Army's needs could be better served by placing the city in the U.S. zone. This he ordered, effective the next day.[43]

To a sensitive General de Lattre, removing his troops after their achievement in capturing Stuttgart was an affront. While protesting to General Devers, he reported the situation to the chief of the French Provisional Government, General de Gaulle. De Gaulle replied promptly and firmly. De Lattre was to

maintain a French garrison in Stuttgart, institute a military government, and tell the Americans that the French intended to hold and administer all territory conquered by French troops until the interested governments had fixed a French zone of occupation.[44]

In passing the word to General Devers, de Lattre added that Stuttgart was available nonetheless to all needs of the 6th Army Group. To Devers, use of Stuttgart was no longer the issue; the issue was a direct violation of orders by a subordinate, a situation he found "intolerable." [45] Tales emanating from the city of wanton rape and looting further strengthened his resolve. After reporting the matter to General Eisenhower on 26 April, Devers reiterated his order to relinquish the city and told the 100th Division to move in.

As American troops began to arrive, the local French commander treated them amicably but declined to evacuate the city. While informing de Gaulle of this development, de Lattre again notified General Devers that because of contrary instructions from his government, he was unable to comply with the 6th Army Group's order.[46]

General Devers himself went into Stuttgart on the 27th to check the tales of rape and looting. The reports, he found, had been exaggerated. Rather than 50,000 rape cases, as rumored, there had been fewer than 2,000; and most of those, as well as considerable looting and "misbehavior," were attributable to for-

[42] SUSA Diary, entry of 24 Apr 45. See also Brief of Events Having to Do With the Advance on Ulm by First French Army, 26 Apr 45, in SHAEF SGS Post-OVERLORD Planning file, 381, IV, and comments by General Morris on the draft MS for this volume.

[43] 6th AGp Msg BX 13260, 22 Apr 45, as found in Hq, 6th AGp, History, p. 269; 6th AGp TWX, 23 Apr 45, in SHAEF SGS Post-OVERLORD Planning file, 381, IV; Seventh Army Report, pp. 803–04.

[44] De Lattre, Histoire de la Première Armée Française, pp. 569–70.

[45] Devers to Eisenhower, B–13494, 26 Apr 45, in SHAEF SGS Post-OVERLORD Planning file, 381, IV.

[46] De Lattre, Histoire de la Première Armée Française, p. 570.

eign laborers and Germans themselves. Conditions were, in any event, markedly improved. Deciding that the city was too badly damaged to be of use to the 6th Army Group, Devers readjusted the interarmy boundary, giving Stuttgart—"and the conditions there," he noted wryly—back to the French.[47]

The Supreme Commander, for his part, protested officially to General de Gaulle. "Under the circumstances," General Eisenhower wrote, "I must of course accept the situation, as I myself am unwilling to take any action which would reduce the effectiveness of the military effort against Germany . . . ." He protested nevertheless that the issuance of direct orders to the First French Army counter to operational orders given through the military chain of command violated the understanding with the United States Government under which the United States had armed and equipped French divisions to serve under the Combined Chiefs of Staff. He had no choice, he concluded, but to refer the matter to the Combined Chiefs.[48]

In reply General de Gaulle put the blame on a lack of agreement and liaison between France and the Allied governments relating to war policy in general and the postwar occupation in particular. As for arms for French troops, he noted, those had been furnished under lend-lease, for which French services had been given in return.

When news of the incident reached Washington, President Truman was shocked. If the time had come, he wrote

General de Gaulle, when the French Army was to carry out only the political wishes of the French Government, then the command structure would have to be rearranged. De Gaulle in reply expressed the wish that situations of this nature would not arise and suggested that they could be avoided if the Allies would consult the French on matters involving French interests.

There the matter rested. It would be finally settled early in May when the Allies at last agreed on a French zone of occupation and a French role in the control machinery for Germany.

From the Danube Into Austria

In reaching Lake Constance on 21 April, the First French Army had failed to snare the commander of the *Nineteenth Army,* General Brandenberger, and his staff. The French had nevertheless trapped most of Brandenberger's remaining troops, the entire *XVIII SS Panzer Corps,* in the southern half of the Black Forest. (*Map XVII*) Beginning the night of the 24th, the Germans tried to break out to the southeast, giving rise to violent combat, but when French air and artillery pummeled them mercilessly by day, the Germans quickly weakened. Only individuals and small groups escaped, leaving some 27,000 to wend their way into prisoner-of-war enclosures. By 27 April the Black Forest was calm.[49]

The demise of the *XVIII SS Panzer Corps* left the *Nineteenth Army* with the remnants of two corps, that part of the *LXIV Corps* that had avoided the French near Stuttgart (*OB WEST* assigned a new corps commander) and General Beyer's

---

[47] Devers Diary, 27 Apr 45. See also SUSA Diary, entry of 25 Apr 45.

[48] Aspects of the incident at higher levels are discussed and annotated in Pogue, *The Supreme Command,* pp. 459–61.

[49] See de Lattre, *Histoire de la Première Armée Française,* pp. 561–67.

LXXX Corps, the latter minus some 2,000 men trapped in the Swabian Highland by the 10th Armored Division's crossing of the Danube and left to the 103d Division to mop up. Also under the *Nineteenth Army* was a force of little more than division size deceptively called the *"Twenty-fourth Army."* These were mainly headquarters troops fleshed out with *Volkssturm* and frontier battalions that had manned posts along the Swiss border to discourage any Allied plan to enter Germany by way of neutral Switzerland. The *Twenty-fourth Army* had escaped the French trap by crossing Lake Constance by boat.[50]

As for General Foertsch's *First Army,* all corps headquarters and most divisional formations—such as they were— got across the Danube a step ahead of their pursuers, but all inevitably lost large numbers of men in the process. During the week ending 26 April, each of the U.S. Seventh Army's three corps averaged well over a thousand prisoners a day.

The Third Army's southeastward turn had created an unremediable rupture between the German *First* and *Seventh Armies,* throwing the *Seventh Army* back against the Czechoslovakian frontier where General von Obstfelder and his staff could do little but await eventual capitulation.[51] Although Kesselring at *OB WEST* ordered a counterattack into the Third Army's eastern flank, the meager forces available for commitment had no fuel. When on the 26th Kesselring ordered the *LXXXV Corps,* which con-

tained remains of the *11th Panzer Division,* to move to the *First Army* to cover the gap by defending the Danube along the Austrian frontier near Passau, lack of gasoline again prevented compliance. Two days later Kesselring formally recognized the split between the *First* and *Seventh Armies* by removing the *Seventh Army* from *Army Group G's* control and placing it directly under his own command.[52] So disorganized were the German defenders along the seam between the armies that the U.S. XII Corps in a week took from the sector more than 25,000 prisoners.

Forced behind the Danube and patently incapable of preventing Allied troops from crossing wherever they chose, the Germans in the south at last were as disorganized and impotent as those who had tried to stem the eastward surge of the 12th Army Group. They still might muster an occasional counterattack, sometimes in as much as battalion strength, and they might yet delay Allied advance at strategic points, particularly in cities, but the end was near. As someone at General Eisenhower's headquarters put it, the Allied forces now were engaged in "the disarming, by battle, of the German armies."[53]

One American crossing of the Danube after another quickly eliminated that river as a factor in the operation. The 12th Armored Division (XXI Corps) crossed over a captured bridge at Dillingen on the 22d; the 10th Armored and 44th Divisions (VI Corps) over three captured bridges near Ehingen on the 23d. After the 42d Division had captured Donauwoerth on the 25th, both the 42d and 45th Divisions (XV Corps) made

[50] MSS # B-102 and # B-103, *Twenty-fourth Army,* 17 Oct 1944-5 May 1945 (General der Infanterie Hans Schmidt). See also MS # B-191, The *LXIV Army Corps* in the Time from 21.IV.45 to 5.V.45 (Generalleutnant Helmuth Friebe).

[51] MS # A-893 (Gersdorff).

[52] MS # B-703 (Wilutzky).

[53] As quoted in Seventh Army Report, p. 805.

assault crossings near that old city before daylight on the 26th. At the same time, the 65th and 71st Divisions (XX Corps) crossed on either side of Regensburg, in the process prompting the combat commander of the old south-bank fortress city (Napoleon had known it as Ratisbon) to flee, leaving to a retired general the ignominy of surrender without fight. The 103d Division (VI Corps) crossed northeast of Ulm at daylight on the 26th; and finally, the 86th Division (III Corps), after capturing Ingolstadt, made an assault crossing the night of the 26th. (Advancing southeast between the Danube and the Czechoslovakian border, the XII Corps would face a crossing of the river only after reaching the Austrian frontier.)

Only one new component of appreciable size joined the German order of battle, a *Division Nibelungen,* originally intended but readied too late for General Wenck's *Twelfth Army* on the Elbe. Committed on 27 April in the path of the U.S. III Corps southeast of Ingolstadt, the division was almost at full strength in men, but some 40 percent lacked weapons. Aside from a few pre-World War II tanks, the heaviest weapon on hand was the *Panzerfaust.* In a matter of only three days, the division ceased to exist.[54]

As the drive toward the Austrian border began, the now familiar pattern of an armored division out front, followed by infantry divisions for the mop-up, quickly developed everywhere except in General Haislip's XV Corps. Having relinquished his armor to the incoming III Corps, Haislip would be able to commit the replacement, the inexperienced 20th

Armored Division (Maj. Gen. Orlando Ward), only on 28 April.

The assault spread rapidly through the picturesque Bavarian villages and countryside. If the villagers displayed white flags and no one fired, the columns raced rapidly on. If the Germans made a stand, tanks, artillery, and planes tore the houses to bits. The message apparently got through, for time after time civilians prevailed upon the German soldiery to leave.

A pattern of no resistance in cities, too, began to emerge. Before attacking Memmingen, just east of the Iller River midway between Ulm and the Austrian frontier, the 10th Armored Division sent ahead burgomasters of towns already captured to warn that only white flags and absence of resistance could spare the city from destruction. The stratagem worked; on 26 April, nobody fought back in Memmingen.

At Landsberg, site of another of the incredibly bestial Nazi concentration camps, a garrison of almost a hundred Hungarian troops lined up in parade-ground formation to surrender. Men of the 103d Division, occupying the town in the wake of the tanks of the 10th Armored Division, claimed as a souvenir a bronze plaque on a building commemorating the spot where Hitler had been imprisoned following the abortive Munich Putsch in 1923 and where he had dictated the bible of the National Socialist movement, *Mein Kampf.*

In Augsburg, on the Lech River midway between Ulm and Munich, arose the first tangible evidence of an active German underground resistance organization. As the 3d Division approached the city on 27 April, word came from an adjacent unit that two civilians had ar-

---

[54] MS # B-348 (Wolf Hauser); III Corps AAR, Apr 45.

rived to arrange surrender and avoid destruction. Despite shelling from anti-aircraft batteries ringing the city, the division commander, General O'Daniel, put a moratorium on artillery fire pending further developments.

Within Augsburg the combat commander, Generalmajor Franz Fehn, intended to fight, but he refused to sanction demolishing bridges and overpasses. He also early began to evacuate German soldiers from the city's hospitals and distributed several hundred tons of military rations to the civilian population.

Small underground groups, none yet aware of the existence of others, meanwhile prepared to stage a coup. Members of one group calling itself the "Freedom Party of Augsburg" reached one of the American regiments by telephone with word that the city wanted to surrender. Others who counseled surrender spread the word that the authorities had already capitulated and that everybody should display white flags. A civilian patrol reached one of the American columns to lead a battalion commander and a small group to a bunker shared by General Fehn and civilian functionaries of the city. Given five minutes to surrender, General Fehn marched dutifully out to view a city already fluttering with white flags.[55]

Munich, capital of Bavaria, Germany's third city and another shrine of nazism, was next. En route, contingents of the 42d and 45th Divisions overpowered some 300 SS guards and unveiled another of Germany's most notorious concentra-

tion camps, Dachau. Delirious with joy, some of the pitiful survivors of the camp rushed the electrically charged wire enclosure and died in their moment of liberation. Others hunted down their wardens, many of whom had changed into prison garb to hide among the inmates, and beat them to death with stones, clubs, fists. More than 30,000 prisoners clinging precariously to life, and great piles of grotesque, starved cadavers crammed the camp. At the crematorium was the usual grim evidence of the efficiency of Nazi extermination methods.

Leaving to medics the task of trying to save the typhus-infested inmates, the 42d and 45th Divisions pushed on to join a four-division assault against Munich stage-managed by General Haislip's XV Corps. With the 20th Armored and 42d and 45th Divisions approaching the city from the northwest and north, the Seventh Army's General Patch altered corps boundaries to put the 3d Division, which was approaching from Augsburg in a position to swing to the south of Munich, temporarily under Haislip's command. Anxious to have a hand in seizing the prize, the 12th Armored Division of the neighboring XXI Corps sent its reconnaissance troops on an unauthorized foray toward the city from the southwest.

As at Augsburg, a delegation of civilians bought word that residents of Munich were trying to prevail on military leaders to spare the city. During the night of 27 April, a variety of groups ranging from sincere anti-Nazi underground workers to war-weary burghers and common opportunists rose in a series of unconnected revolts. At the center of the uprising were three platoons of troops from *Wehrkreis VII,* reinforced

---

[55] Seventh Army Report, pp. 828–30; MS # B–186, Report by *407 Replacement Division* About the Construction and Organization of the Donau-Iller Defense (Generalmajor Franz Fehn).

by contingents from a panzer replacement battalion stationed in a nearby town and little groups of dissident infantrymen. As street fighting broke out, the insurgents captured the Nazi gauleiter of Bavaria and the Munich radio station, but they failed to seize military and Nazi party headquarters.

Bolstered by SS troops from a caserne in the northern fringe of the city, troops loyal to the Nazis fought back. They failed to squelch the rebellion in Munich entirely, for the insurgents managed to save the city's bridges and to provide considerable assistance when the Americans arrived forty-eight hours later. Neither could the insurgents claim victory. Although some units of the 3d and 42d Divisions reached the center of the city before midday on 30 April to the welcome of small groups of civilians waving both white flags of surrender and Bavarian flags of celebration, other contingents had to clear stubborn nests of resistance, and the 45th Division faced a determined fight for the SS caserne. For most of the day it was a question of pouring in heavy artillery fire, attacking behind smoke screens across city streets, dodging deadly fire from antiaircraft guns or persistent machine guns—all the usual accouterments the men had come to expect in clearing rubble-strewn German cities. Even as a big white streamer flew from the highest building in Munich, troops of the 45th Division were fighting from room to room in the SS caserne to dislodge die-hard defenders. By nightfall of 30 April, it was finally over.

Those two corps of the Third Army that had crossed the Danube meanwhile were running a day or so behind the Seventh Army, primarily because of the late commitment of the III Corps. Before armor could begin to exploit from the bridgeheads, heavy rains set in. The 13th Armored Division of the XX Corps nevertheless crossed the Isar River near Landau on the 29th, then two days later reached the Inn River where it forms the Austrian border around Braunau. The 14th Armored Division of the III Corps took Landshut on the Isar on 30 April, then caught up with its neighbor to reach the Inn the next day. Advancing down the corridor between the Danube and Czechoslovakia, the 11th Armored Division of the XII Corps put patrols across the Austrian frontier near Passau as early as the 26th.

Both here and in the zone of the Seventh Army a feature of the advance was the liberation of thousands of American and Allied prisoners of war. At long last the Germans had abandoned all efforts to march the prisoners out of reach of the rampaging Allied columns.

While these thrusts were getting under way, the Supreme Commander, General Eisenhower, reaffirmed final objectives for the Third Army and the 6th Army Group.[56] As before, the goal of the Third Army was to link with the Russians inside Austria, in the process seizing Salzburg and thus blocking passes leading from Salzburg into the Austrian Tirol. The 6th Army Group was to capture all other routes into the Alps—that at Bregenz at the eastern end of Lake Constance leading into the Vorarlberg, others in the vicinity of Fuessen and Garmisch-Partenkirchen leading to Landeck and Innsbruck, and that at Kufstein, in the valley of the Inn River,

---

[56] See SCAF 316, 27 Apr 45, as reproduced in Hq, 6th AGp, History, pp. 286–87. The 6th Army Group received the instructions orally on the 25th.

leading to Kitzbuehel—then to push on to the passes on the Italian frontier.

As General Devers transmitted these instructions to his army commanders, it appeared likely that the French would beat the Seventh Army to the Austrian border and thus might advance not only beyond Bregenz but also to Landeck. Although Devers did not yet assign Landeck to the French, he did alert de Lattre to "be prepared to continue the advance to capture Landeck." [57] This was clearly but a warning order, for the interarmy boundary remained at the town of Hoefen, south of Fuessen, according the main Alpine highway leading via the Fern Pass to Landeck to the Seventh Army. While the nearby Oberjoch Pass fell within the French zone, it afforded, without recourse to the main road that belonged to the Seventh Army, only roundabout passage to Landeck.

To de Lattre the warning order was license enough; he directed one of his armored divisions to head immediately for Landeck. De Lattre was anxious to have the town in order "to seal the victory at the Italian frontier" with a linkup with Allied forces in Italy. Only through Landeck to the Resia Pass was there any route by which the French might reach the Italian border. [58]

The desperate attempt by the German *XVIII SS Panzer Corps* to break its entrapment in the Black Forest interfered with de Lattre's plan. By the time he could spare troops to head for Landeck, the U.S. VI Corps had broken free, on 27 April dashing into Kempten, a little over twenty miles from Fuessen and less

than that from the Austrian frontier. The next day, as de Lattre urged his troops to advance with "vigor and speed," the U.S. 10th Armored Division with help from the 44th Division captured Fuessen and crossed into Austria. On the 29th the armor got almost to the Fern Pass before German-induced landslides blocking a precipitous Alpine highway forced a halt.

With the *XVIII SS Panzer Corps* contained, the French on the 30th cleared Immenstadt and got within eight miles of the Oberjoch Pass. Then came what was to de Lattre distressing news. American troops, word had it, were already beyond the Fern Pass, little more than a stone's throw from Landeck.

General de Lattre promptly fired off a message to the Seventh Army's General Patch:

"... I expect to reach Landeck, *my objective,* the evening of 30 April and there make contact with your elements. In the event your troops arrive first in the area of Landeck, I request that *just as I withdrew from Ulm to leave you free passage in your sector . . . ,* so you in return take necessary measures to leave in my control the Road Junction at Landeck and the road leading to the Resia Pass." [59]

Although de Lattre's information on the location of American troops was erroneous—they had yet to clear the Fern Pass—a message from headquarters of the 6th Army Group, received by General Patch only two hours before de Lattre's, just as effectively denied what de Lattre wanted. By that message, General Devers extended the interarmy boundary beyond Hoefen to the Resia

---

[57] 6th AGp Msg, BX 13351, 24 Apr 45, in Hq, 6th AGp, History, p. 270.

[58] De Lattre, *Histoire de la Première Armée Française,* pp. 572–73; Quotation is from page 575.

[59] SUSA Diary, entry of 30 Sep 45. Italics supplied.

Pass and specifically assigned Landeck and the pass to the Seventh Army. In an ill-disguised artifice not lost on General de Lattre, the 6th Army Group directed a change in the map co-ordinates given in earlier communications to designate the town of Hoefen. The new co-ordinates referred not to the town called Hoefen that was located south of Fuessen but instead to another, smaller town by the same name not quite seven miles to the northwest. The effect was to deny the French not only the Fern Pass but the Oberjoch Pass as well.[60]

Since American troops already blocked the limited roadnet, General de Lattre had no choice but to accede to Devers's order and abandon the cherished goal of linking with the Allied troops in Italy. He had begun to reconcile himself to the inevitable when word came that the Americans were having trouble getting through the Fern Pass. At the suggestion of the corps commander, de Lattre seized upon the idea of a raid south from Immenstadt over a snow-blocked back road leading up the imposing massif of the Arlberg to the Arlberg Pass and the town of St. Anton. If the Americans still had not made is to Landeck, he intended to beat them to it by the back door, going from St. Anton to Landeck and the Resia Pass.

Hastily equipped with skis, a reinforced platoon began an arduous twenty-mile trek through the snow on 5 May. Reaching the Arlberg Pass during the afternoon of the 6th, the commander placed a telephone call over the civilian network to Landeck. To the French officer's chagrin, an American voice answered. Men of the 44th Division had reached the town late the day before.[61]

Unconcerned with this kind of internecine rivalry, tanks of the 10th Armored Division on the left wing of the VI Corps during the last days of April had cleared Oberammergau, site in less troubled days of the world-renowned Passion Play, and entered the twin resort towns of Garmisch-Partenkirchen. Heading up winding roads dominated by towering white peaks, one column of armor on the 30th crossed the Austrian border to the southwest and established contact with troops of the 44th Division. Aiming for the Isar River and the Mittenwald Pass leading to Innsbruck, another column could make no such headway because of one obstacle after another—a deep crater in the road, a demolished bridge over a gorge, two minefields, 250 officer candidates defending a defile with machine guns and *Panzerfausts,* another blown bridge over a cascading mountain stream. The job of the final drive into Austria at this point would pass to infantry of the 103d Division as it did at the Fern Pass to the 44th Division.

The Seventh Army's other two corps meanwhile ran several days behind in their drive to reach the frontier because they had to make wider swings to the southeast than did the VI Corps. The presence of towering mountains short of the border between the Isar and Inn Rivers, denying the XXI Corps ready access to the objective of the Inn valley, further complicated the thrust.

Seeking a natural approach into the Inn valley, the XXI Corps commander,

---

[60] Hq, 6th AGp, History, p. 272; de Lattre, *Histoire de la Première Armée Française,* p. 576.

[61] De Lattre, *Histoire de la Première Armée Française,* pp. 580–81; 44th Div AAR, 1–10 May 45. The 44th Division's action is covered in Chapter XIX below.

TANKS OF THE 20TH ARMORED DIVISION FORD THE INN RIVER *en route to Salzburg.*

General Milburn, sent his 12th Armored Division down the Munich-Salzburg autobahn toward the Inn near Rosenheim, thirty miles southeast of Munich. That threw Milburn's armor into the natural line of advance of General Haislip's XV Corps, conqueror of Munich. Without some adjustment in boundaries and objectives, converging drives of the XXI Corps into the southeastern tip of Germany and of the right wing of the Third Army on Salzburg soon would pinch out the XV Corps.

At the same time, from General Eisenhower's headquarters came pressure to speed the closing of all Alpine passes to eliminate even a remote possibility of the Germans' forming a National Redoubt. With concurrence of the Third Army's General Patton, who needed to bring more infantry divisions forward before he could begin a push on Salzburg, General Devers on the first day of May asked General Eisenhower to alter the interarmy group boundary to give Salzburg to the 6th Army Group. Displaying a measure of disdain for normal security precautions, Devers negotiated the change by radio, telephone, and liaison plane in a day, then ordered Hais-

PARATROOPERS OF THE 101ST AIRBORNE DIVISION APPROACH BERCHTESGADEN

lip's XV Corps to drive swiftly for Salz-burg.[62]

If any chance still existed for the Germans remaining in southeastern Germany to enter the Alps for a final stand, Eisenhower's decision killed it, so swiftly did both the XV and XXI Corps advance. Bavaria seemed to be one endless array of white flags, and those towns and villages that failed to conform usually fell in line after only a few bursts of machine gun fire. In many cases, so rapid

was the advance that artillery and even tanks were left behind. Rubber-tired reconnaissance cars and jeeps, capable of greater speed than tanks, often took the lead.

It was not even pursuit warfare any more; it was more a motor march under tactical conditions. Unseasonable cold and heavy rain, often mixed with snow, gave more concern than did the enemy. Even had the weather made tactical air support possible, nobody needed it any more. The main roads were clogged with Germans—entire units—trying to surrender. The 106th Cavalry Group in a

---

[62] Hq, 6th AGp, History, p. 318; Seventh Army Report, p. 852.

hasty ceremony accepted surrender of an entire Hungarian division, 8,000 strong.

At the music shrine of Salzburg, a delegation of military and civilian functionaries offered surrender to the same cavalry group. No sooner had that happened early on 4 May than General Patch authorized General Haislip's XV Corps to turn to the southwest and come on Hitler's mountain retreat at Berchtesgaden from the rear. The order failed to halt units of the XXI Corps, in whose sector the town lay; and while the 3d Division of the XV Corps approached from the rear, grounded paratroopers of the 101st Airborne Division and recently attached men of the 2d French Armored Division, old allies of the Seventh Army, sped toward the objective from the northwest.

It was congestion, not resistance, that slowed entry into Berchtesgaden. "Everybody and his brother," said one message, "are trying to get into the town." [63] Motorized troops of the 3d Division got there first, in late afternoon of 4 May. The last temple of nazism still standing in an area of American responsibility had fallen.

Capture of Salzburg and Berchtesgaden, sealing the last passes leading into the Austrian Alps, spelled an absolute end to any possibility of a National Redoubt. To the men of the 6th Army Group and the Third Army, the feat was hardly necessary to convince them that the end of the war was near. Even if there was to be no formal surrender of the German nation, or even if the forces of *Army Group G* made no formal surrender, the time was at hand when every square inch of territory in which the remains of the Wehrmacht might hide would be overrun in a matter of days, perhaps even in hours.

---

[63] Seventh Army Report, p. 855.

CHAPTER XIX

Goetterdaemmerung

Although the Germans had no formal plans for a National Redoubt, Adolf Hitler had intended leaving Berlin on 20 April, his fifty-sixth birthday, to continue the fight from southern Germany. By mid-April the bulk of the ministerial staffs already had abandoned the capital in a frantic exodus to the south, though Hitler himself began to procrastinate. While conscious of the difficulty of holding Berlin indefinitely, he persisted in the self-delusion that time remained, and even that his armies might achieve a spectacular victory before Berlin.

The atmosphere in the *Fuehrerbunker* beneath the ruined city ranged alternately from despair to blind hope. One moment Hitler railed that the German people had failed him; they deserved the cruel fate they would suffer at the hands of the conqueror from the east. The next moment it was his generals—incompetent, negligent, spineless; they were fools, fatheads. Yet when a general occasionally dared to speak the truth, to reveal that the end was near, Hitler seized on some new scheme designed to set everything right again—previously uncommitted (and untrained) Luftwaffe and naval troops thrown into the line, a counterattack here, a shift of forces there.

The early moments of 13 April brought news that elated many of Hitler's coterie, if not the Fuehrer himself. Goebbels, the propagandist, reported it

to Hitler by telephone while an air attack raged over the city. As it had been written in the stars, the miracle Goebbels had been awaiting to save the Third Reich, as in an earlier day another had saved Frederick the Great, had come to pass.

"My Fuehrer!" Goebbels exclaimed. "I congratulate you! Roosevelt is dead."[1]

The events that followed—among other reverses, Vienna fell that day to the Russians—hardly confirmed Goebbels's expectations of deliverance from the enemies of the Reich. Hitler nevertheless used the President's death to exhort his troops to supreme effort. In an order of the day on 15 April, he proclaimed: "At the moment when fate has removed the greatest war criminal of all time from the earth, the turning point of this war shall be decided."

As the military high command and the party hierarchy gathered in the bunker to pay obeisance to the leader on his birthday, Hitler repeatedly professed faith that the Russians were about to incur their worst defeat in front of Berlin. Even though the generals warned that Russians and Western Allies soon would link to cut all escape routes to the south, he declined to leave the capital. Should the linkup occur, he decreed, the

---

[1] Toland, *The Last 100 Days*, p. 377. For details and documentation of events during the last days of Berlin, see sources cited in ch. XV.

front was to be divided into two commands, to be headed in the north by Grossadmiral Karl Doenitz, the naval chief; in the south by someone else, perhaps Kesselring or the Luftwaffe's Hermann Goering.

Hitler then sanctioned the departure of various commanders and party leaders from Berlin, which most were happy to leave in desperate hope of saving their skins or at least postponing the end. The SS chief, Himmler, scurried north to continue peace negotiations he had recently opened in secret with Count Folke Bernadotte, head of the Swedish Red Cross. Doenitz too moved north. In a truck caravan loaded with luxuries, Goering turned south. Foreign Minister von Ribbentrop also got out, as did most of the staff officers and clerks of OKW and OKH, though Keitel and Jodl remained with a small staff in a western suburb to keep OKW functioning. The faithful Goebbels was invited to move with his wife and children into the bunker, to which Hitler's mistress, Eva Braun, already had repaired.

The next day, 21 April, Hitler hit on a new scheme to set everything right. From the north an SS corps was to counterattack to break through Russian columns and relieve the city. Yet twenty-four hours later even Hitler had to admit that this offered no hope. At the daily situation conference, he exploded in what may have been the greatest of many notable rages. This was the end. Everybody had deserted him; lies, corruption, cowardice, treason. They had left him no choice but to remain in Berlin to direct the defense of the capital himself and die.

Then hope stirred again as General Jodl proposed that Wenck's *Tweflth*

Army turn its back on the Allies at the Elbe and come to the relief of Berlin. That Hitler ordered, along with a drive on Berlin from the south by the *Ninth Army,* already threatened by Russian encirclement. Keitel and Jodl were to direct the converging attack. When the stratagem inevitably failed, continued Russian advances forced the remnants of OKW to displace farther and farther to the north.

Learning on the 23d of Hitler's decision to stay in Berlin, Reichsmarshal Goering, whom Hitler long ago had designated to be his successor, believed the time had come for him to take over and try to salvage something by peace negotiations. From Berchtesgaden, he radioed Hitler for instructions, noting that if he received no answer by late evening, he would assume that Hitler had lost freedom of action, whereupon he would take control.

That same evening, in the north, Heinrich Himmler was usurping the powers of dictatorship without even asking. Concluding his negotiations with Count Bernadotte, Himmler signed a letter to General Eisenhower. Germany, he wrote, was willing to surrender to the Western Powers while continuing to fight the Russians until the Allies themselves were ready to assume responsibility for the campaign against bolshevism.

Goering's message threw Hitler into another rage, as would the news of Himmler's act when it reached the bunker several days later by way of a monitored broadcast of the BBC. Accusing Goering of "high treason," Hitler demanded his resignation from command of the Luftwaffe and from the Nazi party. Before dawn the next day, the heir-apparent of the Third Reich found himself under arrest by the SS.

By that time, 23 April, the Russians had completed encircling Berlin. Although linkup between Russians and Allies was yet to come, the encirclement, in effect, split the German command. As Jodl notified all senior commanders that the fight against bolshevism was the only thing that mattered and that loss of territory to the Western Allies was secondary, Hitler on 24 and 25 April approved a new command structure for the Wehrmacht. Abolishing OKH, Hitler made OKW responsible, subject to his authority, for operations everywhere. As head of OKW, Keitel reserved for himself control of all army units in the north until such time as communications with Hitler might be severed, whereupon he would submit to the authority of Admiral Doenitz. He designated another commander for those forces opposing the Russians south of Berlin, General der Gebirgstruppen August Winter, and directed Field Marshal Kesselring to assume command of German forces in Italy, Austria, and the Balkans in addition to his command of *Army Group G* and the *Nineteenth Army*.

OKW's primary mission, Hitler directed, was to re-establish contact with Berlin and defeat the Soviet forces there. Making his first specific reference to creating a redoubt, he issued a half-hearted directive to units in the south to prepare a defense of the Alps "envisioned as the final bulwark of fanatical resistance and so prepared." Just how either of those assignments was to be accomplished, he did not say.[2]

The Meeting at Torgau

As these futile efforts to keep up a pretense of hope persisted on the German side, a fever of expectation that contact with the Russians was imminent had begun to grip Allied troops and commanders, particularly those of the First and Ninth U.S. Armies holding the line of the Elbe and Mulde Rivers. Eager to go down in history as the unit that first established contact, divisions vied with each other in devising stratagems to assure the honor for themselves. Which unit was the leading contender at any given time might have been judged from the size of the press corps that flitted from one headquarters to another in an impatient wait to report the event.

What would happen when Allied and Russian troops came together had been on many minds on the Allied side for a long time. Because the Russians throughout the war had treated the Western Powers with suspicion and distrust, creating a workable liaison machinery had proved impossible; even where makeshift arrangements had been established, the Russians had disrupted them constantly by procrastination and delay.[3] While the disruption was merely exasperating in early stages of the war, it became as the war neared an end potentially dangerous. Misunderstandings, even collisions resulting in casualties, were possible among U.S. units fighting side by side; as Allied and Russian troops devoid of liaison approached each other in fluid warfare where even division commanders were not always sure within

---

[2] Ziemke, *Stalingrad to Berlin,* ch. XXI. Quotation is from page 481.

[3] Detailed discussion and annotation of arrangements with the Russians, including decisions on zones of occupation, are to be found in Pogue, *The Supreme Command,* pp. 461–69.

twenty to forty miles where their forward troops were located, serious clashes might ensue, resulting not only in casualties but possibly in postwar recrimination.

The problem for the air forces had long been acute. As early as the preceding November, U.S. fighters attacking what they identified as a German column in Yugoslavia had killed, the Soviets charged, several Russian soldiers, including a lieutenant general. Despite the incident, efforts to establish effective co-ordination with the Russians by means of a flexible bomb line had been basically unproductive until March 1945, when the Russians at last agreed to a bomb line 200 miles short of forward Russian positions. The line was not to be violated by Allied planes except on 24-hour notice, which the Russians might veto.

Although the Western Allies and the Russians had sealed an agreement on zones of occupation at the Yalta Conference, no one pretended that the demarcation lines corresponded with military requirements, though the Russians from time to time expressed concern about Allied intentions to withdraw from the Soviet zone once hostilities ceased. In a series of exchanges lasting past mid-April, the Combined Chiefs of Staff, General Eisenhower, and the Red Army's Chief of Staff finally agreed that the armies from east and west were to continue to advance until contact was imminent or linkup achieved. At that point adjustments might be made at the level of army group to deal with any remaining opposition while establishing a common boundary along some well-defined geographical feature.

Since the arrangement did little to forestall the possibility of Allied-Soviet clashes, General Eisenhower began, even

as the exchanges proceeded, to negotiate on recognition signals. At Eisenhower's request, the Red Army's Chief of Staff suggested as an over-all recognition signal, red rockets for Soviet troops, green rockets for Allied. Eisenhower concurred. To a Russian proposal that Soviet tanks be identified by a white stripe encircling the turret, Allied tanks by two white stripes, and that both place a white cross atop the turret, General Eisenhower suggested instead that to avoid a delay in operations while putting on new markings, the Soviet troops be acquainted with existing Allied markings. The Russians agreed, and by 21 April identification arrangements were complete.[4]

General Eisenhower also proposed exchanging liaison officers, which the Russians neither refused nor encouraged, and asked the Russians for details of their operational plan while expanding on his own, which, to the chagrin of the British, he had revealed broadly not quite a month before. Repeating the intent stated earlier to stop his central forces on the Elbe-Mulde line, Eisenhower noted that the line could be changed to embrace upper reaches of the Elbe should the Russians want him to go as far as Dresden. His northern forces, he made clear, were to cross lower reaches of the Elbe and advance to the Baltic Sea at the base of the Jutland peninsula, while forces in the south drove down the valley of the Danube into Austria.

The Russians responded with unusual alacrity. Agreeing to the line of the Elbe-

---

[4] U.S. Military Mission to War Dept, 14 Apr; Eisenhower to U.S. Military Mission, 17 Apr; and U.S. Military Mission to SHAEF, 21 Apr; all in OPD IN file 1–30 Apr 45.

Mulde as a common stopping place, they noted that the Soviet armies, in addition to taking Berlin, intended to clear the east bank of the Elbe north and south of Berlin and most of Czechoslovakia, at least as far as the Vltava (Moldau) River, which runs through Prague.

Co-ordination with the Russians would come none too soon for commanders of units that were hourly anticipating contact. General Hodges of the First Army, for example, spent much of the morning of 21 April trying to get instructions from SHAEF on procedures to be followed, only to obtain little guidance other than to "treat them nicely."[5] It was past midday when confirmation from the Russians on recognition signals arrived and word went out to subordinate units.[6]

As finally determined, whoever made the first contact was to pass word up the chain of command immediately to SHAEF, meanwhile making arrangements for a meeting of senior American and Russian field commanders. To the vexation of the small army of excited war correspondents, no news story was to be cleared until after simultaneous announcement of the event by the governments in Washington, London, and Moscow.[7]

First word was that bridgeheads already established over the Elbe (the 83d Division's at Barby) and the Mulde

(those of the 69th Division east of Leipzig; the 2d Division southeast of Leipzig; the 6th Armored and 76th Divisions near Rochlitz, northwest of Chemnitz; and the 87th and 89th Divisions west of Chemnitz) might be retained; but another message from the Russians early on the 24th changed that.[8]

Beginning at noon that day, the Russians revealed, they were to start an advance on Chemnitz by way of Dresden. During the advance, their air force would refrain from bombing or strafing west of the line of the Mulde as far south as Rochlitz, thence along a railroad from Rochlitz to Chemnitz, then to Prague. General Eisenhower promptly ordered all bridgeheads across the Mulde withdrawn as far south as Rochlitz with only outposts to protect bridges and small patrols to make contact with the Russians remaining on the east bank. Patrols were to venture no more than five miles beyond the Mulde.

Excitement among First and Ninth Army units was mounting all along the line. Rumor piled upon rumor; one false report followed another. Russian radio traffic cutting in on American channels convinced almost everybody that contact was near. Word was on the 23d that a staff sergeant in the 6th Armored Division actually had talked by radio with the Russians. Unit after unit reported flares to the east, attaching to them varying interpretations. A battalion of the 69th Division on 23 April reported sighting a Russian tank with a white stripe around the turret, then had to admit

---

[5] Sylvan Diary, entry of 21 Apr 45. See also Gay Diary for the same day.

[6] Eisenhower to AGp Comdrs, FWD 19604, 21 Apr 45, in SHAEF SGS 322.01–1, Liaison with the Russians.

[7] Eisenhower to AGp Comdrs, FWD 19624, 21 Apr 45, and Eisenhower to CCS, FWD 19737, 23 Apr 45, both in SHAEF SGS 322.01–1, Liaison with the Russians.

[8] U.S. Military Mission to Eisenhower, MX 24032, 24 Apr 45, in SHAEF SGS 373.5, Bomb-line, Liaison, and Co-ordination of Fronts. I.

that it was actually a grassy hummock with a clothesline stretched across it.[9]

Men of the 84th Division painted signs of welcome in Russian. The division canceled all artillery fire beyond the Elbe lest it hit Russian troops, but rescinded the order when German soldiers on the east bank began blatantly to sunbathe. At General Hodges' command post, a specially outfitted jeep was ready by the 23d for presentation to the army commander of the first Russian troops encountered.[10]

After pilots of tactical aircraft reported numerous (but erroneous) sightings of Russian columns east of the Elbe, almost all divisions sent their frail little artillery observation planes aloft for a look. The pilot of a plane belonging to the 104th Division was convinced of success late on the 23d when far beyond the Mulde he spotted a column of troops. Landing, he found only Germans with a few British prisoners heading west in hope of surrendering. Another pilot from the 104th Division flew fifteen miles east of the Elbe beyond the town of Torgau on 24 April, where he observed what appeared to be an artillery duel between Russians and Germans. Although he tried to land behind Russian lines, antiaircraft fire turned him back. Other units on the 24th reported seeing Russian planes over American positions.

Although the 83d Division in its bridgehead over the Elbe readied a task force that included tanks, tank destroyers, and a company of infantry to probe eastward to find the Russians, the force dutifully awaited approval from higher command before setting out. There were few other units that did not, in the meantime, violate the order on depth of patrols. Some patrols of the 2d Division probed in vain up to seven miles beyond the Mulde. One from the 104th Division's reconnaissance troop, composed of three men under 1st Lt. Harlan W. Shank, roamed more than twenty miles and reached the Elbe at Torgau late on April 23d, spent the night in the town under occasional Russian artillery fire, and finally departed at noon on the 24th after seeing no Russian troops.

Through it all, the men along the line of the Mulde still had a war to fight— after a fashion. As late as the 22d, part of the 69th Division's 271st Infantry was fighting hard to clear the town of Eilenberg, astride the Mulde, and after night fell had to repulse a determined counterattack by as many as 200 Germans. Company-size counterattacks also hit some units of the 2d Division. Meanwhile, other German soldiers in small groups and in large poured into American lines, eager to surrender. Every division handled thousands each day, as well as hundreds of American and Allied prisoners released by their captors. At the same time hordes of civilians gathered at bridges over the Mulde, terrified of the Russians, tearfully hopeful of refuge within American lines. Although the official word was to turn back German civilians, many an American soldier looked the other way as the refugees tried to pass, or liberally interpreted the proviso that foreign laborers might cross.

Unwittingly setting the stage for momentous events to follow, the burgomaster of Wurzen, on the Mulde's east bank east of Leipzig, begged permission late

---

[9] Unless otherwise noted, events during this period are from official unit records and from Capt. William J. Fox, The Russian-American Linkup, a historical narrative supported by combat interviews with members of the 69th Division.

[10] Sylvan Diary, entry of 23 Apr 45.

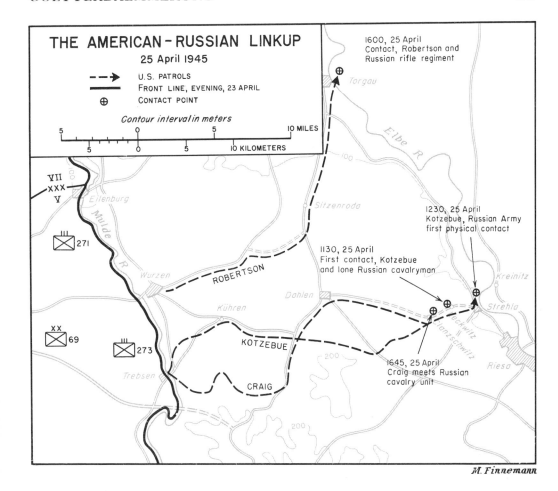

THE AMERICAN - RUSSIAN LINKUP
25 April 1945

- - - ➔   U.S. PATROLS
━━━━━   FRONT LINE, EVENING, 23 APRIL
⊕   CONTACT POINT

Contour interval in meters

1600, 25 April
Contact, Robertson and
Russian rifle regiment

Torgau

Elbe R.

VII
XXX
V

Eilenburg

Sitzenroda

Mulde R.

271

1230, 25 April
Kotzebue, Russian Army
first physical contact

Kreinitz

1130, 25 April
First contact, Kotzebue
and lone Russian cavalryman

Wurzen   ROBERTSON

Dahlen

Kühren   *Strehla*

69   273   *Lanzschwitz*

KOTZEBUE

Trebsen   *Riesa*

CRAIG   1645, 25 April
Craig meets Russian
cavalry unit

M. Finnemann

MAP 7

on the 23d to surrender his town to the 69th Division's 273d Infantry. Since the burgomaster's purpose was to release thousands of American and Allied prisoners and to surrender hundreds of German troops in the town, and since a restraining order on bridgeheads over the Mulde was yet to come, commanders up the chain of command sanctioned the move. The bulk of a battalion crossed the Mulde in early evening into Wurzen to participate in a chaotic night

of processing both the liberated and the newly captured.

By the afternoon of 24 April nobody yet had any definite word of the Russians. Nor could anyone know that contrary to the agreement with General Eisenhower, Russian troops approaching that part of the Elbe which runs some eighteen to twenty miles east of the Mulde were under orders to halt, not at the Mulde but at the Elbe. Word on the Mulde as a demarcation line had yet to pass down the Russian chain of command.[11]

Frustrated by the prolonged wait, the commander of the 273d Infantry, Col. Charles M. Adams, in midafternoon of 24 April directed 1st Lt. Albert L. Kotzebue of Company G to lead a jeep-mounted patrol of thirty-five men "to contact the Russians." Lieutenant Kotzebue was to go only as far as Kuehren, a village four miles beyond the Mulde; but when he reached Kuehren after encountering only a few hospitalized Allied prisoners and hundreds of docile Germans anxious to surrender, he gained permission to proceed another three miles, technically two miles beyond the five-mile limit. (*Map 7*) That Kotzebue did, encountering only the usual German groups trying to escape the Russians, then returned to Kuehren to bed down for the night. Although he received two messages ordering his patrol to return before dark, Lieutenant Kotzebue ignored them because it was already well after dark.

With no further word from Kotzebue, Colonel Adams that night ordered two more patrols to depart the next morning, 25 April. The orders were the same, "to contact the Russians," again within the five-mile limit. Members of one patrol made up of the regiment's intelligence and reconnaissance platoon apparently accepted the limitation without question. Those of another commanded by a platoon leader of Company E but accompanied by the 2d Battalion's executive officer, Maj. Frederick W. Craig,

took the restriction less seriously. To a man they entered into a kind of humorous conspiracy to meet the Russians, regardless. As the two patrols left in jeeps mounting machine guns early on the 25th, no one yet had heard anything more from Lieutenant Kotzebue in Kuehren.

Later in the morning, at Wurzen, the 1st Battalion's S–2, 2d Lt. William D. Robertson, awoke from a deep sleep occasioned by staying up the previous night to help process the surrendering Germans and liberated Allied prisoners in the town. With three men, Lieutenant Robertson left by jeep in midmorning to scout neighboring towns and villages for other Allied prisoners and other Germans wanting to surrender. Having no radio with him, Lieutenant Robertson had no intention of contacting the Russians as he headed eastward.

In Kuehren, in the meantime, Lieutenant Kotzebue and his men had awakened to a breakfast prepared by villagers eager to please in fear that if the Americans left, the Russians would come with the reign of terror that rumor promised would follow. Caught up in the general expectation that the Russians were on their way, Lieutenant Kotzebue saw no reason why he should not be the one to meet them first. His orders, "to contact the Russians," he deemed sufficiently broad to warrant continuing toward the east. Leaving his radio jeep in Kuehren to serve as a relay point for messages, he headed east with the bulk of his patrol.

Thus, in midmorning of 25 April, four separate groups of the 69th Division's 273d Infantry were moving eastward. Only one, the intelligence and reconnaissance platoon, was concerned enough

---

[11] The Russians had acknowledged it to General Eisenhower only on 24 April. See U.S. Military Mission to Eisenhower, MX 24032, 24 Apr 45, *op. cit.*

with the five-mile restriction to comply with it.[12]

Encountering dispirited German soldiers, jubilant American and Allied prisoners, apprehensive German civilians, and exuberant, sometimes intoxicated foreign laborers, Lieutenant Kotzebue and his men advanced almost due east through the town of Dahlen toward the Elbe in the vicinity of Strehla, a few miles northwest of Riesa, some seventeen miles southeast of Torgau. It was almost noon as the jeeps slowed to enter the farming village of Leckwitz, less than two miles from the Elbe.

Far down the main street, the men spotted a horseman just as he turned his mount into a courtyard and passed from view. At a glance, the man's costume seemed unusual. Could it be? Was this it?

Spinning forward, the jeeps came to a halt at the entrance to the courtyard. Inside, among a crowd of foreign laborers, was the horseman. There could be no doubt. He was a Russian soldier.

The time was 1130 on 25 April, the setting inauspicious, but the moment historic: the first contact between Allied armies from the west, Soviet armies from the east.

Through Russian-speaking Tech. 5 Stephen A. Kowalski, Lieutenant Kotzebue asked directions to the soldier's commander; but the Russian was suspicious and reserved. Waving his arm to the east, he suggested that one of the foreign laborers, a Pole, could lead them better than he. With that, he galloped away.

Taking the Pole as a guide the patrol continued to the Elbe, a few hundred

yards north of Strehla. Seeing uniformed figures on the east bank milling about the wreckage of a column of vehicles close to the remains of a tactical bridge, Lieutenant Kotzebue raised his binoculars. Again there could be no doubt. They were Russians. The rays of the sun reflecting off medals on their chests convinced him.

At the lieutenant's direction, his driver fired two green signal flares. Although the figures on the far bank gave no answering signal, they began to walk toward the edge of the river. As Kotzebue's driver fired another flare for good measure, the Polish laborer shouted identity across the water.

Using a hand grenade, Lieutenant Kotzebue blasted the moorings of a sailboat and with five of his men rowed across the Elbe. A major and two other Russians, one a photographer, met them. The meeting was at first restrained, but as Kotzebue explained who he was, the Russians relaxed.

Minutes later, Lt. Col. Alexander T. Gardiev, commander of the 175th Rifle Regiment, arrived. Making clear that he intended to take the Americans to meet his division commander, he suggested that the men return to the west bank of the Elbe and proceed northward to a hand-operated cable ferry opposite the village of Kreinitz. There the Russians would meet them again, presumably at the pleasure of two motion-picture cameramen who by that time also had arrived on the scene.

Returning to the west bank, Kotzebue sent one of his jeeps accompanied by his second-in-command back to Kuehren with a message to be transmitted by radio to headquarters of the 273d Infantry. Making a mistake he would come to rue,

---

[12] The story of all patrols is based on detailed combat interviews in Fox, The Russian–American Linkup.

the lieutenant gave the wrong map co-ordinates for his location.

Lieutenant Kotzebue signed his message at 1330. His regimental commander, Colonel Adams, received it not quite two hours later: "Mission accomplished. Making arrangements for meeting between CO's. Present location (8717). No casualties."

Hardly had Colonel Adams telephoned that information to the division's chief of staff when the division commander, General Reinhardt, picked up the phone. Reinhardt was irate. As late as that morning he had been at Adams's command post where he had reiterated the order that patrols were to go no more than five miles beyond the Mulde. If Kotzebue was where the map co-ordinates indicated, he was far beyond the Mulde at the Elbe itself on the fringe of the town of Riesa.

General Reinhardt's first reaction was to clamp a blackout on the news until Colonel Adams could verify it by a meeting with the Russians himself. On second thought he telephoned the V Corps commander, General Huebner, who reacted much as had Reinhardt but passed the word to General Hodges at First Army. Hodges passed it on to General Bradley at 12th Army Group, who took it calmly.

Mollified by this reaction near the top and rationalizing that Lieutenant Kotzebue might not have known of the five-mile restriction, General Reinhardt still was reluctant to publicize the contact without some confirmation. Time for proof was short, for despite all efforts to contain the news, rumors of a meeting with the Russians were rife throughout the division, and correspondents already were deserting neighboring di-

visions to rush to the 69th's command post. To speed confirmation, Reinhardt directed Adams to cancel arrangements for a personal meeting with the Russians pending a flight by the division G–3 in an artillery spotter plane to the site Lieutenant Kotzebue had specified.

The results of the flight further confused the issue. Taking along an interpreter in a second plane, the G–3 flew to Riesa, which marked the co-ordinates Kotzebue had mistakenly given. Antiaircraft fire at Riesa turned both planes back.

On two occasions, in late morning and early afternoon of 25 April, Colonel Adams ordered Major Craig and the 47-man patrol from the 273d Infantry's 2d Battalion to advance no farther. Both times he qualified the order with authority "to scout out the area" near where the patrol was located. Both times Major Craig used this authority to justify continuing toward the east.

Craig and the men with him, like Lieutenant Kotzebue and his men, were caught up in the elation of the moment. Abroad in what was technically enemy territory, they were welcomed by jubilant foreign laborers and Allied prisoners as liberators, by the German populace and soldiers as saviors from some ephemeral dread called "the Russians are coming." Only occasionally did a German soldier display any inclination to fight. One word and white flags appeared in the villages as if by magic.

Craig had another incentive to continue. With him was a historian, Capt. William J. Fox, operating out of headquarters of the V Corps. Rationalizing that he was not subject to the five-mile restriction, Fox insisted that if Craig felt obligated to turn back, he personally would continue to contact the Russians.

Two hours after the second stop order from Colonel Adams, Major Craig and his patrol still were traveling eastward. The patrol's radio was delightfully void of any more orders, and Craig sent no further reports on his position lest they generate a new directive to halt.

By midafternoon the patrol had reached a point less than three miles from the Elbe when two jeeps overtook the column. They carried men from Lieutenant Kotzebue's patrol on their way forward from Kuehren after having relayed the message telling of Kotzebue's meeting with the Russians.

All doubts about continuing to the Elbe erased by this news, Craig's patrol was heading for Leckwitz, the village where Kotzebue had first encountered the lone Russian, when a cloud of dust revealed the approach of horsemen. Craig halted his jeeps and the men piled out, eager and excited at the prospect of meeting what obviously was Russian cavalry interspersed with a few men on motorcycles and bicycles.

"I thought the first guy would never get there," one soldier recalled. "My eyes glued on his bicycle, and he seemed to get bigger and bigger as he came slower and slower towards us. He reached a point a few yards away, tumbled off his bike, saluted, grinned, and stuck out his hand." [13]

The time was 1645, 25 April.

After a few self-conscious speeches from both sides extolling the historic moment, the Russians went on their way south toward Dresden, while Craig and his patrol hurried on to the Elbe to join

---

[13] Combat interview with men of Craig's patrol.

Lieutenant Kotzebue on the east bank. There the commander of the 58th Guards Infantry Division, Maj. Gen. Vladimir Rusakov, whose 175th Regiment had made the first contact with Kotzebue, saw it his duty for the second time in the same afternoon to welcome an American force with toasts in vodka to Roosevelt, Truman, Churchill, Stalin, the Red Army, the American Army, and, it seemed to some Americans present, to every commander and private soldier in each army.

Back at headquarters of the 273d Infantry on the Mulde, a radio message from Major Craig arrived shortly before 1800: "Have contacted Lieutenant Kotzebue who is in contact with Russians." To Colonel Adams, that confused the issue more than ever.

Having left Wurzen in midmorning of 25 April in a jeep with three men in search of Allied prisoners and surrendering Germans, Lieutenant Robertson, the 1st Battalion S-2, experienced much the same reactions to the arrival of Americans in the German towns and villages as did the patrols of Kotzebue and Craig. Although Robertson had no intention at first of trying to find the Russians, he kept moving from one town to the next until at Sitzenroda, a little past the midpoint between Mulde and Elbe, a group of released British prisoners told him there were many American prisoners, some of them wounded, in Torgau on the Elbe. Already exhilarated by the ease with which he was moving across the no man's land between the two rivers, Robertson used the information to justify his continuing to Torgau, rescuing the prisoners, and if possible, meeting the Russians.

Entering Torgau in midafternoon, Lieutenant Robertson searched for the reported American prisoners to no avail, though he did find a group of released prisoners of various nationalities that included two Americans, a naval ensign and a soldier. The two joined Robertson's little band. The few German troops encountered appeared to be preparing to leave the town and readily gave up their weapons.

Hearing small arms fire from the direction of the Elbe, Robertson and his men headed through the center of the town toward a castle on the river's west bank. Assuming that the fire came from Russians east of the Elbe, Robertson yearned for an American flag to establish his identity. As he passed an apothecary shop, the idea came to him that he could make a flag. Inside the shop, he found red and blue water paint with which he and his men fashioned a crude flag from a white sheet.

With the flag in hand, Robertson climbed into a tower of the castle. Although the firing had stopped, he could see figures moving about on the east bank of the Elbe. Displaying the flag outside the tower produced no fire, but when one of Robertson's men showed himself, the figures on the east bank began again to shoot.

At long last the firing stopped, and a green signal flare went up from the other side of the river. Robertson was elated. That, as he remembered it, was the agreed recognition signal to be fired by the Russians. (The Russians should have fired a red signal.) Certain that the figures on the east bank were Russians and not having a flare with which to answer, Robertson sent his jeep back to the Allied prisoners found earlier to bring up a Russian who had been among the lot.

Climbing the tower, the Russian shouted across to the east bank. Almost immediately the figures beyond the Elbe began to mill about. They understood, the freed prisoner shouted from the tower, that Robertson and his men were Americans.

With that, Robertson and his little group rushed to a destroyed highway bridge and slowly began to climb across the river on twisted girders. A Russian soldier from the far bank began to climb toward them. The soldier and the released prisoner met first, then Robertson reached the soldier. The lieutenant could think of nothing to say. He merely grinned and pounded the Russian exuberantly.

The time was 1600. Although word of Major Craig's contact reached the 273d Infantry command post before that of Robertson's, the meeting on a girder above the swirling waters of the Elbe was by some forty-five minutes the second contact between the armies from east and west.

Once on the east bank, Americans and Russians pounded each other on the back, everybody wearing a perpetual grin, then drank a series of toasts in wine and brandy provided by the Russians. They had fired on Robertson's flag, the Russians explained, because a few days earlier a group of Germans had displayed an American flag to halt Russian fire and make good their escape. The impromptu celebration went on for an hour. When Robertson at last announced a return to his own headquarters, a Russian major, two lesser officers, and a sergeant volunteered to go

LIEUTENANT ROBERTSON (*extreme left*) *shows General Eisenhower the make-shift flag displayed at the Elbe.*

with him. They were from the 173d Rifle Regiment.

Shortly after 1800, Lieutenant Robertson and his overloaded jeep arrived at the 1st Battalion command post in Wurzen. As soon as he could convince his battalion commander that the Russians were genuine soldiers, not released prisoners, word passed up the line to regiment.

To Colonel Adams this development was more startling than the others. He had ordered no patrol from the 1st Battalion, yet the battalion had four Rus-

sians as living proof of contact. He ordered them brought to his headquarters, where they successfully ran a gantlet of war correspondents and photographers who had almost inundated the 273d Infantry command post.

When the division commander, General Reinhardt, learned of the new development, he was more irate than ever. The corps commander obviously was getting the impression that nobody in the 69th Division followed orders, and Reinhardt could hardly blame him. Reinhardt even toyed briefly with the idea of a court-martial for Robertson. (Someone noted in the 273d Infantry journal: "Something wrong with an officer who cannot tell 5 miles from 25 miles.")

The fact that Robertson's exploit had produced tangible evidence entitling the 69th Division to the acclaim of first contact with the Russians apparently had something to do with Reinhardt's decision to play it straight. Once he himself had talked with the Russians at his command post, he interrupted the inevitable toasts and photographs to report the news to the V Corps commander. General Huebner in turn told Reinhardt to proceed with arrangements for a formal meeting of division commanders the next day, 26 April, and of corps commanders on the 27th. Since nobody yet had any specific information on the site of Lieutenant Kotzebue's meeting, the formal linkup celebrations would be held at Torgau.

General Reinhardt met General Rusakov, the man of many welcomes, on the east bank opposite Torgau at 1600 on the 26th. Camaraderie, photographs, toasts, dancing in the street, and a hastily assembled feast with a main dish of fried eggs were the order of the day. General Huebner conducted a second ceremony on the 27th with his opposite, the commander of the 34th Russian Corps, and General Hodges a third on the 30th with the commander of the First Ukrainian Army. The American, British, and Soviet governments officially announced to the world at 1800 on the 27th that east and west had met on the Elbe at Torgau.

In the meantime, somebody at last had remembered to do something about Lieutenant Kotzebue, Major Craig, and their men waiting on the east bank upstream near Kreinitz. Late on the 26th, a patrol brought them the news that history had passed them by. On the same day, Lieutenant Shank of the 104th Division, who also had had a close brush with history, returned to Torgau, this time actually to meet the Russians he had failed to wait for long enough two days before.

A few problems of co-ordination with the Russians remained on the northern and southern portions of the front. The British Chiefs of Staff were particularly concerned lest the Russians intended the Elbe as a stopping point in the north as well as the center of the front. A Russian drive to the Elbe would jeopardize the British drive to the Baltic. Urging General Eisenhower to make the distinction clear, the British Chiefs also pointed out that by seeking to halt on a well-defined geographical line, Eisenhower might be forgoing remarkable political advantages to be gained by liberating Prague and much of the rest of Czechoslovakia. If possible without detracting from the main drives to the Baltic and into Austria, they believed the Allies should exploit any opportunity to drive deep into Czechoslovakia.

When the U.S. Army Chief of Staff, General Marshall, passed the latter view to General Eisenhower for comment, the Supreme Commander responded: "Personally and aside from all logistic, tactical or strategical implications I would be loath to hazard American lives for purely political purposes." [14] Right or wrong from a political standpoint, the decision was in keeping with the U.S.

---

[14] Marshall to Eisenhower, W–74256, 28 Apr 45, and Eisenhower to Marshall, FWD 20225, 29 Apr 45, both in SHAEF cable log.

GENERAL HODGES MEETS THE RUSSIANS AT THE ELBE

military policy followed generally throughout the war—to concentrate everything on achieving military victory over the armed forces of the enemy.[15]

First priority, Eisenhower told Marshall, was to be accorded the drives to the Baltic and into Austria. The thrust to the Baltic, he said, was to forestall Russian entry into Denmark (a departure from the stated military policy which no one officially remarked); the

thrust into Austria to deny a National Redoubt. If additional means should be available, he intended to attack enemy forces that still might be holding out in Czechoslovakia, Denmark, and Norway. Both the latter, he believed, should be the province of the Allies; but the Red Army was in perfect position to clean out Czechoslovakia and certainly to reach Prague in advance of U.S. troops. "I shall not attempt any move I deem militarily unwise," he assured Marshall, "merely to gain a political prize unless I receive specific orders from the Com-

[15] For a detailed discussion of the point, see Pogue, *The Supreme Command*, p. 468.

bined Chiefs of Staff." [16] As in the case of going to Berlin, such orders never came.

In an even fuller explanation of plans to the Russians, General Eisenhower on the last day of April allayed British fears about lower reaches of the Elbe. In the north, the Supreme Commander noted, he intended to clear the Baltic coast as far east as Wismar and build a line south to Schwerin, thence southwest to Doemitz on the Elbe, 23 miles downstream from Wittenberge. From headwaters of the Mulde River southward, he intended to hold a line approximately along the 1937 frontier of Czechoslovakia, though he might advance as far into Czechoslovakia as Karlsbad, Pilsen, and Ceské Budějovice. Farther south he planned to halt in the general area of Linz.

The Russians accepted these proposals, but four days later, on 4 May, when General Eisenhower said he was willing not only to advance to the Elbe in the vicinity of Dresden but also to clear the west bank of the Vltava within Czechoslovakia, which would bring his forces in the center as far east as Prague, generally on a line with those in the south at Linz, the Red Army Chief of Staff strongly objected. To avoid "a possible confusion of forces," he asked that the Allies confine their advance in Czechoslovakia to the Karlsbad-Pilsen line as earlier stated. He added pointedly that the Russians had stopped their advance toward the lower Elbe in accordance with Allied wishes.

General Eisenhower promptly agreed to the Russian request.[17]

The End in Berlin

Linkup by the enemies of the Third Reich was but one more thorn in a bristling crown of troubles pressing hard on Adolf Hitler's brow. Indeed, amid the welter of sad tidings pouring into the *Fuehrerbunker,* the meeting on the Elbe may have passed unremarked.

Since Hitler's decision on the 22d to stand and die in Berlin, an air of aimless resignation had hung over the bunker, relieved more and more rarely by some vain flurry of hope. It was common knowledge among the sycophants in the bunker that Hitler intended suicide, as did Eva Braun. Late on the 26th, Russian artillery fire began to fall in the garden of the Reich Chancellery above the bunker, reminder enough for any who still might have doubted that the end was near. Yet the Fuehrer's military chiefs, Keitel and Jodl, even though now removed from Hitler's presence, persisted either in coloring their reports on the military situation or in refusing to face the facts themselves.

General von Manteuffel, who earlier had been transferred from the west for the twilight of the campaign in the east, told Jodl late on the 27th that anyone who wanted a true picture had but to stand at any crossroads north of Berlin and observe the steady stream of refugees and disheartened troops clogging the roads to the rear. What the soldier could do had been done, Manteuffel insisted; now the time had come for

---

[16] Eisenhower to Marshall, FWD 20225, 29 Apr 45, SHAEF cable log, as cited by Pogue, *The Supreme Command,* p. 468.

[17] For details and documentation, see Pogue, *The Supreme Command,* p. 469.

political action, for negotiations with the Western Powers.[18]

Yet both Keitel and Jodl could persist in their belief that more still might be done. Relieving the army group commander north of Berlin, they ordered General Student, commander of the *First Parachute Army,* to fly from the Netherlands to assume command.

On the 28th, grim news poured into the bunker in a torrent. Italian partisans, Hitler learned, had arrested his erstwhile partner, Mussolini, and there were distressing rumors of army leaders in Italy negotiating surrender. He learned too of the uprising in Munich. On that day also, telephone communications with OKW failed.

The 29th was grimmer still. Hitler himself would not be notified until the next day, but on the 29th the last thin hope of relieving Berlin evaporated when the turnabout attack of General Wenck's *Twelfth Army* stalled near Potsdam, seventeen miles southwest of the capital. Only some 30,000 men of the *Ninth Army* south of Berlin had escaped Russian encirclement; so exhausted were they, so depleted their arms and ammunition, that they would be of no help to Wenck.

Mussolini and his mistress, Hitler learned, had been executed the day before and strung up by their heels. Yet the most crushing blow was the word that Heinrich Himmler had turned traitor. As with Goering, Hitler expelled Himmler from the party and stripped him of all claim to the succession. When

his fury had passed, he drew a will and testament appointing Admiral Doenitz as head of the German state and Supreme Commander of the Armed Forces. Then, before daylight the next morning, he married Eva Braun.

Field Marshal Keitel finally sent a message by radio early on the 30th telling of the failure of Wenck's *Twelfth Army,* in effect admitting that all hope was gone. Although the message may never have reached the bunker, Hitler apparently already had concluded that it was time to die. He spent much of the morning saying farewells to his staff, seemingly unmoved by the news that Russian troops were little more than a block away, then in midafternoon retired with Eva Braun to his suite.

Eva Braun killed herself by biting on a cyanide capsule. Hitler shot himself with a pistol. In accordance with prior instructions, members of the household staff burned the bodies outside the bunker.[19]

News of the Fuehrer's death was slow to emerge. Most likely those in the bunker delayed in order to await the outcome of a Goebbels-inspired attempt to negotiate the surrender of Berlin in exchange for safe passage of those in the bunker. When the Russians predictably declined any accommodation, word went out at last—more than twenty-four hours after the suicide—that Hitler was dead. Admiral Doenitz announced it publicly by radio that evening, 1 May, in the process giving the impression that Hitler had died a hero's death.

---

[18] In addition to sources previously cited for events in Berlin, see Magna E. Bauer, MS # B–69, The End of *Army Group Weichsel* and *Twelfth Army,* 27 April–7 May 1945, prepared in OCMH to complement this volume.

[19] The evidence that Hitler shot himself appears to be conclusive, despite a report by a former Soviet intelligence officer that Hitler too bit on a cyanide capsule. See Lev Aleksandrovich Bezymensky, *The Death of Adolf Hitler* (New York: Harcourt, Brace & World, 1968).

That same day Goebbels and his wife, after poisoning their six children, arranged their own deaths at the hands of an SS guard. Three of Hitler's military entourage also killed themselves. The others tried to escape. Few made it.

The Drive to the Baltic

As these melodramatic events occured, two major Allied offensives were continuing, one by Montgomery's 21 Army Group to clear northern Germany and the Netherlands, the other by Devers's 6th Army Group and the Third Army into Austria.

The 21 Army Group's offensive evolved from the bridgehead established over the Rhine near Wesel. While the First Canadian Army on the left drove generally north to reach the IJsselmeer and the North Sea, the Second British Army attacked northeast to seize the line of the Elbe from Wittenberge to the sea. Those goals achieved, the Canadians were to turn west to clear the Netherlands and east to sweep the littoral from the Dutch border to the estuary of the Weser River. The British were to attack across the Elbe to capture Hamburg and make a 45-mile drive to the Baltic in the vicinity of Luebeck.[20]

Benefiting much as had the First and Ninth U.S. Armies from the great gap created in the German line by encirclement of *Army Group B* in the Ruhr, the British south wing alongside the Ninth Army made the most rapid gains. There the 8 Corps had a four-day brush with contingents of Wenck's *Twelfth Army* near Uelzen but reached the Elbe the next day, 19 April, opposite Lauenberg, some thirty miles upstream from Hamburg. Another corps in the center reached the Elbe opposite Hamburg four days later on the 23d. Both this corps and another on the left that was advancing on the great port of Bremen fought against the essentially makeshift force, *Army Blumentritt,* formed in early April as a component of *OB NORDWEST,* the new command under Field Marshal Busch which had been created as the Allied armies threatened to split the Western Front.[21] Strengthened by sailors fighting as infantry, the Germans made a stand for a week in front of Bremen, but by nightfall of 26 April the British were in full control of the city.

The First Canadian Army at the same time was facing the remains of General Student's *First Parachute Army* and the *Twenty-fifth Army,* which was subordinate to *OB NEDERLANDER,* the new command under General Blaskowitz who formerly had headed *Army Group H.* Comprising two of the more cohesive forces remaining to the German Army in the west, the troops drew added strength from readily defensible positions along one canal or river after another. Contingents of one Canadian corps nevertheless reached the North Sea near the northeastern tip of the Netherlands on 16 April, thereby splitting the German front. Another corps on the 14th took Arnhem on the Neder Rijn, an objective that had eluded British troops in the preceding September's big airborne attack, and on the 18th ended a 40-mile trek to the IJsselmeer.

One corps turned east to clear the

---

[20] Montgomery, *Normandy to the Baltic.* For plans, see pages 261–63; for operations, pages 264–66.

[21] See above, ch. XVIII.

coast between the Dutch border and the Weser, but little reason remained for the other to make the planned assault to erase the Germans trapped in the western portion of the Netherlands. If the Canadians attacked, the Germans in all probability would flood the low-lying countryside, increasing the suffering of a Dutch population already facing a food shortage that was close to famine. Even the Nazi high commisssioner in the Netherlands, Arthur Seyss-Inquart, had by early April become concerned that a catastrophe was in the making. Word that Seyss-Inquart might be amenable to a relief operation reached the Canadians in mid-April, resulting in conferences with the Germans that led to an agreement for the Allies to provide food for the Dutch by land, sea, and air. Airdrops began on 28 April while negotiations were still going on.[22]

During the conferences, General Eisenhower's representative tried to persuade Seyss-Inquart to agree either to a truce or to unconditional surrender. Seyss-Inquart refused on the grounds that it was the duty of the Germans in the Netherlands to fight until ordered to do otherwise by the German government. As Dutch relief operations got underway, a lull not unlike a truce nevertheless settled over the front.[23]

For the British attack across the Elbe to reach the Baltic, General Eisenhower provided assistance by General Ridgway's XVIII Airborne Corps with three U.S. divisions. Although the corps was attached to the Second British Army for the operation, the Ninth Army provided administrative and support services. Under the British plan, the 8 Corps was to make an assault crossing of the Elbe, whereupon the 12 Corps and the XVIII Airborne Corps were to cross into the bridgehead, the former to mask and later capture Hamburg, the latter to clear additional bridging sites upstream and protect the right flank of the 8 Corps in a northward drive to the Baltic.[24]

The rapid deterioration of German forces everywhere on the Western Front prompted Field Marshal Montgomery to advance the date of the river crossing two days, to 29 April. It also prompted General Ridgway to propose that instead of waiting six or seven days to cross British bridges, the XVIII Airborne Corps make its own assault crossing before daylight on 30 April. The commander of the Second Army, General Dempsey, approved.

General Ridgway's problem was to get an assault force ready in time. Although one division, the 8th, had arrived by nightfall of the 28th from mop-up operations in the Ruhr, its regiments were concentrated near the British crossing site in keeping with the original plan. Of the 82d Airborne Division, assembling near the bridge sites reserved for the U.S. corps, only a battalion had arrived by dawn of the 29th, and a full regimental combat team was not scheduled to arrive until late afternoon of the same day, a few hours before the time for the assault. A third division, the 7th Armored, was not to complete its move until the 30th.

In the interest of speed and in a belief

---

[22] For details and annotation, see Stacey, *The Victory Campaign*, pp. 581–87, 606–09, and Pogue, *The Supreme Command*, pp. 457–58.

[23] Pogue, *The Supreme Command*, pp. 458–59; Stacey, *The Victory Campaign*, pp. 607–08.

[24] This account is based on official records of the XVIII Airborne Corps and its divisions. See also Montgomery, *Normandy to the Baltic*, pp. 269–73.

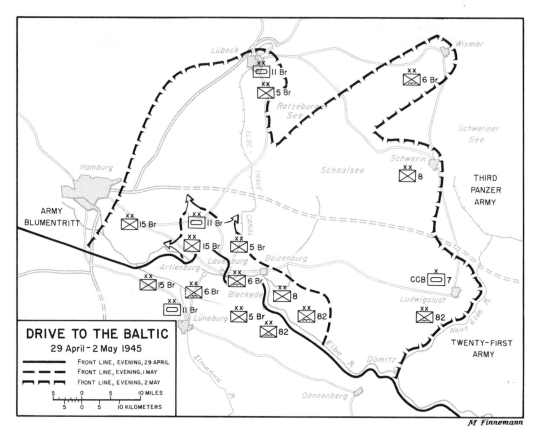

MAP 8

that resistance would be light, Ridgway named the airborne division for the assault even though at the start only one battalion of the 505th Parachute Infantry would be available. To provide a ready follow-up force, he attached four battalions of the 8th Division to the 82d.

Following an almost unopposed crossing by British commandos near Lauenburg before daylight on the 29th, the battalion of the 505th's paratroopers moved silently in assault boats across the sprawling Elbe at Bleckede, six miles upstream from Lauenburg, at 0100, 30 April. (*Map 8*) As rain mixed with snow

prompted the Germans on the far bank to seek cover, only an occasional flurry of small arms fire swept the river.

The paratroopers fanned out against sporadic resistance, though artillery fire began to fall in heavy volume at the crossing site. The shelling harassed succeeding waves and hampered engineers constructing a heavy ponton bridge, but a 1,110-foot bridge was nevertheless ready for traffic before dark on the first day, fifteen hours after work had begun.

The next day, 1 May, the bridgehead expanded rapidly. Having crossed a British bridge at Lauenburg, the 6th

IN THE AUSTRIAN ALPS *a nest of resistance confronts men of the 103d Division.*

British Airborne Division was attached to General Ridgway's command to form the left wing of the corps. Four battalions of the 8th Division and an additional parachute infantry regiment of the 82d participated in the day's attacks amid increasing indications that all resistance was about to collapse. By the end of this second day, the American bridgehead was six miles deep, contact was firm with the British on the left, and a second bridge was in operation eight miles upstream from Bleckede. Contingents of British armor to assist the British airborne division and a combat command of the 7th

Armored Division to help the 82d were crossing the river.

On 2 May, as news of Hitler's death spread, the enemy's will to fight disappeared. In rare instances was a shot fired. The problem became instead how to advance without running down hordes of German soldiers and civilians who appeared to have only one goal: to get out of the way of the Russians.

With attached armor, the 82d Airborne Division moved east to Ludwigslust and southeast along the Elbe to Doemitz to anchor the 21 Army Group's right flank on the line General Eisenhower had specified to the Russians. The 8th Division drove forty-five miles to the northeast to occupy Schwerin. While British troops before Hamburg began negotiations for the fire-gutted city's surrender and while a British armored division entered Luebeck without a fight, the 6th British Airborne Division dashed all the way to Wismar on the Baltic. The drive sealed off the Jutland peninsula, trapping German forces in the nation's northernmost province and barring the way to Denmark. Two hours later the first Russian troops arrived.

Piecemeal Surrenders

The second of the continuing Allied offensives, a prolongation into Austria of the drive through southern Germany by the 6th Army Group and the Third Army, also became closely involved in the growing German dissolution. Hardly were the first troops across the Austrian frontier when the news broke that on 29 April the German command in Italy had surrendered. The capitulation was effective at noon on 2 May and included the Austrian provinces of Vorarlberg, Tirol, Salzburg, and part of Carinthia (Kaernten), the areas into which troops of the 6th Army Group were moving.[25]

On the same day, 2 May, Admiral Doenitz, new head of the Third Reich, convened his advisers in a headquarters established in the extreme north of Germany. Anxious to end the bloodshed, Doenitz just as fervently wanted to save

as many German soldiers and civilians as possible from the grasp of the Russians. Aware that agreements between the Western Powers and the Soviet Union precluded his surrendering all to the Western Allies alone, he believed that the only chance of saving more Germans lay in opening the front in the west while continuing to fight in the east, meanwhile trying to arrange piecemeal surrenders to the Allies at the level of army group and below.

As Doenitz surmised, the way was open for such surrenders. Basing their conclusions on indications reaching General Eisenhower's headquarters in mid-April that German commanders in Norway, Denmark, and the larger north German cities might be induced to surrender, the Combined Chiefs of Staff on 21 April had notified the Russians that surrender of large formations was a growing possibility. They suggested that Britain, the Soviet Union, and the U.S. be represented on each front in order to observe negotiations for surrender. The Soviets had promptly agreed.

Word went out from Doenitz's headquarters during 2 May to commanders facing the Russians in the north to move as many men as possible behind the line Wismar-Schwerin-Ludwigslust-Doemitz and to exploit any opportunity to negotiate local surrenders to the Allies.[26] General der Infanterie Kurt von Tippelskirch, commander of the *Twenty-first Army*, complied that afternoon, contacting General Gavin, commander of the 82d Airborne Division, in Ludwigslust. Tippelskirch surrendered his command unconditionally, though in deference to the Russians, Gavin speci-

---

[25] See Ernest F. Fisher, Cassino to the Alps, in preparation for the series UNITED STATES ARMY IN WORLD WAR II. Unless otherwise noted, the surrender story is based on Pogue, *The Supreme Command*, pp. 478–94; Ziemke, *Stalingrad to Berlin*, ch. XXI; and Royce L. Thompson, Military Surrender in the ETO, MS in OCMH.

[26] See Bauer, The End of *Army Group Weichsel* and *Twelfth Army*.

fied that the capitulation was valid only for those troops who passed through Allied lines.[27]

A formal surrender was hardly necessary in any case. By the afternoon of 2 May the bulk of the German troops and their commanders were falling over themselves to get into Allied prisoner-of-war enclosures. That the Germans in the area north of Berlin were squeezed into a corridor only some twenty miles wide between Russian and Allied troops hardly could have eluded anybody. Great columns of motor vehicles, horse-drawn carts, foot troops, even tanks, moved in formation to surrender. Other soldiers straggled in individually, many with their women and children and pitiful collections of personal belongings. To the 8th Division alone at Schwerin more that 55,000 Germans surrendered that day.

The next day, 3 May, Tippelskirch himself entered an enclosure of the 82d Airborne Division along with some 140,000 other Germans of the *Twenty-first Army,* while farther north, at Schwerin, some 155,000, mainly of the *Third Panzer Army,* including the commander, General von Manteuffel, surrendered to the 8th Division. The headquarters of the army group controlling these two armies apparently disintegrated. Having narrowly escaped capture when men of the 8th Division entered Schwerin, the newly assigned commander, General Student, went into hiding but would be apprehended later in the month.

As Tippelskirch surrendered on 2 May, Admiral Doenitz was sending emissaries to Field Marshal Montgomery with a view to surrendering all German forces remaining in northern Germany. Under instructions from General Eisenhower, Montgomery on 4 May accepted the unconditional surrender effective the next day of all Germans in the Netherlands, the Frisian Islands, Helgoland, and all other islands, north Germany, and Denmark. (Norway, Eisenhower ruled, would constitute a political rather than a tactical surrender and thus would have to await negotiations at which Russian representatives would be present.) Although Montgomery refused to accept withdrawal into his zone of German civilians or military formations still opposing the Russians, he agreed to accept individual soldiers. Since the bulk of those opposing the Russians already had entered Allied lines in any case, the restriction made little difference.

General Wenck's *Twelfth Army* and the 30,000 survivors of the *Ninth Army* meanwhile entered negotiations with the Ninth U.S. Army on 4 May in hope of gaining approval for troops and a mass of civilians accompanying them to cross the Elbe and surrender. The Ninth Army's representatives agreed to accept the troops so long as they brought their own food, kitchens, and medical facilities, but forbade the civilians to cross. Actually, the Ninth Army's troops imposed no ban on civilians. On a catwalk spanning the ruins of a railroad bridge, on ferries, boats, and rafts, or by swimming, some 70,000 to 100,000 men of the *Ninth* and *Twelfth Armies* got to the west bank of the Elbe.[28]

---

[27] 82d Abn Div AAR, Apr–May 45.

[28] Details of the negotiations for the surrender may be found in Maj. Gen. James E. Moore (Chief of Staff, Ninth Army), Memorandum for the Commanding General, 7 May 1945, copy in OCMH through courtesy of General Moore.

In Austria, first indications that Field Marshal Kesselring might be ready to surrender his *Army Group G* and the *Nineteenth Army* developed on 3 May when General Devers learned through SHAEF that Kesselring had asked the German command in Italy to whom he should surrender.[29] On the same day Kesselring asked Admiral Doenitz for authority to surrender, which Doenitz granted.

As Kesselring began his overtures, the war in Austria went on amid an aura of unreality—not really war, yet not quite peace. There were three main drives, that of the French into the Vorarlberg, that of General Patch's Seventh Army toward Landeck and Innsbruck, and that of General Patton's Third Army toward Linz.

The 13th Armored Division of General Walker's XX Corps in the Third Army's center was the fiirst of Patton's troops to reach the Austrian frontier in strength, doing so on the first day of May along the Inn River opposite Braunau (Hitler's birthplace). The next day, as divisions of the XX Corps bridged the Inn at three places, in the process capturing both Braunau and Passau, the latter at the juncture of the Inn with the Danube, a new order and another that was pending forced General Patton to alter and broaden his plan of attack.

The first order was the boundary change according Salzburg to the Seventh Army. The change pinched out the III Corps along that part of the Inn River that flows inside Germany, ending participation of General Van Fleet's command in the fighting. The second was based on a plan to withdraw headquar-

ters and special troops of the First Army from the line, a first step in projected deployment of General Hodges' command to the Pacific. As part of the plan, General Huebner's V Corps on 2 May began relieving northernmost units of General Irwin's XII Corps along the Czechoslovakian frontier, a preliminary to transfer of the V Corps two days later to the Third Army. Irwin's corps was thus freed to join the drive on Linz down the north bank of the Danube. The scene was also prepared for an operation to which General Eisenhower had alerted the Russians a few days earlier, an advance of up to forty miles inside Czechoslovakia to Karlsbad, Pilsen, and Ceské Budějovice.[30]

Under the new arrangement, Walker's XX Corps was to press from its bridgehead over the Inn to the line of the Enns River southeast of Linz while the right wing of Irwin's XII Corps moved along the north bank of the Danube to capture Linz. Irwin's left wing meanwhile was to attack into the southwestern corner of Czechoslovakia toward Klatovy and Ceské Budějovice, while Huebner's V Corps advanced eastward to take Karlsbad and Pilsen.

The divisions of the XX Corps drew only occasional enemy fire as they moved swiftly to reach the Enns River on 4 May and there awaited the Russians. The 11th Armored Division of the XII Corps at the same time reached a point only a few miles north of Linz, where an official of the city offered to surrender on condition that the German garrison be allowed to march east against the Russians. The armor refused that priviso, and a column advanced swiftly the next morning to

---

[29] Hq, 6th AGp, History, p. 320.

[30] See 12th AGp Ltr of Instrs 22, 4 May 45.

find a bridge across the Danube intact, the city almost devoid of Germans. Another column uncovered more evidence of German atrocities in concentration camps near Mauthausen and Gusen. The armor then moved to the Linz-Ceské Budějovice highway to join neighbors of the XX Corps in a watch for the Russians.

For the rest of the XII Corps and for the V Corps, the drive into Czechoslovakia was at first an anticlimax. The fighting was unreal, a comic opera war carried on by men who wanted to surrender but seemingly had to fire a shot or two in the process. The land, too, was strange, neither German nor Czech. The little towns near the border, with their houses linked by fences and their decorated arches over the gates, had the look of Slavic villages, but the population was unquestionably hostile. This country was the disputed Sudetenland.

The monotony—an occasional burst of small arms fire along roads, a rocket from a *Panzerfaust* at a roadblock, a stray round of artillery fire in fields—was broken for the 90th Division on 4 May when out of the wooded hills emerged an old foe of the Third Army, the *11th Panzer Division*. This time the panzers were bent not on attack but on surrender. With an odd conglomeration of tanks and other vehicles, the remnants of the division marched with their commander, General von Wietersheim, to prisoner-of-war cages.

Two days later General Patton sent the 4th Armored Division through the 90th in the hope that General Eisenhower would agree to an advance down the valley of the Vltava River to Prague, but approval never came. Patrols had advanced as far as Pisek on a tributary of

the Vltava northwest of Ceské Budějovice when the armor came to a halt.

On 6 May men of the 2d and 97th Divisions and a new unit, the 16th Armored Division (Brig. Gen. John L. Pierce), came upon an entirely new scene. Early in the day the armor began unsuspectingly to pass through the infantry along the highway leading to Pilsen. Past silent, undefended forts of Czechoslovakia's western fortifications, the "Little Maginot Line," again untested in battle as it was after the Munich Pact, the troops burst suddenly from the Sudetenland with its apathetic, sometimes sullen German sympathizers into a riotous land of colorful flags and cheering citizenry.

As if they had stepped across some unseen barrier, the men found themselves in a new land of frenzy and delight. War and nonfraternization lay behind. It was Paris all over again, on a lesser scale and with different flags, but with the same jubilant faces, the same delirium of liberation. Past abandoned antiaircraft guns that had protected the big Skoda industrial complex on the outskirts of the city, the armor raced into Pilsen. *"Nazdar! Nazdar!"* the people shouted.

Except for the 1st Division, advancing on Karlsbad, the V Corps had joined the growing list of American units for which the shooting war was over. It was almost over for the 1st Division as well. Karlsbad surrendered by telephone early the next afternoon, the staff of the opposing *Seventh Army* the day after that.

In the Tirol, in the meantime, the Alpine terrain restricted the forces the Seventh Army could employ in drives on Innsbruck and Landeck to two divisions. Although only a few Germans resisted,

AUSTRIAN CIVILIANS *line a street in Innsbruck to welcome American troops.*

they drew added strength from their positions in the precipitous, narrow Alpine passes. Snow mixed with freezing rain and great drifts of the preceding winter's snow also slowed the advance. Nor were the men and their commanders eager, in view of the approaching end of the war, to take undue chances.

Relieving the armor of the VI Corps before the Mittenwald Pass leading to Innsbruck, the 103d Division during 1 May established telephone contact with the German garrison in the Tirolean capital, but the lines went out before surrender negotiations could be completed. Further negotiations were underway when, during the afternoon and evening of 2 May, Austrian partisans seized control of Innsbruck. Although the partisans begged for American entry lest SS troops counterattack, the 103d Division still had to fight through occasional German delaying groups to get to the city. During midmorning of 4 May, in a driving snowstorm, the Americans entered.

From Innsbruck, General McAuliffe sent his 411th Infantry hurrying southward in trucks to gain the Brenner Pass. In hope of speeding the advance over a

Cᴢᴇᴄʜᴏsʟᴏᴠᴀᴋɪᴀɴ Vɪʟʟᴀɢᴇʀs Wᴇʟᴄᴏᴍᴇ Tᴀɴᴋ Cʀᴇᴡ *of the 16th Armored Division.*

treacherous Alpine road, McAuliffe sent the convoy forward the night of 3 May with headlights blazing. Without firing a shot, the 411th Infantry took the town of Brenner just before 0200, 4 May, while a mounted patrol continued through the pass and across the Italian frontier to Vipiteno, there making contact at 1051 with reconnaissance troops of the 88th Infantry Division. A Seventh Army that had invaded Sicily long months before, then had left the fighting in the Mediterranean to the Fifth Army while detouring by way of southern France to Germany, joined hands with those men who had fought up the long, mountainous spine of Italy. That the troops belonged to the VI Corps was appropriate, for long ago the VI Corps had fought in Italy in a besieged beachhead at Anzio.

At the Fern Pass, where men of the 44th Division relieved other contingents of the armor of the VI Corps, a 300-man German detachment stanchly defended a serpentine highway blocked by deep craters and a landslide. A battalion of the 71st Infantry began to attack the

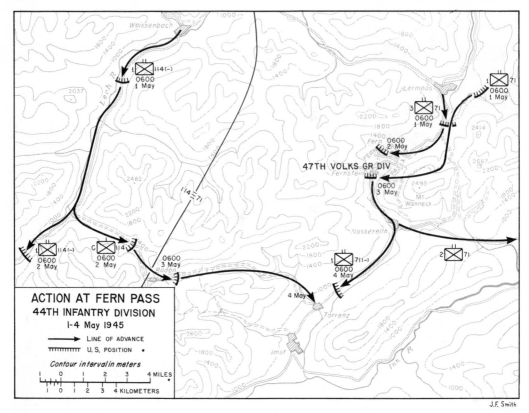

MAP 9

position early on 1 May. (*Map 9*) Anticipating difficulty getting through the pass, the division commander, General Dean, at the same time sent a reinforced company on a circuitous 40-mile outflanking maneuver, back almost to the Oberjoch Pass, then southwestward up the valley of the Lech River to another route—more a trail than a road—leading across a high mountain range to the vicinity of Imst, some eight miles behind the Fern Pass.

The company was still bucking fresh snow and old drifts when around midday on 2 May the commander of the 71st Infantry sent a second battalion to help

in reducing the defenses at the Fern Pass. As the battalion was moving up, five Austrian partisans appeared with an offer to guide the men along a little-known secondary road that would put them in rear of the pass. Led by the Austrians, the battalion moved swiftly along a road that cut through forests and over a steep crest south of the Fern Pass. The men seized the town of Fernstein behind the pass, then before dark, came upon the Germans at the pass from the rear. Resistance collapsed.

The next day men of the 44th Division pushed on foot toward Imst, to make contact there with the reinforced company that two days before had begun the wide outflanking maneuver; but resumption of a full-scale advance to Landeck and the Resia Pass beyond had to await repair of the road through the Fern Pass and the coming of tanks and other vehicles. It was this delay that prompted the commander of the First French Army, General de Lattre, to try to beat the Americans into Landeck by way of the Arlberg Pass.[31]

Unaware that de Lattre had begun a race for Landeck, the 44th Division was in no rush, particularly not in view of other developments on 4 May. Through the division's lines at Imst that day passed emissaries of General Brandenberger's *Nineteenth Army* on their way to open negotiations for surrender. Not far away, other emissaries on the night of 4 May approached troops of the 3d Division of the XV Corps to begin arrangements for capitulation of General Schulz's *Army Group G.*

The *Nineteenth Army* surrendered in keeping with a detailed scenario worked out at headquarters of the VI Corps. The enemy commander, Brandenberger, was to present himself at the Landsrat in Innsbruck at a specified time on 5 May. The scenario spelled out how Brandenberger was to be met, that no salutes or handshakes were to be exchanged, even the times when conferees would stand and when they would be seated.

Except that Brandenberger reached the scene some minutes late, all went according to plan. Shortly before 1500 the VI Corps commander, General Brooks, afforded Brandenberger and his staff a brief period in which to confer privately upon condition that they return

to the conference room at 1500. At that time the *Nineteenth Army* surrendered unconditionally, effective at 1800 the same day.[32]

A regiment of the 44th Division meanwhile had resumed the advance on Landeck when in midmorning of the 5th, the German commander in the region suggested a truce pending the outcome of Brandenberger's negotiations. On the condition that the arrangement include evacuation of Landeck, General Dean agreed, and a battalion of the 44th Division occupied the town that afternoon, in the process unwittingly thwarting General de Lattre's effort to reach Landeck first. Not until two days later, on the 7th, would anyone bother to proceed to the Resia Pass, which de Lattre so earnestly wanted to attain. At 1900, 7 May, the 44th Division established contact there with contingents of the 10th Mountain Division.

In the broader surrender of *Army Group G,* an element of surprise was present in that General Devers had anticipated, on the basis of Field Marshal Kesselring's query as to whom he should surrender, that Kesselring would be surrendering his entire command. Kesselring had intended to do that, but the new German government had granted authority only for *Army Group G,* not for those troops opposing the Russians in Austria and the Balkans, which by Hitler's order of 24 April were at that point under Kesselring's command.[33]

Thus it was that the commander of the *First Army,* General Foertsch, representing the commander of *Army Group G,* General Schulz, appeared the night of

---

[31] See above, ch. XVIII.

[32] See AAR's of VI Corps, 44th and 103d Divs, May 45, and Seventh Army Report, pp. 848–49.
[33] Kesselring, *A Soldier's Record,* p. 342.

4 May before troops of the XV Corps. The 3d Division commander, General O'Daniel, accompanied the delegation to an estate at Haar, near Munich, where negotiations began on the rainy fifth day of May. Among those present, in addition to Devers, were Patch of the Seventh Army and Haislip of the XV Corps. No representative of the First French Army was included.

Although General Foertsch made no objection to terms, he felt impelled to point out that even with the best of intentions, it would be difficult for the Germans to comply with some provisions in the time allowed. Such was the state of German communications, for example, that many hours might pass before all German troops received word of the surrender. He also asked if the Allies would hand over prisoners to the Russians.

With these points answered, usually noncommittally, General Devers stated firmly that General Foertsch's action was no armistice; it was unconditional surrender.

"Do you understand that?" he asked.

Foertsch stiffened. After nearly a minute, he responded.

"I can assure you, sir," he said, "that no power is left at my disposal to prevent it."

At approximately 1430, representatives of both sides signed the terms to become effective at noon the next day, 6 May.[34]

The surrender affected all German troops between Army Group G's eastern boundary near the Austro-Czech border and the western border of Switzerland, thus excluding General von Obstfelder's

Seventh Army in Czechoslovakia, which a week earlier had been subordinated directly to OB WEST, but including Brandenberger's Nineteenth Army and its shadow appendage, the Twenty-fourth Army, even though Brandenberger, apparently without the knowledge of General Foertsch, had begun negotiations ahead of Foertsch. The duplication probably resulted from Kesselring's authorizing both army group and army commanders to enter negotiations, from a breakdown in communications within Army Group G, or from the on-again, off-again nature of the Nineteenth Army's subordination to Army Group G during the preceding month, this last apparently having depended either on the whim of Kesselring or on the state of communications among the three headquarters. Troops of the Nineteenth Army, in any event, generally observed the earlier effective hour of surrender specified in Brandenberger's negotiations with the VI Corps.

The same was not true of the shadow force, the Twenty-fourth Army, though only partially through the fault of the Germans. Representatives of the commander of the force, General der Infanterie Hans Schmidt, had approached the French at noon on 4 May with a request for terms of surrender, but before word could reach General de Lattre, the French commander received a request from the 6th Army Group to send a parliamentary to the VI Corps to treat with the Nineteenth Army. When General Schmidt's delegation reached de Lattre's headquarters with word that Schmidt had authority to treat independently, de Lattre theorized that the French had been invited to participate in the Nineteenth Army's surrender be-

[34] Hq, 6th AGp, History, pp. 321–33. See also XV Corps AAR, May 45, and Seventh Army Report, pp. 856–60.

cause soldiers of that army faced both French and Americans but that he was free to treat alone with Schmidt since only French troops faced the *Twenty-fourth Army*.[35]

By the time General Schmidt's emissaries returned from contacting the French, Schmidt had learned that *Army Group G* was surrendering to the 6th Army Group. Deciding against presenting himself to de Lattre, Schmidt sent instead a letter noting the broader surrender and suggesting that the French get in touch on the matter with the 6th Army Group.

Shocked by the "insolence" of Schmidt's letter, General de Lattre demanded that General Devers send on to him any plenipotentiaries from the *Twenty-fourth Army* who might approach American forces. He intended to continue hostilities, he said, until the moment German representatives presented themselves at his headquarters.

General Devers's chief of staff replied that *Army Group G* had surrendered in entirety effective at noon on 6 May, including the troops opposing the French. Devers's orders were that all troops of the 6th Army Group stop in place and cease fighting immediately, the word to be transmitted without delay to both Germans and French.

De Lattre was not satisfied. If the *Nineteenth Army* as a part of *Army Group G* had surrendered individually with an effective hour different from that for the entire army group, then the same conditions should be applied, he rea-

soned, to the *Twenty-fourth Army*. Failing to take cognizance of the fact that Schmidt's command was attached as a subordinate unit to Brandenberger's, he rationalized that if the *Twenty-fourth Army* had been included in the surrender, it would have been mentioned by name. Defying the directive from Devers, de Lattre sent a courier to General Brandenberger to demand that he send Schmidt to surrender to the French. In the meantime, he said, the French would continue to fight.

Hostilities ostensibly were continuing in the French sector when late on 6 May General Devers sent a liaison officer to explain to de Lattre how, even as negotiations had been underway with Brandenberger, a delegation from *Army Group G* had arrived to surrender the entire command. De Lattre was still not to be placated. Ignoring the fact that the *Twenty-fourth Army* bore the name of an army command purely for purposes of deception, he pointed out that neither in the surrender of *Army Group G* nor of the *Nineteenth Army* had the *Twenty-fourth Army* been specifically mentioned. Besides, he maintained, not without logic, if the Germans on his front were included in *Army Group G*'s surrender, then the First French Army should have been represented at the ceremony.

When the liaison officer asked him at this point to sign his name to the surrender document, de Lattre refused on the grounds that General de Gaulle had named him as an official representative of the French government to accept the over-all German surrender and that a governmental representative should not affix his signature to an operational document originating in the field. In de-

---

[35] The account of this incident is based on de Lattre, *Histoire de la Première Armée Française,* pp. 583–93; Seventh Army Report, pp. 850–51; and Devers Diary, entry of 13 May 45.

clining, he again demanded that General Schmidt be turned over to the French. General Devers refused. There the matter rested, with hostilities on the French front coming to an end from a combination of a lack of anybody to fight back and of general German surrender.

Elsewhere on the 6th Army Group's front, some fanaticism on the part of lower echelon German units and individuals lingered at various points. SS troops, who as members of the *Waffen-SS* constituted an arm of the Nazi party not subject to army command except for operational orders when attached to army units in the field, caused particular trouble. As General Foertsch was returning to German lines following the surrender ceremony, for example, SS troops blew craters in the road in front of the delegation and allowed only Foertsch himself to pass. After dark on 6 May, SS troops seized three men of the 101st Airborne Division, then released them the next morning with word to send officer representatives to accept surrender of an SS command. After German Army guards surrendered a castle near Woergl, northeast of Innsbruck, in which prominent Frenchmen were imprisoned (former Premiers Edouard Daladier and Paul Reynaud and Marshals Maurice Gamelin and Maxime Weygand), SS troops attacked but were beaten off by a combined effort of the German guards and men of the 36th Division's 142d Infantry. As late as 8 May arrangements were being completed for separate surrenders of the *XIII SS* and the *LXXXII Corps*.[36]

Surrender at Reims

As the piecemeal surrenders occurred, the new head of the Third Reich, Admiral Doenitz, was exploring the possibilities of over-all surrender while striving somehow to continue the exodus of German troops from in front of the Russians.[37] As a first step, he instructed the officer heading the delegation to Field Marshal Montgomery to establish contact with General Eisenhower to explain why surrender was not yet possible and to explore the chances of further partial capitulations.

That the Germans were trying to gain time to save their troops facing the Russians could hardly be lost on General Eisenhower, nor would the stratagem receive any more encouragement that had Himmler's presumptive effort to surrender only to the Western Powers. Eisenhower promptly cabled Moscow that he intended to inform the Germans that they would have to surrender all forces facing the Red Army to the Russians and that he wanted the surrender on both Eastern and Western Fronts to be made simultaneously. The Russians in turn authorized Maj. Gen. Ivan Susloparoff, long their liaison officer at SHAEF, to represent Soviet interests in any negotiations with the Doenitz government.

The German party arrived at General Eisenhower's headquarters in Reims in late afternoon on 5 May. There the Germans learned quickly that the Allies would sanction no separate surrender for the Western Front. The head of the delegation cabled this information to

---

[36] Seventh Army Report, pp. 860–61; 142d Inf AAR, May 45.

[37] This account is based on Pogue, *The Supreme Command*, pages 483–492, which provides details and annotation.

Doenitz, requesting permission either to sign an unconditional surrender for all fronts or to have someone else come to Reims for that purpose.

Shocked by Eisenhower's stand, Admiral Doenitz the next day sent General Jodl, strong opponent of surrender in the east, to continue the negotiations. When Allied conferees quickly discerned during conversations the night of 6 May that Jodl was merely dragging out the talks to gain time, they put the problem directly to the Supreme Commander. If the Germans did not speedily agree to terms, Eisenhower responded, "he would break off all negotiations and seal the Western Front, preventing by force any further westward movement of German soldiers and civilians."

Impressed with Eisenhower's determi-
nation, Jodl telegraphed Doenitz for authority to make a final and complete surrender on all fronts. Although Doenitz deemed the Supreme Commander's demand "sheer extortion," he felt impelled to accede since it was Jodl, only the day before strongly opposed to surrender in the east, who insisted that over-all surrender was the only way out. In the early minutes of 7 May, he granted Jodl authority to sign.

In the War Room of General Eisenhower's headquarters in a red brick boy's school at Reims, Jodl signed the surrender at 0241, 7 May, to become effective at 2301, 8 May. (*Map XVIII*) For the benefit of the Russians, the Germans did it again on the 8th in Berlin with Keitel substituting for Jodl.

CHAPTER XX

Epilogue

With the lights going on again all over Europe, the United States and its allies on 8 May celebrated V–E (Victory in Europe) Day. To the troops in the field, the end brought a flush of relief but with it a dulling sense of anticlimax.

A myriad of taxing jobs remained before Allied troops everywhere could turn full attention to occupation duties. The Allies had to disarm and control all German forces, many of them sizable, as in Denmark, Norway, and Czechoslovakia, and discharge them as quickly as possible in order to reduce the strain on food stocks and facilities. They had to continue to evacuate Allied prisoners of war; control, feed, and eventually evacuate foreign laborers and other displaced persons; assert authority over the Doenitz government and OKW, then disband them along with the headquarters of the Luftwaffe and the Navy. They had also to collect German records and documents; arrest ranking German officers and others who might be charged with war crimes; begin redeploying some units through the Suez Canal to the Pacific, others to the United States, both for projected commitment in the war against Japan; weed out individuals with long overseas and combat service for early return to the United States; prepare for disbanding SHAEF and shifting to military government in four national zones of occupation; withdraw American and British forces from the Russian zone; arrange for four-power occupation of Berlin and Vienna—these and more.[1]

The thorniest of all problems with German forces still under arms was in Czechoslovakia where large German units continued to fight against the Red Army in hope of withdrawing into American lines. Yet once the general surrender became effective at 2301 on 8 May, haven in American lines was denied by stipulation of the terms of surrender signed at Reims. As German troops, many with their families in tow, continued to flock toward American positions, U.S. divisions assembled them in "concentration areas" immediately in front of their defensive line, there eventually to turn them over to the Russians. At Russian insistence, SHAEF also directed that higher commanders of those forces presumed to have been responsible for continued defense and thus for violation of the surrender agreement, also be turned over to the Russians even though they might have entered American lines before the deadline. Many was the pitiable scene enacted, for most of the Germans were desperately fearful of what the Russians would do to them.[2] For

---

[1] Greater detail on post-D-day activities may be found in Pogue, *The Supreme Command*, ch. XXVI.

[2] See AAR's of 4th Armd and 26th Divs, May 45; V Corps Operations in the ETO, p. 465; Gay

some million and a quarter German officers and men who became prisoners of the Russians after the surrender, the way home would be long and toilsome.[3]

The last days of the war in Czechoslovakia also brought appeals from Czech partisans and the Czech government-in-exile for Allied units to march to relief of partisans in Prague. Although the partisans liberated their capital on 5 May, German armor promptly converged on the city. On the basis of the prior Soviet request that Allied troops advance no farther than the line Karlsbad-Pilsen-Ceské Budějovice, Eisenhower declined to send troops but passed the appeals on to the Russians.[4]

Other than in Czechoslovakia, the surrender of German forces produced few problems except those of an administrative and logistical nature. With assistance from small U.S. units, British forces undertook the surrender and evacuation of German troops from Denmark and Norway; the Canadians, those Germans in the Netherlands. A garrison that held out on the French coast at Dunkerque surrendered on 9 May to the Czech Independent Armored Brigade Group that had been containing them. The British accepted surrender of German forces in the Channel Islands, also on 9 May, and the last Germans holding out along the southwestern coast of France capitulated to the French on the same day. The garrisons of Lorient and St. Nazaire on the coast of Brittany surrendered on 10 May to troops of the

U.S. 66th Division (Maj. Gen. Herman F. Kramer). Having earlier assumed the assignment of containing these garrisons from the 94th Division, the 66th was one of only two U.S. divisions in the European theater that failed to enter the enemy's country before hostilities ended.[5] The other, the 13th Airborne Division, was the only division to see no combat.

Although General Eisenhower's Supreme Headquarters, Allied Expeditionary Force, continued to function until 14 July, the combat phase of World War II in Europe ended with the final German capitulations. The campaign from the D-day landings in Normandy on 6 June through the surrenders had taken just over eleven months.

In those eleven months Allied armies had driven some 475 to 700 miles from the beaches of Normandy and those of the Côte d'Azur to the Baltic, the Elbe, and into Czechoslovakia and Austria. From the Dutch coast near the mouth of the Rhine to the Baltic near Luebeck, thence south to the Brenner Pass and westward to the Swiss frontier, the final Allied positions encompassed some 900 miles. As of V–E Day General Eisenhower had under his command more than four and a half million troops, which included 91 divisions and several independent brigades and cavalry groups (61 of the divisions were American), 6 tactical air commands, and 2 strategic air forces. At peak strength in

---

Diary, entries of 10 and 11 May 45; SHAEF SGS 322.01–1, Liaison with the Russians, *passim;* and Koyen, *The Fourth Armored Division* (first edition), p. 151.

[3] Ziemke, *Stalingrad to Berlin,* ch. XXI.

[4] See Pogue, *The Supreme Command,* pp. 504–05.

[5] In one of the few instances of the sinking of a loaded U.S. troopship during World War II, the 66th Division had lost 800 men on Christmas Eve 1944, when a German submarine sank the Belgian ship *Léopoldville* in the English Channel. See Jacquin Sanders, *A Night Before Christmas—The Sinking of the Troopship Léopoldville* (New York: MacFadden Books, 1964).

April, the Allies had 28,000 combat aircraft, of which 14,845 were American, including 5,559 heavy bombers and 6,003 fighters. Between D-day and V–E Day, a total of 5,412,219 Allied troops had entered western Europe along with 970,044 vehicles and 18,292,310 tons of supplies.[6]

Allied casualties from D-day to V–E Day totaled 766,294. American losses were 586,628, including 135,576 dead. The British, Canadians, French, and other allies in the west lost approximately 60,000 dead.[7] How many of the three million Germans that were killed during the entire war died on the Western Front is impossible to determine, but exclusive of prisoners of war, all German casualties in the west from D-day to V–E Day probably equaled or slightly exceeded Allied losses. More than two million Germans were captured in the west.[8]

---

[6] SHAEF G–3 War Room Daily Sum, 11 May 45, and AAF Statistical Digest, World War II, p. 156.

[7] Department of the Army, *Army Battle Casualties and Nonbattle Deaths in World War II: Final Report, 7 December 1941–31 December 1946,* and SHAEF's final cumulative casualty report in the G–3 War Room Daily Summary, 29 May 1945.

[8] The only specific figures available are from *OB WEST* for the period 2 June 1941–10 April 1945 as follows: Dead, 80,819; wounded, 265,526; missing, 490,624; total, 836,969. (Of the total, 4,548 casualties were incurred prior to D-day.) See Rpts, *Der Heeresarzt im Oberkommando des Heeres Gen St d H/Gen Qu, Az.: 1335 c/d (IIb) Nr.: H.A./263/45 g. Kdos.* of 14 Apr 45 and *1335 c/d (IIb)* (no date, but before 1945). The former is in OCMH X 313, a photostat of a document contained in German armament folder *H 17/207;* the latter in folder *OKW/1561 (OKW Wehrmacht Verluste).* These figures are for the field army only, and do not include the Luftwaffe and *Waffen-SS.* Since the Germans seldom remained in control of the battlefield in a position to verify the status of those missing, a considerable percentage of the missing probably were killed. Time lag in reporting probably precludes these figures' reflecting the heavy losses during the Allied drive to the Rhine in

In many respects the last offensive had been a replay on a grander scale of the Allied victory in France. Following the difficult close-in fighting during the fall of 1944 in the Netherlands, along the West Wall, and in Alsace and Lorraine, which could be likened to the early weeks in Normandy, the Germans had counterattacked in the Ardennes as they had in Normandy at Mortain, and in the process so weakened themselves that great slashing Allied drives across their homeland were as inevitable as had been the swift Allied thrusts across France and Belgium. Nor was there anything new in Hitler's adamant refusal to authorize withdrawals; he had done the same in France.

Being, in effect, a replay, the campaign had produced little that was new in American tactics, doctrine, or techniques. The efficacy of the American tank-infantry-artillery team, of methods of air-ground co-operation, of the regimental combat team and combat command concepts, and of the "lean" division with attachments provided as needed, the role of the tank as an antitank weapon, the general excellence of American arms and equipment, the ability to motorize infantry divisions on short notice—all these had been demonstrated and proved long before. The campaign merely emphasized the general efficacy and professionalism of the American forces. The same shortcomings that had been evident before also were again

---

March, and the cut-off date precludes inclusion of the losses in the Ruhr Pocket and in other stages of the fight in central Germany. SHAEF records list 2,057,138 Germans as "prisoners of war" and another four million as "disarmed enemy personnel," the former presumably taken before formal capitulation began, the latter afterward. SHAEF G–3 War Room Daily Sum, 23 Jun 45.

apparent: the basic obsolescence of the Sherman tank, the relative uselessness of the towed 57-mm. antitank gun, the relative ineffectiveness of the tank destroyer as compared with the tank as an antitank weapon, the redundance of a regimental cannon company in view of the close relationship éxisting between infantry and supporting artillery, the need for combat experience before a division functioned smoothly.

In view of the length of time and the tremendous power on the ground that was required to bring the foe finally to his knees, it was apparent that the new air arm for all its staggering blows against the enemy's production, economy, and morale had failed to achieve decision. It was not until December 1944 that German production of essential military items dropped off sharply, and not until late January and early February 1945 were indications of eventual collapse present in the German economy. Had Allied airmen known from the start what they learned later—that persistent blasting of a select group of targets critical to the entire economy may be more effective in less time than occasional strikes against a host of targets—the aerial campaign well might have critically influenced an earlier decision. As it was the Western Allied armies in league with the ally from the east, and with essential air and naval power in support, had broken the back of the German armies in the field before the aerial bombardment could build to an intensity capable of decision in its own right. Indeed, that air power alone can bring decision has yet to be demonstrated.[9]

Despite the overwhelming nature of the victory on the ground, many a provocative event had emerged. The First and Third Armies in the Ardennes, for example, might have trapped large numbers of the enemy had the main effort shifted after relief of Bastogne to the drive Patton wanted along the base of the bulge. The drive would have speeded German withdrawal if nothing else. Had General Bradley been allowed to continue a full-blooded attack from the Ardennes into the Eifel, the First and Third Armies probably would have gained the Rhine in short order, thus unhinging German defense west of the Rhine without the direct confrontation of the First Canadian Army with German strength in the flooded Rhine lowlands to the north. Perhaps the most striking result of the enemy's Ardennes offensive was the general apprehension and concern for German capabilities that it engendered in the Allied command, whereas once the counteroffensive was over, the Germans in reality had little but defensive capability left.

In several cases Allied commanders seemingly passed up opportunities that might have speeded the end: Field Marshal Montgomery's decision, for example, to deny Simpson's Ninth Army a quick jump of the Rhine early in March; or the failure to trap all German forces in the Saar-Palatinate, despite superb tactical strokes by the Third Army.

Yet there were moments, too, that seemed inspired: not only Remagen but also Oppenheim; the campaign to encircle the Ruhr, particularly that part staged by the First Army; the dashes by

[9] *The United States Strategic Bombing Survey— Summary Report (European War)*, 30 September 1945, pages 15–16, appears to have overstated the case in saying, "Allied air power was decisive in the war in Western Europe. . . ."

the Ninth Army's 2d Armored and 83d Divisions to the Elbe.

There were others to be regretted, particularly Patton's ill-starred foray to Hammelburg, which was too ambitious for the force assigned and was unfortunate regardless of whether Patton knew his son-in-law was a captive there. The 10th Armored Division was overextended at Crailsheim, even for the type of loose-reined warfare that was the order of the day. Given the nature of the opposition, it was unnecessary to go through with the plan to employ airborne divisions in conjunction with Montgomery's Rhine crossing, since the risks and losses attendant on airborne operations hardly could be justified under the circumstances.

The last offensive was nevertheless a brilliant exercise in controlling masses of men and units and in co-ordinating the air and all the ground arms—a demonstration of power never before seen, even in the early German campaigns of World War II or in the offensives of the Red Army. It was, for all the crumbling nature of the opposition, a logistical *tour de force* by the most highly motorized and mechanized armies the world had ever known. No part of General Eisenhower's vast force had to pause at any point for purely logistical reasons, even while driving in slightly more than six weeks over such great distances as the 250 miles from the Roer to the Elbe. It was a campaign to be told in superlatives.

Despite the presence of potentially abrasive personalities in the Allied command—Montgomery, de Lattre, Patton —no serious interference with the conduct of the campaign developed. Montgomery's insistence on keeping the Ninth Army and driving on Berlin was

a disagreement that took place behind the scenes and did nothing to delay the advancing divisions. De Lattre's digressions at Stuttgart, Ulm, and St. Anton took on in the end a character of nothing more serious than an *opéra buffe*. Patton's lamented detour to Hammelburg was painful and costly to the men involved but had little lasting effect on the campaign.

On the matters of major controversy with the British—Berlin and Prague— the Supreme Commander could hardly be faulted. On Berlin, there seemed little point in driving deeper into territory already allocated for Russian occupation merely for the sake of prestige, and since arrangements for Allied access to Berlin during the occupation had already been made at governmental level, dashing to the capital would have had no effect on them. As for Prague, the Supreme Commander might have relented on humanitarian grounds, but since the Western Allies had no intention of staying long in Czechoslovakia, the effect on postwar developments could hardly have been lasting.

The German attempt to stem the last offensive was an exercise in futility. Once the Germans had failed in the Ardennes, there could be no longer any doubt that they had lost the war. Had Hitler acquiesced in an early withdrawal behind the Rhine, as his field commanders apparently urged, they might have prolonged the end; but so empty was the threat of miracle weapons, so unlikely a démarche between the Western Allies and the Soviet Union, that prolongation would have been the sole result.

The only basic matter to be decided

by the last offensive was not whether the Germans would be reduced to total defeat, but when. Given the stranglehold and almost mystic fascination that Hitler and his coterie exercised over the German people and the incredible loyalty of German military commanders to a régime that long had been discredited, perhaps it was inevitable that the end would come only when the nation was prostrate, almost every square inch of territory under the control of the victors. In those circumstances, whether the invaders insisted on unconditional surrender or came shouting mercy and forgiveness probably would have had little effect on the outcome.

As the last offensive came to an end, few if any who fought in it could have entertained any doubts as to the right of their cause—they had seen at Buchenwald, Belsen, Dachau, and at a dozen other places, including little Ohrdruf, what awful tyranny man can practice on his fellow man. To erase those cruel monuments to evil was reason enough for it all, from bloody OMAHA Beach to that bridgehead to nowhere over the Elbe.

Appendix A

Table of Equivalent Ranks

U.S. Army	German Army and Air Force	German Waffen-SS
None	Reichsmarschall	None
General of the Army	Generalfeldmarschall	Reichsfuehrer-SS
General	Generaloberst	Oberstgruppenfuehrer
Lieutenant General	General der Infanterie	Obergruppenfuehrer
	Artillerie	
	Gebirgstruppen	
	Kavallerie	
	Nachrichtentruppen	
	Panzertruppen	
	Pioniere	
	Luftwaffe	
	Flieger	
	Fallschirmtruppen	
	Flakartillerie	
	Luftnachrichtentruppen	
Major General	Generalleutnant	Gruppenfuehrer
Brigadier General	Generalmajor	Brigadefuehrer
None	None	Oberfuehrer
Colonel	Oberst	Standartenfuehrer
Lieutenant Colonel	Oberstleutnant	Obersturmbannfuehrer
Major	Major	Sturmbannfuehrer
Captain	Hauptmann	Haupsturmfuehrer
Captain (Cavalry)	Rittmeister	
First Lieutenant	Oberleutnant	Obersturmfuehrer
Second Lieutenant	Leutnant	Untersturmfuehrer

Appendix B

Recipients of the Distinguished Service Cross

All who were awarded the Medal of Honor for individual actions during operations described in this volume have been mentioned either in text or footnotes. Space limitations precluded similar mention of all who were awarded the Distinguished Service Cross. The following list of recipients of the DSC is as complete as possible in view of the fact that no single Army file listing DSC awards was maintained. Ranks are as of the date of the action cited. (P) indicates a posthumous award; * indicates DSC with Oak Leaf Cluster.

Pfc. Patsy A. Aiezza, Jr. (P)
1st Lt. Marshall Alexander
Pfc. Rex Anderson (P)
Pfc. Thomas E. Ankesheiln, Jr.
1st Lt. Ray F. Axford
S. Sgt. Everett E. Baker (P)
S. Sgt. James F. Baker
1st Sgt. Charles A. Baldari
S. Sgt. Ernest L. Barber
1st Lt. Lee J. Barstow
Pfc. Virgil E. Barton (P)
Capt. Abraham J. Baum
Sgt. William T. Baxter
S. Sgt. Paul Beck (P)
Cpl. Leslie M. Belden
Pfc. Edward M. Bell, Jr.
Pfc. Sherle E. Bellard
2d Lt. John L. Beranek
Capt. Robert H. Bertsch (P)
1st Lt. Lawrence P. Bischoff, Jr.
Tech. 4 Clarence E. Bowman (P)
2d Lt. Dale E. Bowyer
Tech. 5 Eli M. Bozickovich (P)
2d Lt. Archer L. Bradshaw (P)
1st Lt. Neil F. Brennan
Lt. Col. John P. Brewster (P)
Pfc. Raymond J. Brisson (P)
2d Lt. Raymond E. Broadbent (P)
Pfc. William J. Brooks (P)
S. Sgt. Fred H. Brown (P)

S. Sgt. Henry C. Brown
Capt. Ralph T. Brown
Sgt. Wallace E. Brown
Capt. Peter P. Buescher
T. Sgt. Woodrow Bugg (P)
Pfc. Gene P. Burks
2d Lt. Virgil S. Burks
Pfc. Edward C. Burnshaw
Pfc. Herbert H. Burr
Pvt. Raymond O. Butts
Pvt. Everett M. Callaway
1st Lt. William H. Callaway
S. Sgt. Harry W. Caminiti (P)
Pvt. Sam Capri
2d Lt. William M. Capron
1st Lt. James R. Carpenter (P)
S. Sgt. Clair R. Carr (P)
S. Sgt. Edward J. Carroll (P)
Pfc. James R. Carroll
Pfc. Vernon E. Cassady
T. Sgt. James T. Chapman
Lt. Col. Henry T. Cherry, Jr.
T. Sgt. Michael Chinchar
Capt. Paul Chmar
Cpl. Angelus M. Christiana (P)
1st Lt. Edward C. Christl (P)
Pfc. Thomas E. Churchill
Lt. Col. Wadsworth P. Clapp (P)
Pfc. John T. Clements (P)
Lt. Col. Robert B. Cobb

S. Sgt. Raymond O. Cocannouer
S. Sgt. Travis P. Collins
Tech. 5 Almon N. Conger, Jr.
2d Lt. Alwyn D. Conger
Pvt. James F. Cousineau
Pfc. John J. Coyle
Pvt. Jack C. Cunningham
S. Sgt. Francis J. Daddario
2d Lt. George Dail (P)
Tech. 5 Wilman T. Daley (P)
1st Lt. Thomas A. Daly (P)
Tech. 5 Donald K. Davis
Pfc. Ted R. Davis
Capt. Robert S. Dayton
Pfc. Frederick S. DeBenedetto (P)
S. Sgt. Joseph A. Delisio
Pfc. Joseph A. Demay
Cpl. Harold Denham (P)
Lt. Col. William E. Depuy
Capt. Billy J. DeVault
Capt. Robert B. Dexter
Pfc. Warner S. Deyoe
Lt. Col. Francis H. Dohs (P)
2d Lt. Glenn J. Doman
Sgt. Eugene Dorland
1st Sgt. Jack J. Dorsey
S. Sgt. Harold D. Douglas (P)
2d Lt. James B. Dozier
Sgt. Alexander A. Drabik
Pfc. Robert C. Driscoe
Pfc. Allen D. Druckenboard
2d Lt. William A. Dunlap
1st Lt. Frederick Eastman
Pfc. Henry T. Ebersole
1st Lt. Clyde W. Ehrhardt
2d Lt. Archibald A. Farrar
Capt. William H. Feery
S. Sgt. Joseph G. Feiley (P)
S. Sgt. William A. Flesch
T. Sgt. Peter H. Fleury
Pvt. Michael J. Fortuna (P)
Lt. Col. Leroy E. Frazier
Pfc. Russel M. Frederick
1st Lt. Robert L. French (P)
Sgt. Kenneth L. Gaines
Maj. Charles F. Gaking
Sgt. Wallace M. Gallant
1st Lt. Glenn H. Gass (P)

2d Lt. Emmette F. Gathright
S. Sgt. George Gaydush (P)
Capt. Albert C. Geist
1st Lt. Frank T. Gerard, Jr. (P)
Sgt. John Gilman
S. Sgt. William J. Glynn
Sgt. William J. Goodson
2d Lt. Malcolm B. Gott
S. Sgt. William E. Graves (P)
1st Lt. John Grimball
S. Sgt. Fred Grossi
Pfc. Harry Gubino
Pfc. Green D. Hadley
2d Lt. Claude J. Hafner
2d Lt. Frank J. Hagney
T. Sgt. Joseph W. Hairston
Pfc. Christy A. Hampe, Jr.
T. Sgt. James L. Hansen
1st Lt. Glen W. Harman
Chaplain (Capt.) Edward H. Harrison
T. Sgt. William B. Hawk, Jr. (P)
Sgt. Leonard B. Haymaker (P)
Pfc. Earl Hensel (P)
S. Sgt. William Hess
Pfc. Ralph H. Higby (P)
Cpl. Robert H. Hill (P)
Lt. Col. Clarence K. Hollingsworth (P)
2d Lt. William J. Honan
Pfc. Henry T. Hopper
Sgt. James I. Hoppes
1st Lt. Marion L. Howard
1st Lt. Norman R. Hughes
1st Lt. Galen C. Hughett
Sgt. Charles M. Huntington
T. Sgt. Alvin A. Hyman
Pfc. Robert L. Ifland (P)
S. Sgt. Wiley J. Ingram
1st Lt. Ned T. Irish
Capt. Orval D. Irvin (P)
Lt. Col. Albin F. Irzyk
1st Lt. William N. Jackson
Pvt. Jackson J. James
S. Sgt. Maynard M. Jerome (P)
1st Lt. Clark E. Johnson
Sgt. Glenn N. Johnson
Capt. Neil O. Johnson
Capt. Lennis Jones
1st Lt. Vernon C. Jordan

Pfc. Wilbur A. Jurries
T. Sgt. Francis E. Kelley
Sgt. James R. Kellogg
Lt. Col. John E. Kelly
Pfc. William H. Kendall (P)
Pfc. Carl J. Kistel
Pfc. Leonard F. Krause (P)
Lt. Col. Robert L. Kriz
T. Sgt. Chester E. Kroll
Pfc. Jerome L. Kucinski (P)
S. Sgt. Abe M. Kuzminsky (P)
S. Sgt. Maurice R. Kyne
1st Lt. John E. Lance, Jr.
S. Sgt. Oscar M. Langenkamp
Pfc. William G. Lanseadel (P)
S. Sgt. John F. Larson
Pfc. Leroy S. Law (P)
Sgt. Delbert D. Lee (P)
Lt. Col. Lewis W. Leeney
Capt. Victor C. Leiker
Pfc. Edward J. Lesinski
Capt. Jerry H. Lewis (P)
1st Lt. Richard S. Lewis
Sgt. Hugh P. Lockhart
Col. Jay B. Loveless
1st Lt. Henry F. Luehring
S. Sgt. Melvin N. Lund
Col. Carl E. Lundquist
2d Lt. Willard H. Maas (P)
S. Sgt. Ova I. Madsen (P)
Pfc. Alexander Maluchnik (P)
1st Lt. Thomas J. Mann
Sgt. John R. Mantville (P)
Pfc. Raymond Manz (P)
Pfc. Anthony L. Markovich (P)
S. Sgt. Thomas E. Martin
1st Sgt. Lawrence Marzella
T. Sgt. William W. Masters (P)
Cpl. Robert L. Mathis
Cpl. Walter W. Mathis
Pfc. Abraham Matza (P)
Lt. Col. Robert C. McCabe
Pfc. Charles W. McCartney
S. Sgt. Hal H. McColl
Capt. Boyd H. McCune
1st Lt. William E. McInerney
T. Sgt. Charles W. McKeever
Pfc. John F. McKeon, Jr.

S. Sgt. Charles S. McMillian
Cpl. William P. McPherson
2d Lt. Myron A. Mears
1st Lt. Norman J. Mecklem, Jr.
1st Lt. Charles W. Miller
Pvt. Harvey L. Miller, Jr. (P)
Capt. Barber C. Mills
1st Lt. Charles C. Misner
Capt. John Mitchell
S. Sgt. Henry A. Moen (P)
Pfc. George R. Mohn (P)
Pfc. Stevenson W. Moomaw (P)
Lt. Col. Robert B. Moran
Pvt. Patrick H. Moreschi
1st Lt. George H. Morgan
Pfc. William H. Moriarity
1st Lt. Hugh B. Mott
Tech. 4 Charles E. Mueller
2d Lt. Milton J. Munch
Capt. Patrick F. Murphy (P)
1st Lt. Samuel J. Murray
2d Lt. William L. Nelson
2d Lt. George P. Nestor
1st Lt. Eugene M. Nettles (P)
S. Sgt. Clemens G. Noldau (P)
1st Lt. Andrew G. Nufer, Jr.
1st Lt. Henry O. Odegard
Lt. Col. Delk M. Oden
S. Sgt. Alvin G. Olson
Pfc. Halbert E. Olson (P)
Sgt. Leo E. O'Mara
2d Lt. Albert I. Orr, Jr.
Sgt. Thomas E. Oxford
Sgt. Alfred B. Padilla
Tech. 4 Frank E. Palco, Jr.
Pfc. Max Y. Parker (P)
T. Sgt. Rowdy W. Parker
Pvt. Donald L. Parta
Brig. Gen. Herbert T. Perrin
Tech. 5 Leslie R. Perry (P)
S. Sgt. Jacob M. Peter (P)
Pfc. Dale J. Peterson (P)
S. Sgt. Joseph S. Petrencsik
2d Lt. Charles M. Phillips, Jr.
Col. James H. Phillips
Capt. Carl E. Pister
Pvt. Anthony F. Pistilli (P)
Pvt. Ronald G. Pomerleau

Capt. Frank M. Pool
Pfc. Harlan J. Porter
1st Lt. Raymond A. Porter
1st Lt. Marvin H. Prinds (P)
Sgt. Vito C. Pumilia
2d Lt. Walter J. Pustelnik (P)
Pfc. Srecko F. Radich (P)
S. Sgt. Donald N. Radtke
Capt. Edward R. Radzwich
S. Sgt. John T. Ramer (P)
Sgt. Paul E. Ramsey
Pfc. Robert G. Randall (P)
Tech. 5 Calvin J. Randolph (P)
Pfc. William H. Ratliff
2d Lt. William S. Read
Maj. Edward J. Regan
Pfc. Patsy Retort
S. Sgt. John A. Reynolds
Tech. 3 John F. Riskey
Pfc. Johnny C. Rodriguez
Brig. Gen. James S. Rodwell
Sgt. Francis N. Rogowicz
Pfc. Guillermo Rosas
Pfc. Loren E. Rowland (P)
S. Sgt. Samuel A. Rowland
2d Lt. Stanley S. Sadaj (P)
T. Sgt. Charles D. St. John
S. Sgt. Anthony L. Samele
Pfc. Leo W. Satterfield (P)
2d Lt. Alton Sawin, Jr.
S. Sgt. Frederick O. Sawyer (P)
Pfc. Roy D. Sawyer, Jr. (P)
T. Sgt. Charles E. Scabery
1st Lt. Jerome E. Scanlon (P)
S. Sgt. Harold F. Schaefer
Pvt. Charles H. Schroder (P)
Tech. 5 Florn W. Schutt (P)
Capt. Reed L. Seely (P)
S. Sgt. Dale H. Seggerman (P)
T. Sgt. Osborne F. Sellars*
Sgt. Robert L. Sellers
Sgt. James T. Semradek
Pfc. Edward F. Servis, Jr.
1st Lt. Julian R. Sheehy
Cpl. Russell W. Shoff
Pfc. Warren H. Shorey (P)
1st Lt. John G. Sinclair, Jr.
S. Sgt. Frank L. Sirovica

1st Lt. Earle R. Smedes
Lt. Col. John F. Smith
T. Sgt. Joseph J. Smyth
Pfc. Eugene Soto (P)
Capt. George P. Soumas
Cpl. Thomas M. Spaulding
Pfc. William H. Steen
Pvt. Ernest J. Steineker
Capt. John M. Stephens, Jr.
Pvt. Sampson J. Stephens (P)
Maj. Alexander C. Stiller
2d Lt. August A. Storkman, Jr.
1st Lt. Harold D. Swan (P)
T. Sgt. Deesie H. Talley
Sgt. Albert B. Taylor (P)
S. Sgt. Elmer D. Tener
Lt. Col. Evert S. Thomas, Jr.
S. Sgt. George D. Thomas (P)
Pfc. Jack Thomas
Maj. Claire A. Thurston
Capt. John P. Tice
2d Lt. Karl H. Timmermann
S. Sgt. Edward M. Transue
T. Sgt. Clifford C. Turner (P)
Pfc. Roy B. Turner
1st Lt. Frederick L. Tyler
Maj. Gen. James A. Van Fleet
S. Sgt. James A. VanHooser (P)
Capt. Keith G. Van Neste (P)
S. Sgt. Daniel B. Vannice
Pfc. Romanus Wagner (P)
Capt. Howard J. Wall (P)
Pfc. Jimmie D. Walton (P)
1st Lt. Horace K. Ward
1st Lt. Sammie L. Warren
S. Sgt. Ivan B. Waterbury
Capt. James M. Watkins (P)
Pvt. Harlen W. Way (P)
T. Sgt. Frank L. Wease (P)
Tech. 5 Forrest L. Webb (P)
S. Sgt. Arthur D. Webber (P)
2d Lt. Herbert J. Welch, Jr. (P)
Pfc. Henry V. White (P)
Pfc. Theodore White (P)
S. Sgt. Hassell C. Whitefield (P)
S. Sgt. Charles F. Whitlow
Capt. David H. Wiggs*
Lt. Col. Leonard S. Wilhelm (P)

Cpl. Carl Wilson (P)
Capt. Weldon W. Wilson
Capt. Charles A. Wirt
S. Sgt. Edward J. Wisniewski (P)
Tech. 5 George R. Wolff
Pfc. Harold L. Wood
2d Lt. Leon M. Wood

Col. Sidney C. Wooten
1st Lt. Wilbur F. Worthing
S. Sgt. Willis D. Wyatt
Pfc. Manuel R. Zabala
Pfc. Paul A. Zaring
Sgt. William E. Zarnfaller

Bibliographical Note

As with all campaign volumes in the series UNITED STATES ARMY IN WORLD WAR II, the most important documentary sources for *The Last Offensive* are the official records of U.S. Army units. Each headquarters in the European theater, from army through regiment and separate battalion, submitted a monthly after action report, accompanied by supporting daily journals, periodic reports, messages, staff section reports, and overlays. Although the records vary in quantity and quality, they are essential to any detailed study of operations. Those most valuable to the historian of combat operations are housed in the historical reports files in the World War II Records Division, National Archives. Almost all are without security classification.

The after action reports are in effect monthly compendiums of all the other documents, but the chance of error or the introduction of a commander's hindsight makes it imperative that these reports be checked against the supporting documents. Journals, when carefully prepared, are invaluable. In the manner of a ship's log, they of all the documents most nearly reflect the events and thinking in the headquarters at the time.

Much the same pattern of official records was followed at headquarters of the 6th and 12th Army Groups. The 6th Army Group also kept a command diary and the 12th Army Group a planning file labeled 12th Army Group, Military Objectives, 371.3.

The basic SHAEF files used for this volume are the richest of the official SHAEF collection, that of the SHAEF G-3, labeled Future Operations, and that of the Secretary of the General Staff (SHAEF SGS 381, Volumes I through IV). In addition, the author has drawn on the definitive experience with the SHAEF records of Dr. Forrest C. Pogue, author of *The Supreme Command*. While preparing his volume, Dr. Pogue collected transcripts or photostats of documents from General Eisenhower's wartime personal file. This material, cited as the Pogue files, is located in OCMH. Also falling under the category of SHAEF records are those of the airborne units, which are housed in the World War II Records Division under the heading SHAEF FAAA files.

Four of the tactical headquarters published official consolidated versions of their after action reports for limited distribution. Two of these—the 12th Army Group Report of Operations and V Corps Operations in the ETO—provide in addition to the narrative report a convenient assimilation of pertinent orders, periodic reports, and other documents. The First Army Report of Operations, 1 August 1944–22 February 1945 and 22 February–8 May 1945, and the Seventh Army Report of Operations are more strictly narrative.

Unofficial Records

Most records falling in the category of unofficial records are combat interviews conducted by teams of historical officers working under the European Theater Historical Section. In addition, there are narratives written by the field historians to accompany the interviews and occasionally field notes and important documents collected by the historical officers. The footnotes in this volume should provide an adequate guide to the available combat interview material, which is housed in the historical reports files in the World War II Records Division.

Unit Histories

Soon after the war, almost every division, some corps, and some regiments published unofficial unit histories. Many of these works are heavy on the side of unit pride, but some are genuinely useful. A brief analysis of each is usually included in this volume in the footnote where the work is first cited. In a special class is *Conquer: The Story of Ninth Army* (Washington: Infantry Journal Press, 1945), a sober and valuable volume.

German Sources

The account of German operations has been based primarily on monographs prepared in OCMH by Mrs. Magna Bauer specifically to complement this volume and on a series of manuscripts prepared after the war by former German commanders working under the auspices of the U.S. Army. Mrs. Bauer's monographs are based on these manuscripts and on official German records captured or seized by the U.S. Army.

Most of the comtemporary German records have been returned to Germany, but microfilm copies are available in the World War II Records Division. The German manuscripts, numbering more than two thousand, are filed in the World War II Records Division and have been adequately catalogued and indexed in *Guide to Foreign Military Studies 1945-54*, published in 1954. The quality of the manuscripts varies, reflecting the fact that almost all are based only on the memories of the writers, yet they are invaluable in supplementing the official records, particularly for latter stages of the war, when many records were destroyed and many were sparse and often inaccurate because of the fluid and usually retrograde nature of the German operations.

Published Works

Two previously published volumes in the series UNITED STATES ARMY IN WORLD WAR II were of particular value: Dr. Pogue's *The Supreme Command* and Roland G. Ruppenthal, *Logistical Support of the Armies, Vol. II*. In addition to those and unofficial unit histories, published works of special value in preparation of this volume are as follows:

Ambrose, Stephen E. *Eisenhower and Berlin, 1945–The Decision to Halt at the Elbe.* New York: W. W. Norton and Co., 1967.

Bradley, Omar N. *A Soldier's Story.* New York: Henry Holt and Co., 1951.

Brereton, Lt. Gen. Lewis H. *The Brereton Diaries.* New York: William Morrow and Co., 1946.

Bullock, Alan. *Hitler: A Study in Tyranny.* New York: The Macmillan Co., 1947.

Butcher, Capt. Harry C. *My Three*

Years with Eisenhower. New York: Simon and Schuster, 1946.

Churchill, Winston S. *Triumph and Tragedy.* Boston: Houghton Mifflin Co., 1953.

Donnison, F. S. V. *Civil Affairs and Military Government, North-West Europe 1944–1946.* London: Her Majesty's Stationery Office, 1961.

Ehrman, John. *Grand Strategy.* London: Her Majesty's Stationery Office, 1957.

Eisenhower, Dwight D. *Crusade in Europe.* New York: Doubleday and Co., 1948.

Feis, Herbert. *Churchill, Roosevelt, and Stalin.* Princeton: Princeton University Press, 1957.

Gilbert, Felix. *Hitler Directs His War.* New York: Oxford University Press, 1950.

Goudsmet, Samuel T. *ALSOS.* New York: William Morrow and Co., 1964.

Guderian, Heinz. *Panzer Leader.* New York: E. P. Dutton and Co., 1952.

Hechler, Ken. *The Bridge at Remagen.* New York: Ballantine Books, 1957.

Irving, David. *The Destruction of Dresden.* London: William Kimber, 1963.

Kesselring, Field Marshal Albert. *A Soldier's Record.* New York: William Morrow and Co., 1954.

Lattre de Tassigny, Marshal Jean de. *Histoire de la Premiére Armée Française.* Paris: Librairie Plon, 1947.

McGovern, James. *CROSSBOW and OVERCAST.* New York: William Morrow and Co., 1964.

Minott, Rodney G. *The Fortress That Never Was.* New York: Holt, Rinehart and Winston, 1964.

Montgomery, Field Marshal the Viscount of Alamein. *Normandy to the Baltic.* Boston: Houghton Mifflin Co., 1947.

Morison, Samuel Eliot. *The Invasion of France and Germany.* Boston: Little, Brown and Co., 1957.

Pash, Boris T., *The ALSOS Mission.* New York: Award House, 1966.

Patton, George S. *War As I Knew It.* Boston: Houghton Mifflin Co., 1947.

Rundell, Walter, Jr. *Black Market Money.* Baton Rouge: Louisiana State University Press, 1964.

Ryan, Cornelius. *The Last Battle.* New York: Simon and Schuster, 1960.

Shirer, William L. *The Rise and Fall of the Third Reich.* New York: Simon and Schuster, 1960.

Smith, Walter Bedell. *Eisenhower's Six Great Decisions.* New York: Longmans, Green and Co., 1956.

Stacey, Charles P. *The Victory Campaign.* Ottawa: W. Cloutier, Queen's Printer, 1960.

Toland, John. *The Last 100 Days.* New York: Random House, 1966.

Wilmot, Chester. *The Struggle for Europe.* New York: Harper and Bros., 1952.

Ziemke, Earl F. *Stalingrad to Berlin: The German Defeat in the East.* Washington: Government Printing Office, 1968.

Glossary

AAA	Antiaircraft artillery
AAF	Army Air Forces
AAR	After action report
Abn	Airborne
Actg	Acting
Admin	Administrative, administrator
AGp	Army group
AM	Amplitude modulated
Armd	Armored
Asst	Assistant
Bailey bridge	Portable steel bridge of the "through" type. The roadway is supported by two main trusses composed of 10-foot sections called "panels" pinned together to form a continuous truss. Capacity may be increased by adding extra trusses alongside the first, by adding an extra truss on top of the first to make a second story, or by both means.
BAR	Browning automatic rifle
Bazooka	2.36–inch rocket launcher
BBC	British Broadcasting Corporation
Bn	Battalion
Burp gun	German submachine gun
C–47	American transport plane
CCA	Combat Command A
CCB	Combat Command B
CCR	Combat Command Reserve
CCS	Combined Chiefs of Staff
CG	Commanding general
CO	Commanding officer
Co	Company
CofS	Chief of Staff
Comdr	Commander
Conf	Conference
CP	Command post
DD	Duplex drive (tank)
D-day	Day on which an operation commences or is to commence
Dept	Department
Dir	Directive, director
Div	Division
Dragon's teeth	Concrete pillars or iron posts erected as tank barriers
Dukw	2 1/2–ton amphibious truck

"88"	German 88–mm. high-velocity dual-purpose antiaircraft and antitank piece
Ersatzheer	German Replacement Army
ETO	European Theater of Operations
ExecO	Executive officer
FA	Field artillery
Feldheer	German Field Army
Flak	Antiaircraft
FM	Frequency modulation
FO	Field order
Fuesilier battalion	Separate infantry battalion performing both reconnaissance and support in German division
FUSA	First United States Army
FWD	Forward headquarters
G–1	Personnel officer or section of divisional or higher staff
G–2	Intelligence officer or section
G–3	Operations officer or section
G–4	Supply officer or section
Grazing fire	Fire which is approximately parallel to the ground and does not rise above the height of a man, standing
Half-track	Combination wheeled and tracked armored personnel carrier
H-hour	Exact time on D-day at which a specific operation commences
Hilfswillige	Volunteer auxiliaries (non-German)
Hist	History
Hp	Horsepower
Hq	Headquarters
Incl	Inclosure
Inf	Infantry
Info	Information
Intell	Intelligence
JCS	Joint Chiefs of Staff
JIC	Joint Intelligence Committee
Jnl	Journal
Jump-off	Start of a planned ground attack
Kampfgruppe	German task force
Kampfkommandant	German combat commander
Kampfstaerke	Combat effective strength
Landesschuetzen	Home Guard battalion sometimes employed outside Germany
LCM	Landing craft, medium
LCVP	Landing craft, vehicle and personnel
Ltr	Letter
Luftwaffe	German Air Force
LVT	Landing vehicle, tracked

M1 (Garand)	American semiautomatic rifle
M4 (Sherman)	American medium tank
M10	American tank destroyer with 3–inch gun
M26 (Pershing)	American medium tank mounting a 90–mm. gun
M36	American tank destroyer mounting a high-velocity 90–mm. piece
Marching fire	Firing by troops while erect and advancing
Mark IV	German medium tank
Mark V (Panther)	German medium tank with heavy armor and high-velocity gun
Mark VI (Tiger)	German heavy tank
Min	Minutes
Mm	Millimeter
MS (S)	Manuscript (s)
Msg	Message
NAF	Symbol for messages from the Combined Chiefs of Staff to the Commander in Chief, Allied Expeditionary Force
Nebelwerfer	Multiple-barrel 150–mm. mortar or rocket launcher mounted on wheels and fired electrically
NUSA	Ninth United States Army
OB NEDERLANDER	*Oberbefehlshaber Nederlander* (Headquarters, Commander in Chief Netherlands)
OB NORDWEST	*Oberbefehlshaber Nordwest* (Headquarters, Commander in Chief Northwest [northwest Germany, Denmark, and the Netherlands])
OB NW	See *OB NORDWEST.*
OB SUED	*Oberbefehlshaber Sued* (Headquarters, Commander in Chief South [southern Germany and several army groups on the Eastern Front])
OB WEST	*Oberbefehlshaber West* (Headquarters, Commander in Chief West [France, Belgium, and the Netherlands])
OCMH	Office, Chief of Military History
OKH	*Oberkommando des Heeres* (Army High Command)
OKW	*Oberkommando der Wehrmacht* (High Command of the Armed Forces)
OPD	Operations Division
Opn (s)	Operation(s)
Opnl	Operational
Panzerfaust	One-shot, shaped-charge antitank weapon
Plunging fire	Gunfire that strikes the earth's surface at a high angle
POZIT	Proximity fuze
PX	Post Exchange
RAMPS	Recovered Allied Military Personnel
Ranger	Soldier specially trained to make surprise attacks on enemy territory
Ret	Retired

Rpt	Report
S–2	Intelligence officer or section of regimental or lower staff
S–3	Operations officer or section
SACMED	Supreme Allied Commander, Mediterranean Theater
SCAF	Designates cables from Supreme Headquarters, Allied Expeditionary Force, to the Combined Chiefs of Staff
SCR	Set complete radio
Seamule	38–foot tug powered by two 143–hp. engines
Sec	Section
SGS	Secretary, General Staff
SHAEF	Supreme Headquarters, Allied Expeditionary Force
Sitrep	Situation report
S-mine	German antipersonnel mine
SS	*Schutzstaffel* (Elite Guard)
Storm boat	Metal ponton propelled by 50–hp. outboard motor
Sub	Subject
Sum	Summary
SUSA	Seventh United States Army
T26	See M26.
TAC	Tactical Air Command
Tagesstaerke	Present for duty strength
TD	Tank destroyer
Telecon	Telephone conversation
T-forces	Special forces designated to search for items of scientific value
TM	Technical manual
TOT	Time on target, a method of timing artillery fire from various points to fall on a given target simultaneously
Tree burst	Explosion of shells against trees, designed to destroy troops underneath
TUSA	Third United States Army
TWX	Teletypewriter exchange
USA	United States Army
USAF	United States Air Force
USAREUR	United States Army, Europe
USNR	United States Naval Reserve
V–2	German supersonic rocket
Volksdeutsche	"Racial Germans" from border areas of adjacent countries
Volks Grenadier	Honorific accorded by Hitler to certain infantry divisions
Volkssturm	A people's militia, partially organized in one of the last steps of German mobilization for total war
VT	Variable time (fuze)
Waffen-SS	Military arm of the Nazi party

Wehrkreis   German Army administrative area, for the most part
                                       inside greater Germany
Wehrmacht   German Armed Forces
WFSt   *Wehrmachtfuehrungsstab* (Armed Forces Operations
                                       Staff)

Code Names

ALSOS — Allied mission made up of special intelligence forces which sought information on German developments in nuclear fission

ECLIPSE — Name given Operation TALISMAN after a presumed compromise of security

FLASHPOINT — Ninth U.S. Army assault crossing of the Rhine in March 1945 (part of Operation PLUNDER)

GRENADE — Ninth U.S. Army assault crossing of the Roer followed by a northeastward drive to link with the First Canadian Army along the Rhine, February 1945

KAPUT — Ninth U.S. Army assignment of defeating an incursion into the zone of the XIII Corps and of clearing a sector along the Elbe, April 1945

LUMBERJACK — Converging thrust by U.S. First and Third Armies to create a pocket of trapped Germans in the Eifel, February and March 1945

MARKET — Phase of Operation MARKET-GARDEN that involved seizure of bridges in the Nijmegen-Arnhem area

MARKET-GARDEN — Combined ground-airborne operation intended to establish a bridgehead across the Rhine in the Netherlands, September 1944

NEPTUNE — Actual operations within Operation OVERLORD; used for security reasons after September 1943 on all OVERLORD planning papers that referred to target area and date

NORDWIND — German counteroffensive launched on New Year's Eve 1944 near the southern end of the Allied line in Alsace

OMAHA — Normandy beach assaulted by troops of U.S. V Corps, 6 June 1944

OVERLORD — Plan for invasion of northwest Europe, spring 1944

PLUNDER — Assault crossing of the Rhine by the 21 Army Group, March 1945

TALISMAN — Early name for post hostilities plans for Germany

UNDERTONE — Seventh U.S. Army operation to breach the West Wall and establish a bridgehead over the Rhine in the Worms area, March–April 1945

VARSITY — First Allied Airborne Army operation in support of Operation PLUNDER

VERITABLE — 21 Army Group plan for a Canadian attack between the Maas and the Rhine, January–February 1945

Basic Military Map Symbols*

Symbols within a rectangle indicate a military unit, within a triangle an observation post, and within a circle a supply point.

Military Units—Identification

Antiaircraft Artillery . . . .

Armored Command . . . .

Army Air Forces . . . .

Artillery, except Antiaircraft and Coast Artillery . . . .

Cavalry, Horse . . . .

Cavalry, Mechanized . . . .

Chemical Warfare Service . . . .

Coast Artillery . . . .

Engineers . . . .

Infantry . . . .

Medical Corps . . . .

Ordnance Department . . . .

Quartermaster Corps . . . .

Signal Corps . . . .

Tank Destroyer . . . .

Transportation Corps . . . .

Veterinary Corps . . . .

Airborne units are designated by combining a gull wing symbol with the arm or service symbol:

Airborne Artillery . . . .

Airborne Infantry . . . .

*For complete listing of symbols in use during the World War II period. see FM 21–30, dated October 1943, from which these are taken.

Size Symbols

The following symbols placed either in boundary lines or above the rectangle, triangle, or circle inclosing the identifying arm or service symbol indicate the size of military organization:

Squad . . . . •

Section . . . . ••

Platoon . . . . •••

Company, troop, battery, Air Force flight I

Battalion, cavalry squadron, or Air Force squadron . . . . I I

Regiment or group; combat team (with abbreviation CT following identifying numeral) . . . . I I I

Brigade, Combat Command of Armored Division, or Air Force Wing X

Division or Command of an Air Force XX

Corps or Air Force XXX

Army XXXX

Group of Armies XXXXX

EXAMPLES

The letter or number to the left of the symbol indicates the unit designation; that to the right, the designation of the parent unit to which it belongs. Letters or numbers above or below boundary lines designate the units separated by the lines:

Company A, 137th Infantry . . . . A⊠137

8th Field Artillery Battalion . . . . •⎵8

Combat Command A, 1st Armored Division . . . . A⬭I

Observation Post, 23d Infantry . . . . ⧊23

Command Post, 5th Infantry Division . . . . ⊠5

Boundary between 137th and 138th Infantry . . . . —|||—

137 / 138

Weapons

Machine gun . . . . ●→

Gun . . . . ●

Gun battery . . . . ⊔⊔⊔

Howitzer or Mortar . . . . ◆

Tank . . . . ◇

Self-propelled gun . . . . ⬡

UNITED STATES ARMY IN WORLD WAR II

The multivolume series, UNITED STATES ARMY IN WORLD WAR II, consists of a number of subseries which are planned as follows: The War Department, The Army Air Forces, The Army Ground Forces, The Army Service Forces, The Western Hemisphere, The War in the Pacific, The Mediterranean Theater of Operations, The European Theater of Operations, The Middle East Theater, The China–Burma–India Theater, The Technical Services, Special Studies, and Pictorial Record.

The following volumes have been published or are in press:*

The War Department
  Chief of Staff: Prewar Plans and Preparations
  Washington Command Post: The Operations Division
  Strategic Planning for Coalition Warfare: 1941–1942
  Strategic Planning for Coalition Warfare: 1943–1944
  Global Logistics and Strategy: 1940–1943
  Global Logistics and Strategy: 1943–1945
  The Army and Economic Mobilization
  The Army and Industrial Manpower

The Army Ground Forces
  The Organization of Ground Combat Troops
  The Procurement and Training of Ground Combat Troops

The Army Service Forces
  The Organization and Role of the Army Service Forces

The Western Hemisphere
  The Framework of Hemisphere Defense
  Guarding the United States and Its Outposts

The War in the Pacific
  The Fall of the Philippines
  Guadalcanal: The First Offensive
  Victory in Papua
  CARTWHEEL: The Reduction of Rabaul
  Seizure of the Gilberts and Marshalls
  Campaign in the Marianas
  The Approach to the Philippines
  Leyte: The Return to the Philippines
  Triumph in the Philippines
  Okinawa: The Last Battle
  Strategy and Command: The First Two Years

---

*The volumes on the Army Air Forces, published by the University of Chicago Press, are not included in this list.

Special Studies

Chronology: 1941–1945
Military Relations Between the United States and Canada: 1939–1945
Rearming the French
Three Battles: Arnaville, Altuzzo, and Schmidt
The Women's Army Corps
Civil Affairs: Soldiers Become Governors
Buying Aircraft: Matériel Procurement for the Army Air Forces
The Employment of Negro Troops

Pictorial Record

The War Against Germany and Italy: Mediterranean and Adjacent Areas
The War Against Germany: Europe and Adjacent Areas
The War Against Japan

Index

U.S. GOVERNMENT PRINTING OFFICE: 1973 O—470—928